# DIAGRAM FOR THE CLASSIFICATION OF WORLD LIFE ZONES OR PLANT FORMATIONS

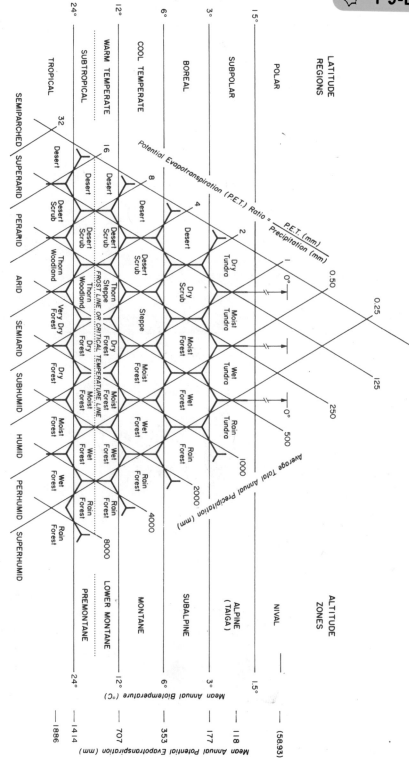

Redrawn from L.R Holdridge, Life Zone Ecology,
Tropical Science Center, San Jose, Costa Rica

# INTRODUCTION TO FOREST SCIENCE

# INTRODUCTION TO
# FOREST
# SCIENCE

## Raymond A. Young

EDITOR

University of Wisconsin

## John Wiley & Sons

New York    Chichester    Brisbane    Toronto    Singapore

**Library of Congress Cataloging in Publication Data**
Main entry under title:

Introduction to forest science.

   Includes index.
   1. Forests and forestry.  I. Young, Raymond
Allen, 1945–    .  II. Title: Forest science.
SD373.I57        634.9        81-16031
ISBN 0-471-06438-6        AACR2

Printed in the United States of America

10 9 8 7 6 5 4 3 2 1

**DEDICATED TO MY SONS, TIM AND ERIC**

*To waste, to destroy, our natural resources, to skin and exhaust the land instead of using it so as to increase its usefulness, will result in undermining in the days of our children the very prosperity which we ought by right to hand down to them amplified and developed.*

**Theodore Roosevelt**

# AUTHORS AND AFFILIATIONS

**John D. Aber**
Department of Forestry
University of Wisconsin
Madison, Wisconsin

**Robert H. Becker**
Department of Recreation and Parks Administration
College of Forest and Recreation Resources
Clemson University
Clemson, South Carolina

**Daniel M. Benjamin**
Department of Entomology and Forestry
University of Wisconsin
Madison, Wisconsin

**James G. Bockheim**
Department of Soil Science and Forestry
University of Wisconsin
Madison, Wisconsin

**Thomas M. Bonnicksen**
Department of Forestry
University of Wisconsin
Madison, Wisconsin

**Joseph Buongiorno**
Department of Forestry
University of Wisconsin
Madison, Wisconsin

**Gordon R. Cunningham**
Department of Forestry
University of Wisconsin
Madison, Wisconsin

**John W. Duffield**
School of Forest Resources
North Carolina State University
Raleigh, North Carolina

**Alan R. Ek**
College of Forestry
University of Minnesota
St. Paul, Minnesota

**Robert D. Gale**
Forest Service
U.S. Department of Agriculture
Washington, D.C.

**Ronald L. Giese**
Department of Forestry
University of Wisconsin
Madison, Wisconsin

**Gordon W. Gullion**
Department of Entomology, Fisheries and Wildlife
Cloquet Forestry Center
University of Minnesota
Cloquet, Minnesota

**Raymond P. Guries**
Department of Forestry
University of Wisconsin
Madison, Wisconsin

**George J. Hajny**
Forest Products Laboratory
Forest Service
U.S. Department of Agriculture
Madison, Wisconsin

**Jan Henderson**
Department of Forestry and Outdoor Recreation
Utah State University
Logan, Utah

**Bjorn F. Hrutfiord**
College of Forest Resources
University of Washington
Seattle, Washington

**Alan Jubenville**
School of Agriculture and Land Resources Management
University of Alaska
Fairbanks, Alaska

# AUTHORS AND AFFILIATIONS

**W. David Klemperer**
School of Forestry and Wildlife Resources
Virginia Polytechnic Institute and State University
Blacksburg, Virginia

**Theodore T. Kozlowski**
Department of Forestry
University of Wisconsin
Madison, Wisconsin

**Hans Kubler**
Department of Forestry
University of Wisconsin
Madison, Wisconsin

**William A. Leuschner**
School of Forestry and Wildlife Resources
Virginia Polytechnic Institute and State University
Blacksburg, Virginia

**Craig G. Lorimer**
Department of Forestry
University of Wisconsin
Madison, Wisconsin

**John N. McGovern**
Department of Forestry
University of Wisconsin
Madison, Wisconsin

**Robert F. Patton**
Department of Plant Pathology and Forestry
University of Wisconsin
Madison, Wisconsin

**R. Max Peterson**
Forest Service
U.S. Department of Agriculture
Washington, D. C.

**Roger M. Rowell**
Forest Products Laboratory
Forest Service
U.S. Department of Agriculture
Madison, Wisconsin

**Jeffrey C. Stier**
Department of Forestry
University of Wisconsin
Madison, Wisconsin

**Harold W. Wisdom**
School of Forestry and Wildlife Resources
Virginia Polytechnic Institute and State University
Blacksburg, Virginia

**Raymond A. Young**
Department of Forestry
University of Wisconsin
Madison, Wisconsin

# PREFACE

The science of forestry is a complex amalgamation of the biological, physical, managerial, social, and political sciences. Few if any forestry professionals are able to treat all aspects of forest science with complete authority. An edited book on forestry is thus the best alternate method for conveying the science of forestry in one text. *Introduction to Forest Science* is intended to provide beginning and intermediate students with a comprehensive introduction to important aspects of the field of forestry. The book represents a joint effort by different authors to present a broad view of the field. The authors give general coverage of their specialized fields within forestry and emphasize the important factors that forest managers must consider in their decisions affecting the forest ecosystem. References to other works that explore certain aspects of forest science in more depth are provided for the interested student.

In the book an attempt is made to maintain a flow from the basic cell and individual trees to the forest stand, followed by management of the forest stand, and finally the acquisition of goods and services from the forest. To this end, the book is arranged into four major parts. After the *Introduction* (Part 1), the *Forest Biology* section (Part 2) contains information on factors affecting individual tree growth through growth of the forest stand. The management of forest stands for multiple uses is treated in the *Forest Management* section (Part 3). Finally the commodities obtainable from the forest are described in the last section, *Forest Products* (Part 4). The separation of the field of forestry into these distinct sections is very difficult because of the interdependence of the many factors affecting the forest. Therefore the reader is encouraged to refer to other sections or chapters where appropriate. Cross references are indicated in the text to designate when a specific subject is given more detailed treatment in another chapter. A glossary is also included to aid

the reader less familiar with the specialized terminology used in forestry.

The level of presentation provided in the text is more advanced than previously offered in introductory forestry books. This was intended because the modern student should be aware of the level of sophistication that the broad field of forestry has achieved in the present-day technological context. Therefore concurrent enrollment in such courses as freshman botany and chemistry would provide valuable background and interplay for maximum benefit from *Introduction to Forest Science*.

Forestry in the United States has gone through a number of gradual changes in the past century. However, significant events in the 1960s and 1970s caused a dramatic reassessment of the role of forestry and forestry practices in America. For example, some people indicated they could no longer tolerate the expansive clearcuts in the national forests; the Forest Service, in the face of court injunctions, developed sweeping new policies to correct for restraints imposed by legislation dating as far back as 1897. The use of insecticides and herbicides also came under careful scrutiny, which was reinforced with environmental legislation during this period. The events leading up to and including the policy changes of the 1970s are documented in two chapters: Chapter 1, "Development of Forest Policy in the United States," and Chapter 12 "Forestry at the National Level." Important forestry legislation is treated in more detail in a number of other chapters in the *Forest Management* section of the book.

The present composition and location of forests in the world are described in Chapter 2 in the *Introduction* section. The economic and social values of forest trees in each of the major regions are presented with an emphasis on North American forests.

The complex nature of forest ecosystems and the dramatic influence people can impose on them, either willfully or inadvertently, are presented in the

*Forest Biology* and *Forest Management* sections. The *Forest Biology* section emphasizes the important biological factors that influence the health and growth of trees. The basic "Physiology of Tree Growth" is presented in Chapter 3 with a description of growth characteristics of trees and important internal requirements for growth such as carbohydrates, minerals, and water.

Additional critical factors to tree growth include environmental and hereditary potential. In Chapter 4 the physical and chemical properties of soils are given with a description of how these important factors influence tree growth. Chapter 5, "Forest Genetics and Forest Tree Breeding," documents natural variation in forest-tree populations and outlines the potential of genetics for producing "supertrees." These biological factors contributed strongly to the patterns of ecological succession of the world's forests. Chapter 6 discusses the impacts of natural and artificial forces on succession in forest stands. Chapter 6 also introduces a broader "ecosystem" perspective through the concept of computer modeling and describes how a systems-analysis approach can be used for scientific assessment of an ecosystem. Thus the individual contributions of water, temperature, nutrients, light, etc., are integrated by computer-modeling techniques to give an overview of the forest ecosystem and to show how the components interact to affect the overall viability of the forest community.

The health and vigor of a forest are affected by other outside factors such as insects and disease. Indeed, insects inflict the highest levels of tree mortality, and the greatest growth loss of trees is due to fungus attack. The complex "Interaction of Insects and Forest Trees" is described in Chapter 7, and the "Diseases of Forest Trees" are discussed in Chapter 8. Both chapters present a number of management options such as silvicultural, biological, and chemical techniques as alternate or integrated methods of pest management.

The next section, *Forest Management,* incorporates the concept of multiple-use management of the forest. Chapter 9 is involved with the biological aspects of managing forests, a science commonly referred to as "Silviculture." Chapter 10 gives details on modern methods of "Measurement of the Forest" and the development of important forest surveys. The complex subject of "Multiple-Use Management of the Forest" is then treated in Chapter 11, which describes the application of administrative, organization, economic, and social principles in combination with physical and biological principles and practices to the planning, budgeting, and decision-making process in forest management. The special role of "Private Nonindustrial Forests," which comprise almost 60 percent of commercial forestland, is treated in Chapter 13.

Management of forests for multiple use includes timber, recreation, wildlife, watersheds and rangelands. The methods utilized in watershed, rangeland and timber management are discussed in Chapter 11; while separate chapters are devoted to "Forest-Recreation Management", "Forest-Wildlife Interactions" and "Behavior and Management of Forest Fires". Emphasis is placed on methods of integrating silvicultural management schemes for enhancement of each of the multiple uses, for example, timber, recreational values and certain wildlife populations.

The last major section of the book, *Forest Products*, deals with the conversion of forests to usable commodities. The special properties of wood that make it valuable as solid material are described in Chapter 17. A continually greater percentage of wood is used for conversion to paper, and Chapter 18 describes the "Chemistry and Pulping of Wood" for papermaking.

A topic currently of major concern to the nation is our energy supply. Chapter 19, "Energy and Chemicals from Wood," discusses the role that woody biomass can play in the overall energy picture for the United States. The chapter describes the methods for conversion of wood to liquid fuels, such as ethanol and methanol, and other chemical commodities. The final chapter, "The Forest-Products Economy," gives an overview of the market value of forest products and their place in the national and world economies. The chapter gives special treatment to the critical fuelwood crisis in underdeveloped countries.

The approach taken in *Introduction to Forest Science* was designed to give students a broad overview of the field of forestry but with sufficient detail that they might be able to assess their specific role as practicing forestry professionals. The book should serve as a ready reference in upper-level forestry courses and should be retained for later use by professional foresters. Indeed, current forestry professionals would find the text a convenient method for updating their knowledge of forest science. Certainly the book conveys the broad scope of forestry and the great challenges that lie ahead.

**Raymond A. Young**

# ACKNOWLEDGMENTS

The chapter authors and I have received many constructive comments on the chapters and the book by both our colleagues and outside reviewers. I would especially like to thank Ronald Giese, chairman of the Department of Forestry, University of Wisconsin—Madison, for his sustained support and encouragement throughout the editing process. Craig Lorimer also deserves special acknowledgment for help with several of the biology and management chapters. Appreciation is expressed to Norah Cashin for constructive comments throughout the book and preparation of the glossary and Appendix I, "Seed Plant Structure: A Review." Valuable proofreading was also performed by Tim and Terry Young and Trenten Marty. I am grateful to the departmental secretaries, Pauline Meudt, Barbara Kennedy, Janet Blucher, and Marian Jacobs, for many tedious hours of typing and other clerical assistance. Dawn Alder also provided expert typing services. The quotation by Theodore Roosevelt in the dedication was kindly located by Renie Giese.

We are grateful to the following additional people for reviews or assistance: Chapter 1, Robert G. Lee, University of Washington; John A. Zivnuska, University of California—Berkeley, Susan L. Flader, University of Missouri; Chapter 4, Tim Ballard, University of British Columbia, David Grigal, University of Minnesota—St. Paul, James Love, University of Wisconsin—Madison; Chapter 5, Reinhard Stettler, University of Washington, Nicholas Wheeler, University of Wisconsin—Madison; Chapter 7, Mary Schneider, University of Wisconsin—Madison; Chapter 8, John Berbee and John Andrews, University of Wisconsin—Madison; Chapter 9, David Smith, Yale University, William Leak, Northeast Forest Experiment Station, Forest Service, James Guldin, University of Wisconsin—Madison; Chapter 10, Ralph Meldahl, Auburn University, Anne LaMois (illustrations); Chapter 11, Thomas A. Walbridge, Virginia Polytechnic Institute and State University; Chapter 14, David Erickson, University of Kentucky; Chapter 15, Bruce M. Kilgore, National Park Service, Robert W. Mutch, Forest Service, Richard C. Rothermel, Northern Forest Fire Laboratory, Forest Service, Ronald H. Wakimoto, University of California—Berkeley; Chapter 16, Cindy Mankowski (typing), Cloquet Forestry Center; Chapter 18, Jean Holland (illustrations); Appendix I, Susan E. Eichhorn, University of Wisconsin—Madison.

**R.A.Y.**

# CONTENTS

# CONTENTS

# CONTENTS

# INTRODUCTION TO
# FOREST SCIENCE

# PART 1

## INTRODUCTION

Throughout history forests have been of importance to humans. Forests provided shelter and protection, and trees provided many products such as food, medicine, fuel, and tools. For example, the bark of the willow tree, when chewed, was used as a painkiller in early Greece and was the precursor of the present-day aspirin; acorns from oak trees were an important food base to the American Indian. Wood served as the primary fuel in the United States until about the turn of the century; indeed, over one-half of the wood now harvested in the world is used for heating fuel. Today over 10,000 products are made from wood.

Forests provide many other benefits, such as control of erosion and flooding and reduction of wind erosion. In addition to many utilitarian uses, the forest provides important aesthetic features which cannot be assigned quantitative values. The amenities include forest wildlife such as songbirds, fall coloration, wildflowers, and beautiful landscapes (Figure P1.1). Urbanized society has placed increasing emphasis on preserving the natural qualities of the forest for recreational purposes, escape, and solace. This has led to the ultimate designation of ''wilderness areas'' intended to be unaltered by humans.

Obviously a conflict of interest has arisen over the use of the forest in modern American society. What a member of a preservationist group such as the Sierra Club defines as proper management of the forest will probably be in direct conflict with how a paper industry executive views the use of the forest. The forest manager, while recognizing this conflict, must understand both views and develop a management plan that reflects the values involved in both viewpoints.

We can now define forestry as the art, science, and practice of managing the natural resources that occur on and in association with forestland for human benefit. This definition necessitates that the forest manager consider not only the trees in the forest, but also such things as protecting wildlife and preserving water systems for drinking and for aquatic life. Foresters are often involved with the control of fire, insect pests, and diseases in the forest, and they can also assume the broad role of protecting the forest environment. The forester is a land manager responsible for all the goods, benefits and services that flow from the forest (1).

The Multiple Use—Sustained Yield Act of 1960 recognized the many benefits derived from the forest: outdoor recreation, rangeland, timber, watershed protection, and wildlife and fish habitat. All need not be available at every location, but the value of each should be given equivalent recognition on a nationwide basis. Thus, a clearcut for timber in a national forest should, in some way, be balanced by opportunities for the wilderness-type experience at another location. The importance of the legislative process in forestry is further discussed in the first chapter, ''Development of Forest Policy in the United States.'' In the 1970s we witnessed a dramatic increase in forestry legislation important to the future of forestry practices in the United States.

In conformation with legislation, managers of forests on public lands must strive to have a continual supply of the products, services, and amenities available from the forest. To do this they must have a solid knowledge of science and society. A broad background in physical, biological, and social sciences is a necessity. To this must be added administrative skills and an element of diplomacy

**1**

**Figure P1.1** A majestic, mature stand of western red cedar in western Washington. Lichens clothing dead branches attest to humid climate. (Courtesy of U.S.D.A. Forest Service.)

for resolving conflicts. Clearly the task of the forest manager is a complex one requiring insight and many learned skills (2, 3).

## THE FOREST

The forest is a biological community of plants and animals existing in a complex interaction with the nonliving environment, which includes such factors as the soil, climate, and physiography. A continuous canopy of large trees usually distinguishes forests from other types of communities. Forests are widespread, representing almost 30 percent of the earth's land surface, and typically have a predominant species composition; thus there are many *forest types*. The distribution of forest types around the world is discussed in Chapter 2, "Forest Regions of North America and the World." The remainder of the land surface of the earth is composed of desert (31%), grasslands (21%), polar icecaps and wasteland (11%), and croplands (9%) (1).

Although trees are the predominant woody vegetation in terms of *biomass*[1], trees represent only a small proportion of the total *number* of species present in the forest. There are thousands, perhaps millions, of different types of plants and animals in the forest. Shrubs, herbs, ferns, mosses, lichens, and fungi are present beneath the forest canopy and in the gaps of the forest cover. Large animals such as deer and bears coexist with smaller birds, insects, and tiny microorganisms. Each component makes a contribution to the flow of energy and materials through the system.

The forest is a dynamic ecosystem that is continually changing in structure and composition. Disturbances such as fire, windfall, and harvesting produce sites where new communities of trees, plants, and animals can exist and differ from the original forest. Fallen leaves and woody material that reach the forest floor decay and continue the cycling of energy and nutrients through the system. The forest

[1]Terms that may be unfamiliar to the reader are defined in the Glossary.

community is a complex unit divided into many areas of study, which are treated in specific chapters in the text.

## TREE CLASSIFICATION

Trees are generally classified into two categories as seed plants: *angiosperms* with encased seeds and *gymnosperms* with naked seeds (Figure P1-2). The angiosperms are the dominant plant life of this geological era. They are the products of a long line of evolutionary development that has culminated in the highly specialized organ of reproduction that we know as the flower. Their seeds are enclosed in the matured ovary (fruit).

Two classes exist for the angiosperms, the Monocotyledones and the Dicotyledones (Table P1.1). Palms are classified as monocots, while the woody dicots are what we usually refer to as *broad-leaved* trees. Because the broad-leaved trees

**Table P1.1**
Scientific and Common Nomenclature of Forest Trees

| Angiosperms (encased seeds) | Gymnosperms (naked seeds) |
|---|---|
| Monocotyledones (parallel-veined leaves) | Cycadophyta |
| | Ginkgophyta |
| | Gnetophyta |
| Grasses | Coniferophyta |
| Palms | (conifers) |
| Other | Softwoods |
| | Evergreen trees |
| | Needlelike leaved trees |
| Dicotyledones (net-veined leaves) | |
| Dicotyledonous herbs | |
| Dicotyledonous shrubs | |
| Dicotyledonous trees | |
| Hardwoods | |
| Deciduous trees | |
| Broad-leaved trees | |

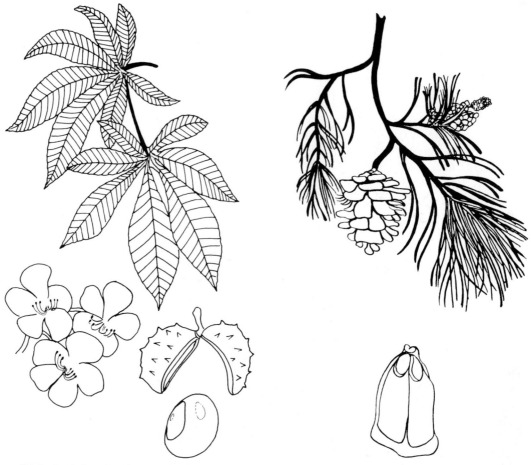

**Figure P1.2** Depiction of angiosperms (encased seed) and gymnosperms (naked seed).

typically lose their leaves each fall, they are also often referred to as *deciduous* trees. However, a number of exceptions occur, such as southern magnolia or pacific madrone, both of which retain their leaves all year. The broad-leaved or deciduous trees are also often referred to as *hardwood* trees, although this is a misnomer and does not refer to wood texture. Many broad-leaved trees such as basswood (linden), have soft-textured wood.

The other major class of trees is the gymno-sperms, which bear their seeds in cones. The major-ity of the trees in this classification fall into the division Coniferophyta or *conifers*. A notable ex-ception is the ginkgo tree, the only living species in the division Ginkgophyta. Some of the last living ginkgo trees were located by a botanical expedition in China in 1690. Subsequently seeds from the tree have been planted worldwide (Figure P1.3).

The conifers generally do not lose their needle-like leaves annually in the fall and therefore are

**Figure P1.3**  The ancient ginkgo tree thrives in polluted urban environments and is planted as an ornamental worldwide. (Photograph by R. A. Young.)

termed *evergreens*. Again, there are exceptions such as the larch, a conifer that loses its needles each year like the broad-leaved trees. The conifers are also referred to as *softwoods,* but, like the hardwoods, the designation does not refer to the texture of the wood but to the *class* of tree. The terminology of hardwoods and softwoods probably originated in the early sawmills when most of the conifers used for timber were the soft-textured pines, while the broad-leaved trees were hard-textured maples and oaks. It is important to recognize the synonymous terms since they are used interchangeably in both the literature and the common language.

## REFERENCES

1. H. L. Shirley, *Forestry and Its Career Opportunities,* Third Edition, McGraw-Hill, New York, 1973.
2. C.H. Stoddard, *Essentials of Forestry Practice,* Third Edition, John Wiley & Sons, New York, 1978.
3. G.W. Sharpe, C.W. Hendee, and S.W. Allen, *Introduction to Forestry,* Fourth Edition, McGraw-Hill, New York, 1976.

# 1

# THE DEVELOPMENT OF FOREST POLICY IN THE UNITED STATES

## Thomas M. Bonnicksen

All residents of the United States derive benefits from forests either indirectly as consumers of forest products or directly as participants in outdoor activities within forest settings. Americans are also making increasingly varied and heavy demands on their forests. Although forest resources are renewable, there is only so much forestland from which to produce these resources, so as demand rises, competition for resources also rises. This competition for resources has led to the formation of interest groups that try to influence elected officials and government agencies on the allocation and management of forest resources. The policymaking process is the means by which these differences are resolved. Understanding this process, and the forest policy it generates, is the principal focus of this chapter.

According to Boulding, a policy "generally refers to the principles that govern action directed toward given ends" (1). But policies are more than this. They are also hypotheses concerning what is thought will happen in the future if certain actions are taken. Whether or not a policy will achieve the ends specified is always open to question until the results of implementing the policy are actually observed. If the policy does not perform as expected, the whole policy process might be reinitiated. Thus policymaking is a continuous process that is constantly attacking new problems as well as problems generated by past policies (2).

All of a society's history, philosophy, beliefs, attitudes, values, contemporary problems, and hopes are woven into the policymaking process. Furthermore, what is an acceptable forest policy to one society in a given physical setting may be inconceivable to another society in a different physical setting. Although U.S. forest policy incorporates many European forestry principles, it still represents a unique blend of approaches and goals tailored to American needs and circumstances. American forest policy is also continually developing to accommodate change. Thus the forest policies adopted in the late 1800s differ significantly from those adopted in the latter half of the 1900s. Which policies were better at one time cannot be judged using the standards of another time, just as forest policies appropriate to a given society cannot be judged according to the standards of another society.

## A PROFILE OF FOREST POLICY DEVELOPMENT

Throughout the remainder of this chapter the policy process will be used as the framework for visualizing the historical development of U.S. forest policy. We will look at the broad periods that characterize major shifts in our policies toward forests. In addition, we will describe the environmental context and goals of the policy process within each period, and we will evaluate the results of a policy in terms of those goals.

Because the topic of American forest policy is vast, it was necessary to limit the scope of this analysis. Therefore, we emphasize the federal government's role in forestry and the management of national forests. We also emphasize policies that are stated as legislative statutes, executive orders and decrees, administrative rules and regulations, and court opinions.

### Native Americans and Forests (to 1607)

The relationship between American Indians and forests varied from place to place. In some cases the forest provided building materials, food, or both; in other cases it was an obstacle to cultivation. For instance, in the pre-Columbian period the heavily forested northwest coast of North America was occupied by seafaring people who were highly skilled woodworkers (3, 4). Although many Indian tribes of the eastern deciduous forests also obtained raw materials from forests, the forest was principally an obstacle to the cultivation of maize, beans, and squash (5).

In some cases, American Indians made a conscious effort to favor certain species of trees over others. In California, for instance, the widespread and abundant oak trees produced acorns, which were the staff of life for the Indian. The Miwok Indians inhabiting Yosemite Valley burned the grass under the black oak trees in the fall to prevent the growth of other trees that could grow taller and shade out the black oak. They also burned to clear the ground so that acorns could be gathered more readily.

American Indians who resided in the forests of North America abided by certain rules while deriving their living from the land. These rules or guidelines were handed down from one generation to the next by word and action. Such an agreed pattern of behavior, which is designed to accomplish a specified goal, fits the definition of a policy. Consequently, although aboriginal peoples did not have forest policies that were explicitly recognized as such, they did have rules that governed their relationship to forests. Whether modern people agree or disagree with these rules is unimportant. What is important is that American Indians had the equivalent of forest policies that were successful in helping them survive.

## Colonial Settlers and Forests (1607–1783)

Although the world known to Europe expanded to include North America in 1492, it was not until 1607 that Europeans successfully colonized what is now the United States. The site selected by the Virginia Company of London was Jamestown on the wooded banks of the James River in what is now Virginia.

Forests were the dominant feature of the colonial landscape and became one of its most valued resources. The forests surrounding Jamestown were used not only to construct the town but also as a source of fuel for a thriving glass industry. However, the thick forests made a good hiding place for unfriendly Indians, so the forests had to be cleared to make the area safe and to make room for farms and roads. Thus two attitudes toward forests developed that profoundly influenced forest policies for many generations. First, forests were a nuisance, and the citizen who made the greatest improvement in the land was the one who cut down the most trees. Second, the seemingly unending supply of trees led

to an acceptance of waste and a view that forests were inexhaustible.

Wood was the primary fuel and energy source for colonial America and remained so until 1870 (see Figure 19.1). Because the colonists lacked transportation, wood for fuel and building material had to be cut near settlements. As the forest receded from the settlements it became increasingly difficult to haul wood. Although the forests as a whole seemed inexhaustible, local timber supplies were limited. As a result, the first American forest policy on record was established on March 29, 1626, by Plymouth Colony. The policy forbade the transport of any timber out of the colony without the consent of the governor and council. Similar policies were adopted by Rhode Island, New Hampshire, and New Jersey. In 1681 William Penn directed that in Pennsylvania ("Penn's woodland") 0.4 hectares (1 acre) be left forested for every 2 hectares (5 acres) cleared of forest.

Colonial policymaking included political rule by a distant monarchy. This meant that forest policies had to reflect the perceived needs of a distant society as well as the immediate needs of the colonists themselves. The tension between these two interests presented serious limitations for England's forest policies for the New World.

The abundance of large trees made it possible for the colonists to develop a shipbuilding industry. The "Blessing of the Bay," launched at Medford, Massachusetts, in 1631, marked the beginning of both this industry (6) and a direct conflict with British interests in America's forests. As early as 1609 the first shipment of masts was sent from Virginia to England (6) (Figure 1.1). Trees of sufficient size for masts were scarce, and supply lines from northern and central Europe could be easily disrupted by hostile countries. Furthermore, Great Britain was competing with other countries for masts, so America became its principal source of supply. In order to protect its interests, a new charter granted to the Province of Massachusetts Bay in 1691 reserved for the crown all trees 61 centimeters (24 inches) or more in diameter on lands that were not in private

**Figure 1.1**  A sheer hulk stepping a mainmast. (Courtesy of Mr. Jack Coggins and Stackpole Books.)

ownership. This became known as the Broad Arrow policy because the reserved trees were marked with a broad arrow blaze—the symbol of the British Navy. By 1721 the Broad Arrow policy covered all colonial lands from Nova Scotia to New Jersey.

Although little is known about how well these policies worked during this period, it is probable that local wood supplies increased. Similarly, the British did obtain a relatively steady supply of masts and other naval timbers during the period. However, the Broad Arrow policy had to be enforced with large fines because it was vigorously opposed by the colonists. In 1772, for instance, in Weare, New Hampshire, Sheriff Benjamin Whiting arrested Ebenezer Mudgett for cutting the king's white pine. The colonists seized the sheriff in the night, beat him with rods, and forced him to ride out of town. This event was known as the "Pine Tree Riot" (6). The Broad Arrow policy was possibly one of the events that led to the American Revolution.

## Building and Defending the Republic (1783–1830)

The British formally recognized the independence of the United States with the signing of the Treaty of Paris in 1783. This marked the beginning of America's control of her own forests, but it also served as the beginning of a set of new social and economic problems. The old belief that forests were inexhaustible remained unchanged, however.

The most significant change in the context of the forest policy process that occurred in the aftermath of the revolution was the development of a new government. The first government was based on the Articles of Confederation, a document designed to preserve the states as free and independent sovereignties while granting Congress limited authority to act on behalf of all the states. The two most important powers denied to Congress were the authority to levy taxes and the authority to regulate commerce. Thus Congress under the confederation was purposely designed to be weak.

Approving the Articles of Confederation required the unanimous consent of all thirteen states. Six states were reluctant to sign because they did not have claims to large tracts of unsettled western lands. States with such lands had an advantage because they could sell them to defray debts incurred during the revolutionary war. Landless Maryland refused to sign the Articles of Confederation unless the other states abandoned their land claims. Maryland held out until March 1, 1781, when New York surrendered its western land claims to the federal government and Virginia appeared ready to do the same. Thus, ratification of the confederation also marked the beginning of the public domain. (The public domain included all lands that were at any time owned by the United States and subject to sale or other transfer of ownership under the laws of the federal government).

Congress pledged to dispose of the public domain for the ''common benefit,'' partly to create new states and partly to make good on its promise to grant land to revolutionary soldiers and officers. Since Congress could not levy taxes, it had to use the public domain as a source of revenue to discharge the national debt and operate the government.

Although Congress was weak under the Articles of Confederation, it still managed to pass two major laws that have left their imprint on the landscape to this day. The first of these laws was the Land Ordinance of 1785. It provided that the Old Northwest, a territory lying between the Ohio and Mississippi rivers and the southern shores of the Great Lakes, should be sold to help defray the national debt. The land was also to be surveyed before sale using the now familiar rectangular grid system of townships and sections. Only the thirteen original states and Texas, whose admission to the union was contingent on state ownership of public lands, were not subjected to this survey system. The Northwest Ordinance of 1787 further provided that when a territory could claim 60,000 residents it might be admitted by Congress as a state. This scheme worked so well that it was ultimately carried over to other areas of the public domain (Figures 1.2 and 1.3).

One of the problems facing the new Congress was the need to build and maintain a strong navy. Thus Congress authorized the construction of six frigates in 1794 and established a Department of the Navy in 1798 (6). Congress passed an act on February 25, 1799, that appropriated $200,000 for the purchase of timber and lands growing timber suitable for naval construction. Two islands supporting live oak were promptly purchased off the coast of Georgia.

At the outbreak of the War of 1812, the United States had only sixteen ships in its entire navy to throw into battle against the 800 men-of-war in the British navy. By the end of the war the United States had only two or three ships left (7). Congress reacted by passing an act on March 1, 1817, authorizing the secretary of the navy to reserve from sale public-domain lands that supported live oak and red cedar to rebuild the navy. However, the presi-

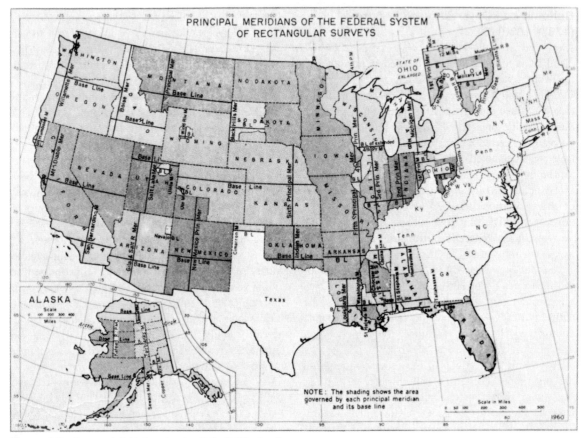

**Figure 1.2** States subdivided under the U.S. Public Land Survey and principal meridians and baselines. (U.S. Dept. of Interior.)

dent had to approve each reservation. An act on March 19, 1828, appropriated an additional $10,000 for the purchase of lands bearing live oak.

The timber reserves set aside by Congress received no more support from the public than did the earlier Broad Arrow policy of the British. Looting, or timber trespass, was common. In 1821 the commissioner of the General Land Office instructed his agents to stop illegal cutting on the reserves (6), but the officials responsible for carrying out the order were political appointees with little interest in confronting thieves in the forest. Congress tried to help by passing an act on February 23, 1822, authorizing the president to use the army and the navy to prevent timber depredations in Florida, but there was little improvement.

**Important Features of the Period 1783–1830.**
Forest policies adopted between 1783 and 1830 produced a mixed result. First, the revenues derived from the sale of public lands did not reach the expected amount. The Land Ordinance of 1785 provided that the lands should be sold in blocks of at least 640 acres (259 hectares) to the highest bidder, but at not less than $1 per acre. Unfortunately, land could be purchased elsewhere at lower prices, and the $640 required as a minimum purchase price proved difficult for most people to raise at the time.

12

Subsequent laws providing for credit sales and a reduction in the minimum area did not improve the situation. As a result, people needing land "squatted" on the public domain in increasing numbers, and efforts to remove them met with little success.

The naval timber-reserve policies had a similar result. Since forests were generally regarded as inexhaustible and the public domain was expanding, interest in the reserves gradually declined. Nevertheless, the policy of reserving forestlands as a source of timber set an important precedent for future forest policy decisions. The right of Congress to control the use of public lands in the national interest was also established during this period. Perhaps the most undesirable consequence of these policies was the failure to prevent timber stealing in sparsely settled areas of the frontier.

## The Erosion of a Myth (1830–1891)

In 1830 Andrew Jackson was elected president, and control of government by the common people was securely established. Many people in the upper classes sneered at the "New Democracy," referring to "coonskin congressmen" and enfranchised "bipeds of the forest" (7). Nevertheless, politicians who could boast of birth in a log cabin had a real advantage in an election. The sturdy pioneer and settler of the forest was clearly in command.

By 1867, when Alaska was purchased, the public domain had grown an additional 405 million hectares. There was a great need to people these lands with settlers who could protect them and make them productive. In fact, during this period, more than any other, the nation's policy was to transfer the bulk of the land, including forestland, into private ownership and rely on market forces as a primary means for allocating natural resources.

**Exploitation of the Forests.** With a seemingly inexhaustible supply of forests, and a government dominated by people sympathetic to the need for western settlement and economic expansion, a

period of rapid exploitation of resources was inevitable. Furthermore, pressure on timberlands was increased by the demand for wood to build towns on the treeless Great Plains, for railroad construction, to fight the Civil War and repair what it destroyed, and to rebuild 10.4 square kilometers of the city of Chicago that burned in the Great Fire of 1871.

Settlers occupying lands on the Great Plains had to import most of their timber. Tree planting was thought to be a reasonable solution and might have the additional benefit of increasing rainfall. In 1866, Commissioner Joseph S. Wilson of the General Land Office supported the idea and recommended that homesteaders be required to plant trees in areas lacking timber (6). Congress responded in 1873 by enacting the Timber Culture Act. Under the law settlers could receive 65 hectares (160 acres) of public land by planting 16 hectares (40 acres) of it with trees.

With the exception of railroad land grants, most of the policies enacted during this period focused on the development of agriculture. However, by 1878 it became obvious that large areas of the public do-

**Figure 1.3** An original witness tree marked by the Land Office in 1843, Ouachita National Forest, Arkansas. (Photography courtesy of U.S.D.A. Forest Service.)

main were more suitable for timber production than agriculture, and no provision had been made for the acquisition of these timberlands, or the timber, by the public. Congress tried to remedy the situation by passing two laws in 1878: the Free Timber Act and the Timber and Stone Act. The Free Timber Act stipulated that residents of nine western states could cut timber for building, mining, and other purposes without charge to aid in the development of their farms and mineral claims (Figure 1.4). Although this act was well intentioned, and undoubtedly provided substantial aid to deserving settlers, it was

nevertheless widely abused. Enforcement of both the act and regulations issued by the secretary of the interior for its administration was nearly impossible.

The Timber and Stone Act provided that unoccupied, surveyed land that was principally valuable for timber production or stone, but not agriculture, could be purchased in 65-hectare (160-acre) tracts for $2.50 per acre in Washington, Oregon, California, and Nevada. The purchaser had to swear that the land was for personal use and not for speculation.

Throughout this period two major forest policy

**Figure 1.4** Native Americans used wood under provisions of the Free Timber Act, Black Hills National Forest, South Dakota, in 1931. (Photograph courtesy of U.S.D.A. Forest Service.)

problems existed. First, speculation and fraud in the acquisition of public lands was rampant. Speculators and lumber executives interested in accumulating large holdings of timberland took advantage of almost every policy for the disposal of the public domain. Most of these policies were designed to encourage small owner-operator farms, but there was little control over what the owner did with the land after purchasing it. Military land bounties, for example, were granted to soldiers for their service and to encourage them to enlist. However, many soldiers were not interested in settling the frontier and sold their land to speculators and large companies. The volume of sales became so great that bounty warrants were quoted on the New York Stock Exchange (6).

Some timber operators made no pretense of purchasing timberlands but simply set up lumber mills on the public domain and began cutting trees. In other cases they purchased 40-acre (16-hectare) plots and proceeded to cut all the surrounding public timber on as much as a section of land. These were known as "round forties" or "rubber forties" because of the flexibility of the boundaries.

The beginning of the end of timber stealing occurred in 1877 with the appointment of Carl Schurz as secretary of the interior. Schurz immigrated to America from Germany where forest resources were scarce and carefully husbanded. He advocated a similar approach to forest management in the United States. He also took exception to the popular belief that timber resources were inexhaustible. In his first annual report Schurz predicted that within 20 years the timber supply would not be capable of meeting national needs (8).

Schurz began vigorously to enforce laws against timber stealing (6). His authority was based primarily on an act of March 2, 1831, known as the Timber Trespass Law, which imposed both fines and imprisonment on those who cut timber from the public lands without authorization. In 1850, the U.S. Supreme Court upheld the act and extended it to include any trespass on public lands.

## Conservation and Preservation of the Forests.

The period from 1830 to 1891 was characterized primarily by rapid disposal and exploitation of the public domain. But the myth that timber and other resources were inexhaustible, although still widely held, was gradually eroding, and a concern for conservation and preservation was intensifying. As early as 1801 publications by Andre Michaux and his son, after their travels through the forests of the United States, noted "an alarming destruction of the trees" and warned that an increasing population would make timber scarce (6). By 1849 the commissioner of patents was also warning of timber shortages (6); in 1864, George Perkins Marsh published his famous book *Man and Nature*, which pointed out the undesirable consequences of forest destruction. Beginning about 1866 annual reports from the secretary of the interior and the commissioner of the General Land Office regularly included an expression of concern about the exhaustion of forest resources.

In 1867, this concern was translated into action at the state level when the legislatures of both Michigan and Wisconsin appointed committees to investigate the potential long-term consequences of deforestation. The most dramatic state action was taken in 1885 by New York, when it created a "forest preserve" on state-owned lands in the Adirondack and Catskill mountains. In 1894, the new state constitution of New York forbade timber cutting on the preserve. Also in 1885, California established a State Board of Forestry and granted it police powers two years later.

Federal action aimed at forest conservation began about this same time. In 1874, a committee of the American Association for the Advancement of Science (AAAS) prevailed on President Ulysses S. Grant to ask Congress to create a commission of forestry (6). Congress responded by attaching an amendment to the Sundry Civil Appropriations Bill of 1876, which provided $2000 to hire someone to study forest problems in the United States. This act also established a precedent by assigning the position to the Department of Agriculture. Henceforth, federal forest management would be primarily a responsibility of this department.

Franklin B. Hough, who had chaired the AAAS committee on forest preservation, was appointed to the job of studying America's forests. He discharged his duties by publishing three monumental reports containing most of what was known about forestry in the United States at that time. Later he became chief of the Division of Forestry, which was subsequently given statutory permanence in the Department of Agriculture by an act on June 30, 1886. This division was the precursor of the Forest Service. In that same year, Bernard E. Fernow, who had studied forestry at Muenden in western Prussia, followed Hough as chief of the division.

The preservation movement, which was to have a profound effect on forest policy, also developed during this period. In 1832, George Catlin, a painter and explorer of the American West, called for establishment of "a nation's park" in the Great Plains, "containing man and beast, in all the wild and freshness of their nature's beauty!" (9). Catlin's plea for preservation was echoed by Henry David Thoreau in 1858, when he asked in an article in the *Atlantic Monthly*, "why should not we . . . have our national preserves . . . for inspiration and our true re-creation?" (10). Catlin and Thoreau were followed by other well-known preservationists such as Frederick Law Olmsted and John Muir. Together they helped to found our present system of national parks and monuments beginning with Yellowstone National Park, which was set aside in 1872 "as a public park or pleasuring-ground for the benefit and enjoyment of the people," Sequoia and General Grant (now Kings Canyon) national parks followed in 1890.

## Important Features of the Period 1830–1891.

The period from 1830 to 1891 included three separate movements. Disposal of the public domain and intensive cutting of forests characterized an exploitive movement that occurred at the same time as—and in part caused—two other

movements: scientific management of resources and preservation of natural scenery. One major success in meeting the goals of the period stands out clearly. About 405 million hectares, which was nearly the same amount of land as entered the public domain during this period, were sold to private owners (6). However, much of this land did not end up in the hands of small farmers but was added to large corporate holdings. Another major success was the encouragement of western expansion and settlement, but here, too, the benefits were mixed with problems. A quarter-section of land that was just the right size for the East, where water was plentiful, was completely inadequate for sustaining a farmer in the arid West. Thus many farms were abandoned and abused. Finally, prodigious amounts of timber products were produced, but a legacy of cutover and deteriorated land was handed to subsequent generations. Nevertheless, this period ended with a rapidly growing and prosperous nation that had already taken major steps toward improving the use of its forests.

## Crystallizing a Philosophy (1891–1911)

The circumstances that affected forest policy in the United States between 1891 and 1911 were different from those of any previous period in American history. The shift from rural to urban life was accelerating. In 1790 only 2.8 percent of the population lived in cities with 10,000 or more people; by 1900 it was 31.8 percent (7). An urban population often perceives natural resources differently than a rural population, whose livelihood is directly and visibly dependent on the land. Thus this period clearly contains the conflict between urban residents of the Eastern Seaboard and their strong desire for preservation, and the rural residents of the West who wanted to expand their economy by developing resources.

This was the first period that began without a geographic frontier. In 1890, the superintendent of the census in Washington announced that a frontier line no longer existed (3). All of the United States and its territories contained settlements. Although the myth of inexhaustible resources had been eroding for decades, the loss of the frontier and the scalped land of the once heavily forested East made it obvious that something had to be done to conserve forests and other resources. A "timber famine" was seen as a real possibility.

Three general domestic goals of residents of the United States during this period strongly affected forest policies: defend the rights of the people, maintain a continuous supply of timber, and prevent waste in the exploitation of natural resources, particularly timber.

**Creation of Forest Reserves.** Perhaps the single most important forest policy ever enacted in the United States was the General Revision Act of 1891. Important provisions of the act included the repeal of the Timber Culture Act of 1878 and the Preemption Act of 1841, as well as the imposition of restrictions on the Homestead Act of 1862 to discourage speculation and fraud. What made this act so important to forestry was Section 24, which provided that "the President of the United States may, from time to time, set apart and reserve any part of the public lands wholly or in part covered with timber or undergrowth, whether of commercial value or not." Thus, the authority granted to the president by Section 24 (also known as the Forest Reserve Act) to set aside forest reserves from the public domain served as the basis for the U.S. system of national forests.

Less than a month after the Forest Reserve Act passed, on March 30, 1891, President William Henry Harrison established the Yellowstone Park Forest Reservation. Over the next two years he proclaimed an additional fourteen forest reserves, bringing the total to over 5.3 million hectares. A storm of protests from western interests followed these proclamations, in part, because the Forest Reserve Act did not include any provision for using the reserves. Consequently, the argument made by westerners that the forest reserves were "locked up" and could not be used was absolutely correct.

Logging, mining, or any other activity could not be legally conducted on the reserves. Nevertheless, there were too few agents and too little money to enforce the law, so timber stealing proceeded unobstructed.

Just a few months before the Forest Reserve Act passed Congress, Gifford Pinchot, the most famous person in the history of American forest policy, returned home from Europe where he had been studying forestry under Dr. Dietrich Brandis in France. Pinchot's motto, from the beginning of his career until the end, was "forestry is tree farming" (11). He did not believe in preserving forests but in using them "wisely."

Pinchot emerged on the national scene in forest policy when he joined a forest commission of the National Academy of Sciences, which was formed at the request of Secretary of the Interior Hoke Smith. The commission was charged with studying the question of forest reserves and their administration. In addition, it was supposed to make recommendations for new legislation that would help break the deadlock in Congress over the management of the reserves.

The commission submitted a list of proposed forest reserves to President Grover Cleveland without a plan for their management. Pinchot argued, to no avail, that such a plan should accompany the list so that western congressional representatives would know that the commission wanted to use the forests and not simply lock them up. Cleveland had only ten days left in office and was forced to act on the commission's recommendation. On February 22, 1897, he set aside an additional 8.6 million hectares of forest reserves.

Once again a storm of criticism arose in Congress, and legislation was introduced to nullify Cleveland's actions. Congress acted quickly to resolve the issue. On June 4, 1897, the Sundry Civil Appropriations Act was passed with an amendment (known as the Organic Administration Act) introduced by Senator Richard Pettigrew of South Dakota, providing that "no public forest reservation shall be established except to improve and protect the forest . . . for the purpose of securing favorable conditions of water flows, and to furnish a continuous supply of timber.'' The act excluded lands principally valuable for mining and agriculture, and it authorized the secretary of the interior to make rules for the reserves ''to regulate their occupancy and use and to preserve the forests thereon from destruction.''

The language in this act dated back as far as 1893 when Representative Thomas C. McRae introduced the first in a long series of bills for the management of the forest reserves. Early opposition to these bills came from western senators whose constituents were accustomed to obtaining their timber from the public lands without paying a fee. When a compromise was finally reached to handle western criticism, eastern senators continued to block passage of the bill because they feared that opening up the reserves would lead to more abuses by timber owners. Cleveland's bold action in setting aside reserves served as the catalyst to overcome the impasse in Congress. Enough votes were obtained to pass the bill because even some eastern senators thought the new reserves created a hardship for people in the West.

The forest reserves were placed in the hands of the General Land Office, which was still, as Pinchot put it, governed by ''paper work, politics, and patronage'' (11). Reform seemed impossible, so when Pinchot became head of the Division of Forestry on July 1, 1898, he immediately set out to gain control of the reserves.

Pinchot was aided in his quest by his good friend Theodore Roosevelt, who became president in September, 1901, after President William McKinley was assassinated. Roosevelt and Pinchot were both master politicians—persuasive, dedicated, and equipped with boundless energy (Figure 1.5). They were both driven by the same ideas about the meaning of conservation, epitomized by such words and phrases as *efficiency, wise use, for the public good,* and *the lasting good of men.* To them conservation was the ''antithesis of monopoly'' and, although wealthy themselves, they both abhorred

''concentrated wealth,'' which they viewed as ''freedom to use and abuse the common man'' (11).

With the help of Roosevelt, Pinchot accomplished his goal to gain custody of the forest reserves. The reserves were transferred from the Department of the Interior to the Department of Agriculture by the Transfer Act of 1905. One month later, March 3, 1905, the name of Pinchot's agency was changed to the Forest Service. In 1907, the forest reserves were renamed the national forests.

Management of the forest reserves changed dramatically under the new regime. On the day the Transfer Act was signed, Secretary of Agriculture James Wilson sent a letter to Pinchot outlining the general policies he was to follow in managing the reserves. Actually, the letter was written by Pinchot (6). In keeping with the philosophy of the time, the letter required that the reserves be used ''for the permanent good of the whole people, and not for the temporary benefit of individuals or companies.'' It also stipulated that ''all the resources of the reserves are for use'' and ''where conflicting interests must be reconciled the question will always be decided from the standpoint of the greatest good of the greatest number in the long run'' (6). These lofty, although somewhat ambiguous, goals still serve to guide Forest Service administration.

Many additional landmark policies affecting U.S. forests were enacted during this period. For example, the precedent set by the Forest Reserve Act was copied in the American Antiquities Act of 1906. This act authorized the president ''to declare by proclamation . . . objects of historic or scientific interest'' on the public lands ''to be national monuments.'' This gave the lands protection against commercial utilization and opened them up for scientific, educational, and recreation purposes. By the end of his administration Roosevelt had used the act to set aside eighteen national monuments, including what later became Grand Canyon, Lassen Volcanic, and Olympic national parks.

Roosevelt enlarged the area of the forest reserves more than any other president. At the beginning of his term there were 41 reserves totaling 18.8 million

**Figure 1.5**   Chief forester Gifford Pinchot (right) with President Theodore Roosevelt on the riverboat *Mississippi* in 1907. (Photograph courtesy of U.S.D.A. Forest Service.)

hectares, and by 1907 he had increased the number of reserves (now called national forests) to 159, bringing their total area up to 61 million hectares (12). Roosevelt's zealous expansion of the forest reserves moved Congress to pass an act on March 4, 1907, revoking his authority to establish reserves in six western states. Roosevelt left the act unsigned until after he had signed proclamations reserving an additional 30.4 million hectares of forestland (12).

The end of this period is marked by a controversy between Pinchot and Secretary of the Interior Richard A. Ballinger that led President William Howard Taft to fire Pinchot as chief of the Forest Service on January 7, 1910. Actually, Pinchot had decided several months earlier to "make the boss fire him" (12). He was upset by the policies of the Taft administration that, in his view, did not carry on the traditions of Roosevelt and the philosophy of conservation.

**Important Features of the Period 1891–1911.** The period from 1891 to 1911 was undoubtedly one of the most colorful and active in the history of American forest policy. The goals that were formulated were clearly followed throughout the period. Nevertheless, eliminating waste—and bringing the management of national forests up to the standard hoped for by Pinchot and Roosevelt—was too great a task to be accomplished with meager funding and little time. The greatest forest policy accomplishments of the period were the creation of the Forest Service, the establishment of a system of national forests, and the crystallization of a utilitarian philosophy of conservation to guide their management.

## Organization, Action, and Conflict (1911–1952)

The United States and most of the rest of the world faced enormous difficulties and hardships during the period from 1911 to 1952. The world went to war twice, taking a frightening toll in human lives and property, and underwent the agonies of the Great Depression. In the United States disastrous floods regularly ripped through some settled valleys, while large expanses of potentially good agricultural land in the West remained unused for lack of water. Intolerable working conditions and low wages drove urban laborers out into the streets to protest. At the same time, on the Great Plains, a lack of understanding of drought cycles and proper farming practices drove farmers off the land as the soil and their livelihood blew out of the region during the dust-bowl era.

These were difficult years, but they were also relatively simple years in the sense that the problems faced were clearly understood by most people, and the goals, although always controversial, were also fairly clear. In forest policy, these goals included: (1) keeping the watersheds of navigable streams and rivers covered with vegetation so that flooding and sedimentation could be reduced, (2) keeping sufficient wood flowing out of the forests to meet the nation's requirements for building its industries and successfully ending its wars, (3) protecting the nation's forests from overexploitation and losses due to insects, diseases, and fire, and (4) using the production of forest resources from public lands to aid in reducing unemployment during the Great Depression and in stabilizing the economies of communities dependent on local forests. In addition, a small but influential segment of society was also inspiring the public to preserve tangible parts of the United States' cultural and natural heritage.

**Conservation versus Preservation.** Toward the end of Pinchot's term in the Forest Service, the conservation philosophy of people such as Catlin, Thoreau, and Muir was gaining ground. Private organizations were rapidly forming to represent this view. These "aesthetic conservationists," or preservationists, differed significantly from "Pinchot" or "utilitarian conservationists." Preservationists concentrated their efforts on protecting natural beauty and scenic attractions from the lumberjack's axe and miner's pick by placing them within national parks. On the other hand, the utilitarian conservationists' philosophy was rooted in the idea that resources must be "used." They referred to preservationists as "misinformed nature lovers" (12). This difference of opinion finally led preservationists to break away from the organized conservation movement because it was dominated by the utilitarian philosophy.

When conservationists and preservationists ceased to be allies, conflict over the disposition and management of the public lands was inevitable. This conflict has grown in intensity over the years. By the late 1960s and 1970s, it dominated American forest policy.

During the early 1900s the conflict between preservationists and conservationists centered on dividing up the public lands. At first, preservationists focused their efforts on creating a separate agency to manage the national parks. Pinchot countered this move by trying to consolidate the national parks with the national forests. Although the preservationists succeeded in gaining the support of Taft and Ballinger, Pinchot, arguing that such an agency was "no more needed than two tails to a cat" (12), carried enough influence in Congress to block the proposal. However, Secretary of the Interior Franklin K. Lane came to the rescue of preservationists. He placed all national parks and monuments under the jurisdiction of an assistant to the secretary. He then filled the post with Steven T. Mather, a wealthy preservationist who helped usher the National Park Act of 1916 through Congress and was later selected as director of the Park Service. Thus preservationists obtained an administrative home in the Department of the Interior for their parks and monuments, and they gained a champion to expand and protect the national park system.

Pinchot was no longer chief of the Forest Service, but his successors during the early 1900s, Henry S. Graves (1910–1920) and William B. Greely (1920–1928), were utilitarian conservationists. Furthermore, Pinchot continued to be influential with Congress, both as an individual and through the National Conservation Association. Thus the adversaries were firmly entrenched in two separate agencies within two separate departments of the federal government, and each had its own constituency. Their first contest centered on the fact that the national forests contained most of the public land suitable for national parks, and the Park Service was anxious to take these lands away from the Forest Service.

The Forest Service was not really hostile toward national parks, but as Chief Forester Graves said, "the parks should comprise only areas which are not forested or areas covered only with protective forest which would not ordinarily be cut" (8). The problem was philosophical and, of course, territorial. The Forest Service, like any other government agency, did not want to give up land it was already managing. Therefore, the Forest Service countered Park Service advances by vigorously resisting the withdrawal of national forest land for park purposes. The Forest Service also continued its efforts to develop a recreation program that it hoped would make new national parks unnecessary.

**Forest Recreation.** The formulation of a recreation program by the Forest Service also represented a response to a technological innovation—the automobile—and the expansion of roads pleasure-seekers could use to gain access to the national forests. In 1907, there were about 8000 kilometers (4,971 miles) of roads in all the national forests. The need for roads increased with automobile use and, as a result, between 1916 and 1921 over $33 million was spent on roads in and near national forests (10). These roads brought in so many recreationists that rangers, concerned about fire hazards and other conflicts with commodity uses, sought to discourage them by concealing entrances to new trails and leaving roads unposted (10). The tide of recreationists could not be turned, however, and the Forest Service reluctantly began providing for their needs.

One of the most celebrated accomplishments in national forest recreation was the establishment of the nation's first designated wilderness area. In 1918, a road was proposed that would cut through the watershed of the Gila River in New Mexico. Aldo Leopold, an assistant district forester for the Forest Service, protested against building the road, claiming that "the Gila is the last typical wilderness in the southwestern mountains" (10). He then proposed designating the watershed a "wilderness" without roads or recreational developments. No action was taken on his proposal and, in 1921, when an appropriation of $13.9 million for developing forest roads and highways passed Congress, he publicly expressed his concern for wilderness protection. He defined wilderness as "a continuous stretch of country preserved in its natural state, open to lawful hunting and fishing, big enough to absorb a two weeks pack trip, and kept devoid of roads, artificial trails, cottages or the works of man" (10). This definition has remained relatively unchanged until the present.

It took nearly three more years for Leopold to convince the district forester of New Mexico and Arizona to approve the Gila Wilderness plan. This was only a local decision. However, with mounting criticism of the Forest Service from preservationists, and Park Service acquisition of national forest lands on the increase, Greely established a national wilderness system in 1926.

Although the Forest Service had to spend part of its time defending itself against incursions from the Park Service, it was still a popular and aggressive agency. The momentum of the Roosevelt-Pinchot era had slowed somewhat, but the Forest Service maintained a strong sense of mission. It advanced on four fronts: expanding national forests in the East; promoting forest research; developing the national forests; and regulating forest practices on private land.

Agitation from preservationists for adding lands to the national forest system in the East continued. As early as 1901 the Appalachian National Park Association joined with other private organizations to petition Congress for the preservation of southern Appalachian forests. By that time, however, most public lands in the East had already passed into private ownership. This meant that additional na-

tional forests would have to be purchased. Congress responded by authorizing studies of the question, but no purchases were made. A few years later the Society for the Protection of New Hampshire Forests joined forces with the Appalachian group and together they succeeded in securing passage of the Weeks Act of 1911 (11).

The Weeks Act specified that the federal government could purchase lands on the headwaters of navigable streams and appropriated funds for their acquisition. This restrictive language reflected a congressional view that the federal government only had the power to purchase national forests if it appeared that the purchase would aid navigation. Naturally, the advocates of eastern forest reserves, including Pinchot, shifted their arguments from an emphasis on the forests themselves to the role of forests in preventing floods and reducing sedimentation. These arguments worked, and, influenced by the great Mississippi flood of 1927, Congress accelerated the acquisition of forestland when it passed the Woodruff-McNary Act of 1928 (13). By 1961 over 8.1 million hectares of forestland, mostly in the East, had been purchased under this act (8).

**Forestry Research.** The second major task of the Forest Service was expanding its efforts in forest research. Documenting the relationship between forests and streamflow was part of the reason for the rise in forest research activity. However, reforesting cutover lands, increasing yields, and reducing waste through greater utilization of trees were also important goals of research.

Raphael Zon deserves much of the credit for the organization of research within the Forest Service. His emphasis was on applied research; he stated that "science . . . must serve mankind" (13). In 1908, he presented a plan to Pinchot for establishing forest experiment stations on key national forests. Pinchot, recalling his response, said that "I had seen forest experiment stations abroad and I knew their value. The plan, therefore, was approved at once" (11). When Pinchot left office in 1910, he had established two forest experiment stations and he had authorized the construction of the Forest Products Laboratory in Madison, Wisc.

Over the next fifteen years Congress was extremely tightfisted with research funding. A big boost came in 1925, when enough funds were appropriated to add six new experiment stations. Yet funding was haphazard at best, severely limiting research activities. With Greely's enthusiastic support, the Forest Service obtained the assistance of private groups to campaign in Congress for long-term research funding. Their efforts paid off in 1928 with passage of the McSweeney-McNary Act. This act raised research to the same level of importance as other Forest Service functions, such as timber and grazing. Furthermore, the act not only increased appropriations for forest research but also authorized a nationwide survey of timber resources in the United States.

**Civilian Conservation Corps.** Development of the national forests received increased attention when President Franklin D. Roosevelt established the Civilian Conservation Corp (CCC) by executive order on April 5, 1933, as part of his New Deal. In a March 21, 1933, document asking Congress for its support of the CCC, Roosevelt detailed his goals as not only "umemployment relief" during the Great Depression but also advance work in "forestry, the prevention of soil erosion, flood control and similar projects." He also thought of the CCC's work as an investment "creating future national wealth" (9).

Between 1933 and 1942, when the CCC started to disband because of World War II, over two million people had worked in the program with as many as one-half million enrolled at one time (Figure 1.6). The Forest Service received nearly half the projects, but the Park Service and other federal agencies also

**Figure 1.6**   CCC Camp in the territory of Alaska. (Photograph courtesy of U.S.D.A. Forest Service.)

received substantial aid from the program (8). Although the CCC was criticized for hiring enrollees from lists of Democrats (8), its accomplishments outweighed its problems. Young people built trails, thinned forests, fought fires, planted trees, and constructed campgrounds and other facilities. Their efforts substantially advanced the development of the national forests.

**Regulation and Control of the Forests.** The final and most controversial action by the Forest Service during the period was its attempt to regulate private forest management. The agency had played an advisory role in private timber management until passage of the Transfer Act of 1905, when much of its attention shifted to managing the newly acquired national forests. This cooperation with private owners was generally accepted as beneficial by all concerned at the time. However, Pinchot later recalled that he had been ''misled'' into thinking that timber owners were interested in ''practicing forestry'' (11).

The regulation issue created a split in the ranks of professional foresters. Pinchot led the faction in favor of federal control, and Graves and Greely led the fight for state control. Pinchot argued that ''forest devastation will not be stopped through persuasion'' and his solution was ''compulsory nation-wide legislation'' (6). Pinchot firmly believed that state legislatures were too easily controlled by the lumber industry. Only the federal government, in his view, had the power to enforce regulations. The Forest Service argued that federal regulation was unconstitutional and that the federal role should be aimed more at cooperation than at direct intervention in private forest management.

The line was drawn and Congress became the battlefield. Bills were introduced favoring each position and both sides stood firm. Pinchot said it was ''a question of National control or no control at all'' (8). The two bills were stalemated in Congress. Greely then proposed to break the deadlock with a compromise measure that dropped regulation entirely and emphasized fire control. After all, he

contended, timber cutting was ''insignificant'' in comparison to wildfires as a cause of deforestation (8). Pinchot agreed (8), and Congress passed the Clarke-McNary Act of 1924.

Although the Weeks Act previously authorized state and federal cooperation in fire control, the Clarke-McNary Act expanded this cooperation and extended it into other areas as well. For example, it enabled the secretary of agriculture to assist states in growing and distributing planting stock, and in providing aid to private owners in forest management. These two acts stimulated the establishment of state forestry organizations throughout the country.

The Clarke-McNary Act also set a precedent by authorizing the purchase of land in the watersheds of navigable streams for timber production as well as streamflow protection. The purchase of timberland, particularly after it had been logged, was one approach to solving the deforestation problem on which most parties could agree. Overall, the Clarke-McNary Act is one of the most important pieces of legislation in the development of American forest policy.

World War II increased the nation's appetite for timber. Not only was it necessary to harvest great quantities of timber from both public and private lands, but certain important species were also in short supply. For example, Sitka spruce was needed for airplane construction, and at one point loggers were almost allowed to move into Olympic National Park to cut the necessary trees. Rapid cutting to satisfy wartime timber requirements intensified the public regulation controversy. Timber executives mounted a major publicity campaign to thwart further attempts at federal regulation. They were particularly concerned that conditions might be attached to cooperative funds allocated under the Clarke-McNary Act.

The heightened pressure on forest resources induced by the war, and the regulation controversy, motivated passage of a number of pieces of forestry legislation. The continued threat of federal control helped lumber interests decide to support state laws as the least offensive alternative. By 1939 five states had enacted legislation to curtail destructive cutting practices, but they were generally ineffective. The Oregon Forest Conservation Act of 1941 set the precedent for more effective state action. This law was aimed primarily at securing and protecting tree reproduction, and it included several specific and even quantitative guidelines. Lumber owners could only deviate from practices specified in the law if they first obtained state approval for an alternative timber management plan. The state forester was also authorized to correct problems on timberlands caused by violating the law and to charge the cost to the owners. Similar acts were passed in Maryland (1943), Mississippi (1944), Washington (1945), California (1945), and Virginia (1948). Other states, such as Massachusetts (1943), Vermont (1945), New York (1946), and New Hampshire (1949), relied more on incentives and voluntary actions to control timber cutting on private land (6).

At the federal level, two major forest policies were enacted. In 1944, federal income tax laws were amended to allow any timber owner to declare net revenue from timber sales as capital gains instead of as ordinary income. This law reduced taxes for timber owners to encourage them to retain forestland in timber production. It was also supposed to discourage them from abandoning the land to avoid paying delinquent taxes. Roosevelt vetoed the bill, but his veto was overridden by Congress (8).

The second measure passed by Congress was the Sustained Yield Forest Management Act of 1944. Sustained yield, in a general sense, means that a particular area is managed to produce roughly equal annual, or regular periodic, yields of a resource such as timber. This concept can be traced back hundreds of years in Europe where timber resources were scarce, and predictable and steady yields were essential. The U.S. frontier economy made such an approach politically difficult to adopt until war-induced shortages helped to make the idea more acceptable.

The Sustained Yield Forest Management Act was not aimed at national needs. Instead, it focused on safeguarding the economies of forest-dependent communites from local timber shortages. The act authorized the secretaries of interior and agriculture to establish sustained-yield units composed of either federal timberland alone or, where ownerships intermingled, a mixture of private and public timberland. Thus, the secretaries could enter into long-term agreements with private forest owners to pool their resources with the government to supply timber to local mills. Opposition from small companies and labor unions prevented the establishment of more than one cooperative sustained-yield unit. However, the Forest Service did manage to establish five federal sustained-yield units on national forests (8).

The rapid and destructive cutting practices associated with the need to pursue a war left millions of hectares that were not reproducing timber. Equally troubling was the fact that timber cutting during and immediately after the war exceeded forest growth. The Forest Service again laid the blame squarely on the shoulders of private timberland owners. The debate became more acrimonious as each side argued its position. Often technical arguments were set aside and the issue degenerated into an emotional debate. One timber industry spokesperson accused the Forest Service of leading the country into "totalitarian government and ultimately socialism" and even called the assistant chief of the Forest Service, Edward C. Crafts, a "dangerous man" because Crafts felt the public had the right to protect its interests in private land (8).

The debate was settled when Dwight D. Eisenhower let it be known during his presidential campaign that he was against "federal domination of the people through federal domination of their natural resources" (8). Eisenhower was elected president in 1952 and made Governor Sherman Adams of New Hampshire his presidential assistant. Adams had been a lumberman and had stated a year earlier that natural resources could be conserved and distributed "without succumbing either to dictatorship or national socialism" (8). The Forest Service, sensing that the election might bring a philosophical change, moved to have Richard E. McArdle appointed chief, in part because he was not identified with the regulation issue (14). The decision proved to be sound. McArdle dropped the Forest Service campaign for regulation and retained his position through the change of administrations.

## Important Features of the Period 1911–1952.

An evaluation of forest policies between 1911 and 1952 shows the usual mixture of successes and failures. The goal of preventing over-exploitation of forest resources conflicted with furnishing the armed forces with the wood needed to help fight World Wars I and II. Maintaining a forest cover in the headwaters of navigable streams was only partially accomplished. All such watersheds could not be purchased, and cutover lands that were purchased were not always reforested. Similarly, technological constraints and shortages of money and workers during much of the period made it difficult to protect forests adequately from insects, diseases, and fire.

Nevertheless, at least four major accomplishments can be cited for this period, although none of them were considered major societal goals when the period began in 1911. The national park system grew in size to include some of the nation's most scenic areas, and a new agency was established to coordinate their management. Next, a wilderness system was established by the Forest Service. Another important accomplishment was the development of cooperative arrangements in forest management among state, federal, and private timberland owners. Finally, the CCC converted the adversity of the Great Depression into one of the most positive contributions ever made to the development of U.S. forests.

## Adjusting to Complexity (1952–1980)

Although the forest policy problems of previous periods were never really simple, they still seem more comprehensible then the problems faced by contemporary society. Since World War II, the United States has experienced unparalleled material affluence and technological advances that, along with a burgeoning population, have heightened competition for essential natural resources. After World War II came a rapid growth in demand for timber, particularly for housing construction. This demand resulted in a continuation of destructive logging practices. Timber needs were too great to be satisfied from private lands alone, so heavy logging also reached into the national forests.

At the same time, the prosperity that was supported by the rapid exploitation of natural resources also made it possible for people to spend more of their leisure time in the nation's forests. Extractive use and recreational use, other than hunting, generally conflict with each other. However, the issues were broader than those that produced the debates between preservationists and utilitarian conservationists. Preservation was only one of many environmental issues which society faced both then and now. All of these issues influenced the development of U.S. forest policy.

Forest policies were also influenced by such global events as the cold war, the war in Vietnam, and Watergate. The government's lack of candor concerning these problems caused a large segment of society to become more suspicious of many public officials. Consequently, distrust of those in authority, including professional foresters, was widespread. Public demands for citizen participation in resource-management decision making were largely a result of this lack of trust. Professional foresters were unprepared for this intense public scrutiny.

Most of the forest policy goals of the period between 1911 and 1952 were carried over into this period as well. In addition, there was a great need to find ways to minimize conflicts over the allocation of resources, and to provide a growing nation with more raw materials and services from a fixed land base. Unfortunately, achieving these goals had become more difficult because of the complexity of the period.

The termination of Forest Service efforts to impose federal regulation on private forest management in 1952 was a major turning point for the forestry profession. Foresters were accustomed to strong public support for their aggressive actions to improve forest management. Now they were on the defensive.

**Multiple Use of the Forests.** Recreational use of the national forests grew steadily during the pre-World War II years, but it never reached parity with timber production as an objective of forest management. Recreation was formally recognized as an objective in 1935 when the Division of Recreation and Lands was created in the Forest Service. Nevertheless, the main reason for spending money on recreation was to build campgrounds and other facilities to keep recreationists confined and out of the way of commodity uses. Fire prevention was also an important reason for concentrating people in campgrounds (15), particularly in southern California.

The huge demand for timber products after the war dominated the attention of professional foresters, so they tended to overlook the implications of the equally enormous growth in recreation that was also taking place. For example, recreation visits on national forests climbed from fewer than 30 million in 1950 to about 200 million in 1972 (16). The explosive rise in recreation spurred competition between government agencies over the authority to administer recreation on public lands. Again, the two agencies principally involved in the dispute were the Park Service and the Forest Service. The old idea, promoted in the 1930s, was revived that recreation should be separated from other forest uses and administered by the Park Service. By 1961, the Park Service and its supporters had plans to remove 57 areas from the national forests (15). In spite of its vigorous defense, the Forest Service lost a number of areas to the Park Service. For example, Kings Canyon and Olympic National Parks were both carved out of national forests.

Forest Service attempts to increase its recreation budget met with limited success. Part of the problem could be traced to a lack of statutory responsibility for providing recreational facilities on the national forests (15). The Forest Service had to find some way to increase its recreational budget and, at the same time, protect itself against what it viewed as unacceptable demands of the timber industry, the grazing industry, and the Park Service for exclusive use of certain national forest lands. The concept adopted for defending the agency was multiple use. In other words, the Forest Service felt that obtaining congressional endorsement to manage these lands for several uses, including grazing, wildlife, recreation, and timber, would both legitimate the agency's management of all of these resources and enhance its position when asking Congress for funds. The vehicle for the concept was the Multiple Use–Sustained Yield Act of 1960. Through this act Congress directed that the national forests should be managed for outdoor recreation, range, timber, watershed, and wildlife and fish purposes.

Although, in Edward C. Crafts's words, "the bill contained a little something for everyone" (18), it was nevertheless opposed by the timber industry, the Sierra Club (a preservationist group), and the Park Service. People in the lumber industry thought that timber had always been given the highest priority in national forest management and that the bill would eliminate this preferential treatment by placing all resources on an equal level. Their opposition to the bill was subsequently turned into mild support when the bill was amended to include the following phrase: "The purposes of this Act are declared to be supplemental to, but not in derogation of, the purposes for which the national forests were established as set forth in the Act of June 4, 1897" (10). In other words, they felt that since the Organic Administration Act of 1897 specified timber and water as the resources which forest reserves were meant to protect, these resources would be given a higher priority than other resources. However, today it is generally agreed that this ranking only covers establishing national forests and does not extend to their management (17, 18).

The Sierra Club opposed the multiple-use bill for two reasons. First, the members wanted wilderness added to the list of resources so that it would be considered equal to, but separate from recreation. Second, they believed that the real purpose of the multiple-use bill was to stop the Park Service from taking lands out of national forests to make national parks. The former issue was partially resolved when the bill was amended at the request of the Wilderness Society to state that the wilderness was "consistent with the purposes and provisions" of the bill (19). However, the Sierra Club and the Park Service were blocked in their attempt to include an amendment stating that creation of new national parks would not be affected by the bill (18). The Sierra Club and the Park Service were never satisfied with the bill. Nevertheless, only four months after the administration's recommendation was sent to Congress, the Multiple Use−Sustained Yield Act of 1960 was passed and signed into law by Eisenhower.

The Multiple Use−Sustained Yield Act has been eminently successful in accomplishing the Forest Service's goals. The Forest Service preserved its broad constituency; its political flexibility; and its varied responsibilities. However, the boost in congressional funding for nontimber resources that was expected to follow passage of the act did not materialize. Only wildlife management received a significant average increase in funding relative to Forest Service requests (17) (Figure 1.7).

One of the unresolved issues in the multiple-use concept involves priorities for allocating land to various uses. The Multiple Use−Sustained Yield Act evades the issue of priorities entirely. What it mandates is that all the uses mentioned are appropriate for the administration of the national forests; that all uses will be given equal consideration, that all uses will be managed according to sustained yield principles, and that the productivity of the land will not be impaired.

**The Wilderness System.** Forest Service problems with single-use advocates were not completely eliminated by the Multiple Use−Sustained Yield Act. There was still the matter of wilderness to be faced. The creation of a wilderness system may have aided the agency somehat in defending its boundaries, but it also created a preservation-oriented constituency that wanted to protect scenic and roadless areas of the national forests against the commodity-use programs of the Forest Service.

Over the years the Forest Service had been adding areas to its wilderness system and refining its administrative regulations. The agency also developed a classification scheme that included a continuum of levels of protection extending from primitive areas, where some roads and logging were permitted, to wild and wilderness areas where these activities were prohibited. However, in 1940 the Forest Service extended greater protection to primitive areas as well (10).

Wilderness enthusiasts watched as the Forest Service gradually reduced the size of wilderness, wild, and primitive areas. Logging roads advanced, and technology increased the feasibility of utilizing timber in remote areas, so pressures to open protected lands to harvesting also increased. Since the Forest Service could readily change the boundaries of protected lands, preservationists sought the increased security of congressional action for wilderness designation. In addition, they wanted to establish wilderness areas on other federal lands, particularly within national parks and monuments. After eight years of debate and eighteen public hearings the Wilderness Act of 1964 was passed by Congress (Figure 1.8).

The wilderness system created by the Wilderness Act began with setting aside 3.7 million hectares of land, within 54 areas, which the Forest Service originally identified as wilderness and wild areas. Bureau of Land Management (BLM) lands were not included under the Wilderness Act until passage of the Federal Land Policy and Management Act of 1976 (20). This act not only included wilderness among uses of the public domain, but also legislatively created the BLM and gave it land management responsibilities after more than 30 years had passed since the bureau was established by executive reorganization (20).

28

**Figure 1.7**    Bull moose on the Gallatin National Forest, Montana. (Photograph courtesy of U.S.D.A. Forest Service.)

One of the more interesting debates that emerged concerned whether or not wilderness was a renewable resource. The Forest Service stated that wilderness could not be renewed. In other words, the wilderness character of a piece of land could not be reestablished once it had been used for other purposes. On the other hand, preservation groups contended that "certain areas not wilderness . . . if given proper protection and management can be restored and regain wilderness qualities" (21). This was an important issue in the eastern United States because much of the public land had been used for timber production and agriculture.

The Forest Service resisted attempts to classify wilderness areas in the East because it felt that most of these lands no longer retained their original character. Instead, it proposed a new eastern roadless area system that would be less restrictive and separate from the national wilderness preservation system. Preservationists refused to accept this alternative and succeeded in pressuring Congress to pass the Eastern Wilderness Act of 1975. The act added

**Figure 1.8** Packing into the Pecos Wilderness Area of the
Santa Fe National Forest, New Mexico. (Photograph by Harold
Walter, courtesy of U.S.D.A. Forest Service.)

sixteen new areas to the wilderness system totaling nearly 83,772 hectares. An additional 50,587 hectares in seventeen areas were also set aside so that the secretary of agriculture could evaluate them for possible inclusion in the wilderness system. All of these areas were within national forests.

The nearly insatiable appetite of wilderness advocates for land was, and continues to be, far from satisfied. They broadened their sights to include all national forest roadless areas as well as congressionally designated wilderness study areas. The Forest Service responded in 1967 by conducting a nationwide inventory of roadless lands within national forests. To evaluate these lands for wilderness suitability, a procedure was devised known as RARE (Roadless Area Review and Evaluation). A total of 1449 sites, containing approximately 22.7 million hectares, were identified. In 1973, the chief of the Forest Service designated 235 of these sites for further study as possible wilderness areas.

Many criticisms of the RARE process were voiced by preservationists, so a new RARE II process was initiated in 1977. On January 4, 1979, Secretary of Agriculture Bob Bergland made public the results of RARE II. The department recommended to Congress that 6.1 million hectares of national forestlands be added to the wilderness system and that an additional 4.5 million hectares be held for "further planning" because of the need for more reliable information on mineral deposits. It was hoped that this recommendation would help to bring a rapid resolution to the question of how much more land should be classified as wilderness. However, preservationists reacted with "acute disappointment" to the recommendation. While preservationists were concerned that the recommendations fell short of what was needed, the timber industry argued that they were excessive (22). Clearly, the wilderness issue will be around for some time.

**The Clearcutting Issue.** The consumption of wood was increasing at the same time that environmental constraints, such as air and water pollution

control standards and restrictions on the use of pesticides and herbicides, were inhibiting the amount of timber that could be produced and harvested. Furthermore, nationwide net losses of timberland in all ownerships to nontimber purposes was averaging about 2 million hectares per decade. Consequently, foresters believed that at some point in the future, wood shortages could develop. Both preservationists and professional land managers recognized this problem. They disagreed, however, over which methods were best for producing timber.

The focal point of the debate over timber management practices centered on clearcutting. Clearcutting is a harvesting method that involves cutting all the trees on a certain area of land and then regenerating the site by natural seeding, seeding from aircraft, or planting. Preservationists claimed that clearcutting had "an enormously devastating environmental effect which includes soil destruction, stream siltation, and a stinging blow to the aesthetic sense" (23). Where properly applied clearcutting was not destructive, but little could be done to correct the unpleasant appearance of a recent clearcut.

Concern over management practices in the national forests erupted into a national debate on November 18, 1970, when the report *A University View of the Forest Service,* commonly known as the Bolle Report, was released by Senator Lee Metcalf of Montana and published in the *Congressional Record.* The report was prepared by a committee of scientists from the University of Montana at Metcalf's request. The committee's final report not only was highly critical of Forest Service management practices, but also showed that a deep division existed within the ranks of professional foresters.

The problem began in 1968 when residents of the Bitterroot Valley in Montana complained that the national forest surrounding them was being abused because of oversized clearcuts. Most disturbing to local residents, was the Forest Service practice of terracing steep mountain slopes to prevent erosion and improve reproduction where the timber had been removed. The Forest Service received a torrent of letters demanding that these practices be stopped.

The Forest Service responded by appointing a task force to conduct an impartial analysis of management practices in the Bitterroot National Forest. The task force was working on its study at about the same time that the Bolle committee was conducting its own investigation. However, the task force released its findings in April 1970, a full six months before the Bolle committee.

The task force report was remarkably candid relative to what would ordinarily be expected from a government agency that must evaluate its own actions. Task force members found, for example, that the attitude among many people on the national forest staff was "that resource production goals come first and that land management considerations take second place" (24). The Bolle committee concurred with many of the findings in the task force report, but it also found that "the Forest Service is primarily oriented toward timber harvest as the dominant use of national forests" (24). In short, the Forest Service had done an outstanding job of organizing itself to harvest timber, but it had failed to adjust to changing social values.

The Forest Service modified its forest management policies on the Bitterroot National Forest. However, the agency tended to disregard the national implications of public concerns over clearcutting. A few months after the Bolle committee report was released, the Subcommittee on Public Lands of the Senate Interior and Insular Affairs Committee, chaired by Senator Frank Church of Idaho, held hearings on management practices on the public lands. The Church subcommittee's attention was directed primarily at clearcutting in the national forests, especially in Montana, West Virginia, Wyoming, and Alaska. The subcommittee concluded that clearcutting had to be regulated. It also found that the Forest Service "had difficulty communicating effectively with its critics, and its image has suffered" (25). Although the Forest Service had taken some actions to adjust to public concerns over clearcutting, the subcommittee felt they "have made

little impact" (25). The Forest Service lost the opportunity to make widespread and forward-looking revisions in its management policies. Instead, it found itself in the position of accepting the timber-harvesting guidelines recommended by the Church subcommittee.

The most important timber-harvesting policies adopted after 1952 were generated by the issue of clearcutting hardwood forests in the Monongahela National Forest in West Virginia (Figure 1.9). Clearcutting replaced selective cutting on the forest in 1964, and the reaction was almost immediate. Concerned citizens rose up and pressured the West Virginia legislature to pass resolutions in 1964, 1967, and 1970, requesting investigations of Forest Service timber management practices. A Forest Service special review committee appointed to investigate the problem confirmed that some abuses had occurred (26). As a result, timber management policies were changed to encourage a wide variety of harvesting techniques. In addition, where clearcutting was necessary, the area cut was limited to 10 hectares or less, and the distances between clearcuts were regulated. Since many timber sales had already been contracted under the old 32-hectare limit, the reforms made by the Forest Service could not show immediate results on the ground (27).

Preservationists were not satisfied with these reforms. They wanted all clearcutting stopped immediately. On May 8, 1973, the Izaak Walton League of America and other preservation organizations filed suit alleging that clearcutting violated a provision in the Organic Administration Act of 1897 stating that only "dead, matured, or large growth of trees" could be cut and sold from the national forest. On December 3, 1973, Judge Robert Maxwell of the Northern District Federal Court of West Virginia accepted this interpretation of the act. His ruling had the effect of banning clearcutting on the national forests. The Fourth Circuit Court of Appeals unanimously upheld the lower court's decision in 1975, and the Forest Service halted all timber sales on national forests within the jurisdiction of the court. In 1976, the U.S. District Court of Alaska

**Figure 1.9**  Clear-cuts (background) on the Monongahela National Forest (Gauley district), West Virginia. (Photograph by R. L. Giese.)

used the same reasoning to issue a permanent injunction against timber harvesting on a large area of Prince of Wales Island. These and similar lawsuits essentially halted timber sales on national forests in six states (28).

Numerous bills were introduced in Congress to overcome the bottleneck in timber production that resulted from the Monongahela decision. A key provision in the preservationist-sponsored bill would have substituted legislative prescriptions on timber harvesting for the judgment of professional foresters. Acting with unusual speed, Congress passed the National Forest Management Act on September 30, 1976, and it was signed into law on October 22, 1976.

This act contained many important provisions that have yet to be fully evaluated. Nevertheless, the act did repeal the section of the Organic Administration Act of 1897 that served as the basis for the lawsuits against clearcutting within national forests. It also authorized the use of clearcutting in situations where it was found to be the ''optimal'' (''optimal'' was left undefined in the act) silvicultural treatment. The National Forest Management Act did not completely resolve the clearcutting controversy; however, it did bring about a period of calm in which all interests were willing to wait and see how the national forests would actually be managed.

**Judicial Involvement in Resource Policymaking.** The Monongahela decision illustrated the growing importance of the courts in forest policy development. Traditionally the courts have been restrained in both the number and scope of their reviews of administrative decisions. The judiciary gradually became more involved with administrative review as more and more preservationists, frustrated in their dealings with administrators, turned to the courts for relief. The number of suits was increased dramatically by the "Scenic Hudson" case of 1965, where the court decided that an organization whose principal interest was scenic beauty could sue government agencies (29). This decision opened the door to the courts and ushered in the age of judicial involvement in resource policymaking, including the Monongahela case.

Lawsuits are expensive, time consuming, and often embarrassing to the agency involved. Thus, threats of a lawsuit also increased direct participation by citizens in formulating agency policy. However, lawsuits were used most frequently as a delaying tactic to permit government agencies to make more informed decisions. Preservationists were aided materially in their ability to delay decisions by passage of the National Environmental Policy Act of 1969 (NEPA) and similar legislation enacted by various states. NEPA established a detailed procedure for assessing the environmental consequences of "federal actions significantly affecting the quality of the human environment." Legal challenges of noncompliance with these procedures had delayed decisions and, in many cases, brought about changes in forest policy. The large volume of environmental legislation passed by Congress and the states during the late 1960s and 1970s also provided increased opportunities for lawsuits.

**Additional Recent Legislation.** The Forest and Rangeland Renewable Resources Planning Act of 1974 (RPA) was, perhaps, the most far-reaching forest policy enacted during this period. RPA was part of a congressional effort to gain greater control of the budgetary process. Congress was reacting to what it perceived as a decline in its authority relative to the executive branch (30). Furthermore, Congress had always shown greater support for resource programs than the executive branch, particularly the Office of Management and Budget (OMB), and RPA was one means of pressuring the president to raise budget requests for natural resources management.

RPA initiated a procedure for setting goals and formulating forest policies. The act requires that the secretary of agriculture make periodic assessments of national needs for forest and rangeland resources. Then, at regular intervals, the secretary must make recommendations for long-range programs that the Forest Service is required to carry out in order to meet those needs. The assessment and program had to be transmitted to Congress in 1976 and again in 1980. A new assessment is required every ten years thereafter, and the program is to be revised every five years. In addition, the president is required to submit a statement to Congress with each annual budget explaining why the funding request differs from the program approved by Congress.

The Forest Service took advantage of the opportunity provided by RPA. In its first budget request under RPA, the agency asked for substantial increases in funds for managing all of the resources on the national forests. Congress responded favorably and President Jimmy Carter signed the appropriations bill for the 1978 fiscal year. The Forest Service budget was raised $275 million over the funding level of the previous fiscal year (31). Subsequent budgets, however, did not include such large increases.

**Important Features of the Period 1952–1980.** Although many important policies were developed during this period that dealt specifically with forest resources, a series of laws adopted for other purposes have also had a profound effect on forest management. These policies include enactment of NEPA, the Clean Air Act of 1970, the Federal Water Pollution Control Act of 1972, the Federal Environmental Pesticide Control Act of 1972, the Endangered Species Act of 1973, the Toxic Substances Control Act of 1976, and the Clean Water Act of 1977. Two major attributes of these policies are particularly important. First, they rely on complex and detailed processes of federal-state regulation and the exercise of police powers. Second, they were adopted to achieve broad environmental goals not specifically focused on forestry, yet they are becoming the dominant influence in forest policy development. For example, Section 208 of the Federal Water Quality Act amendments of 1972 required the establishment of "best management practices," which are enforceable, to control water pollution. These practices apply to timber harvesting and silvicultural treatments on public and private forestlands (32). Each of these policies has further complicated the forest policy process.

An evaluation of the development of American forest policy since 1952 shows a gradual transition to a more balanced and environmentally aware approach to resources management. The growing strength of groups with an interest in nontimber resources had helped to bring about this change, but timber production still remains paramount in the management of the nation's forests. Similarly, citizen participation in resource decision making has increased, yet no completely effective means, other than the traditional routes through the legislative and judicial processes, have been developed to reduce resource management conflicts. Much work remains to be done if equity is going to be achieved. In spite of the conflicts, however, nearly all groups have received substantially more forest resources, including timber products, than they obtained in any previous period. In addition, a legislative framework was provided for making even greater improvements in the years ahead. The current operations of the Forest Service are further discussed in Chapter 12, "Forestry at the National Level."

## CONCLUSION

In this chapter we have traced the historical development of forest policy in the United States as seen through the policy process. This approach necessarily simplifies history by focusing on certain aspects that conform to stages in the policy process while ignoring other potentially important aspects of policy development. Nevertheless, from this analysis certain general principles about forest resource policymaking emerge, principles that can be expected to remain unaltered into the foreseeable future.

First, the forest policy process is inherently subjective. What is the preferred forest policy of some groups is considered disastrous by other groups. Thus far, at least, the search for objective measures to set goals and assess forest policies has proved futile. No single criterion of what is "best" exists that, if satisfied, can ensure agreement among all contending interests. Everyone uses different standards to judge forest policies. Therefore it is highly unlikely that the policy process will be converted to science, nor will the authority to practice policymaking be delegated entirely to scientists and professionals. Active citizen participation will remain an essential part of the forest policy process.

Second, both the lack of objective criteria for assessing policies and citizen participation ensure that debate and compromise will also continue to be the central means for making decisions in the forest policy process. Clearly, anyone ambitious to become a professional forester must be prepared not only to engage in these debates but also to compromise. The time has passed, if indeed it ever existed, when the judgment of a professional will be accepted without question.

Finally, the forest policy process is growing more complex. As demands for forest resources increase, and the diversity of interests widens, the problem of providing for these needs in an equitable manner becomes more difficult. Important strides have been made toward solving this problem, but its ultimate resolution remains the major challenge of American forest policy.

## REFERENCES

1. K. E. Boulding, *Principles of Economic Policy*, Prentice-Hall, Englewood Cliffs, N.J., 1958.
2. J. E. Anderson, *Public Policy-Making*, Holt, Rinehart and Winston, New York, 1979.
3. G. F. Carter, *Man and the Land—A Cultural Geography*, Holt, Rinehart and Winston, New York, 1975.
4. H. E. Driver, *Indians of North America*, Univ. of Chicago Press, Chicago, 1961.
5. G. M. Day, *Ecol., 34*, 329 (1953).
6. S. T. Dana, *Forest and Range Policy: Its Development in the United States*, First Edition, McGraw-Hill, New York, 1956.
7. T. A. Bailey, *The American Pageant*, D. C. Heath, Boston, 1961.
8. H. K. Steen, *The U.S. Forest Service: A History*, Univ. of Washington Press, Seattle, 1976.
9. R. Nash, ed., *The American Environment*, Addison-Wesley, Reading, Mass., 1968.
10. J. P. Gilligan, "The development of policy and administration of Forest Service primitive and wilderness areas in the western United States," Vol. I and Vol. II, Ph.D. dissertation, Univ. of Mich., 1953.
11. G. Pinchot, *Breaking New Ground*, Harcourt, Brace, New York, 1947.
12. S. P. Hays, *Conservation and the Gospel of Efficiency*, Atheneum, New York, 1975.
13. D. C. Swain, *Federal Conservation Policy 1921–1933*, Univ. of California Press, Berkeley, 1963.
14. E. C. Crafts, "Forest Service researcher and Congressional liaison: An eye to multiple use," Forest History Society Pub., Santa Cruz, Calif., 1972.
15. F. W. Grover, "Multiple use in U.S. Forest Service land planning," Forest History Society Pub., Santa Cruz, Calif., 1972.
16. President's Advisory Panel on Timber and the Environment, Final report, U.S. Govt. Print. Office, 1973.
17. R. M. Alston, "FOREST—goals and decision-making in the Forest Service," U.S.D.A. For. Serv., Intermountain Forest and Range Exp. Sta. Res. Pap. INT-128, 1972.
18. E. C. Crafts, *Amer. For., 76*, 13, 52 (1970).
19. E. C. Crafts, *Amer. For., 76*, 29 (1970).
20. S. T. Dana and S. K. Fairfax, *Forest and Range Policy: Its Development in the United States*, Second Edition, McGraw-Hill, New York, 1980.
21. T. M. Bonnicksen, *California Today, 2*, (1974).
22. R. Pardo, *Amer. For., 85*, 10 (1979).
23. N. Wood, *Sierra Club Bulletin, 56*, 14 (1971).
24. A. W. Bolle, "A university view of the Forest Service," U.S. Govt. Print. Office, Doc. No. 91-115, 1970.
25. U.S. Senate Report, "Clearcutting on federal timberlands," Public Lands Sub-Committee, Committee on Interior and Insular Affairs, 1972.
26. G. O. Robinson, *The Forest Service*, Johns Hopkins Univ. Press, Baltimore, 1975.
27. L. Popovich, *J. For., 74*, 169, 176 (1976).
28. J. F. Hall and R. S. Wasserstrom, *Environ. Law, 8*, 523 (1978).
29. C. W. Brizee, *J. For., 73*, 424 (1975).
30. D. M. Harvey, "Change in Congressional policy-making and a few trends in resource policy," *In: Centers of Influence and U.S. Forest Policy*, F. J. Convery and J. E. Davis, eds., School of Forestry and Environmental Studies, Duke Univ., 1977.
31. L. Popovich, *J. For., 75*, 656, 660 (1977).
32. J. A. Zivnuska, *J. For., 76*, 467 (1978).

# 2

# FOREST REGIONS OF NORTH AMERICA AND THE WORLD

## John W. Duffield

Forestry is practiced where forests exist or may be created. Thus forestry has a geographic dimension, and this chapter deals with a specialized area of the science of plant geography. The general characteristics of forest regions around the world are discussed, with special emphasis on the forests of North America.

## CLASSIFICATION OF FOREST AREAS

Forests are classified in several different ways. Perhaps the simplest is the division of forests into two broad categories: *commerical* and *noncommercial*. The U.S. Forest Service classifies forests as commercial if they are capable of yielding at least 1.4 cubic meters of wood per hectare per year and are suitable now or prospectively for timber harvesting. Obviously, people in regions where wood and other forest resources are scarce make economic use of forests and woodlands that would not be classified as commercial by this definition.

More detailed classifications consider whether the forests are available for economic use and their general composition—that is, whether coniferous or broad-leaved. Table 2.1 gives the forest areas of the world according to a broad classification scheme of this type.

Plant ecologists have developed other classifications of forests. A recent scheme recognizes four principal types of closed high forests, as follows:

1. Mainly evergreen forests.
   (a) Broad-leaved evergreen forests (mainly in warmer climates).
   (b) Coniferous forests (mainly in cooler climates).
2. Mainly deciduous forests.
   (a) Drought deciduous forests (leaves shed in dry season).
   (b) Cold deciduous forests (leaves shed in winter).

The scheme outlined here is a great simplification of the system, which recognizes more than twenty kinds of high forest (10).

Trees grow in a wide range of climates and on a wide variety of soils, in all the continents except Antarctica. They will not grow unless the annual rainfall is more than about 300 millimeters, or in the absence of soil, or where the soil is permanently frozen, or where animal and human activities prevent their reestablishment. Where trees grow closely together, and this happens only where the annual rainfall is 400 millimeters or more, they form the principal or dominant component of *forests*. Where

**Table 2.1**
Forest Areas of the World (million km²)

| Region | Total Land Area | Forest Area | | | Percent of Total Forest |
|---|---|---|---|---|---|
| | | Coniferous | Broad-leaved | Total | |
| North America | 18 | 4.0 | 2.6 | 6.6 | 18.2 |
| Latin America | 20 | 0.3 | 7.4 | 7.7 | 21.3 |
| Europe (excl. Soviet Union) | 5 | 0.9 | 0.6 | 1.5 | 4.1 |
| Africa | 30 | 0.1 | 6.9 | 7.0 | 19.1 |
| Asia (excl. Soviet Union and Japan) | 27 | 0.7 | 4.1 | 4.8 | 13.3 |
| Japan | 1 | 0.1 | 0.1 | 0.2 | 0.6 |
| Soviet Union | 21 | 6.0 | 1.7 | 7.7 | 21.3 |
| Pacific area | 8 | 0.1 | 0.8 | 0.9 | 2.2 |
| World (excl. Antarctica) | 130 | 12.2 | 24.2 | 36.4 | 100.0 |

*Source.* "Outlook for timber in the United States," U.S.D.A. For. Serv., Res. Rept. No. 20, 1973.

trees occur in drier regions, they are more widely spaced, dominating plant communities known as *woodlands*.

## Effect of Physiography and Climate on Forest Types

The amount of soil moisture available to trees depends first on the amount of annual rainfall, and second, but almost as important, on the seasonal distribution of this rainfall. The physical properties of the soil and the evaporative loss of soil moisture also determine availability of soil moisture to the roots of the trees. In very general terms, the availability of soil moisture determines both the height that trees attain (more moisture = taller trees) and the spacing between trees (more moisture = closer spacing), so that if we seek a simple general explanation for the distribution of forest and woodland on the earth's surface, we can find it by comparing maps of vegetation types with maps showing distribution of precipitation. We can find a somewhat closer relationship between forests and climate if we take into account temperature and wind movement as they affect the effectiveness of precipitation in supplying moisture to trees. Warm air, especially when it is in rapid motion, causes rapid water loss from vegetation and soil and thus increases trees' demands for water while at the same time decreasing the availability of soil moisture to the trees. But cold, dry winter winds, especially in areas such as the North American Great Plains, can also subject trees to severe drying.

The elements of climate that determine the existence and productivity of forests—namely, precipitation, temperature, and wind movement—are in turn largely influenced by geographic position, such as latitude and the relative placement of water and land masses, and by physiographic position including elevation, steepness of slope, and the direction in which the slope faces (aspect). These geographic and physiographic features interact and compensate. The climate and vegetation found at high elevations but low latitude (near the equator) resemble those

found at lower elevations but higher latitude. Thus the forest vegetation at 2500 meters in the southern Appalachians at 35 degrees north latitude closely resembles that found near sea level at the mouth of the St. Lawrence River at 50 degrees north latitude. South-facing slopes in the Northern Hemisphere are generally warmer and drier than north-facing slopes so that the elevational limits of a given vegetation type are higher on south-facing slopes. Finally, proximity to oceans and other large bodies of water lowers summer temperatures and raises winter temperatures, so that the vegetation of a mild maritime climatic region such as the Pacific northwest is quite different from that of a harsher climatic region such as central Montana, at the same latitude. Moreover, temperature changes are generally smaller and less sudden in the coastal or maritime climates than in the continental climates, and we find that trees are generally less tolerant of sudden temperature change than grasses, herbs, and annual vegetation.

## Effect of Soils on Forest Types

Trees, like most dry-land vegetation, are rooted in soil. Soils, like the vegetation they support, vary from place to place, depending on: the parent material from which they are derived; the local climate as it affects weathering of rock to form soil; the manner in which soils are transported by wind, water, or volcanic action; the effects of vegetation and soil-inhabiting animals; and the length of time over which these factors have operated. In fact, distribution of vegetation types is both a cause and an effect of distribution of soil types. Vegetation type is influenced by soil texture (whether sandy or clay), by soil aeration, by chemical composition, and by various combinations of these and other soil properties. A striking effect of soil properties on forest vegetation type shows up in the distribution of loblolly, longleaf, and shortleaf pines, which are abundant east and west of the lower Mississippi River, but are absent from a wide zone of river-deposited soils in western Mississippi and northeastern Louisiana. Such soils are generally poorly aerated but of high fertility, often high in calcium, and favorable to the growth of grass and deciduous trees. In the forests of the Pacific slope of North America, soils derived from serpentine rocks support high proportions of such species as Jeffrey pine and incense cedar. In the southeastern United States, bald cypress grows in wet, poorly aerated soils that are unsuited to yellow poplar. A more detailed description of soils and how they affect forest types is given in Chapter 4.

In the following descriptions of the forest regions, certain species of trees are listed as important. Some species, such as Douglas-fir, loblolly pine, or sugar maple, are important as timber producers. Others, such as giant Sequoia or Montezuma cypress, are listed because of their large size, great age, or historical significance. Whitebark and limber pines make the lists because they provide scenic accents at high elevations.

## FOREST REGIONS OF NORTH AMERICA

### Northern Coniferous Forest

**Location and Extent.** Plant geographers refer to the northern coniferous forest as the boreal or northern forest, and in Eurasia by its Russian name, *taiga.* The northern coniferous forest is the largest forest region in North America; as shown in Figure 2.1 it stretches across Canada from eastern Quebec, its southern limit cutting across southern Quebec and Ontario, skirting along the north shore of Lake Superior, and then turning northwest across central Alberta and British Columbia. This forest reaches almost to the Bering Sea, and beyond this barrier continues westward across Siberia and the northern part of the Soviet Union, reaching almost to the Atlantic again in northern Sweden. North of this world-circling forest is the treeless tundra. The transition from forest to tundra is a woodland of scattered trees and shrubs, extending northward to Hudson Bay, and in western Canada almost to the Arctic Ocean. The northern coniferous forest

clothes a region of relatively low elevation, with many rivers, lakes, and swamps (7).

Forest regions can be mapped in general outline simply, but only by overlooking some of the interesting details. The northern coniferous forest appears in many places south of its generally described southern limits, at higher elevations. Examples are the White Mountains of Maine and New Hampshire, the Adirondacks of New York, and the southern Appalachians as far south as North Carolina.

**Principal Species.** Cold regions are notorious for having relatively few species of plants and animals, but large numbers of individuals representing each species. The northern coniferous forest is predominantly a spruce forest, with birches, poplars, and willows making up the broad-leaved component. In North America, the white spruce essentially defines the region, but black spruce is almost as commonly found, occupying the colder and wetter sites (Figure 2.2). Paper birch, quaking aspen, and willows (many species of *Salix,* both trees and shrubs) provide color for the traveler and browse for wildlife. Tamarack, the north's only deciduous conifer, is found throughout most of the region, but balsam fir drops out of the northwestern section. Jack pine, like balsam fir, is limited to the eastern and central portions of the region.

**Economic and Social Importance.** Until fairly recently, the chief economic importance of the boreal forest in North America was the population of mammals on which the fur trade was based. In the East, mineral resources and water power have been developed at the same time as the rise of the pulp and paper industry, based largely on spruce, but more recently on fir and jack pine.

The vast extent of the northern coniferous forest makes it an important actual and potential source of wood and fiber despite the fact that the growth rate of many of the forests in the region is severely limited by short growing seasons, thin and infertile soils, and poor soil drainage. Nevertheless, this

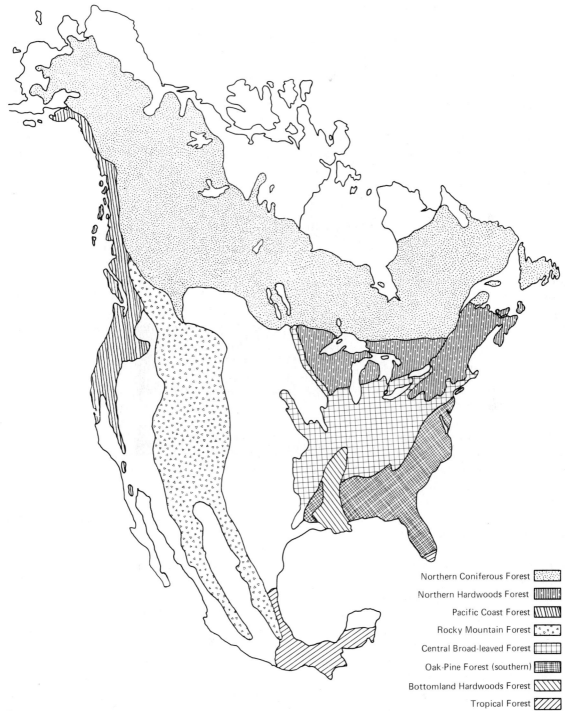

**Figure 2.1** Forest regions of North America.

Northern Coniferous Forest
Northern Hardwoods Forest
Pacific Coast Forest
Rocky Mountain Forest
Central Broad-leaved Forest
Oak-Pine Forest (southern)
Bottomland Hardwoods Forest
Tropical Forest

**Figure 2.2** Vast natural forests of white and black spruce occupy the southern part of the Alaskan interior. (Photograph by Henrich Gohl © Magnum Verlag AG, Basel/Switzerland.)

region offers values greater than those of commodity production. To the extent that wilderness still exists on our planet, the greatest expanses of wilderness are here. Nowhere else in North America is wildlife, from large animals such as moose to the smallest insects, so near to the levels of abundance found by the first European invaders. A major portion of the wildlife of the region is an international resource, for the waterfowl and other migra- tory birds that winter in the United States and Mexico breed in the north woods and the tundra.

## Northern Hardwoods

**Location and Extent.** In eastern North America, the northern hardwoods region lies to the south of the northern coniferous forest. The northern hardwoods reach their strongest development in the northern Great Lakes states, southeastern Canada, and northern New York and New England, and reach down the northern Appalachians into Pennsylvania. A more descriptive name for this region is the hemlock−white pine−northern hardwoods region (Figure 2.1).

**Principal Species.** In the northern hardwoods region, all the principal species of the northern coniferous forest are found, plus a good many more. Table 2.2 lists the principal species of the northern hardwoods region, omitting those found in the northern coniferous forest. The species are listed in the table more or less in the order of their abundance throughout the region. The first four give one of the commonly used names for the region—"beech, birch, maple, hemlock" (Figure 2.3). All of the species listed in the table are important timber producers, except possibly red maple and northern white cedar. Red maple is important because it is both widely distributed and abundant throughout the

**Table 2.2**
Some Important Species of the Northern Hardwoods Region

| Scientific Name | Common Name |
| --- | --- |
| *Fagus grandifolia* | American beech |
| *Betula allegheniensis* | Yellow birch |
| *Acer saccharum* | Sugar maple |
| *Tsuga canadensis* | Eastern hemlock |
| *Pinus strobus* | Eastern white pine |
| *Acer rubrum* | Red maple |
| *Pinus resinosa* | Red pine |
| *Populus grandidentata* | Bigtooth aspen |
| *Quercus rubra* | Northern red oak |
| *Fraxinus americana* | White ash |
| *Ulmus americana* | American elm |
| *Thuja occidentalis* | Northern white cedar |
| *Tilia americana* | American basswood |
| *Prunus serotina* | Black cherry |
| *Picea rubens* | Red spruce |
| *Pinus banksiana* | Jack pine |

region. White cedar is included for its wildlife and horticultural values.

White pine was found by the European explorers and settlers throughout the northern hardwoods region, but most abundantly in areas that had been cleared of hardwoods by ancient fires or blowdowns and on areas of sandier soils. It was particularly abundant on sites in Maine and the western Great Lakes states. In New England, it came in as an old-field "pioneer" following land abandonment in the last third of the nineteenth century. Many present-day hardwood or spruce fir forests in the region stand on land once occupied by white pine (1).

**Economic and Social Importance.** White pine was the first economic prize that European explorers, who would have preferred gold, found on the north Atlantic coast. White pine became a strategic material, vital for providing masts for the ships of England's navy and merchant fleets, especially during the frequent wars that cut off supplies of Scotch pine from the Baltic regions. Another early contribution of the northern hardwoods forest to Europe was northern white cedar, first brought to the attention of Jacques Cartier as a cure for scurvy (because of the vitamin C extracted by boiling the foliage) in the winter of 1535−1536 on the lower St. Lawrence River, and one of the first North American trees imported to the gardens of the Old World.

Until about 1900, white pine was North America's most important producer of timber, particularly along the southern and eastern edge of the northern coniferous forest. It was gradually replaced either by farms (some of which reverted to white pine as farmers moved west) or by spruce, fir, birch, and other broad-leaved species. The importance of white pine as a timber species diminished partly as the result of the fires and land clearing that followed the logging, partly because of the competition with southern pines and later with Douglas-fir, and partly because of the damage caused by a native insect, the white pine weevil, and a disease, white pine blister rust. The development of the pulp and paper indus-

**Figure 2.3** Mature sugar maple on the Nicolet National Forest, Wisconsin. (Courtesy of U.S.D.A. Forest Service.)

try extended into the northern hardwoods region, taking advantage of the older spruce-fir forests in the region and of the younger ones that in places followed the white pine.

Red pine, which is not as widely distributed as white pine, nor as useful for such a range of products, has had a similar history, but remains an important source of saw timber. Jack pine, once regarded as a sort of forest weed by timber owners interested only in white and red pine, has now become an important source of pulpwood. Red and jack pines are especially important in the western part of the region.

Although historically the northern hardwoods region was once one of the world's most important timber producers, its forests are of much greater importance today as places for people to enjoy outdoor recreation of all types and at all seasons. The northern hardwoods forest contains many of the animal species found in the northern coniferous forest—although less abundantly, to be sure. Moreover, the region is accessible to North America's greatest concentration of human population; it seems that recreation and water supply will be the dominant values of these forests, which will, however, remain important suppliers of wood and fiber.

## Pacific Coast Forests

**Location and Extent.** West of the Great Plains, the forests follow the mountain ranges of the Cordillera until they reach the northern coniferous forest in northwestern Canada. In general, the more westerly of these mountain ranges catch more rain and snow and have less extreme winters. These climatic differences account for denser, taller forests nearer the Pacific and are a cause of some contrasts in species composition between the Pacific slope and the Rocky Mountain forests.

The Pacific Coast forests extend from southeast Alaska along the coast ranges to Baja California and in a parallel chain farther inland include the Cascade-Sierra range in Washington, Oregon, and

California and the mountains of southern California. In the north, these forests extend upward from sea level; the most southerly sea-level forests are found in the vicinity of Monterey, California (Figure 2.1).

**Principal Species.** Conifers predominate in the Pacific Coast forests, but there are several important broad-leaved species, particularly in the southern portion of the region. At lower elevations in the foothills surrounding the Sacramento and San Joaquin valleys in California and the Willamette Valley in Oregon, the forest grades into woodland in which oaks and other broadleafs are intermixed with conifers (3).

Table 2.3 lists important trees of this region according to their occurrence in four subregions: the Coast Ranges, the Cascades, the Sierra Nevada, and the Sierra de San Pedro Martir in Baja California. From the table, it is evident that the number of species decreases in the more inland and southerly subregions. It is also true that, in general, the height of the trees decreases inland and southward (the northern coastal forests have been called oceanic or giant evergreen forests by some plant geographers). The forests of the Coast Ranges include the coast redwoods, some of which reach more than 110 meters in height. Other "giants" in the coastal forests are Sitka spruce, Douglas-fir, and western red cedar. The only other forests in the world where trees taller than 90 meters may be found are the stands of eucalyptus in the well-watered mountains of Tasmania and Victoria in Australia (8).

Monterey pine has been listed as important despite its restricted occurrence in California because it has been so widely planted in mild climates of Mediterranean type, particularly in the Southern Hemisphere.

**Economic and Social Importance.** The forests of the Pacific Coast are among the most important in the world. The climate of this region favors extremely high rates of production of wood, and proximity to the Pacific Ocean facilitates water shipment of logs and finished products overseas and

**Table 2.3**
Some Important Species of Pacific Coast Forests[a]

| Scientific Name | Common Name | Coast Ranges | Cascades | Sierra Nevada | Baja California |
|---|---|:---:|:---:|:---:|:---:|
| *Abies amabilis* | Pacific silver fir | + | + | | |
| *Abies concolor* | White fir | | + | + | |
| *Abies grandis* | Grand fir | + | + | | |
| *Abies lasiocarpa* | Subalpine fir | + | + | | |
| *Abies magnifica* | California red fir | × | + | + | |
| *Abies procera* | Noble fir | + | + | | |
| *Acer macrophyllum* | Bigleaf maple | + | + | + | |
| *Alnus rubra* | Red alder | + | + | | |
| *Arbutus menziesii* | Pacific madrone | + | + | + | |
| *Chamaecyparis nootkatensis* | Alaska cedar | + | + | | |
| *Juniperus occidentalis* | Western juniper | × | + | + | |
| *Libocedrus decurrens* | Incense cedar | + | + | + | × |
| *Picea sitchensis* | Sitka spruce | + | × | | |
| *Pinus contorta* | Lodgepole pine | + | + | + | × |
| *Pinus jeffreyi* | Jeffrey pine | × | + | + | × |
| *Pinus lambertiana* | Sugar pine | × | + | + | × |
| *Pinus monticola* | Western white pine | + | + | + | |
| *Pinus ponderosa* | Ponderosa pine | × | + | + | |
| *Pinus radiata* | Monterey pine | × | | | |
| *Populus trichocarpa* | Black cottonwood | + | + | + | × |
| *Pseudotsuga menziesii* | Douglas-fir | + | + | + | |
| *Quercus kelloggii* | California black oak | + | + | + | |
| *Sequoia sempervirens* | Redwood | + | | | |
| *Sequoiadendron giganteum* | Giant sequoia | | | × | |
| *Thuja plicata* | Western red cedar | + | + | | |
| *Tsuga heterophylla* | Western hemlock | + | + | | |

[a] + indicates widespread ocurrence.
   × indicates localized occurrence.

to East Coast U.S. markets. Douglas-fir is rivaled only by loblolly pine of the southeastern United States as a timber producer (Figure 2.4). The forest products industry is one of the leading employers in British Columbia, Washington, and Oregon.

Forest watersheds supply the region with some of the least costly hydroelectric power in North America as well as major irrigation projects in the Columbia Basin and the Central Valley of California. Recreation, wildlife, and scenic resources are available to the public in a chain of four provincial parks in British Columbia and nine national parks, three national monuments, and innumerable state parks and national forest campgrounds in the Pacific Coast states. Big-game hunting and sport fishing are major uses of public and industrial forests through-

**Figure 2.4** (*a*) Old-growth Douglas-fir in western Washington with an understory of mostly western hemlock, (*b*) A 79-year-old second-growth Douglas-fir stand in western Washington. (Courtesy of U.S.D.A. Forest Service.)

**Figure 2.4** (continued)

The forests of the Rocky Mountain region do not form the continuous cover found in some of the other forest regions; however, many of the individual forest stands, particularly of such species as lodgepole pine and Engelmann spruce, often become quite dense (Figure 2.5). The patchy nature of the Rocky Mountain forest is a consequence of the uneven distribution of precipitation in this region, the generally rough topography lying to the leeward, and the coastal ranges, which catch a large share of the moisture drawn from the Pacific Ocean.

**Principal Species.** In the Rocky Mountain forests, even to a greater extent than in those to the west, conifers predominate. Quaking aspen nevertheless forms extensive stands in the forests of the northern and central Rockies and in a number of the forests at higher elevations in the southern Rocky Mountains. As the forests thin out at lower elevations, the woodlands in the southern Rockies are dominated by piñons and junipers.

Table 2.4 lists the important trees of the region according to their occurrence in three subregions: the northern Rockies in western Canada, eastern Washington, northeastern Oregon, Idaho, Montana, and Wyoming; the central Rockies in Wyoming, Utah, and Colorado; and the southern Rockies in Arizona and New Mexico and the northern states of Mexico.

Perhaps the most striking feature of the forest composition of the region as a whole is the large number of pine species. The forests of the Rocky Mountains provide a good illustration of the difficulty of mapping forest regions in a simple manner, for in this region the compensating effects of altitude, latitude, and aspect are most evident. For example, the high mountains of Arizona have forests that, if not in detailed species composition, at least in general appearance closely resemble those of the northern Rockies.

In the discussion of the Pacific Coast forests, it was pointed out that the diversity of species decreases from west to east. This trend continues, as indicated by the comparison of the number of

out the region. Puget Sound and the Strait of Georgia, with their many forested islands and shores, float large fleets of boats for fishing and sailing all year.

## Rocky Mountain Forests

**Location and Extent.** South of the Canada–United States border, the Cordillera is divided by the Columbia basin and plateau and farther south by the Great Basin. To the east of this dry region with few forests lie the Rocky Mountains, which extend southward into Mexico as the Sierra Madre, divided into the eastern and western ranges in the drier north of Mexico.

**Figure 2.5** Stand of 200-year-old lodgepole pine in the Tar-
ghee National Forest, Idaho. (Courtesy of U.S.D.A. Forest
Service.)

species listed for the northern Rockies subregion in
Table 2.4 with the number listed for the three
Canadian and U.S. subregions listed in Table 2.3.

**Economic and Social Importance.** Throughout the region, the chief importance of forests is the
protection of water resources. This is true even in
the relatively well-watered northern Rockies, where
an important forest-products industry exists. Farther
south, the importance of the forests for watershed

protection increases. Forest grazing of cattle and
sheep is also important in this region, particularly in
the more open stands of ponderosa pine. No other
forest region in North America can equal the Rocky
Mountains in diversity of wildlife, including big
game. Some of the best bird-watching areas of the
continent are located here. The recreational importance of the region is very important, as exemplified
by the chain of more than two dozen national parks
in Canada and the United States, in addition to a

**Table 2.4**
Some Important Species of the Rocky Mountain Forests[a]

| Scientific Name | Common Name | Northern Rockies | Central Rockies | Southern Rockies |
|---|---|:---:|:---:|:---:|
| *Abies concolor* | White fir | | + | + |
| *Abies lasiocarpa* | Subalpine fir | + | + | × |
| *Larix occidentalis* | Western larch | + | | |
| *Picea engelmannii* | Engelmann spruce | + | + | + |
| *Picea glauca* | White spruce | + | | |
| *Picea pungens* | Blue spruce | | + | + |
| *Pinus albicaulis* | Whitebark pine | + | | |
| *Pinus contorta* | Lodgepole pine | + | + | |
| *Pinus engelmannii* | Apache pine | | | × |
| *Pinus flexilis* | Limber pine | + | + | |
| *Pinus leiophylla* | Chihuahua pine | | | × |
| *Pinus monticola* | Western white pine | + | | |
| *Pinus ponderosa* | Ponderosa pine | + | + | + |
| *Pinus strobiformis* | Southwestern white pine | | | + |
| *Populus tremuloides* | Quaking aspen | + | + | × |
| *Prunus serotina* | Black cherry | | | × |
| *Pseudotsuga menziesii* | Douglas-fir | + | + | + |
| *Thuja plicata* | Western red cedar | + | | |
| *Tsuga heterophylla* | Western hemlock | + | | |

[a] + indicates widespread occurrence
× indicates localized occurrence

large number of provincial parks, state parks, winter-sports developments, and dude ranches.

## Central Broad-leaved Forests

To a much greater extent than is true of the forests of northern and western North America, the forests of the eastern United States have been modified in various ways by human activities. The most obvious of these changes has been clearing for farming, which converted some of the finest hardwood forests to the present-day corn belt. In many areas such as New England and the Piedmont, the soils cleared early eventually proved unprofitable for farming and were naturally reforested by pines and other pioneer tree species. Moreover, many mixed forests were selectively logged for white pine and hemlock and were thus converted to broad-leaved forests with little or no coniferous component. Finally, artificial reforestation has played a large role in the constitution of the forests in many parts of this large area.

The most detailed classification of the eastern deciduous forests of North America recognizes eight distinct regions south of the northern hardwoods. For the purposes of this brief chapter, six of these will be dealt with as the central broad-leaved forests, a regional grouping recognized also in the somewhat similar climates of western Europe and eastern Asia.

**50**

**Location and Extent.** The central broad-leaved forests are found in twenty-four of the states east of the Great Plains and south of the Northern hardwood forests. The region does not include the pine-oak (Southern) and bottomland forests of the south Atlantic and Gulf coasts or the lower Mississippi Valley. Although the region at present includes much nonforested land, it is by far the largest forest region in the United States. Forest ownerships in the region are generally small in comparison with those in other forest regions, and there are comparatively few large federal forest areas such as national forests and national parks.

**Principal Species.** More than 100 species of native trees are found in the central broad-leaved forests (Figure 2.6). In terms of both number of species and economic value, the oaks are the most important group. During this century, the most important change in the species composition of this forest is the extinction (for practical purposes) of the American chestnut as the result of chestnut blight, and its replacement by oaks and yellow poplar. Table 2.5 lists some of the more important species of this forest.

**Economic and Social Importance.** With the exception of the Pacific Coast, eastern Canada, and central Mexico, most of the concentrations of population and industry in North America are located within the central broad-leaved forest region. Thus these forests are much more directly influenced by the needs and desires of urban centers than are the forests of any other region on the continent. Production of industrial raw materials by the central broad-leaved forests is by no means trivial, although it is not as intensive in any particular locality as in, for example, the Pacific Coast region. The hardwoods of the central broad-leaved region supply a large furniture industry and, particularly in recent years, a growing demand for pallets for mechanized handling and storage of materials. In some portions of this region, hardwood stands on poorer soils are being replaced by pine plantations for the production of pulpwood. Increasingly, the importance of these forests lies in their role in protecting water supplies, providing wildlife habitat, and affording opportunities for outdoor recreation. State, county, and municipal parks provide the major share of recreational facilities, but the Park Service, the Forest Service, and the Corps of Engineers have numerous recreational areas throughout the region. Freshwater fishing and boating are among the most popular recreational activities.

## Oak-Pine (Southern) Forests

**Location and Extent.** The oak-pine region lies along the south Atlantic and Gulf coasts, extending westward into eastern Texas and Oklahoma. It includes the Piedmont region and the sandhills region of the Carolinas. Along the coasts, it is penetrated by the bottomland hardwoods forests, which lie along the river courses, most notably along the lower Mississippi River (Figure 2.1).

**Principal Species.** There has been a major shift in the species composition of the forests of the oak-pine region since the invasion by Europeans. The first change was occasioned by clearing mixed pine-hardwoods forests and planting clean-cultivated row crops, a type of agriculture that proved destructive to the soils of the Piedmont region, which are highly erodible and are subjected to rainstorms of tropical intensity. Widespread farm abandonment was followed by natural reforestation of the worn-out lands, first by the light-seeded pines, with rapid invasion of these pine stands by oaks and other hardwoods such as sweet gum. In many areas on the poorer upland soils, intensive forest management took the form of selective elimination of the low-value hardwoods from pine-hardwood stands by girdling, herbicide use, or prescribed burning. Finally, the harvesting of "old field" pine (Figure 2.7) or pine-hardwoods stands has been followed by large-scale planting of pines. More than half of the pines currently being

**Figure 2.6**  Beech growing with eastern hemlock in Pennsylvania. (Courtesy of U.S.D.A. Forest Service.)

**Table 2.5**
Some Important Species of the Central Broad-leaved Forest

| Scientific Name | Common Name |
| --- | --- |
| *Acer rubrum* | Red maple |
| *Acer saccharum* | Sugar maple |
| *Aesculus octandra* | Yellow buckeye |
| *Betula allegheniensis* | Yellow birch |
| *Carya cordiformis* | Bitternut hickory |
| *Carya ovata* | Shagbark hickory |
| *Carya tomentosa* | Mockernut hickory |
| *Cornus florida* | Flowering dogwood |
| *Diospyros virginiana* | Common persimmon |
| *Fagus grandifolia* | American beech |
| *Fraxinus americana* | White ash |
| *Juglans nigra* | Black walnut |
| *Liquidambar styraciflua* | Sweet gum |
| *Liriodendron tulipifera* | Yellow poplar |
| *Magnolia acuminata* | Cucumber magnolia |
| *Nyssa sylvatica* | Black tupelo |
| *Pinus strobus* | Eastern white pine |
| *Quercus alba* | White oak |
| *Quercus macrocarpa* | Burr oak |
| *Quercus marilandica* | Blackjack oak |
| *Quercus prinus* | Chestnut oak |
| *Quercus rubra* | Northern red oak |
| *Quercus stellata* | Post oak |
| *Quercus velutina* | Black oak |
| *Robinia pseudoacacia* | Black locust |
| *Tilia americana* | American basswood |
| *Tilia heterophylla* | White basswood |
| *Tsuga canadensis* | Eastern hemlock |
| *Ulmus americana* | American elm |

planted in the region are grown from seed produced in seed orchards made up of selected superior trees. Table 2.6 lists some of the more important species of this forest region.

**Economic and Social Importance.** The oak-pine region has the most intensively managed forests in North America, and is one of the leading producers of pulp and paper in the world. To a large extent, the pulp and paper industry has been based on the pine stands that followed agricultural failures, but more recently pine plantations have become an important source of raw materials. A current development in the industry is a growing use of various hardwood species for pulpwood production. Loblolly pine is the leading species throughout most of the region, but in the Deep South slash pine is a major timber resource. The wildlife resources of the region are quite diverse. Two of the major game species—quail and deer—can be managed compatibly with intensive timber production. Wild turkey has been successfully reestablished in many parts of the region. The numerous water impoundments are heavily used for boating and fishing.

### Bottomland Hardwoods Forests

**Location and Extent.** The bottomland hardwoods forests are scattered along the central and south Atlantic and Gulf coasts and in the lower Mississippi Valley. Although many types of bottomland forests are recognized in this region, depending on soil type and drainage pattern, they may be grouped in two broad categories: swamps such as the Great Dismal and the Okefenokee, and floodplains, of which the Mississippi delta is the most extensive.

**Principal Species.** Three conifers are found in these otherwise hardwood forests. Bald cypress, often associated with water tupelo, is found in swamps and frequently flooded bottoms. Atlantic white cedar and pond pine occur, often in pure stands, on peat soils in swamps. Table 2.7 lists some of the important species of this region.

**Economic and Social Importance.** Hardwood lumber and veneer logs for the furniture industry and for paneling are leading products of the bottomland hardwoods forests. Along the lower Mississippi, the "batture" lands between levee and river are planted with cottonwoods for the production of pulpwood. In recent years, pulpwood plantations of sycamore have been installed on bottomland soils.

**53**

**Figure 2.7** Stand of 80- to 90-year-old loblolly pine that colonized an abandoned field in North Carolina. (Courtesy of U.S.D.A. Forest Service.)

**Table 2.6**

Some Important Species of the Oak-Pine (Southern) Forest

| Scientific Name | Common Name |
| --- | --- |
| Acer rubrum | Red maple |
| Carya cordiformis | Bitternut hickory |
| Carya ovata | Shagbark hickory |
| Carya tomentosa | Mockernut hickory |
| Cornus florida | Flowering dogwood |
| Juniperus virginiana | Eastern red cedar |
| Liquidambar styraciflua | Sweet gum |
| Liriodendron tulipifera | Yellow poplar |
| Nyssa sylvatica | Black tupelo |
| Pinus clausa | Sand pine |
| Pinus echinata | Shortleaf pine |
| Pinus elliottii | Slash pine |
| Pinus palustris | Longleaf pine |
| Pinus taeda | Loblolly pine |
| Pinus virginiana | Virginia pine |
| Quercus alba | White oak |
| Quercus coccinea | Scarlet oak |
| Quercus falcata | Southern red oak |
| Quercus marilandica | Blackjack oak |
| Quercus nigra | Water oak |
| Quercus phellos | Willow oak |
| Quercus rubra | Northern red oak |
| Quercus velutina | Black oak |

The bottomland forests are particularly rich in wildlife, including such large animals as the black bear. The region has a large number of wildlife refuges and public recreation areas. Recreational resources are largely water-based.

## Tropical Forests

**Location and Extent.** The tropical forests of North America are located in Mexico and southern Florida. In Mexico, there are three characteristic types of tropical forests, the distinctions arising from differences in topography and seasonal distribution of rainfall. The tropical rain forest is located principally near the Gulf of Mexico in the south, where ample rainfall occurs every month. A winter dry season characterizes the second type, the tropical deciduous forest that extends mostly along the Pacific Coast, but with representatives in the northeast. The third type, the oak and pine forests, with a winter dry season, occur at higher elevations in the Sierra Madre (oriental and occidental) and in the south. The tropical forests of Florida are restricted to the extreme southern tip of the peninsula and to the keys and have well-distributed rainfall (Figure 2.8).

**Principal Species.** To an even greater extent than in the account of the central hardwoods forest, the listing in Table 2.8 of the principal species of the

**Table 2.7**

Some Important Species of the Bottomland Hardwoods Forests

| Scientific Name | Common Name |
| --- | --- |
| Acer negundo | Box elder |
| Acer rubrum | Red maple |
| Acer saccharinum | Silver maple |
| Betula nigra | River birch |
| Carya cordiformis | Bitternut hickory |
| Carya illinoensis | Pecan |
| Celtis laevigata | Sugarberry |
| Chamaecyparis thyoides | Atlantic white cedar |
| Fraxinus pennsylvanica | Green ash |
| Gleditsia triacanthos | Honey locust |
| Liquidambar styraciflua | Sweet gum |
| Magnolia grandiflora | Southern magnolia |
| Nyssa aquatica | Water tupelo |
| Nyssa sylvatica biflora | Swamp tupelo |
| Pinus serotina | Pond pine |
| Platanus occidentalis | American sycamore |
| Populus deltoides | Eastern cottonwood |
| Populus heterophylla | Swamp cottonwood |
| Quercus falcata pagodaefolia | Cherrybark oak |
| Quercus lyrata | Overcup oak |
| Quercus michauxii | Swamp chestnut oak |
| Quercus palustris | Pin oak |
| Quercus virginiana | Live oak |
| Taxodium distichum | Bald cypress |

**Figure 2.8** Mangrove trees with arching prop roots (adventitious roots) in the Florida Keys. As sand, mud, and debris are lodged in the maze of prop roots, the shallows eventually become dry land and an islet is formed. (Photograph courtesy of Michael and N. J. Berrill.)

tropical forests is a very small sample of the great diversity of species present in these forests. Eastern white pine is one of the several species of Mexico's tropical forests that are of major importance in the eastern United States, two others being black cherry and sweet gum.

### Economic and Social Importance.
The pines of the mountainous oak and pine forests are an important source of lumber and pulpwood. Charcoal produced locally from the oaks is used as a cooking fuel in many rural areas. With the rapid urbanization of the population, water has become the dominant resource of Mexico's forests. The principal—and very great—value of the tropical forest of south Florida is as a unique ecosystem in the continental United States, most of it within the Everglades National Park.

## FOREST REGIONS OF THE WORLD

Climate and soil determine the general appearance of a forest—whether it is open or closed; tall or short; evergreen or deciduous; coniferous, broad-leaved, or mixed. These various broad forest types may be found in all continents, but the species that constitute the forests of a given broad type usually differ from place to place. On the other hand, genera often are common to widely separated forests of the same general type. This is particularly true of the cooler, more northerly forest regions. Southern Hemisphere forests, however, differ markedly in their composition from Northern Hemisphere forests.

Because it is possible to recognize these broad general types of forest, we can make a comprehensive survey of world forest regions in a relatively short account (Figure 2.9).

### Northern Coniferous Forest

**Location and Extent.** In Eurasia, the northern coniferous forest or *taiga,* as in North America, is the most extensive forest region, stretching from Sakhalin and Hokkaido in the Pacific across Siberia and European Russia to the Scandinavian peninsula.

**Principal Species.** The Eurasian *taiga* resembles its North American counterpart in the general composition of its forests, but differs in two important respects. In Eurasia, particularly in Scandinavia, Finland, and European Russia, the *taiga* extends, in the form of low open woodland, north of the Arctic Circle, whereas in North America the conifer woodland barely reaches the Arctic in the west. Moreover, the Eurasian *taiga* is somewhat richer in number of species of larch, spruce, and fir and is especially notable for the northern extension of Scotch pine, the world's most widely distributed pine, and for the occurrence in the far north of several small white pines. As in North America, the Eurasian *taiga* has numerous species of birch, poplar, and willow.

**Economic and Social Importance.** As indicated in Table 2.1, the Eurasian *taiga,* most of which is within the borders of the Soviet Union, is the world's largest native coniferous forest region (Figure 2.10). It is an important producer of lumber

**Table 2.8**

Some Important Species of the Tropical Forests[a]

| Scientific Name | Common Name | Rain Forests | Deciduous Forests | Oak-Pine Forests | Southern Florida |
|---|---|:---:|:---:|:---:|:---:|
| *Abies religiosa* | Oyamel | | | + | |
| *Acacia farnesiana* | Huisache | | + | | |
| *Alnus jorullensis* | Aliso | | | + | |
| *Avicennia nitida* | Black mangrove | | | | + |
| *Alvaradoa amorphoides* | Camaron | | + | | |
| *Bumelia celastrina* | Rompezapato | | + | | |
| *Bursera simaruba* | Gumbo-limbo | + | + | | + |
| *Ceiba pentandra* | Silk cotton tree | + | + | | |
| *Cecropia mexicana* | Trumpet wood | + | + | | |
| *Coccoloba diversifolia* | Doveplum | | | | + |
| *Dialium guianense* | Ironwood | + | | | |
| *Eugenia confusa* | Redberry eugenia | | | | + |
| *Ficus aurea* | Florida strangler fig | | | | + |
| *Gilbertia arborea* | Hoja fresca | + | | | |
| *Guaiacum sanctum* | Lignum vitae | | | | + |
| *Krugiodendron ferreum* | Leadwood | | | | + |
| *Lysiloma bahamensis* | Wild tamarind | | | | + |
| *Pinus ayacahuite* | Pinabete | | | + | |
| *Pinus leiophylla* | Piño chino | | | + | |
| *Pinus montezumae* | Piño de Montezuma | | | + | |
| *Pinus oocarpa* | Piño prieto | | | + | |
| *Pinus strobus* | Eastern white pine | | | + | |
| *Pinus teocote* | Piño colorado | | | + | |
| *Piscidia piscipula* | Florida fish poison tree | | | | + |
| *Pistacia mexicana* | Achin | | + | | |
| *Poulsenia armata* | — | + | | | |
| *Rhizophora mangle* | Red mangrove | | | | + |
| *Roystonea elata* | Florida royal palm | | | | + |
| *Sapindus saponaria* | Wingleaf soapberry | | | | + |
| *Sideroxylon foetidissimum* | False mastic | | | | + |
| *Sterculia mexicana* | Castano bellota | + | | | |
| *Swietenia humilis* | Caoba | | + | | |
| *Swietenia mahagoni* | West Indies mahogany | | | | + |
| *Taxodium mucronatum* | Montezuma cypress | | + | | |
| *Zanthoxylon fagara* | Lime prickly ash | | + | | |

[a] + indicates widespread occurrence.

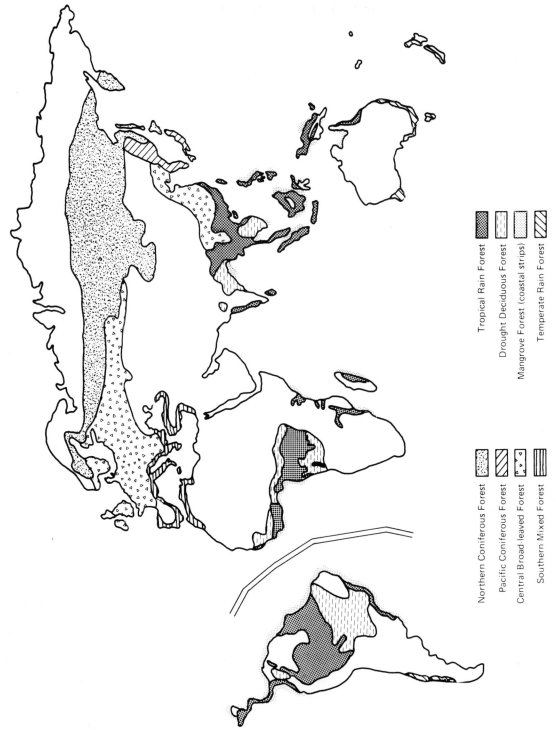

**Figure 2.9** The world's forests.

Tropical Rain Forest

Drought Deciduous Forest

Mangrove Forest (coastal strips)

Temperate Rain Forest

Northern Coniferous Forest

Pacific Coniferous Forest

Central Broad-leaved Forest

Southern Mixed Forest

**Figure 2.10** Timber floating on the Mana River, Krasnozarsk region, Soviet Union. (Photograph courtesy of Novosti Press Agency, Soviet Union.)

large number of coniferous and broad-leaved species. The conifers include most of the genera found in western North America, the species of fir, larch, spruce, pine, and hemlock being especially numerous. Douglas-fir is also represented. *Cryptomeria* (sugi), the principal native conifer of Japan, is intensively cultivated.

**Economic and Social Importance.** Heavy pressure for agricultural production limits commercial forests to steeper and higher lands. Despite intensive cultivation of commercial forests in Japan, these are insufficient to supply the demands for lumber and paper, which are increasingly met by importation from the forest regions surrounding the Pacific. The forests of Japan and Korea are important for watershed protection and for recreational use. Japanese horticulturists have developed many interesting and beautiful varieties of their native trees, which are now found in gardens throughout the world.

and pulpwood, particularly in its western sections, where Scotch pine is the leading commercial species. The rivers and lakes of the region are important in the transportation of sawlogs and pulpwood.

The region has abundant wildlife, from mosquitoes to moose and, like the North American northern forest, continues to be important in the fur trade. In Scandinavia, recreational use of the northern forest is important.

## Pacific Coniferous Forest

**Location and Extent.** The Pacific coniferous forest region is relatively small in extent and is scattered in Japan, Korea, and southern coastal Siberia.

**Principal Species.** The region is mountainous, with a relatively mild coastal climate, and therefore provides a variety of habitats that are occupied by a

## Central Broad-leaved Forest

**Location and Extent.** The central broad-leaved forest of Eurasia is divided into two quite distinct regions by the immense steppe and desert areas of central Asia and eastern Europe. The western broad-leaved forest originally covered western Europe and Britain, while the eastern region constitutes much of eastern China. As in North America, the broad-leaved forest of western Europe and Britain has been substantially reduced in extent by clearing for farming and for urban and industrial development (Figure 2.9).

**Principal Species.** Most of the principal species of the central broad-leaved forest of Britain and Europe have closely related counterparts in the forests of eastern North America and have, moreover, been commonly planted as ornamentals in the United States. In Table 2.9, which lists the principal forest tree species of the broad-leaved forests of

**Table 2.9**

Some Important Species of the Central Broad-leaved Forest of Europe and Britain[a]

| Scientific Name | Common Name |
| --- | --- |
| *Abies alba* | Silver fir |
| *Larix decidua** | European larch |
| *Picea abies** | Norway spruce |
| *Pinus sylvestris** | Scotch pine |
| *Taxus baccata** | Common yew |
| *Acer platanoides** | Norway maple |
| *Acer pseudoplatanus** | Sycamore maple |
| *Alnus glutinosa* | Common alder |
| *Betula verrucosa** | Silver birch |
| *Carpinus betulus* | Hornbeam |
| *Fagus sylvatica** | Common beech |
| *Fraxinus excelsior* | Common ash |
| *Populus tremula* | Aspen |
| *Quercus petraea* | Durmast oak |
| *Quercus robur** | English oak |
| *Tilia cordata** | Small-leaved linden |
| *Ulmus procera** | English elm |

[a] Trees well known in eastern North America are marked with an asterisk.

Europe and Britain, species well known in eastern North America are marked with an asterisk. Three of the conifers (Scotch pine, Norway spruce, and European larch) have been planted for timber production fairly extensively in parts of the northeastern United States, while Scotch pine is commonly planted for the production of Christmas trees.

The central broad-leaved forests of western Europe have conspicuously fewer species than those of eastern Asia and eastern North America. More than two dozen genera of trees and shrubs that are found in the North American and east Asian forests are absent from the western European forests, which were seriously depleted of species as a consequence of the last glaciation.

In strong contrast to those of western Europe, the central broad-leaved forests of eastern Asia contain a fascinating array of species. Indeed in recent times western botanists have been surprised to discover two hitherto unknown genera of conifers: *Cathaya* and *Metasequoia*. Table 2.10 lists a few of the more commonly planted trees introduced into North America from China, but a more complete list of trees and shrubs introduced into Europe and North America from east Asia numbers more than 100 species.

**Economic and Social Importance.** The central broad-leaved forest of western Europe continues, after hundreds of years and several drastic deforestations, to play an important role in the production of solid wood and fiber, as well as providing habitat for large populations of game and other wildlife. With a large urban population distributed throughout the region, the recreational use of the forest is heavy.

The science and practice of forest management and silviculture were born in the broad-leaved forests of western and central Europe, and forest managers in all parts of the world continue to look on European forestry as a model (Figure 2.11).

Much of the broad-leaved forest in east Asia has, so far, played a comparatively small part as a source of industrial raw materials because of inaccessibility, although local populations make extensive use of the forests. Areas of China long ago deforested

**Table 2.10**

Some Species Introduced into North America from China

| Scientific Name | Common Name |
| --- | --- |
| *Ailanthus altissima* | Tree of heaven |
| *Albizzia julibrissin* | Silk tree |
| *Ginkgo biloba* | Ginkgo |
| *Koelreuteria paniculata* | Goldenrain tree |
| *Lagerstroemia indica* | Crape myrtle |
| *Melia azedarach* | China tree |
| *Metasequoia glyptostroboides* | Metasequoia |
| *Paulownia tomentosa* | Paulownia |

**Figure 2.11** Selective cutting in a spruce-fir forest in the mountains near Zalusina, Yugoslavia. (Photograph by R. A. Young.)

are currently being restored to forest productivity by massive tree-planting programs.

## Southern Mixed Forest

The general designation of southern mixed forest covers a number of forest and woodland formations in the warmer but subtropical regions of both Northern and Southern Hemispheres. The principal forest regions in this category are the Mediterranean forest, small areas in coastal California and Chile, and several coastal areas in Australia. What these forest regions have in common are mild maritime climates in which snowfall is infrequent, tempera-

tures seldom fall below −10°C, and precipitation is moderate to slight and occurs mostly in winter. Such a climate is often referred to as Mediterranean.

**Mediterranean Forest.** When the French essayist Chateaubriand wrote, ''Forests precede people; deserts follow them,'' he could well have had the Mediterranean Basin in view (Figure 2.12). This region, with its relatively mild climate, is adjacent to early centers of agricultural production in the Fertile Crescent and the Nile Valley. It became a cradle for civilizations that engaged in breeding livestock and shipbuilding—activities that made heavy inroads into the forests. The effect was

**Figure 2.12** Typical Mediterranean vegetation near Delphi, Greece. (Photograph by R. L. Giese.)

**Table 2.11**

Some Important Trees and Large Shrubs of the Mediterranean Forest[a]

| Scientific Name | Common Name |
| --- | --- |
| *Arbutus unedo\** | Strawberry tree |
| *Carpinus orientalis* | Eastern hornbeam |
| *Castanea sativa* | Spanish chestnut |
| *Celtis australis* | European nettle tree |
| *Ceratonia siliqua\** | Carob tree |
| *Cercis siliquastrum* | Judas tree |
| *Cornus mas* | Cornelian cherry |
| *Corylus avellana* | European hazel |
| *Fraxinus ornus* | Flowering ash |
| *Juniperus oxycedrus* | Prickly juniper |
| *Laurus nobilis\** | Laurel |
| *Olea europaea\** | Olive |
| *Ostrya carpinifolia* | Hop-hornbeam |
| *Pinus halepensis* | Aleppo pine |
| *Pinus nigra* | Black pine |
| *Pinus pinaster* | Maritime pine |
| *Pinus pinea* | Stone pine |
| *Platanus orientalis* | Oriental plane |
| *Quercus cerris* | Turkey oak |
| *Quercus frainetto* | Hungarian oak |
| *Quercus ilex\** | Holm oak |
| *Quercus pubescens* | Pubescent oak |
| *Quercus suber\** | Cork oak |

[a] Evergreen broad-leaved species are marked with an asterisk.

particularly severe in the summer-dry Mediterranean climate, where soil moisture is barely sufficient to sustain closed forests even when they are not subjected to the added stresses of grazing, burning, and heavy cutting.

*Location and Extent.* The Mediterranean forest extends around the Mediterranean littoral, with the exception of the coasts of Libya and Egypt, which are essentially desert or steppe. It extends also to portions of the south and east coasts of the Black Sea and along the Atlantic coasts of Morocco and of southern Portugal and Spain. At lower elevations, the Mediterranean forest (or rather its remains) is often in fact woodland and scrub, termed variously *maquis, macchia, shikara,* and *chaparral.* At higher elevations (with heavier precipitation), closed forests resembling the central hardwoods forest are found.

*Principal Species.* In Table 2.11, which lists some of the important species of the region, evergreen broad-leaved species are marked with an asterisk. The prevalence of evergreen broad-leaved trees is generally high in warm climates.

*Economic and Social Importance.* Timber production is no longer an important use of the Mediterranean forest, except for certain stands at the higher elevations. Nevertheless, these forests and woodlands are heavily exploited for various products. Most of the species listed are utilized for fuel, but this is especially true of the oaks, which are the raw material for local charcoal producers. Many of the species are important as food plants, most notably the olive, which also yields a wood outstandingly suited to fine wood carving. Other food plants are the chestnut, cornelian cherry, hazel or filbert, carob or St. John's bread, and stone pine. Cork oak is the basis for a large cork industry, active mostly in the western Mediterranean and in Portugal, and maritime and black pines are tapped to produce rosin, tar, and turpentine. Grazing by sheep and goats is increasingly recognized as an abuse of these forests and woodlands. At present, the amenity values of these forests eclipse all others as the region's tourist industry attracts visitors to Europe's sun belt (10).

**Coastal Forests of California and Chile.** The central California coast and a relatively short stretch of the coast of Chile, at about the same distance from the equator, share the mild summer-dry winter-wet Mediterranean climate.

In both areas, the dominant vegetation is composed of hard-leaved (sclerophyllous) shrubs with patches of open woodland in situations with adequate soil moisture and shelter from the wind. The forest in California is notable as a scenic and recreational area, in part because of the rugged beauty of two tree species, Monterey pine and Monterey cypress, which are restricted in their natural distribution to this area. Coast live oak is the dominant large broadleaf in this forest. Monterey pine has attained worldwide renown as a highly productive timber species in various areas of Mediterranean climate, and has been particularly successful in the region south of Santiago and Valparaiso in Chile.

**Coastal Forests of Australia.** The summer-dry forests of Australia are restricted to a fairly narrow zone that extends from approximately the Tropic of Capricorn in Queensland southward and around the coasts of New South Wales and Victoria to eastern South Australia. Between Adelaide in South Australia and the southern tip of Western Australia, the coastal zone is treeless or open woodland. About half of the island state of Tasmania is in the summer-dry high forest zone. Two genera, *Eucalyptus* and *Acacia,* dominate these forests, and both include many species. About 600 species of *Eucalyptus* have been described. Many of these are shrubs or small trees, as are most of the species of *Acacia.* Nevertheless, some of the world's tallest trees are eucalyptus. *Eucalyptus diversicolor* (karri) in Western Australia attains 75 meters, and trees of *E. regnans* (mountain ash) of 100 meters have been measured in Victoria (Figure 2.13). These heights are attained only in forests at higher elevations where the rainfall is higher than occurs in a strictly Mediterranean climate. The eucalypts are the principal producers of timber and fiber in Australia, but in the drier portions of the coastal forests, eucalypts are being replaced by highly productive plantations of Monterey pine and, in Western Australia, of maritime pine. The Australian coastal forests are not only importers of these exotic pines; they also have exported hundreds of species of eucalypts, acacias, and other trees and shrubs to the forest plantations and gardens of those parts of the world with similar climates (8).

## Tropical Rain Forest

The tropical rain forest is restricted to a belt within 22 degrees north and south of the equator and is found at low to moderate elevations. Rainfall varies from 2000 to 4000 millimeters, evenly distributed throughout the year.

The most extensive area of tropical rain forest is found in the Amazon Basin of northern Brazil and adjacent portions of Ecuador, Venezuela, and the Guianas. Other areas in the Western Hemisphere are

**Figure 2.13** Virgin karri (*Eucalyptus diversicolor*) in Western Australia. (Courtesy of Forests Department of Western Australia.)

in south coastal Brazil, the Central American countries, some of the islands of the Caribbean, and the southern tip and keys of Florida. In Africa, the tropical rain forest is restricted to the Congo Basin of the western equatorial region and to the eastern side of Madagascar. Southeast Asia, Indonesia, New Guinea, the Philippines, and the northeast coast of Australia constitute the largest extent of tropical rain forest in the Eastern Hemisphere (Figure 2.9).

The outstanding characteristic of the tropical rain forest is extreme diversity of all life forms. Among the plants, diversity is evident not only in number of species, but also in growth forms, resulting in a many-layered high forest, the leaves of which so

efficiently trap radiation that even at noon on a sunny day, the forest floor is in a much deeper shade than one experiences in the densest temperate-region forest (Figure 2.14). This forest is therefore the earth's most productive ecosystem in terms of fixation of carbon as biomass. So far, it has not been possible to utilize this productivity by temperate-region silvicultural and industrial techniques. Sporadic and partial utilization in the form of extraction of certain tree species of high value, such as mahogany and rosewood, has been practiced for centuries, but the complex species composition of these forests has frustrated conventional temperate-region utilization modes. Current attempts to utilize the productive potential of these areas take the form

**Figure 2.14** A dense tropical forest in Indonesia. (Courtesy of S. Hadi.)

of replacing the native forest with simpler communities by planting subtropical pines or exotic broadleafs such as gmelina. It remains to be seen whether this strategy will prove successful in terms of industrial production and protection of the soil and water resources and the indigenous human and animal populations dependent on these resources.

## Drought-Deciduous Forest

Adjacent to several of the areas of tropical rain forest are regions with heavy rainfall restricted to summer, with extreme drought in winter and spring. In these climates, various so-called drought-deciduous forests have developed. Examples are along the central western coast of Mexico, in outliers of the northern Andes, adjacent to the extensive rain forests of Brazil, and the forests north and south of the rain forest of western Africa. The extreme development of this climate is in India, Burma, and Thailand, where the name *monsoon* is applied to the heavy seasonal rains that break the winter drought. The forests within this region have long been of great commercial importance as sources of teak, sal, and bamboo.

## Mangrove Forest

The mangrove swamp forest, although restricted to coastal saltwater areas and brackish streams in the humid tropics, is in the aggregate a large and important forest formation. A number of genera of saltwater-adapted trees and shrubs compose these low forests. The most common are *Rhizophora*, with stilt roots, and *Avicennia*. Human populations are heavy in the areas adjacent to the mangrove forests, which are important sources of fuel and shelter varied wildlife populations.

## Temperate Rain Forest

The temperate rain forest, growing in a temperate climate with abundant, well-distributed precipitation, is found largely in New Zealand, southern Chile, and a few coastal areas in Australia. The native species are a number of gymnosperms including members of the families *Podocarpaceae* and *Araucariaceae* as well as the angiosperm genus *Nothofagus* (southern beech). These have been producers of valuable timber, but have so far not proved adaptable to conventional modes of forest management, with the possible exception of some of the araucarias and eucalypts in Australia. In consequence, this forest region, particularly in New Zealand and Chile, has been the scene of large-scale conversion to plantations of Northern Hemisphere conifers such as Monterey pine and Douglas-fir, and in the warmer parts of the region in Australia, to plantations of slash pine, loblolly pine, and Caribbean pine.

## "New" Forests

Portions of southern Africa, South America, and New Zealand, previously unforested or with woodland of low productivity, have over the past few decades been forested with nonindigenous species of trees, with the object of providing raw materials for local industries. The species used include Monterey pine, slash pine, loblolly pine, Caribbean pine, the tropical Asian *Pinus merkusii* and *kesiya,* and species of *Acacia* and *Eucalyptus*.

## REFERENCES

1. E. L. Braun, *Deciduous Forests of Eastern North America,* Hafner, New York, 1950.
2. R. F. Daubenmire, *Plant Geography With Special Reference to North America,* Academic Press, New York, 1978.
3. J. F. Franklin and C. T. Dyrness, "Natural Vegetation of Oregon and Washington," U.S.D.A. For. Ser., Gen. Tech. Rept. PNW-8, 1973.
4. H. A. Gleason and A. Cronquist, *The Natural Geography of Plants,* Columbia University Press, New York, 1964.
5. H-L. Li, *The Origin and Cultivation of Shade and Ornamental Trees,* Univ. of Pennsylvania Press, Philadelphia, 1974.

6. E. L. Little, Jr., "Atlas of United States Trees. Vol. 1. Conifers and Important Hardwoods," U.S.D.A. For. Ser., Misc. Pub. No. 1146, 1971.

7. J. S. Rowe, "Forest regions of Canada," Dept. of Northern Affairs and National Resources, Canadian Forestry Branch, Bulletin 123, 1959.

8. A. Rule, *Forests of Australia,* Angus & Robertson, Sydney, 1967.

9. V. E. Shelford, *The Ecology of North America,* Univ. of Illinois Press, Urbana, 1963.

10. H. Walter, *Vegetation of the Earth,* Springer-Verlag, New York, 1973.

# PART 2

## FOREST BIOLOGY

Trees are the largest and oldest of the known living plant species in the world today (Figure P2.1). Starting as a minute seed, they can grow to heights over 120 meters accumulating as much as 1500 cubic meters of wood in the process. In addition, trees possess a water-transporting system so powerful that it can raise water about a hundred times as efficiently as the best suction pump ever made by humans (1). Truly, trees are remarkable mechanisms of nature.

Like all other plants, trees are constructed solely of cells, the basic units of life. However, the cells in a leaf, for example, are quite different from those in the trunk and different again from those in the root. Each kind of cell is usually found in association with similar cells; groups of similar cells make up tissue, and tissues combine into even more complex groups known as organs (1). Clearly, the specialized organs serve different purposes in the tree. The complex functions of the tree

**Figure P2.1** One of the oldest known living plants in the world: 3000-year-old bristlecone pine sculptured by wind, sand, and ice. (Courtesy of U.S.D.A. Forest Service.)

and its component parts are treated in detail in Chapter 3, "Physiology of Tree Growth."

The growth and vigor of trees are a function of many factors. Certainly the bountiful diversity in form and style of trees is related to their genetic constitution. Chapter 5, "Forest Genetics and Forest-Tree Breeding," discusses the heritable variation of trees and the application of genetic principles to the development of lines of trees of increased value to humans.

Environmental factors can have a profound influence on tree growth. Minerals in the soil, water shortages, wind and climate, sunlight availability, and attack by insects and disease all affect the patterns of tree growth (Figure P2.2). The impact of these factors and human interaction for control of tree growth and vigor are treated in the following chapters. Integration of the many factors that affect tree and stand growth is discussed in Chapter 6, "Forest Ecology and the Forest Ecosystem." New methodologies for studies on the forest ecosystem through computer-modeling techniques are also described in this chapter.

A forest community must be considered as a

**Figure P2.2** Twisted aspens are called "The Crooked Forest" on the Grand Canyon's northern rim in Arizona. The resilient trees were bent as saplings by winter winds and deep snowdrifts. (Courtesy of Life Picture Service.)

**Figure P2.3** The blast from the eruption of Mt. Saint Helens in the State of Washington flattened previously lush, green forests. Ecologists are closely monitoring the return of plant and animal life. (Photograph by R. L. Giese.)

dynamic structure that responds to the laws of cause and effect where all organisms intertwine to form a harmonic ecosystem (2). The forest has evolved through *plant succession*, the orderly replacement of one plant community or forest stand with another. Generally a temporary plant community is replaced by a relatively more stable community until a dynamic equilibrium is attained between the plants and the environment. The factors affecting succession of forests and the characteristics of the successional stages are further described in Chapter 6.

Disturbances in the forest can be either natural (wind, fire, insect and disease outbreaks) or caused by humans (forest harvesting and fire) and can result in destruction of small or large segments of the forest. The effect of disturbance is to produce sites where new communities of the trees, plants, and animals can exist and may differ from those of the native forest (Figure P2.3). Thus disturbances can alter the biological succession of the forests. These and other effects are considered in the following chapters on forest biology.

## REFERENCES

1. P. Farb, *The Forest*, Time-Life Books, New York, 1969.

2. H. W. Hocker, Jr., *Introduction to Forest Biology*, John Wiley & Sons, New York, 1979.

# 3

# PHYSIOLOGY OF TREE GROWTH

## Theodore T. Kozlowski

Tree physiology deals with the biological processes that control growth of trees.[1] A physiologist thinks of a tree as consisting of three parts: leaves, stem, and root system, each with important functions. The *leaves* synthesize carbohydrates and hormonal growth regulators, and they give off water vapor to the atmosphere. The *stem* supports the crown and conducts water, mineral nutrients, and hormones upward from the roots. It also transports downward the carbohydrates and hormones synthesized in the crown to tissues and organs that require them for growth. The stem also stores large amounts of reserve carbohydrates. The *roots* are important for anchorage, absorption of water and minerals from the soil, synthesis of certain hormones, and storage of reserve carbohydrates (see Figure 17.2).

The importance of tree physiology lies in the fact that physiological processes are the critical intermediaries through which heredity, environmental factors, and cultural practices interact to influence tree growth. This is shown by the following diagram (1).

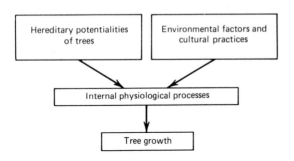

From a developmental viewpoint, increase in size of trees can be considered to be the end result of cell division and expansion. Cell enlargement is followed by differentiation and structural changes in which specialized organs are formed. These sequential phases of growth are regulated by a series of coordinated physiological processes such as: synthesis of carbohydrates; nitrogen and fat metabolism; absorption and loss of water; digestion by enzyme action of complex or insoluble forms of food, such as starch, into simple, soluble compounds; redistribution of carbohydrates, hormones, water, and minerals; and assimilation (the conversion of food into new protoplasm and cell walls) and storage of reserve foods. To a physiologist a tree is a fascinating and complex piece of biochemical machinery that starts from a small seed and builds into a massive organism that may weigh many tons. The important forestry problems of seed production, seed germination, wood production, wood quality, seed and bud dormancy, and flowering all involve control by the linking together of various regulatory physiological processes. Furthermore, growth inhibition or death of trees following catastrophic environmental events, insect attack, or disease is preceded by abnormal physiological events. It cannot be emphasized too strongly that environmental changes, cultural treatments, and disease and insect attacks alter tree growth only through a sequential pathway of physiological change.

## GROWTH CHARACTERISTICS OF TREES

Trees exhibit a number of common growth characteristics. For example, they all grow in height and girth. However, the mechanisms providing for stem and branch elongation and increasing thickness are very different. Elongation of the branched cylindrical axis of a tree is traceable to division and expansion of cells at many terminal growing points (called *apical meristems*[2]). Such growth, called primary growth, occurs at all stem, branch, and root tips. It also provides for branching. Growth in diameter of stems and branches is traceable to

---

[1]Some prior knowledge of botany is presumed for this chapter. To aid the reader a brief review of seed plant structure is given in Appendix I. For a more thorough treatment any basic botany text is recommended.

[2]Meristematic tissue is generative tissue and is distinguished from permanent tissue, which is fully differentiated and incapable of cell division.

division and expansion of cells of a cambium layer located between the bark and wood (Figure 3.1).

Trees also exhibit many interesting individual characteristics. There are marked hereditary variations among trees in crown form, ultimate size, longevity, branching habits, growth rates, shoot growth patterns, root growth characteristics, reproductive growth, autumn coloration, etc. Marked differences in growth characteristics may be found between tropical- and temperate-zone trees, between evergreen and deciduous trees, and even among different species of the same genus.

Another interesting observation is that different parts of trees grow at different rates and at different times. Hence, the general ideas we have about the nature of tree growth and what controls it will depend to a large extent on the aspect of growth we observe or measure—increase in shoot growth,

diameter growth, or root growth. Actually, in many trees of the temperate zone, the roots start to elongate in the spring before the shoots do, and annual cambial growth in the lower stem begins later than either of these (Figure 3.2).

## Shoot Growth

Growth of shoots is the result of bud expansion and involves cell division, elongation, differentiation, and maturation. A bud is an embryonic axis together with some appendages. It is essentially a telescoped shoot or part of a shoot. Buds are variously classified on the basis of their location, contents, or activity. Hence, we may speak of terminal or lateral buds; vegetative, flower, and mixed buds; and active or dormant buds. Vegetative buds contain a small growing point, nodes (parts of the stem at which one or more leaves or

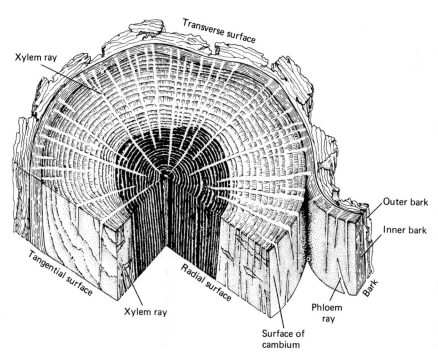

**Figure 3.1** Portion of a red oak stem. The dark area in the center of the stem is heartwood, the lighter wood (note: wood is also called xylem) surrounding the heartwood is sapwood.

(From Raven, Evert and Curtis, *Biology of Plants*, Worth Publishers, New York, 1976)

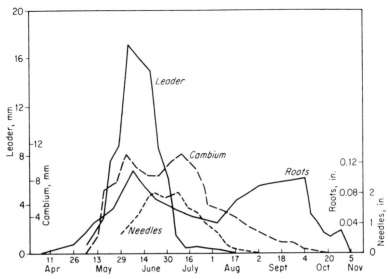

**Figure 3.2** Amount and seasonal duration of height (leader) growth, root elongation and cambial growth of 10-year-old eastern white pine trees in New Hampshire (11). (Courtesy of University of Chicago Press.)

branches are attached), internodes, and unexpanded leaves. Flower buds contain embryonic flowers, whereas mixed buds contain both flowers and leaves.

One of the remarkable features of shoot growth is that its seasonal duration varies greatly among species. Expansion of shoots of some species occurs in only 2 to 6 weeks during the early part of the frost-free season, and of other species in up to several months. Yet in most trees in the United States, elongation of shoots begins before the threat of frost is over and is completed relatively early in the frost-free season (Figure 3.3).

Seasonal duration of shoot expansion is correlated with hereditary patterns of formation of shoot components. At least three different patterns of shoot formation and expansion are recognized.

**Fixed Growth.** In some species, such as red pine, white pine, and beech, an annual shoot is the result of expansion of a bud that contained a preformed shoot. All of the leaves of the mature shoot were already present in the unexpanded bud. Shoot

growth of such species consists of differentiation of shoot components in the bud during one year and expansion of the preformed parts into a shoot during the second year. Shoot elongation in species with fixed growth occurs relatively rapidly and involves only the early part of the frost-free season. For example, elongation of shoots of red pine in Wisconsin is essentially completed by early July. Sometimes shoot growth of species that exhibit fixed growth is complicated when they produce abnormal late-season "lammas," shoots from opening of current-year buds that are not expected to open until the following year (2).

**Free Growth.** Some shoots of poplars and birches are not fully preformed in the winter bud. Shoot growth involves expansion of leaves that were present in the winter bud (early leaves) as well as additional leaves (late leaves) that formed after seasonal shoot expansion started. The continuous formation of leaf primordia in species exhibiting free growth resembles leaf growth of many herbaceous plants. Expansion of shoots by

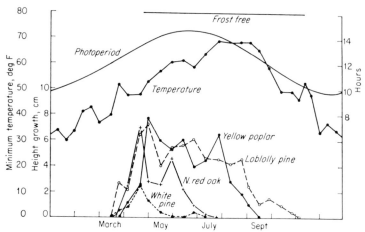

**Figure 3.3** Variations among species in seasonal duration of height growth in North Carolina (16).

free growth occurs over a much longer part of the summer than does expansion of shoots with fixed growth.

**Recurrently Flushing Growth.** Some species, such as the southern pines, many tropical pines and tropical broad-leaved trees, and temperate-zone shrubs, produce shoots in a series of waves or "flushes." This involves the recurrent formation and expansion of a series of buds at the tip of the same elongating shoot. For example, in loblolly pine of the southern United States, the overwintering bud opens in the spring and rapidly expands into a shoot. Then a new bud rapidly forms at the apex of the same shoot, and very shortly thereafter its contents expand also, so the shoot continues to elongate. On any one shoot additional buds may also form and expand within the same growing season. Most individual shoots may have up to three major growth flushes, but as many as seven buds have been shown to form and elongate on the terminal leader of a recurrently flushing pine. Shoots in the upper crown generally exhibit more seasonal growth flushes than do those in the lower crown. Height growth of recurrently flushing species, such as loblolly pine, continues throughout much of the summer.

So far the discussion has been directed to elongation of internodes or shoot axes. Duration of leaf expansion sometimes is correlated with internode expansion and sometimes not. In most deciduous trees the individual leaves expand in a period of days to a few weeks. By comparison, expansion of needles of pines requires a relatively long time. In red pine, for example, the shoot axis or "candle" usually expands in Wisconsin by early July, whereas the needles continue to elongate into late summer.

**Tree Form.** The shapes of many tree crowns are related to the degree of inhibition of growth of lower shoots by those higher up on the stem, a characteristic called *apical dominance*. For example, in many conifers with strong apical dominance, such as pines, the central stem (terminal leader) elongates more each year than the branches below it (Table 3.1). Furthermore, the amount of annual shoot elongation in different whorls of branches tends to decrease from the top of the tree downward. Also, branches attached to the main stem (secondary axes) elongate more than their own branches (tertiary axes). This very orderly pattern of shoot-growth inhibition produces a conical tree form that is often described as *excurrent*. Christmas

75

**Table 3-1**

Apical Dominance in 6-Year-Old Conifers as Shown by Variations in Shoot Elongation on Different Stem Locations[a]

| | Primary Axis (Terminal Leader) | Secondary Axis Whorl Number | | | | Tertiary Axis Whorl Number | | | | | Quarternary Axis Whorl Number | |
|---|---|---|---|---|---|---|---|---|---|---|---|---|
| | | 1 (Terminal) | 2 | 3 | 4 | 2 | 3 Upper Set | 3 Lower Set | 4 Upper Set | 4 Lower Set | 3 | 4 |
| Red pine | 57.7 | 34.6 | 32.5 | 27.7 | 15.4 | 17.1 | 15.3 | 13.7 | 11.5 | 8.1 | 6.2 | 4.7 |
| White pine | 44.3 | 25.5 | 24.8 | 19.1 | 14.1 | 12.3 | 10.5 | 9.5 | 7.8 | 7.3 | 4.3 | 3.0 |
| White spruce | 33.5 | 19.8 | 17.4 | 15.3 | 11.8 | | | | | | | |
| Black spruce | 23.8 | 17.3 | 16.5 | 14.1 | 10.0 | | | | | | | |

*Source.* T. T. Kozlowski and R. C. Ward, *For. Sci.*, 7, 357 (1961).
[a] All measurements are in centimeters.

tree growers often take advantage of such apical dominance by shaping trees through shearing. By removing tips of lateral shoots they stimulate expansion of subordinate shoots and formation and expansion of new buds into additional shoots. The end result of such treatment is a well-shaped, bushy Christmas tree (2).

Many deciduous trees do not show an orderly variation in shoot growth. Instead, they branch and rebranch until sometimes it is difficult to identify the main stem. In such *decurrent* or *deliquescent* trees, many shoots may elongate at about the same rate. Different deliquescent trees often have characteristic crown shapes. For example, beech and oak tend to have ovate to elongate crowns, whereas American elm has a vase- or umbrella-shaped crown.

## Cambial Growth

Growth in thickness of trees is traceable to activity of the cambium, a thin sheathing meristem located between the *xylem* (wood) and *phloem* (inner bark) of the stem, branches, and major roots. (Figure 3.1). Cambial cells divide tangentially to cut off

xylem cells to the inside and phloem cells to the outside. These cambial derivatives then undergo *differentiation* in a series of overlapping phases consisting of cell enlargement, secondary wall formation, lignification, and loss of protoplasts. As a consequence of cambial growth, new layers of wood and inner bark are inserted each year between the previous year's layer of wood and bark, causing increase in stem diameter. More wood than bark is laid down each year, the bark cells eventually collapse and die, and old outer bark is sloughed off from the tree.

The annual rings of wood as seen in cross sections of tree stems are the result of variations in growth rate and in the type of wood produced early and late in the growing season. The wood formed early (earlywood or springwood) has large cells with relatively thin cell walls and is much less dense than the wood formed late in the season (latewood or summerwood). Annual rings stand out in stem cross sections because of the differences in density of earlywood of one year that is adjacent to the last-formed latewood cells of the previous year (Figure 3.4).

In the temperate zone one ring of wood is usually

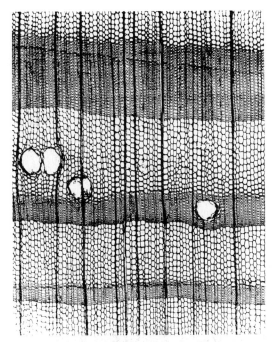

**Figure 3.4.** Variations in wood of longleaf pine produced early in the growing season (earlywood) and wood produced late in the growing season (latewood). The earlywood cells are much larger in diameter and have proportionally thinner walls. Resin canals are present in some annual rings. (Courtesy of U.S.D.A. Forest Service.)

produced each year. In some years, however, more than one ring may form. Hence, we recognize "false" or "multiple" rings. Also when cambial dormancy occurs on one side of a tree, as in trees with injured crowns or in very old trees, partial or "discontinuous" rings, which do not complete the branch or stem circumference, will form. Sometimes frosts that occur after annual growth starts injure the cambium and cause 'frost" rings to form. These sometimes are mistaken for annual rings. Under a microscope, frost rings can be identified by the presence of abnormal cambial derivatives, collapsed cells, and displaced ray cells. Variations in ring formation emphasize that ring counts do not always indicate the true age of a tree.

The amount of wood laid down in the stem varies considerably with stem height (Figure 3.5). Usually the width of the annual sheath of wood laid down by the cambium is near the stem height of greatest leaf volume. Below the crown the thickness of the annual growth ring varies greatly with tree vigor. In vigorous trees the annual growth ring becomes progressively narrower down the stem, but widens again near the base. In slow-growing suppressed trees, the whole growth ring is thinner than in vigorous trees, and little or no wood is laid down in the lower stem. In contrast, open-grown trees with large crowns often show increases in ring thickness all the way down to the base of the stem.

## Root Growth

The most common types of roots are taproots as found in oaks and hickories and fibrous or *heterorhizic* root systems such as those in pines. However, rooting characteristics of some species

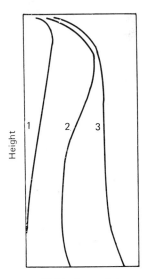

Width of annual ring

**Figure 3.5** Variations in thickness of the annual ring produced at different stem heights in (1) suppressed trees with small crowns, (2) dominant trees with large crowns, and (3) open grown trees with larger crowns than in (1) or (2) (17). (Courtesy of Canadian Institute of Forestry.)

often cannot be rigidly classified because the environment greatly alters the pattern of root growth. Red maple, for example, has a very plastic root system. It develops many shallow laterals in swamps and a deep taproot in dry upland soils. A few species have root systems that are strongly fixed by heredity.

The root system of a tree consists of large perennial roots and many small ones that are short-lived. Death of many small roots occurs normally, mostly during the winter, but can take place at other times as well because of unfavorable environmental conditions or attacks by various pests. Complete defoliation of a tree may cause rapid death of most of the small feeding rootlets. The absorbing surface of small feeder roots of many species is increased by the presence of root hairs. The majority of these live only for a matter of days or weeks. As old root hairs die new ones form behind the growing tip of a root.

The rate of root elongation is quite variable during the season, and in many species it occurs in cycles that are responsive to environmental changes. As might be expected, the rate of root growth varies at different soil depths because of differences in water supply, aeration, mineral supply, temperature, etc. Seasonal cambial growth in roots begins first near the soil surface, and then the growth wave moves downward. Cambial growth in roots is much more irregular than it is in stems. False and double rings in roots, as well as roots that are eccentric in cross section, are common.

Some trees produce various interesting specialized roots such as grafted roots (Figure 3.6), knee roots (pneumatophores), and mycorrhizae (described in the following paragraph) (1). When trees are connected by root grafts there often is transfer, from one tree to another, of carbohydrates, growth hormones, water, and minerals. Sometimes stumps stay alive for many years because they are supplied with growth requirements by a living tree through root grafts. Herbicides injected into one tree can also move through grafted roots and kill another tree by "backflash." In addition, serious fungus diseases

**Figure 3.6**  Grafted roots of balsam fir trees (12). (Courtesy of Society of American Foresters.)

can be translocated through root grafts. For example, local spread of Dutch elm disease and oak wilt has often been associated with root grafting (see Figure 8.5).

Roots of many species of trees are invaded by soil fungi to form root-fungus associations called *mycorrhizae*. These associations are of two kinds: the *ectocellular* mycorrhizae, in which the fungus exists both inside and outside the root, and the *endocellular* forms, in which the fungus exists within root cells. The presence of mycorrhizae is necessary for establishment and growth of many trees. The mycorrhizal relation appears to be a reciprocal one in which the tree supplies carbohydrates and other growth requirements to the fungus, and the fungus increases mineral uptake by the host tree (3). Mycorrhizae are further discussed in Chapters 4 and 8.

## Reproductive Growth

Development of seeds and fruits involves several orderly stages including floral induction, enlargement of the inflorescence, flowering, pollination, fertilization (fusion of male and female gametes), and growth and ripening of fruits and seeds. Failure to produce seeds or fruits often results from internal blocks at one of these essential phases of reproductive growth.

Reproductive growth of some trees is fairly regular, and in others it is very irregular and unpredictable. Biennial bearing of fruit trees is a good example of predictable reproductive growth. Some varieties bear a heavy flower and fruit crop one year and little or none the following year. Two species of the same genus may have different patterns of reproductive growth. For example, sugar maple tends to have good seed crops at several-year intervals, whereas red maple and silver maple are more likely to have good seed crops annually.

When a heavy fruit or seed crop occurs, both shoot growth and cambial growth are reduced during the same year or the following year. This has been shown rather dramatically in biennially bearing fruit trees. Decreases in shoot growth of up to half in years following heavy fruit crops have been authenticated. Inhibition of shoot growth by reproductive growth has also been shown in forest trees. For example, in balsam fir the shoots of flowering trees were only about half as long as those of nonflowering trees. Furthermore, the shoots of flowering trees had poorly developed needles. Years of abundant seed production in both conifers and broad-leaved trees have also been correlated with reduced diameter growth. During good seed years, for example, the width of annual rings of beech was only about half of that in years of low seed production. Heavy seed production also reduced diameter growth for two years thereafter. Such observations emphasize that the reproductive phase of growth monopolized substances required for growth. When a fruit is set it becomes a powerful sink or mobilizer of available carbohydrates, which are then not readily available for vegetative growth. Hence, an interesting internal competition for metabolites goes on between reproductive and vegetative tissue, with the vegetative tissue usually unable to compete successfully.

**Vegetative Reproduction.** Most forest stands reproduce by seeds, but vegetative propagation by stump sprouts and root suckers is important for reproducing certain species of trees. Sprouting is the most important type of vegetative propagation of broad-leaved forest trees, especially various species of oaks and birches (see Figure 19.7). Although sprouting occurs much less commonly in conifers than in broad-leaved trees, a few conifers do sprout readily. These include redwood, pitch pine, shortleaf pine, and bald cypress.

A distinction should be made between stump sprouts and root suckers. Stump sprouts, which arise from root collars, develop from dormant buds that formed early, remained suppressed, and grew outward with the cambium. Root suckers arise from recently formed adventitious buds on roots. Reproduction by root suckers is characteristic of a few broad-leaved species only, following disturbance of a stand of trees by harvesting or fire, for example. Reproduction by root suckers is best known in aspen but it occurs also in beech, sweetgum, black locust, and sassafras.

## Aging of Trees

Like other organisms, trees show aging characteristics. During their early development, trees pass from a juvenile to an adult stage. The juvenile stage differs considerably from the adult stage in growth habit and vigor, capacity for flowering, ease of rooting of cuttings, stem anatomy, leaf retention, leaf shape, and other characteristics. The length of the juvenile stage varies greatly among species from less than a year to many years. Perhaps the best-known indicator of adulthood in trees is the capacity for flowering. Juvenile woody plants do not flower. Once the capacity for flowering is reached, however, individual trees still may not flower annually because their reproductive growth is then modified by various environmental and internal factors.

Among the remarkable mysteries of tree growth is the wide variation in longevity of different species. Perhaps the oldest living trees are the bristlecone pines growing in California. Some of these are in excess of 4000 years old (see Figure P2-1 redwoods achieve an age in excess of 3000 years, some junipers 2000 years, some oaks 1500 years, and sugar maple up to 500 years. By comparison, gray birch is old at 40 years.

The infirmities of old age in trees can be seen in decreases in metabolism and growth, slow wound healing, and decreases in resistance to diseases and insect attacks. Heartwood formation is also associated with aging. Wood of young trees consists entirely of sapwood, which contains mostly dead cells but approximately 10 percent of its cells are alive. When a tree reaches a critical age, which varies with species and environmental conditions, heartwood (Figure 3.1) is produced from the living cells in the central core of the stem that die and become physiologically inactive. Once heartwood formation starts it usually continues, so the innermost sapwood rings turn into heartwood. Changes involved in heartwood formation include death of ray cells and vertically oriented axial parenchyma cells, darkening of wood as a result of deposition of extractive substances (including dyestuffs, tannins, oils, gums, resins, salts, etc.), decrease in metabolic rate, and changes in wood density. The moisture content of heartwood usually is considerably lower than that of sapwood, but sometimes exceptions occur.

**Aging and Growth Characteristics.** Beginning with the seedling one can measure an increase in amount of shoot growth each year for several years and then a progressive annual decline in shoot growth of an aging tree. Some trees such as ginkgo and larch produce a higher proportion of short shoots to long shoots as they age. In ginkgo this results in changing the tree from having an *excurrent* form when it is young to a *globose* form when it is old. As the rate of growth of a tree decreases in the old tree, the leaves become smaller and dead branches are more prevalent.

Cambial growth declines as an aging phenomenon, and annual rings tend to become narrower each year in aging trees. However, a consistent pattern of narrowing annual rings can be altered from year to year by environmental influences, especially variation in rainfall. As trees grow old, they tend to have more discontinuous and missing rings, toward the base of the stem. The rate of root growth also decreases in aging trees. In addition, the capacity of both intact trees and stem cuttings for producing *adventitious roots* declines rapidly after some critical tree age is reached. Anyone who has ever tried to root cuttings from old trees knows that it is essential to cut from young trees only, as soon as the desirable characteristics one wishes to propagate are evident.

## INTERNAL REQUIREMENTS FOR GROWTH

To survive and grow, trees must have adequate supplies of carbohydrates, water, minerals, and hormonal growth regulators. Internal control of growth of both vegetative and reproductive tissues involves close interdependency between roots and shoots as sources of the essential growth-controlling factors. Through its life span a tree is supplied by its leaves and roots, over increasingly longer translocation paths, with substances needed for growth. This requires a delicate balance and precise correlations in rates of physiological processes.

### Carbohydrates

Inasmuch as over two-thirds of the dry weight of trees consists of transformed sugars, their dry weight increment depends fundamentally on control of synthesis of foods and their orderly and efficient assimilation by *vegetative* and *reproductive tissues*. Because carbohydrates are direct photosynthetic products and materials from which proteins and fats are synthesized, they are considered the most important class of foods in growth of woody plants (4). Although most carbohydrates are synthesized in leaves, small amounts may also be produced in other tree tissues, including twigs, flowers, and developing fruits. It should be remembered that trees are not always self-sufficient in production and use of foods; many examples can be cited of carbohydrate transfer among woody plants. For example, some trees obtain carbohydrates from neighboring trees through root grafts. Parasitism is also shown by accumulation of carbohydrates from host trees by mistletoes.

**Photosynthesis.** In photosynthesis, simple sugars are manufactured from carbon dioxide and water in the chlorophyll-containing tissues of plants exposed to light. Photosynthesis undoubtedly is the most important physiological process in trees. It occurs only in green tissues because chlorophyll plays an essential role in the absorption of light energy and its conversion into chemical energy. The photosynthetic process may be summarized as follows:

$$\text{light energy}$$
$$6\ CO_2 + 6H_2O \rightarrow C_6H_{12}O_6 + 6O_2$$
$$\text{carbon dioxide} + \text{water} \rightarrow \text{sugar} + \text{oxygen}$$

In trees sugars are converted to starch whenever a high level of sugar builds up—and starches are transformed to sugars when amounts of sugars are low and at low temperatures. Sucrose is the predominant translocated sugar in trees. Glucose and fructose also occur commonly. Several other sugars may be present, usually in small amounts.

**Utilization of Foods.** A large proportion of the carbohydrate pool is *translocated* to the numerous stem and root tips and along the entire cambial sheath where carbohydrates are converted into new protoplasm and cell walls of vegetative and reproductive tissues. (A further discussion of the development of polysaccharides and cell wall structure from sugars is given in Chapter 18). Large amounts of carbohydrates are consumed in respiration, providing energy for synthesis and growth, and the remainder is accumulated in various tissues and subsequently used. These uses of carbohydrates will be discussed separately.

*Vegetative Growth.* Both stored and currently produced carbohydrates are used in apical and cambial growth. Because various parts of trees grow at different rates and at different times of the year, the utilization of carbohydrates is extremely variable over the tree axis. For example, shoot expansion of most species consumes foods for a shorter period than does cambial growth in the same tree. Seasonal duration of root elongation is greater than the period of cambial growth or shoot expansion; hence it depletes available carbohydrates for a very long time. The rate and duration of carbohydrate depletion along the stem and main branches also vary considerably.

The amount of food that is used in vegetative growth varies among species and from year to year partly because of the large differences in amounts channeled to reproductive tissues. During years of heavy fruiting or seed production, a very large percentage of the available food supply is diverted from vegetative to reproductive tissues.

Opening of buds and expansion of shoots involve utilization of large quantities of carbohydrates. When buds open in the spring, carbohydrates move upward in the growing shoots through reactivated phloem. Marked seasonal depletion of carbohydrate reserves from adjacent tissues as shoot growth begins has been demonstrated for many trees. In the literature the generalization is often made that shoot growth utilizes primarily stored carbohydrates in contrast to cambial growth, which depends mostly on very recently produced photosynthetic products. However, the variety of shoot-growth patterns observed among species, among age classes of the same species, and even among different shoots on the same tree indicates that various degrees of utilization of reserve and currently produced carbohydrates occur (1). In considering the use of food in shoot growth, it is important to distinguish between utilization of carbohydrates in *leaf expansion* and in *internode elongation*. These two components of shoot growth are often out of phase and sometimes use different proportions of current and reserve carbohydrates.

Carbohydrates are used in production of new cambial cells and in xylem and phloem development. Both reserve carbohydrates and current photosynthate are used in cambial growth, with the latter probably most important. Cambial growth generally appears to be limited more by the rate of carbohydrate conversion to new tissues than by the amount of available food. For example, cambial growth can be rapidly checked by late-summer droughts when trees have substantial carbohydrate reserves.

*Reproductive Growth.* Production of seed and fruit crops consumes large amounts of carbohydrates. Growing reproductive tissues are able to divert foods from vegetative tissues. Mobilization of carbohydrates into flowers, fruits, and seeds of many orchard and forest trees has been demonstrated. However, it is difficult to compare the proportional amounts used in vegetative and reproductive growth because these vary greatly among trees, and especially from year to year when seed crops are irregular.

*Respiration.* Respiration, the oxidation of foods resulting in release of energy, occurs in all living cells during the day and night and throughout the dormant and growing seasons. Therefore a very significant portion of the total amount of food produced is consumed in respiration. Various investigators have calculated respiratory losses of carbohydrates in trees. These usually were determined as daytime rates during the growing season and were compared with rates of food production over the same period. However, realistic appraisals of total respiratory losses should account for additional losses during the night and throughout the dormant season when photosynthesis does not occur.

Respiration rates vary greatly among species and tissues and they differ greatly with time. The important internal factors that control respiration are age of tissues, amount of substrate, and tissue hydration. Respiration also is influenced by changes in temperature, light, gaseous composition of the atmosphere, injury, and various biocides (1).

Research has shown that approximately 60 percent of the gross photosynthate of beech trees was lost by respiration in roots, stems, branches, and leaves and by abscission of roots, branches, and leaves (5). Hence only about 40 percent was available for growth. The amount of respiratory loss by trees varied with age, with 40 percent used by 25-year-old trees and 50 percent by 85-year-old trees. Under the high temperatures of tropical forests, the losses of foods by respiration are tremendous and greatly exceed those in trees of temperate zones. For example, in tropical rain forests of the Ivory Coast, respiration may consume almost three-fourths of the dry matter produced.

*Accumulation.* Starch, which is formed by condensation of many glucose molecules, is the major storage form of carbohydrate. In stems the vertically oriented *axial parenchyma cells* and laterally oriented *ray parenchyma cells* in xylem rays (see Figure 3.1) are the major sites of starch storage. In the bark starch is deposited in parenchyma and albuminous cells, which are distributed in a variety of patterns.

The xylem sap of some species contains appreciable amounts of sugar, whereas the sap of others contains only negligible amounts. The outstanding example of a species with a sap high in sugar content is sugar maple, which is tapped annually to make maple syrup. In this species xylem sap usually has a sugar content of 2 or 3 percent, but high-yielding trees may contain up to 8 or even 10 percent. The sugar represents a supply of carbohydrates including starch, sucrose, and hexoses that accumulated during the late summer. Much of the starch is converted to sugar in early winter. The sugar concentration of maple sap is low early in the spring, rises rapidly to a maximum, and then decreases toward the end of the summer. Tapping the stem of mature trees usually produces 40 to 80 liters of sap from a tree, but up to 160 liters may be obtained from some trees.

It is important to distinguish between the total amount and concentration of carbohydrates in different parts of trees. Carbohydrate distribution is often presented in terms of percentage of dry weight in various tissues. Such data sometimes are misleading because carbohydrate concentrations often are high in tissues that comprise a low proportion of the total dry weight of a tree. For example, the concentration of carbohydrates usually is higher in roots than in stems. Nevertheless, in many trees the parts above ground are the primary carbohydrate reservoir because the stem, branches, and leaves make up more of the total dry weight of a tree than do the roots. The carbohydrates in stems are concentrated in living cells, but living plus dead cells, and mostly the latter, are usually used as the dry-weight base for calculating carbohydrate concentrations. This tends to give a very low concentration and is rather misleading with respect to total amounts. The concentration of carbohydrates in the bark often is very high but in many species the total amount in the bark is less than in the wood.

## Water for Tree Growth

The importance of water supply cannot be overemphasized because in many areas water undoubtedly controls growth and survival of trees more than any other factor. Only rarely are soil moisture supplies at optimal levels during the growing season, and tremendous losses in growth result each year because of water deficits in trees. The staggering amounts of such losses are not realized because data usually are not available to show how much more growth would occur if trees had favorable water supplies throughout the growing season. The importance of water is emphasized by the fact that many deserts and grasslands would support trees if an adequate supply of water were available.

Water is indispensable for trees. It is the following:

1. The primary constituent of *protoplasm*. Water content is high in growing tissues (comprising 80 to 90 percent of their fresh weight) and low in tissues that are not actively growing.

2. A reagent in important *biological reactions*. Water is a reactant in the process of photosyn-

thesis. It should be emphasized that only a small amount of water, perhaps less than 5 percent of the total taken up by a tree, is used in metabolism. Most of the absorbed water is subsequently lost from the leaves and does not enter into biological processes.

3. A *solvent* in which materials necessary for growth are transported into and through trees; for example, minerals move in the water stream.

4. A maintainer of *turgidity*. Enough water must be present in leaves to keep the cells turgid for cell enlargement and growth to occur.

**Sources of Water.** Most of the water that trees use is obtained from the soil, but some trees also obtain some water from the atmosphere and from adjacent trees if their roots are grafted together. In certain arid regions, dew and fog are absorbed by leaves and contribute significantly to the water economy of trees.

**Loss of Water.** Trees are constructed such that they lose large amounts of water. In the first place their leaves are perforated with many stomata. These are microscopic pores, each surrounded by two specialized guard cells (Figure 3.7). Stomata average from about 10 to 20 microns in length, and there are about 10,000 to 100,000 of these per square centimeter of leaf surface. In most broad-leaved trees stomata occur only on the undersurface of leaves, but in a few species, such as poplars and willows, they occur on both the upper and lower surfaces. In addition to serving as passages through which water is lost, stomata also provide a path through which the carbon dioxide used in photosynthesis enters leaves.

*Transpiration*, the loss of water from trees in the form of vapor, is basically an evaporation process. It is modified somewhat by plant structure and by stomatal control. In leaves it occurs in two stages involving: (1) evaporation from the wet walls of mesophyll cells into intercellular spaces, and (2) diffusion of water vapor from the intercellular

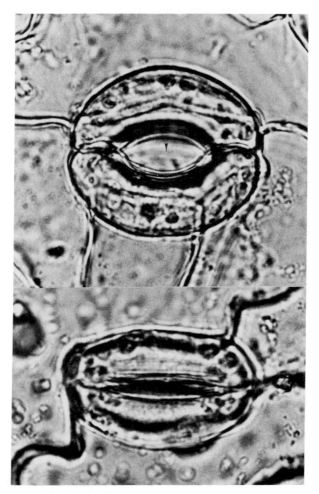

**Figure 3.7**  Open stoma (upper photo) and closed stoma with collapsed guard cells (lower photo). (Photograph courtesy of J.E. Pallas.)

spaces into the outside air. Small amounts of water are lost directly through the epidermal layers of leaves depending on the thickness of the waxy layer on leaf surfaces, and very small amounts are lost through lenticels of twigs, even from deciduous trees in winter. Lenticels are small pores in the tree bark that permit diffusion of gases between the plant and the atmosphere.

The amounts of water taken up by trees and lost by transpiration are very high. It is not uncommon for a large tree to lose as much as a barrel of water a day. The rate of water loss is exceedingly variable, however, and differs greatly with species, site, age of tree, depth and extent of rooting, and even different parts of the same tree. The rate of transpiration also varies greatly with such environmental factors as soil moisture, humidity of the air, wind, light intensity, and temperature.

Adding to conditions for high rates of water loss is the very extensive leaf area developed by trees and exposed to the atmosphere. Trees differ greatly in the number of leaves they bear, with conifers having many more than broad-leaved trees of comparable age. Whereas individual mature broad-leaved trees have leaves numbering in the tens of thousands, individual conifers often have millions. One study showed that a 36-year-old white spruce tree had over 5 million needles. In general, leaf size and leaf number are negatively correlated. But whether trees have very many small leaves or fewer large ones, the central fact remains that in both cases they expose an extensive leaf surface that constantly evaporates water that must somehow be replaced.

**Absorption and Conduction of Water.** The water-absorbing surface of roots of many species of trees is increased by development of *root hairs*. These tubular outgrowths form just behind a growing root tip. Most root hairs live only a few days or weeks. The zone of root hairs migrates because, as old root hairs die, new ones are formed behind the growing point of an elongating root. In a few species, the old root hairs persist for a long time but these are not very efficient in absorbing water. As root systems age, an increasing proportion of their total surface becomes covered with a fatty or waxy material called *suberin*. Only the most recently formed roots are unsuberized, and it often has been assumed that suberized portions of roots do not absorb water. This is not necessarily true. In fact, one study showed that less than 5 percent of the total water absorbed by trees was taken up through unsuberized roots. The very large quantity of water that was taken up by suberized roots entered through lenticels, crevices around branch roots, and openings left by death of branch roots.

After soil water is absorbed through the small roots, it goes through several root tissues (epidermis, cortex, pericycle) before it enters the vertically oriented water-conducting elements of tissue called the xylem. In mature *ring-porous* hardwood trees, such as oak, upward water movement is confined to a thin cylinder of the outer sapwood and often to the outermost annual ring. In *diffuse-porous* hardwoods, such as maple and poplar, and in many conifers, the path of ascent of water occupies several rings of sapwood (the characteristics of ring- and diffuse-porous wood are described in Chapter 17). Deviation from a strictly vertical path of upward water movement is common. In many species, water spirals as it moves upward because of spiral grain in trees. The central core of heartwood does not conduct water.

When water reaches the crown it enters the many branches and finally goes into the leaves through a complex system of veins (Figure 3.8). It then evaporates into the intercellular spaces of the leaves and diffuses outward through the stomatal pores into the atmosphere.

**Figure 3.8** System of major and minor veins in leaf of grey birch (X125). (Photograph courtesy of D. H. Franck.)

**Development of Water Deficits.** Droughts affect tree growth by causing water deficits in their tissues. Internal water deficits are controlled by relative rates of absorption of water and transpiration and by internal redistribution of water. During the day more water is lost from the leaves by transpiration than is taken in by absorption through the roots because of resistance to water movement through the tree (Figure 3.9). The resulting internal water deficits usually are eliminated by a high rate of absorption overnight. At night stomata are closed and transpiration is low or negligible.

For the reasons just cited, water contents of leaves vary daily, with the highest water contents occurring in the early morning. Leaf moisture contents decrease throughout the morning, reach a minimum sometime in the early afternoon, and then begin to increase sometime in the late afternoon. Moisture contents of tree trunks also vary daily and seasonally. Tree trunks generally have the highest water contents in the spring, sometime around the time of beginning of bud opening. When the buds open and leaves emerge, transpiration begins and tends to deplete the stem of water throughout the summer. Water lost is replaced by absorption through the roots, but a general seasonal trend is toward a steady depletion of stem water during the summer until a minimum moisture content is reached, often just before leaf-fall. This seasonal trend of declining water content of tree stems is interrupted by temporary replenishing of stem water during rainy periods.

It should be clear from the foregoing discussion that internal water deficits in trees can be the result of either: (1) excessive transpiration; (2) slow absorption of water from dry, cold, or poorly aerated soil; or (3) a combination of both.

**Effects of Water Deficits.** When the internal moisture content of trees decreases, many physiological processes are affected adversely, resulting in growth loss. Among the processes influenced by water deficits are absorption of water, stomatal aperture, transpiration, photosynthesis, respiration, and mineral uptake. Very severe water stresses often injure and kill trees.

*Stomatal Aperture.* One of the very early responses to leaf-water stress is *stomatal closure*. As guard cells are dehydrated the stomata close (Figure 3.7), often during very early stages of a drought and long before leaves wilt. Even where the soil is wet, the stomata often close temporarily in the middle of

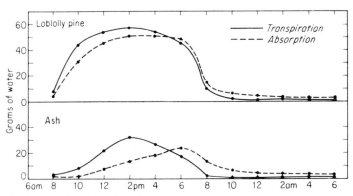

**Figure 3.9** Diurnal variation in rates of water loss from leaves (transpiration) and water uptake through the roots (absorption) (13). (Courtesy of American Journal of Botany.)

the day because the rate of transpiration exceeds the rate of absorption of water.

***Shrinking and Swelling.*** Various tissues and organs of trees usually shrink slightly during the day, when transpiration exceeds absorption, and they expand at night as trees rehydrate (Figure 3.10). Afternoon stem shrinkage occurs often even in trees that are in well-watered soil.

It has been shown that leaf shrinkage and expansion are closely related to environmental conditions affecting stomatal aperture and transpiration of trees (6). Both diurnal and seasonal shrinkage of tree stems has been well documented. In addition to reversible daily stem shrinkage, progressive seasonal shrinkage of tree stems occurs commonly during droughts. Fruits also shrink during the day and expand at night. Diurnal shrinking and swelling of fruits as a result of their dehydration and rehydration have been recorded in lemons, oranges, apples, peaches, pears, walnuts, and even oak acorns. Both seasonal and diurnal shrinkage of pine cones occurs. Young cones show a progressive increase in diameter with little or no superimposed midday shrinkage. In a midstage of development cones tend to shrink during the day and swell at night. When cones approach maturity they show predominant continuous shrinkage (7).

***Growth Inhibition.*** Droughts inhibit both shoot and diameter growth during the year of occurrence of the drought, but the effect often carries over to the next year or years. The degree to which growth is inhibited varies with the severity and duration of the drought and with growth characteristics of trees (1). During a dry year trees produce a narrow ring of wood. Because of resumption and cessation of cambial growth in response to rain followed by severe drought in the same growing season, false or multiple rings of wood may be laid down during one year. In addition to influencing the width of the annual ring, summer droughts influence earlywood-latewood relations. Trees respond to summer drought by earlier-than-normal initiation of formation of small-diameter latewood cells. Thereafter continued drought shortens the period during which latewood forms. Symptoms of severe drought include desiccation injury in the form of "scorch" of foliage, premature shedding of leaves, dieback of shoots, cracking of stems, and death of trees (8).

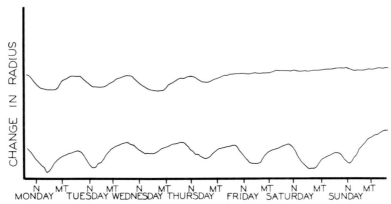

**Figure 3.10** Dendrograph traces showing shrinkage of red pine stems in the afternoon followed by swelling during the night. The upper curve is for the week of July 10−17; the lower curve for August 20−21. The upper curve does not show stem shrinkage and swelling during the latter part of the week when clouds and rainy weather prevailed (18). (Courtesy of International Institute of Arboriculture.)

## Minerals

Mineral nutrients have many functions in trees. They are constituents of plant tissues, catalysts in various reactions, osmotic regulators, constituents of buffer systems, and regulators of membrane permeability (1). An essential element has been defined as one whose absence will prevent completion of the normal life cycle of a plant. The present state of our knowledge includes the following mineral elements as essential for trees: nitrogen (N), phosphorus (P), potassium (K), sulfur (S), calcium (Ca), magnesium (Mg), iron (Fe), manganese (Mn), copper (Cu), zinc (Zn), boron (B), molybdenum (Mo), chlorine (Cl), and cobalt (Co). Of these, the first six are required in relatively large amounts and are called the major elements or *macronutrients*; the last eight are required in very small amounts and are called the minor elements or *micronutrients*.

**Effects of Mineral Deficiency.** The most important general effect of mineral deficiency is reduced growth, but the earliest and most conspicuous response is leaf yellowing, a condition called *chlorosis*, caused by reduced synthesis of chlorophyll. The rate of photosynthesis is greatly reduced in chlorotic trees. Other common symptoms of mineral deficiency include leaf spots, marginal scorching, dieback of shoots, rosetting, fusion of needles, and injury to reproductive structures. Mineral-deficiency symptoms vary with plant species, the deficient element or elements, and the degree of deficiency.

**Absorption, Translocation, and Cycling of Minerals.** The mineral nutrients enter a tree from the seed or as ions taken in from the soil. A small amount of dissolved ions in rainwater also is absorbed through the leaves. Mineral elements represent a relatively small proportion of total tree biomass. However, without an adequate supply of any of the essential mineral elements, tree growth

and function are impaired. The accumulation and availability of minerals in the soil are discussed in Chapter 4.

Ions that are absorbed by young roots move into the xylem and are translocated upward to the leaves by mass flow in the sap stream. Because all of these minerals cannot be stored or used by leaves, some of them enter the phloem and are redistributed. Movement of ions in the phloem occurs chiefly downward, but some upward movement also occurs. The more mobile elements move out of old leaves to young ones and into meristematic regions. There is also considerable lateral movement of minerals from the phloem to the xylem. Hence, at least some of the minerals circulate within the tree. A large proportion of ions in leaves of deciduous trees move back into the twigs shortly before the leaves are shed. Figure 3.11 summarizes the main features of mineral absorption and translocation by trees.

There is a continuous cycling of minerals between forest trees and the soil in which they are growing. As may be seen in Figure 3.12, some of the absorbed minerals are retained by trees and others eventually returned to the soil, largely by decomposition of litter. A smaller amount of loosely held minerals in leaves is washed out by rain and returned to the soil (see Chapters 4 and 6).

**Fertilizers.** Forest nursery soils often become deficient in mineral nutrients because large amounts are removed with the harvested trees and lost by leaching. The use of fertilizers to alleviate mineral deficiency in seedlings and transplants and to accelerate growth is standard practice in forest nurseries (Figure 3.13). Demands for increased wood production have led to application of fertilizers by airplanes over large areas of forest land. Addition of too much fertilizer sometimes results in reduced growth and injury in trees. High concentrations of salts in the soil solution may plasmolyze young roots and reduce water absorption, which, in turn, leads to desiccation of leaves, stomatal closure, reduction in photosynthesis, and inhibition of growth.

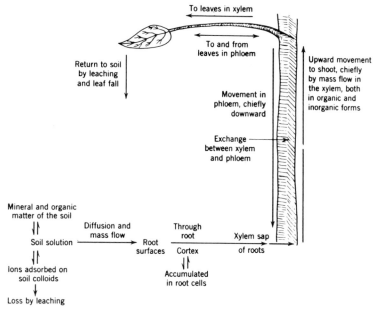

**Figure 3.11** Absorption and translocation of minerals in trees (14). (Courtesy of McGraw-Hill Books.)

## Hormonal Growth Regulators

Trees synthesize a number of plant-growth hormones that serve as chemical messengers and direct cells of widely separated tissues and organs to carry out the functions of growth and differentiation. The five groups of hormones that are involved in such integrative roles include auxins, gibberellins, cytokinins, ethylene, and a growth inhibitor called abscisic acid (ABA). Each of these has been identified with control of specific plant processes, yet each can influence several aspects of growth and development including cell division, cell expansion, and differentiation. A characteristic of growth hormones is that they exert a regulatory role while present in minute concentrations.

Much evidence shows that various growth processes are coordinated by interactions among two or more plant-growth hormones, rather than by the influence of a single hormone. In these interactions one hormone may reinforce the influence of another (synergism) or it may counteract it (antagonism). The effect of hormones on initiation and subsequent control of growth is initiated by external factors such as light intensity, day length, water, and temperature.

**Hormonal Regulation of Growth.** This section will give examples of hormonal involvement in important growth processes.

*Dormancy.* To germinate, many seeds require specified environmental conditions such as cold or light. The hormonal growth inhibitor, ABA, is present in many seeds that are physiologically dormant. As the seed begins to germinate, the ABA level is reduced and the level of gibberellin, a growth promoter, is increased. Seed dormancy often can be broken with applied gibberellins. The obvi-

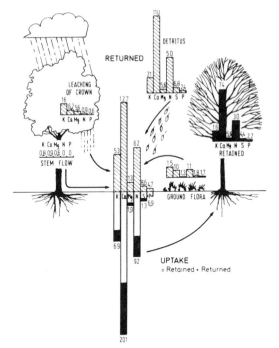

**Figure 3.12** Mineral cycling in a mixed hardwood forest in Belgium. Amounts of minerals cycled are given in kilograms per hectare per year. Yearly uptake of minerals is shown by the amounts retained by plants (solid bars) and those returned to the soil (cross-hatched bars) by leaching, stem flow, and litter (15). (Courtesy of Springer-Verlag.)

ous practical application of such control is that seed germination may be stimulated with applied hormones without long environmental requirements of stratification at low temperatures.

Dormancy of buds is usually broken in the field by many hours of exposure to low winter temperatures. After release from dormancy by chilling, buds require exposure to high temperature for a critical period before normal growth begins. Both induction of bud dormancy and its release are regulated by balances between endogenous growth promoters and inhibitors. During development of bud dormancy, the growth-regulator balance shifts in favor of inhibitors, such as ABA, over growth promoters

(auxins and gibberellins). In contrast, the release of bud dormancy is associated with an increase in growth promoters, a decrease in growth inhibitors, or both.

*Shoot Growth.* Both auxins and gibberellins regulate shoot expansion, with gibberellins playing a dominant role. The importance of gibberellins is shown by correlation of internode expansion with endogenous gibberellin levels, increase in shoot

**Figure 3.13** Response of black spruce seedling to fertilizer. The greatly increased growth of the terminal shoot followed application of a complete fertilizer. (Photograph courtesy of Pulp and Paper Research Institute of Canada.)

**90**

expansion after applying gibberellins, and counteracting the effects of applied growth retardants by application of gibberellins.

*Cambial Growth.* Plant hormones regulate several phases of cambial growth including division of cambial cells to produce xylem and phloem, increase in size of cambial derivatives, thickening of cell walls of cambial derivatives, beginning of formation of latewood, and termination of seasonal cambial growth. There is a close relationship between shoot activity in the spring and initiation of seasonal cambial growth. Growth-promoting hormones, which are produced in expanding buds, are translocated down the branches and main stem to stimulate cambial activity and production of wood and bark tissues.

*Reproductive Growth.* The initiation and development of flowers, fruits, and seeds are controlled by a series of hormonal signals. Although regulatory effects of hormones on reproductive growth are synergistic, several individual hormones appear to have very important roles at different stages of the reproductive cycle.

This chapter has presented only a generalized review of the physiology of tree growth. Readers interested in expanding their knowledge of each of the sections in this chapter are referred to the book *Physiology of Woody Plants* by Kramer and Kozlowski (1).

## REFERENCES

1. P. J. Kramer and T. T. Kozlowski, *Physiology of Woody Plants*, Academic Press, New York, 1979.
2. T. T. Kozlowski, *Growth and Development of Trees.* Vol. I, Academic Press, New York, 1971.
3. G. C. Marks and T. T. Kozlowski, eds., *Ectomycorrhizae*, Academic Press, New York, 1973.
4. T. T. Kozlowski and T. Keller, *Bot. Rev., 32*, 293 (1966).
5. C. M. Möller, M. D. Müller, and J. Nielsen, *Det Forstlige Forsögsväsen i Danmark, 21,* 327 (1954).
6. W. R. Chaney and T. T. Kozlowski, *Ann. Bot., 33,* 691 (1969).
7. D. I. Dickmann and T. T. Kozlowski, *Can. J. Bot., 47,* 839 (1969).
8. T. T. Kozlowski, ed., *Water Deficits and Plant Growth.* Vols. 1−6, Academic Press, New York, 1968−1981.
9. T. T. Kozlowski and R. C. Ward, *For. Sci., 7,* 357 (1961).
10. P. H. Raven, R. F. Evert, and H. Curtis, *Biology of Plants*, Worth Publishers, New York, 1981.
11. R. Kienholz, *Bot. Gaz., 96,* 73 (1934).
12. T. T. Kozlowski and J. C. Cooley, *J. For., 59,* 105 (1961).
13. P. J. Kramer, *Amer. J. Bot., 24,* 10 (1937).
14. P. J. Kramer, *Plant and Soil Water Relations: A Modern Synthesis*, McGraw-Hill, New York, 1969.
15. W. Larcher, *Physiological Plant Ecology*, Springer-Verlag, New York, 1980.
16. P. J. Kramer and T. T. Kozlowski, *Physiology of Trees*, McGraw-Hill, New York, 1960.
17. J. L. Farrar, *Forestry Chron., 37,* 323 (1961).
18. T. T. Kozlowski, "Water balance in shade trees," *Proc. 44th Int. Shade Tree Conf.*, 1968.

# 4

# FOREST SOILS

## James G. Bockheim

Forest-soil science is a broad field involving chemistry, physics, geology, forestry, and other disciplines. Because soils have a profound influence on both the composition and productivity of a forest, it is important for the forester to understand the basic character of soils. Possibly the most significant contributions that soil science has made to forestry are: (1) matching tree species to soil type so that increases in survival and growth rate of trees can be realized, and (2) evaluating hazards or limitations to forest management based on soil properties. In this chapter the properties of forest soils will be treated through a comparison of the forest soil and the agricultural soil.

## CONCEPT OF FOREST SOIL

The forest soil has been defined as "a portion of the earth's surface which serves as a medium for the sustenance of forest vegetation; it consists of mineral and organic matter permeated by varying amounts of water and air and is inhabited by organisms. It exhibits peculiar characteristics acquired under the influence of the three factors uncommon to other soils—forest litter, tree roots, and specific organisms whose existence depends on the presence of forest vegetation" (1). Soil has also been defined as a natural body with physical, chemical, and biological properties governed by the interaction of five soil-forming factors: initial material (geologic substratum), climate, organisms, and topography, all acting over a period of time. A third view of the soil is that it is the interface of the atmosphere, lithosphere, and biosphere where materials are added, transformed, translocated, and lost because of natural cycling mechanisms. Nikiforoff (2) described the soil as the "excited skin of the sub-aerial portion of the earth's surface."

Soils are important to trees because they: (1) offer mechanical support, (2) retain and transmit water and gases, (3) serve as a habitat for macro- and microorganisms, and (4) hold, exchange, and fix nutrients.

## STRUCTURE AND PROPERTIES OF SOILS

### Soil Morphology

A soil profile[1] is a two-dimensional section or lateral view of a soil excavation. The *soil profile* is divided into a number of sections termed *soil horizons,* which are distinct, more or less parallel, genetic layers in the soil (Figure 4.1). The forest floor (*0* horizon) is a layer of partially decomposed and humified organic matter that overlies a series of mineral horizons. In contrast to most forest soils, the agricultural soil features a plow layer over a thin compacted zone known as the plow sole (Figure 4.2). *A* horizons are those that have accumulated organic matter or that have lost clay, iron, or aluminum with resultant concentration of quartz or other resistant minerals of sand or silt size. *B* horizons are those that have accumulated clay, iron, aluminum, or humus, alone or in combination, either from leaching of overlying layers or from weathering in place. The *C* horizon is a mineral horizon, excluding bedrock, that is relatively little affected by soil formation.

The forest floor is important as a "slow-release" source of nutrients, as an energy source for organisms, and as a covering for protecting the soil against runoff, erosion, and temperature extremes. There are three types of forest floors. The *mor* contains an organic layer that is sharply differentiated from the underlying mineral soil. The *mull* consists of an intimate mixture of organic matter and mineral soil. The *duff mull* or *moder* possesses some of the characteristics of both mulls and mors.

Whereas agricultural crops tend to be less deeply rooted (0.5 to 2.5 meters), trees may root to depths of 5 to 7 meters. This distinction is important, because trees are able to obtain water and nutrients more deeply within the soil. However, tree roots

---

[1]Soils are also viewed in three dimensions. A pedon is the smallest volume of soil that can be called an individual. It commonly ranges from 1 to 30 cubic meters in volume.

Figure 4.1 A soil profile occurring beneath a northern hardwoods forest near L'Anse, Michigan. The profile contains a thin forest floor followed by an organic-enriched Al horizon, a bleached A2 horizon, an iron-enriched B horizon (being pointed out by the observer), and a relatively unaltered sandy C horizon. (Photograph by J. Bockheim).

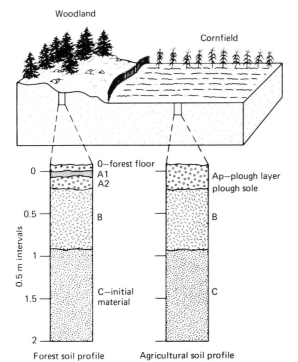

Figure 4.2 Contrasting soil profiles under forest and agricultural vegetation showing several major soil horizons.

occupy a lesser percentage of the total soil volume than do roots of agricultural crops.

## Physical Soil Properties

Soil can be differentiated according to a range of physical properties. These properties include soil texture, structure, porosity and bulk density, and hydrophobicity. Each of these physical properties is described in some detail below.

**Soil Texture.** Soil texture refers to the relative proportion of the various mineral particles, such as sand, silt, and clay in the soil. The U.S. Department of Agriculture developed a common classification system where the particle-size fraction of sand ranges between 2 and 0.05 millimeters, silt particles range between 0.05 and 0.002 millimeters; and clay particles are less than 0.002 millimeters in diameter. Soil texture may be estimated in the field by trained people by simply feeling the soil in moist and dry states. However, the soil is measured in the laboratory using a number of more sophisticated techniques such as sedimentation, centrifugation, and sieving. After such analyses are completed, particle size data are often plotted on a soil textural triangle as shown in Figure 4.3. Thus, for example, a soil that contains 60 percent sand, 30 percent silt, and 10 percent clay by mass is termed a sandy loam. Texture of the soil is important because it influences such things as soil structure and aeration, water retention and drainage, ability of the soil to hold, exchange, and fix nutrients, root penetrability, and seedling emergence.

Sandy forested soils often support pines, hemlocks, scrub oaks, and other trees with low moisture and nutrient requirements. In contrast, silt-and clay-enriched soils usually support trees of high moisture and nutrient requirements, including Douglas-fir, maple, hickory, ash, basswood, oak, elm, spruce, fir, tulip poplar, and black walnut. Soil texture is thus an important consideration in reforestation, in selection of silvicultural treatment and

**95**

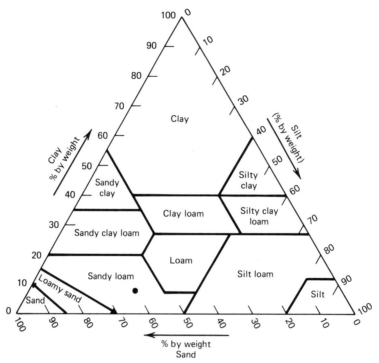

**Figure 4.3** A soil textural triangle using the classification scheme of the U.S. Department of Agriculture. A soil with 60 percent sand, and 30 percent silt, and 10 percent clay (designated by the point within the triangle) is classified as a sandy loam. (Courtesy of U.S. Department of Agriculture.)

system (Chapter 9), and in establishment of forest nurseries.

**Soil Structure.** Soil structure refers to the arrangement of primary soil particles into secondary units called *peds*. Peds are characterized on the basis of size, shape, and degree of distinction. Common ped shapes include prisms or columns, blocks, plates, and crumbs or granules (Figure 4.4). The major causes for such differences of soil structure are chemical reactions, the presence of organic matter and organisms, and wetting and drying cycles.

**Soil Porosity and Bulk Density.** *Porosity* refers to the volume percentage of the total soil bulk not occupied by solid particles. These air spaces or pores within the soil are distributed in various sizes. If the mass of a sample of dry soil is measured and divided by the total (bulk) volume of the soil (including pores), then a measure of *bulk density* is obtained. Total porosity, pore-size distribution, and bulk density of a soil are influenced by a variety of soil parameters such as soil texture and structure, stone and organic matter content, and degree of compaction due to forest management practices. Soil porosity and bulk density are very important factors because they influence water retention and water movement, soil aeration, and root penetrability. It has been found that total porosity generally is greater and bulk density is less in forest soils than in agricultural soils of the same texture (Table 4.1). This may be because of the following: (1) a greater amount of organic matter in the forest floor, (2) less

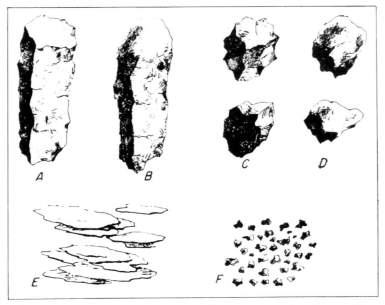

**Figure 4.4** Examples of several types of structure commonly found in soils (A) prismatic; (B) columnar; (C) angular blocky; (D) subangular blocky; (E) platy; (F) granular. (From U.S. Soil Survey Staff, 1951.)

compaction by machinery on forest soils, and (3) the loosening effects of tree roots and other forest soil organisms. Forest soils commonly contain about 40 to 60 percent pore space. The bulk density of mineral horizons of forest soils usually ranges between 0.8 and 1.6 grams per cubic centimeter, while organic horizons may have bulk density values as low as 0.1. A number of factors can dramatically alter the density of a soil; for example, logging during wet conditions and repeated tractor trips may markedly diminish pore space in forest soils. Excessive recreational use may cause a reduction in total porosity and may result in diminished tree growth. However, compacted soils may return to their pretreatment bulk density levels as a result of normal biological activities such as extension of plant roots, and wetting-drying and freezing-thawing cycles. Mechanical loosening is also employed in some areas to reduce the bulk density of a soil.

**Hydrophobicity.** The tendency of certain soils to be water repellent is commonly referred to as hy-drophobicity. Hydrophobicity is controlled by the amount and composition of organic matter, nature of the microorganisms, and forest management practices. Forest litter in the natural state commonly is water repellent, particularly after drying; and intensive forest fires may accentuate hydrophobicity of the soil. If water repellency is high, there may be excessive runoff and erosion of soil, soil water retention and movement may be reduced, and seed germination and plant growth may be inhibited. Hydrophobicity can be controlled by a number of techniques such as using cool-burning fires during prescribed burning, by mechanical breakup of the water-repellent layer, and by application of chemical wetting agents.

## Organic Matter

Organic matter in the forest soil serves several important functions. It improves soil structure and increases soil porosity and aeration. In addition, organic matter influences the soil temperature re-

**Table 4-1**

Physical Properties of a Dodge Silt Loam (Typic Hapludalf) under White Oak – Mixed Hardwoods and under Agriculture, Southern Wisconsin

| Horizon | Depth (cm) | Sand (%) | Silt (%) | Clay (%) | Bulk Density (g/cm$^3$) | Total Porosity (%) |
|---------|-----------|----------|----------|----------|------------------------|--------------------|
| | | | *Forest*[a] | | | |
| A1 | 0–10 | 13 | 73 | 14 | 0.96 | 64 |
| A2 | 10–28 | 12 | 74 | 14 | 1.30 | 46 |
| B1 | 28–40 | 11 | 64 | 25 | 1.37 | 45 |
| B2t | 40–60+ | 8 | 59 | 33 | 1.50 | 42 |
| | | | *Agricultural* | | | |
| Ap | 0–15 | 14 | 70 | 16 | 1.26 | 51 |
| A2 | 15–28 | 12 | 69 | 19 | 1.31 | 50 |
| B1 | 28–40 | 13 | 62 | 25 | 1.45 | 46 |
| B2t | 40–60+ | 9 | 56 | 35 | 1.50 | 42 |

*Source.* Original data.

[a] Data for forest floor not shown.

gime, serves as a source of energy for soil microbes, and increases the moisture-holding capacity of forest soils. Soil organic matter holds and exchanges nutrients, and upon decomposition it is a source of tree nutrients.

Most organic matter is added to the forest soil in the form of litter, which includes freshly fallen leaves, twigs, stems, bark, cones, and flowers. Many factors influence litter production. Annual production in temperate latitudes is 1000 to 4000 kilograms per hectare. Litter is comprised predominantly of cellulose and hemicellulose (which are carbohydrates), lignins, proteins, and tannins, the characteristics of which are treated in more detail in Chapter 18. Many nutrient elements are supplied by litter, including calcium, nitrogen, potassium, and magnesium, in descending order of abundance.

Once litter reaches the forest floor, a host of macro- and microorganisms act on it. As litter is decomposed, carbon dioxide, water, and energy are released. A byproduct of litter decomposition is humus, which is a dark mass of complex amorphous organic matter. Organic matter is incorporated into the mineral soil by soil organisms such as rodents,

earthworms, roots, and microorganisms and is produced at greater depths by decomposition of tree roots. Organic matter is also translocated as chemical complexes with iron oxides and with clay. The organic-matter content of an undisturbed, mature forest soil represents the equilibrium between the agencies supplying fresh organic debris and those leading to its decomposition. The ratio of carbon (C) to nitrogen (N) is stable in soils where this equilibrium exists. Whereas the C:N ratio of agricultural soils commonly ranges from 8:1 to 15:1, the ratio is wider in forest soils, usually 15:1 to 30:1.

The organic matter content of the upper 15 centimeters of the forest soil may be greater than that of a similar soil under agriculture because: (1) the forest soil contains a forest floor, (2) tillage or cultivation and intensive cropping tend to reduce organic matter, particularly where manuring and crop rotation are not practiced, and (3) removal of organic matter by erosion is less in an undisturbed forest than in an intensively managed agricultural soil.

Organic matter may be regulated in the forest soil by careful selection of a silvicultural system (i.e.,

**98**

strip-cutting versus clearcutting) and of a utilization practice (i.e., harvesting of only the merchantable stem versus the entire aboveground portion of the tree), and by leaving the slash on the ground following pruning or thinning (see Chapters 9 & 10). Burning may be prescribed in some areas for release of nutrients from thick, undecomposed humus and slash.

## Soil Water

Moisture supplies in the forest soil are rarely at optimal levels during the growing season, as described in Chapter 3. Studies with forest trees invariably have shown growth responses to changes in soil moisture. Not only does soil water influence the distribution and growth of forest vegetation, but it also acts as a solvent for transporting nutrients to the tree root. Soil-water content influences soil consistency, soil aeration, soil temperature, the degree of microbial activity, the concentration of toxic substances, and the amount of soil erosion.

The ability of the soil to retain water is influenced by adhesive and cohesive forces associated with soil matrix and by the attraction of water molecules for ions produced by soluble salts in the soil. Often soil scientists speak of "available" water—the proportion of water in a soil that can be readily absorbed by tree roots. Several factors have been shown to influence the ability of the forest soil to hold water and make it available to trees.

1. Soil texture is strongly related to available-water holding capacity. A fine-textured soil, such as a loam or a silt loam, will hold twice as much water as an equal depth of sand or sandy loam. Mean tree height in a 44-year-old red pine plantation was 60 percent greater on a fine sandy soil than on a coarse sandy soil (3).

2. Stones may take up a considerable portion of the soil volume and reduce soil water storage and tree growth. Whereas a soil with 5 percent stones held 38 centimeters of water in the upper 120 centimeters of the profile, a soil with 75 percent stones held only 5 centimeters of water (4). One-hundred-year-old Douglas-fir growing on similar soils with 5 and 75 percent stones attained heights of 54 and 43 meters respectively (5).

3. Fine-textured bands of soil can cause "perching" or a raising of the water table. Fine-textured bands within the upper 2 meters of soil resulted in a 60 percent increase in growth of red pine in a 25-year-old plantation, in contrast to areas where the subsoil lamellae were deeper or absent (6).

4. Sandy forest soils containing an abundance of free iron oxides and organic matter have a greater moisture-holding capacity than soils with lower amounts of these substances in northern Michigan (7). Annual merchantable volume growth of jack pine and northern hardwood species was nearly threefold greater on soils enriched in free iron and organic matter.

Water moves in forest soils under *saturated* and *unsaturated* conditions and as water vapor. Saturated flow occurs predominantly in old root channels, along living roots, in animal burrows, and in other macropores of the subsoil (8). Saturated flow also occurs in smaller soil pores in the surface soil during and immediately following heavy rainstorms. Unsaturated flow occurs by capillarity at the upper fringe of the water table, from the soil matrix to the tree root, and in small to medium pores in the soil matrix whenever moisture gradients exist in the available water range.

A mode of water loss from the soil is through *transpiration*. In a humid temperate environment, trees transpire nearly as much water as will be evaporated from an open body of water (Table 4.2). Agricultural crops transpire less than a forest because of a lesser vegetative surface area and a shorter growing period. However, during the peak period of growth, agricultural crops may consume more water than a forest. During the peak period of growth, agricultural crops will utilize from 60 to 120

**Table 4-2**

Relationship between Vegetation and Annual Evapotranspiration, Central Wisconsin

| Vegetation | Annual Evapotranspiration (cm) |
|---|---|
| Water | 75−80 |
| Forest | 65−75 |
| Alfalfa-brome | 55−65 |
| Corn | 45−55 |
| Bluegrass | 30−45 |
| Bare soil | 40−50 |

*Source.* C. B. Tanner, unpublished data.

cubic meters per hectare of water per day from the soil (9). In contrast, loblolly pine in Louisiana consumed from 25 to 64 cubic meters per hectare of water per day (10). A measure of the efficiency of water consumption is the transpiration ratio, which is the grams of transpired water required to produce a gram of dry matter. Whereas transpiration ratios of trees commonly range between 150 and 350, those of agricultural crops generally range between 400 and 800 (11). Therefore trees, particularly conifers, are more efficient in their use of water than are agricultural crops.

Excessive amounts of soil water may be controlled by ditching, ridging, or bedding, mechanical breakup of barriers such as a hardpan, and underplanting with species requiring high amounts of soil moisture. Flooding and irrigation have been used on a limited scale in areas where water deficiencies exist. Silvicultural treatments, such as thinning and herbicide application to control weed growth, may be an economical way to increase soil moisture in some areas.

## Soil Organisms

Soil organisms play an important role in forest soils and tree growth. Soil organisms decompose organic matter and release nutrients for consumption by trees. They incorporate organic matter into the soil, thereby improving soil physical properties, soil moisture, temperature, and aeration. It has also been found that soil organisms influence soil profile development, particularly the nature of the forest floor.

Perhaps the most important organisms in the forest soil are the roots of higher plants. These roots do the following: (1) add organic tissue to the subsurface and subsoil, (2) stimulate microorganisms via root exudates, (3) produce organic acids that solubilize certain compounds that are relatively insoluble in pure water, (4) hold and exchange nutrients within the soil, (5) give off toxic compounds that inhibit the establishment and growth of other plants, (6) act as an important soil-forming agent, and (7) protect against soil creep and erosion.

Another group of important soil organisms are *mycorrhizae* ("fungus root"), which are associations, usually symbiotic, of specific fungi with the roots of higher plants. Mycorrhizae increase the absorbing surface area of tree roots, and roots infected by mycorrhizae fungi usually live longer than uninfected roots. Mycorrhizae may also increase the ability of trees to take up nutrients, particularly nitrogen, phosphorus, potassium, calcium, and magnesium. Other types of fungi also are important in forest soils; for example, saprophytic-type fungi decompose forest litter, and parasitic fungi may cause "damping off" or killing of young seedlings by decay of the stem or roots. The influence of certain fungi on growth of forest trees is further discussed in Chapter 8. The bacteria, which are microscopic unicellular organisms of different forms, are also important soil organisms. Some types of bacteria break down organic matter and others utilize nitrogen directly from the atmosphere or mutually with higher plants. A variety of other organisms occur in forest soils, such as protozoa, algae, nematodes, earthworms, insects, and small vertebrates. In terms of soil organisms, forest soils tend to contain an abundance of fungi, while agricultural soils often have a greater number of bacteria. This is mainly because fungi are favored by the more acidic forest soils, while bacteria respond more favorably to the neutral or alkaline agricultural soils (see section on Soil Reaction).

## Chemical Soil Properties

**Cation-Exchange Capacity.** Cation exchange is the ability of the soil to hold and exchange positively charged forms of plant nutrients. These positively charged ions or cations are held on "exchange sites" on the surfaces of clay particles and humus. Dominant cations in most forest soils are hydrogen ($H^+$), aluminum ($Al^{3+}$), calcium ($Ca^{2+}$), magnesium ($Mg^{2+}$), potassium ($K^+$), and sodium ($Na^+$), in order of relative abundance. Cation-exchange capacity (CEC) depends on the amount of organic matter, the amount and type of clays, and soil acidity or alkalinity. Cation-exchange capacity is low in sandy soils but higher in fine-textured soils.

**Soil Reaction (pH).** The acidity or alkalinity of a soil solution is often measured according to the pH; a pH of less than 7 indicates an acidic solution, while a pH between 7 and 14 indicates an alkaline solution. pH is extremely important in forest soils, because it influences the microbial population of the soil, the availability of phosphorus, calcium, magnesium, and trace elements, and the rate of nitrification—that is, biological oxidation of ammonium to nitrate.

Forest soils often are more acid than grassland or agricultural soils (Table 4.3). This is because tree litter commonly is acid and releases hydrogen ions upon decomposition. Because of *liming* (i.e., replacing hydrogen on the exchange sites with calcium or magnesium), pH and exchangeable calcium are greater in the soil managed for agriculture. While pH is mainly a function of internal mechanisms in the soil, it is important to recognize that acid precipitation occurs in forested regions downwind from industrial centers and may ultimately affect soil pH.

*Buffering capacity* of the soil is the ability of the soil to resist sudden changes in pH of the soil solution. Buffering is greatest in forest soils containing an abundance of organic matter or clay particles. pH may be altered in managed stands by fertilizer application, burning of litter and slash, and thinning. Opening the stand by thinning raises the soil temperature and increases soil moisture, thereby stimulating microbial activity and the release of base-forming cations.

**Plant Nutrient Elements.** In addition to carbon, hydrogen, and oxygen, which constitute the bulk of the dry matter of plants, fourteen elements are considered essential for normal growth processes and development of trees. Nitrogen, phosphorus, potassium, calcium, magnesium, and sulfur are referred to as *macronutrients,* since they are absorbed in comparatively large amounts by trees. Iron, manganese, boron, copper, molybdenum, zinc, chlorine and cobalt are called trace elements, or *micronutrients,* because they are taken up in comparatively small but important quantities. The plant nutrients are converted to forms available to trees by the processes of *mineralization* (see later discussion), decomposition of litter, and chemical weathering.

Nitrogen is present largely in the organic form in forest soils, although it may also be present as "fixed" ammonium or as soluble ammonium ($NH_4^+$) and nitrate ($NO_3^-$). The latter two forms are taken up by trees. The conversion of organic nitrogen to ammonium is carried out by microorganisms and is an example of mineralization. Nitrogen is often limiting in intensively managed stands, particularly in conifer plantations.

Phosphorus is present in organic forms and also as secondary inorganic compounds in combination with calcium, iron, and aluminum as phosphates; $H_2PO_4^-$ and $HPO_4^{2-}$ are soluble forms taken up by trees. Phosphorus is most available under near-neutral conditions.

Potassium, calcium, and magnesium are contributed mainly by soil minerals. Potassium is present largely in minerals such as micas and orthoclase feldspar. Calcium and magnesium are present in

**Table 4-3**

Chemical Properties of a Dodge Silt Loam (Typic Hapludalf) under White Oak–Mixed Hardwoods and under Agriculture, Southern Wisconsin

| Horizon | cm | pH | Organic Matter (%) | Total Nitrogen (%) | Carbon: Nitrogen | Extractable Phosphorus (mg/l) | Exchangeable Cation (meq/100 g) | | | |
|---|---|---|---|---|---|---|---|---|---|---|
| | | | | | | | Calcium | Magnesium | Potassium | Total |
| *Forest*[a] | | | | | | | | | | |
| A1 | 0–10 | 4.7 | 2.6 | 0.14 | 11 | 77 | 3.3 | 2.0 | 0.33 | 5.6 |
| A2 | 10–28 | 4.8 | 1.2 | 0.058 | 12 | 103 | 2.1 | 1.2 | 0.26 | 3.6 |
| B1 | 28–40 | 5.0 | 0.71 | 0.043 | 10 | 88 | 3.5 | 1.7 | 0.31 | 5.5 |
| B2t | 40–60+ | 5.1 | 0.69 | 0.045 | 9 | 92 | 4.9 | 4.1 | 0.39 | 9.4 |
| *Agricultural* | | | | | | | | | | |
| Ap | 0–15 | 6.5 | 2.4 | 0.13 | 11 | 125 | 7.4 | — | 0.23 | — |
| A2 | 15–28 | 6.5 | 2.2 | 0.13 | 10 | 112 | 7.2 | 3.2 | 0.24 | 10.6 |
| B1 | 28–40 | 6.7 | 0.89 | 0.058 | 9 | 76 | 7.0 | 2.0 | 0.29 | 9.3 |
| B2t | 40–60+ | 6.5 | 0.55 | 0.040 | 8 | 90 | 9.2 | — | 0.44 | — |

*Source.* Original data.

[a] Data for forest floor not shown.

dolomite, olivines, pyroxenes, and amphibole minerals. Potassium, calcium, and magnesium are available to trees as exchangeable and as water-soluble ions in the form, $K^+$, $Ca^{2+}$, and $Mg^{2+}$, respectively.

Sulfur is present in organic and mineral forms and can be taken up by trees as exchangeable and as water-soluble sulfate, $SO_4^{2-}$. In addition, sulfur dioxide ($SO_2$) gas may be taken up directly by trees through their stomata (see Figure 3.7).

Micronutrients are present in mineral forms and as complexes with organic matter. Acid sandy soils, organic soils, and intensively cropped soils, such as those in forest nurseries, may be depleted in micronutrients.

# EDAPHOLOGY OF FOREST SOILS

Edaphology (from the Greek *edaphos*, "soil" or "ground") is the study of the soil from the standpoint of higher plants. It considers the various properties of soils as they relate to plant production. The edaphologist is practical, having the production of food and fiber as an ultimate goal, but at the same time must be a scientist to determine reasons for variation in the productivity of soils and to find means of conserving and improving this productivity (11a).

## Forest Soil Fertility

Soil fertility is defined as the ability of the soil to supply nutrient elements for plant growth. One way in which nutrients in the soil are taken up by trees is through root interception, which is nutrient absorption by root extension. Mass flow is also involved in nutrient uptake from the soil and is the movement of the soil solution bearing nutrients in the direction of the plant root. A third factor for nutrient supply to plants is ionic diffusion, which involves ion movement from a zone of high ion concentration to a zone of low concentration. Rapid diffusion caused by steep gradients may also occur in the vicinity of plant roots, where some ions are being absorbed and others are being released (12).

In general, agricultural crops have greater nutrient uptake rates and requirements than forest crops. This is particularly true in the case of potassium, which is taken up by agronomic crops in "luxury" amounts. Deciduous tree species require greater amounts of nutrients than coniferous species. Table 4.4 gives a comparison of nutrient demands of both hardwood and conifer forests and agricultural crops; however, the table does not show nitrogen, which is also taken up in greater amounts by agricultural crops than by trees.

Approximate minimum *nutrient requirements* for satisfactory growth of major commercial tree species

**Table 4-4**

Nutrient Demands of Forest Compared with Agricultural Crops

| Crop | Total Nutrient Demand During 100 Years of Growth (kg/ha) | | |
| --- | --- | --- | --- |
| | Calcium | Potassium | Phosphorus |
| Pines | 82 | 37 | 8.5 |
| Other conifers | 177 | 95 | 17 |
| Hardwoods | 356 | 91 | 20 |
| Agricultural crops[a] | 397 | 1215 | 174 |

*Source.* P. J. Rennie, *Plant Soil*, 7, 49 (1955).
[a] Four-source rotation of oats, grass, potatoes, and turnips over a 100-year cropping period.

in plantations are given in Table 4.5. Whereas pines have comparatively low nutrient requirements, hardwood species have high nutrient requirements. These data are important relative to matching tree species to soil type for maximum survival and yield following reforestation.

Three methods are commonly used to diagnose *nutrient deficiencies* and to predict tree growth: (1) visual tree symptoms, (2) soil analysis, and (3) plant analysis. Visual nutrient-deficiency symptoms include chlorosis and necrosis of foliage, unusual leaf structure, deformation or rosetting of branches, and tree stunting. Although many of these symptoms are relatively easy to recognize, nutrient-deficiency symptoms of tree species are difficult to isolate from those due to disease, insects, or other site limitations, such as a moisture deficiency. Thus it is important to combine such analyses with soil testing. Soil testing· involves determining the "available" nutrient content of the soil and relating it to productivity of a particular tree species. The third category for identifying nutrient deficiencies is plant analysis, which is the determination of the nutrient content of a particular plant tissue, usually the foliage, and relating it to visual deficiency symptoms, to biomass yield, or to fertilization responses.

Use of fertilizers in the forest is increasing in North America. Forest fertilization may increase not only fiber yield and quality, but also insect and disease resistance and aesthetic quality of the vegetation. However, use of fertilizers in the forest constitutes a depletion of nonrenewable resources for perpetuating a renewable resource. Fertilization is also expensive and may contribute to environmental pollution when not applied judiciously. Rate of fertilizer application depends on: (1) initial soil fertility level, (2) tree species, (3) age of stand, and (4) type of fertilizer. The most commonly applied nutrient to forests is nitrogen. Nitrogen is applied at rates of 100 to 400 kilograms per hectare to stands of Douglas-fir in the Pacific Northwest and at rates of 5 to 100 to southern pines in the southeastern United States. Phosphorus is applied to pines in the Southeast at rates of 30 to 100 kilograms per hectare. Fertilizer generally is applied to open land or young

**Table 4-5**

Approximate Minimum Contents of Nutrients Essential for Satisfactory Growth of Commercial Tree Species of North America in Plantations

| Trees Planted at Spacing of 1.5 m | Content of Nutrients in 0−15 cm Layer of Soil | | | | |
| --- | --- | --- | --- | --- | --- |
| | Total Nitrogen (%) | Extractable Phosphorus (kg/ha) | Extractable Potassium (kg/ha) | Exchangeable Calcium (kg/ha) | Exchangeable Magnesium (kg/ha) |
| Species with low requirements[a] | 0.02 | trace | 30 | 220 | 55 |
| Species with moderate requirements[b] | 0.05 | 10 | 50 | 560 | 130 |
| Species with high requirements[c] | 0.10 | 25 | 120 | 1300 | 340 |

*Source.* S. A. Wilde, *Forest Soils: Their Properties and Relation to Silviculture*, Ronald Press, New York, 1958.

[a] Includes longleaf pine, slash pine, jack pine, red pine, lodgepole pine, ponderosa pine, eastern red cedar.

[b] Includes white pine, white and black spruce, Douglas-fir, western hemlock, balsam fir, northern red oak, yellow birch, largetooth and trembling aspen.

[c] Includes black walnut, white ash, sugar maple, basswood, white oak, beech, tulip poplar, black locust, Norway spruce, northern white cedar, bald cypress, loblolly pine, black cherry.

plantations using mechanical spreaders. In established stands and stands occupying large land areas, aerial application is used. Research is now in progress to determine if municipal and industrial effluents and sludges can be applied as a fertilizer substitute in some forested areas.

## Soil-Site Factors Related to Tree Growth

Soil-site evaluation involves the use of soil properties (as discussed earlier in the chapter) and of other site factors, such as topographic and climatic features, to predict tree growth (13). The ability to *predict* tree growth is of great value to the forester and for planning in the forest-products industry. In order to use the method, plots are located in older forest stands representing the range of sites and soils found within a particular region. Measurements of tree growth and soil properties are then taken and correlated using statistical methods. The resulting equations can be used to predict site quality of stands that are heavily cut, of uneven age, or too young for tree measurements.

Soil features most important in soil-site studies usually are those dealing with depth, texture, and drainage. It has been found that surface soil depth is particularly important for growth of southern pines and eastern hardwoods. This may be because the soil-surface mineral horizon contains many of the roots and often features the greatest concentration of soil nutrients. In addition, effective depth or thickness of the soil profile (A + B horizons) is especially important for growth of western conifers and eastern hardwoods. The importance of this parameter may be related to differences in depths of rooting barriers, such as a hardpan, bedrock, or a water table. Surface and subsoil texture are commonly related to forest productivity, particularly for eastern hardwoods. Southern pines and eastern hardwoods have been found to be especially responsive to differences in depth of the water table.

It is difficult to select chemical extractants that approximate the form of nutrient "available" to trees. Therefore chemical properties do not enter soil-site equations as commonly as the more readily measurable morphological and physical properties of soils and site factors. Quantitative measurement of available water holding capacity of forest soils is time-consuming. Therefore available soil-water indexes, as with chemical properties, seldom enter soil-site equations.

*Site factors* are very important to tree growth. Eastern hardwoods, particularly oaks, respond to differences in slope position, aspect, and slope steepness. These factors influence soil moisture and temperature relations and the degree of geologic erosion. For northern conifers and eastern hardwoods, soil drainage has been determined to be an important variable. Elevation and rainfall vary considerably in the western United States and influence productivity of western conifers.

## PEDOLOGY OF FOREST SOILS

Certain aspects, such as the origin of the soil, its classification, and its description, are involved in pedology (from the Greek *pedon*, "soil" or "earth"). Pedology considers the soil as a natural body and places minor emphasis on its immediate practical utilization. The pedologist studies, examines, and classifies soils as they occur in their natural environment; the findings may be as useful to highway and construction engineers as to farmers or foresters (11a).

## Soil Survey and Classification

A *soil survey* involves the systematic examination, description, classification, and mapping of soils in a particular area. Mapping of soils requires a knowledge of the interaction of the soil-forming factors: climate, initial material, relief, organisms, and time.

A soil-survey report contains soil maps at scales commonly ranging from 1:10,000 to 1:60,000 and the following information: descriptions, use and management, formation and classification of soils, laboratory data, and general information pertaining to the area. The resulting soil surveys provide the forester with valuable information for planning forestry activities. The soil surveys can be used to locate roads and landing areas, to match harvesting systems with soil conditions in order to minimize site degradation, and to match tree species with soil type during reforestation in order to maximize yield. These soil surveys also enable the forester to plan silvicultural treatments, such as thinning and fertilization more efficiently. Finally, soil surveys are useful for planning recreational facilities, for evaluating potential impacts of mining, grazing, and waste disposal, and for predicting water yield and quality in forested watersheds.

An example of the type of soil interpretation information that is available to foresters in some areas is the *woodland-soil site study* of the U.S. Soil Conservation Service (14). A team consisting of a forester and a soil scientist selects plots for measuring reliable tree-growth data on a specific soil taxonomic unit. Site index, an expression of the tree-growth potential of a site (Chapter 10), is also measured on each plot. The soils of a given region are then placed in woodland suitability groups to assist in planning land use for wood crops. Each group is made up of soils that are suited to the same kind of trees—that is, sites that will need the same kind of management when the vegetation on them is similar and that have about the same potential productivity. Each woodland group is identified by a three-part symbol, such as 2d1 or 3r2. The first symbol (woodland suitability class) indicates the relative potential productivity of the soils in the group, based on site index: 1 = high, 2 = medium high, 3 = medium, 4 = medium low, 5 = low, 6 = unproductive. The subclass, designated by a small letter, indicates an important soil property that imposes a slight to severe limitation in managing the soils for a wood crop: w = excessive wetness, d = restricted rooting depth, c = clayey soils, s = dry, sandy soils, f = fragmental or skeletal soils, r = relief or slope steepness, and o = slight or no limitations. The third symbol, a number, indicates a group of soils having similar hazards or degree of limitation affecting tree growth or woodland management.

In addition to woodland suitability groups, each soil is rated according to hazards presented to forest management, such as erosion hazard, equipment restrictions, seedling mortality, plant competition, and wind-throw hazard. Recommendations can then by given as to which tree species should be planted and which species should be favored in existing stands on a given soil taxonomic unit.

Numerous schemes have been used to classify forest soils and to predict site quality. *Multiple-factor systems* have been used extensively in the western United States and in Canada. An example is the Land Systems Inventory of the U.S. Forest Service (15). The aim of this system is to differentiate and classify ecologically significant segments of the landscape using landform, soil initial material, forest cover type, and soil taxonomic unit.

The United States *soil taxonomy method* (16) is an example of a single-factor (soil) system used to classify forestland. It is an attempt to classify all of the soils of the world into various categories, based on soil properties. There are seven categories of classification in the system: (1) order (broadest category), (2) suborder, (3) great group, (4) subgroup, (5) family, (6) series, and (7) type.

The following discussion describes each of ten soil orders and the associated forest cover types. Three soil orders of importance to North American forestry are ultisols, alfisols, and spodosols. *Ultisols* are forest soils with less than 35 percent of the exchange sites containing calcium, magnesium, potassium, and sodium. These soils occur in areas with moist, warm to tropical climates, with an average annual temperature more than 8°C. They are reddish in color because of an abundance of iron oxides, and they have a clay-enriched horizon. Ultisols support loblolly and shortleaf pines in the southeastern United States and oak-hickory and oak-pine in the south-central United States.

*Alfisols* are forest soils with greater than 35 percent of the exchange sites containing calcium, magnesium, potassium, and sodium. They contain a gray surface mineral horizon and a brown, clay-enriched B horizon. These soils feature oak-hickory in the central United States, northern hardwoods in northern New York, aspen-birch in the northern Great Lakes states, and ponderosa and lodgepole pines in the Inland Empire.[2]

*Spodosols* contain a grayish A horizon and dark reddish brown B horizons that are enriched in organic matter and/or iron oxides. These soils develop from coarse-textured, acid initial materials under cold humid climates. Major forest cover types are spruce-fir, eastern white pine, and northern hardwoods in New England and eastern Canada, and northern hardwoods and aspen-birch in the Great Lakes region. In southwest Alaska, spodosols support western hemlock-Sitka spruce, and in Florida poorly drained spodosols support longleaf and slash pines.

*Entisols* are mineral soils without B horizons. They occur predominantly on floodplains, steep slopes, or shifting sands. Entisols occur on excessively drained sands supporting jack pine and scrub oaks in the Great Lakes region and on poorly drained sands supporting slash pine in Florida. *Inceptisols* are also poorly developed but contain slight alteration of the initial material. They contain a weak B horizon. They support oak-pine in the Appalachian Mountains, oak-gum-cypress in the southern Mississippi River valley, ponderosa pine, western white pine, and larch in the northern Rocky Mountains, spruce-hardwoods in interior Alaska, and western hemlock-Sitka spruce in the Pacific Northwest and western Canada. *Aridisols* are desert soils and do not feature commercial forest vegetation in North America. *Mollisols* contain a deep, dark-colored surface horizon with strong granular structure and an abundance (50 percent) of potassium, calcium, and magnesium on the exchange sites.

They occur predominantly under grassland. However, some mollisols have developed under forests, such as brown forest soils, that contain ponderosa pine in the southwestern United States and oak-hickory in the central United States. *Vertisols* have been subjected to excessive shrinking, cracking, and shearing due to an abundance of swelling clays. These soils are of limited extent in North America. *Histosols* are organic soils that support spruce-fir, aspen, and swamp conifers in the northern Great Lakes states. *Oxisols* are intensively weathered soils enriched in iron oxides and depleted in weatherable minerals. They occur in tropical areas and are absent in North America. In Hawaii, introduced species such as Norfolk Island pine, monkeypod, silk oak, and eucalyptus do well on oxisols.

## Nutrient Cycling in the Forest

Nutrient cycling refers broadly to the movement of nutrients throughout the various components of the forest ecosystem, including the trees, understory vegetation, the forest floor, and the underlying mineral soil (see Figures 3.11 and 3.12). Nutrients are continually added and removed from a forest ecosystem by a number of mechanisms. Nutrients are added to the forest soil via precipitation, atmospheric fallout, stemflow (flow of precipitation down the stem of the tree), throughfall (movement of precipitation through the tree canopy), litterfall, and chemical weathering of the soil. Nutrients leave the ecosystem via runoff, erosion, leaching or translocation below the rooting zone, and timber harvesting. Once nutrients reach the soil, they may be held on exchange sites or taken up by trees, understory vegetation, and soil organisms.

A *nutrient budget* for a 36-year-old Douglas-fir stand appears in Table 4.6. The biomass of most commercial tree species contains nutrients in the following order: calcium > nitrogen > potassium > magnesium > phosphorus. The percentage concentration of total nutrients in the tree is in the order: foliage > bark > branches > stem > roots. Fortu-

---

[2]The Inland Empire is the area lying between the crests of the Cascade and Bitterroot mountains, extending from the Okanogan Highlands to the Blue Mountains of northeastern Oregon.

**Table 4-6**
Distribution of Nutrients and Organic Matter in a 36-Year-Old Douglas-Fir Ecosystem (kg/ha)

| Component | Nitrogen | Phosphorus | Potassium | Calcium | Organic Matter |
|---|---|---|---|---|---|
| Tree | | | | | |
|   Foliage | 102 | 29 | 62 | 73 | 9,097 |
|   Branches | 61 | 12 | 38 | 106 | 22,031 |
|   Wood | 77 | 9 | 52 | 47 | 121,687 |
|   Bark | 48 | 10 | 44 | 70 | 18,728 |
|   Roots | 32 | 6 | 24 | 37 | 32,986 |
|   Total tree | 320 | 66 | 220 | 333 | 204,529 |
| Subordinate vegetation | 6 | 1 | 7 | 9 | 1,010 |
| Forest floor | 175 | 26 | 32 | 137 | 22,772 |
| Soil (cm) | | | | | |
|   0−15 | 809 | 1,167 | 79 | 313 | 38,372 |
|   15−30 | 868 | 1,195 | 66 | 196 | 36,935 |
|   30−45 | 761 | 980 | 52 | 152 | 28,290 |
|   45−60 | 371 | 536 | 37 | 80 | 7,955 |
|   Total soil | 2,809 | 3,878[a] | 234[b] | 741[b] | 111,955 |
| Total ecosystem | 3,310 | 3,971 | 493 | 1,220 | 339,863 |

*Source.* D. W. Cole, S. P. Gessel, and S. F. Rice, "Distribution and cycling of nitrogen, phosphorus, potassium and calcium in a second-growth Douglas-fir ecosystem," In: *Primary Productivity and Mineral Cycling in Natural Ecosystems,* Univ. of Maine Press, Orono, 1967.
[a] Soil portion is extractable.
[b] Soil portion is exchangeable.

nately, most commercial tree species generally have their biomass distributed in approximately an inverse sequence: stem > roots > branches > bark > foliage. Therefore, harvesting of the stem—that is, leaving branches and foliage in the woods—does not deplete the ecosystem of plant nutrients to the same degree as harvesting the entire aboveground portion of the tree or the complete tree. The forest floor contains the lowest proportion of plant nutrients. However, many of the transport processes are regulated by products formed during biological decomposition on the forest floor, and therefore retention of the forest floor is important to a healthy forest. The greatest proportion of nutrients can be found in the mineral soil.

Nutrient-cycling studies provide a wealth of information useful to the forest manager. For example, such studies give information on: (1) distribution of nutrients and biomass among components of the ecosystem, (2) annual transfer of nutrients among components of the ecosystem, (3) annual uptake and return of nutrients by trees, (4) annual accumulation of nutrients, and (5) impacts of forest management practices on soils and water quality. The movement of nutrients through the forest ecosystem is further treated in Chapter 6.

## FOREST SOILS AND ENVIRONMENTAL QUALITY

Soil erosion from forested land ranges between 0.11 and 0.22 tons per hectare, which is less than the geologic norm (18). In contrast, soil erosion for agricultural land usually ranges between 2.2 and 11 tons per hectare. Improper road-building practices are most often cited as the major cause of sedimentation in forest environments, particularly in steep mountainous areas. Timber harvesting may also contribute to sediment in streams, lakes, and reservoirs by exposing surface soil, particularly during skidding and yarding operations (Figure 4.5). Factors influencing the effect of timber harvesting on soil disturbance include (see Chapter 11 for methods of timber harvesting): (1) silvicultural system, (2) yarding method, (3) intensity of utilization, (4) season of year, (5) slope, and (6) soil type. Turbidity of mountain streams following progessive strip-cutting of northern hardwoods was less than that recorded after conventional clearcutting in the White Mountains of New Hampshire (19). Skidding of logs with tractors and rubber-wheeled vehicles is more likely to cause soil disturbance and subsequent erosion and sedimentation than when high-lead cable, skyline cable, balloon, or helicopter systems are

**Figure 4.5**  Skidding during logging operation. (Photograph courtesy of U.S.D.A. Forest Service.)

employed (see Chapter 11) (20). Some amount of soil destruction can be avoided by harvesting only the merchantable stem instead of removing the entire tree, because the logs are then suspended on a bed of slash. Severe soil disturbance may also be reduced by harvesting during the winter in areas where soils freeze. Obviously wet-weather logging is especially detrimental to soils and should be avoided if at all possible. In addition, slopes greater than 70 percent are particularly susceptible to disturbance in the Pacific Northwest (20). The most highly erodible soils include those with an abundance of silt and very fine sand, low amounts of organic matter and of coarse sand, a very fine granular structure, and low permeabilities (21). Furrowing, scalping, disking, and other forms of site preparation for reforestation may expose mineral soil to erosion, particularly on steep slopes.

While soil erosion and sedimentation are important water-quality problems, much concern has been expressed over nutrient losses following timber harvesting, slash burning, forest fertilization, and biocide application. Clearcutting of a northern hardwoods ecosystem on thin soils in New Hampshire resulted in large increases in streamwater concentrations of calcium, magnesium, potassium, sodium, and nitrate (see Chapter 6) (22). Whereas the annual net export of some of the nutrients recovered in three or four years, calcium and nitrogen losses may require 60 to 80 years to recover (23). This is an important consideration because future forests may become less productive if continual clearcutting practices are carried out in the same location. Progressive stripcutting of northern hardwoods in New Hampshire may be a more reasonable alternative because this method resulted in lower nutrient losses than those occurring after conventional clearcutting (19).

In a 16-year-old loblolly pine plantation, harvesting of the complete tree (i.e., aerial and below-ground biomass) resulted in four times as much nutrient loss due to removal of the biomass than harvesting of pulpwood restricted to an 8-centimeter top (24). Debarking loblolly pine pulpwood in the woods would save 10 percent of the nitrogen removed in the biomass. In a study with the same species, one complete tree harvest after 40 years removed 40 percent less nitrogen from the biomass than two 20-year harvests (25).

Burning oxidizes slash and portions of the forest floor, leaving an alkaline ash at the soil surface. As much as 62 percent of the nitrogen contained in litter is lost as gases to the atmosphere by such burning (26). In recent investigations it has been found that concentrations of nutrients in the soil solution at the base of the rooting zone may be fourfold greater in a burned area than in an unburned control (27). Nitrogen can also be returned to the forest ecosystem artificially through fertilization. However, forest fertilization with nitrogen resulted in an increase in nitrate levels in streams of the Pacific Northwest (28) and in the northeastern United States (29). Fortunately, these nitrate levels rarely persisted or exceeded public water-quality limits.

Biocides are used in the forest ecosystem to control vegetation competing for soil moisture and nutrients. Concern has been expressed regarding the effect of biocides on water quality in forested areas. Biocide levels were high in streams of the Pacific Northwest shortly after treatment but did not persist for more than a few days (30). In addition, soil organisms are capable of degrading biocides, and soil colloids may adsorb biocides.

## REFERENCES

1. S. A. Wilde, *Forest Soils: Their Properties and Relation to Silviculture*, Ronald Press, New York, 1958.
2. C. C. Nikiforoff, *Science, 129,* 186 (1959).
3. W. A. Van Eck and E. P. Whiteside, "Soil classification as a tool in predicting forest growth," In: *First North American Forest Soils Conf. Proc.*, T. D. Stevens and R. L. Cook, eds., Michigan State Univ., East Lansing.
4. C. T. Dyrness, "Hydrologic properties of soils on three small watersheds in the western Cascades of Oregon," U.S.D.A. Forest Service, Res. Note PNW-111, 1969.

# REFERENCES

5. W. H. Carmean, *Soil Sci. Soc. Am. Proc.*, *18*, 330 (1954).

6. D. P. White and R. S. Wood, *Soil Sci. Soc. Am. Proc.*, *22*, 174 (1958).

7. S. G. Shetron, *Soil Sci. Soc. Am. Proc.*, *38*, 359 (1974).

8. G. M. Aubertin, "Nature and extent of macropores and their influence on subsurface water movement," U.S.D.A. Forest Service, Res. Paper NE-192, 1971.

9. R. L. Donahue, R. W. Miller, and J. C. Shickluna, *Soils: An Introduction to Soils and Plant Growth,* Fourth Edition, Prentice-Hall, Englewood Cliffs, N.J., 1977.

10. D. M. Moehring and C. W. Ralston, *Soil Sci. Soc. Am. Proc.*, *31*, 560 (1967).

11. W. Larcher, *Physiological Plant Ecology*, Springer-Verlag, New York, 1975.

11a. H. O. Buckman and N. C. Brady, *The Nature and Properties of Soils,* Seventh Edition, Macmillan, New York, 1969.

12. P. J. Rennie, *Plant & Soil, 7,* 49 (1955).

13. W. H. Carmean, *Adv. Agron., 29,* 209 (1975).

14. P. E. Lemmon, "Grouping soils on the basis of woodland suitability," In: *Tree Growth and Forest Soils,* C. T. Youngberg and C. B. Davey, eds., Oregon State Univ. Press, Corvallis, 1970.

15. G. E. Wendt, R. A. Thompson, and K. N. Larson, "Land Systems Inventory Boise National Forest, Idaho," U.S.D.A. Forest Service, Intermountain Region Report, Ogden, Utah, 1975.

16. U.S. Soil Survey Staff, "Soil taxonomy: A basic system of soil classification for making and interpreting soil surveys," *U.S.D.A. Soil Conserv. Serv., Agric. Handbook 436,* 1975.

17. D. W. Cole, S. P. Gessel, and S. F. Dice, "Distribution and cycling of nitrogen, phosphorus, potassium and calcium in a second-growth Douglas-fir ecosystem," In: *Primary Productivity and Mineral Cycling in Natural Ecosystems,* Univ. of Maine Press, Orono, 1967.

18. J. H. Patric, *J. For., 74,* 671 (1976).

19. J. W. Hornbeck, G.E . Likens, R. S. Pierce, and F. H. Bormann, "Strip cutting as a means of protecting site and stream-flow quality when clearcutting northern hardwoods," In: *Forest Soils and Forest Land Management,* B. Bernier and C. H. Winget, eds., Les Presses de l'Université Laval, Quebec, 1975.

20. J. G. Bockheim, T. M. Ballard, and R. P. Willington, *Can. J. For. Res., 5,* 285 (1975).

21. W. H. Wischmeier and J. V. Mannering, *Soil Sci. Soc. Am. Proc., 33,* 131 (1969).

22. R. S. Pierce, C. W. Martin, C. C. Reeves, G. E. Likens, and F. H. Bormann, "Nutrient losses from clearcutting in New Hampshire," In: *National Symp. on Watersheds in Transition,* Am. Water Resour. Assoc. Proc. Ser. No. 14, 1972.

23. G. E. Likens, F. H. Bormann, R. S. Pierce, and W. A. Reiners, *Science, 199,* 492 (1978).

24. J. R. Jorgensen, C. G. Wells, and L. J. Metz, *J. For., 73,* 400 (1975).

25. C. G. Wells and J. R. Jorgensen. *Tappi, 61,* 29 (1978).

26. D. S. DeBell and C. W. Ralston, *Soil Sci. Soc. Am. Proc., 34,* 936 (1970).

27. D. W. Cole, W. J. B. Crane, and C. C. Grier, "The effect of forest management practices on water chemistry in a second-growth Douglas-fir ecosystem," In: *Forest Soils and Forest Land Management,* B. Bernier and C. H. Winget, eds., Les Presses de l'Université Laval, Quebec, 1975.

28. D. G. Moore, "Fertilization and water quality," *Proc. Annual Meeting Western Reforestation Coord. Comm.,* West. For. Conserv. Assoc., 1971.

29. G. M. Aubertin, D. W. Smith, and J. H. Patric, "Quantity and quality of stream-flow following urea fertilization on a forested watershed," *Forest Fertilization Symp. Proc.,* U.S.D.A. Forest Service, Gen. Tech. Rep. NE-3, 1973.

30. R. L. Fredriksen, D. G. Moore, and L. A. Norris, "The impact of timber harvest, fertilization, and herbicide treatments on streamwater quality in western Oregon and Washington," In: *Forest Soils and Forest Land Management,* B. Bernier and C. H. Winget, eds. Les Presses de l'Université Laval, Quebec, 1975.

# 5

# FOREST GENETICS AND FOREST-TREE BREEDING

# Raymond P. Guries

Forest genetics is the study of the *heritable variation* in forest trees. Like other fields of genetics, it is grounded in the dogma of classical genetics and molecular biology. Thus, at the level of the gene, what is true for garden peas and fruit flies is true for forest trees. While the exact details of origin and evolution vary from organism to organism, the mechanics of inheritance transcend species lines, providing a common denominator for the study of life. Research in forest genetics provides information on the genetic properties of trees, both as individuals and as populations. Such information is needed for the wise utilization of forest resources.

*Forest-tree breeding* is the application of genetics principles to the development of lines of trees that will have increased value for humans. It is primarily a domestication process that involves the *selection* and *propagation* of trees possessing desirable characteristics. Specific details of the process vary depending on whether the primary goal is increased wood production, pest resistance, amenity values, or some combination of such traits.

It might be possible to infer from the above definitions that there is relatively little overlap between these "basic" and "applied" lines of research. Nothing could be further from the truth. In fact, much of the basic forest genetics research being conducted today was initiated in response to problems encountered in applied breeding programs. The flow of information and ideas is very definitely a two-directional process.

## SOME PROBLEMS UNIQUE TO FOREST GENETICS

The use of trees as research organisms poses a number of problems. For example, their *large size* makes them poor objects for most studies in laboratory settings. Because the basic cellular processes and the mechanics of inheritance are remarkably similar among most plants and animals, many questions pertaining to metabolic functions, the mutation process, and other topics requiring precise experimental control are investigated with organisms other than trees.

The large size of most trees poses additional problems to forest geneticists. Seed or cone collection, or the need to make control pollinations, frequently requires spending long hours in the crown of a tree, thereby limiting the number of trees that can be collected or worked with in any one season (Figure 5.1).

The *long life cycle* of many trees poses the problem of long intervals between generations in a research program. Many species commonly do not attain sexual maturity for fifteen, twenty, or more years. This slows the progress of a breeding program to a pace commensurate with the life cycle of the species, so that the possibility of breeding more than a few generations of trees during an individual researcher's lifetime is remote.

An associated feature of this size-longevity problem is the *large land area* needed to complete many genetics experiments. Once established, such experiments are impossible to relocate and are subject to destruction by natural catastrophes such as drought, storm, or pests. Highway construction, fire, and vandalism also take a toll. In addition, much valuable information may be lost following personnel changes because plantings frequently outlive their originator.

All of these problems serve to reduce the pace at which reliable genetics information becomes available on forest trees. While human knowledge of crop-plant genetics is encyclopedic, knowledge of forest-tree genetics is still extremely limited. The tremendous gains achieved by many grain and vegetable crop breeders in the last few generations is due largely to an increased understanding of the genetics of these crops as well as to their having relatively short life cycles. While such gains in plant breeding are both important and impressive, research in forest genetics does offer certain advantages that few agronomic crops can match. One of the most important is the opportunity to work with an enormous and as yet relatively unexploited genetic resource.

**Figure 5.1** Making control pollinations in the crown of a Norway spruce tree. Note the steel pole with guy wires to permit the worker to reach the top of the tree. (Photograph courtesy of Hans Nienstaedt, U.S.D.A. Forest Service, Rhinelander, Wisconsin.)

# FOREST GENETICS

## Natural Variation in Forest-Tree Populations

The existence of considerable stores of natural genetic variation in forest-tree populations is one of the major findings of forest genetics research during the last century. Numerous studies of such variation have provided evidence for the operation of evolutionary processes and adaptation in trees. Although the evidence is usually indirect, there is little doubt that this variation is a key to long-term species survival and continued evolution. Natural genetic variation provides the "buffer" that has permitted trees to adapt to variable and changing environments and thereby dominate the landscape (Figure 5.2).

From the standpoint of tree breeding, the presence of considerable variation is a particularly pleasing circumstance because it enhances the prospect of locating individuals that are well above average in economically important traits. Whether selection is imposed by nature, or artifically by humans, variation must be present if the resultant populations are to be different from the preselected ones, and this variation must be genetically based. In the absence

Finally, it should be noted that trees possess other unique features, such as the capability of wood production, or the facility for long-distance transfer of photosynthate, water, and nutrients between roots and branches. Despite the obvious importance of such features to tree growth, very little is known concerning their genetic control or evolution. But it is recognized that such subjects can be studied only in trees despite the technical difficulties involved.

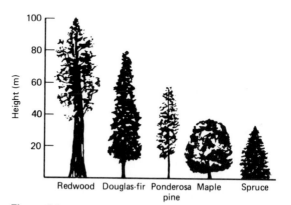

**Figure 5.2** Tree characteristics such as height and shape are inherited, but environmental factors may also play a significant role.

of such variation, no selection is possible, by either humans or nature.

### Continuous versus Discontinuous Variation.

During the formative years of plant genetics, considerable attention was paid to characters that appeared to be inherited as discrete units in discontinuous fashion. Characters such as flower or seed color of the type studied by Gregor Mendel in peas during the nineteenth century could be shown to be controlled by a single "factor," or *gene*. During the early twentieth century, it became increasingly obvious that many, perhaps most, plant characters did not display this *discontinuous* either-or pattern of variation. Characters such as plant weight, leaf length, fruit weight, numbers of veins in leaves, and numerous others displayed a *continuous* pattern of variation. Such patterns typically approximate a "normal distribution" when the frequency of occurrence is plotted against a range of performance or size classes (Figure 5.3).

Most of the individual measurements are clustered about the mean with smaller numbers of observations falling into classes further removed from the mean. Geneticists now recognize that these metrical (or quantitative) characters are controlled by a large but unknown number of genes. Most characters of interest to tree breeders are of this metrical type.

The inability to identify precisely the genes responsible for producing a particular character in many instances led to the origination of the terms *genotype* and *phenotype*. The term *genotype* refers to the genetic constitution of an individual. It is the sum total of all the genetic information that an individual possesses. The term *phenotype* refers to the external appearance of an individual. The stature, girth, and various other qualities are the end product of the interaction of the individual genotype and the environment in which it develops. The phenotype of an individual can be seen and measured, but this is almost never possible for an individual's genotype. A useful concept may be to consider a genotype as a potential phenotype. At the

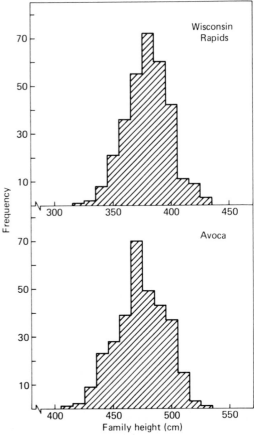

**Figure 5.3** Average height growth of 310 red pine families raised at two locations in Wisconsin. While the exact shape of the curve is different at each location, both approximate a normal distribution.

start of development, an enormous array of possible phenotypes may be produced, but the one that ultimately develops is the product of a genotype developing in a certain environment.

A great deal of effort has gone into attempts to separate "nature from nurture" during the course of development. For traits of economic interest such as growth rate, geneticists would like to know the extent to which a particular character is inherited. If the variation observed has little or no heritable basis, then efforts to improve it will be unfruitful, or at least very inefficient. On the other hand, characters under strong genetic control generally are more amenable to rapid improvement because a good phenotype is more apt to reflect a good genotype.

**Extent and Patterning of Variation.** Most information on the amount and distribution of natural genetic variation in forest trees has come from *provenance studies*. In such studies, seeds from a number of geographic origins or stands are collected and grown together in one or more locations under conditions that make it possible to compare the relative performance of each seed source with all others (Figure 5.4). The original aim

**Figure 5.4** An indication of the magnitude of growth-rate differences between two provenances of lodgepole pine in the nursery at Redrock, British Columbia. Both rows of trees are 6 years old. (Photograph courtesy of Nicholas Wheeler, British Columbia Forest Service.)

of provenance testing was to identify superior seed sources for reforestation needs, but in the process a great deal has been learned about the *evolution* of many tree species.

The first tests to establish that *seed origin* was an important factor in determining the ultimate form of a tree were initiated by Phillipe-André de Vilmorin in France. Between 1820 and 1850 de Vilmorin set out plantations of Scotch pine on his estate using seeds collected from a number of stands throughout Europe. Although poorly designed by today's standards, these tests documented that Scotch pine from different geographic origins varied considerably in height and diameter growth, needle length, stem form, and other characters. Because all the trees were grown at the same location, de Vilmorin concluded that the differences among seed sources were due to factors inherent in the trees. De Vilmorin's work was repeated and confirmed with Scotch pine and other species by a number of foresters in Europe and the United States from 1885 to 1920.

Provenance studies demonstrated that many tree species were genetically quite variable, but the patterning of variation was not considered until Olof Langlet's analysis of Scotch pine during the 1930s. Langlet collected seeds from 582 populations throughout Sweden and raised them under carefully controlled conditions. His studies showed that certain patterns of variation were closely related to climate because the characters he studied changed *systematically* with increasing altitude and latitude of origin. Such patterns of variation appeared to be established and maintained in response to environmental factors such as the length of the growing season or minimum winter temperature.

The *adaptation* of tree populations to climate is well documented, especially for coniferous species. Pines and spruces have been studied especially well because of their economic importance. Results for a number of species indicate that patterns of continuous variation (*clinal variation*) are quite common for survival and growth-related traits, as well as certain wood-quality traits such as specific gravity. Such patterns are generally correlated with length of grow-

**117**

ing season, date at which spring temperature exceeds a certain level, or other environmental features that have a dramatic influence on physiology and that also exhibit clinal variation. Such geographic patterns of variation are most easily explained as optimal (or near optimal) growth strategies that develop in response to selection imposed by the environment (1).

Some very complex adaptations have evolved in tree species as a result of *competitive interactions* for light, moisture, and even for pollinators such as bees and small mammals. Even within the crown of a single tree, morphological differences among leaves are apparent and greatly affect the overall "capture" of light energy. Botanists have recognized two different leaf forms, "sun leaves" and "shade leaves," each with a characteristic size, thickness, and chlorophyll content. "Sun leaves," those on the outer shell of branches, tend to be smaller, thicker, and have a higher concentration of chlorophyll on a leaf-weight basis than "shade leaves." This adaptation permits plants to take best advantage of the filtering effect that leaf canopies have on light quantity and quality.

Adaptations to special soil conditions, to fire, to heavy snow and ice conditions, to insect and disease attack, for pollination and seed dispersal, and other factors have been described and form part of a rich botanical literature on the subject. Today, adaptations are recognized as a general feature of the interactions that occur between organisms and their environment. Patterns of variation may be quite local, as could be expected if they arose in response to some physical or biological feature of the environment that changed rapidly over short distances. Some patterns are more regional in nature, perhaps reflecting gradual changes in one or more climatic variables such as temperature or moisture variation. Some patterns are quite obvious, while others can be more cryptic or complex, requiring careful analysis before they become apparent. But to understand the nature of adaptation and the factors that control it, the mechanisms responsible for bringing about evolutionary change must be considered.

## The Origin and Modification of Natural Variation

Almost all evolutionary change can be attributed to certain causal factors or mechanisms that are responsible for changing the frequencies of different genes in populations. These factors can be assigned to one of two classes: those that create or release natural variation, and those that subsequently modify this variation. Much of the work of population genetics has involved an elaboration of evolutionary mechanisms from a theoretical standpoint followed by laboratory field studies to support their operation. At times, certain concepts have to be modified or refined to bring them into agreement with observations made in the natural world. But there is no doubt concerning the general validity of these mechanisms and their importance in bringing about evolutionary change. A number of excellent introductory texts on population genetics and evolution are available for those desiring a more complete treatment (2−4).

**Mutations as a Source of Variation.** Mutations are the ultimate source of all genetic variation. While most mutations are generally harmful, they are still a vital part of the evolutionary process because they provide the "raw material" upon which natural and artificial selection may act. Mutations may involve the alteration of a single gene by way of the addition, deletion, or substitution of one of the "building blocks" of the DNA molecules. The end result may be completely undetectable, or it may lead to a gross change in the morphology or development of an organism. Mutations affecting cotyledon and leaf pigments, seedling stature, branching habit, and other traits that appear to be controlled by one or a few genes have been observed in a number of tree species.

Mutations may also involve a major alteration in the genetic material, such as the loss or addition of a whole chromosome or a set of chromosomes. Such changes in chromosome number or patterning are more rare than single gene mutations, but have

**118**

occurred in many plant species at one time or another. Just as in the case of single gene mutations, these changes are sudden and irreversible. Naturally occurring and artificially produced triploid aspen is a good example of such a mutation.

Forest trees are relatively poor organisms for studying the mutation process, however, because of their large size and long life cycle. Mutation rates for most well-studied organisms range from $1 \times 10^{-4}$ to $1 \times 10^{-6}$ per gamete per generation, and this is probably correct for trees as well. Mutation rates vary depending on the site of the change in the DNA molecule, the organism involved, and the specific environment in which the organism is placed. Radiation and certain chemicals are known *mutagens* and can greatly increase the rate of mutation. However, humans have essentially no control over the exact kinds of mutations produced. *Mutation breeding*, a practice seldom employed in forest genetics, can be used to create new variation by increasing the frequency of new mutations. The vast bulk of these mutations are still harmful, but a small number may be useful. While the thought of somehow directing the mutation process has considerable appeal, especially to breeders of agronomic crops, this subject is fraught with moral and ethical issues concerning possible extensions to other organisms, especially humans. However, genetic engineering at this level still eludes even the most ingenious scientist although enormous progress has been made in this field in recent years.

## Recombination as a Source of Variation.

While mutations provide the initial source of genetic variation, genetic recombination appears to be a more immediate source of variation in sexually reproducing populations. In trees, as in most other sexual organisms, new combinations of genes are created each generation by the segregation, assortment, and recombination of genes and chromosomes during *meiosis*. The pollen and eggs produced can then reunite at fertilization and eventually develop into seed. The vast array of new genotypes produced in this way provides the successors to the parent generation and contains the variation required for coping with a potentially new or changing environment. Because virtually all tree species are capable of sexual reproduction, it is probable that recombination is an extremely important evolutionary mechanism in forest-tree populations.

**Migration or Gene Flow as a Source of Variation.** The migration of genes from one population to another via seed and pollen dispersal is another way in which variation can be introduced into populations over a period of time. Unlike mutation, however, the genes in question already exist in some populations. Obviously, for migration to have a significant effect, these genes should be absent, or present at a low frequency, in the population into which they are introduced. Seed and pollen dispersal are the obvious modes of migration for forest trees.

*Seed dispersal* distances of most forest-tree species are rather small, but occasional propagules may travel considerable distances. Reports of long-distance dispersal have been made for seed such as coconuts carried by ocean currents. Such dispersal is obviously quite important in colonization events, especially where suitable habitats are widely dispersed. In general, though, it appears that gene migration via seed dispersal is slow in most forest trees.

*Gene flow* via pollen dispersal is a somewhat more difficult process to measure, at least in part because some estimates of pollen-dispersal distance may be biologically irrelevant. That is, simply knowing that pollen grains of a particular species can be detected many kilometers from their point of release does not mean that they are capable of or likely to effect a fertilization. This question is particularly important from the seed-orchard perspective, because orchard managers are concerned that pollen contamination from outside the orchard may seriously hinder the production of improved seed.

As with seed, when a single tree serves as a point source, the vast bulk of any pollen released falls within a short distance of the tree. When a forest is

**119**

considered as the pollen source, however, the relatively small, widely dispersed contribution from each tree is summed over a large number of trees. This total volume may be considerable inasmuch as the pollen production of a forest of large trees must total billions or trillions of grains. *Pollen dispersal* probably is more effective than seed dispersal as a migration mechanism, especially in insect-pollinated species, but little data are actually available on forest trees to confirm this point. However, theoretical calculations indicate that the rate of gene migration required to prevent populations from becoming sharply differentiated is very low, so even limited gene flow may be important.

### Random Processes that Modify Variation.

Random processes as well as directional ones can produce changes in gene frequencies from one generation to the next. Random genetic drift occasioned by a restriction of population sizes or isolation of populations by distance could play a major role in the evolution of many tree species.

The seed produced in any year carries only a sample of the genes available in the parental population, so small population size can lead to large and unpredictable changes in gene frequencies. As population sizes become very small, the operation of such chance factors may assume considerable importance in the evolution of these populations. It seems likely, then, that species such as bristlecone pine, knobcone pine, or others with small, patchy distributions have been considerably influenced by such random processes.

The *"founder effect,"* or the establishment of a population from one or a few individuals, is another example of the operation of chance factors that can occur in tree populations. It is quite easy to envision how natural catastrophes such as fire may decimate a forest leaving a scattered few individuals to reproduce and create the next generation. An analogous situation would be the long-distance dispersal of a few seeds to a new habitat. As a sample, these seeds may not represent accurately the distribution of gene frequencies that existed in the original population.

Because of chance alone, some genes present in the original population may be absent from this new population.

While the likelihood that such events will occur can be predicted, the direction and magnitude of change in any one instance is indeterminate. In the absence of any directional forces, the net effect of such chance occurrences over a long period of time would be to create a mosaic of populations, each with a gene-frequency distribution quite different from any other. It is more likely, though, that some combination of directional and random factors operates together to establish patterns of variation in natural populations.

### Selection: The Directional Modification of Variation.

*The power of Selection, whether exercised by man, or brought into play under nature through the struggle for existence and the consequent survival of the fittest, absolutely depends on the variability of organic beings. . . . The importance of the great principle of Selection mainly lies in this power of selecting scarcely appreciable differences, which nevertheless are found to be transmissible, and which can be accumulated until the result is made manifest to the eyes of the beholder (5).*

Charles Darwin clearly recognized the importance of heritable variation to selection in his studies of wild and domesticated plants and animals. Darwin saw natural selection as a process that could account for the enormous diversity of adaptations he observed in natural populations. He also realized that the development of domesticated plants and animals was an analogous process wherein humans, not natural processes, exercised control over survival and reproduction via *artificial selection*. But the role of heritable variation was clearly central to both natural and artificial (or "methodical") selection.

Darwin's theory is still central to the understanding of evolutionary processes and the origin of adaptations, but it has undergone much refinement since its conception a century ago. One source of refinement was the work of Gregor Mendel, which blossomed into the science of genetics during the twentieth century and provided the mechanism of inheritance that Darwin's theory needed. This merger of Darwinism and Mendelism forms the basis for the present understanding of organic evolution.

Despite its obvious importance, *natural selection* has proved to be a difficult phenomenon to study. Indeed, a great deal of evidence for the existence of natural selection is indirect. Lerner addressed this problem when he noted:

*natural selection is not an* a priori *cause of any phenomenon observed in nature, in the laboratory, or on the farm. Natural selection is a term serving to say that some genotypes leave more offspring than others. Natural selection has no purpose. It can be deduced to have existed and its intensity can be measured only* ex post facto. *For any given generation, natural selection is a consequence of the differences between individuals with respect to their capacity to produce progeny (6).*

Viewing natural selection as a consequence instead of a cause of differences—and one that can be studied only after the fact—we can appreciate the problem potential researchers face in studying it.

Artificial selection is somewhat easier to approach, at least from the standpoint of choosing traits of human value, and the hundreds of lines of domesticated plants and animals serve as testimony to the effectiveness of such selection. Humans are the selective agents here, and within the bounds established by natural variation, artificial selection can proceed toward the development of lines of increased value. However, it is important not to lose sight of the fact that natural selection still operates whether we practice artificial selection or not. Human desires may be counter to those that have

guided evolution over a long period of time, and compromises may have to be struck between the intensity of our breeding activities and biological factors, which work to ensure the long-term survival of the species.

## FOREST-TREE BREEDING

"It is therefore very desirable, before any man commences to breed either cattle or sheep, that he should make up his mind to the shape and qualities he wishes to obtain, and steadily pursue this object" (5). This remark, attributed to Lord Spencer in 1840, is obviously true for trees as well. Tree-breeding programs are long-term, expensive propositions into which one does not lightly enter. The development of appropriate guidelines at the formative stages is essential if the program is to be successful. Major concerns include the selection of a suitable species and characters to be improved, an assessment of the biological, technical, and financial resources available to support the program, and the formulation of a working plan to guide program development.

### Some Economic Concerns

Most tree-improvement programs have developed around a species that was historically the mainstay of the forest industry in that region. The loblolly pine program in the southeastern United States, as described by Zobel (7), is a good example of such an effort. Such an approach can be advantageous, especially if a good deal is already known about the amount and patterning of genetic variation within the species. This information is very useful in directing our selection strategies toward particular characters or toward particular regions. This early phase of a tree-improvement program, where large numbers of stands or individual trees are being examined, is one of the most expensive owing to time and travel costs. Some prior knowledge of the native variability permits a more efficient use of funds in exploiting this variation.

The concerns of the wood-using industries also must be addressed at the formative stage. These industries are generally familiar with most species from a wood-properties standpoint, but may have particular interests in only a few species. While more volume per unit land area is certainly one of their concerns, different industries may have a preference for wood with high or low specific gravity, wood with long or short fibers or tracheids, wood with more or fewer extractives, and other properties depending on their products. The ability to accommodate their specific interests could have a significant impact on the products industry and make the improvement program economically viable.

A major concern, particularly with regard to financing, involves how much improved material is needed and at what date, depending, of course, on the areas to be reforested and the reproductive biology of the species. Neither of these can be considered a constant when a number of years must pass between program initiation and the time at which improved planting stock becomes available. Typically, an agency will develop seed orchards of a size to satisfy just its own needs, unless the market price of improved seed is attractive. Estimates of the number of seeds produced per seed orchard tree per year, together with estimates of the number of seedlings needed per acre per year, permit one to equate supply with demand, but the vagaries of local climate, insect attack, and numerous other problems that influence seed production make such estimates far from perfect. Like other factions in agriculture, breeders are reduced at present to stockpiling seed during the good years to provide for the lean years that inevitably follow. Good seed-orchard management practices should provide the stimulating environment needed for adequate, predictable seed crops. Many major problems in the area of seed-orchard management remain to be solved at this time.

Finally, it should be obvious that tree-breeding activities can abbreviate but not circumvent the long rotation period needed to produce a crop of trees. Money invested now will not be recovered for

decades. If growing trees is not a profitable operation for a particular set of circumstances, the substitution of improved material may not alter this situation. Tree improvement is not a ''cure-all'' for forestry's ailments. Sound management practices are still required, and careful examination will show that in certain instances good silvicultural practices will be more beneficial than conversion to improved planting stock.

## Approaches to Forest-Tree Domestication

Several alternative avenues can be followed in developing improved lines of trees. At the start of an improvement program there may be little or no information available on the genetic biology of a species. Some rather questionable assumptions (or outright guesses) may have to be made concerning the extent and patterning of heritable variation within a species. In addition, improvement strategies may have to vary considerably depending on the characters to be improved. For example, some early attempts at developing elms in the United States that were truly resistant to Dutch elm disease involved a search for resistance within the American elm. Unfortunately, levels of resistance to Dutch elm disease were limited within the American elm, with the result that several elm-improvement programs now are based on breeding exotic elms (Figure 5.5). Similar examples could be cited for the American chestnut, a number of poplars (especially in Europe), and other species of forest trees.

**Provenance Selection.** As discussed earlier, the practical side of provenance testing involves the identification of suitable seed sources for reforestation needs. Once such provenances have been identified, the seed needed for reforestation can be collected from specific stands or areas. In some species such as Scotch pine, which has a large natural range covering much of Eurasia, and which also has been studied well, growth-rate differences vary by as much as 400 percent between the fastest- and slowest-growing provenances when planted in a

**Figure 5.5** (*a*) An urban American elm with Dutch elm disease (note dying, defoliated branches at top). (*b*) A Dutch elm disease-resistant hybrid of Japanese and Siberian elms (Saporo Autumn Gold) developed at the University of Wisconsin. (Photographs by R. A. Young.)

given locale. Sizable differences also exist among provenances for foliage color (of importance to Christmas-tree growers), cold-hardiness, resistance to various insect defoliators, and other biochemical and morphological characters (8). For many tree species, the simple movement of seed a few hundred kilometers has resulted in the improvement of growth rate or other traits by 5 to 10 percent or more. Because the differences between stands or provenances may be several times as large as differences between trees within a stand, the results of provenance tests are usually quite useful to an agency planning a more intensive improvement program. It is almost always more efficient to select the best stands before selecting the best trees within a stand. An especially good account of provenance selection is given by Wright (8).

**Exotic Introduction.** The term *exotic* might conjure up images of bizarre or wondrous plants, but for breeding purposes it refers only to a plant growing outside of its native range. Sugar maple trees planted in California are exotic by this definition. The use of exotic plants becomes a more comfortable notion when it is realized that almost all of the domesticated crops raised in the United States—corn, wheat, oats, barley, rice, potatoes, tomatoes, and beans, to name just a few—are exotics introduced for satisfying human food needs. While North America may be blessed with an abundance of valuable forest-tree species, many other countries are not so fortunate. For biological or historical reasons, many countries have had to

**123**

rely on exotics to enrich otherwise limited forest resources. South Africa, like many Southern Hemisphere regions, lacks good softwood species and has relied on exotic introductions of conifers from North America to satisfy its softwood and fiber needs.

Other countries may have only one or a few species suitable for their wood needs, and introduce exotics that grow faster or produce high-quality wood. For this reason, several European countries have developed large-scale testing and breeding programs using conifers from the western United States and Canada, especially Douglas-fir, Sitka spruce, and lodgepole pine (Figure 5.6).

Finally, as noted earlier, the search for disease or pest resistance may lead to introduction of exotics. An important or wide-ranging species may be virtu-

ally destroyed when a new or exotic pest is suddenly introduced. This was the case with American elm when Dutch elm disease was introduced from Eurasia. Although little or no natural resistance to the disease existed in American elm, a number of Eurasian elms are moderately to highly resistant, presumably because they evolved together with the pathogen for millenia. The development of disease-resistant elms will certainly be based on this naturally occurring resistance.

In the introduction of exotics, provenance testing is a logical starting point. However, a number of factors that govern successful introductions permit us to select species with a high probability of success. Perhaps the most important indication of usefulness elsewhere is performance in the native

**Figure 5.6** Douglas-fir seedlings grown for industrial plantation development in Banja Luka, Yugoslovia. (Photograph by R. A. Young.)

range. A tree that is slow-growing, has very poor form, and produces poor-quality wood is not likely to improve markedly in new surroundings.

*Environmental similarity* is an important consideration for successful introductions. Species adapted to warm, dry summers and cool, wet winters probably will perform poorly, or fail to survive, if moved to a region with wet summers and dry winters. Minimum winter temperature, soil types, amount of annual rainfall, and other climatic and edaphic factors should be checked to obtain an approximate match between environment and species adaptability. While some latitude can be tolerated for variation between environmental features in the native and exotic locations, the more the two regions differ in this regard, the greater the probability of disappointing performance.

**Interspecific Hybridization.** Hybrid breeding has a special appeal in most areas of applied plant science that is akin to the alchemist's changing base metal into gold. Most people think only of "hybrid vigor" whenever they see the word *hybrid*. However, increased vigor (or "heterosis," as it is sometimes called) may or may not result from crossing two different species. In most hybrid-breeding programs involving agronomic crops, different lines of the same species are crossed, instead of different species. In such crops, uniformity of performance or disease resistance may be the objective, rather than increased vigor.

Some hybridization programs have been quite successful in plant breeding, but the number of documented successful hybrids in forestry is actually quite small. In fact, certain hybrids such as black × red spruce, once considered superior to either parental species, are actually inferior in growth rate to either parental species (9). The rate of growth syndrome that fascinated many early tree breeders has slowly given way to the belief that hybridization will find its greatest use in the development of trees resistant to pests and pathogens, or tolerant to adverse environmental conditions.

One example of a currently successful hybridiza-tion program involves the production of the pitch pine × loblolly pine hybrid in Korea. Pitch pine possesses a relatively poor form with large branches, but is quite hardy in northern climates. Loblolly pine has a much better form and is faster growing than pitch pine, but is not especially cold-hardy. The hybrid performs quite well in Korea, apparently because it combines some of the cold-hardiness of pitch pine, as well as the better form and growth rate of loblolly pine (10).

**Plus-Tree Selection.** Perhaps the most common approach to tree improvement involves the selection of trees from wild populations based on their apparent superiority in one or more traits of interest. Either seeds or cuttings (scions) are collected from these trees and propagated in one or more locations to serve eventually as seed orchards (Figure 5.7). Genetically improved seed will be obtained from such orchards to satisfy reforestation needs.

No one selection method is suitable for all species under all conditions. For example, a method known as "comparison-tree selection" has been widely employed in the southern pine region with apparent success. In this system, a "candidate" tree is compared to a number of neighboring trees and is included in the selections only if it exceeds these neighbors by an arbitrary amount in the characters examined. The fact that most stands of southern pine tend to be even-aged, and that such stands occur in large blocks on relatively homogenous sites, operates in favor of this selection method.

A number of species, especially hardwoods, tend to occur in uneven-aged or uneven-sized stands, and individual trees may be widely separated, making direct comparison with neighbors impossible. In such cases, a system known as "baseline selection" may be employed wherein a "candidate" is compared to a regional average (or baseline) for the species calculated from a composite of measurements on a number of trees within the region. To be selected, the candidate must exceed this regional average by some arbitrary amount.

In making the original selections, it is possible,

**Figure 5.7** A superior tree selection of lodgepole pine near Babine Lake, British Columbia. Note the excellent stem form and crown characteristics. (Photograph courtesy of Nicholas Wheeler, British Columbia Forest Service.)

depending on available resources, to screen greater or lesser numbers of candidate trees. Obviously, the more trees examined,the greater the probability of locating more extreme or desirable types. However, at some point a balance must be struck between the number of trees examined and the number of trees actually selected. Selection criteria must be rigorous enough that candiate trees are likely to be *genetically superior*, but not so stringent that only one or a few trees is actually included. In short, we need an adequate genetic base on which to build.

Once a selection approach has been chosen, it generally proves convenient to collect and assemble the selected materials in one or a few places so that further evaluation and breeding can proceed efficiently. *Scions* can be propagated in an orchard by grafting or rooting so that the original parent genotype is retained intact. In some instances, it may be easier or more desirable to collect seed instead of (or in addition to) scions and raise the seed in a plantation or orchard setting. In this case, the genes of the selected tree are preserved but the original genotype is no longer intact. Each seedling contains a different sample of the genes of the selected tree, the other genes coming from whichever tree provided pollen for fertilization.

The decision to use clonal versus seedling material can have some effect on the level of improvement obtained during the first generation, but various testing schemes can largely compensate for most differences. Many tree breeders would prefer not to be concerned with the propagation effort, considering it the domain of the horticulturist. But the success of many applied tree-improvement programs depends on the successful propagation of selected materials for seed-orchard establishment. This is one area where an applied program has been the catalyst for renewed research in propagation techniques, especially hormone physiology.

Eventually, the propagation effort culminates in the development of seed orchards (Figure 5.8). Now the geneticist must be concerned with problems involving flowering, cone or fruit protection, harvesting, processing, and storing seed. In many instances, tree nurseries are located at or near the orchard site, so raising the improved seedlings is an attendant responsibility. Obviously, the more seed produced, or the earlier seed production begins,the more profitable the orchard becomes. Cooperation with soil scientists, plant physiologists, entomologists, and others is necessary if the expected level of improvement is to be realized.

**Evaluation of Select Trees.** Our initial selection procedure is somewhat limited, as we noted earlier, by our inability to equate phenotype with

**Figure 5.8** A portion of the seed-orchard/provenance test complex of the U. S. Forest Service/Wisconsin Department of Natural Resources in northern Wisconsin. (Photograph courtesy of Hans Nienstaedt, U.S.D.A. Forest Service.)

genotype. Wild-tree selection serves as a first approximation of an individual tree's genetic worth to a breeding program. Subsequent observations on the performance of the candidate tree or its relatives are needed to refine our original evaluation.

Many tree-breeding programs have relied on a separate testing phase wherein the offspring of selected parents are raised and compared. The practice of evaluating a parent's genetic worth on the basis of progeny performance is termed *progeny testing*. This test is used to rank selected trees so that undesirable genotypes may be eliminated from the seed orchard, and also to serve as a check on the level of genetic gains achieved to date. Progeny tests may serve other functions as well, such as a political demonstration to management that its investment has been well spent, but alternative procedures for this and other functions are usually more desirable. In recent years, the use of large, expensive plantings that serve the primary purpose of ranking candidate trees has diminished. In their place, breeding designs that mate selected parents have led to the creation of new populations in which further selection can be practiced.

**Genetic Gain.** The term *genetic gain* is an apt synonym for the term *improvement* in the breeder's language; both have the connotation of economic benefit to the producer in particular and society in general.

Symbolically, the expression for genetic gain is

$$G = S \times h^2$$

where $G$ is gain, $S$ is selection differential, and $h^2$ is heritability. Because they are based on estimates that vary from species to species and population to population, neither term on the right side of the equation is fixed. It is possible to alter the level of gain obtained by manipulating these terms. For example, it may be possible to change the selection differential for a character by merely selecting a smaller fraction of the total population for inclusion in the breeding population. If this reduced fraction represents a significant shift from the population mean, then the process will be successful. In practice, there are limits to just how small a fraction can be included, and *inbreeding depression*, or loss of vigor due to matings among closely related individuals, could become a serious problem if the breeding population is severely reduced. A viable alternative, at least with forest trees, is to expand the number of stands in which selections are made. This serves the purpose of expanding the base population but avoids the cost of screening billions of trees.

One alternative way (there are others) to increase the expected gain is to increase the *heritability estimate*. We will not dwell on the statistical details, but such an increase need not be as difficult as it may seem. Keep in mind that a heritability estimate is not a fixed quantity, but varies from population to population; this quantity can be changed by including selections from a larger geographic area, or by crossing parents from a large number of stands and selecting progeny prior to testing. Both of these procedures tend to increase genetic variability in the population of interest, leading to increased heritability estimates. Specific details concerning these methods can be found in Wright (8).

Any or all of the above methods can lead to increased gains in tree-improvement programs. Current estimates of genetic gain based on the selection of wild trees are on the order of 10 to 20 percent, depending on the species and trait in question (7, 11). It is likely that subsequent generations of breeding and selection will lead to additional gains of at least this magnitude.

**Advanced-Generation Breeding.** There will be a continuing need for breeding and further selection and evaluation activites beyond this first generation. Certainly the gains produced by this first generation are important, but continued progress will require that appropriate mating and evaluation designs become a part of all tree-improvement programs. This will be essential for continuing advances via artificial selection, as well as the maintenance of a broad genetic base for future generations.

Many tree-improvement programs are now at the point where advanced-generation breeding can begin. The prospects and problems associated with this phase are formidable and have received considerable thought (12). We are essentially at the point of creating new, synthetic populations that will be tailored to meet growing needs for fiber and energy. The lines developed to this end will stem largely from the new genotypes generated by crossing among our select trees. To be sure, new variability will have to enter the breeding program from time to time, either from additional wild-tree selections or from lines developed in other programs or geographic regions. But the bulk of the materials finding their way into production seed orchards will be one to several generations removed from the wild.

## DOMESTICATION OF THE FOREST

### Plantation Forests—Pro and Con

Forests that originated by natural processes are rapidly being replaced. In some instances they are being harvested and replanted with native or exotic trees. In many more instances they are yielding to the crush of humanity, as it expands its urban and agricultural activities on an ever-widening scale. While the need for food and shelter is very real, many environmental groups are alarmed at the rapid replacement of natural forests with *monocultures*. Certainly the process has shortcomings. In the case of agriculture there appear to be no easy choices for increasing food production, but many people view forest plantations with a suspicious eye. At times their fears are well placed, and breeders should attempt to minimize potential problems before they arise.

Natural populations are generally well adapted to their sites because their ancestors evolved on or near the same site. Replacement with trees originating from a distant source may produce a poorly adapted population with resultant low survival and inferior growth. However, these new forests may be very productive if care is taken to use seed from local sources, or from provenances that evolved under very similar ecological conditions. This is the basis for the establishment of seed zones to control the movement of seed and planting stock into areas where performance will be acceptable. Large tree-improvement programs with species such as Douglas-fir also control the movement of improved planting stock by developing seed orchards for specific regions within the species range.

Many people perceive *plantation forests* to be ecologically unstable monoculture systems tottering on the brink of disaster. In this regard, it is worth noting that many tree species such as jack pine, lodgepole pine, and Douglas-fir form naturally occurring monocultures (Figure 5.9). Pest epidemics occur here and in other forest types as well. Real cause for concern should not be directed at species monocultures *per se,* but at the genetic uniformity that often accompanies monocultures. Almost all documented examples of devastated monoculture systems involve *clones* (for example, the nineteenth-century destruction of the French wine industry, which used clonal varieties of rootstock), or highly inbred lines. Almost all forest-tree plantations are produced from seed arising from large numbers of parents. Even in seed orchards producing improved seed, the numbers of parents are considerable, thereby ensuring a broad array of genotypes. In those few species, such as some poplars, where clonal propagation is used, steps can be taken to mix cuttings from a number of clones

into the planting, thereby minimizing this monoculture hazard.

Perhaps a more objectionable feature of plantation forests is their *visual uniformity.* Such forests are even-aged and established at a regular spacing. Mechanized planting equipment and ease of maintenance during the early life of the stand necessitate the regular spacing, and it seems unlikely that current procedures will change in the near future. An irregular thinning process could mitigate this problem, but not before the stand is ten to twenty or more years old. A more permanent solution to this aesthetics problem could be the development of techniques for raising *mixed-species plantings.* Mixtures of species, either by rows or by plots, was once common practice in forestry, but has generally been abandoned. Species or provenance selections were usually such that one species overtopped and eliminated the other before any merchantable harvest was possible. Perhaps if more were learned about mixed-species culture, and how to select compatible species, the variety that such mixed plantings could create would make plantation culture more attractive. Opponents of monoculture would feel that such plantings also were "more stable" ecologically.

The advantages of plantation forests can be enormous if the breeding process has progressed to the point where significant improvement in growth rate, pest resistance, wood quality, or other traits has been achieved. For example, an adequate level of pest resistance may represent the difference between a crop of wood and nothing at all. Breeding progress in other areas can result in increased yields of forest products in a shorter period of time from forests occupying a diminishing land base. The concept of forest plantations as sources for energy is further developed in Chapter 19.

## Preserving Natural Variation—The Case For Genetic-Resource Conservation

The need for genetic-resource conservation is widely recognized by plant and animal breeders.

**Figure 5.9** Many natural forests such as this virgin stand of Douglas-fir in California (Seskiyou Mountains) are comprised of a single species—like many planted monocultures. (Photograph by C. G. Lorimer.)

The original wild populations from which most important crops and breeds of animals were developed were lost centuries ago. These *progenitor populations* could be of great value today as sources of variation for breeding, especially in the area of pest resistance. Vulnerability to pests is a real danger in widely planted crops that have a narrow genetic base.

Most forest-tree species still occupy large ranges and appear to be genetically quite variable. Many people, then, would conclude that concern for genetic-resource conservation in tree species is unnecessary. However, a species need not be pushed to the brink of extinction before a serious reduction of the genetic resource has occurred. Either directly or indirectly, many human activities have depleted the genetic base of forest-tree populations. Harvesting practices that systematically remove the best trees in a forest (high-grading), or the replacement of natural stands of one species with plantations of another species both operate to reduce genetic variability. The inadvertent introduction of pests, which caused the chestnut blight and Dutch elm disease in North America, has also resulted in the enormous loss of genetic resources that can never be recovered. These and similar events that occur during a relatively short period of time can have enormous long-term consequences.

The problem of preserving genetic resources can be approached in several ways. Certain measures could provide for the preservation of *"gene pools"* using existing natural populations or populations created to serve this specific role. These latter populations may be far removed from their native range. Alternatively, we can preserve genes via the *storage* of seed, pollen, or other plant parts in special collection facilities such as those already established for agronomic crops.

Natural scientific or preservation areas offer some promise as genetic-resource conservation sites, especially those containing large populations of trees occurring in a number of different habitats. Appropriate management practices could ensure that even pioneer species that require occasional disturbances to perpetuate themselves are maintained on such areas. Fortunately, the national forests and parks in many countries also serve a genetic-resource conservation function to some degree, even though management practices on such areas must meet other priorities. Whether such areas are plentiful enough, or large enough to isolate natural stands effectively from gene migration effects, is an open question. Certainly they are a start, but are inadequate to satisfy the entire conservation need.

The breeding orchards, clone banks, provenance and test plantings, and other collections of trees brought together during the conduction of tree-improvement activities also serve a conservation function. Although the size of such populations is small relative to those in national parks and forests, these plantings represent some of the most valuable genetic materials for breeding purposes. Selections included in such plantings were obtained in many instances following an intensive examination of millions of trees in thousands of stands. Such collections may also contain representative samples of many populations to enhance further their usefulness as genetic reserves. Finally, it might be pointed out that many such collections are located outside their native range and therefore might be free from pollen or seed migration emanating from domesticated forests.

# FUTURE DIRECTIONS FOR FOREST GENETICS AND FOREST-TREE BREEDING

## Anticipating Tomorrow's Needs

History provides countless examples of human failure to anticipate accurately the long-term consequences of our actions. National and international strife, recessions and depressions, and overpopulation with all its attendent problems are among the more conspicuous examples of such short-sighted behavior. Given the potential for disaster, it will be of paramount importance that forest geneticists avoid possible blind alleys in *tree-domestication programs*. This will generally call for adopting conservative yet creative approaches in programs of selection, testing, and breeding. The time and effort required may occasionally be considerable, but the eventual impact of a wrong decision at a central point may be disastrous.

The problems of forecasting anticipated needs and demands one, two, or more generations into the future are difficult even with accurate information on past trends. The forest-products industry fluctuates wildly in its demands for raw materials. In addition, there are continuing changes in quality of the raw materials available and in the nature of goods being produced. All of these factors impinge on tree-improvement activities.

The presettlement forest of large, long-boled trees is a thing of the past, replaced by regrowth forests established by natural and artificial means. As demand for forest products increases, trees will be harvested at an increasingly smaller size and younger age. The principal change in wood quality will be the relatively high proportion of less desirable juvenile wood contained in small-size trees. While it may prove possible to manipulate juvenile wood volume and characteristics genetically, it is obvious that the products industry will also have to adapt its technology to a changing resource.

The kinds of products being manufactured have also changed since colonial times. Veneer and particleboard panels have replaced sawed lumber in many uses for a variety of economic and technological reasons. The development of new and better products, some of which cannot be foreseen even one generation ahead, requires that the forest resource not be modified to the point that new technologies cannot be accommodated. This does not mean that a status quo situation must exist, only that wood characteristics suitable for a variety of uses be selected, with the occasional development of "specialty" strains of trees to satisfy particular needs while still maintaining a broad genetic base.

Fortunately, many of the directed changes advocated by forest geneticists, such as increased volume per unit time or area, or increased disease or pest resistance, need not alter inadvertently other characters. It may be difficult to envision circumstances in which seemingly well-advised manipulations of growth rate or other characters of economic importance could ultimately prove to be liabilities. But this is not certain, and provides one strong argument for "*gene banks*" and the maintenance of natural populations. However, fail-safe mechanisms are no substitute for clear insights and a job done well the first time.

## Prospects for Continued Improvement

Present tree improvement programs are only the beginning of efforts to provide more and better products from our forests. The genetic gains being obtained today are the result of only one generation of selection. Theoretical arguments, as well as early results from second-generation tests, indicate that additional gains will be possible for a number of generations in the future. These gains will not come effortlessly, however, and it will be imperative that breeders exercise good judgment in planning and conducting future research.

In addition to the steady pace of improvement resulting from the selection, propagation, and testing of candidate trees, forest-genetics research has provided a number of important and exciting developments. The finding that flowering can be induced in juvenile trees, either directly by application of plant growth hormones or indirectly by manipulating photoperiod and temperature, will permit a reduction in the length of time between flowering in successive generations. Where breeders once had to wait ten to fifteen years for young trees to begin flowering, such flowering can be induced in trees only one or two years old. This will permit greatly accelerated breeding and testing programs when the characters of interest, such as disease resistance, can be evaluated in young plants.

Considerable interest has also been devoted to a comparison of *mating designs* in recent years as the need for creating advanced-generation populations from original selections became evident. In general, a large number of possible crossing schemes could be employed to produce progeny of known and related parentage. The problem is primarily to determine precisely what information or other use can be obtained from these populations and then which designs are most efficient at providing this information. Like most other tree-improvement problems, some sort of compromise is generally struck between adopting a complex, elegant design and the cost and likelihood of actually completing such a design in the field. Fortunately, the large number of mating-design variations available virtually ensures that the creation of populations needed for advanced-generation breeding will be accomplished. However, at this time there is no final consensus on just what those designs should be.

Finally, it is worth mentioning one additional line of research that has not yet come of age, the *cell-culture production* of forest trees. Despite the current controversy surrounding the cloning of humans, plant biologists have carried on cloning research for a number of years with many notable accomplishments. Unfortunately, a bit of "magic" is still associated with this work, and it is not yet possible to propagate large numbers of plantlets from one or a few cells for most species of interest. Eventually it should be possible to produce unlimited numbers of plants from selected genotypes without concern for the problems of rooting or graft incompatibility that have annoyed breeders in the past. In the meantime, the limited production of plantlets cloned from plant tissue is useful, but also creates impatience for the research breakthroughs that will usher in the age of the clone.

Forest genetics has been and continues to be a stimulating area for research and development directed toward increasing forest yields. Agriculture has provided the precedent for domestication programs; if the breeder keeps an eye to the past and its painful lessons, as well as an eye to the future, the prospects for continued improvement are enormous.

## REFERENCES

1. K. Stern and L. Roche, *Genetics of Forest Ecosystems,* Springer-Verlag, New York, 1974.
2. D. Briggs and S. M. Walters, *Plant Variation and Evolution,* McGraw-Hill, New York, 1969.
3. L. E. Mettler and T. G. Gregg, *Population Genetics and Evolution,* Prentice-Hall, Englewood Cliffs, N. J., 1969.
4. T. Dobzhansky, *Genetics of the Evolutionary Process,* Columbia University Press, New York, 1970.
5. C. Darwin, *The Variation of Animals and Plants Under Domestication,* Vol. 2., Second Edition, D. Appleton & Co., New York, 1900.
6. I. M. Lerner, *The Genetic Basis of Selection,* John Wiley & Sons, New York, 1958.
7. B. J. Zobel, *So. J. Appl. For., 1,* 3 (1977).
8. J. Wright, *Introduction to Forest Genetics,* Academic Press, New York, 1976.
9. S. M. Manley and F. T. Ledig, *Can. J. Bot., 57,* 305 (1979).
10. S. K. Hyun, *Silvae Genetica, 25,* 188 (1976).
11. R. Porterfield, B. J. Zobel, and F. T. Ledig, *Silvae Genetica, 24,* 33 (1975).
12. M. Arbez, ed., "Advanced Generation Breeding," *Proceedings of the I.U.F.R.O. Joint Meeting of Genetic Working Parties,* Bordeaux, France, 1976.

# 6

# FOREST ECOLOGY AND THE FOREST ECOSYSTEM

# John D. Aber    Jan Henderson

135

Ecology is the study of the interactions between organisms and their environment. Such interactions are understandably varied and complex. However, the application of the results of ecological studies has helped to change forestry from a custodial-exploitive business to a sophisticated profession. Depending on one's perspective, ecology focuses on the individual and its relationship to the environment *(autecology)* or on a community of organisms and the interaction between the community and the environment *(synecology)*. It is important for the synecologist to recognize the difference between the community (the organisms) and the ecosystem (the community plus its physical environment). Although the community is always linked to the environment in a very definite way, it is sometimes worthwhile to study or talk about the community by itself—hence the distinction (1, 2).

Other perspectives have given rise to different areas of ecology. Foresters and forest ecologists have a patent interest in the structure and function of forest ecosystems. The structure of the ecosystem is the organizational pattern of a community. As a simple example, a forest of many small trees packed closely together would represent quite a different structure from one with a few large trees widely spaced. The function of the forest ecosystem relates to biological activities or processes associated with the community. This represents the dynamic as opposed to the static (structural) aspects of the ecosystem.

We also distinguish between theoretical and applied ecology. *Theoretical ecology* is the development of ecological principles such as succession, nutrient cycling, energy exchange, etc., all of which will be subsequently described. *Applied ecology* uses ecological principles to solve particular land-management problems. Studies of fertilization of forest stands, for example, are done with the express purpose of trying to find a way to grow timber or other forest crops bigger, better, or faster. Such studies rely on the ecological principles developed by the theoretical ecologist but represent ecology applied to solve a particular problem.

## FOREST COMMUNITY DEVELOPMENT

Forestry can be distinguished from other wildland-management professions by the fact that it deals with ecosystems with long developmental periods. The time periods required to produce a mature forest vary from as little as 35 years in the Southeast to over 100 years in the Rocky Mountains. The developmental process is not only long but also complex. It involves establishment of young individuals of pioneer species,[1] growth, and replacement by other species through a complex set of interactions that form the basis of the science of ecology. The ecological development is called *succession*.

Through the practices of silviculture (Chapter 9) foresters may affect the succession of a forest. Their treatments may be designed to maintain the status quo, speed succession (i.e., move the stand ahead to a later successional stage), or set it back to an earlier stage. The ecological development of a forest ecosystem, however, implies much more than the establishment and growth of the trees that dominate it. Many other organisms are involved, and many emergent properties may only be indirectly tied to the trees. Understory plants comprise an important part of any forest ecosystem. Insects and fungi play an important role by consuming or infecting vascular plants. Birds and mammals nest, mate, and obtain their food and shelter from the resources of the forest and in turn affect many of the functional aspects of the ecosystem such as energy flow and nutrient cycling. Bacteria, insects, and fungi in the soil may fix nitrogen or contribute to the cycling of all the nutrients through decomposition.

The forester can affect succession by every treatment made to the forest. A planting may speed succession by establishing a species that is characteristic of later stages in the successional sequence. An improvement cut will either speed or set back succession depending on whether earlier or later successional species are favored. Selective harvest

[1] Pioneer species are those present in the first stage of the ecological development of a community—that is, the pioneer stage.

of scattered trees will maintain a mature stand's structure and composition without allowing succession to proceed to an overmature or climax situation.

Intelligent management of a forest demands that management decisions be based on knowledge and understanding of the ecosystem. With a large degree of certainty, one can predict the probable outcomes of a treatment. If a prescribed fire is the treatment, what will be the outcome? How will the forest be affected? We should try to know the answers to these questions before deciding to implement such a treatment. In order to do this we need to understand quite fully the ecological development of the forest.

## FOREST-TREE GROWTH AND DISTRIBUTION

A question raised in the study of forest ecology is "Why are there so many species of trees in a forest region and why do certain species tend to occur on sites with similar characteristics?" The earliest settlers in the New World recognized that certain species in the primeval forest, such as sugar maple, tended to grow on the richest soils that allowed the best crop growth. Other species, for example, hemlock, meant poor soils and poor crops and were to be avoided. The relationship between the distribution and abundance of tree species and characteristics of the sites on which they grow will be described in this section.

### Tolerance, Competition, and Succession

What determines tree-species distribution? We have seen in earlier chapters that different species have different physiological responses to the availability of a given growth-promoting resource. For example, Figure 6.1 shows the relative rates of growth for three different species at various levels of light intensity (3). The curves in this figure express the concept of shade tolerance, which has traditionally been a key to forest ecology and management. A *tolerant species* is one that can grow comparatively well at low light availability but does not show large

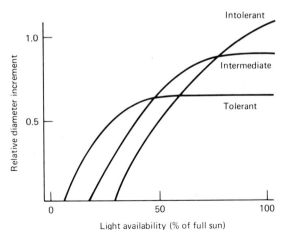

**Figure 6.1** Relative rates of growth as a function of light availability for tolerant, intermediate, and intolerant species (3).

increases in growth with increasing light levels. An *intolerant species* shows the opposite trends: very poor growth at low light levels but faster growth rates than tolerant species at light levels approaching full sun exposure. Trees of different tolerance levels are expected to grow under different conditions in natural forests. The relative tolerances to shade of some North American tree species are given in Table 6.1 (4).

Imagine a mature forest with tall trees whose crowns completely occupy the upper canopy levels. In deciduous forests of this type, only 2 to 5 percent of the light striking the top of the canopy will reach the forest floor. From Figure 6.1 it can be seen that trees of intolerant or intermediate species growing below the canopy will not be able to have a positive growth rate because light levels are below the *compensation point,* or the level where a net positive energy gain is possible. Only tolerant species will be able to grow in this dense shade. The tolerant species will be the only ones represented in the understory and the only species in a position to grow up into the canopy later (see Figure 6.2a). Thus, unless some sort of disturbance occurs, this stand will continue to be dominated by the same tolerant species and will not change much in species composition.

**Table 6-1**
Relative Tolerance to Shade of Some North American Tree Species (arranged in order of tolerance among groups but not within groups)

| Eastern Conifers | Eastern Deciduous | Western Conifers | Western Deciduous |
|---|---|---|---|
| | | Very Tolerant | |
| Balsam fir | American beech | Western red cedar | |
| Eastern hemlock | American hornbeam | Silver fir | |
| | Flowering dogwood | Western hemlock | |
| | American holly | California torreya | |
| | Eastern hophornbeam | Pacific yew | |
| | Sugar maple | | |
| | | Tolerant | |
| Northern white cedar | Rock elm | Alaska yellow cedar | California laurel |
| Red spruce | Blackgum | Incense cedar | Canyon live oak |
| White spruce | Sourwood | Port Orford cedar | Tanoak |
| | Red maple | Grand fir | |
| | Hickory spp. | Subalpine fir | |
| | | California red fir | |
| | | White fir | |
| | | Mountain hemlock | |
| | | Redwood | |
| | | Englemann spruce | |
| | | Sitka spruce | |
| | | Intermediate | |
| Eastern white pine | Ash spp. | Douglas-fir | Red alder |
| Black spruce | Basswood | Monterey pine | |
| | Sweet birch | Sugar pine | |
| | Yellow birch | Western white pine | |
| | Buckeye | Blue spruce | |
| | American elm | Giant sequoia | |
| | Sweetgum | Noble fir | |

Imagine that a hurricane, tornado, or fire sweeps through this stand, felling large numbers of the old tolerant trees and flooding the forest floor with light. Conditions are now much better for intolerant species; if a source of seed is available and ground surface conditions are suitable, intolerant species will germinate and grow at a much faster rate than the established seedlings (called "*advance regeneration*"). The intolerant trees will soon overtop the tolerant species because of their faster rate of growth in full sun and will soon dominate the stand (Figure 6.2b). However, they will not cast shade that is darker than their compensation point. This leaves light levels below their crowns sufficient for the growth of intermediate species and in turn for tolerant species. Thus a stratified canopy may develop with intolerant species at the highest level, intermediate species below them, and tolerant species lower still (Figure 6.2c). Eventually, as the tolerant trees slowly grow taller and the intermediate and intolerant trees die, a stand dominated by tolerant trees will be reestablished (Figure 6.2d).

**Table 6-1** *(continued)*

| Eastern Conifers | Eastern Deciduous | Western Conifers | Western Deciduous |
|---|---|---|---|
| | | Intermediate | |
| | Hackberry | | |
| | Cucumber magnolia | | |
| | Silver maple | | |
| | Black oak | | |
| | Northern red oak | | |
| | Southern red oak | | |
| | White oak | | |
| | | Intolerant | |
| Bald cypress | Paper birch | Bigcone Douglas-fir | Madrone |
| Loblolly pine | Butternut | Juniper spp. | Big-leaf maple |
| Pitch pine | Catalpa spp. | Bishop pine | Oregon ash |
| Pond pine | Black cherry | Coulter pine | California white oak |
| Red pine | Chokeberry | Jeffrey pine | Oregon white oak |
| Shortleaf pine | Kentucky coffeetree | Knobcone pine | Golden chinkapin |
| Slash pine | Honeylocust | Limber pine | |
| Virginia pine | Pin oak | Lodgepole pine | |
| | Scarlet oak | Piñon pine | |
| | Pecan | Ponderosa pine | |
| | Persimmon | | |
| | Yellow poplar | | |
| | Sycamore | | |
| | | Very intolerant | |
| Jack pine | Aspen spp. | Alpine larch | Quaking aspen |
| Longleaf pine | Gray birch | Western larch | Cottonwood spp. |
| Sand pine | River birch | Bristlecone pine | Willow spp. |
| Eastern red cedar | Black locust | Digger pine | |
| Tamarack | Post oak | Foxtail pine | |
| | Turkey oak | Whitebark pine | |
| | Blackjack oak | | |
| | Willow spp. | | |

*Source.* Adapted from H. W. Hocker, Jr., *Introduction to Forest Biology,* John Wiley & Sons, New York, 1979.

What has just been described is an example of the process of *succession,* a central concept in the field of ecology. Succession can now be more specifically defined as the orderly replacement of species through time in a given location, leading eventually to a generally stable plant community. This end point has been called the "*climax community*"; however, some scientists feel that even late successional communities will change in composition through time. The type of succession described is called *secondary succession.* This results from the destruction of an established plant community without severe disturbance of the site, mainly the soil in which the new plants will grow. *Primary succession* occurs when plants invade an area in which no plants have grown before, such as bare rocks or new lakes created by the retreat of glaciers. In primary succession on land, the plants must build the soil; a much

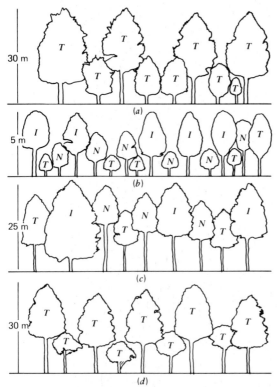

**Figure 6.2** Schematic view of the distribution of tree crowns by tolerance class and height for four stages of succession initiated by severe disturbance. (*a*) Before disturbance. (*b*) Immediately after disturbance (5 years). (*c*) Midpoint of succession (50–75 years). (*d*) Full recovery and return to predisturbance conditions. (*T* = tree of tolerant species, *N* = tree of intermediate species, *I* = tree of intolerant species.)

longer time is required for the process—hundreds to thousands of years. Secondary succession usually takes only decades to perhaps hundreds of years (5). Before we continue with the treatment of secondary succession, we will describe the basic principles and classification schemes for primary succession.

**Primary Succession.** Three basic types of primary succession correspond to the character of the substrate on which succession is initiated: *xerarch, mesarch,* and *hydrarch* succession. It is important to recognize that these types represent only nodes or reference points along a gradient of site conditions

from dry to wet, including many intermediate situations. *Xerarch succession* is illustrated by the bare rock to juniper shrub sequence (6). In this successional sequence (sere), invading plants, lichens, and mosses, together with the strong influence of weathering forces of the climate, modify the substrate so that the other plants can develop. This sere is characterized by dry conditions and a lack of soil even though the site may occur in an area of ample rainfall. The substrate has little water-holding capacity, and therefore water is available only intermittently as precipitation falls, and shortly thereafter. The successional sequence in this case is very closely tied to the development of the soil. The time involved for ultimate development of the juniper-dominated community is thousands of years, a time span too long to be of much consequence to the forestland manager.

*Mesarch succession* is illustrated by community development following glacial retreat in Southeast Alaska (6–8). The climate of the area is cool and moist. The parent material of the soil is glacial rubble deposited at different times, and therefore a series of plant communities with different ages have become established. The soil material itself is raw and unweathered as it is laid down by the retreating glacier.

Pioneer species in this sere are those with specialized mechanisms for transport, such as feathery plumes or wings to be carried by the wind or barbs or burrs to be carried (inadvertently) by animals. These include such species as Drummonds dryas, Sitka alder, dwarf fireweed, willows, and cottonwood. Notably two of these pioneers are also nitrogen fixers (dryas and alder). A lichen-moss stage is essentially absent here, being swamped out by the much more rapidly growing vascular plants.

Some vascular plants do not appear to enter the sere until these pioneers have improved the nutrient and organic matter status of the soil. The mature pioneer stage, dominated by alder and willow, gives way to cottonwoods, hemlocks, and spruces, the latter of which eventually overtop and replace the former species. The conifers will assume dominance of the site after about 170 years following glacial retreat.

Beneath the new overstory of hemlock and spruce, regeneration of the species is going on, seeming to ensure the replacement of this type of climax forest. However, mosses and litter are building up under the conifer canopy, and eventually sphagnum will dominate, as it does inland in white spruce forests (9), and may slowly eliminate the hemlock and spruce creating a muskeg. What happens after muskeg formation is uncertain but there are some indications that an alder-willow community might eventually be reestablished, possibly allowing this whole cycle to occur again. This sere is illustrated in Figure 6.3.

*Hydrarch succession* is illustrated by community development in cold, freestanding water, as occurs frequently in the Great Lakes region. In this sere, floating vegetation such as water lilies and pondweed and mat-forming sedges or other grasslike plants initiate the sequence. These species invade a bog, often from around the edges, and by means of vegetative reproduction creep out farther into the freestanding water. Sphagnum moss often invades after the sedge mat has been formed, which helps bind the vegetation together. At this point the vegetation is floating on what may be several meters of water. Later in the sere, shrubs such as bog rosemary, labrador tea, or cranberries invade the area, and tall shrubs such as willow, birch, or alder will eventually replace the low shrubs. Last, conifer trees such as tamarack or black spruce will become established. While all this is going on the sedge mat or floating pond-lily type of vegetation pushes farther out into the bog. What one often sees, therefore, is a sequence over space from the pioneer sedges and pond lilies near the center of a bog to shrubs and tree-dominated bog around the edges (Figure 6.4). This sequence in space is interpreted as a sequence in the ecological development of a community over time (i.e., it is a sere). Such a succession from sedge mat to conifer bog appears to be a reasonable interpretation of the sequence; however, the statement that this sere will ultimately yield

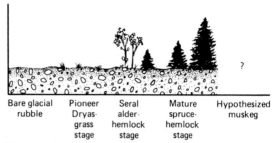

| Bare glacial rubble | Pioneer Dryas-grass stage | Seral alder-hemlock stage | Mature spruce-hemlock stage | Hypothesized muskeg |

**Figure 6.3** Successional sequence illustrating mesarch succession from Alaska. Pioneer stages rapidly invade freshly exposed glacial rubble. Shrubs including alder and tree seedlings of hemlock and spruce invade the pioneer community. The mature (climax?) conifer forest develops after the spruce and hemlock grow through and replace the shrub stage.

a closed conifer forest similar to those that develop on adjacent glacial soils is probably misleading. The organic soil formed in the bog will never resemble the inorganic (usually derived from glacial rubble in this area) soil of a well-developed spruce forest.

Examples of primary succession *per se* are infrequently encountered in forestry. However, all places on earth have yielded a primary succession at some time in history and some have had several, such as places that have been repeatedly glaciated and deglaciated. Events that disrupt successional development and set the sere back to an earlier stage, thus initiating a secondary succession, are called *perturbations*.

**Secondary Succession.** Secondary succession can be considered as a modification of the longer-lasting primary succession. One way of viewing succession is that for any place on earth, a primary succession (actually several may be in progress at the same time but at different scales) began at the last time that place was completely divested of biota and biotic influences. Secondary successions complicate the series by "setting back" parts of the system to an earlier or less-developed stage. When the disturbance is over, succession begins again, and the community develops toward some theoretical end point called the climax.

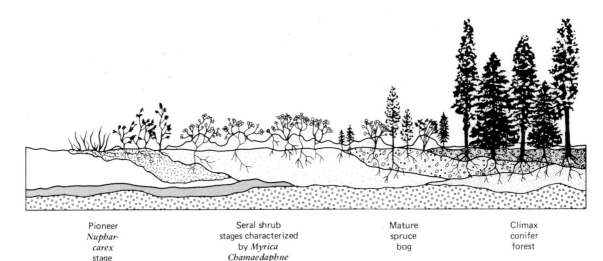

| Pioneer | Seral shrub | Mature | Climax |
|---|---|---|---|
| *Nuphar-* | stages characterized | spruce | conifer |
| *carex* | by *Myrica* | bog | forest |
| stage | *Chamaedaphne* | | |
| | and *Ledum* | | |

**Figure 6.4** Successional stages of a hydrarch sere from the Great Lakes region. Pioneer stages are characterized by floating plants that invade open water, followed by shrubs that invade the floating mat and then water tolerant conifers (black spruce and tamarack), which characterize the mature spruce bog. The mature climax spruce-fir forest that develops on inorganic soil substrate is shown to the right to complete the transect from the pond (left) to *terra firma* (right). (Reproduced with permission of the National Research Council of Canada from the *Canadian Journal of Botany, 30,* 490–520, 1952.)

A special case of secondary succession occurs when a natural forest is cleared and the land is farmed for several years. The plowing and lack of plant cover cause substantial changes in the soil, particularly the loss of organic matter and nutrients. If the field is then abandoned, the succession that follows is quite different from that after a natural disturbance. Such an *old-field succession* usually begins with herbaceous instead of tree species and takes longer to reach the climax state. Because most forestry practices deal with some form of secondary succession, the remaining emphasis of this section will be on this phase of plant community development.

*Small-Scale Disturbance or Gap-Phase Regeneration.* Disturbance in the forest is not always on the large scale previously described for tornados or fires that clear large tracts of land. Lesser storms or the natural death of older trees that fall and crush smaller trees in their path may create small gaps on the order of tens to hundreds of square meters (Figure 6.5a). Light levels in these gaps are not as high as in the open because of partial shading by the remaining trees surrounding the gap. Frequently these gaps are filled by intermediate species that grow well at moderate light levels (Figure 6.5b). Species of intermediate tolerance, such as tulip poplar and yellow birch, are often called gap-phase reproducers for this reason. *Gap-phase succession* is a form of secondary succession, but few if any intolerant trees will be present and the size of the area is smaller. Because this type of small-scale disturbance (usually attributed to natural mortality) is very common in otherwise undisturbed forests, species of intermediate tolerance can become established and will often be present in old, mature or "climax" stands (figure 6.5c).

*Relationship Between Tolerance and Life-History Phenomena.* In addition to light responses, natural selection has acted on many other aspects of plant growth to allow adaptation for different sizes, frequencies, or intensities of disturbance. Selection

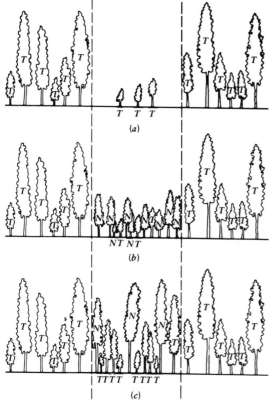

**Figure 6.5** Schematic view of distribution of tree crowns by tolerance class and height during succession in canopy gaps (gap-phase regeneration). (a) Immediately following creation of gap. (b) After initial regeneration of gap-phase intermediate species. (c) At end of gap succession with few remaining intermediate species. (T = tolerant tree species, N = intermediate tree species, I = intolerant tree species.)

may produce quite different results in different forest regions; therefore, it is very difficult to make general conclusions for all forest ecosystems. The following discussion emphasizes relationships which occur in the *eastern deciduous forest region*.

We have mentioned the need for a seed source if intolerant species are going to grow in a newly disturbed area. If this area is surrounded for any distance by mature forests without intolerant species, how will the seeds get to the area? Two main methods have evolved. As mentioned previ-

ously many of the earliest successional species (such as cottonwood and aspen) produce large quantities of light seeds, often with large networks of filaments, that can be dispersed for miles by air movements. This has been called the *"fugitive strategy."* A species must maintain only a small number of stems over a fairly large area to be able to reach any disturbed site with fresh seed. A second method of having seeds available in an area where no trees of the same species are currently growing is the *"buried-seed"* strategy. Some species (such as pin cherry and many of the blackberries) produce heavy seeds in large numbers, most of which fall directly beneath the parent plant. These seeds can remain dormant but alive in the forest floor for 100 years or more. Succession can occur on the site, leading to the elimination of all trees of the intolerant buried-seed species, but if disturbance occurs again while the seeds are still viable, new trees of this species will appear even though no parent tree exists for miles around. Species having this method of reproduction often produce fleshy fruits surrounding the seeds so that birds will consume them and carry some of each seed crop into new areas (10).

At the other extreme, tolerant species are most likely to reproduce successfully within the stands occupied by the parent tree where little or no change will occur. Many of these species (such as beech and sugar maple) tend to have heavier seeds that are not transported any great distance by either wind or animals, although there are many exceptions such as hemlock and spruce.

Intermediate species tend to either have seeds of intermediate weight or some means of catching a wind to assist in dispersal. This results in dispersal distances that are intermediate between the fugitive species and the tolerant trees.

A number of other characteristics also tend to coincide with the tolerance of eastern deciduous forest tree species (see Table 6.2). All of these characteristics reflect the need for intolerant trees to reach disturbed areas, grow quickly, and reproduce prolifically at a young age. Tolerant species occupy the other extreme; they live longer, grow more

**Table 6-2**

Tolerance versus Relative Life-History Characteristics for the Eastern Deciduous Forest (5).[a]

| Characteristic | Intolerant | Tolerant |
|---|---|---|
| Maximum size | Small | Large |
| Longevity | Short | Long |
| Growth rate | Fast | Slow |
| Age at first reproduction | Young | Old |
| Seed weight | Light or fleshy fruits | Heavy |
| Number of seeds per year | Many | Few |

[a]Western conifers show a distinctly different relationship.

slowly and to greater size, reproduce at a later age, and have fewer, larger seeds. Intermediate species lie between these extremes for seed characteristics and rate of growth, but tend to be fairly long-lived since this is their method of maintaining a seed source in an undisturbed area (a few large stems along with many tolerant species in a mature stand) (see Figure 6.5c).

Life-history characteristics (rate of growth, size at maturity, etc.) are important not only in understanding the function of plant communities and ecosystems but also for the management of forests. Different characteristics make different species more or less attractive as crop trees. For example, fast growth is very important for high yields, which would indicate that managers should favor intolerant species. The managers would therefore want to create the type of environment favorable to reproduction and growth of intolerant trees, usually by clearcutting practices (see Chapter 9). However, some intolerant species do not grow large enough to be harvestable for timber. If dominant intolerant trees die before harvest, the energy captured by the leaves during their lifetime is lost as the wood decomposes. In the more controlled conditions of *plantation forestry,* the need for faster growth and the possibility of early harvests (shorter rotation lengths or thinnings) often leads to the use of the most intolerant species (red pine, aspen (as hybrid poplars), loblolly pine, etc.). The manipulation of forest stands to achieve specified objectives is treated in more detail in Chapter 9, "Silviculture."

***Competition for Resources Other than Light–The Niche Concept.*** So far most of our attention has been given to the effects of light on growth rates and the related implications for natural succession and forest management. However, plants have other requirements for growth; the ability of different sites to provide these factors influences tree-growth rates. Chief among these are water and nutrients, as discussed in Chapters 3 and 4 on tree physiology and forest soils.

The production of the *macronutrients* (nitrogen, phosphorus, sulfur, potassium, calcium, and magnesium) in forest soils was described in Chapter 4. Extensive tests with various types of fertilizers that increase the availability of different combinations of nutrients have shown that forests are almost always limited by a low availability of nitrogen or phosphorus, with *nitrogen* being by far the most common.

Interestingly, species responses to nitrogen availability can be described in much the same way as their response to light. In a classic study in the 1930s (11) it was determined, through response to fertilizer trials, that tree species could be grouped as tolerant, intermediate, or intolerant of low nitrogen availability. The response curves looked almost identical to those in Figure 6.1 with the *x*-axis labeled as nitrogen availability instead of light availability. However, species that are tolerant of low light levels are not necessarily also tolerant of low nitrogen availability. Figure 6.6 lists the species examined in this classic study with their tolerance ratings for both

Tolerance class for light

| | Tolerant | Intermediate | Intolerant |
|---|---|---|---|
| **Tolerant** | Closed canopies—poor sites<br><br>Hickory | Gaps—poor sites<br>White oak<br>Chestnut oak | Open—poor sites<br><br>Bigtooth aspen |
| **Intermediate** | Closed canopies—moderate sites<br>Beech<br>Red maple | Gaps—moderate sites<br><br>Basswood | Open—moderate sites<br><br>Trembling aspen |
| **Intolerant** | Closed canopies—rich sites<br>Sugar maple<br>Black gum | Gaps—rich sites<br>White ash<br>Northern red oak | Open—rich sites<br><br>Tulip poplar |

Tolerance class for nitrogen

**Figure 6.6** Separation of several deciduous tree species in the northeastern United States by tolerance classes for light and nitrogen. (Adapted from Mitchell and Chandler, reference 11.)

145

nitrogen and light. The data in this table indicate where each species might be dominant within a large forested area containing young, disturbed and old, undisturbed stands. For example, white ash is intermediate for light and intolerant for nitrogen, and it tends to occur in small (gap-phase) disturbances on rich sites. The type of site where each species group would be found is also listed in Figure 6.6.

It may now be apparent why there are so many species of trees in a given forest region. Nine distinct types of environments that occur because of light and nitrogen availability have been designated. Through competition and natural selection, each species tends to specialize for a certain type of environment where it can outcompete other species, dominate the stand, and reproduce successfully. This is the basic concept of the *ecological niche*. A species niche is that set of environmental conditions where the species can survive, compete, and reproduce. Using white ash as an example, its niche is defined as high nitrogen and moderate light availability. Many ecologists believe that no two species can occupy the same niche, so no two species in a region should be identical in their responses to environmental conditions. In Figure 6.6 there are still some boxes with more than one species, which indicates that more than one species occupies the same niche with regard to light and nitrogen. However, there are other growth-limiting resources to which species may respond differently.

*Water* is crucial to plant life, and forest trees frequently experience moisture stress and suffer growth reductions as a result. Species responses to water availability usually follow a bell-shaped curve (Figure 6.7) with growth fastest at some point between the wettest and driest conditions. Figure 6.7 shows that this optimal point can be at different levels for different species (12). This water gradient could separate red maple and beech in Figure 6.6 because the maple tends to occur on wetter sites, even into swampy conditions.

Length of growing season and average tempera-

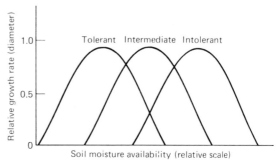

**Figure 6.7** Relative rates of growth (to maximum potential for each species) as a function of moisture availability. (*Tolerant species* in this figure refers to tolerance to low moisture levels). The bell-shaped curve may result from lack of oxygen in the rooting zone at high moisture content (12). (Absolute growth rates may vary).

ture during the growing season also affect tree growth differently for different species. The growth exhibits a similar bell-shaped response to temperature (Figure 6.8). Species with optimal growth at levels closer to the origin (Species A), such as yellow birch, would be expected to occur either farther north or at higher elevations than species with optimal growth farther along the $x$-axis (Species B and C), such as white ash (12).

By combining species responses to all four of these growth-limiting resources and expanding Figure 6.6 into three (and then four!) dimensions, species could be divided until each box in the figure contained only one species. This would represent that species niche as defined by these four growth-limiting resources. If we had three classes of responses (tolerant, intermediate, and intolerant) to each resource, with four resources (light, nitrogen, water, temperature), there would be $3^4$ or 81 boxes allowing 81 separate species to coexist with different niche descriptions.

In a complete niche analysis, reproductive strategies (fugitive strategy versus buried-seed strategy) and life-history characteristics (life expectancy, age at reproduction, etc.) would be considered as well, increasing the number of potential niches still

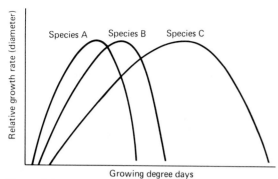

**Figure 6.8** Relative rates of growth (to maximum potential for each species) for three species as a function of the number of growing degree days (summation of the number of days with mean temperature above 40° F times the difference between mean temperature and 40° F; a measure of length and average temperature of the growing season) (12). (Absolute growth rates may vary).

further. We can begin to understand the occurrence of several hundred species of trees in the eastern deciduous forest region. Another factor (chemical) that may affect associations or absence of certain species at a particular site will be discussed in the next section.

***Competition through Chemical Alteration of the Soil Environment–Allelopathy.*** Certain associations of trees and other plant species have been noted in the forest throughout history. In 1832, De Candolle (13) suggested that some plants may excrete from their roots chemicals that are harmful to other plants. This effect, known as *allelopathy,* is more generally defined as the inhibition of germination, growth, or metabolism by one plant on another through the production of chemical compounds that escape into the environment (14). This form of inhibition is distinct from competition, which acts through the depletion of resources. The importance of allelopathy lies in its capacity to alter the structure, function, and diversity of plant communities.

Through allelopathy a dominant species may speed its invasion of a previous community and delay its replacement by other species. Chemical effects of a species on the soil may limit the number and kinds of species able to coexist with it. In mixed-species stands, a mosaic of differing chemical effects may form on the soil and contribute to the patterning and species diversity of the forest stand. Together with competition for light, soil moisture, and nutrients, allelopathic effects appear to be among the most probable causes for the spatial distribution of tree species (15).

Probably the most well-documented allelopathic effect of trees is the suppression of plant growth exhibited by established black walnut trees (Figure 6.9). As early as 1881, Stickney and Hoy (16) observed very sparse vegetation under black walnut trees and pointed out that no crop would grow under or near the trees. Later reports verified that neither alfalfa nor tomatoes could grow near black walnut; the growth of red pine, yellow birch, and apple trees was inhibited by this tree species (14,15).

An active substance, *juglone,* was isolated and identified as the major inhibitory chemical compound responsible for the allelopathic effects. Juglone is present in the roots, leaves, and fruit hulls of the tree. Thus the chemical can accumulate in the soil in a variety of ways—for example, through rain washing the compound from the leaves to the forest floor or by leaf and hull litter accumulating on the ground (14).

Allelopathy is apparently of widespread occurrence in forest communities. It has been reported that the growth of yellow birch is restricted by the presence of sugar maple, and a pattern where yellow birch grows in the presence of beech but not sugar maple has been proposed (17, 18). The abundance of each of these species in the beech-birch-maple climax association may therefore depend on the abundance of the other two species. It has been observed that relatively bare areas occur under sycamore, hackberry, white oak, and northern red oak in a bottomland forest in Missouri even though herbaceous species grow well under American elm trees in the same area (19). After detailed analyses,

**147**

**Figure 6.9** Growth inhibition of shrubs under black walnut tree possibly due to the allelopathic substance juglone.

the reduced understory growth was ascribed at least in part to allelopathy. Additional tree species suspected of exhibiting allelopathic effects include black cherry, sassafras, ailanthus, eucalyptus, white pine, lodgepole pine, Scotch pine, European larch, and winged sumac.

It is clear that allelopathic effects occur in the forest and affect species composition. How widespread this effect may be is still a matter of conjecture. Research is active in this field today, and future results may aid the forester in development of proper management schemes compatible with natural forces.

***Species-Site Interactions.*** So far the effect of light, water, nutrients, and chemicals on succession of forest stands has been discussed. It was noted that deficiencies or excesses in any of these important factors can dramatically alter tree growth and species composition of a site. However, availability of these factors is not constant over time. In the example of the old-field succession previously described, severe disruption of the forest soil for agriculture reduced soil organic matter and nitrogen availability. Less severe disturbances such as harvesting or changes in species composition can also change nutrient availability. A constant interaction between the species and the site determines the overall rate of movement of nutrients, water, and energy between plants and the soil and between the plant-soil system and the surrounding atmosphere, groundwater, streams, and lakes. This brings us into the realm of forest ecosystem studies, the next section of this chapter.

## OPERATION OF THE ECOSYSTEM

Solar energy is the driving force for all the acitivities of the forest ecosystem. It powers photosynthesis in the leaves, which creates chemical energy for the production of wood, roots, and next year's leaves. The sunlight also heats the surfaces of the leaves, causing evaporation from the moist cells and establishing the force that pulls water out of the soil, through the roots, stem, and branches, and out to the leaf. Some of the energy from photosynthesis is transported to the roots where it is used to extract nutrients from the soil. The nutrients then move through the tree with the flow of water. In the soil, billions of microbes and larger animals feed on decaying plant and soil material, releasing essential nutrients for plants to take up. A fresh batch of litter material is made available to these decomposers each autumn with leaf-fall or whenever roots, stems, or other plant parts are shed by the tree. Many of the nutrients can thus continuously cycle between plant and soil without leaving the system.

All of the nutrients do not, however, remain in the cycle. A summer rainstorm might add new water to the system; while we think of both rainwater and forest streamwater as pure, they both contain variable concentrations of nutrients and possibly pollutants as well, and these concentrations change as the water passes through the system. First, rainwater impinging on leaves and stems usually leaches nutrients from the plant and increases the nutrient concentration of the solution. In the soil, the concentration can increase further as nutrients released by decomposition or from soil minerals go into solution. On the other hand, plant roots create a thick network of absorbing surfaces, which take these nutrients out of solution and carry them back up to the plant. The water percolating below the rooting zone and into streams or groundwater can be either more or less concentrated in different chemicals than

the rainwater that entered the system. In large part we rely on this "processing" of water and air by forests and other vegetation types for our clean supplies of both.

The processes just described encompass the scope of *ecosystem studies,* which concentrate on the movement of energy, water, and nutrients (or other chemicals including pollutants) into, out of, and through ecosystems. It differs from ecology in that forest ecology emphasizes the *interactions* between species and site in determining the distribution and abundance of species. Light, water, and nutrients were considered important in this context but were not the main focus. In ecosystem studies, the focus is on how species and soils function *together* as a unit to determine overall patterns of movement for energy, water, and nutrients.

What is an *ecosystem?* The emphasis on inputs and outputs makes the boundaries of the system crucial. An ecosystem can be as large or as small as fits the purposes of the study. Some have used a single leaf as the system under study and looked at the inputs and outputs of energy, plus changes in temperature that represent energy storage (3). At the other extreme, one of the first and now classic studies in environmental science centered on the movements of the pesticide DDT through food chains around the world. Finding traces of this chemical in animals far removed from areas where DDT had been applied demonstrated that the entire globe can be seen as a single interconnected ecosystem (20).

The definition of the extent of an ecosystem is determined by the nature of the study and the type of information desired. For forest ecosystems, one of two definitions is generally used: the *watershed* or the *stand.* A *watershed* is a topographically defined unit of land such that all the precipitation falling into it flows out in a single stream. Watersheds can range in size from a few hectares near ridgetops in mountainous area with extreme topography to thousands of square kilometers, as in the case of the Mississippi River watershed, which drains nearly one-third of the United States. The advantage of using a watershed is that, as presented previously, most of the movement of nutrients in and out of forests occurs in water, and a watershed simplifies the measurement of the water budget or the quantities of water that enter and leave the system.

A *stand* is any area of forest vegetation with site conditions, past history, and current species composition sufficiently uniform to be managed as a unit. This definition indicates the importance of both current vegetation and past human or natural disturbance on processes within the system, as discussed in the next section.

It should be clear that the measurement of the processes that effect the transformations of energy, water, and nutrients in the ecosystem must encompass many disciplines such as plant physiology, soil science, microbiology, hydrology, and geology. This raises a second basic property of ecosystem studies. It is an *integrative science,* synthesizing knowledge from various specialties into a unified, coherent picture of system dynamics. This picture often takes the form of a computer program or model, which allows the systems ecologist to describe the best current view of the workings of the entire system and then test the implications by running the model under different conditions.

This brief introduction might be concluded with some discussion of why ecosystem studies have become increasingly popular and productive in the past decade. The first is that the basic processes studied involve important products we expect from forests and the assessment of *potential impacts* of internal management or external pollution stresses on forest productivity. Energy transformation from sunlight to wood for fuel and fiber is probably the most obvious effect, but purification of air and water by these processes is also crucial in many areas. Management practices can simultaneously affect the quantity and quality of water leaving a forested area either directly or as a side effect of management for wood production. Many important environmental pollutants such as those in "acid rain" are carried to forest ecosystems in the atmosphere and deposited

by rainfall. This change in precipitation chemistry could affect all the processes determining production or water quality.

The second reason for the rise of ecosystem studies is their *integrative nature*. The results of many workers from different disciplines can be synthesized into a single coherent view of the dynamics of a given ecosystem. This synthetic view, again often in the form of a computer model, can then be used to produce the type of quantitative predictions required either for detailed management decisions or for environmental impact statements.

## EXAMPLES OF ECOSYSTEM STUDIES

Perhaps the best example of an ecosystem-level study of a forested watershed is the one carried out at the Hubbard Brook Experimental Forest in New Hampshire (5, 21, 22). The Hubbard Brook valley contains six small watersheds (those studied range from 12 to 43 hectares) with very similar soils, vegetation, and geology (Figure 6.10). Each watershed represents a separate ecosystem, but all are so similar that they are considered replicates for the purposes of comparing results. These replicate watersheds offered a unique opportunity to test the effects of different experimental management treatments at the ecosystem level. Because the six watersheds were essentially identical to begin with, any differences between watersheds could only be attributed to the treatment.

Another important characteristic of the Hubbard Brook watershed ecosystems is that they are all characterized by shallow soils over watertight bedrock. This meant that all the water entering as precipitation either evaporated to the air or appeared in the stream that drained the watershed. Losses to groundwater by deep seepage were found to be negligible, which was crucial because the first characteristics examined in the watersheds were the chemical and hydrological balances over the study area. Precipitation gauges were installed throughout the watershed (see Figure 6.10), and a *V*-notch weir (Figure 6.11) was put in the stream. The difference

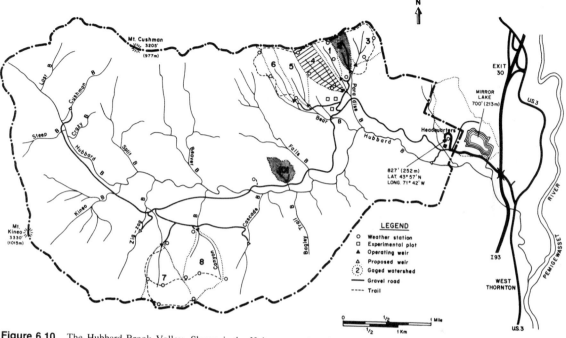

**Figure 6.10** The Hubbard Brook Valley. Shown is the Hubbard Brook Experimental Forest (HBEF) with its gauged watersheds, weirs, weather stations, roads, experimental treatments, and drainage streams tributary to Hubbard Brook (Reproduced with permission of Springer-Verlag from *Biogeochemistry of a Forested Ecosystem,* G. E. Likens, *et al.,* 1977.)

between precipitation and streamflow was assumed to be equal to evaporation from soil and plants (i.e., evapotranspiration). By measuring the concentration of chemical elements in precipitation and streamflow and multiplying by the amount of water, total input and output for each element could be obtained.

The results of these studies provided fresh insight into the function of forested ecosystems that were essentially unavailable from studies of the individual parts of the system (e.g., soils, trees, etc.), Figure 6.12 shows seasonal and annual patterns of variation for water and for the essential nutrient nitrogen. These data demonstrate a number of important characteristics of many undisturbed ecosystems. First, Figure 6.12*a* shows that the yield of water from the forest ecosystem in streamflow is highly predictable from the amount of precipitation coming

into the system. Such predictability can be important in management of urban or agricultural water supplies downstream. The ecosystem also exhibits a large degree of control over the nitrogen balance. It was found that the nitrate ($NO_3^-$) concentration in the precipitation exhibited no definite pattern through time; however, Figure 6.12*b* shows very marked seasonal changes in nitrate concentrations in the streamwater. Again, this demonstrates that the forest ecosystem dramatically influences the water and nutrient balances. An additional characteristic of this system is that it is gaining more nitrogen from precipitation than it is losing in streamflow. Most undisturbed forests gain nitrogen in this way (5, 21).

Comparisons of results between the six replicate watershed ecosystems showed very similar patterns indicating that they were indeed nearly identical with respect to hydrology and the nitrogen balance.

**Figure 6.11**  Stream-gauging weir. The metal flume on the left measures high streamflows; the 90 degree, sharp-edged, V-notch weir on the right measures low streamflows. The gauging station is built on bedrock so that all streamflow is channeled first through the flume and then into the weir. Recording instruments for both flume and weir monitor streamflow continuously. Propane burners are used during the winter to prevent freezing. Large particulate matter transported by the stream during high flows is caught either in the screen as the flow cascades from the flume over the trough, bypassing the V-notch, or in the ponding basin behind the V-notch (Reproduced with permission of Springer-Verlag from *Biogeochemistry of a Forested Ecosystem*, G. E. Likens, *et al.*, 1977.)

The next step was to carry out an experiment at the ecosystems level. In one watershed (number 2), all of the vegetation was cut down and herbicides were used to suppress regrowth for three years (starting in 1965). The purpose of this experiment was to determine the effect of the biological activity of trees and shrubs on the hydrological and chemical patterns of watersheds. With the plant material removed, any differences between watershed 2 and a control (undisturbed) watershed (number 6) could be related mainly to the suppression of plants. The differences were extreme, as shown in Figure 6.13. The increase in streamflow (Figure 6.13*b*) was somewhat predictable because transpiration by plants was removed, but the increased nitrogen output (6.13*d*) was many times higher than the

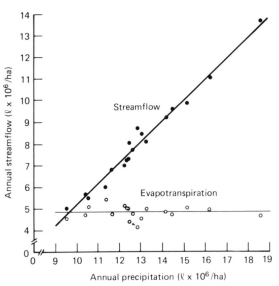

**Figure 6.12 *a***  Relationship between precipitation and streamflow for the Hubbard Brook Experimental Forest (HBEF) during 1956–1974 (Reproduced with permission of Springer-Verlag from *Biogeochemistry of a Forested Ecosystem*, G. E. Likens, *et al.*, 1977.)

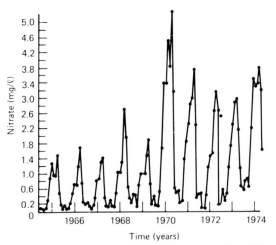

**Figure 6.12 *b***  Nitrate levels at HBEF during 1965–1974 in streamflow (Reproduced with permission of Springer-Verlag from *Biogeochemistry of a Forested Ecosystem*, G. E. Likens, *et al.*, 1977.)

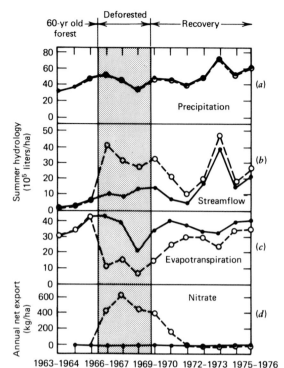

**Figure 6.13** Effects of deforestation on hydrology and nitrate concentrations in an experimentally deforested northern hardwood forest ecosystem (HBEF) (o - - - o, watershed 2) compared with a forested reference ecosystem (●——●, watershed 6). The 60-year-old forest was devegetated during autumn of 1965, maintained bare for three growing seasons, and then allowed to revegetate during the growing season of 1969. (Adapted from reference 22 (*Science*) with permission of the American Association for the Advancement of Science.)

increase in streamflow and indicated strong biological control over the accumulation and loss of this element. Nitrate concentration in the stream actually exceeded U.S. public health standards for drinking water during parts of this experiment. However the nitrate level did return to normal after revegetation of the watershed (22).

The initial results of this study were very timely because they coincided with the national debate on clearcutting as a means of harvesting national forestlands. It was argued by some that the complete

devegetation on watershed 2 was similar to clearcutting and that therefore this practice would reduce water quality substantially. Others argued that the total suppression of all plant growth was an extreme treatment and that commercial clearcutting with immediate regrowth would yield lower nitrogen losses. Still others said that clearcutting might be even more severe than the watershed-2 experiment because in the experiment the cut trees were left on the site and no roads were built into the watershed as would be the case in an actual logging operation.

To settle this controversy, stream chemistry studies were carried out on a number of other watersheds with different harvesting histories (23, 24). Increases in nitrogen losses were measured under all conditions, but the amounts were less than on watershed 2 and were directly related to how much of the watershed was harvested. This information begins to allow prediction of the effects of different harvesting practices on local and regional water quality.

During the clearcutting debate, results from similar experiments in other forest types began to show that not all forests exhibited the large nitrogen losses seen at Hubbard Brook. For example, studies in the Douglas-fir forests of Washington demonstrated a negligible enhancement of nitrogen loss after clearcutting (25). Other studies showed intermediate results. Unfortunately, the different investigators used different methods to measure nitrogen losses, and therefore the results were not always directly comparable.

In a recent study (26), which involved six researchers from around the United States, a standardized disturbance was applied to nineteen forest types in the six regions and all were analyzed for nitrogen losses. A complete range from high to essentially no losses was found spread across forest types and regions (Table 6.3). The only general conclusion was that "rich" sites with relatively fertile soils tended to lose nitrogen more rapidly.

As a result of these studies, and also because it is known that reduced availability of nitrogen to plants

**Table 6-3**

Nitrogen Losses Caused by Disturbance in Nineteen Forest Ecosystems Throughout the United States

| Site | Nitrogen Losses |
|------|-----------------|
| Indiana | |
| Maple, beech | Very high |
| Oak, hickory | High |
| Shortleaf pine | Low |
| Massachusetts | |
| Oak, pine | Medium |
| Red pine | Low |
| Oak, red maple | Low |
| New Hampshire | |
| Maple, beech | High |
| Balsam fir | Medium |
| New Mexico | |
| Ponderosa pine | Very low |
| Mixed conifer | Medium |
| Aspen | Medium |
| Spruce, fir | Very low |
| North Carolina | |
| Mixed oak | Low |
| White pine | Medium |
| Oregon | |
| Western hemlock | Medium |
| Washington | |
| Alder | Very high |
| Douglas-fir (low site quality) | Low |
| Douglas-fir (high site quality) | Medium |
| Pacific silver fir | Very low |

*Source.* Adapted from P. M. Vitousek, et al., *Science, 204,* 469 (1979).

limits growth in many forest types, a considerable amount of research effort has been expended to determine what factors control the rate of nitrogen loss from forest ecosystems and the rate at which nitrogen cycles within the system.

## THE NITROGEN CYCLE

Figure 6.14 outlines the important components of the *nitrogen cycle* in two very different forest ecosystems. In the previous discussion we were concerned with only the nitrogen introduced into the ecosystem in precipitation and that moving out with streamflow. The streamflow losses result not just from inputs in precipitation but also from the processes that control the cycling of nitrogen within the system (27–30).

The processes are just the same as were described in the opening paragraphs of this section, but each has a specific name. When rainfall hits the forest canopy and then drips through, it is called *throughfall.* Thus, the nitrogen content of precipitation changes as a result of contact with the leaf and stem surfaces. This nitrogen then enters into the soil and is available for *uptake* by plants. Uptake rates are very different in the two forest types, and this

**154**

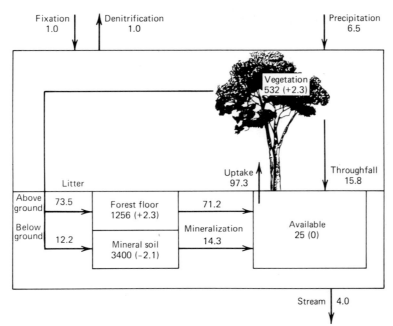

**Figure 6.14 a** Nitrogen cycle (kg/ha/year) for a typical deciduous forest in the northeastern United States (adapted from 25, 26).

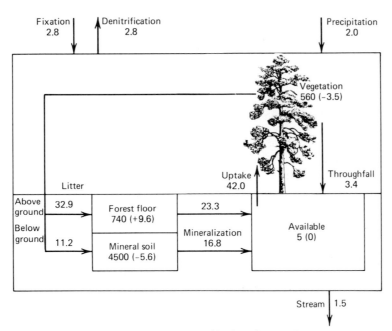

**Figure 6.14 b** Nitrogen cycle (kg/ha/year) for a typical coniferous forest of the Pacific Northwest (adapted from 27, 28). (Numbers in parentheses are the change in storage level per compartment per year.)

**155**

difference is fairly characteristic of deciduous compared to coniferous forests. The coniferous forest is not less productive in terms of weight of material synthesized from sunlight in a year, but has lower nitrogen concentrations in leaves, needles, and wood and therefore apparently needs less nitrogen to produce the same amount of material.

Much of the nitrogen taken up is returned in the same year to the *forest floor* through *litter fall,* which is the shedding of leaves or needles, roots, and branches plus toppling of whole live or dead trees, and throughfall (the loss from the vegetation is the difference between throughfall value and precipitation). However, some of the nitrogen is retained in the growing vegetation. This is true for the hardwood stand in Figure 6.14, which is younger and still increasing in total biomass (live weight of trees), but not for the conifer stand, which in this example is losing more live biomass through tree mortality and litter fall than it is producing each year. Aboveground litter falls on top of and becomes part of the forest floor, the mostly organic uppermost soil horizon. A considerable amount of root litter also occurs in the forest floor. Input to the mineral soil is mostly through root litter. This nitrogen is not immediately available to plants because it is still bound up in organic materials. Plants require nitrogen in simple ionic compounds such as nitrate ($NO_3^-$) and ammonia ($NH_4^+$). Decomposition of the organic material in the litter and soil releases the nitrogen in ionic form, which the plants can then utilize. This process is called *mineralization* and occurs much more rapidly in the hardwood stand (see Chapter 4). In both stands, the forest floor is increasing in total nitrogen content while the amount in the mineral soil is decreasing.

The total amount of nitrogen in the available pool at any one time is very small. Once it is in the simple ionic forms, it is either taken up very quickly or washed away (leached) below the rooting zone and into the stream.

Two additional processes make the nitrogen cycle even more complex. *Nitrogen fixation* is the uptake of $N_2$ gas from the atmosphere by certain microorganisms living either free in the soil and litter (nonsymbiotic) or in a mutually beneficial relationship with plant roots (symbiotic). The opposite process, the release of nitrogen-containing gases to the atmosphere, can occur simultaneously and is called *denitrification.* These processes have not been studied as extensively as other transfers within forest ecosystems, but the quantities appear to be fairly small and nearly equal in most undisturbed forests.

## Systems Analysis

The simple diagrams shown in Figure 6.14 represent "models" of the nitrogen cycles in the two forest types and can be put into computer form. However, the data from these diagrams can also be utilized for simple calculations to determine how fast nitrogen is moving through each part of the system and possibly which factors limit the overall rate of nitrogen cycling. This is a very important bit of information because total tree growth is often limited by the amount of nitrogen available, and any management practice that speeds this rate of movement through the whole system would increase the amount passing through the available pool.

This approach to the analysis of ecosystems is part of a relatively new science called *systems analysis,* which deals with many kinds of complex sets of interacting parts or systems. These can be production systems such as factories, information systems such as telephones and computers, or biological systems such as forests. In general, systems analysis deals with the movement or transfer of energy or materials to different parts of the system. In our forest ecosystems shown in Figure 6.14, the compartments are vegetation, forest floor, mineral soil, and available nitrogen. The transfers are precipitation, throughfall, leaching, litter fall, mineralization, fixation, and denitrification. Systems analysis is a complex and highly mathematical field, but we can use two simple measurements from this discipline to compare the nitrogen cycles in the two forest types: *turnover rate* and *residence time.* Both relate to how much nitrogen passes through a compartment versus how much is in the compartment at any one time.

*Residence time* is calculated as the sum of all the inputs to a compartment divided into the total in the compartment. For example, the residence time for nitrogen in the forest floor of the hardwood stand is 1256/73.5 kilograms per hectare per year or 17.1 years. We could calculate a residence time for the whole ecosystem by dividing all the nitrogen in all the compartments (5213 kilograms per hectare) by precipitation and fixation inputs (7.5 kilograms per hectare per year), which gives 695.1 years. Residence time is the average retention time of nitrogen in a particular compartment.

*Turnover rate* is just 1 divided by the residence time. For the hardwood-forest floor, turnover rate is $1/17.1 = 0.058$ or 5.8%. This is the fraction of the nitrogen in the compartment to enter in that year.

Table 6.4 lists the turnover rates for all the compartments in both forest types. The results are very different for the different compartments and indicate where nitrogen cycles quickly and where it cycles slowly. In both stands, the fastest turnover is in the *available pool* and the slowest is in the *mineral soil*. Turnover is intermediate in the vegetation and forest floor. These numbers express quantitatively what was stated previously in this chapter—that nitrogen is made available relatively slowly from the soil and is either taken up or leached quickly from the available pool. We might conclude that the decomposition rates limit the total rate of nitrogen cycling in both stands, but to a greater extent in the conifer forests.

Looking at these models also gives some clues as to why Hubbard Brook watershed 2, with a nitrogen cycle similar to that in Figure 6.14*a* before devegetation, exhibited such large losses of nitrogen after devegetation. Uptake was completely cut off, and therefore all the nitrogen made available by mineralization either remained in the available pool or leached to the stream. In addition, removing the forest canopy results in both higher temperatures in the soil and increased soil moisture content because transpiration is reduced. This in turn leads to faster decomposition rates, greater mineralization, and more total available nitrogen for leaching. On the other hand, the coniferous forest may lose less nitrogen after harvesting because of the generally slower cycling of this element and additional differences in the effect of the species on turnover rates for nitrogen. One very interesting question currently under study is whether or not the species on a site determines the rate of nitrogen cycling by its uptake rates and type and quantity of litter (e.g., conifer litter generally decomposes more slowly than hardwood litter) or whether the nitrogen availability on the site determines the type of vegetation and its uptake rate (27, 28).

## COMPUTER MODELS AND MANAGEMENT OF FOREST ECOSYSTEMS

The complexity of forest ecosystems is such that building computer models is nearly the only way to predict quantitatively the effects of different management practices. The kind of information presented in Figure 6.14 is complicated in itself, but for management decisions we must also know how all of these transfers change with different species at

**Table 6-4**

Turnover Rates for Nitrogen in Different Compartments of Two Contrasting Forest Ecosystems

| Compartment | Deciduous | | Coniferous | |
|---|---|---|---|---|
| Vegetation | $\dfrac{103.8}{532}$ | 0.195 | $\dfrac{44.0}{560}$ | 0.079 |
| Forest floor | $\dfrac{73.5}{1256}$ | 0.058 | $\dfrac{32.9}{740}$ | 0.044 |
| Mineral soil | $\dfrac{12.2}{3400}$ | 0.0036 | $\dfrac{11.2}{4500}$ | 0.0025 |
| Available | $\dfrac{101.3}{25}$ | 4.05 | $\dfrac{43.5}{5}$ | 8.70 |

*Source.* Prepared from data in references 27–30 and Figure 6.14.

different ages under different soil conditions, and so on. Thus we need to know not only how fast nitrogen moves through the system but also what controls that rate. The results of different studies on rates of litter decomposition as a function of the type of material plus growth rates of different species for different mineralization rates and other important interactions within the system are combined in the computer model, which represents a synthesis and summary of everything quantitatively known about the system.

## Construction of an Ecosystem Model

The construction of a model of forest ecosystem dynamics follows four basic steps.

1. *Model structure*. The general outline of the data and information available is translated into a series of computer language statements.
2. *Parameterization*. The specific data are entered in the general structure of the program. The difference between these first two steps is that the outline or structure of the model may be identical for different forests, but the specific data or parameters will be different. For example, the structures of the models in Figure 6.14 are identical but the data are different.
3. *Validation*. The model is used to predict the results of an experiment that was not used in building the model. This tests the accuracy of the completed model.
4. *Prediction*. The model can now be used to predict the effects of experiments not made in the field or the effects of potential management practices.

## Forest Ecosystem Models

Several models of forest ecosystems have been developed, and some have been used to predict the effects of different management practices. An example is the model developed from the Hubbard

Brook study (12, 31, 32), which predicts the movement of organic matter and nitrogen through these northern hardwoods forest ecosystems.

The structure of this model is similar to that presented in Figure 6.14, but with greater detail included regarding types of litter and types of species in the system. The *parameters* for the model are too lengthy to present here but result from many different studies in this forest type.

*Validation* is a key process because it allows the appraisal of the accuracy of the model. If it cannot predict the results of past experiments, then it cannot be relied on to predict effects of new management practices. Two examples of validation are shown in Figure 6.15, where the model predictions are matched with data measured in the field but not used in building the model. These data are for changes in the weight of organic matter in the forest floor and the basal area of all living trees.

Once we are satisfied with the accuracy of the model through validation, then it can be used for *predictive purposes*. For example, recent increases for demand in wood yields from a shrinking forest-land base have in some cases led to more intensive

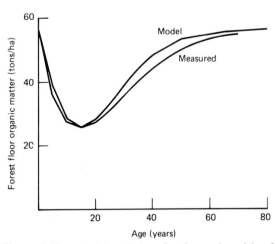

**Figure 6.15 a**   Model predictions for changes in weight of organic matter in the forest following clearcutting and measured values (Reproduced by permission of the National Research Council of Canada from the *Canadian Journal of Forest Research, 8*, pp. 306–315, 1978.)

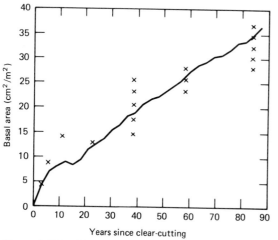

**Figure 6.15***b* Model predictions (solid line) for changes in basal area over time following clearcutting with measured values (x).

as stem only (clearcutting), whole tree (including branches and leaves), and different rotation lengths (frenquency of cutting) were simulated with the models. Table 6.5 shows projected results of these more frequent and intensive harvests on total productivity and total harvestable yield. Under the conditions in the model, the more intensive harvesting (whole tree and complete forest), especially on short rotations, actually *reduces* the yield of wood instead of increasing it (31, 32). Such projections are only as accurate as the model itself, and a critical assessment of the outline and parameters of the model is an absolute necessity before projections based on the model can be accepted.

Models such as this can also predict the impacts of pollution on forest ecosystems. One pollution problem of current interest is the incidence of "acid rain" due to the burning of fossil fuels, which creates sulfuric and nitric acids in the atmosphere. Acid rain in this form can cause numerous problems in the forest including direct damage to plants and a decrease in mineralization rate under increasingly acid conditions. However, the acid rain can also act as fertilizer since low nitrogen availability can limit growth and nitrogen is a component of acid rain. Again, a computer model can combine all of these effects and predict which might be the greater, growth reduction or growth enhancement.

harvesting—removing more of each cut tree from the site and harvesting more frequently. Because these are new practices, no field trials are available to test their long-term consequences. An accurate model can predict these consequences and avoid costly mistakes.

The Hubbard Brook models have been used to make these predictions for the northern hardwoods forest type. Different intensities of harvesting, such

**Table 6-5**

Estimates of Total Net Production and Total Yield (Harvested) Obtained from the Forest Floor–Forest Growth Model for Seven Harvesting Regimes Over a 90-Year Period

| Type of Cutting | Length and No. of Rotations | Total Net Productivity (tons/ha/90 years) and Rank | Total Yield (tons/ha/90 years) and Rank | Percent of Total Productivity Harvested |
|---|---|---|---|---|
| Clearcutting | 90 (1) | 1090 (2) | 154 (4) | 14 |
| Whole tree | 90 (1) | 1120 (1) | 197 (2) | 18 |
| Whole tree | 45 (2) | 853 (4) | 108 (6) | 13 |
| Whole tree | 30 (3) | 478 (6) | 93 (7) | 19 |
| Complete forest | 90 (1) | 1055 (3) | 252 (1) | 24 |
| Complete forest | 45 (2) | 841 (5) | 171 (3) | 20 |
| Complete forest | 30 (3) | 476 (7) | 150 (5) | 32 |

*Source.* J. D. Aber, D. B. Botkin, and J. M. Melillo, *Can. J. For. Res., 9,* 10 (1979).

In summary, the study of forests as ecosystems is an attempt to place all of the major processes in the system (for example, production of plant parts or decomposition of litter and soil) in a single unified framework, to show how they all *interact* and how the entire system will *respond* to different disturbances, pollution impacts, and management practices. It has been called a *"holistic"* science in that the emphasis is on the cumulative response of the entire system instead of on any single component. As such it draws from many traditional disciplines and places them in the framework of the ecosystem.

## REFERENCES

1. E. P. Odum, *Fundamentals of Ecology,* W. B. Saunders, Philadelphia, 1971.
2. S. H. Spurr and B. V. Barnes, *Forest Ecology,* Third Edition, John Wiley & Sons, New York, 1980.
3. W. Larcher, *Physiological Plant Ecology,* Springer-Verlag, New York, 1979.
4. H. W. Hocker, Jr., *Introduction to Forest Biology,* John Wiley & Sons, New York, 1979.
5. F. H. Bormann and G. E. Likens, *Pattern and Process in a Forested Ecosystem,* Springer-Verlag, New York, 1979.
6. H. J. Oosting and L. E. Anderson, *Bot. Gaz., 100,* 750 (1939).
7. W. S. Cooper, *Ecol., 20,* 130 (1939).
8. R. L. Crocker and J. Major, *J. Ecol., 43,* 427 (1955).
9. P. E. Heilman, *Ecol., 47,* 825 (1966).
10. F. B. Salisbury and C. W. Ross, *Plant Physiology,* Wadsworth, Belmont, Calif., 1978.
11. H. L. Mitchell and R. F. Chandler, "The nitrogen nutrition and growth of certain deciduous trees of northeastern United States," *Black Rock For. Bull. 11,* 1939.
12. D. B. Botkin, J. F. Janak, and J. R. Wallis, *J. Ecol., 60,* 849 (1972).
13. N. A-P. DeCandolle, *Physiologie Vegetale,* Bechet Jerene, Lib. Fac. Med., Paris, 1832.
14. E. L. Rice, *Allelopathy,* Academic Press, New York, 1974.
15. R. H. Whittaker and P. D. Feeney, *Science, 171,* 757 (1971).
16. J. S. Stickney and P. R. Hoy, "Timber culture," *Trans. Wis. State Hort. Soc., 11,* 156 (1881).
17. L. K. Forcier, *Science, 189,* 808 (1973).
18. C. H. Tubbs, "Effect of sugar maple exudate on seedlings of northern conifer species," U.S.D.A. For. Serv., Res. Note NC-213, Washington, D.C., 1976.
19. M. A. K. Lodhi, *Am. J. Bot., 64,* 260 (1976).
20. G. M. Woodwell, *Sci. Am., 216,* 24 (1967).
21. G. E. Likens, F. H. Bormann, R. S. Pierce, J. S. Eaton, and N. M. Johnson, *Biogeochemistry of a Forested Ecosystem,* Springer-Verlag, New York, 1977.
22. G. E. Likens, F. H. Bormann, R. S. Pierce, and W. A. Reiners, *Science, 199,* 492 (1978).
23. R. S. Pierce, C. W. Martin, C. C. Reeves, G. E. Likens, and F. H. Bormann, "Nutrient loss from clearcutting in New Hampshire," In *Proc. Symp. Watersheds in Trans.,* Ft. Collins, Col., 1972.
24. J. W. Hornbeck, G. E. Likens, R. S. Pierce, and F. H. Bormann, "Strip cutting as a means of protecting site and streamflow quality when clearcutting northern hardwoods," *Proc. 4th N.A. Forest Soils Conf.,* 1975.
25. D. W. Cole and S. P. Gessel, "Movement of elements through a forest soil as influenced by tree removal and fertilizer additions," In: *Forest-Soil Relationships in North America,* Youngberg, ed., John Wiley & Sons, New York, 1965.
26. P. M. Vitousek, J. R. Gosz, C. C. Grier, J. M. Melillo, W. A. Reiners, and R. L. Todd, *Science, 204,* 469 (1979).
27. J. M. Melillo, "Nitrogen cycling in deciduous forests," In: *Nitrogen Cycling in Terrestrial Ecosystems.* Ecological Bull., Stockholm, in press.
28. F. H. Bormann, G. E. Likens, and J. M. Melillo, *Science, 196,* 981 (1977).
29. G. S. Henderson, W. T. Swank, J. B. Waide, and C. C. Grier, *For. Sci., 24,* 385 (1978).
30. P. Sollins, C. C. Grier, F. M. McCorison, K. Cromack, Jr., and R. Fogel, "The internal element cycles of an old-growth Douglas-fir stand in western Oregon," *Ecological Monographs, 50,* 261 (1980).
31. J. D. Aber, D. B. Botkin, and J. M. Melillo, *Can. J. For. Res., 8,* 306, 1978.
32. J. D. Aber, D. B. Botkin, and J. M. Melillo, *Can. J. For. Res., 9,* 10, 1979.

# 7

# INTERACTION OF INSECTS AND FOREST TREES

# Ronald L. Giese    Daniel M. Benjamin

Insects and trees have complex interactions in forest habitats; insects create impacts on forest trees, and, conversely, forests have important influences on insects. Thus *forest entomology* is concerned with the influences of insects on forests and their products. It is a biological discipline that deals with insects and their associates, and their effects on trees, forests, and forest products. It also provides a means of quantification and management of insects and insect damage within the forest ecosystem.

## INTRODUCTION

Attention to forest insects is an ancient phenomenon; ravages have been noted for centuries. Linnaeus, in the mid-eighteenth century, formally named and described many insects we know as forest pests today. Just as forestry had its roots in Europe, modern forest entomology found its beginnings there in the last century. A classical treatise on forest insects was published by the German J. T. C. Ratzeburg; in France, A. de La Rue wrote on the natural history of forest insects in the mid-nineteenth century. Modern forest entomology literature is very extensive, and current American reference books usually emphasize either principles (1, 2) or taxonomic—life-history approaches to forest entomology (3, 4).

## Beneficial Effects of Insects in Forest Ecosystems

Although the destructive activities of forest insects are well known and are sometimes dramatic, it is best to realize that many insects play a beneficial role in forest ecosystems. Were it not for parasitic and predacious insects, outbreaks of pest species would be even more common. We will see how elimination of these advantageous species, or disruption of the predator-prey relationships, can have massive biological consequences. Insects are also primary pollinators of some tree species (e.g., maples and willows). They play a key role in the decomposition of dead trees and leaves and conse-

quently aid in nutrient cycling. Insects help to thin dense forest stands by eliminating overmature trees; this thinning promotes the growth of young seedlings and the regeneration of an "old" forest. Insects aid in the development of mixed stands, thereby prompting succession toward more climax states.

## Importance and Mode of Action of Destructive Agents

Accidental fire damage extracts a large toll on forest resources, yet insects remove even larger volumes of timber. Such destructive events can be assigned to any of three categories depending on duration, extent, and predictability. When the destruction is a widespread, unpredictable event of dramatic proportions, it is classified as a *catastrophe*. Examples include massive windstorms, fires, extensive damage caused by insects, and contagious diseases of trees. During this century over 123 million cubic meters of timber were destroyed during forest-insect catastrophes.

Perhaps more important, although less spectacular than catastrophic phenomena, is *growth impact,* which is a pervasive, ongoing feature in forests. Growth impact has two components: it is the sum of *growth loss* and *mortality,* which are the second and third categories of destructive events. Growth loss is the cumulative and continuous absence or reduction of normal growth caused by destructive agents, such as insects, whereby tissue (e.g., terminal length or diameter) may not achieve its potential dimensions. Insects are present in every forest ecosystem, whether they be wood borers or bark beetles, and their toll, no matter how subtle, proceeds at all times. The other element of growth impact is mortality, which implies the removal of trees from growing stock or sawtimber through death from natural causes. Just how momentous these destructive, yet quite natural, forces are is shown in Table 7.1, which reflects the comparative losses attributable to the major destructive agents. Although updated information is needed in a resource-short society,

**Table 7.1**

Estimated Losses to Forests Caused by Destructive Agents in 1952

| Loss Factor | Total Volume Reduction[a] | Percent of Total Volume Loss Resulting from Various Agents | | | |
|---|---|---|---|---|---|
| | | Insects | Diseases | Fire | All Other[b] |
| Mortality | | | | | |
| Growing stock | 99.4 | 28 | 22 | 7 | 43 |
| Sawtimber | 29.9 | 40 | 18 | 6 | 36 |
| Growth loss | | | | | |
| Growing stock | 217.7 | 10 | 56 | 19 | 15 |
| Sawtimber | 73.5 | 11 | 57 | 21 | 11 |
| Catastrophe[c] | | | | | |
| Volume | 286.8 | 43 | 15 | 26 | 16 |

*Source.* "Timber resources for America's future," U.S. D.A. For. Serv., Res. Rept. No. 14, 1958.

[a] Million cubic meters.
[b] Includes weather, animals, suppression, logging damage.
[c] Cumulative for first half of century.

the table suggests the immense importance of insects in terms of relative losses incurred, as well as total volume consumed by these small organisms.

Regional tree mortality estimates for the United States were provided for 1962 and 1970 (Table 7.2). For 1970, the mortality loss was calculated to be 130.2 million cubic meters of growing stock and 36.3 million cubic meters of sawtimber; about one-fifth of all annual growth was nullified by mortality. (For these data, catastrophic losses were included with other forms of mortality.) Unfortunately, of the total volume of dead timber, only about 7 percent of the softwood and 3 percent of hardwood were salvaged. To indicate the importance of protecting our forests against destructive agents, "the annual mortality and growth reduction attributable to only three pests . . .—western dwarf mistletoes, western bark beetles, and southern pine beetles— . . . are estimated to equal about 13 percent of the current timber harvest" (6).

## The Geographic Origin of Forest Insects

While most insects affecting North American trees are native to the continent, a number of significant pests are exotics; that is, they were introduced from foreign countries. For example, of 37 major North American pests (7), over one-fifth were inadvertently imported; among these were the European pine shoot-moth, gypsy moth, larch casebearer, European pine sawfly, and the smaller European elm bark beetle (which is the principal vector of the Dutch elm disease pathogen). Six of the eight introduced pests on this partial list arrived in North America during the twentieth century.

## ECOLOGICAL CONSIDERATIONS

### Theoretical Numerical Increase

Outside of their environmental context, we can examine the inherent capability of forest pests to

163

**Table 7.2**

Recent Estimates of Volume Losses From Mortality

| Region | Softwoods | | Hardwoods | |
|---|---|---|---|---|
| | 1962 | 1970 | 1962 | 1970 |
| | Growing Stock Volume Loss (million cubic meters) | | | |
| East | 19.8 | 25.5 | 39.6 | 45.3 |
| West | 56.6 | 56.6 | 2.8 | 2.8 |
| Total | 76.4 | 82.1 | 42.4 | 48.1 |
| | Sawtimber Volume Loss (million cubic meters) | | | |
| East | 3.8 | 4.7 | 8.0 | 8.5 |
| West | 23.8 | 22.2 | .7 | .9 |
| Total | 27.6 | 26.9 | 8.7 | 9.4 |

*Source.* "The outlook for timber in the U.S.," U.S. D.A. For. Serv., Res. Rept. No. 20, 1973.

expand their numbers. In its simplest general form, $N = I (EF)^n$, where $N$ = final number of individuals, $I$ = initial number of insects, $E$ = number of eggs produced per female, $F$ = decimal fraction of females in the population, $n$ = number of annual generations. For example, if an initial population consists of six female and four male European pine sawflies on a pine tree, and if each female produces 80 eggs, then there will be $10(80 \times 0.6) = 480 = N$ individuals at the end of a single generation, and 23,040 in two generations. By the fifth year there would be $2.55 \times 10^9$ sawflies. This concept, termed *reproductive potential,* provides an estimate of the pest's ability to multiply in the absence of countervailing forces.

## Population Fluctuations

In natural situations, however, numerous factors reduce an insect population's innate capacity to increase *ad infinitum.* Collectively called *environmental resistance,* these factors are both physical and biological. The balance between reproductive potential and environmental resistance is an extraordinarily important and dynamic interaction that determines the distribution of forest insects and whether populations will rise or fall.

If insect numbers were represented over time, the resulting graph would probably be a series of peaks and valleys representing periods of population growth and decline (Figure 7.1). We can broadly classify the condition of a population with respect to the amplitude and frequency of these peaks. Populations maintained at low levels are termed *endemic* or *latent;* this is the normal situation for most insects in forest ecosystems. In some areas, abnormal forest conditions (e.g., tree plantations) may permit insect numbers to stabilize at high densities, resulting in serious, though not necessarily fatal, injury to trees. The white pine weevil and European pine shootmoth are two pests characterized by populations balanced at high densities.

When the amplitude of a population exceeds its general equilibrium position and produces economic losses above some minimum threshold, the population is considered to be in an outbreak or epidemic phase. Outbreaks may be either *sporadic* or *periodic* depending, as the terms imply, on whether they can be anticipated. Pests that persist at economically insignificant numbers for years, then suddenly

**164**

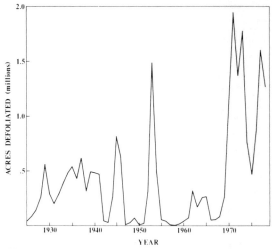

**Figure 7.1** Population fluctuations of the gypsy moth. When actual numbers of insects are impossible to measure, the degree of damage inflicted may be used as an index of population levels.

explode to outbreak proportions because of lowered environmental resistance, cause sporadic outbreaks.

Periodic outbreaks constitute some of the most difficult and challenging problems of contemporary forest entomology. They are the result of the interactions of several factors, including favorable weather conditions over a period long enough to launch the outbreak, and an insect population whose cycles of increase and decline occur at fairly regular intervals. Periodic outbreaks are most common in monotypic stands and tend to produce their most significant effects in mature stands.

## Physical Factors of the Environment

**Temperature.** Because forest insects are exposed to the atmosphere during some of their life stages, they are greatly influenced by elements of the physical environment. Although other environmental factors may ameliorate the effects of temperature, or modify them through interaction, temperature itself is regarded as the single most important physical environmental factor. Insects as a class

have no mechanisms for controlling their internal body temperature as do higher animals—that is, they are cold-blooded. Since body temperatures of insects vary with ambient conditions, metabolism and developmental processes are directly related to "outside" temperature; consequently, successful development is dependent on favorable temperatures. Each forest insect species has a thermal preferendum. This is a temperature continuum that includes an optimum temperature range for the insect's life activities, and upper and lower thresholds beyond which development ceases. These developmental thresholds are bounded by lethal thresholds, or limits, that cause mortality when exceeded. When the temperature limits of an insect species are known, zones of potential population levels can be illustrated on a map as irregular contour lines. If based on climatic history, and on both empirical and experimental knowledge of the insect's behavior, these zones can be useful for predicting the distribution and population levels possible in different geographic areas.

An example of contoured zones of abundance resulted from a study of the European pine shoot-moth at a time when Wisconsin was being newly invaded by this pest (Figure 7.2). To assess potential problem areas, frequencies of occurrence of the lower lethal threshold for the overwintering stage (−28°C) were determined for the state. Although the moth's hosts are distributed throughout Wisconsin, it was predicted that about half of the state state would remain free of serious infestation. In the twenty years since its original publication, the map has been proved correct: one known outbreak occurred in zone III, with all remaining major infestations in zone II.

Most north-temperate forest insects are endowed with a fail-safe mechanism that prevents continued development into periods of extreme temperatures. Termed *diapause*, this mechanism is a physiological state of arrested development resembling hibernation. Insects in diapause, however, do not respond immediately to temporary changes in the physical environment. The advantages of diapause include

**165**

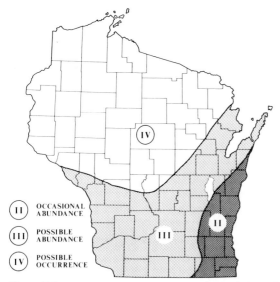

**Figure 7.2** Zones of abundance for Wisconsin populations of the European pine shoot-moth based on low lethal temperature probability. The normal zone of abundance (I) would appear to the southeast of the map.

study of the relation of a periodic biological phenomenon to climate is called *phenology*. These phenological maps are of practical value in forestry, especially when a temperature-dependent event is to be managed on a regional level. Using one phenological event to predict a second event is another tool of forest managers; for example, shoot elongation of balsam fir closely corresponds with development of the larval stages of the spruce budworm and is often used to schedule surveys and the initiation of aerial spray programs against this pest.

**Moisture.** Although secondary to temperature as a predominant, driving force, moisture levels are nevertheless crucial outside a rather narrow zone of acceptability. Insects can tolerate only small fluctuations in the amount of water maintained in their bodies. These fluctuations are controlled by balancing moisture intake and loss. Larvae typically regu-

resistance to severe weather, synchronization of the insect's life cycle with that of its food supply, and synchrony with seasonal temperatures favorable for its rapid development and reproduction.

Generally, springtime insect activities are later as one proceeds north, east, and upward; the opposite is true for fall activities. It is often useful to combine the physical environmental factors affecting development of a particular population of animals or plants. This is most efficiently done by measuring the result of all these interacting factors—namely, the phenological development of individuals in the population. When this information is transferred to a map, contour lines can be drawn to denote areas where environmental conditions have combined to produce similar results—that is, the same stage of plant-animal development at the same point in time (Figure 7.3). If the average of several years of data is mapped, the resulting contours are a reliable indication of areas of equal development, and of the annual developmental lagtime between areas. The

**Figure 7.3** Isophenes (contours based on phenology) showing locations of equal biological development. Isophenes pass through areas 5, 10, 15, and 20 days later in spring phenology than the 0 line.

late evaporation by seeking favorable moisture levels—for example, by moving into or out of the direct rays of the sun.

Just as insects have a thermal preferendum, they also exhibit a preference for a particular range of moisture levels, or evaporation rates during each developmental stage. Representing these ranges graphically produces curves that are often helpful in classifying insects according to their adaptations for dry, mesic, or wet conditions; adults of the white pine weevil are most active in dry habitats (20 percent relative humidity), while nymphs of the Saratoga spittlebug live only in a nearly saturated atmosphere.

Insects cannot always choose their accommodations, however; weather events with inadvertent, indirect effects often transpire. Driving rain, for instance, can dislodge insects from their feeding sites. Long periods of rainfall can coincidentally result in lower than favorable temperatures for feeding or development. Higher than normal relative humidity can promote fungus diseases, which act as insect pathogens or competitors for food.

**Light.** The response of insects to light is well known, although it is generally of less importance than temperature and moisture. Natural light (day length) often acts as a *token stimulus* to insects; that is, it indicates the parallel occurrence of biological events important to the insects' survival, such as the "readiness" of host plants for feeding. Day length is a consistent and reliable indicator of seasonal changes in temperature and food availability. It is also the stimulus for other important events. An insect's "biological clock" is a physiological mechanism that, when stimulated by changes in photoperiod, triggers a biological response such as the spring termination, or fall initiation, of diapause.

Some insects have a particular attraction for discrete light sources; the most typical examples are moths. The attraction of many flying insects to light is the principle behind the scientific use of light traps. These traps are employed to assess the presence of certain species, to estimate population levels, or to indicate proper timing of control measures.

**Wind.** The movement of air significantly influences the behavior and location of forest insects. Wind affects insects in three general ways. Depending on its speed, wind can act as a deterrent or as a positive stimulus to active, directed flight of adult forms. It also serves as a carrier for olfactory stimulants, enabling insects to find suitable host material or, in the case of pheromones, a mate. Sometimes wind causes the passive, mass displacement of insects. This displacement might involve a small distance—such as dislodging larvae from their feeding sites—that nevertheless could cause mortality by starvation or increased vulnerability to predators. Displacement over large distances—sometimes hundreds of miles—can occur when a cold front passes over an area, picks up insects, and deposits them at other locations. This phenomenon is known as *convective transport*. The result in the "new area" is the presence of more individuals than the resident population could have produced and, hence, the possibility of an "instant outbreak." This phenomenon suggests that even careful quarantine enforcements cannot always confine pests to rigid geographic boundaries.

**Bioclimatology.** The integrated workings of all these factors of the physical environment over a period of years at a given locale, comprise *climate*. Relating climate to living organisms is the study of bioclimatology. Recent technology, especially in the areas of synoptic meteorology and the movements of large air masses, has helped elucidate many of the ecological relationships of forest insects. By concomitantly studying the population trends and climatic patterns of a region backward in time, it may be possible to build a methodology for predicting population trends forward in time.

Two forest pests of the Great Lakes states serve as an interesting example: the spruce budworm and the forest tent caterpillar. Both species are residents of the same region, but their populations never reach outbreak proportions at the same time. In fact, because of differing physiological requirements and behavioral attributes, the two pests respond to quite different climatic patterns: spruce budworm populations are nurtured by prolonged sunny, dry weather; forest tent caterpillars develop better under partly cloudy, warm, humid conditions (8). If polar air masses predominate for several years in succession, conditions become increasingly favorable for a surge of spruce budworm numbers. If, however, tropical air masses of maritime origin prevail for successive years, the potential for an outbreak of forest tent caterpillars greatly increases. Conditions favorable to one species are actually detrimental to the other; hence, only one of these pests will be a threat to forests at a given time.

Studies of this nature led to the formulation of the theory of *climatic release* (8): no initial increase of indigenous populations occurs until seasonal climatic control is relaxed, and favorable weather recurs for several years in succession. The population's reproductive potential is then realized, and its growth proceeds so rapidly that even adverse physical and biotic factors cannot bring it under control immediately. Understanding such climatic influences enables practicing foresters to monitor ecological conditions in view of their entomological consequences, and to initiate preventive, ameliorative, or salvage operations before potential consequences become history.

## Biological Factors of the Environment

We have discussed some of the physical environmental factors that influence population levels of insects. Equally important, however, are the biological mechanisms affecting insect numbers. These may be internal, such as intraspecific competition, or external, such as biological control factors.

**Intraspecific Competition.** Intraspecific competition (i.e., within the species) acts as a function of density or crowding and operates within the biological life processes of each individual in a population. Competition for food or space is a key element in determining population levels of the mountain pine beetle. Studies of this pest on lodgepole pine in the western United States have revealed that numbers of new adult beetles are drastically reduced when density increases. Similarly, the Douglas-fir beetle of the Pacific Northwest produces the greatest number of progeny when its population density is low; as crowding increases, fewer eggs are laid and mortality among those that are produced is higher. In general, when food supplies or space diminish, the size of adult insects declines, as well as the number of eggs produced per female; the sex ratio may be strongly influenced, and migration could be provoked. This form of self-regulation is well known among defoliating insects, such as the gypsy moth, and is one of the factors contributing to density fluctuations, or cycles.

With respect to spatial competition, many insects must feed and develop singly. Even with sufficient food, group rearing is deleterious to these species because of mutual interference. Examples of two such pests are the elm spanworm and the walkingstick. Other insects, like the pine sawflies, must feed in colonies to complete larval development successfully (Figure 7.4).

**Biotic Control Mechanisms.** Natural control of insect populations also results from external factors such as parasites, predators, disease organisms, and natural host resistance. Although they may act individually, these factors exert their greatest influence when they act in concert, or in sequence, with each other. They are primarily responsible for maintaining forest insects at their normal, endemic levels.

A parasite typically requires one host to serve as its food supply while it completes its development. It normally lives on or in the host for its entire larval stage; the death of the host insect follows some time after the initial attack. Many species of flies and wasps, for example, deposit their eggs in or on other insect species. After hatching, the developing larvae

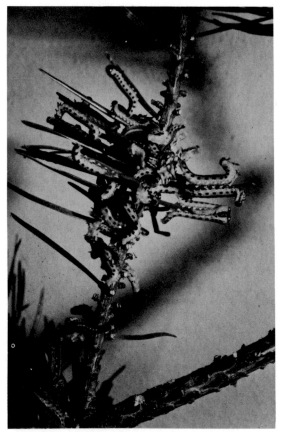

**Figure 7.4** Red pine sawfly larvae are defoliators that must feed gregariously for normal growth and development to occur.

feed on their host until they are ready to pupate; eventually the host dies. Most parasites are members of the orders Diptera (flies) and Hymenoptera (wasps); others are found among the Coleoptera, Lepidoptera, and Strepsiptera.

Predators (as opposed to parasites) are free-living and require numerous prey for food, killing each host at the time of encounter. Ants and ladybug beetles are common predacious insects. A wide variety of birds and small animals, such as mice and shrews, also function as entomophagous organisms. In particular, woodpeckers, nuthatches, and chickadees have been known to reduce populations of

larch casebearers, bark beetles, cankerworms, and sawflies. Moles, mice, and shrews feed voraciously on insects that must spend a portion of their lives on or in the soil.

Forest insects are subject to infection by many pathogenic microorganisms, some of which can produce widespread insect diseases that result in the population collapse of the host species. Viruses, bacteria, rickettsia, protozoa, and fungi are typical "micro" control agents. Many insect species are particularly susceptible to viruses; among them are: eastern tent and forest tent caterpillars, Douglas-fir tussock moth, European pine sawfly, red-headed pine sawfly, linden looper, and the white-marked tussock moth. A virus (nuclear polyhedrosis) sometimes plays a major role in controlling gypsy moth numbers in the northeastern United States and Europe. An outbreak of the European spruce sawfly in eastern Canada and the United States was halted by a similar virus in the 1930s.

Naturally occurring bacteria infect several species of forest insect pests. The "milky disease" of larvae of the Japanese and June beetles is so effective at reducing beetle populations that once the soil is infected no further beetle outbreaks can occur. Several varieties of the *Bacillus thuringiensis* bacterium appear to be efficient in controlling insect numbers, and these are currently being cultured for use in microbial control strategies.

Fungi (entomophagous) take a continuing, modest toll among forest insects, but mortality attributable to fungi rarely rises above a few percent. Exceptions are noteworthy, however. In 1958, fungus disease caused 97 percent mortality in a population of European elm bark beetles in Connecticut (9); in Ontario, between 1949 and 1952, fungi were responsible for a high degree of control of a forest tent caterpillar outbreak.

Another type of biotic control agent is the *nematode* (roundworm), which infests the gut and haemocoel of an insect host. Grasshoppers, bark beetles, and wood wasps often succumb to nematode attacks; other insects may not die as a result of roundworm infestation, but they may become sterile or produce fewer eggs. Nematodes have also been influential in reducing the effects of insect outbreaks, but their importance has generally been less than the previously mentioned organisms. The sirex wood wasp in New Zealand and the fir engraver in New Mexico are pests whose upward population trends have been reversed primarily by nematode infestations.

Deliberate manipulation of insect parasites, predators, and microorganisms is called *biological control* or biocontrol. A form of biological control using microorganisms is microbial control. Sometimes referred to as biological pest suppression, biocontrol is usually a long-term preventive endeavor to maintain pest populations at low levels.

Biocontrol has distinct advantages over the use of chemical pesticides. Once established, biotic agents may be self-perpetuating, relatively permanent, and more economical in the long run. If properly chosen, they are not hazardous to use and do not create harmful pollution or persistent toxic side effects. Experience with synthetic organic insecticides has shown that we must use great caution when infusing potent toxicants into the complicated communities that comprise forest ecosystems.

## INTERACTIVE CONSIDERATIONS

We have discussed a few of the environmental and biological aspects of insect populations in a forest community. We should remember that the forest ecosystem is comprised of a complex mixture of interacting factors. The position of a beetle on a leaf or in a tree is not due simply to any one factor in the mixture. Although temperature, light, predators, etc., have been treated as individual factors, it is the interplay of these and all the other known and unknown elements that creates a "dynamic stability" in the forest—a condition that nurtures both continuity and change. The intricacies of the ecosystem necessitate the study of elemental parts as an entree to understanding, but it should be remembered that the simple addition of parts bears no semblance to the whole. With this in mind, we will consider some of the parts that deal with the kinds of damage forest insects do, individually and collectively, on trees.

## Impact of Insects on Forest Trees

**Defoliators.** Defoliators are insects that eat needles and leaves; they include caterpillars, cankerworms, tussock moths, webworms, sawflies, leaf beetles, walkingsticks, skeletonizers, and leafminers (Figures 7.4 and 7.5). Understanding the impact of defoliation on forest trees is a prerequisite to the intelligent management of these pests. In some instances, complete defoliation may cause tree death in a single season; in another situation, trees might withstand complete foliage destruction and not die.

As a general rule, partial defoliation (50–90 percent) of both broad-leaved and coniferous trees results in reduced terminal and radial growth. Tree branch mortality rarely occurs until after several seasons of severe defoliation. Tree response to complete destruction of its needles or leaves varies greatly depending on the individual characteristics of the species. In the case of the Pinaceae[1] with persistent leaves, complete defoliation in one growing season can cause immediate tree death (Figure 7.6). Two major exceptions to this generality exist: several southern pines (shortleaf and longleaf pines) can be completely defoliated and refoliate with only rare mortality; the annually deciduous larch and bald cypress also can withstand complete defoliation for several years with little or no mortality.

Complete defoliation rarely causes mortality among the broad-leaved trees. Exceptions are hard maple and yellow birch, which may die if completely defoliated during mid-July to mid-August (10).

Insect defoliators vary greatly in their seasonal histories, biologies, and methods of feeding. Some species are *polyphagous* and include many tree species in their host list. The red-headed pine

[1]The Pinaceae include the pines, spruces, firs, hemlocks, sequoias, cedars, cypresses, junipers, and larches.

**Figure 7.5** The walkingstick belongs to the group of pests known as defoliators.

sawfly, for example, feeds on over 20 species of conifers. The gypsy moth, too, has a long host list. Other defoliators are *oligophagous* and feed only on a few hosts—examples are the European pine sawfly, which prefers to feed on about half a dozen pine species, and the red pine sawfly, which will feed on three hard pine species. Defoliators that seek out a single host species are *monophagous*; some, like the Swaine jack pine sawfly, further restrict their feeding to needles only one or more seasons old.

**Figure 7.6** Jack pine mortality resulting from defoliation by the pine tussock moth.

Some defoliators consume entire needles or leaves; others mine tunnels between the epidermal layers of the tree's foliage. One group, the skeletonizers, feed on leaf tissue between the veins and produce "skeleton" leaves with an almost lacy appearance.

Defoliators often cause indirect destruction by weakening their hosts and rendering them susceptible to invasions by other insects such as bark beetles and borers whose damage can be severe or fatal. For example, defoliation by budworms may predispose spruces and pines to the attacks of *Ips* and *Dendroctonus* bark beetles; cankerworms have so weakened oaks that the two-lined chestnut borer can often successfully colonize these otherwise resistant trees. The hemlock looper begins the collapse of mature-overmature hemlock forests of eastern North America by defoliating and weakening its host, and making it vulnerable to subsequent attacks by the hemlock borer, which then delivers the coup de grâce.

Defoliator outbreaks are often spectacular and may cover thousands of hectares of forest. The larch sawfly outbreak of 1920–1930 involved the entire tamarack type of eastern North America; the 1956–1957 outbreak of the forest tent caterpillar encompassed most of the aspen type of north-central North America; budworm outbreaks on spruce-fir types have covered the North American continent. Because of the vastness of these outbreaks, emergency controls could be applied only to high-value forests.

**Bark Beetles.** Bark beetles are among the most devastating forest insects in the world; they have been responsible for the stunting and killing of vast areas of forests (Figure 7.7). Although many species attack and kill trees in overmature forests, or those under environmental stress, other bark beetle species are capable of successfully infesting healthy, vigorously growing forests, where they often inflict serious damage.

Bark beetle adults may be attracted to their hosts, or they may arrive by random dispersal. Adult

**171**

**Figure 7.7** Tree mortality on a Colorado mountainside resulting from tunneling activity of the Douglas-fir beetle. (Courtesy of W. E. Waters.)

beetles bore through the bark and, after mating, females lay their eggs either along their boring tunnels or in special galleries cut in the region between the bark and the wood (Figure 7.8).

After hatching, the larvae feed in the phloem and xylem and eventually girdle the trunk or branch with their tunnels. This girdling interrupts the translocation of nutrients and moisture, and the tree may soon wilt and die. Trees that are growing vigorously often "pitch out" or drown the adult bark beetles in resin or sap; however, overmature trees and those weakened by drought or insect defoliators may not be able to repel the mining adults or larvae.

Some beetle species also act as the carriers or vectors of a variety of lethal tree pathogens. The pine bark beetle, for example, frequently carries the spores of a blue-stain fungus and inadvertently inoculates its host tree as it tunnels beneath the bark. Spores of blue-stain fungi produce mycelia that block the conducting (xylem) tissue and kill the tree. The pine engraver, the western pine beetle, and the mountain pine beetle are also vectors of blue-stain fungi. (The wood is stained blue by the fungus, but its structural strength is not impaired.)

Another group of bark beetles vector pathogens of the deadly Dutch elm disease, which was responsible for killing most of the American elms in cities and villages of the entire eastern half of North America in recent years.

Ambrosia beetles (Figure 7.9) are classed as bark beetles even though many species bore directly through the bark and into the solid wood of their host. Ambrosia adults carry with them ambrosia fungi that infest their galleries and serve as food for the young larvae. The larvae and fungus inflict little direct physiological damage to the tree; however, the galleries may become stained dark gray, brown,

**Figure 7.8** Galleries excavated by larvae of the smaller European elm bark beetle. Not only does this beetle inflict damage from its feeding activities, but it is also a major vector of the Dutch elm disease fungus.

**Figure 7.9** Adult stage of the ambrosia beetle, *Xyloterinus politus*. These individuals have recently emerged from their pupal cases and will soon disperse to infest other trees.

or black and reduce the economic value of the tree. In higher-value species such as mahogany the stained pinhole galleries enhance the value. Still another group of bark beetle species infests cones and seeds of pines and can cause nearly complete destruction of seed crops.

## Sucking Insects.

Both coniferous and deciduous trees are subject to assaults from sucking insects, such as aphids, scales, and spittlebugs (Figure 7.10). These pests have modified mouthparts that enable them to pierce the foliage, tender twigs, or roots of trees and suck the sap or resin as food. These pests create a continuous drain on the vitality of healthy trees, and, if their numbers are great enough, they may cause serious stunting or death of their hosts.

Aphids or plant lice usually attack a tree's tender new foliage or twigs, withdrawing sap and secreting honey dew, which then becomes infected with sooty mold. Sooty mold is a diagnostic to foresters, indicating the presence of sucking insects.

## Wood Borers.

Wood borers are found in a variety of insect groups, including beetles, moths, and wasps. Most wood borers attack trees that are overmature, dying, or suffering from environmental stress. Also, they may invade cut pulp wood, logs, and fire-scarred trees. Borers are among the most serious enemies of forests under stress. A few species even attack healthy, vigorous trees.

Two major groups of wood-destroying beetles are the *long-horned* or *round-headed borers* (Figure 7.11), and the *short-horned* or *flat-heated borers*. These latter insects are often called metallic borers. As their name implies, the long-horned/round-headed borers have long filamentous antennae, and they emerge from deep in the wood through a circular hole. The short-horned borers generally are flat and metallic in appearance, with short antennae; they emerge through an oval or lens-shaped hole. Females of both groups lay eggs in notches cut into the bark, and the new larvae mine for a period in the phloem. They then turn inward to feed in the wood where they construct large and damaging tunnels. The white spotted sawyer, a transcontinental enemy

**Figure 7.10** Spittle masses, formed by immature stages (nymphs) of the pine spittlebug, help the insect maintain a high-humidity environment while feeding on sap extracted from the tree. This feeding results in necrotic areas on the stem or branch and causes stunting or death of many coniferous species in the eastern United States.

**Figure 7.11** Larval (left) and pupal (right) stages of the poplar borer.

of pines, spruce, and fir, is an example of a typical long-horned borer; the bronze birch borer is a short-horned borer that seriously infests birches throughout the continent.

**Shoot and Bud Insects.** The growing meristem—the buds and shoots of trees—is often seriously infested by insect pests. Although death of the tree rarely occurs, stunting, distortion, and forking of the main bole of the tree are common. The pine tip moths are the best known of these pests and they occur throughout the world. They are especially damaging in even-aged forests, plantations, and in ornamental beautification plantings. One species, the European pine-shoot moth, has spread across eastern North America and into Washington, Oregon, and British Columbia since its introduction in New York in 1914.

The white pine weevil is the most injurious pest of the white pine in northeastern North America (Figure 7.12). Damage is of two types: first, infestation may result in a permanent forking of the main bole and render the tree unmarketable; second, the recoverable volume often is of low quality. Severe stunting occurs also in plantations of jack and Scotch pines and in Norway spruce.

**Root Weevils.** The root weevils comprise an insidious group of insects that infest the roots and root-collar regions of planted conifers. Habits of these pests vary greatly with regard to the host species, age, and mode of attack, but tree stunting and killing often occur.

Adult Pales weevils are attracted to areas where pines are being harvested in eastern and southern North America. Females lay their eggs in stumps of the harvested trees, and the emerging adults debark newly replanted seedlings; mortality of entire plantations is common. In the same parts of the country, a second species, the pine root collar weevil, infests the trunks of hard pines from 3 to 20 years old between the soil surface and the root system. Feeding by the larvae causes stunting, and severely

injured trees often break off at the soil surface or die suddenly during windy periods.

White grubs, the larvae of May and June beetles, pose serious problems to forest nurseries and new plantings. The adults feed mainly on broad-leaved trees nearby and lay eggs in areas of heavy grass and sod. Larvae feed on the roots and stunt or kill seedlings.

## Impact of Insects on Forest Stands

Insects are an essential component in the continuing ecological succession of the forest from its pioneer status to maturity, and they are intimately involved in the recycling of nutrients within the forest ecosystem. The dense growth of seedlings and saplings occupying recently burned or harvested pine stands often are naturally thinned by root weevils, scales, and defoliating sawflies. As competition intensifies among the young trees for nutrients and sunlight, defoliators and scales enter the picture to reduce stand density further. As the monotypic pioneer forest reaches maturity, then begins to decline in vigor, bark beetles, borers, and defoliators complete its destruction and set the stage for the entry of more tolerant and aggressive forest trees. This cycle may be repeated sequentially, each time with a slightly different mix of tree species, or it may be interrupted and repeat itself innumerable times with the same species. Ultimately the climax forest is developed—but this, too, succumbs, with insects often providing the major impetus for this marvel of natural succession.

An example of the influence of insects on forest stands is found in the pioneer jack pine monotype following catastrophic fires. Mineral soil is exposed, the serotinous cones have opened and seedlings rapidly cover the area. Not uncommonly, 40,000 to 100,000 saplings per hectare survive the first few years. Then the onslaught of insects and competition begins. During the first 10 years, insects that reduce the stand may include: pine tortoise scale, red-headed pine sawfly, Swaine jack pine

**Figure 7.12** A 13-year-old spruce tree with evidence of numerous white pine weevil attacks. The weevil kills the terminal shoot causing lateral shoots to assume dominance. The attack history is shown schematically on the right. Dead leaders appear as black crooks.

sawfly, pine anomela beetle, pine shoot borer, white pine weevil, and the pitch nodule maker.

In the next 10 to 30 years, the faunal picture may change as a result of the actions of the following species: pine tortoise scale, jack pine sawfly, red pine sawfly, and the pine tussock moth.

In the last phase of the succession, from 40 years onward, the following insect species will predominate and be instrumental in the ultimate collapse of the jack pine monotypic forest: pine engraver, jack pine budworm, pine sawyer, and the Swaine jack pine sawfly.

With the demise of the dominant jack pine, the more tolerant pines and firs surviving, but sup-

**175**

pressed, in the understory can begin to occupy the area as ecological succession proceeds.

The walkingstick, a defoliator of deciduous hardwoods in east-central North America (Figure 7.5), is another insect often associated with alterations in forest species composition. It prefers black oaks, basswood, elm, and wild cherry, but the walkingstick will also feed on white oak, aspen, ash, paper birch, and hickory. Walkingstick outbreaks frequently develop in mixed hardwoods forests of the Great Lakes states, and the resulting defoliation of oaks may cover large areas. The insect's inherent preference for black oaks benefits the less-preferred white oak, which gradually gains greater dominance in the forest canopy. This process has not gone unnoticed by forest managers, for white oaks generally are more valued than black oaks for lumber. In fact, the walkingstick has been suggested as a management tool to encourage the predominance of white oak over black oak in mixed hardwood forests.

As will be discussed later, stand structure may be manipulated in order to control damage by particular insects, but sometimes this can result in species compositions different than originally intended. For example, as a defensive strategy against the white pine weevil, red, white, and jack pine can be interplanted beneath a light hardwood overstory. While these conditions reduce damage caused by the weevil, they create a favorable environment for the red-headed pine sawfly. The sawfly exhibits a feeding preference for jack pine and, during outbreaks, may completely eliminate this tree species from the understory, leaving only red and white pines beneath the hardwood canopy.

Besides changes in species composition, the age class distribution of forest trees may also be altered as a result of insect activity. This usually results from the selective feeding of insects on trees of specific ages in the mixed forest.

## The Spruce Budworm Situation—An Overview.

As a practical illustration of many of the topics discussed in this chapter, a synopsis of the spruce budworm situation in the northeastern United States and southeastern Canada is included. The intensity and duration of problems directly and indirectly related to this pest merit special attention.

The spruce budworm exhibits both species- and age-specific feeding preferences. Under natural conditions, the spruce budworm usually remains at endemic levels in spruce-fir forests, and erupts to outbreak levels roughly every 40 years if weather and food conditions are favorable. This pest has a distinct preference for balsam fir trees, or spruce 50 to 75 years old. When fir trees account for approximately 50 percent of the forest stand, or when young spruces have matured to a palatable age, food conditions are favorable for budworm outbreaks.

Before the advent of pesticides, and before the harvesting of forest resources became an economic necessity, spruce budworm populations were natural "thinners" of spruce-fir forests, promoting the vitality of the forest as a whole by eliminating the mature spruces in the overstory and releasing young trees from their restrictive sunlight/nutrient regimes. When the supply of fir or mature spruce was exhausted, or when weather conditions became unfavorable, the inflated insect populations collapsed, and numbers of budworms returned to endemic levels.

Whereas the density of an endemic budworm population is extremely low (it is often difficult to trap even a single specimen), budworm densities in some areas of southeastern Canada have been maintained at artificially high levels for many years by attempts to control the insect's damage chemically. Spray operations have largely been aimed at protecting trees instead of controlling or eradicating budworms; in this regard, they have been effective at maintaining defoliation at about one-third of the total foliage. This condition, however, provides more than ample food for the budworm larvae that survive the chemical treatments. "[A]lthough chemical control has the ability to prolong the life of trees and prevent loss, it may also prolong the duration of the outbreaks" (11). Spray operations aimed at reducing budworm numbers to endemic levels were attempted in the western United States in the mid-1950s; however, the amount of pesticide required, the vast areas needing spraying, the ecological consequences on other forest life, and the lack of funds combined to make this goal unfeasible.

The spruce budworm problem is further complicated by the mobility of the moths. The passage of a cold front over an infested area in the late evening hours has been known to carry massive numbers of moths as far as 70 miles in a single night, and adults may fly on more than one night. In particular, the behavior of female moths predisposes them for extensive dispersal and propagation. Females usually deposit only a portion of their full egg complement in the evening before they are drawn to the airstreams above the forest canopy by phototropic responses and favorable weather conditions (12).

There is some evidence that, "more recent outbreaks have apparently been more severe than those prior to 1900" (13), possibly due to the predominance of balsam fir in previously clearcut areas. There is also some indication in New Brunswick that the intervals between outbreaks may be decreasing, the last two being 37 and 22 years (outbreaks in 1912, 1949, and 1971) (14). (Aerial spraying of DDT first began in 1951.) If this seeming trend toward increasing frequency and severity of outbreaks is valid, it is clear that much more foresight and caution are needed in selecting harvest methods and control strategies than have been exhibited in the past.

It becomes obvious that the control measure for a given region must take into account the measures adopted by adjacent regions, especially those "upwind." In dealing with outbreak or potential outbreak conditions, the immediate alternatives are to spray, or not to spray and let the outbreak take its course (15). Salvaging dead or dying trees, especially in the latter option, would help mitigate the economic loss in the short run, but could do nothing to sustain the pulp and timber industries in the long run should an outbreak become severe or extensive. These industries have declared their inability to recover from the economic consequences of a do-nothing policy and, hence, have devoted much time and money to protecting trees via pesticide applications. However, as mentioned earlier, this spraying has sustained artificially high budworm populations that, in turn, have necessitated more spraying. At present, some areas of New Brunswick have become locked indefinitely into extensive, annual programs of aerially applied chemical controls. Ironically, the reduction in growth rate of budworm-stressed trees could eventually create another economic crisis for the forest industry within the next 20 to 30 years because of an overall decrease in the volume of harvestable timber.

As one can see, there is neither a simple statement of, nor a simple solution to, the spruce budworm situation. Many aspects have not even been mentioned in this brief section. In recognition of the complexities, controversies, and lack of adequate knowledge in many areas surrounding the spruce budworm problem in both the United States and Canada, a six-year international program (CANUSA) was established in 1978 to coordinate and focus research in both countries toward the cooperative development of a workable, integrated approach to pest management. As explained in a later section, this approach to insect control is based on sound ecological principles and makes use of a variety of control strategies as needed.

## Impact of Forest Trees and Stands on Insect Populations

**Stand Attributes.** A primary determinant of insect population levels is the availability and condition of food—that is, the species composition and stand structure of the forest are influencing factors in the population growth of insects. As a general rule, forests with the greatest diversity of tree species are more resistant to outbreaks of forest insects.

Uniform age distribution functions much like species composition in that even-aged stands are more vulnerable to insect assaults than those composed of a mixture of ages. Trees are subject to attack from different insects at different stages of their growth, in addition to those pests that attack host trees by species. It follows, then, that the greater the mix of tree species and ages, the more varied the mixture of insect species that can be supported—but the fewer individuals of each species. It is an accepted ecological premise that stability is proportional to diversity.

Biotic catastrophes were unknown in the climax forests of upland northern hardwoods in Wisconsin until maple blight appeared several decades ago. Researchers were at first surprised to observe damage of major consequences in these "climax" stands, but later discovered that previous selective cutting had created almost pure stands of maple. Consequently, through the interactions of trees, insects, disease organisms, and humans, the ecological groundwork had been laid for increasing vulnerability to insect outbreaks (16).

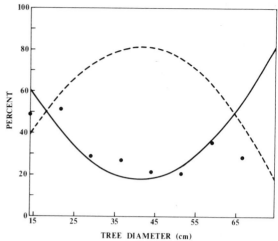

**Figure 7.13** The relative mortality of different-sized sugar maple trees in defoliated northern hardwoods stands. The solid mortality curve may be equated with susceptibility in order to show its complement, resistance (dashed curve).

**Tree Attributes.** Individual host trees exhibit varying degrees of pest susceptibility depending largely on their size. Small trees, particularly those that are suppressed (i.e., have strong competitors for sunlight and nutrients), and the very large, overmature trees are most apt to succumb to insect attacks. This *bimodal mortality* distribution occurred in the maple blight situation (Figure 7.13). When measured against a tree-diameter gradient, the highest death rates were found at the high and low ends of the continuum, with mortality lowest in the middle range.

Certainly other elements, such as genetic and morphological factors, affect a tree's resistance to damage; but growth rate, indirectly measured by tree size or age, is of primary importance. The dominant and codominant individuals undergoing vigorous growth will be most able to offset major pest damage.

Many of a tree's physiological processes interact with insect pests. The *oleoresin phenomenon* is an excellent example of a physiological defense mechanism of softwood trees. Oleoresin is widely recognized as a major factor in the resistance of conifers to bark beetle damage. Oleoresin, or "pitch," is stored in canals in the sapwood and serves to seal wounds that penetrate the phloem layer. When a boring beetle ruptures a resin canal, the reduced pressure causes the pitch to flow into the tunnel created by the insect, often pushing the intruder completely back out of the tree. The rate and duration of resin flow vary among conifer species, and even among individuals of the same species, making it difficult to anticipate which trees are most vulnerable to beetle attack. Recent experimental work, however, has demonstrated that oleoresin exudation pressure (OEP) varies with the season, time of day, weather conditions, and age of the tree. By measuring OEP, researchers discovered a close correlation between it and water relations in the tree. In fact, OEP is now recognized as a criterion of a tree's physiological condition and is an effective quantitative measure of tree resistance to bark beetles. Trees with low OEP may succumb to persistent attack by bark beetles; trees with high OEP are more resistant. Large infestations of the pest are usually associated with older conifers or stands subjected to drought or defoliation.

**178**

# TASK AND SCOPE OF FOREST ENTOMOLOGY

## Qualitative Methods

Among the responsibilities of the forest entomologist is the development of techniques and procedures for conducting *surveys* to detect harmful species and populations of insects in the forest and to predict future population levels of pest species. Surveys have many designs depending on the kind and degree of information that is sought. Qualitative survey methods are used to detect tree injury and determine its cause—that is, identify the pest responsible. First-line defenses also include detecting the presence of new insect species or a change in numbers of a particular resident pest species. These observations may be casual and unscheduled, as in the case of a backpacker reporting dead or dying trees to a ranger, or they may be part of a regular, planned survey to keep track of changes in the forest's condition.

Periodic surveillance is often conducted by airplane where forests are extensive. Aerial surveillance can vary from simple visual inspection to use of color-infrared photography or computer-enhanced satellite images. Aerial photographs are used to detect and map defoliation; this technique, along with satellite imagery, is being developed in conjunction with control measures for the gypsy moth, spruce budworm, forest tent caterpillar, larch sawfly, and the Douglas fir tussock moth.

On the ground, many sampling and survey techniques are designed to provide qualitative and/or quantitative information. In many cases, qualitative information is obtained from insect surveys at semipermanent sample stations in various forest types. Survey and measurement techniques utilized in forestry are also discussed in Chapter 10, "Measurement of the Forest."

## Quantitative Methods

When qualitative surveys indicate a disturbance in the population level of a pest species, more refined and definitive surveys are undertaken to produce numerical descriptions of the changes. *Numerical surveys* follow a regimen specifying the locations, number, and frequency of samples to be taken. In some areas, these numerical assessments are made on a regular basis in order to keep close surveillance on pest species with potentially explosive populations. During one such survey in Wisconsin, which monitored overwintering stages of the jack pine budworm, it was discovered that the percentage of parasitization of *Apanteles* was very high. This indicated that defoliation in late spring and summer would be greatly reduced. Consequently, an aerial spray operation scheduled to cover 81,000 hectares was reduced by 85 percent. This not only resulted in a significant monetary savings, but also encouraged continued parasitization by beneficial insects.

The methods and techniques used to measure insect populations depend on the biological and ecological characteristics of the species, the proposed use of the information, the size of the area to be surveyed, the nature of the terrain, the availability of skilled personnel and funding, and the value and intended use of the threatened resources. If the survey is in response to a newly discovered infestation or outbreak, sampling may be intensive and extend well past estimated boundaries in order to determine borders accurately and to calculate intensity.

Survey procedures have been standardized for most major forest insect pests. The life stage(s) that provides the criterion for estimating population levels depends on the species being measured. For many species, eggs serve as a population indicator (eggs are particularly useful because of their immobility); in other cases, larvae are counted. Symptoms and signs provide indirect population information; for example, the number of exit holes of bark beetles or wood borers in a standardized area of bark surface implies internal beetle densities and tree damage. Whatever the survey technique used for the life stage sampled, the goal of quantitative surveys is to provide an estimate of the pest's population or tree damage on a per-unit-area or per-tree basis—that is, *density*. The survey information is later used in conjunction with biological and ecological knowledge to predict future population levels or damage impact. Hence, if we know how many insects are present in a given stand via a quantitative survey, and have prior knowledge of the density of insects that will cause stand mortality (i.e., economic damage levels), we can make management decisions regarding the necessity of future pest-control measures.

Specific survey techniques are too numerous to detail here, but we will focus on two recent innovations that have increased efficiency and reduced survey costs. Traditionally, surveys have been employed using a fixed sample size—for example, 10 percent of the trees in a plantation may be examined to determine the number of sawfly colonies per tree. A modern variation of this approach uses a flexible sample size based on the principle of *sequential sampling*. Sequential techniques require extensive prior knowledge and are based on sophisticated statistical methods. In its simplest form the sequential survey is conducted in conjunction with a table or graph. For example, a graph (Figure 7.14) used for classifying population levels of the Douglas-fir tussock moth is employed in an egg-count survey. To begin, twig samples are taken from four trees and the number of eggs counted: a total of 50 eggs is found (point A, Figure 7.14). The numbers of eggs found on twig samples from five more trees are 15, 70, 55, 20, and 90. The points given by using the successive, cumulative numbers of trees as the *x*-coordinates, and the corresponding cumulative numbers of eggs as the *y*-coordinates (points B through F), are plotted on the graph. The area in which a point falls determines whether more samples must be taken. Whereas it took nine samples to denote a "heavy" classification in our example, it might take twenty samples to determine a light population level. Likewise, if the first twig sampled contained 200 eggs, no further sampling would be necessary. As long as the point resulting from the coordinates for cumulative trees and eggs falls in the "no decision" band, surveying must be continued

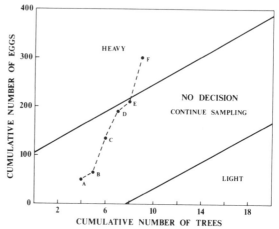

**Figure 7.14** Sequential sampling graph for classifying Douglas-fir tussock moth populations. (Modified from Mason (17), U. S. D. A. Forest Service.)

(up to a predetermined maximum number of samples) because it is not statistically possible to classify the level with certainty. Depending on the particular objectives, the terms *heavy* and *light* on the graph might be replaced with *control* and *no control*, or other decision paradigms.

A second innovative approach to damage/insect surveys concerns managing white pine plantations in eastern North America to control the *white pine weevil*. As mentioned earler, this weevil kills the terminal shoot of sapling- and pole-sized white, red, jack, and Scotch pines, and causes a permanent crook or fork to develop in the main bole of the tree. These forked trees often are of limited value, for they rarely produce high-quality lumber when they reach the marketable age of 75 to 150 years. Obviously, the objective of a sound forest management plan is to grow white pines that produce straight and clear lumber. White pine plantations generally are planted at a mean density of about 3000 trees per hectare; harvest of saw-log sized trees is aimed at 250 to 370 trees per hectare. The final crop trees are selected early in the life of the plantation according to criteria of rapid growth and good form. Slow-growing, stunted, and weevil-injured trees are gradually removed during intermediate harvesting and thinning.

**180**

Under this procedure, white pine plantations are scheduled for control only if they are approaching the limit of tolerable injury by the weevil. This requires assessing the annual decrease in the number of unweeviled trees and charting the information, as shown in Figure 7.15. When the decreasing number of healthy, well-formed, unweeviled trees approaches the critical level of 300, then controls will be applied to protect these final crop trees. The investment required for weevil control is based on affording protection to the final crop trees—control of weevil injury to trees producing less valuable products is not accepted as good management.

## Control of Forest Insects

The decision to control insects infesting natural forests and plantations must be based on a comprehensive review of all factors bearing on the

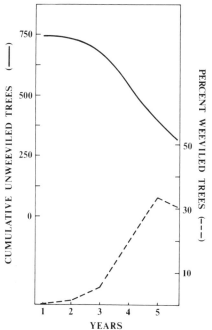

**Figure 7.15** White pine weevil damage indices, used as criteria for control decisions. (Modified from Waters (18), U. S. D. A. Forest Service.)

management and culture of these multiple-use, renewable, natural resources. Ecological, sociological, and economic implications must be weighed carefully. The perpetuation of forests involves long-term management of insects that are a natural force in the ecological succession of living biological systems. It is inevitable that periodically the forest environment may become favorable to some species of pest insects. It is the responsibility of the forest entomologist to acquire sufficient basic information concerning the pest species in the region to be able to recommend sound practices that will temper the effects of these population eruptions. The tools available for this task, as well as their effectiveness, are being steadily improved and expanded.

**Silvicultural Control.** The objective of silvicultural control is to reduce the adverse impact of pest insects through the implementation of various forest management practices. (Silvicultural practices are discussed in more detail in Chapter 9.) To be effective, methodologies must be based on a fundamental understanding of the biology and ecology surrounding the pest species and the ecological requirements of the forest type being managed.

The use of silvicultural methods for controlling insect pests is *preventive* instead of corrective, and the effect may be reflected some years beyond the time the practice is initiated. For example, delaying the replanting or reseeding of an eastern North American coniferous forest immediately after a clearcut harvest will avoid a devastating outbreak of the Pales weevil among the new seedlings one to two years later. Adult weevils are drawn to the odor of pitch from the harvested trees and feed on bark of the newly established seedlings. Successive generations of weevils, hatching from eggs laid in the cut stumps, may destroy the entire crop of young pines.

Many silvicultural techniques are the result of careful study and experience.For example, it was found that planting hard pines in eastern North America too deeply results in abnormally long distances between tree roots and the soil surface. This condition predisposes the trees to serious injury by the pine root collar weevil 5 to 20 years after planting. The solution to the problem has been simply to plant less deeply.

In the Great Lakes region, the adult Saratoga spittlebug causes substantial tree mortality of hard pines by sucking the sap from twigs. The spittlebug requires an alternate host during the nymphal stage, and this information has been put to use in the three options currently employed to alleviate the problem: (1) avoid establishing hard pines in areas of dense alternate hosts; (2) reduce density of alternate hosts with herbicides prior to planting; or (3) establish plantations at a minimum density of 3000 stems per hectare to effect early crown closure to shade out alternate hosts.

Likewise, the ravages of bark beetles may be curtailed in a variety of ways. The pine engraver and pine sawyer can be controlled in cutting sites by "hot logging"—that is, removal of cut logs and pulp within 30 days during spring and summer and removal of all winter-cut wood from the forest by May 15. The western pine beetle, a problem among more mature trees and those of less vigor, is controlled by thinning. Low vigor, thin-crowned, and overmature ponderosa pines that are likely to succumb to the beetle before the next scheduled thinning are removed during a special cut.

**Chemical Control.** The application of chemical insecticides for insect control in the forest is an emergency undertaking, designed to avoid or reduce damage immediately. Except for rare instances, the objective is not to eradicate the pest. If properly planned and carefully executed, application of the pesticide should have a negligible effect on the environment or natural control factors such as parasites and predators. The latter are subsequently expected to exert sufficient influence to hold the pest population at endemic levels.

Most insect-control programs involving forest insects are directed against defoliators like the spruce and pine budworms, tussock moths, tent caterpillars, cankerworms, gypsy moths, and

sawflies. Among the sucking insects, controls have been applied for scales, spittlebugs, and balsam wooly aphids. Bark beetles also have been subject to controls, the major targets being the western pine beetle, the spruce weevil, the southern pine beetle, and the pine engravers. Shoot moths, seed and conefeeders, and the white pine weevil also have received special attention.

The habits of the pest species, the area involved, the proximity to water, and the potential for adverse impacts on area wildlife all must be taken into account when considering if, which, when, how, and how much pesticide is to be applied. These decisions are among the most serious facing the forest manager, for their consequences are often felt for many years afterward.

Pesticides can act on an insect in a variety of ways, and they are therefore often classified according to how the poison enters the insect's body:

1. Stomach poison—taken in by mouth parts (includes poison baits, systemics).
2. Contact poison—absorbed through the body wall.
3. Fumigant—taken in through respiration.

Pesticides can also be classified according to their chemical makeup: (1) inorganic poisons, (2) chlorinated hydrocarbons, (3) carbamates, (4) organophosphates, and (5) natural plant products.

Methods of pesticide application in the forest depend on the vulnerability or exposure of the pest and the magnitude of the area involved. Most defoliators are exposed while feeding, and stomach poisons applied to the foliage will be taken into the body along with their food. On individual trees or small forest areas (1 to 10 hectare), pesticides are usually applied by hydraulic sprayers or mist blowers. For large areas (more than 10 hectares), airplanes or helicopters are more efficient. Trees infested by bark beetles and wood borers often are treated with insecticide by hand or machine spraying of the tree trunk. The same technique has been used successfully to treat pulpwood and log piles that must be left in the forest for long perods.

For insects feeding inside buds, shoots, seeds, and foliage that are not exposed to external sprays, systemic pesticides are employed. These are either applied externally to the foliage where they are absorbed and translocated throughout the tree, or they may be applied on the soil around the tree as granules,which are dissolved and washed into the root zone. The pesticide is then absorbed by the roots and translocated to all parts of the tree.

A large number of pesticides are available for forest insect control. It is worth emphasizing that the user of pesticides must very carefully read and follow the instructions on the package label—almost all pesticides are poisonous to humans as well as insects. The label specifies which insects the pesticide may be used against, the dosage rate, best method of application, and the major safety precautions required. A casual attitude toward pesticide handling and use may not only be a violation of state or national pesticide-use regulations, but could also endanger the health and lives of all who come in contact with the chemical. Pesticides can be used safely and effectively if the required precutions are heeded.

## Novel Chemical Approaches.

Among the chemicals available for forest pest control are several that exploit an insect's particular biological characteristics. Most insect species require mating before the female is able to lay fertile eggs. In some species like the gypsy moth, males find females by following the particular identifying "odor" of a chemical substance called a *pheromone* that is secreted by the females. Chemists have synthesized this pheromone, and it is now used as a lure to detect male moths in areas of low density and in areas beyond the species' normal range. Forests infested with gypsy moths might also be sprayed with this sex attractant to confuse the males and prevent their finding and fertilizing females.

A similar biological exploitation involves raising a large number of males in the laboratory and sterilizing them prior to their release in the infested area. These males mate with virgin females but, because there is no fertilization, only infertile eggs are produced.

A recent innovation in insect control involves a chemical that inhibits chitin formation and deposition. (Chitin is a major component of the insect's exoskeleton.) This chemical is not toxic to insects, but causes weaknesses to develop in the body wall during molting. The exoskeleton does not develop properly, and the insect fails to complete its life cycle or dies when its exoskeleton ruptures.

Other chemicals, called feeding inhibitors, are not poisons but are used to inhibit or stop an insect's feeding. These chemicals eventually result in starvation of the target pest.

Novel chemicals and methods are developing rapidly, and each must be carefully examined for its impact on target insects and on the flora and fauna of the entire forest ecosystem.

## Biological Control.

As mentioned earlier, biological control is the planned use of living organisms and their products in the abatement of noxious insects. Even though organisms of many types have been studied as potential control agents, the vast number of insect species, viruses, fungi, etc., makes it evident that research in this area is still in its infancy. Current research focuses on control agents that are naturally associated with a pest species (or closely related species), especially when the pest has been introduced from another area or country. In such cases the natural enemies of the introduced species are also imported, and the possibilities of their establishment are evaluated for the new area. This process requires great care, however, because the introduction of exotic new species into an established ecosystem—or the attempted extermination of a long-time resident species—can have unanticipated, dramatic consequences.

Successful importation and establishment of control agents have been accomplished for a variety of pest insects. Following are several examples of the use of imported controls in the management of insect pests:

1. The *larch casebearer*, a tiny moth whose larvae feed on larch needles, is an exotic pest from Europe. Two of its European parasites were introduced to combat the pest in this country, and they are now considered responsible for reducing larch defoliation to a nominal level.

2. Both native and exotic *sawflies* defoliate conifers throughout North America. The European parasite, *Dahlbominus fuscipennis* (Zett.), was introduced to bolster the control exerted by native beneficial insects. The parasite was successfully established in many parts of Canada and the United States where it has contributed to the control of the red-headed pine, and European pine sawflies.

3. A nematode is being tested as a control agent for the *sirex wasp* in New Zealand and Australia. The sirex wasp is a threat to *Radiata* pine, and during outbreaks the pest kills large numbers of these trees. Female wasps infected by the nematode become sterile. Infected males transmit the nematode to their offspring when they mate with an uninfected female.

4. *Calasoma sycophanta*, a large, iridescent, green beetle, was imported from Europe to control gypsy moths in the northeastern United States. Both the larval and adult stages of the beetle prey on moth populations.

Introductions of parasites and predators are not always successful. One of the most extensive biological control projects in the United States has been in operation since the early 1900s against the gypsy moth. Large-scale importation of natural enemies from Europe and Japan was carried on for almost 30 years, with over 100 million individuals, comprising 40 species of parasites and predators, released in this country. Of these, only 11 species have become established.

**Integrated Pest Management.** Forest-pest control, like agricultural crop protection has a history of environmental abuses due to ignorance. Whatever the vagaries of the past, the maturity of experience now demands establishment of a new system for dealing with pests of all types. A new concept is at hand—called *integrated pest management* (IPM)—and great international efforts are being orchestrated to bring it to a practical reality. IPM is a pest-control strategy based on ecological principles; it integrates methodologies from several disciplines in a management plan designed to be effective, practical, economical, and protective of human health and the environment.

Historically, scientists in different disciplines—entomology, pathology, soils, forestry, chemistry, etc.—approached a pest problem with minimal communication with their colleagues in other fields. Occasionally controls imposed for one pest conflicted with those used against another, or resulted in undesirable effects on the pest population and/or beneficial species. It was finally realized not only that is it feasible to integrate pest control methods, but also that this integration must consider simultaneously the effects on a multitude of other factors, including other organisms, other forest management activities, and other uses of the ecosystem.

Two relatively new fields of study providing information important to the construction of viable IPM programs are *population dynamics* and *forest ecology*. Research in the former has led to a better understanding of how a myriad of factors affect population fluctuations. Forest ecology has expanded its traditional limits to encompass investigations in the interdependency of various organisms, and the quantification of stand dynamics. IPM is making use of modern economic theory and systems analysis. The progression of computer technology and the parallel development of systems concepts were timely events in the human quest for modern pest-management strategies.

IPM, by definition, brings together old knowledge, new ideas, policy considerations, treatment techniques, prediction, monitoring, and decision making in a way only recently possible. The environmental and biological factors discussed in this chapter are used as tools for evaluating pest management needs—thresholds, tree-species composition, climatological concepts, damage impact, etc. IPM's function is to employ the various elements of silvicultural, biological, and chemical control as needed, such that they work in concert, not in conflict, with one another.

A major national effort for IPM was recently sponsored by the federal government in cooperation with universities, states, and private industry. This multimillion dollar research project focused on the gypsy moth, the tussock moth, and the southern pine beetle. Although some problems remain unsolved, major inroads to understanding were made. This program must rank as one of the most intensive national efforts of any country to resolve important forest-pest problems.

IPM is in its infancy; there is still much to learn in many areas. Existing knowledge and creative research can produce a pest-management system that integrates two seemingly incompatible conditions: the economical need to control pest damage, and the ecological necessity of preserving, as nearly as possible, the natural vitality and beauty of forested land.

## REFERENCES

1. K. Graham, *Concepts of Forest Entomology,* Reinhold, New York, 1963.
2. F. B. Knight and H. J. Heikkenen, *Principles of Forest Entomology,* Fifth Edition, McGaw-Hill, New York, 1980.
3. W. L. Baker, "Eastern forest insects," U.S.D.A. For. Serv., Misc. Publ. No. 1175, 1972.
4. R. L. Furniss and V. M. Carolin, "Western forest insects," U.S.D.A. For. Serv., Misc. Publ. No. 1339, 1977.
5. Anon., "Timber resources for America's future" U.S.D.A. For. Serv., Res. Rept. No. 14, 1958.
6. Anon., "The outlook for timber in the United States," U.S.D.A. For. Serv., Res. Rept. No. 20, 1973.
7. A. G. Davidson and R. M. Prentice, eds., "Important forest insects and diseases of mutual concern to Canada, the United States and Mexico," Dept. For. and Rural Development—Canada, Publ. No. 1180, 1967.
8. W. G. Wellington, *Meteor. Mon., 2,* 11 (1954).
9. C. C. Doane, *Ann. Entomol. Soc. Amer., 52,* 109 (1959).
10. R. L. Giese, J. E. Kapler, and D. M. Benjamin, "Studies of mapleblight. IV. Defoliation and the genesis of maple blight," *Univ. Wisc. Agr. Expt. Sta. Res. Bul. 250,* 81 (1964).
11. D. O. Vandenburg, "Protection of selected forest resources (crop protection) as a management strategy," *Proc. Symposium on the Spruce Budworm,* U.S.D.A. For. Serv., Misc. Publ. No. 1327, 1976.
12. G. A. Simmons, "Influence of spruce budworm moth dispersal on suppression decisions," *Proceedings of a Symposium on the Spruce Budworm,* U.S.D.A. For. Serv., Misc. Pub. No. 1327, 1976.
13. J. R. Blais, *For. Sci. 11,* 13 (1965).
14. D. O. Greenbank, "The dynamics of epidemic spruce budworm populations," R. F. Morris, ed., *Memoirs of the Entomol. Soc. Canada,* No. 31, 1963.
15. L. C. Irland, "Notes on the economics of spruce budworm control," Univ. Maine, School of Forest Resources, Technical Notes No. 67, 1977.
16. R. L. Giese, D. R. Houston, D. M. Benjamin, and J. E. Kuntz, "Studies of maple blight. I. A new condition of sugar maple," *Univ. Wisc. Agr. Expt. Sta. Res. Bull., 250,* 1 (1964).
17. R. R. Mason, "Sequential sampling of Douglas-fir tussock moth populations," U.S.D.A. For. Serv., Res. Note PNW-102, 1969.
18. W. E. Waters, "Uninjured trees—a meaningful guide to white pine-weevil control decisions," U.S.D.A. For. Serv., Res. Note No. 129, 1969.

# 8

# DISEASES OF FOREST TREES

## Robert F. Patton

Like all other organisms, forest trees are subject to injury and disease caused by adverse environmental influences and a variety of destructive biotic agents. They may be affected at all stages in their life cycle, from seed to mature tree, and even afterward as the wood product. These agents have a variety of effects on the forest and cause losses in both quality and yield.

The losses we are concerned with in this chapter are those caused by *disease,* as opposed to losses from fire, insects, animals, or weather. Disease can be defined as a malfunction of a metabolic process, or disturbance of normal structure, that is caused by continuous irritation by some abiotic or biotic agent. This activity results in symptoms and signs produced by the suscept and pathogenic agent, respectively, and these evidences of disease are used in characterization and diagnosis of the disease. Injury, as opposed to disease, also may impair vital functions or disrupt the normal structure, but it results from an agent such as fire, insects, or animals, affecting the plant only once or intermittently, and the irritation is discontinuous, temporary, or transient. *Damage* is sometimes used as a synonym for *injury,* but it usually connotes a decrease in quantity or quality of a product that leads to an economic loss.

The study of forest diseases is called *forest pathology.* In its broadest sense it includes the study of diseases that cause damage or loss to the forest as an economic unit, diseases of shade and ornamental trees, and microbiological deterioration of forest products after harvest (1). In forest pathology we are interested in the influence of diseases on forest management practices, and also in the influence of management practices on the occurrence and development of diseases.

## SIGNIFICANCE OF FOREST-DISEASE LOSSES

The total loss, including all the various effects, resulting from tree diseases is referred to as *growth impact.* This includes both *mortality* and *growth*

*loss,* the latter including reduced growth rate, losses of accumulated growth (e.g., by decay), losses of efficiency in utilization of the site, and losses in quality.

Our knowledge of the loss caused by forest-tree diseases is grossly inadequate, and for lack of better figures, we continue to quote the estimates made at the time the concept of growth impact was derived in 1952, as shown in Table 7.1 (Chapter 7). Although insects cause the highest mortality losses of trees, by far the largest growth losses are a result of tree diseases. Such diseases account for over 50 percent or about 170 million cubic meters of the annual growth loss in the forest. Thus losses from disease are indeed enormous. Reductions in such losses would go far toward increasing the timber supply necessary to meet future demand.

Although there are differences in the magnitude of increases, all recent projections indicate substantially larger demands on domestic forests in the future than at present (2). The amount of available timber has increased (through tree growth) faster than total wood consumption, but increased costs of stumpage, processing, and marketing are reducing the economic supply even as the timber inventory grows. Beyond about the year 2000, however, increased forestry effort will be necessary if timber supply is to meet demand. Opportunities for increasing timber supplies appear through intensified forest management. One aspect of more intensive forest management is reduction of the great impact on growth caused by disease. Because of adverse economic and environmental impacts caused by increasing use of wood substitutes, programs to produce increased timber crops are important, and the reduction of losses through the management of disease in our forests represents a challenge and an opportunity for foresters.

## CAUSES OF FOREST DISEASES

The health of forest trees is affected by a number of factors that subject trees to *stress.* At any point in time several stress factors may be operating concurrently so that the general state of health of a tree may be determined by the total effect of all stresses (3). For convenience in study and understanding, however, we separate the treatment of these factors into various disciplines, such as pathology and entomology. In forest pathology the diseases caused by these factors may be classified in several ways: according to the causal agent, the portion of the tree affected, the process or function disrupted, or the stage of development of the tree, such as nursery seedlings.

## Agents that Cause Disease

Agents or factors inducing diseases in plants, including forest trees, are classed as abiotic (noninfectious, nonparasitic) or biotic (infectious, parasitic). A specific biotic agent causing a disease is designated as a *pathogen*.

**Abiotic or Noninfectious Agents.** A number of abiotic agents are causes of diseases in trees, including extremes of moisture and temperature, nutrient excess or deficiency, and toxic substances in the air or soil. Also, mechanical injury may be caused by hail, ice, snow, and windstorms; lightning damage may result in death of individual trees or even trees in groups. Diseases caused by abiotic agents often are difficult to diagnose because the causal agent is no longer present or active, or because the cause-effect relationship is difficult to establish.

Some of the most complex forest-disease problems are those induced by adverse variations in the environment. Pole blight, characterized by severe root and crown decline of second-growth pole-size western white pine, was the result of an abnormally long period of drought superimposed on certain sites having low moisture-storage capacity in the Inland Empire region of Washington, Idaho, and Montana. A number of hardwood declines, blights, or diebacks appeared in the 1950s when drought was implicated as the primary inciting factor. Oak decline, ash dieback, and sweetgum blight are among

such diseases in which the causal relations are extremely complicated, consisting of an interaction of various factors, even to the inclusion of insect defoliation in the cause of oak decline.

Temperature or moisture extremes may cause direct damage to trees or so weaken them that they are predisposed to attack by microorganisms. Sunscald canker of thin-barked trees often results from sudden exposure—for example, after thinning, whereby above-freezing temperatures on sunny days combined with freezing temperatures at night kill the bark and cause cankers to form. Winter injury or winter drying of foliage of conifers results when warm winds cause excessive transpiration, and roots in frozen ground cannot replace the water.

Conditions of deficiency or excess of nutrients or other chemicals in the soil may be encountered in local areas, especially in nurseries and forest plantations. Pine and eucalyptus plantations have failed in Africa because of boron deficiency. In Scotland plantations of Sitka spruce suffering from phosphate deficiency were immediately improved by aerial fertilization with phosphate. As forest management becomes more intensive, forest fertilization may become almost routine, but there is also likelihood of damage from a variety of chemicals such as fertilizers, fungicides, insecticides, herbicides, and others if they are applied at excessive rates or under improper conditions.

In recent decades air pollution has reached such high levels that grave concern has been expressed over the widespread damage to both forests and urban trees in most of the industrialized regions of the world. Many chemicals highly toxic to trees and other plants are introduced into the atmosphere, especially by transportation vehicles, industrial processes, and power plants. Sulfur dioxide, from coal combustion and other industrial processes, and the photochemical pollutants ozone and peroxyacetyl nitrate, the main components of urban smog, are major causes of damage to conifers in particular. In the East white pine has suffered considerable damage from sulfur dioxide and ozone, and the chlorotic decline disease of ponderosa pine in Southern

California is attributed to prolonged exposure to aerial oxidants, mainly ozone. Fluorides have caused local damage to forest and orchard trees when released into the atmosphere from ore reduction, fertilizer, and ceramics installations. The role of acid precipitation in influencing plant growth, especially that of forests, is also attracting considerable attention.

**Biotic or Infectious Agents.** Most diseases of forest trees are caused by various biotic agents. These include viruses, mycoplasmas, bacteria, fungi, parasitic higher plants, and nematodes. Of these the *fungi* cause the largest number of diseases as well as the greatest total loss. Examples of diseases caused by these agents are described in the following sections.

*Diseases Caused by Viruses, Mycoplasmas, Bacteria, and Nematodes.* *Viruses* are extremely small infectious agents visible only in the electron microscope. Although plant viruses cause many major diseases of important agricultural crops, known virus diseases of forest trees such as elm mosaic, birch line pattern, or black locust witches' broom apparently are of minor importance (4). As their incidence becomes better known through research, perhaps they will be considered of greater significance in the future. Also, because vegetative propagation perpetuates viruses, the trend to plantation forestry—and in some species (e.g., poplars) an emphasis on vegetative propagation—will tend to enhance the threat and importance of virus diseases in commercial forest plantings throughout the world.

A few tree diseases, formerly thought to be caused by viruses, are now known to result from infection by the smallest of free-living organisms, commonly referred to as *mycoplasmas*. They lack a cell wall but possess a distinct flexible membrane and are often smaller than bacteria. None are known to cause any diseases of major importance in American forestry, although one tree disease caused by a mycoplasma, phloem necrosis of American elm and winged elm, has caused the death of many elms in

the central United States. Mortality from this disease alone was considerable, but its presence in the area in which Dutch elm disease was introduced has made control efforts for the latter disease, including attempts at breeding for resistance, more difficult than they would have been otherwise.

*Bacteria* cause diseases in species of all the important families of higher plants, but few are direct causes of disease of forest and shade trees. The bacterial canker of poplar is a serious disease in Europe but so far is unknown in North America. New clones for poplar culture are released in European countries only with intensive selection and testing for resistance to this disease. In many species of trees a water-soaked condition of the heartwood, called "wetwood," along with discoloration and production of gas (principally methane), is associated with bacteria, apparently as direct causes of the malady. Bacteria are also significant in the successional processes leading to discoloration and decay in the wood of trees. They are among the principal pioneer microorganisms that invade wounds and initiate the succession of changes that ultimately ends in decay of wood by fungi (5).

Plant-parasitic *nematodes* are microscopic eelworms of great importance as pests of agricultural and ornamental crops, yet there is little knowledge of nematode diseases of forest trees. This situation may be due partly to difficulties in measuring growth loss in trees resulting from damage to feeder roots (6). Economic losses in tree nurseries have resulted from nematode attacks on roots that lead to dieback and abnormalities of roots, stunting of the plant, and even mortality. Most information is on associations of nematodes with forest trees in plantations or natural stands, but evidence of pathogenicity (proof of parasitism) is lacking in most instances. Symptoms may include galling, devitalized root tips, and browning and shriveling of feeder roots, but such symptoms also may be produced by other organisms or soil conditions. Disease results from a decrease in the water- and nutrient-absorbing area of feeder roots resulting in slow decline of the trees. In the southern United States high densities of nematodes often occur in forest plantations established on abandoned farmlands, causing significant root damage and stunting.

*Diseases Caused by Fungi.* The most destructive causal agents of disease in forest trees are the fungi. These organisms are usually classified as plants without chlorophyll and with a very simple structure undifferentiated into stem, leaves, and roots. The basic structural unit of most fungi is a microscopic threadlike filament or tube that contains the cytoplasm. These filaments or hyphae in aggregate make up the mycelium or vegetative body of the fungus, as seen in the fuzzy growth of the common bread mold or the white mycelial fans beneath the bark of a tree root attacked by the shoestring root-rot fungus, *Armillariella (Armillaria) mellea.* Fungi reproduce by spores produced on fruiting structures that vary in complexity from a simple hypha to complex bodies, such as the mushroom that emerges from the soil or the bracket or ''conk'' on the trunk of a tree with heartrot. Most fungus spores are disseminated by wind, but there is also chance distribution by agents such as splashing rain, surface and underground water, insects, birds and other animals, and even humans. On a suitable substrate the spore germinates to form a simple hypha or germ tube, which then elongates and branches to form another mycelium. Fungi live on organic material, either as *saprophytes* on dead material or as *parasites* on living plants or animals.

Most fungi are saprophytes, and the consumption of dead organic material by saprophytic fungi is often designated as rot or decay. The decay of heartwood in living trees in the forest is the result of a succession of activities by saprophytic organisms and is responsible for over 70 percent of the loss attributed to diseases in the forest. The conversion of dead plant and animal remains on the forest floor into humus is a beneficial aspect of saprophytic fungi.

Some fungi are parasites and obtain their food from living plants or animals. The activities of such fungi disrupt the life processes of their hosts, and disease results, as in the girdling of a stem by the white pine blister rust fungus or the spotting and death of longleaf pine needles by the brown spot needle blight pathogen.

The activities of fungi cause both mortality and growth loss in producing the most numerous and most important diseases of forest trees. These diseases vary enormously in the species and parts of tree affected, in the symptoms they produce, and in the type of damage they cause. Consequently, their effects on forest yield and their significance to forest management are also variable; some may be inconsequential, whereas others may be limiting factors in growth and management of a species.

## Decay of Forest Trees

**Heartrot.** A major objective in forestry is wood production. When wood of the tree trunk is utilized as food by fungi, the cell walls deteriorate resulting in changes in color and texture as well as physical and chemical properties of the wood. This process is known as *decay* or *rot*, and a wood rot is the primary decay of wood caused by a particular species of fungus.

Decay is caused primarily by fungi. Most decay occurs in the central core of dead wood, or "heartwood," of the tree and often is termed *heartrot* (Figure 8.1). The sapwood is relatively resistant to decay in the living tree and protects the underlying heartwood against invasion by most decay fungi. Under some circumstances, however, some fungi may decay both sapwood and heartwood.

The wood rots commonly are grouped into two main types, *brown* and *white rots*. These are classified according to the type of decay process that ensues, but the predominant color changes are really incidental accompaniments of the decay process. Brown-rot fungi decompose wood by utilizing primarily the carbohydrates (cellulose) of the cell walls, whereas white-rot fungi utilize both the carbohydrate and lignin components of the cell wall. These differences are important in that they can

**Figure 8.1** Typical brown cubical heartrot in a log of Douglas-fir. (Courtesy of Canadian Forestry Service, Pacific Forest Research Center, Victoria, B.C.)

affect the utilization of decayed wood. Strength is decreased by both types of decay, and rotted wood is of no use for construction. Pulp yields from white-rotted wood may be relatively high and of fairly good quality, whereas brown-rotted wood cannot be used. See Chapter 18 for a further discussion of the chemical nature of wood.

The loss caused by heartwood decay (either loss in volume through unmerchantability or lowering of quality) has the greatest growth impact on forest trees of all destructive agents and accounts for over 70 percent of the total loss attributed to diseases of forest trees. Loss of accumulated wood volume is the most significant factor in this loss, and the activities of decay fungi, since their effects are largely on dead wood cells, are of little importance in causing mortality or reduction in vigor. Of course, structural weakness can lead to increased storm damage.

Many different species of fungi cause heartrot, but each has its own particular manner of behavior and distinctive characteristics. Some attack many different tree species. The shoestring root-rot fungus, *Armillariella (Armillaria) mellea*, which may cause both root rot and heartrot of forest trees, has a host range extending to hundreds of both woody and nonwoody plants. The most important single decay of forest trees, red ring rot caused by *Phellinus (Fomes) pini*, occurs only in conifers. Others, such as the important white trunk-rot fungus of aspen, *Phellinus (Fomes) igniarius*, are restricted to certain hardwood species. In some species, such as trembling aspen, one or a very few species of decay fungi account for most of the volume loss from decay. In other species, such as the oaks and maples, many different fungi contribute significantly to the total decay loss. Interestingly, susceptibility or resistance to decay of wood in the living tree is no indication of durability of that wood in service.

There are many different pathways of entry into the wood of a tree by decay fungi, and these *infection courts* are largely the result of wounding or damage to the protective barriers such as the bark and sapwood of the tree. Infection courts may include broken stems or branches, dead branch stubs, dead branches, and wounds of all kinds including logging wounds and, particularly, fire scars.

In recent years *discoloration* and *decay* in the wood of forest trees have come to be recognized as complex processes involving typical successions of many organisms. A variety of organisms including bacteria, nonwood-rotting fungi, and true wood-rotting fungi all seem to be important in the processes that lead to discoloration and decay, even though the ultimate rotting of the wood may be due only to a certain species of fungus present in a given situation. During these processes the tree itself also makes a response to this invasion; the response may then lead to a compartmentalization or confinement of the decay to a certain limited portion of the tree trunk.

The amount of decay in forest stands is extremely variable. Generally there is an increase in number of trees decayed and in total volume of decay with increasing age of the trees. Events in the stand

**192**

history influence the decay situation in a stand—for example, the occurrence of past fires, severe sleet or ice storms, and past silvicultural practices. Knowledge of the amount of decay in given forest stands is important for the preparation of accurate inventories of present and potential growing stock, which are basic to proper forest management. Foresters can estimate the amount of decay in a stand with information from sample plot measurements and knowledge of external indicators of decay, such as fruiting bodies or "conks," swollen knots, and branch stubs. Gross volume estimates are corrected to net volumes through application of these decay estimates, expressed as cull factors or percentages of gross volume, thus allowing accurate determinations of yields, allowable cuts, sales costs, and other factors necessary in timber management (see Chapter 10).

The control of decay in the forest rests largely in the application of *preventive measures*. There is no "cure" for decay once it develops in the individual tree. Feasible control methods are aimed at (1) securing the greatest return in the harvesting of present merchantable (mostly virgin) stands, and (2) minimizing losses from decay in future stands.

Information on both qualitative and quantitative decay losses can lead to closer utilization, and thus greater yields, from diseased trees. The size and other characteristics of the rot column can influence how the tree is utilized and thus the profit in logging. Decay losses can be reduced by refinement of technological and economic utilization practices, even to the use of decayed material, especially white rots, in pulp or in various specialty products including veneer and plywood.

Reduction of decay losses in our future stands must come from application of silvicultural practices, as described in Chapter 9. One such measure is the adjustment of rotation age and cutting cycles as, for example, a rotation age of 70 years for balsam fir with cutting cycles of about 20 years, and cutting ages for aspen of about 50 years or less in the Great Lakes states and between 80 and 100 years in the West. Considerable attention is being paid now

to avoidance of logging and other operational injuries to trees in the residual stand, such as in selectively logged stands of northern hardwoods. In second-growth stands of ponderosa pine in the Southwest, future losses from red rot can be reduced by controlling size of branches by proper stand density and by pruning. Other silvicultural practices that could help reduce decay might include sanitation or timber-stand improvement cuts to remove cull trees, early selective thinning of hardwood stump sprouts, and especially protection against basal wounding from fire, because basal fire scars are an important infection court for decay fungi. In the future, as forest management becomes more intensive and as trees are grown on shorter rotations, losses from decay may become less of a factor than at present.

**Root Rots.** A substantial portion of a tree exists in the soil, and in this very complex below-ground environment root diseases develop that are among the most important causes of loss and the most difficult to control. *Fungi* are the most important agents of root disease. Some may attack only young, succulent roots such as the feeder roots, essentially causing a decline of the tree through starvation. Others, acting as wood-destroying fungi, cause death of roots by parasitic attack and decay of the killed roots, causing a *root rot* of all or a portion of the root system.

Root diseases may cause mortality, and they can interfere with the vigor of growth, density, form, and composition of a forest stand all the way from the seedling stage to the rotation age. They may kill even dominant and codominant trees that would otherwise form part of the final crop. Some may result in *butt rot*—decay of the basal stem portion—causing growth loss both in volume and quality. Decay of the root system makes trees especially subject to wind-throw. Underground spread of the causal fungus from a focal point of infection frequently causes the occurrence of disease in patches.

One of the most important root rots in forests throughout the world is caused by the *honey mushroom,* or the shoestring root-rot fungus, *Armillariella (Armillaria) mellea* (Figure 8.2). The disease usually reaches its greatest severity in trees of reduced vigor, but the fungus can also attack and kill healthy trees. From one invaded root system the fungus spreads through the soil by black, shoestring-like strands of mycelium—rhizomorphs—that can penetrate healthy bark of living roots. The fungus attacks the living tissue of the roots as a parasite and

**Figure 8.2** Clump of mushroom fruiting bodies produced by the shoestring root-rot fungus, *Armillariella mellea,* at the base of a white pine sapling killed by the fungus. Note the white mycelial fan on the stem and the characteristic resin-infiltrated mass of soil around the root collar.

continues activity as a sapropyte in rotting the dead wood of roots and the butt of the tree.

Root and butt rot caused by *Heterobasidion annosum (Fomes annosus)* is one of the most important forest-tree diseases in Europe, especially in coniferous plantations. In the United States it is especially important as a problem after thinning in pine plantations in the Southeast and in second-growth stands, particularly of western hemlock, in the Pacific Northwest. Infection commonly occurs through germination of the windborne spores on freshly cut stump surfaces. The fungus colonizes the stump and grows down into the root system from which it can infect roots of healthy adjacent trees through root contacts. Colonization of the new root system results in root rot along with subsequent butt rot or mortality of the formerly healthy trees to which the fungus has spread. Prevention of stump infection is often possible in the Southeast by stump treatment with borax immediately after the tree is cut. On hemlock in the Pacific Northwest borax has not been as effective as on southen pines, and other chemicals such as zinc chloride are being tried. Another preventive measure successful on pines, both in the South and in England, is the application to the stump surface of a spore suspension of a competitive fungus, *Peniophora gigantea.* This fungus colonizes the stump and prevents establishment by *Heterobasidion annosum* but does not itself cause disease in the residual trees. This latter technique is an excellent example of the application of *biological control* in forest-disease management.

The reduction of root-disease losses is a formidable task because of the difficulties in diagnosis of root disease and in determining the complex relationships among root pathogens, the tree host, and the soil environment. As information is accumulated, it is integrated with our knowledge of silviculture in the formulation of the best possible management practices. For example, *Phellinus (Poria) weirii* root rot is the most destructive disease of young-growth Douglas-fir in the Pacific Northwest of the United States and in British Columbia (Figure 8.3). The intensity and distribution of the disease influence

**194**

**Figure 8.3** Wind-thrown trees in a *Phellinus weirii* infection center of a 50-year-old stand of Douglas-fir. (Courtesy of G.W. Wallis and Canadian Forestry Service, Pacific Forest Research Center, Victoria, B.C.)

various proposals that are recommended for stand harvest, regeneration, and thinnings of stands; proposals range from land clearing where feasible to a change to less susceptible species for future stands.

**Deterioration of Killed or Injured Timber.** When trees are killed by various agencies such as fire, wind-throw, or insects, the dead sapwood deteriorates so rapidly that within a few years salvage may not be economically possible. In living trees sapwood is relatively decay resistant, but after trees are killed sapwood is readily susceptible to invasion by microorganisms and insects. First, the sapwood is invaded by stain fungi and wood-boring insects and then is damaged by seasoning checks as it dries. Next, the sapwood is attacked by wood-destroying fungi, and later the heartwood is invaded by the same or different fungi. The younger the timber, the more rapidly it deteriorates, because of the smaller size and greater proportion of sapwood to heartwood. On the other hand, much of the wood in stands of overmature, large-sized timber, particularly of species with relatively decay-resistant heartwood such as Douglas-fir, may be salvageable for many years after the trees have been killed. The cause of death, whether insects, fire, or whatever, is an important factor in the rate of deterioration and the succession of organisms involved, both of which influence the time available for salvage to reduce the loss from the catastrophe.

One of the beneficial aspects of decay in the forest is the breakdown and decay of *logging slash*. The economic disposal of logging slash remains a problem in fire protection and stand improvement. The rate of breakdown and decay varies widely in major forest types, and knowledge of slash decay has important implications for forest protection and management, since the amount of slash is closely related to the fire hazard and may have influences on the seedbed for natural reproduction.

**Stain and Decay of Forest Products.** Just as in standing trees in the forest, *stains* and *decays* can develop in wood after the tree is felled, during storage and seasoning, and in service. Extensive losses are produced by such deterioration, involving economic values of hundreds of millions of dollars annually. Most such deterioration can be controlled by relatively simple preventive techniques in handling or using the product. The control methods are derived from knowledge of the causes of wood deterioration and factors that favor the causal agents.

Wood stains are confined largely to sapwood and result in unsightly discolorations of the wood that make it unacceptable for many uses such as furniture, paneling, food containers, and similar products where appearance is of importance. Fungus stains occur mainly during the holding of freshly cut logs and in green lumber and veneer. The most common sap stain is called "blue stain" because of the blue-gray to black color imparted to the wood penetrated by the hyphae of the causal fungi. Surface molds impart various colors to lumber and veneer by masses of their spores that can be brushed or planed off lumber, but cannot be removed as easily from veneer. Less important are stains caused by enzymatic reactions, by excessive heating during processing, and by weathering. Fungus stains and molds develop under favorable moisture and temperature conditions and occur most commonly during warm, humid weather. *Prevention* is the only control for fungus stains, and rapid drying by air-seasoning or in a kiln is the most effective method for preventing stain. Fungicide dips for lumber and chemical treatments of log ends may help prevent staining where drying is ineffective.

Wood-destroying fungi can cause decay in wood products when conditions are favorable for their growth, including the presence of oxygen, temperatures generally in the range from above freezing to about 35°C (95°F), and moisture content of the wood above the fiber saturation point, approximately 25 to 32 percent of the dry weight of the wood. Exclusion of oxygen by storage of logs and pulpwood in water or under sprinkling systems is one method of preventing decay. For most wood products the key to control of decay is to dry wood quickly to a moisture content of 20 percent or less and to keep it dry. Where wood is used in places of low decay hazard, proper construction practices will minimize decay losses. Durability of wood varies with species, and some protection against decay is offered through proper selection of species for particular uses. When decay hazard is high, such as for wood placed in contact with soil, wood *preservation* by chemical toxicants can control decay. A variety of both water- and oil-soluble preservatives are available, and applications vary from brushing or dipping to high-pressure treatment.

## Bark Beetle–Blue-Stain Fungi Complex

An interesting and important relationship between fungi and insects in the forest is the association of *blue stain fungi* with *bark beetles*. Bark beetles have a special repository in which spores of blue stain fungi are carried. The spores are inoculated into trees by activity of beetles beneath the bark, and after their germination mycelium grows in cells of both phloem and xylem. Eventually large sectors of sapwood are colonized, resulting in killing of the cells, blue stain of the wood, girdling of the trunk by nonfunctional sapwood, and eventual decline and death of the tree. Thus, not only are trees killed quickly through successful interaction of the symbiotic insect-fungus complex, but the wood is also degraded by stain. Efforts toward direct control of bark beetle epidemics by chemical sprays, salvage logging, or other techniques have temporary effects only, but these may complement preventive management practices aimed at reducing stand susceptibility, as discussed in Chapter 7 on forest insects.

## Canker Diseases

A number of causal agents, but mostly a variety of fungi, can cause the death of relatively localized areas of bark and cambium tissues on trunks, branches, and even twigs of trees. These lesions are termed "cankers," and even though they may be caused by unrelated incitants, including nonliving agents, many of the more important canker diseases have important similarities. Cankers may be annual or perennial. Perennial cankers continue activity over a period of years. Some may be a diffuse type, whereby the pathogen grows rapidly through the host bark with little or no callus development, resulting in stem girdling and death. Others are long-standing and more limited in extent, with continual production of callus tissue, often in concentric ridges or layers (a "target" canker), and slow progress of the pathogen as it gradually enlarges the lesion. Some canker fungi also extend into the wood beneath the face of the canker and cause decay of the stem, making it susceptible to wind breakage at the canker (see Figure 8.4). Canker diseases occur in both gymnosperms and angiosperms, but they are most numerous and of greatest significance in deciduous hardwoods.

Most of the persistent perennial cankers do not cause mortality, but they are important in causing *stem malformation* and *discoloration* of the wood. They cause quality reduction and may result in a volume loss, often of the lowest, most valuable log of the tree. The characteristics of such canker diseases as *Nectria* canker of many important hardwoods or *Euypella* canker of sugar maple are identifiable and are important for control of these diseases. Stands under intensive management can be handled so that cankers are recognized in their incipient state and young infected trees removed from the stand early.

Perhaps the most notorious of all forest diseases, *chestnut blight,* caused by the fungus *Endothia parasitica,* is a canker disease of the diffuse, rapidly developing type. Apparently introduced on nursery stock imported from the Orient, this fungus was first noticed in 1904 in the New York Zoological Park, and in less than 50 years it had spread throughout the natural range of American chestnut and destroyed it as a commercial species. Chestnut blight caused the most spectacular devastation ever wrought by any known forest tree disease. Today sprouts from persisting stumps and root systems continue to appear but eventually are killed by the disease before they mature. Considerable effort has been expended toward breeding disease-resistant chestnuts by hybridization of resistant Asian species with susceptible American and European species but with limited success in obtaining a resistant tree of good timber type. Since the mid-1960s chestnut blight has again attracted considerable attention with the demonstration that inoculation of certain strains of the pathogen of low virulence (hypovirulent) in trees could result in healing of cankers and protect against infection by the virulent strain. The hope is that this research will lead to practical biological control of the disease.

Another killing canker disease is *Hypoxylon* canker of aspen. It is present throughout the range of aspen and is one the most important tree diseases in the Great Lakes states (Figure 8.4). It can decimate entire young stands, and unfortunately no suitable control methods are known.

## Vascular Wilt Diseases

The vascular *wilt* diseases are caused by fungi that grow principally in the xylem vessels. Their activity reduces or inhibits normal water conduction in the stem, and the tree wilts and dies. Wilt diseases are of primary significance in angiosperms, and some of the most publicized tree diseases are in this group, including *Verticillium* wilt, Dutch elm disease, and oak wilt. With some, such as *Verticillium* wilt, direct infection of roots occurs from soil, but with others the fungi move underground from tree to tree through root grafts and above ground by insect vectors. One approach to control has been through breaking the root connections between trees either mechanically or with soil fumigants. Other efforts have been directed toward the insect vectors, espe-

**Figure 8.4** Stem breakage and cankering (arrows) in a stand of aspen trees severely affected by Hypoxylon canker.

**197**

cially the elm bark beetles for control of Dutch elm disease.

*Dutch elm disease* has killed many elm trees in the forest but its greatest impact has been on shade and ornamental American elms, the most susceptible species, in urban environments. Introduced into the United States from Europe, the disease was discovered first in Ohio and some east-central states in the early 1930s, but it has since spread westward to the Pacific Coast states.

Dutch elm disease is the most destructive shade tree disease in the United States today, and the cost of control, or even of merely removing the killed trees because of the hazard they pose, amounts to millions of dollars annually. The causal fungus is transmitted overland by the European elm bark beetle and the native elm bark beetle. Local spread from a diseased to a healthy tree through root grafts is also very important and is responsible for much of the mortality that has occurred in rows of street trees.

Control efforts have been considered successful where losses in a community can be kept under about 2 percent annually through an organized program that may encompass strict sanitation, spraying to control insect vectors, attempts at preventing root-graft spread, good tree maintenance, and prompt replacement of killed trees with nonsusceptible species. Programs for development of resistant elms have resulted in the release of several selections both here and in Europe. Treatment of individual elms by trunk or root injections of systemic fungicides is also showing promise.

*Oak wilt,* caused by a fungus closely related to the Dutch elm disease pathogen, is a native disease and perhaps the most serious disease of oaks in the north-central United States. All oak species are susceptible, but symptoms and severity vary depending on whether the affected tree is a member of the red oak group, in which killing is relatively rapid, or the white oak group, in which wilt symptoms develop more slowly, over a period of several years. Local spread through root grafts may result in large pockets of killed trees in a forest (Figure 8.5).

**Figure 8.5**  Large oak wilt "pocket" in an oak forest stand continues to enlarge by marginal spread through root grafts.

Overland spread may occur by sap-feeding beetles in the family Nitidulidae and possibly by some other insect vectors that are, however, much less efficient than are the vectors for the Dutch elm disease pathogen. Control of local spread through root grafts is expensive but effective, either by mechanical trenching or killing root sections by soil injection of chemical fumigants, especially Vapam (sodium N-methyldithiocarbamate). Overland spread is difficult to control, and major objectives of such efforts have been directed toward reducing abundance of inoculum by girdling and removing diseased trees and preventing unnecessary wounding.

## Rust Fungi

The *rust fungi,* so-called because of the rusty orange color of so many of their spore forms, comprise a group of highly specialized parasitic fungi, including species that attack cones of certain conifers, leaves of both hardwoods and conifers, and stems of conifers (Figure 8.6). Many, but not all, of the fungi in this group are unique in that they require two different and widely unrelated host plants to complete their life cycle. Also most of the rusts produce five different spore stages, which appear in a definite sequence, although some species have as few as one. Thus *Cronartium ribicola,* the cause of the *white pine blister rust* disease, produces pycniospores (spermatia) and aeciospores on white pines, and three other spore forms (urediospores, teliospores, and basidiospores) on the alternate host plants: currants and gooseberries in the genus *Ribes*. Stem rusts of conifers, especially white pine blister rust and fusiform rust of southern pines, are diseases of major importance in natural forests and plantations.

White pine blister rust, along with chestnut blight and Dutch elm disease, is another example of the dangers resulting from introduction of foreign diseases. This fungus, a native of Asia, spread to Europe and from there was introduced to North America on imported white pine planting stock in about 1900. On this continent it found a number of highly susceptible hosts in the white pines (five-

**Figure 8.6** Aecial pustules or "blisters" containing orange masses of aeciospores on a branch canker of white pine blister rust.

needle pines) and has spread to become their most serious disease and one of the limiting factors in growth and management of our commercially important white pines.

For many years, and at a cost of millions of dollars, control was attempted in both the East and the West by large-scale *eradication* of currants and gooseberries. Theoretically this approach seemed possible, as explained later in the section on influences on disease occurrence and development. But after many years of trial it proved not to be feasible, especially in the West. It was impracticable because of the high susceptibility of western white and sugar pines, the extremely favorable climatic conditions for spread and infection, and the impossibility of completely eliminating the alternate host plants. Sufficient spores were still produced on remaining plants to cause highly damaging levels of infection in the pine stands. By about 1970 ribes eradication had been abandoned in the West, and in the East ribes ''suppression'' is being used only to protect eastern white pine in some forest nurseries and forest stands in a few restricted areas.

The most promising hope for control of white pine blister rust lies in selecting and breeding resistant trees (7). Programs for development of resistant planting stock of eastern white pine for the East and of western white and sugar pines for the West are making good progress, and some seed orchards already have been established (see Chapter 5). In management of present natural stands of western white pine, recommendations have been proposed for selecting ''leave-trees'' that have a high probability of producing progeny for the next generation that will exhibit increased resistance to blister rust.

The *fusiform rust* of southern pines is a good example of a disease that has become important as a result of human activities in the forest. Loblolly and slash pine, the main pine hosts, are killed by development of fusiform-shaped galls or ''cankers,'' whereas longleaf pine is relatively resistant and shortleaf pine essentially immune. Oaks are the alternate hosts on which the spores that infect the pines are produced. Unlike the introduced white pine blister rust, this fungus had developed through the ages as a part of the natural forest ecosystems in the southern United States. Prior to 1900 it was rare and little more than a curiosity. After logging of the virgin forest, distribution of the pine hosts was markedly altered. With extensive clearcutting of stands of longleaf pine, its replacement by other species, especially the highly susceptible slash pine and loblolly pine, was favored by the introduction of fire protection and the artificial restocking of the site by planting. Such extensive cutting also favored the release of oaks, which increased in abundance. This combination of circumstances favored buildup of the rust to a level such that we are now in the midst of a major epidemic. In 1975 annual losses were estimated at around $28 million (8).

The management of fusiform rust in southern pine forests is a major component of southern pine forest management and represents a synthesis of available knowledge about the disease and practical methods of forest management. Principal strategies are to prevent the disease in pine nurseries and young stands and to minimize losses in diseased stands. Seedlings in nurseries can be protected by the application of fungicides, and various silvicultural procedures are recommended to minimize losses in rust-infected stands. The primary effort in avoiding rust in young stands is directed toward the development and use of resistant planting stock. A cooperative rust-resistance testing center (U.S. Forest Service Resistance Screening Center) has been established near Asheville, N.C., to evaluate resistance in slash and loblolly pine progeny. Seed orchards for production of seed as a source of resistant seedlings for planting are continually being established and improved in quality throughout the South (9).

Numerous other stem rusts occur on conifers, some of which may cause extensive damage in local areas. Of somewhat less importance are many *foliage rusts* of both conifers and hardwoods. The *Melampsora* rusts of poplars have received increased attention as the threat of high losses from premature defoliation has increased with greater emphasis on plantations of cottonwood, particularly in the South.

## Foliage Diseases

Diseases of the foliage of hardwoods are numerous, but most of these are seldom considered serious. Leaf diseases are mainly important when major defoliation results or when most of the leaves are attacked and damaged so that their normal functioning is impaired. Reduction in growth and vigor may result, but *time of year* of the attack and shoot and foliage characteristics of the tree greatly influence the amount of damage caused. Sometimes leaf diseases can become limiting factors in growth of a species. Since about 1960 the *Marssonina leaf blight* has become of considerable significance in the culture of hybrid poplars in Europe. The *Melampsora leaf rust* also has been of major concern in hybrid poplar culture, and for both of these diseases systems have been developed for evaluating disease resistance of clones. In the United States Melampsora leaf rust has been most important on hybrid poplars. As emphasis on growing hybrid poplars and cottonwood increases in this country, there is evidence that both diseases represent potential threats that must be met by breeding for disease resistance, as discussed in Chapter 5.

Extensive foliage injury to conifers may result in severe damage or death. Generally defoliation reduces tree growth increment in proportion to the degree of defoliation, and there is usually an accompanying reduction in vigor. Quality reduction is also important in ornamentals, especially Christmas trees, where attack in a single year may completely destroy the marketability of the crop. The *needle cast fungi*, as exemplified by *Lophodermium*, often cause rather spectacular epidemics, especially in nurseries and plantations. Relative success has been achieved by fungicidal sprays applied to protect nursery seedlings, and in the north-central states, Scotch pine trees in Christmas tree plantations. The *brown spot needle blight*, caused by *Scirrhia acicola*, also has produced extensive damage in Christmas tree plantations of Scotch pine, especially in the Great Lakes states (Figure 8.7). Furthermore, it has proved to be a major obstacle to production of longleaf pine in the South, where it defoliates seedlings and causes mortality or greatly delays growth of young trees, keeping them in the "grass stage" for unacceptably long periods. Because longleaf pine possesses a fire-resistant terminal bud, control is often possible by prescribed burning in young, established plantations in the dormant season. In New Zealand another needle disease, caused by *Dothistroma pini*, once threatened the forest industry based on the planting of exotic pine species, especially two American species that are highly susceptible to this fungus: Monterey and ponderosa

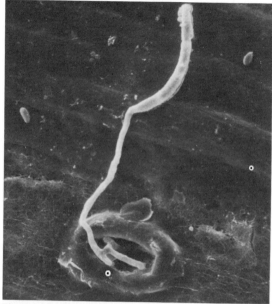

**Figure 8.7** Growth of a germ tube of a conidiospore of the brown spot fungus, *Scirrhia acicola*, on a needle of Scotch pine and development in the stomatal antechamber as seen with the scanning electron microscope.

pine. This was one instance in forestry where control by protective chemical sprays proved feasible. Aerial sprays of copper fungicide on a large scale have been both effective and economical in controlling a disease that might otherwise have had disastrous consequences.

## Mistletoes

Mistletoes are true seed plants, perennial evergreens that are parasitic on stems or branches of trees or shrubs. The leafy, or so-called true mistletoes, are really semiparasites and are well known largely for their ornamental and sentimental uses at Christmas time. They occur chiefly on hardwoods, but some grow on a few conifer species, especially juniper, cypress, and incense cedar. They are most abundant in warmer regions and especially in the arid Southwest. In general, the true mistletoes have not caused major economic damage in forest stands of the United States.

The numerous *dwarf mistletoe* species, however, in the genus *Arceuthobium,* have come to be recognized as the single most important disease problem in conifer forests of the western United States, and damage ranks second to that caused by heartrot. Once remaining virgin stands are cut, losses from dwarf mistletoe effects are expected to exceed those from decay. Management of affected stands is a major silvicultural problem (10). In the East, especially in Minnesota, only one species occurs, causing problems in management of black spruce.

The parasitic growth of these tiny plants results in extreme growth reduction in the host—often the development in the crown of abnormal branch growths known as *witches' brooms,* dieback of the leader and branches, and eventual death of the tree. Local spread of the parasite in the stand occurs by forcible ejection of sticky seeds for distances of 12 meters or more. Isolated new infection centers may be established when seeds are carried by birds.

Management of affected stands to reduce losses is aimed largely toward direct control measures: physical removal of infected trees or their parts by pruning, poisoning, burning, or cutting. Treatments of sawtimber or pole-size stands are designed to incorporate dwarf mistletoe eradication with silvicultural practices with the objective of obtaining and retaining stands free of dwarf mistletoe after the harvest cutting. For some areas computer simulation programs have been developed that enable foresters to examine a number of alternatives for managing dwarf mistletoe-infected stands and help them decide on the best treatment to meet management objectives.

## INFLUENCES ON DISEASE OCCURRENCE AND DEVELOPMENT

The forest is a dynamic community of plants and animals interacting in a constantly changing environment. It follows a successional development governed by the interactions among all the living organisms and the site. Moreover, the site will also change with the successional development of the forest, as discussed in Chapter 6.

During the course of development of a forest there is also a succession of diseases. These may influence not only the early survival of individual trees but also the later development of the forest (11). This principle of dynamic interaction of the forest and its environment emphasizes a major concept relating to disease. A disease does not necessarily result from the mere juxtaposition of a *susceptible host* and a *virulent pathogen;* there also must be a *favorable environment.* Further, these must interact in relation to *time.* The disease triangle of host-pathogen-environment is given a three-dimensional aspect when these components are related to time to form a disease *pyramid* (12). This concept of the disease pyramid is well illustrated by the environmental influences on the white pine blister rust disease. The causal fungus, *Cronartium ribicola,* requires two different types of host plants for completion of its life cycle: the white pines and currants and gooseberries in the genus *Ribes.* Spores produced on leaves of ribes plants infect the pine through the needles, and the fungus grows into branches and stems where it forms girdling lesions or cankers (see Figure 8.6). The spores produced in the blisters that erupt from stem cankers cannot reinfect pines but can only infect the leaves of ribes plants, thus completing the cycle. The fungus is delicately adjusted to seasonal changes and weather conditions, so that unfavorable conditions at one period may prevent any significant number of new pine infections for that year. In general, moist growing seasons favor intensification and spread of blister rust, and dry seasons are unfavorable. The most critical periods are those influencing germination of the spores that infect pine and ribes. For formation and germination of basidiospores, which infect the pine needle, a period is required of at least 18 hours of high moisture conditions, either relative humidities above 96 percent or contact with a film of free water, and temperatures within reasonable limits, above freezing but below about 20°C (68°F). A period of hot, dry weather before this time also unfavorably affects development of the fungus on the ribes leaves, and chances for pine to escape infection are increased. One method of control has been to remove the alternate host from the vicinity of pines to protect the pines from infection. The protection zones for ribes eradication are based on the extreme susceptibility of basidiospores to drying and on evidence that infection of pines decreases rapidly as distance from ribes bushes, the source of the spores, increases. Knowledge of microclimatic relations of blister rust has made possible predictions of blister rust potential of various sites and delineation of infection hazard zones in the Great Lakes states. This information has made possible modifications of approaches to control of the disease by ribes eradication and by silvicultural procedures such as pruning of a portion of the lower crowns of crop trees. Pruning protects trees from infection in the high-hazard zone by removing needles likely to be infected within about 6 to 10 feet of the ground, where a great majority of infections occur on young trees. Thus, consideration of the interrelated components of disease helps the pathologist and the forest manager determine the major factors governing occurrence and development of a particular disease and develop an appropriate disease-management strategy that will minimize losses.

Our continuing efforts to make timber supply meet timber demand inevitably result in more intensive forest-management practices. More intensive forest management brings both dangers and benefits. Disease hazard may be greater through increased wounding of residual trees or from stumps in thinned stands serving as infection courts for root-rot fungi. On the other hand, in short-rotation management, salvage or disease-preventive measures may result in better protection and reduced losses. Silvicultural operations may change the interrelationships of the components of the disease pyramid so that the

probability of disease and consequent loss is either favored or lessened.

## DISEASE COMPLEXES

Reference was made earlier to the concept that the forest is a dynamic community in which organisms interact under influence of a constantly changing environment. Often the trees are affected by a number of stress factors acting in concert or in succession, so that it is sometimes difficult to assign priority to one more than another as a disease-producing agent. Thus diseases may result from action of joint causal agents. Also, the activity of, or the result of activity by, a specific causal agent may be so modified by environmental influences that disease initiation and development may or may not occur.

The *beech bark disease* is an example of a disease that has more than one causal agent. It is caused by fungi that infect minute feeding wounds made by scale insects in the bark of beech. The principal fungus is *Nectria coccinea* var. *faginata,* although other species of *Nectria* also may be involved. The fungus may infect large areas on the trunks of some trees, completely girdling and killing them, whereas on other trees narrow strips of bark are infected, parts of the crown become chlorotic and die, and the tree survives in a weakened state for many years. Little injury is caused by each organism attacking separately.

A different type of disease complex is illustrated by the *littleleaf disease* of shortleaf and loblolly pines in the southeastern states. In this disease chlorosis and decline of the crown, and eventually death of the tree, results from attack of the feeder rootlets by the fungus *Phytophthora cinnamomi*. But disease only develops in heavy and wet soils with poor aeration and low fertility. On such sites trees are of low vigor, and their poor root-regeneration potential following repeated attacks by the fungus prevents recuperation of the root system. As a result, intake of nutrients is hindered, and littleleaf disease follows. On good sites the fungus may be present and may even attack the rootlets, but lost rootlets are quickly replaced and little damage is sustained because of the higher tree vigor and different environmental conditions.

## DISEASE PROBLEMS IN FOREST NURSERIES

Seedlings are subject to a wide range of both noninfectious and infectious diseases. Little is known about diseases of seedlings under forest conditions, but seedling diseases in forest nurseries are known to cause extensive losses at all stages from seed in storage, through sowing, to outplanting. Nursery diseases also pose a threat to forests when infected seedlings are planted in forested areas where the pathogen has not previously existed. The most notorious example of this is the introduction of *white pine blister rust* into North America. Among the most important seedling diseases are the damping-off diseases, root rots, stem and foliage blights, and stem rusts (13).

*Damping-off* is the most important disease problem in nurseries and is one of the chief obstacles in raising coniferous seedlings, although a number of hardwood species are also susceptible. Damping-off is really a group of similar diseases caused by many fungi, but most commonly by species of *Pythium, Rhizoctonia, Fusarium,* and *Phytophthora.* Early attacks, or preemergence damping-off, may kill the seedling before it emerges from the soil. Postemergence infection generally occurs at or just below the groundline; stem tissues collapse and the seedling topples over. *Root rot* in either early or late stages of seedling development is another aspect of the disease, and seedlings may be killed but remain standing. Control is sometimes achieved by cultural practices, but chemical control either by application of seed-protectant fungicides or by soil fumigation is often necessary.

## MYCORRHIZAE

From the emphasis given in this chapter to pathogenic fungi as causal agents of diseases of forest trees, one might get the mistaken impression that all fungi are harmful. Fortunately this is not the case, and one major *beneficial* aspect of saprophytic fungi is their role in conversion of dead plant and animal remains to essential humus of the forest soil. Another important beneficial role of fungi is in the formation of *mycorrhizae* (14), a symbiotic association of mycelium of a fungus with the feeder roots of a higher plant in which a distinctive morphological structure develops.

Mycorrhizae result from infection of cortical cells of short roots by a fungal symbiont. A physiologically balanced reciprocal parasitism is established in a relationship that is mutually beneficial to the host and the fungal symbiont. So prevalent throughout the plant world is this association that nonmycorrhizal plants are proving to be the exception. Without mycorrhizae most plants, including our important forest and horticultural species, could not survive in the highly competitive biological communities in natural soil habitats.

Mycorrhizae benefit the host plant by increasing the solubility of soil minerals, improving uptake of mineral nutrients, facilitating movement of carbohydrates from one plant to another, and even by protecting feeder roots against infection by certain root pathogens. In turn, the host provides the fungal symbiont with carbohydrates, vitamins, and growth factors.

Mycorrhizal development is influenced by the previous history of the site. Most forest soils seem to have sufficient populations of mycorrhizal symbionts, but there are some sites devoid of mycorrhizae and on which trees will not grow until the soils have been inoculated with mycorrhizal fungi. Such sites include, for example, prairie-type soils, surface material left after strip mining, and the artificial "soils" often used for growing containerized seedlings. The great potential benefits of selection of specific symbionts for specific sites have stimulated much research toward developing inoculation techniques for use in growing seedlings with mycorrhizae adapted to selected sites or types of environments.

## PRINCIPLES OF FOREST-DISEASE MANAGEMENT

The "products" provided by the forest depend on the objectives of the managers and users of the land. The various objectives may be included under the broad concept of *multiple use*, which embraces use of forests for many purposes, including timber, wildlife, watershed protection, recreation, and others. On this basis the control of forest pests might be undertaken only when the activity of a pest can be shown to interfere significantly with the management objectives of the particular forest. The goal of forestry is to obtain optimum production from the forest, which means giving increasing attention to the efficiency of the management system. And the management of disease must become an increasingly used component of the broader field of forest management.

More and more we are substituting *"disease management"* for "disease control." Use of the term *management* conveys the concept of a continuous process and implies that diseases are inherent components of the forest ecosystem that must be dealt with on a continuing basis. The goal of disease management is reducing disease damage or loss to economically acceptable levels. Also, there is increasing emphasis on the concept of *integrated pest management*, whereby all aspects of a pest-host system are examined to provide the resource manager with an information base on which to make a decision, as discussed in Chapter 7.

Most methods for control of forest diseases are preventive in nature, instead of being concerned with cure of diseased individuals, and are directed toward protection of the future crop. Also, most forest-disease control is indirect in that it is effected through adjustments in forest-management practices. *Direct control* measures are those where efforts and expenditures are made specifically and solely for the control of a given disease; the activities are separate from normal silvicultural operations, such as the ribes eradication program that was formerly in effect for control of white pine blister rust.

With disease prevention being the most important principle in forest-disease control, most control strategies are *cultural measures* such as site and species selection, choice of proper rotation age, and employment of a variety of timber-stand improvement operations including thinning, burning, or pruning.

The ultimate objective of forest-disease management might be the development of predictive models for forest ecosystems (Chapter 6) through which the management decisions can be made that will give the maximum benefits to the producer, the consumer, and the public at large.

## REFERENCES

1. G. H. Hepting and E. B. Cowling, *Ann. Rev. Phytopathol., 12,* 431 (1977).
2. Anon., "The nation's renewable resources—an assessment, 1975," U.S.D.A. For. Serv., For. Resour. Rep. No. 21, 1977.
3. W. H. Smith, *Tree Pathology: A Short Introduction,* Academic Press, New York, 1970.
4. C. E. Seliskar, "Virus and viruslike disorders of forest trees," *In Documents, FAO/IUFRO Symposium on Internationally Dangerous Forest Diseases and Insects,* Vol. 1, Oxford, FAO, United Nations, 1964.
5. A. L. Shigo and W. E. Hillis, *Ann. Rev. Phytopathol., 11,* 197 (1973).
6. J. L. Ruehle, *Ann. Rev. Phytopathol., 11,* 99 (1973).
7. R. T. Bingham, R. J. Hoff, and G. I. McDonald, eds., "Biology of rust resistance in forest trees," *Proc. NATO-IUFRO Adv. Study Inst.,* U.S.D.A. For. Serv., Misc. Publ. No. 1221, 1972.
8. H. R. Powers, J. P. McClure, H. A. Knight, and G.

F. Dutrow, "Fusiform rust: Forest survey incidence data and financial impact in the South," U.S.D.A. For. Serv., Res. Pap. SE-127, 1975.

9. R. J. Dinus and R. A. Schmidt, eds., "Management of fusiform rust in southern pines," *Symposium Proceedings,* Univ. of Fla., Gainesville, 1977.

10. R. F. Scharpf and J. R. Parmenter, Jr., Tech. Coordinators, *Proc. of symposium on dwarf mistletoe control through forest management,* U.S.D.A. For. Serv., Pac. Southwest For. and Range Exp. Stn., Gen. Tech. Rep. PSW-31, 1978.

11. D. V. Baxter, "Development and succession of forest fungi and diseases in forest plantations," Univ. Mich., Sch. For. and Cons. Circ. No. 1., Univ. of Mich. Press, Ann Arbor, 1937.

12. J. G. Horsfall and E. B. Cowling, eds., *Plant Disease—An Advanced Treatise,* Vol. 1, "How disease is managed," Academic Press, New York, 1977.

13. G. W. Peterson and R. S. Smith, Jr., Tech. Coordinators, "Forest nursery diseases in the United States," U.S.D.A. For. Serv., Agric. Handbook No. 470, 1975.

14. E. Hacskaylo, ed., "Mycorrhizae," *Proc. First North American Conf. on Mycorrhizae,* U.S.D.A. For. Serv., Misc. Publ. No. 1189, 1971.

# PART 3

# FOREST MANAGEMENT

The forests compose one of the earth's greatest reservoirs of renewable natural resources. They can provide us with essential products indefinitely if managed properly and at the same time can remain a home for wildlife and a vital source of water supplies (Figure P3-1). However, the management of the forest for each of the many products, services, and benefits presents a complex problem. This section deals with the methods and practices by which the forest manager obtains these benefits from the forest without adversely affecting the environment. Chapter 9, "Silviculture," discusses the biological management of the forest for regulation of forest regeneration, species composition and growth. The external and internal variables important to forest-management decisions are then outlined in Chapter 11, "Multiple-Use Management of the Forest."

Management of forests for multiple use includes timber, recreation, wildlife, watersheds, and rangelands. The methods utilized in watershed, rangeland and timber management are discussed in Chapter 11 and specific procedures for assessment of the forest and timber resources are further described in Chapter 10, "Measurement of the Forest." Separate chapters are devoted to "Forest Recreation Management" and "Forest-Wildlife Interactions." Possible methods to integrate management decisions for protection of all of the natural resources provided by the forest are discussed in each of the chapters in this section. Extraction of timber from the forest does not necessarily create a harmful effect on other forest-derived benefits. A moderate-size clearcut, for example, gives additional wildlife habitat areas, and selective cutting in the forest creates areas more suitable for recreational activities. These and other methods for coordinated forest management are emphasized.

Although humans cause most forest fires today, fires have probably occurred in the forest as long as there have been lightning storms. The importance of fires in shaping the forest landscape is discussed in Chapter 15, "Behavior and Management of Forest Fires." The use of fire as a management tool (i.e., "prescribed burns") is also described in this chapter.

The viewpoint of forestry at the national level (Chapter 12) can be compared to that of the small, private, nonindustrial landowner (Chapter 13) in succeeding chapters. The effect of attitudes and policies at the national level on the management of private forests can be viewed and assessed. The private nonindustrial forests may hold the future for forest-derived benefits; almost 60 percent of commercial forestland is owned by the private nonindustrial sector.

Industrial forests comprise a small but significant (14 percent) share of the commercial timberland in the United States. These forests are mainly managed for timber and pulpwood production; thus the methods and practices described in this section demonstrate the options available for management of these private lands.

**Figure P3.1**   Our forests compose one of the earth's greatest
reservoirs of renewable resources and if properly managed can
provide us with essential products indefinitely and at the same
time remain a home for wildlife and a vital source of water
supplies. (Courtesy of U.S.D.A. Forest Service.)

# 9

# SILVICULTURE

# Craig G. Lorimer

Under strictly natural conditions, a forest is generally a self-perpetuating system that does not require management, even though cyclical changes may occur. Likewise, under certain conditions, even cutting operations may require little skill or planning to maintain a vigorous, productive forest. Historically, however, humans have attempted to favor those species having desirable commercial characteristics, and this has usually not proved to be an easy task. For example, harvesting operations frequently induce a major change in species composition that more often than not is considered to be undesirable. As early as 1863, Thoreau noted that pure stands of eastern white pine, which were the principal source of construction lumber at the time, were replaced by oak species after logging. Regeneration of white pine was found to be difficult even with human intervention, and the obvious solution of planting pine seedlings was rarely successful except on abandoned fields. Problems with regeneration and insect damage, along with the dwindling supply of mature trees, were enough to lead to a regional decline in the lumber industry in New England, and the industry began to migrate south and west.

Such problems in the regulation of forest regeneration, species composition, and growth fall within the realm of silviculture, a specialty within the field of forestry that deals with the biological aspects of forest management, subject to economic and environmental constraints. The purpose of silvicultural manipulation may be to enhance timber production, wildlife habitat, streamflow, or the aesthetic qualities of the forest. A broad definition of silviculture might therefore be stated as the manipulation of forest stands to accomplish a specified set of objectives.

It was not merely the desire to regenerate certain valuable species that spurred the study of silviculture in this country. During the late nineteenth and early twentieth century, unregulated clearcutting was occurring on an enormous scale throughout eastern North Amercia. Repeated fires often followed. Not only was there concern over how to regenerate many areas that seemed destined to be occupied by brush for several decades, but also there was the problem that cutting was proceeding at a much faster pace than the forests were growing back. If it had not been for the vast reserve of coniferous timber in the West, a shortage of construction lumber would have been probable. Even today, the results of this period of intensive exploitation are apparent in the vast expanses of 60−70-year-old stands that as yet contain relatively few large trees.

More recently, much effort in silviculture has been devoted to increasing the growth rates of forest stands. This has long been a concern of European foresters; in many cases considerable attention has been given to individual trees in a stand. In North America, the vastness of the forests and the relatively low value of individual trees traditionally rendered such an approach impractical on a large scale. But the increasing worldwide demand for forest products in recent decades has altered this situation. It is now the rule, rather than the exception, for forest industries routinely to conduct timber inventories of their holdings, classify the productivity of various sites, make estimates of future growth, and carry on silvicultural practices such as thinning of forest stands. The methods employed for conducting timber inventories and estimating future growth are discussed in the following chapter.

Silvicultural practices are frequently used strictly to enhance nontimber values. Prescribed burning, for example, may be used solely to improve wildlife habitat. Owners of small, private woodlands comprise a major class of landowners whose principal management goal is often recreation, aesthetics, or wildlife. Whatever silvicultural practices are applied to these lands may be designed to enhance their values with timber being produced occasionally as a secondary benefit.

## GROWTH AND DEVELOPMENT OF FOREST STANDS

In many cases silvicultural practices are intended to mimic natural processes in forest development, only in such a way as to hasten the final outcome. The lack of a natural counterpart to a specific management practice does not necessarily mean that it is environmentally unsound, but when in doubt, it is probably wise not to force a radical departure from natural processes. An understanding of the development of natural stands is therefore considered fundamental to the practice of silviculture.

## Even-Aged Stands

Major disturbances of human or natural origin tend to set in motion predictable patterns of forest growth and development. Sudden removal of the tree canopy by clearcutting or fire usually improves the chances of successful seedling establishment, and these sites are often quickly colonized or dominated by a new wave of tree seedlings. By the time these

trees have reached the age of 10 or 20 years, their crowns have usually expanded to the extent that a closed canopy of foliage has developed, creating the appearance and environment of a young forest. Forests of this type in which most canopy trees are approximately the same age are said to be *even-aged*. The existence of even-aged stands always indicates that the previous stand was removed over a fairly short period of time, regardless of whether the cause was a harvest cut or a natural disturbance. Ages of the canopy trees, however, will rarely be exactly the same except in plantations because initial seedling establishment often occurs over more than a decade. The actual range of ages is frequently 20 to 30 years in natural even-aged stands. When even-aged stands are young, the trees often appear remarkably similar in size (Figure 9.1*a*). Variation in tree size increases over time, however, and older

**Figure 9.1** Two even-aged hardwood stands showing the reduction in stem density and increase in average tree size over time due to the natural competitive process. (*a*) A dense 40- year-old stand of oak, birch, and maple. (Courtesy of Harvard Forest, Harvard University.) (*b*) A spacious 250-year-old stand of yellow birch.

even-aged stands usually display a wide range of tree size because of differences in growth rates among individual trees.

Even-aged stands are commonly classified by their stage of development, as reflected by the average size or age of the trees. As arranged by increasing size, these categories are *seedling, sapling, pole, mature,* and *overmature.* In most forest types, the transition between seedling and sapling is considered to occur at a height of about 1 meter (3 feet); the lower limit for a pole stand is generally about 10 centimeters (4 inches) in diameter. The size range of mature stands varies greatly according to species and location; in many temperate regions a stand would be considered mature if most of the trees are between 30 to 60 centimeters (12 to 24 inches) in diameter. Overmature stands, from a commercial point of view, are even-aged stands in which a large proportion of the trees are becoming senescent. Losses from mortality often exceed additions in volume from growth, and a sizable proportion of the total wood volume may show signs of decay and other defects. In managed forests, final harvest cuts are generally carried out many years prior to this stage. The age of the stand at which a harvest is planned is known as the *rotation age.*

As individual trees in a young even-aged stand become larger and older, competition becomes more severe. A young stand may have thousands of small trees on 1 hectare (2.47 acres) of land, but at stand maturity there will be space only for a few hundred trees on the same area. As a result of competition, crowns of the slower-growing trees become increasingly crowded and may finally be overtopped completely by adjacent, faster-growing trees. The stands therefore tend to show a limited amount of vertical stratification, and individual trees in even-aged stands are often classified by their relative position in the canopy. These *crown classes* (Figure 9.2) are defined as follows:

*Dominant.* Trees that project somewhat above the general level of the canopy, having crowns that receive direct sunlight from above and partly from the side.

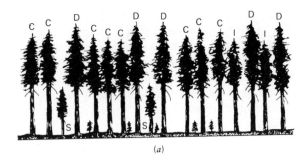

(a)

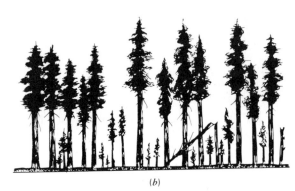

(b)

**Figure 9.2** Diagrammatic profiles of an even-aged and an uneven-aged forest stand. (a) Young even-aged stand shortly after crown closure, showing the various crown classes. D = dominant, CD = codominant, I = intermediate, S = suppressed. (b) Mature uneven-aged stand. Note the irregular profile and small openings.

*Codominant.* Canopy trees of average size that receive direct sunlight from above but relatively little from the sides.

*Intermediate.* Trees with crowns extending into the canopy layer, but crowded on all sides so that only the top of the crown receives direct sunlight.

*Suppressed.* Trees with crowns completely overtopped by surrounding trees so that they receive no direct sunlight except from occasional "sunflecks" that penetrate small gaps in the foliage above.

Once a tree has become suppressed, its chance of regaining a dominant position in the stand is relatively low, and the probability of imminent death is greatly increased. High mortality rates of trees in the lower crown classes result in a progressive decrease in the number of trees per unit area until the stand matures. In 40 years the number of trees may be reduced by 50 to 60 percent or more. This natural decrease in numbers of trees in even-aged stands because of competition is known as the *self-thinning* process. Older stands tend to be more open and spacious as a result of the natural self-thinning process.

From these principles it follows that a small tree growing beneath the main canopy may not always be younger than the larger trees above it. Also, the crown class of many trees will be subject to progressive change. Most suppressed trees in even-aged stands were once in a dominant position, and trees in the intermediate crown class are almost certain to become suppressed in the near future if the stand is still growing rapidly.

## Uneven-Aged Stands

Unless some catastrophe intervenes, even-aged stands tend to give way gradually to *uneven-aged* stands in which three or more age classes are intermixed. Understories of shrubs and tree seedlings begin to develop in even-aged stands usually by the time the pole stage is reached. Understory development accelerates as the stand matures, and when canopy trees become senescent and begin to die singly or in groups, the resulting gaps in the canopy are filled by the saplings and seedlings in the understory. The wide range of age in uneven-aged stands is because of the fact that germination of understory trees and filling of gaps may occur over a long period of time. In contrast to even-aged stands, the suppressed trees in uneven-aged stands are often younger than the larger overstory trees, and some of them may eventually attain canopy status. Differences in the structure and appearance of even-aged and uneven-aged stands are shown diagramatically in Figure 9.2, and actual examples are shown in Figures 9.1 and 9.10.

## Pure versus Mixed Stands

Under natural conditions, trees may occur in nearly pure stands of a single species or in mixtures. Pure stands on productive sites are often even-aged, having developed following some natural catastrophe such as intense fire. Examples are the extensive, nearly pure stands of Douglas-fir or lodgepole pine that often spring up following extensive wildfires. When pure stands are established artificially by planting, they are sometimes referred to as *monocultures.*

The relative merits of pure versus mixed stands have long been a subject of controversy. Those who favor pure stands stress the administrative ease in managing pure stands as well as lower costs of cultural treatments and harvesting. If a site is planted with the most valuable species suited to local conditions, the value of the plantation will often exceed that of a stand containing a mixture of various species. On the other hand, mixed-species forests may be more aesthetically pleasing and may have a greater carrying capacity for wildlife (see Chapter 16). There is good evidence that mixed stands are usually more resistant to insect and disease outbreaks than pure stands. Nevertheless, it is difficult to make valid generalizations, and exceptions can be found. For example, mixed stands of spruce and balsam fir are more susceptible to budworm attack than pure stands of spruce, and mixed conifer-hardwood forests are more susceptible to fire than pure stands of most hardwood species. Clearly the characteristics of the individual species in each case determine the relative susceptibility (1).

## REGULATION OF SPECIES COMPOSITION AND GROWTH

In the early years of American forest management, most forest stands received little or no treatment between the time of establishment and the time of harvest. But the benefits of such manipulation in terms of improved species composition, growth rate, and wood quality can potentially be great. Silvicultural treatments applied between the time of establishment and the time of harvest are called *intermediate treatments*. Objectives of intermediate treatments may include: (1) favoring certain species over others, (2) regulating spacing and stand density, (3) removing poorly formed or diseased trees, (4) improving the wood quality of the remaining trees by pruning branches, (5) salvaging dead or dying trees, and (6) fertilizing the soil to increase growth rates.

Several types of intermediate treatments are designed to regulate species composition and growth rates. *Release cuttings* are performed in young sapling or seedling stands of desired species and remove larger trees of competing species that have suppressed the crop trees or are likely to do so in the near future. If the undesirable species are vigorous sprouters, cutting alone may not be sufficient, and the use of herbicides may be necessary. Release cuttings are often necessary in young coniferous stands that are intermixed with aggressive hardwood species. *Improvement cuts,* on the other hand, are generally understood to apply only to stands of at least pole size and include the removal of trees that are diseased or poorly formed, in addition to the removal of trees of undesirable species. Improvement cuts are especially important in stands that have had a long history of "high-grading"—the selective removal of only the best-quality trees.

Stand density is regulated primarily by *thinning* (Figure 9.3). The purpose of thinning is to reduce the stand density so that the growth of the remaining trees is accelerated. Thinning does not usually increase the total amount of wood produced by a forest; in fact the amount usually remains about the same. But since the available light, water, and nutrients are being used by fewer trees, the remaining trees become larger than they otherwise would have been. This is the principal benefit of thinning, for large trees are more valuable than an equal volume of small trees. At the same time, less vigorous trees that would probably die anyway from competition can be salvaged for usable material. The eventual result of thinning is a more open, spacious stand of larger trees. Thus thinning basi-

cally hastens the natural outcome of competition in forest stands and is a good example of how some silvicultural techniques have natural counterparts.

Several different methods of thinning are possible, but it is useful to recognize three basic approaches. In *low thinning* or "thinning from below," the trees to be cut are mostly from the lower crown classes. If most of the trees removed in a low thinning are suppressed or intermediate, much material may be salvaged, but the remaining trees will not necessarily show a substantial increase in growth. For if the gaps created in the canopy are few and small in size, there is little opportunity for the dominants and codominants to expand their crowns, which is important for increased growth. Thus it is often advisable to remove some codominant trees in a low thinning. In *high thinning,* or "thinning from above," the creation of significant gaps in the canopy by the removal of trees in the upper crown classes is a major objective, and somewhat less attention is given to removing suppressed trees. In *mechanical thinning,* all trees are removed in rows or strips without regard to crown class. The greatest response therefore comes from trees whose crowns are adjacent to the cleared strip. This method is relatively quick and inexpensive and can be easily done in plantations by mechanical tree fellers. In plantations, mechanical thinning is often accomplished simply by removing every third row of trees.

Although a single thinning will usually increase growth rates and upgrade the overall stand quality, such improvements are likely to be short-lived, since continued growth and competition will again render the stand crowded, usually within a decade or two. For this reason, intensively managed stands are usually thinned at periodic intervals such as once every 10 years. The first thinning can be done even before crown closure of the stand, although the first thinning is often delayed until the trees are pole-sized and the logs removed in thinning are marketable as pulpwood or fuelwood.

Thinning can also be a valuable management tool for forests in which recreation or wildlife is the principal goal. Young even-aged stands are often

**Figure 9.3** A stand of longleaf pine in Florida after a pulpwood thinning that removed 30 percent of the original volume, leaving 650 trees per hectare. (Courtesy of U.S.D.A. Forest Service.)

unattractive for both people and wildlife because of the extremely high density of stems, poor visibility, profusion of dead lower limbs, and paucity of undergrowth. A moderately heavy thinning can immediately improve the appearance and wildlife habitat of such stands. Private landowners who value their forests primarily for recreation or wildlife are often understandably reluctant to have any cutting done on their property, but judicious light thinning can actually hasten the development of a

forest of large stately trees, such as shown in Figure 9.1*b*.

A common method of increasing growth rate that does not involve cutting trees is *fertilization* of the soil. Fertilization is apt to be most successful in areas where the soils are known to contain specific nutrient deficiencies. In North America, for example, nitrogen deficiencies are common in the Douglas-fir region and in boreal spruce-fir forests. Standard fertilizer applications may result in 20 to

100 percent increases in growth rate. But a decision to fertilize should be weighed carefully. Fertilizers are energy-expensive to produce and some of the raw materials are in limited supply. The use of fertilizers for food crops will generally be of higher priority than the application to forest stands (2). Furthermore, some forest types show little or no response to fertilization (3, 4).

## PREDICTION OF FOREST GROWTH

Accurate prediction of forest growth has always been one of the major goals of foresters. A reasonable plan of forest management usually requires some estimate of the rate of growth on each site in order to determine how much timber can be cut each year and to estimate the magnitude of response to silvicultural treatments. In the past, growth predictions were obtained by compiling average timber volume statistics for a wide variety of stand ages and sites, and the results were then made available in the form of tables showing the expected timber yields for major species (see Chapter 10). However, this approach had severe limitations. It was generally only feasible to construct yield tables for "pure" even-aged stands of a single species, simply because it would be difficult or impossible to obtain an adequate sample of the staggering number of possible combinations of species, ages, and sites that would occur for mixed-species stands. Thus owners of mixed forests often had no published guidelines for the amount of expected growth. Furthermore, most yield tables predict growth only for unmanaged stands with no history of thinning or other silvicultural treatments. The amount of data that would be required to take into account the wide variety of management options was also too prohibitive to be incorporated into yield tables.

So the modern method of growth prediction has required a radically different approach. The rationale is that if we have sufficient information on the process of tree growth, competition, and mortality, then we can construct an abstract *model* of the forest that can imitate the development of actual forest stands. The term *forest-growth model* is used to signify that our representation of forest development on paper is a simplification of reality, just as a test-model aircraft is a simplified physical representation of a complex machine.

The first step in constructing a forest-growth model is usually to define the basic variables and interactions that are believed to exist. For example, we know that the growth rate of a tree depends on its age or current size, as well as on the inherent productivity of the site and competition induced by neighboring trees. Such a relationship can be expressed by a "word equation" as follows:

$$\text{growth} = f(\text{age, site quality, competition})$$

where $f$ indicates that growth is a function of the variables in parentheses. Such an expression illustrates the important point that biological processes can generally be approximated by equations, which form the heart of most forest-growth models. Equations are frequently superior to our intuitive understandings of forest growth because they can be used systematically to obtain predictions when, as is usually the case in nature, the interactions among variables are exceedingly complex. Of course, the preceding equation does not show how the variables interact and therefore cannot be used to obtain predictions. An example of an actual diameter-growth model with these variables (5) is

$$\Delta D = b_1 + b_2 D + b_3 S + b_4 1/(1+C) - b_5 C$$

This equation states that diameter growth of a tree ($\Delta D$) is proportional to its current diameter ($D$) and site productivity ($S$). In other words, growth rates will be highest for large trees on good sites. Growth is also shown to be inversely proportional to the degree of competition ($C$), so that growth rate decreases as competition increases. In this model competitive stress ($C$) is determined by the size and number of competing trees. The final negative term ensures that at high levels of competition, growth starts to decrease at a linear rate and will drop to 0 at some threshold of severe competition. The $b$'s in this equation are not variables but numerical constants whose values are estimated by standard statistical procedures. Once these have been determined, all we need to know are the tree diameters, site productivity rating, and the size and number of competing trees in order to predict the diameter growth.

How accurate are these forest models? Recent studies have shown that very good predictions of forest growth and future yields are possible. Figure 9.4 for example, shows close agreement between the predicted and observed basal-area growth of a forest that had received periodic light harvest cuts over a span of 26 years. This particular model demonstrated that good predictions were possible for mixed-species stands regardless of the relative proportions of species, the history of silvicultural treatments, and the age structure of the forest. Such a

model therefore provides the forest manager with a powerful tool: instead of having to wait 30 years to see the results of a thinning or harvest cut, a forester can test a variety of options and predict the outcome in a matter of minutes.

It should be emphasized that much of the accuracy of forest-growth models depends on the success of statistical calibration procedures, by which the unknown numerical constants in the equations are adjusted until the equations predict the growth already observed on sample plots as closely as possible. Growth modeling is not an exact science because growth does not "obey" simple natural laws. Therefore, the observed growth on sample plots is used initially to calibrate the model, and subsequently the model can be used to predict growth on other sites for which no growth data are available.

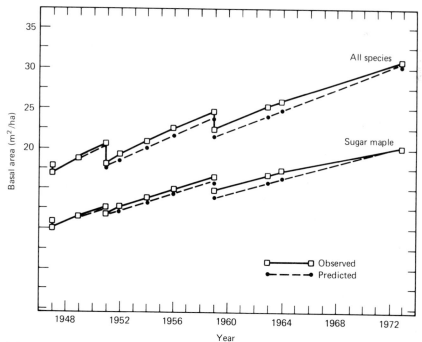

**Figure 9.4** Gradual changes in the basal area of this mixed-species hardwood forest due to growth and timber harvest have been accurately predicted by a growth model called FOREST. The long-term increase in basal area is because of net growth in this even-aged stand. The sharp decreases in 1951 and 1959 reflect light timber harvests in those years (10). (Courtesy of R.A. Monserud.)

# REGENERATION OF FOREST STANDS

In proper forest management, stands are never harvested without careful consideration of how adequate and desirable regeneration can be obtained. Two approaches to *harvest cutting* are to be avoided. The *first* is the temptation to make a "partial cutting" in which most of the high-quality trees are removed and the malformed or defective trees are left to repopulate the stand. Such a practice, commonly called "high-grading," may result in deterioration of the stand, especially when several such cuts are made over a long period of time. Small woodlot owners are sometimes the unwitting victims of high-grading by local logging contractors. The best insurance against such an event is to have a forester develop a management plan for the tract and mark the trees to be cut in each operation with paint, making sure to specify in the contract that only marked trees can be removed by the logging company.

The *second* situation to avoid is any harvest operation that is done without regard to the biological requirements for germination and growth of seedlings of the species to be favored. For example, the inability of aspen to tolerate shade would make any light, partial cutting pointless if aspen is to be maintained. Paper birch also requires full sunlight for adequate survival and growth, but in addition requires exposed soil for good seedling establishment. Therefore clearcutting in itself would be no guarantee of adequate regeneration.

Following a harvest cut, the forester can either accomplish regeneration by artificial means, such as planting, or rely on natural regeneration processes. Clearly the choice will be largely determined by biological requirements of the species in question.

## Natural Regeneration

In some areas of the world, natural regeneration after cutting is very dependable. One source of natural regeneration, of course, is seeds carried by wind or animals into the cut area from adjacent standing trees. But careful observations will often reveal that many of the seedlings present on a recently cut area were already present under the forest stand prior to harvest and are in effect unobtrusive survivors of the harvest operation. Such seedlings or saplings are referred to collectively as *advance regeneration* (see Figure 9.10). In addition, many hardwood species sprout from the stump after cutting, and such sprouts constitute an important source of regeneration in hardwood forests (Figure 9.5). A few species of trees may regenerate from seeds stored in the litter.

Even in regions where natural regeneration of some type is not ordinarily problematical, regeneration of a particular species may be difficult. The success of attempts to favor a single species varies tremendously for the following reasons:

1. Adequate seed production in some species may occur almost every year and in other species only at long or irregular intervals. Good seed crops of red pine, for example, occur only once in seven years on the average. For this reason natural regeneration of red pine is unpredictable and planting is ordinarily recommended.

2. Seedling germination and survival is greatly influenced by the weather in some species. As a result, inadequate regeneration may occur even in years of good seed production.

3. The *microclimate* of the stand must be favorable if good regeneration is to occur. Some species require open, sunny conditions for germination, while seedlings of other species require partial shade and may be killed by high soil temperatures.

4. The condition of the ground surface or *seedbed* is of prime importance. The forest floor under most stands is covered with a thick mat of leaves and partially decomposed organic matter or *duff*. Seedling germination and survival may be adequate when the duff is kept

**Figure 9.5** Dense regeneration from aspen sprouts one year after clearcutting, northern Wisconsin.

shaded and moist. When exposed to the sun as after a heavy cutting, however, duff dries out readily and becomes a formidable barrier to seedling establishment. In such cases removal of the duff by burning or mechanical scarification may be necessary (Figure 9.6). Since this procedure also kills most of the advance regeneration, reliance must then be placed on seed dissemination or planting.

5. If the advance regeneration, shrub layer, and sprout layer are dense, as they often are, they may largely or entirely preclude the establishment of other, perhaps more desirable species.

6. Seed and seedling predators are sometimes partly or largely responsible for regeneration failures. Insect larvae may infest the seeds before or after they have fallen from the tree (Figure 9.7), and mammals such as mice and deer can cause almost complete mortality of

established seedlings. This has been convincingly demonstrated in areas fenced or screened to exclude mammals.

### Artificial Regeneration

Although natural regeneration is often a dependable means of stand establishment, artificial regeneration may be preferable in certain situations, especially those involving highly intensive management of forests harvested at short intervals. Artificial regeneration can be accomplished either by directly applying seeds to a harvested site or by planting nursery-grown seedlings. Planting gives the forester greater control over stand establishment and growth than artificial dispersal of seeds, but both methods have the following advantages over natural regeneration:

1. Stand establishment may be more reliable because it does not depend on the occurrence of a good seed year or the distance to which

**Figure 9.6** Mechanical site preparation reduces competition from advance regeneration and shrubs and provides a more favorable seedbed for natural seedling establishment. This scene shows site preparation for regeneration of western larch in Montana. Logging slash is pushed into piles and burned. (Courtesy of U.S.D.A. Forest Service.)

seeds are dispersed by wind. If large clearcuts are made, artificial regeneration is often necessary to ensure adequate regeneration on the central portion.

2. Artificial regeneration increases the chances of prompt reforestation.

3. The timing of artificial regeneration can be planned to coincide with favorable weather conditions and to avoid drought.

4. There is greater control over species composition. It permits the option of growing pure stands or stands of nonnative or uncommon species in areas where the expected result of natural regeneration would be highly mixed stands of lower value species.

5. There is greater control over tree spacing and subsequent growth. Plantations are often established in rows at a predetermined spacing

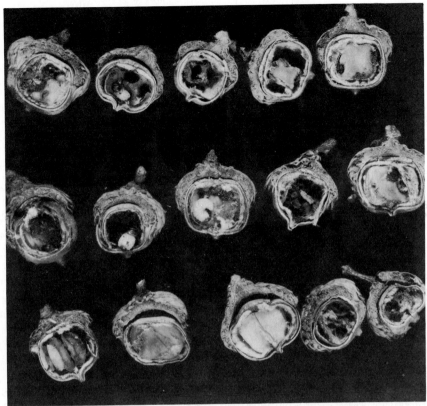

**Figure 9.7** These acorns were damaged by weevils; such insect damage is one of the factors responsible for the scarcity of oak advance regeneration in much of eastern North America. An undamaged acorn is shown for comparison (lower row, center). (Photograph by R.L. Giese.)

to optimize stand growth, reduce variability in growth rates, and allow easier access for mechanized equipment.

6. Seeds or seedlings can be derived from genetically superior trees.

**Direct Seeding.** Artificial dispersal of tree seed is known as *direct seeding*. It may be accomplished on the ground by hand or machine, or from the air by helicopter or fixed-wing aircraft. Direct seeding is usually cheaper than planting, but it offers less control over spacing and usually has a lower success rate. As a minimal precaution, seeds may be treated with chemical repellents to reduce pilferage by rodents and birds. Germination and survival of seedlings tend to be considerably better on sites with some exposed mineral soil than on sites with a thick covering of litter or logging debris. Maximum success with direct seeding is probably achieved by sowing seeds on the ground in such a way that seeds are covered with soil.

Despite its limitations, direct seeding from the air can be very useful when extensive areas must be reforested quickly, as would be the case following a large forest fire. Direct seeding is also useful on steep, irregular terrain where planting by machine would be impossible and hand planting would be difficult.

**Planting.** The fairly high survival rate of planted seedlings and the convenience of managing row plantations has led to a great increase in plantation establishment in recent years, particularly among paper companies. Planting is often done in the spring season when soil moisture is high and root growth is most active, but it is possible at other times depending on the geographic location. Mechanized planting is becoming more and more common, although hand planting is still done in many cases.

Despite the higher success rate of plantations compared to direct seeding, failures and losses sometimes do occur. Mice and other rodents may cause the loss of many seedlings, especially in grassy areas, and browsing by deer and other large herbivores can be a problem. Planted seedlings may face stiff competition from shrubs and stump sprouts of other trees, which may necessitate prior site preparation and perhaps application of herbicides. Furthermore, harsh microclimates on some sites may lead to planting failures, particularly on steep slopes facing south.

Planting often represents a sizable proportion of the total cash investment in a forest stand. The cost of the seedlings reflects the expense of nursery establishment and maintenance. The planting operation itself is a fairly labor-intensive operation, and to this must be added the costs of site preparation and other measures taken to enhance planting success.

### Production of Seedlings in Nurseries.

In nursery operations, seeds are usually sown in rows at a predetermined spacing. After the seedlings have grown in the beds for the desired length of time, they are carefully lifted from the bed (usually by machine) and the soil shaken loose. They are then sorted, graded according to quality, vigor, and age, and packaged in a bare-root condition.

The packaging of bare-root seedlings has traditionally been the most common and inexpensive method, but in recent years the use of *containerized seedlings* has greatly increased in popularity. Containerized seedlings are usually grown in individual tubes containing a specially prepared potting medium instead of soil and are often grown in large greenhouses with a capacity of many thousands of seedlings (see Figure 5.6). They may be planted with or without the container. Container seedlings are more expensive to grow than bare-root stock, but root systems are less likely to be damaged during the lifting and transporting process, and better survival of planted seedlings results in some cases.

## Silvicultural Systems

From the preceding sections it should be evident that the conditions necessary for regeneration of a species, and not merely economics, are often what dictate the method and intensity of harvest cutting. Certain methods of harvesting to achieve adequate regeneration have found favor in silvicultural practice. Although they have become stylized in concept, they can be adapted to the requirements of each species. These *silvicultural systems* are long-range harvest and management schemes designed to optimize the growth, regeneration, and administrative management of particular forest types, usually with the goal of obtaining a perpetual and steady supply of timber. The total forest property is then said to be managed on a *sustained-yield* basis.

The use of silvicultural systems involves making a comprehensive prescription of stand treatments throughout the life of the stand, including the method of harvest, an evaluation of whether or not site preparation is necessary, the use of seeding, planting, or natural regeneration, and a schedule of intermediate stand treatments. Silvicultural systems are generally classified by the method used to harvest and regenerate the stand. These methods vary in cutting intensity but they may readily be grouped under the categories of even-aged or uneven-aged methods.

### Even-Aged Methods.

In even-aged management the trees are removed over a relatively short period of time, creating open, sunny conditions, and leading to the development of even-aged stands.

Many species can be managed by even-aged methods, and for certain species intolerant of shade the even-aged methods may be almost mandatory, since adequate regeneration would not occur under lightly cut stands. The even-aged methods are *clearcutting, seed tree,* and *shelterwood*. Only in the clearcutting method are all trees removed at once. In the other methods, trees are removed over a longer period of time.

Regeneration by the *clearcutting* method is accomplished by natural seeding, direct seeding, or planting. If reliance is placed on natural seeding, the effective dispersal distance of seeds may limit the width of the clearcut. Even with light-seeded species such as western larch and the spruces, most of the seeds fall within three or four tree heights of the windward edge of the clearcut, and the amount of seeds that fall 300 to 400 meters (1000–1300 feet) from the stand margin may be too small for adequate regeneration. Direct seeding or planting, of course, can remove these size restrictions. Nevertheless, large clearcuts will probably be less common in the future than in the past because of their unfavorable aesthetic impact, the limited value of large clearcuts to many wildlife species, and possible erosion hazards. Political opposition has also limited clearcutting practices, as discussed in Chapter 1.

Other even-aged methods are designed to overcome some of the problems inherent in the clearcutting method. In the *seed-tree* method, scattered mature trees are left on the site to serve as a seed source for the new stand and to provide a more uniform disperal of seed. Although this may seem like a good solution to the problem of seed dispersal, experience has shown that the seed-tree method may be unsuccessful in many situations. The most serious difficulty is that the presence of seed trees frequently does not result in adequate numbers of seedlings becoming established, especially in the absence of site preparation and on sites susceptible to rapid invasion by shrubs. In some cases, as with the eastern oaks, whatever seedlings do become established may not be sufficiently vigorous to compete with advance regeneration and sprouts of other species. Second, the seed-tree method does not work well with shallow-rooted species, since many of the seed trees will be blown down by wind. The seed-tree method is best suited to situations in which intensive site preparation is feasible and the species are reasonably wind-firm. Western larch and the southern pines are examples of species well suited to the seed-tree method.

The *shelterwood* method not only provides for seed trees, but also leaves sufficient numbers of trees standing to provide some shade and protection for new seedlings (Figure 9.8). Once the seedlings are firmly established, usually after several years, the residual trees are then cut so that they do not suppress the growth of the new stand. The shelterwood method is ideally suited for species that are intermediate in shade tolerance. Even some of the more intolerant species may benefit from the protection of a shelterwood overstory during the first few years of seedling establishment when seedlings are particularly vulnerable to dessication; this is particularly true on harsh sites. The shelterwood method also has the least visual impact of any even-aged method, since by the time the last of the residual overstory trees are removed, the new stand is already sapling-sized. It therefore bypasses the typically devastated look of recent clearcuts. In many situations it probably reduces the erosion hazard as well.

The *coppice* method differs from all other reproduction methods in that dependence is placed on vegetative regeneration by stump sprouts instead of development of stands from seed. However, since coppice stands are usually harvested by clearcutting, it may be conveniently discussed with other evenaged methods. The coppice method is restricted to species that typically sprout vigorously and have sprouts capable of attaining commercial size. Good examples of such species are aspen (Figure 9.5) and oak. Coppice stands are usually managed on short rotations, and the products may be fuelwood or pulpwood. The use of the coppice method has declined in recent decades because of the decreasing use of wood as fuel, but the energy crisis may

**Figure 9.8** On drier sites, the shelterwood system often results in better natural regeneration than clearcutting. This example shows a shelterwood cut in old-growth Douglas-fir, western Oregon. (Courtesy of U.S.D.A. Forest Service.)

stimulate a revival of its use. Forest plantations for energy are further discussed in Chapter 19.

In all forms of even-aged management, sustained yield is achieved by successively cutting parts of the total property holding at regular intervals, so that when the cycle is completed, trees on the first tract in the sequence are old enough to be cut again. For example, if trees are being grown on a 100-year cycle or *rotation*, we could divide the property into 100 units and cut a different one each year. Or the tract could be divided into 20 units and a cut made every 5 years (Figure 9.9). Such a scheme provides a convenient starting point for management, although biological and economic uncertainties often demand that managers be much more flexible than

this. A further discussion of the development of forest-management schemes is given in Chapter 11.

**Uneven-Aged Methods.** Uneven-aged management is accomplished by the *selection method*, in which scattered trees or small groups of trees are cut. This diffuse pattern of timber removal ensures that all ages of trees will be intermixed (Figure 9.10). The selection method has some unique advantages. There is usually no need for expensive site preparation or planting. Regeneration tends to be reliable and more or less automatic, for new trees are simply recruited from the reservoir of saplings in the forest understory. Selection cutting is the only silvicultural system in which sustained yield can be

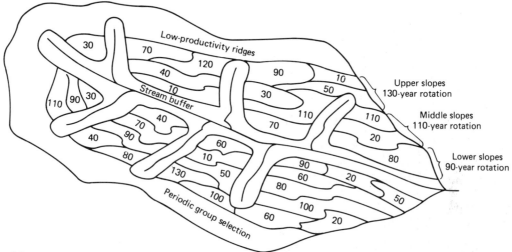

**Figure 9.9** Compartment map of a hypothetical watershed managed by the clearcutting system for sustained yield of timber. The number of each compartment indicates the order and year in which it is harvested. Every 10 years three compartments are cut, one each at lower, middle, and upper elevations. Cuts are made in irregular strips parallel to the contour to minimize erosion and optimize wildlife habitat. A permanent buffer strip is left around streams to protect water quality. The ridgetop lands are of marginal productivity and are managed by periodic group selection cuts. The most productive lower slopes are managed on shorter rotations than the middle and upper slopes.

obtained from a single stand of trees. Provided that cutting is not too intense, trees can be harvested in perpetuity, while the forest canopy remains largely intact with little evidence of manipulation. Erosion and disturbance to the site are minimal. Fire hazard is relatively low because of the lack of extensive piles of logging debris. For these reasons it is highly attractive to owners of small woodlots or managers of multiple-use recreation areas.

Associated with the benefits of selection cutting are some limitations. Generally only the most shade-tolerant species will prosper under such a scheme. The opening created by the removal of a single mature tree usually does not allow enough light for adequate survival and growth of intolerant or intermediate species. The list of such species is considerable and includes most of the pines, larches, oaks, birches, and aspens (see Table 6.1). Light selection cutting in stands of these species will not only fail to regenerate the species in most cases, but will actually tend to hasten the conversion to what-

ever tolerant species happen to be in the understory. Therefore the selection system is most appropriate for tolerant species such as the maples, hemlocks, cedars, spruces, and true firs. The lack of sizable openings may also be unfavorable for certain species of wildlife, including some of the popular game species. A disadvantage that is more or less inherent in the method and difficult to avoid is the injury to some of the standing trees that may occur during felling and hauling operations.

Some of the disadvantages of the selection system can be lessened by modification of the method of harvest. By cutting small groups of trees instead of scattered individuals, the amount of direct sunlight can be increased to the point where some regeneration of intolerant species can occur. This *group selection* method will also improve wildlife habitat for many game species, while still retaining the more or less closed-canopy appearance of the forest as a whole (Figure 9.11). In many cases the problems that might result from the use of the

**225**

**Figure 9.10** With the individual tree selection method of harvest, disturbance is often hardly noticeable, as in this uneven-aged forest of spruce along the coast of Maine. Note the dense advance regeneration of the same species.

individual-tree selection method by small landowners can be circumvented by partial or complete substitution by the group selection method.

**Choice of Even-Aged or Uneven-Aged Management.** The choice between growing trees in even-aged or uneven-aged stands will ordinarily depend on particular management goals and constraints. Many small landowners might consider the tendency for selection cutting to favor shade-tolerant species a trivial concern, especially when measured against the numerous advantages of the selection

system. For forest industries, conversion to tolerant species in some cases could be a serious problem. Most of the reasons are related to the comparative economics of the two management schemes.

The costs of site preparation and planting avoided by using the selection system must be weighed against differences in the market values of the species and their growth rates. There is not always a correlation between the shade tolerance of a species and its commercial value (Table 9.1), but many of the species in high demand for pulp or lumber products are intolerant and not well suited to the selection system. The economic gap is widened by the fact that most shade-tolerant species are inherently slow-growing. Some of the valuable shade-tolerant species do not acquire moderate value until the trees reach a size large enough for lumber or veneer, which entails a commitment to long rotations. There are exceptions to these generalizations. For example, the tolerant spruces of the Northeast are more valuable for pulp, despite their slow growth, than the intolerant, fast-growing paper birch.

Logistics and logging costs must also be considered. Clearcutting is administratively easier than other methods when large areas are involved, and this is undoubtedly a major reason for its popularity among industrial firms. In logging heavy stands of old timber in the Pacific Northwest, which entails the use of expensive cable systems (see Chapter 11), selection cutting may not always be economically feasible. However, in other forest types, selection cutting is not necessarily more expensive or less time-efficient—an objection frequently leveled against the system—when costs are expressed per unit of timber volume harvested (6, 9).

In the final analysis, each case must be considered individually. But there may be no need to decide exclusively on one system. A sizable landholding could easily accommodate even-aged and uneven-aged management involving several different silvicultural systems. It is also probable that most intolerant species could successfully be managed by small patch cuts of one hectare (2.5 acres) or less, a

**Figure 9.11** Group selection cuts near a major road on national forestland. (Courtesy of U.S.D.A. Forest Service.)

management strategy that falls between the realms of group selection and regular clearcutting.

## ENVIRONMENTAL IMPACTS OF SILVICULTURAL PRACTICES

Many people envision a "natural" forest environment as one consisting of an unbroken canopy of trees with a rich and diverse understory of shrubs and herbs. The contrast with a recently harvested area can be striking, especially after clearcutting. The general public may consider clearcutting and other even-aged harvesting methods to be the exploi-

tive use of a resource in the same manner as strip-mining. Concern will often be expressed over the possibility of accelerated soil erosion, site degradation, and loss of wildlife habitat. It is therefore important for the forest manager to be well informed on such issues and to be prepared to arrive at balanced, impartial conclusions. Well-informed opinion is possible only after review of careful experiments designed to measure the environmental effects of silvicultural practices.

### Soil Erosion

Many early small-scale experiments suggested that a necessary condition for soil erosion is the exposure

227

**Table 9.1**
Silvicultural Information for Some Major Forest Types of the United States

| Forest Type | Tolerance (Major Species) | Successional Status | Growth Rate | Current Commercial Value | Methods of Regeneration | Ease of Regeneration |
|---|---|---|---|---|---|---|
| **Western** | | | | | | |
| Douglas-fir | Inter | Variable (site-dependent) | Rapid | High | C, SH (SP,P) | M |
| Hemlock/Sitka spruce | Tol | Climax | Mod-rapid | High | SH, GS, S, C | E |
| Coast redwood | Tol | Climax | Rapid | High | GS,C,SH,S | E |
| Ponderosa pine | Intol | Variable | Mod | Mod-high | SH,GS,S,ST,C (SP,P) | M-D |
| Western larch | Intol | Successional | Rapid | Mod | ST,C,SH(SP) | E-M |
| Engelmann spruce/fir | Tol | Climax | Slow-mod | Mod | GS,S,SH,C | M |
| Lodgepole pine | Intol | Successional | Mod | Low | C,SH | E |
| **Eastern** | | | | | | |
| Spruce/fir | Tol | Climax | Slow-mod | Mod | GS,S,SH,C | E-M |
| White pine | Inter | Successional | Rapid | Mod | SH,GS | M |
| Jack pine | Intol | Successional | Rapid | Mod | C,ST,SH(SP) | M |
| Red pine | Intol | Successional | Rapid | Mod | C,SH(SP,P) | D(Nat), M(Art) |
| Northern hardwoods | Tol | Climax | Slow | Mod | S,GS,SH | E |
| Aspen/birch | Intol | Successional | Rapid | Low-mod | C(SP) | E |
| Oak/hickory | Inter-intol | Uncertain | Rapid | Mod-high | C,GS,SH | M-D |
| Southern pines | Intol | Successional | Rapid | High | C,ST,GS(SP,P) | M |

*Principal Sources.* "Silvicultural systems for the major forest types in the U.S.," Agr. Handbook 445. U.S. D.A. For. Serv., 1973; R. B. Phelps, "The demand and price situation for forest products," U.S. D.A. For. Serv., Misc. Publ. 1357, 1977; and R. D. Forbes and A. B. Meyer, *Forestry Handbook*, Ronald Press, New York, 1955.

*Abbreviations.*
Tolerance: Tol = tolerant, inter = intermediate, intol = intolerant.
Methods of Regeneration: C = clearcutting, SH = shelterwood, ST = seed tree, GS = group selection, S = individual tree selection; (SP, P) = site preparation and planting may be necessary.
Ease of Regeneration: E = easy, M = moderate, D = difficult.

**Figure 9.12** Experimental clearcuts on which erosion levels have been monitored for a number of years. (*a*) In a North Carolina clearcut, erosion over a 15-year period was not appreciably higher than in uncut areas. (*b*) In a western Oregon clearcut, located on inherently unstable slopes, erosion was about three times normal levels. Logging roads were not constructed in either case. (Courtesy of U.S.D.A. Forest Service.)

of bare soil to the impact of rain. This finding has interesting implications for forest management. What would happen if trees are cut and no soil is exposed? The experimental clearcuts shown in Figure 9.12 were designed partly to answer this question. In both cases, the boundaries of the clearcut conform to natural watershed boundaries, so that streamwater draining the clearcut area can be monitored at the stream outlet (see Chapter 6). In the North Carolina watershed shown in Figure 9.12*a* all the trees were cut and left where they fell. No roads were constructed and no timber was removed. Negligible increases in soil erosion occurred, even though the brush was mowed annually for 15 years (11). These results are typical of many regions and indicate that protection of the soil by leaf litter and ground vegetation is usually sufficient to prevent erosion on most sites. Some exceptions can be expected on steep slopes and in areas of unstable soils. Thus, a similar experiment in Oregon shown in Figure 9.12*b* resulted in erosion rates about three times the normal rate of undisturbed watersheds, although the actual magnitude of the increase was still small (12).

Most timber-harvest operations, however, require the construction of roads, and roads often represent a significant area of bare soil susceptible to erosion. In the early stages of logging the litter may be scraped away and bare soil exposed as logs are dragged or "skidded" to a central loading deck (see Figure 4.5). Even the selection methods of harvesting result in the development of skid trails. Roads are also required, of course, for transportation of logs out of the forest by trucks. Erosion may occur from water running along the surface of the road or skid trail, from steep surfaces of the road "cut" and "fill" areas, and from the slumping of slopes into streams where the slope has been weakened by a road cut. In most parts of the country, proper road design can keep soil loss to very low levels. In the more erosion-prone areas, such as the Pacific Northwest, the risk can be greatly reduced by using logging methods that minimize the occurrence of skid trails. With balloon and skyline logging (see Chapter 11), logs can be transported to a loading deck without dragging along the ground. Restricting the intensity, frequency, and extent of cutting is also recommended on unstable sites.

## Nutrient Loss

The generally minor impact of timber harvests on erosion rates does not entirely rule out the possibility of site deterioration. Another problem to consider is the loss of mineral nutrients from the site. Typical harvesting operations remove certain quantities of nutrients from the site that are contained in the logs and other usable woody material. These nutrients are not lost permanently from the site because they are gradually replaced by natural sources such as precipitation and the weathering of rock. As long as the rotations are reasonably long, no net loss will occur. But in recent years there has been a trend toward shorter rotations—for example, 20 years or less in the South—and this clearly accelerates the rate of nutrient withdrawals. In some regions nutrient loss is not merely confined to whatever is removed in the form of wood products. Experimental cuttings in New Hampshire have shown that substantial amounts of nutrients can be leached from the site and flushed into streams, because of accelerated decomposition of organic matter and the subsequent release of stored nutrients (see Chapter 6) (13). Furthermore, the practice of whole-tree harvesting, in which even the branches and leaves are utilized (Figure 9.13), can be expected to increase nutrient loss. The added impact of whole-tree harvesting is more than what a simple tally of additional harvested material might suggest, because branches have higher concentrations of nutrients than stemwood (14).

It is not certain, however, if even whole-tree harvesting on 20- or 30-year rotations will necessarily lead to a decline in fertility, partly due to uncertainties over how much of the total soil nutrient reserves are available to plants. Certainly the amount of nutrients stored in plant biomass is small compared to the total quantity stored in the soil, but additional research will be necessary to resolve questions about the impact of short rotation forestry. It also appears that major nutrient losses from leaching may not be common outside the northern

hardwoods region of the Northeast (15). Some specialists feel that, in general, whole-tree harvesting and regular clearcutting are not likely to cause major problems in soil fertility (15, 16), but others foresee such problems with intensive, short-rotation forestry (13, 14, 17).

## Use of Chemicals

Silvicultural practices do not necessarily depend on the use of chemicals, but herbicides and chemical fertilizers are frequently used in certain situations. Of the two, herbicides are probably of greater importance to silvicultural practice because many conifer species are difficult to regenerate if there is substantial competition from hardwoods and shrubs. Recent concerns about environmental hazards from the use of these chemicals have prompted evaluations of possible harmful effects.

The greatest demonstrated impact of both herbicides and fertilizers is probably on water quality. A few species of fish and other aquatic animals have low tolerance levels to herbicide applications, and concentrations as low as 1 to 10 parts per million can cause high mortality (18). Nitrogen and phosphorous fertilizers can stimulate algal growth in streams and lakes, which in turn reduces the oxygen supply to aquatic animals. However, monitoring of watersheds after typical herbicide and fertilizer applications has shown that concentrations of these chemicals are generally well within safe limits, provided that care is taken to prevent direct application of the chemicals to bodies of water. For example, peak concentrations of herbicides in streams flowing through treated areas seldom exceed 0.1 parts per million, and concentrations rapidly decline over time (19).

Tolerance levels of mammals to herbicides are much higher than those of fish, and the common herbicides persist for a very short time in the bodies of mammals. High rates of ingestion are unlikely because natural breakdown of herbicides occurs rapidly. Thus typical herbicide applications are be-

**Figure 9.13** Mechanized whole-tree harvesting. (Courtesy of U.S.D.A. Forest Service.)

lieved to have little effect on wildlife populations. However, much concern has arisen over possible hazards to human health of two herbicides (2,4,5-T and Silvex) that contain trace amounts of a highly toxic contaminant known as dioxin. In 1979 the Environmental Protection Agency issued an emergency suspension order prohibiting the use of these herbicides based on evidence of a statistically higher rate of miscarriages of women living in an area where the use of 2,4,5-T was common. Further

investigations will be necessary before a final ruling is made.

## Aesthetic Considerations

Silvicultural treatments can be designed to harmonize well with landscape features, but unfortunately this has not been common historically. Stark geometric shapes were often used in the past for western clearcuts. This has understandably caused adverse public reaction, and the tendency of some foresters to appear unconcerned about landscape aesthetics has only compounded the problem. It may be true that once a clearcut site has become reoccupied by dense green vegetation, it ceases to be objectionable to many people. But when a clearcut is being made somewhere in the area every few years, this argument will not necessarily cause objections to subside.

What is needed is a more imaginative approach to silviculture and a willingness to search for acceptable alternatives to clearcut-and-burn prescriptions. Coupled with this must be a recognition that the visual quality of a forest landscape is in itself a resource that can and should be managed. In recent years fruitful collaborations between foresters and landscape architects have been made in developing principles and guidelines for landscape management on national forests. When a management plan is made for an administrative unit of national forest-land, visual considerations are incorporated directly into the plan. The plan may identify certain zones in which aesthetics will be given major consideration. These zones may lie along major roads, near recreation areas or campsites, or in highly scenic areas. Selection cutting may be feasible in many of these areas. If even-aged management is desired, the shelterwood method is often a highly acceptable substitute for clearcutting. In cases where clearcutting is necessary, many techniques can soften the blow to the visual appearance of the area. Narrow cuts with curved contours can be shaped to blend in with natural terrain, and islands of uncut vegetation can be left to break up the view and add visual diversity. Logging debris can be lopped and scattered on the clearcut so that the waste is not as visible and will decay more quickly.

## Natural Precedents for Harvest Methods

It was previously pointed out that thinning imitates the natural process of mortality that occurs in all even-aged stands. Can natural precedents likewise be found for harvest cutting? If this is the case, it clearly has bearing on whether or not silvicultural systems create an unacceptable environmental strain on forest ecosystems.

It is easy to find natural precedents for the selection method in the death of mature trees from old age or disease. It might seem more difficult to find natural precedents to the seemingly drastic methods of harvest such as clearcutting or seed-tree cutting. Yet the evidence of natural counterparts to heavy cutting could hardly be more convincing. Land surveyors traveling through extensive tracts of primeval forest in the mid-1800s often reported large windfalls in which all the trees had been blown down in a tangled mass. In Maine, for example, one group of surveyors laying out a township line reported that "half of the first six miles was of the very worst kind of windfalls, so very bad that we couldn't get more than a mile into Vaughanstown." Storms in recent times have caused similar damage. Large tracts were blown down on the Olympic Peninsula in Washington in a storm of 1921, and the 1938 hurricane in central New England caused heavy damage over 243,000 hectares (600,000 acres). In 1977 strong winds generated by a thunderstorm cut a 300-kilometer (160 mile) swath through the forests of northern Wisconsin (Figure 9.14). The extensive forest devastation (230 sq. miles) caused by the eruption of Mt. Saint Helens in Washington is another timely example (see Figure P3.3). In certain regions insect epidemics and lightning-caused forest fires periodically destroy forest canopies over thousands of hectares (see Chapter 15).

The philosophical issue is therefore not whether clearcutting is "unnatural," but whether or not natural catastrophes are so common that most stands would be even-aged anyway in the absence of humans.

In the early part of the century, when the theory of forest succession was being developed, much emphasis was placed on the classification and study of climax forests. Although these pioneer workers were clearly aware of the occurrence of natural disturbances, it appears that catastrophes were

**Figure 9.14** Aftermath of a 1977 windstorm in an old-growth forest in Wisconsin. Strong downdrafts from a summer thunderstorm reached windspeeds of up to 157 miles per hour (290 kilometers per hour) and caused damage on 850,000 acres (340,000 hectares).

viewed as rare or aberrant events. Yet subsequent workers, in the process of studying remnants of primeval forest, often found them to be even-aged with evidence of catastrophic disturbance in the past (20, 21), and for this reason much skepticism developed as to the validity of the climax concept. This viewpoint was well expressed by Cline and Spurr (20) in 1942:

> *The primeval forests, then, did not consist of stagnant stands of immense trees stretching with little change in composition over vast areas. Large trees were common, it is true, and limited areas did support climax stands, but the majority of the stands undoubtedly were in a state of flux resulting from the dynamic action of wind, fire, and other forces of nature.*

In writing of the forests of northern Minnesota, one investigator has carried this conclusion a step further and considers the local climax type to be "largely unknown to science" (22). For any such forest region the implication is clear: of the various harvesting methods used, the types of heavy cutting used in even-aged management would most closely mimic the predominant process of tree mortality that occurs in nature.

Nevertheless, the existence of relatively stable climax forests is not easily disputed in some forest types. The early government land surveys show that prior to settlement, early successional species comprised only a small proportion of the forest in many parts of eastern North America (23–25). Studies of primeval forest remnants of shade-tolerant species have revealed them to be uneven-aged more often than not (26–28). In fact, some evidence suggests that natural catastrophes may indeed be infrequent in some regions (23, 29).

## A Management Overview

It seems reasonable to conclude that natural parallels can be found for virtually every silvicultural system. Selection cutting imitates the death of scattered individual trees from old age or disease. Parallels to shelterwood and seed-tree cutting are found in stands partially damaged by wind. The effect of clearcutting is not unlike that of the occasional natural catastrophe. Clearcutting will generally have the highest environmental impact of the four systems and selection cutting the least, but in many regions the impact of clearcutting itself appears to be small provided that it is not done repeatedly on the same site at short intervals. It also has certain benefits such as the perpetuation of intolerant tree species and the creation of favorable wildlife habitat for certain species. For these reasons clearcutting cannot be categorically condemned. It is possible that some optimal level of environmental quality can be achieved by a diversity of management systems that create a landscape with a variety of forest types and age classes. Such a mosaic appears to provide near-optimal habitat for many wildlife species (30), and quite possibly was the condition of the North American forest when Europeans arrived.

## REFERENCES

1. D. M. Smith, *The Practice of Silviculture,* Seventh Edition, John Wiley & Sons, New York, 1962.

2. D. M. Smith and E. W. Johnson, *J. For.*, *75*, 208 (1977).

3. D. S. DeBell, "Fertilize western hemlock—yes or no?" In *Global Forestry and the Western Role*, Western Forestry and Conservation Assoc., Portland, Oreg., 1975.

4. D. M. Stone, "Fertilizing and thinning northern hardwoods in the Lake States," U.S.D.A. For. Serv., Res. Pap. NC-141, 1977.

5. G. L. Martin, "A dynamic network analysis of silvicultural alternatives for red pine," Ph.D. thesis, University of Wisconsin–Madison, 1978.

6. S. M. Filip, "Harvesting costs and returns under 4 cutting methods in mature beech-birch-maple stands in New England," U.S. D.A. For. Serv., Res. Pap. NE-87, 1967.

7. Anon., "Silvicultural systems for the major forest types of the United States," *Agr. Handbook 445*, U.S. D.A. For. Serv., 1973.

7a. R. D. Forbes and A. B. Meyer, *Forestry Handbook*, Ronald Press, New York, 1955.

8. R. B. Phelps, "The demand and price situation for forest products," U.S. D.A. For. Serv., Misc. Publ. 1357, 1977.

9. R. D. Nyland, et al., "Logging and its effects in northern hardwoods," Appl. For. Res. Inst., Res. Rept. 31, College Envir. Sci. and Forestry, State Univ. New York, 1976.

10. R. A. Monserud, "Methodology for simulating Wisconsin northern hardwood stand dynamics," Ph.D. thesis, University of Wisconsin–Madison, 1975.

11. J. N. Kochenderfer, "Erosion control on logging roads in the Appalachians," U.S. D.A. For. Serv., Res. Pap. NE-158, 1970.

12. R. L. Fredriksen, "Erosion and sedimentation following road construction and timber harvest on unstable soils in three small western Oregon watersheds," U.S. D.A. For. Serv., Res. Pap. PNW-104, 1970.

13. G. E. Likens, F. H. Bormann, R. S. Pierce, and W. A. Reiners, *Science, 199,* 492 (1978).

14. J. P. Kimmins, *For. Ecol. and Management, 1,* 169 (1977).

15. E. Stone, "The impact of timber harvest on soils and water," In Report of the President's Advisory Panel on Timber and the Environment, Washington, 1973, pp. 427–467.

16. J. R. Boyle, J. J. Phillips, and A. R. Ek, *J. For., 71,* 760 (1973).

17. J. B. Waide and W. T. Swank, "Simulation of potential effects of forest utilization on the nitrogen cycle in different southeastern ecosystems," In *Watershed Research in Eastern North America*, Smithsonian Institution, 1977.

18. Anon., "Vegetation management with herbicides in the Eastern Region," Final environmental statement, U.S. D.A. For. Serv., 1978.

19. W. L. Pritchett, *Properties and Management of Forest Soils*, John Wiley & Sons, New York, 1979.

20. A. C. Cline and S. H. Spurr, "The virgin upland forest of central New England," *Harvard Forest Bull.,* 21 (1942).

21. D. K. Maissurow, *J. For. 33,* 373 (1935).

22. M. L. Heinselman, "The natural role of fire in northern conifer forests," In *Fire in the Northern Environment: A Symposium*, U.S. D.A. For. Serv., Pacific Northwest Forest and Range Exper. Sta., Portland, Oregon, 1971.

23. C. G. Lorimer, *Ecol., 58,* 139 (1977).

24. H. J. Lutz, *J. For., 28,* 1098 (1930).

25. R. P. McIntosh, *Amer. Midl. Natur., 68,* 409 (1962).

26. F. C. Gates and G. E. Nichols, *J. For., 28,* 395 (1930).

27. W. B. Leak, *Ecol., 56,* 1451 (1975).

28. C. H. Tubbs, *J. For., 75,* 22 (1977).

29. F. H. Bormann and G. E. Likens, *Pattern and Process in a Forested Ecosystem*, Springer-Verlag, New York, 1979.

30. R. C. Biesterfeldt and S. G. Boyce, *J. For., 76,* 342 (1978).

# 10

# MEASUREMENT OF THE FOREST

# Alan R. Ek

The multiple uses of forests for such things as timber, wildlife, recreation, and water and the large size of many forest tracts have led to a wide range of resource-assessment practices. For example, the forest-products industry has always had a need for estimates of potential yields of solid wood products and fiber from the forests. There is also a growing need for assessment of forest-stand conditions such as tree density and site quality as the basis for allocation of silvicultural treatments, as described in Chapter 9. In urban areas, tree vigor, removal, and replacement are key factors in management decisions. These various interests provide a need for surveys with a decision orientation; that is, the information that is collected forms the basis for determination of the best courses of action.

Surveys with both a *decision-making* and an *analytical* emphasis are becoming more common. The analytical emphasis has evolved from increased interest in the many individual characteristics of forests and how they relate to a wide range of end uses. Forestry has always been involved with long-range planning, but only in the last several decades has each of the multiple uses of forests been considered explicitly in surveys.

The intent of this chapter is to describe essential concepts in the design of forest resource-assessment efforts and to illustrate common forest-measurement practices. The major emphasis is on the timber resource, but the concepts are applicable to almost any resource characteristic of interest.

## FOREST GROWTH AND CHANGE ESTIMATION

The forests of North America and particularly those of Europe have been surveyed a number of times. Repeated surveys are especially efficient for determining the growth of the forest and the direction of the successional changes in terms of cover types, stand conditions, and other forest characteristics. Repeated forest surveys also allow us to assess the effectiveness of past management. Such surveys are the basis for regulating forests over long time periods—a basic aspect of forestry.

Repeated surveys frequently rely on permanent field plot observations—that is, observations on well-monumented plots. The plots are usually remeasured at intervals of 5 to 10 years. At each visit, the diameters and heights of the live trees originally measured are reassessed. Dead trees (mortality) among those originally measured, plus new stems arising through regeneration (ingrowth stems) are also noted. In most cases, ingrowth is defined as stems growing into the smallest measured size class. Such plot records also provide the necessary data base for developing *computer-based models* to make projections of future forest growth and yields.

Elaborate inventories and related growth-projection models have become common elements of contemporary forest practice. For policy and public-agency budgeting questions, regional surveys are frequently designed to estimate the forest area, product volumes, and associated stand conditions over large areas. The forest growth-projection models facilitate the projection of these variables for several to many decades ahead. The computer-projection models are further used to estimate what the forest will look like in the future under varying forms of management. In some detailed models, lists of individual trees on plots comprising the inventory are updated by projecting future tree diameters, the probable mortality, and sometimes the number and kind of ingrowth trees that may arise over time. Examples of such models are described in a number of recent publications (1, 1a, 1b). Usual predictor variables, which will be subsequently described, are present *tree size, crown condition class, site index* and some measure of individual tree or average stand competition. *Basal area per hectare* is frequently used to express the degree of crowding or competition. Simpler models that increment aggregate stand descriptors such as *basal area* and *volume* instead of individual tree dimensions are also used frequently (2). Planning horizons in forestry with such models are typically in the range of 30 to 100 years duration. These growth models are also augmented by models that attempt to predict future changes in forestland area and the amount of cutting or harvesting that may take place. In some cases they may be used to assess insect and disease impacts, as described in Chapter 7, for example.

This discussion should indicate that there may be many inventories going on at any one time. The details and objectives of these surveys, however, do vary. The major types we should distinguish are: periodic *national forest surveys* primarily for public policy questions, *state inventories* designed for managing state or county lands more effectively, *company or agency organized local inventories* designed to aid management at the operational level by identifying quantity and location of timber, and *timber appraisal* for product or land sales.

## SAMPLING AND MEASUREMENT CONCEPTS

Basic to forestry practice are the concepts of *sampling* and *measurement*. A forest tract may be considered as simply a population of trees. Frequently, however, the tract size or the number of trees is so large that a complete census or count of all trees and their characteristics is impractical. Consequently, foresters have come to rely on techniques for drawing samples of trees from the population—samples that are representative of the population. The samples are then the basis for making inferences about the population. As an example, a survey designed to estimate the total pulpwood volume on a 600-hectare tract might be based on only 200 representative 0.1-hectare sample plots. In most cases such a sample can provide a very accurate estimate of pulpwood volume for the entire tract. The techniques for drawing representative samples and constructing estimates from them are based on statistical sampling theory.

Distinct from the selection of the sample is the practice of measurement applied to the sample. For example, on the sample plots noted above, each tree

might be felled and its volume carefully measured directly. Alternatively, tree heights and diameters can be measured for indirect estimation of volume with a tree *volume table* (see Table 10.1) (3). The latter alternative is a faster and less expensive approach to determining tree volumes; however, it also introduces additional sampling error or variation because the volume table is only an approximation. Use of volume tables is a common practice because the time saved allows for a larger number of plots to be visited, which in turn reduces the variability of estimates of population characteristics. The area of forestry that considers the determination of tree and forest-stand product yields and their relation to forest-stand characteristics is called *forest mensuration* (4, 5).

Sampling and mensurational theory and practice provide the framework for forest-resource survey design. The forester chooses from among many sampling unit sizes (field-plot size), sample selection procedures, measurement tools, and formulas for developing estimates of population characteristics from those observed in the sample. The actual choices in any problem depend in part on what information is available prior to the survey. Common prior information includes maps and aerial photography of the forest stand, experience with field logistics, and the estimated costs and gains of the various alternatives.

### Land Survey

Basic to survey design is an understanding of land-survey systems and units of measure. In one sense, forests are but transient attributes of the land base. Much of the land subdivision in the world is based on the *metes and bounds* system. With this system, property lines and corners are based on physical features such as streams, ridges, fences, and roads. Locating such legal boundaries is often difficult (an understatement), especially when descriptions are vague, corners that were monumented have been obliterated or lost, and lines such as streams have

**Table10-1**

Portion of a Table for Approximating the Merchantable Volume of Commercial Species in the Great Lakes states. (As an example of usage, a tree of measured diameter of 30 centimeters at breast height and a total height of 25 meters would have an estimated usable volume of 0.718 cubic meters.)

| Diameter at Breast Height (cm) | Total Height (m) | | | | | |
|---|---|---|---|---|---|---|
| | 10 | 15 | 20 | 25 | 30 | 35 |
| | Volume (m³)[a] | | | | | |
| 10 | 0.021 | 0.024 | | | | |
| 20 | 0.126 | 0.186 | 0.247 | 0.311 | | |
| 30 | 0.292 | 0.429 | 0.570 | 0.718 | 0.853 | |
| 40 | 0.524 | 0.767 | 1.017 | 1.281 | 1.523 | |
| 50 | | 1.200 | 1.592 | 2.005 | 2.384 | 2.783 |
| 60 | | 1.728 | 2.294 | 2.887 | 3.436 | 4.010 |

*Source.* Adapted from S. R. Gevorkiantz and L. P. Olsen, "Composite volume tables for timber and their application in the Lake States," U.S.D.A. For. Serv., Tech. Bull. No. 1104, 1955.

[a] Inside bark volume from 0.3 m stump height to limit of merchantability; that is, to a point on the stem where the diameter inside bark is not less than 8 cm.

moved over time. In 1784 the United States adopted a *rectangular survey system* that applies roughly from the state of Ohio westward (including Florida, but not Kentucky, Tennessee, and Georgia) (6, 7).

The rectangular survey system uses carefully established baselines and meridians as references for land location. Numerous such lines were established as land acquisition and development progressed westward in the United States (see Figure 1.2). The baselines run from east to west and the meridians run north to south. The starting point for land surveys is the intersection of the *baselines* and the *meridians,* called the *initial point.* Figure 10.1 indicates how land is then described by this system. Progressing from the initial point, square *townships* are laid out north and south of the baseline. Township locations east and west of the meridian are designated by *ranges.* An example of the numbering of the townships, also originating at the initial point, is T3N, R2W, which delineates the area of Township 3 North, Range 2 West (Figure 10.1) (6, 7).

Townships are nominally 9.66 kilometers square (6 square miles) containing 9324 hectares (23,040 acres) and are divided into 36 sections nominally 1.61 kilometers square containing 259

hectares (640 acres). These sections are in turn divided into quarter-sections of 67.75 hectares (160 acres), which are further divided into four sections of 16.19 hectares (40 acres). The latter are referred to as "forties," often written as ¼ − ¼ (quarter − quarter) sections.

Problems arise in the measuring of townships as a result of the earth's curvature. The meridians, following the curvature of the earth, will converge to the north; the closer to the north pole, the greater the convergence. Hence, the northern boundary of a township will be less than the theoretical 9.66 kilometers. Measurement of a township begins in the southeast corner, with progression to the north along one row of forties at a time. This will cause an accumulation of error in the most northern and western tiers of forties. To minimize this error in area measurement, *correction lines* are established 38.62 kilometers (24 miles) north and south of the baseline and east and west of the meridian. This prevents a continuation of this error in subsequent townships. In addition to boundary lines, detailed measurements are also required on specific tree and stand characteristics for comprehensive forest inventories.

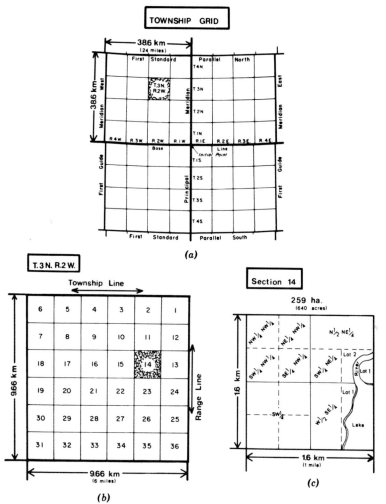

**Figure 10.1** Generalized diagram of the rectangular survey system. (*a*) Township grid showing initial point, baseline, principal meridian, standard parallels and guide meridians, and examples of township and range designations. (*b*) Subdivision of township into sections and the system of numbering sections from 1 to 36. (*c*) Subdivision of a section into quarter sections and forties. (Adapted from the Bureau of Land Management, U.S. Department of Interior.)

## Units of Measure (Forest Stands)

Forests and the individual trees that comprise them are measured for numerous purposes and in a variety of ways. *Height, diameter,* and *age* measurements of trees on plots can characterize the forest in terms of *current volumes, potential productivity* or for *refined management practices.* Regardless of the final objectives, the basic techniques and units of measurement remain the same.

**Tree Diameter (dbh).** The diameter of a tree is commonly measured at breast height and denoted as dbh. Breast height is 1.3 meters or 4.5 feet above the average ground level on the uphill side of the tree. Several instruments are available for measuring tree diameters such as the *caliper* (Figure 10.2) and a *steel tape*. Rough tree-diameter measurements are obtained with a *Biltmore stick,* a solid stick with a graduated scale based on the geometric principle of similar triangles. The stick is held horizontally against the tree at arm's length (63.5 centimeters or 25 inches) with one edge of the stick along one edge of the tree. The diameter is then "sighted" directly on the stick (see Figure 10.14). This method is accurate to within about one-half inch. Tree diameters are frequently used to determine tree *basal area*.

**Basal Area.** Basal area as applied to tree measurement is the area in square meters (square

**Figure 10.2** Measurement of tree diameter at breast height (dbh) with a caliper.

feet) of the cross section of a tree at breast height. Basal area per hectare (acre) is the sum total of the individual tree basal areas and is a frequently used measure of *stand density*.

Tree basal area in square meters is obtained from the formula for the area of a circle or a tree cross section expressed as

$$A = \pi r^2 \text{ or } \pi(dbh)^2/4 \text{ or } 0.7854(dbh)^2$$

Computations in the field are unnecessary because available tables give basal areas for each diameter class.

Basal area per hectare varies with species, timber type, and age. Recommended residual stocking levels for pole and sawtimber stands in the Great Lakes states, for example, may run from 15 to 28 square meters per hectare. Unmanaged forests may possibly run up to 70 square meters, particularly in dense pine stands. With some western species, the basal area per hectare may possibly run over 115 square meters (8).

Basal area in a sapling stand is naturally low but increases rapidly through the small-pole stage and then gradually levels off as a stand reaches 30 to 50 years. The culmination of mean annual basal area growth in red pine, for instance, occurs at about age 25. In a young red pine stand the annual basal area growth may be 1.5 to 1.6 square meters or more per hectare, but as the stand becomes older the annual basal area growth levels off at about 0.5 to 0.7 square meters. Thus, basal area is a more stable measure of stand density in older stands (30 years and older) than it is in vigorously growing immature stands (8).

It has been shown that height growth in general is not greatly affected by stand density. It has also been determined in recent years that there is not as strong a relationship as originally supposed between basal area and site. The main reason for the differences in volume on good sites as against poor sites is height. For many practical purposes, therefore, one can assume that basal area varies little with site except at the extremes (8).

**Tree Height.** There are a number of different methods for obtaining tree heights. For small trees the heights can be measured directly with graduated poles. A variety of single, folding, and telescopic *height poles* are available to suit particular conditions of measurement. The height poles are best suited to trees with branches that allow the poles to pass readily between them but give the poles lateral support. Usually this method is too cumbersome for trees greater than 20 meters in height (9), and this method is mainly restricted to detailed study plots.

The heights of trees are usually measured with instruments called *hypsometers*. Many types of hypsometers have been devised over the years, but all are based on geometric principles involving similar triangles or on trigonometric principles (4, 5). The latter requires knowledge of the distance from the observer to a tree and a device for reading the angles from the horizontal up to the top of the tree and from the horizontal down to the base of the tree. Figure 10.3 illustrates the two basic approaches to tree height measurement based on (a) trigonometric and (b) geometric principles.

Total tree heights are frequently measured (together with diameter at breast height, or dbh) as a basis for estimating tree-product content. Such heights are also used to determine site productivity and age relationships (see "site index" following). *Tree ages* in the temperate region are determined by using an increment borer to extract a core of wood where annual rings of wood increment are counted (Figure 10.4). In temperate regions, with few exceptions, each annual ring corresponds to a year of growth.

When assessment interests are primarily for market-appraisal purposes, merchantable or usable heights instead of total heights are sometimes measured (Figure 10.5). Determination of *merchantable height* involves measuring the height from a usable stump elevation, usually about 0.3 meters above ground, to a point on the bole above which the stem is too small in diameter or too irregular to be used.

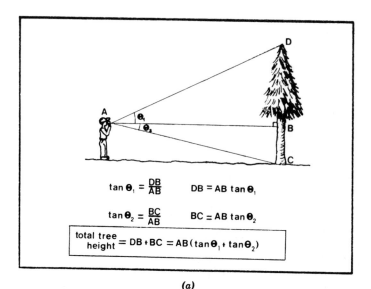

$$\tan \Theta_1 = \frac{DB}{AB} \qquad DB = AB \tan \Theta_1$$

$$\tan \Theta_2 = \frac{BC}{AB} \qquad BC = AB \tan \Theta_2$$

$$\text{total tree height} = DB + BC = AB(\tan \Theta_1 + \tan \Theta_2)$$

*(a)*

**Figure 10.3 *a*** Three measurements are required to determine the total height of the tree using *trigonometric* principles: the angle $\Theta_1$ from horizontal to the top of the tree, the angle $\Theta_2$ from horizontal to the base of the tree, and the horizontal distance *AB* from the observer to the tree.

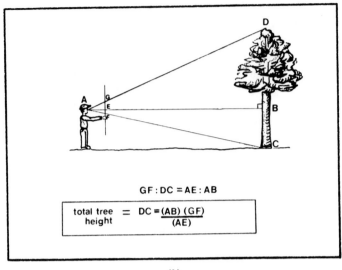

$$GF : DC = AE : AB$$

$$\text{total tree height} = DC = \frac{(AB)\,(GF)}{(AE)}$$

*(b)*

**Figure 10.3 *b*** Measurement of total tree height using *geometric* principles: ratios of distances are constructed using the principle of similar triangles.

Table 10.1 illustrates the use of height measurements. The table uses total height together with diameter at breast height and a specified usable top diameter to estimate the usable stem contents. Similar tables are also available but with product content expressed in terms of merchantable height instead of total height (10). Merchantable heights are generally

**Figure 10.4** Tree-age determination with an increment borer.

expressed in terms of log lengths or in units of log lengths; for example, 15 meters (three 5-meter logs) or simply three logs. The top diameter or merchantable limit of a tree depends on the product involved. In the case of pulpwood, merchantable trees are frequently those from 12 centimeters dbh to a top diameter inside the bark of 7 to 10 centimeters.

After the usable volume has been determined from diameter (breast height) and height measurements, it is usually expressed in terms of cubic meters. Tree volumes, whether of pulpwood, sawlog, or veneer log size, may all be expressed in cubic meters.[1]

Methods other than field measurement of diameters and heights for estimating product volumes also exist. An *optical dendrometer* is sometimes used to

[1]Board-foot units from the English system of measurement are still in use. A board foot is a piece of lumber 1 foot by 1 foot by 1 inch thick (144 cubic inches). With the adoption of the metric system, this unit will likely become obsolete. See section on primary products estimation for further discussion on board-foot estimation.

**242**

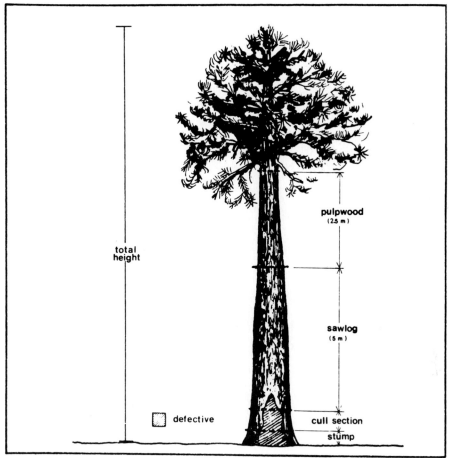

**Figure 10.5** Breakdown of tree stem into merchantable product categories.

observe upper stem diameters, as depicted in Figure 10.6. With diameter measurements taken at various heights on the tree, volumes may be calculated by stem section and then summed. Equations are constructed to describe *diameter-height-volume* relationships from which volume tables are derived. Such equations also facilitate rapid computer-based data processing for large numbers of tree measurements. The final product-volume estimate will obviously be affected both by the accuracy and precision of the specific equation used, and by the accuracy

and precision of the field observations of tree diameters and heights.

**Site Index for Forest Stands.** Forest stands are commonly classified according to "*site quality,*" which indicates the productive capacity of a specific area of forestland for a particular species. Although many species may grow on the same site, they may not grow equally well. The site productivity measure most commonly used is *site index,* the average height of dominant and codominant trees at a expected dominant tree height for this site is 15 meters at the index age of 50 years (4, 5, 11).

Site index has been found to be correlated with soil factors and topography as related to tree growth. For example, the site index can sometimes be predicted from such factors as depth of surface soil, stone, silt and clay content, slope steepness, etc., in the absence of a forest stand. However, the concept of site index is not well suited for uneven-aged stands and areas of mixed-species composition (4).

**Figure 10.6** Observation of upper stem diameter with a Wheeler optical caliper.

specified index age, usually 50 years. Sometimes an index age of 100 years is used for the longer-lived West Coast species and 25 years for southern plantations.

As mentioned above, when the two variables height and age have been determined they are used as coordinates for determining site index from a set of curves (Figure 10.7). Site-index curves and tables have been developed for most commercial species. The plot shows that a white pine stand with an average total height of 20 meters at an age of 70 years has a site index of 15. This means that the

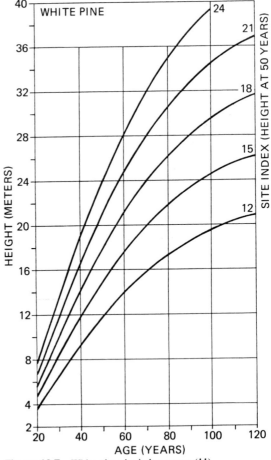

**Figure 10.7** White pine site-index curves (11).

## SURVEY DESIGN CONSIDERATIONS FOR TIMBER RESOURCES

### Use of Remote Sensing Information

The first step in survey design is identifying and specifying the forest area under examination. Remote sensing tools, particularly aerial photographs, are extremely useful for this preliminary step. The aerial photograph provides a picture of the forest much like a detailed map. Foresters are most interested in vertical aerial photographs,[2] or those that are taken with the camera film plane parallel to the ground. The actual flight lines of the aircraft are planned so that the photographs will have an average endlap of 60 percent and an average sidelap of approximately 35 percent. This overlap allows for three-dimensional study of the forest by an interpreter using a stereoscope (see Figure 10.8). Although not a true map, the aerial photograph in conjunction with existing maps provides a basis for identifying and delineating the various forest characteristics of interest. In particular, the forest may be divided into

groups or cover types based on *species, size,* and *stand density* classes. The areas of these cover types may also be measured. This breakdown of the forest is illustrated in Figure 10.9. The example illustrates the breakdown of a tract into two strata according to species composition. This stratification is helpful to survey design in two ways: first, as a means of *identifying* where particular kinds of forest stands lie in an ownership; second, as a statistical tool for increasing the precision of *estimates* of timber volumes and other stand characteristics. Most large regional forest surveys are based on multiphase or multistage sampling designs involving aerial photos at the first stage or phase and ground observations at the last phase (4, 12, 13). Satellite imagery is also receiving increased attention as the basis for first stage or phase observations.

A wide range of aerial photograph scales and combinations of films and filters are used in practice. In particular, for black and white photography,

[2] A vertical photo has its optical axis parallel to vertical or the direction of gravity.

**Figure 10.8** Parallax bar oriented over overlapping vertical aerial photographs under a mirror stereoscope. The stereoscope facilitates three-dimensional study of the photographed scene. The parallax bar is used to determine approximate tree heights and terrain elevations. (Courtesy of Wild Herrbrugg, Inc.)

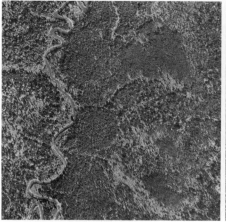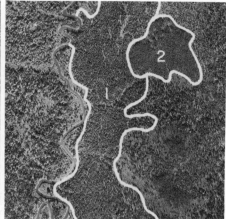

**Figure 10.9** Stereogram illustrating cover-type mapping of balsam fir (1) and black spruce (2) stands, Ontario, Canada.

(From Zsilinszky (13); courtesy Victor G. Zsilinszky, Ontario Centre for Remote Sensing.)

certain film and filter combinations greatly enhance differences between various species groups. Color infrared film is also frequently used and can distinguish hardwood and softwood species groups as well as diseased or otherwise stressed trees. These techniques in turn increase the speed and accuracy of photo-interpretation and mapping.

The separation of tree species and disease conditions on aerial photographs is based on differing reflectance and absorption of the various wavelengths of light energy. Hardwood trees usually reflect more of the longer red and near-infrared wavelengths of light energy than conifers and thus appear lighter on photographs. The effect is enhanced using film sensitive to the near-infrared wavelengths and by using filters to screen out the shorter blue and green wavelengths of light energy where the reflectance of hardwoods and softwoods overlaps. Similarly, diseased or stressed vegetation may exhibit decreased infrared reflectance because of leaf water loss or related factors. This may facilitate detection of the condition on infrared color films when it may not be evident on normal color film or even to the human eye.

Individual tree species also have characteristic crown *size* and *shape* on aerial photographs. For example, eastern white cedar has a rounded shape, black spruce has a cone shape, and white pine has a star-shaped crown. In dense stands, the arrangement of the tree crowns produces a *pattern* and a *texture* that facilitates identification. In area 2 of Figure 10.9, which is composed of a pure stand of black spruce, a smooth, fine-textured pattern is exhibited, in contrast to area 1, which contains a mixed stand of balsam fir and black spruce. Balsam fir has a wider base and grows more erratically than black spruce; thus the stand containing the balsam fir (area 1) appears coarser-textured and more uneven (13, 14).

## Field Observation and Measurement Techniques for Forest Inventory and Appraisal

Once a cover-type map is obtained through photo-interpretation, a frequent subsequent step in the survey is to lay out plots in the field for sampling. Figure 10.10 illustrates a random (*a*) versus systematic (*b*) layout of sample plots in the strata (cover types) comprising a particular forest tract. The sampling intensity differs between the strata because of differing interest, usually economic, in the par-

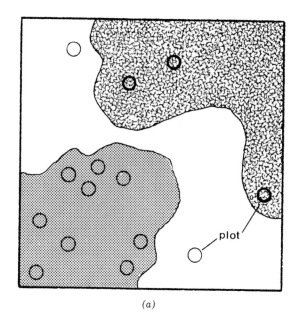

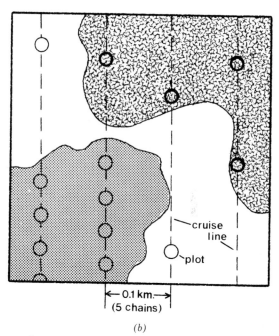

(a)

(b)

|← 0.1 km →|
(5 chains)

**Figure 10.10** Portion of a forest tract illustrating (a) random and (b) systematic allocation of sample plots for three cover types. Sampling intensity (number of plots per unit area) varies by cover type.

ticular cover types and because of differences in the variability of the forest characteristics within the respective strata. A systematic layout of plots (Figure 10.10b) is perhaps the easiest to work with in the field because the cruiser simply travels in a series of parallel straight lines. However, this system of plot layout poses greater problems in the statistical interpretation of the reliability of the survey. For such low-intensity sample surveys, the actual statistical differences between the systematic and the random plot layout designs fortunately are usually small and not of major concern.

The field-sample plots may vary in size as a matter of cruiser preference and between different regions and timber types. Circular or square plots approximately 0.04 to 0.08 hectares in size are frequently used. Generally, all tree sizes encountered on the fixed-size sample plots are tallied. Tally entries may note tree species, size, quality, and other characteristics.

A more rapid and equally accurate method of sampling tree basal area and also obtaining tree volumes was devised by Bitterlich (15). This method does not require measurement of sample plot areas nor does it require measurement of tree diameters. It is referred to here as the *Bitterlich system,* but is also commonly referred to as point sampling, variable plot sampling, plotless cruising, or plotless timber estimating (4, 5, 8, 16). The Bitterlich system involves selection of trees with a probability proportional to their *size* instead of their frequency. With this method, a plot or point center is established and trees are then tallied by rotating the projection of a fixed angle (gauge) around the plot (Figure 10.11). The angle gauge may be in the form of a wedge prism or a stick with a bar at a suitable distance from the observer's eye. Trees with a dbh larger than the projected gauge angle are counted or tallied as ''in'' on the plot. The other trees are considered ''out'' and are not tallied.

**247**

**Figure 10.11** Use of a stick-angle gauge to tally trees on a Bitterlich horizontal-point sample plot. Borderline trees are checked with distance tapes and careful diameter measurement to determine if they are ''in'' or ''out.''

Borderline trees are checked for size (dbh) and distance from the plot center to determine if they are ''in'' or ''out.'' On flat terrain a common practice is to count every other borderline tree as ''in.''

This process effectively counts trees on plots, and the size of the plot for any tree is a direct function of the individual tree's basal area (Figure 10.12). A convenient feature of the method is that when the number of trees on a plot has been tallied, an estimate of the basal area per hectare at the sampling point is found simply by multiplying the tree count by a constant factor (basal area factor, or BAF) related to the specific gauge angle. Because there is a correlation between tree basal area and tree volumes, timber estimates may be obtained when counted trees are tallied by merchantable height classes or when the total number of logs or pulpwood bolts in the counted trees are recorded.

The predetermined *basal area factor* can be any convenient factor. It is determined by the size of the angle that one selects to use for the gauge or by the

strength of the wedge prism. Timber size will determine which factor is most useful. In the average sawtimber stand in the Great Lakes states, an instrument with a basal area factor of 2 (square meters per hectare) is commonly used. In uniform or dense pole-timber stands the 2 factor is also recommended. On the other hand, if one is working with large sawtimber, a 4 factor or larger might be the most convenient. In light-density pole stands a 1 factor instrument may prove to be the most satisfactory since it provides a larger plot size for the small trees (4, 8).

The main criteria in selecting a specific basal-area factor are stand density and the size of the trees normally involved. In dense pole-timber stands some trees are obscured by others, and in large timber the larger trees may be a great distance from the point center, resulting in some trees being overlooked and not counted. For example, using an instrument with a basal area factor of 2, a tree with 1-meter dbh is counted up to a distance of 35 meters

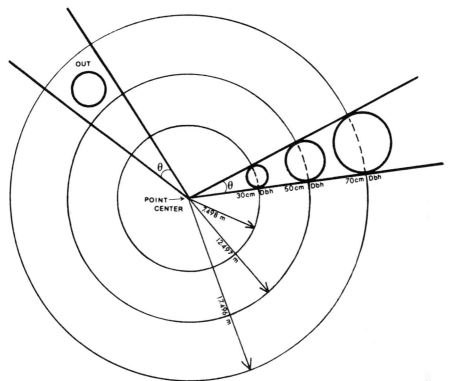

**Figure 10.12** Plot sizes associated with different tree sizes for a 4 square-meter-per-hectare basal-area factor angle gauge. The borderline stems of varying dbh to the right of the point center define the plot size for such tree sizes. The tree to the left is smaller than the projected angle $\Theta$ and is therefore excluded.

from the point center. One can readily see that such trees can be easily missed in areas where there is any amount of underbrush (8).

As an example, a gauge of 137.52 minutes of angle corresponds to a BAF of 4 square meters per hectare. If five trees are tallied as "in" from a point, then the basal area per hectare estimate for that point is BAF × tree tally = 4 × 5 = 20 square meters per hectare. This is also equivalent to multiplying the tree characteristic, in this case its basal area, by the reciprocal of its plot size in hectares. This reciprocal of the tree's associated plot size is frequently called its expansion factor or trees-per-hectare conversion factor—the number of trees per hectare this tree tally represents. Note from Figure 10.12 that this expansion factor can also be obtained by the division BAF/$b$, where $b$ is the individual tree's basal area.

Thus for any observed tree characteristic $v$, say tree volume, the volume (i.e., the amount of that characteristic) per hectare represented by the tallied tree can be written as BAF · $v/b$. If $n$ trees are tallied on a plot, the per-hectare estimate is simply the sum of the $n$ different $v/b$ values times the BAF.

The major time savings in the use of horizontal point sampling arise from three sources: the *high precision* of the plot size selection and estimation procedures, *fewer trees* are tallied on each point, and *plot boundaries need not be established* by the crew in order to tally trees as "in."

When locating the sample plots in the field, the inventory team will gather information much like that illustrated by the *tally sheet* in Figure 10.13. This particular tally sheet is typical of management-oriented surveys by forest industries. A re-

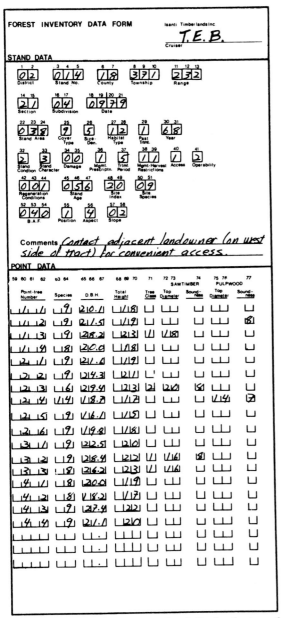

**Figure 10.13** Sample field tally sheet indicating the type of data collected in many management-oriented inventories.

gional forest survey by a public agency usually has a much lower sampling intensity than the one illustrated, but information on many other variables may be collected. Interest in specific variables follows from regional, state, and national planning interests for the development and conservation of the forest resource.

The estimation of timber volumes is generally carried out by a *survey crew* of two persons (Figure 10.14). The crew chief is responsible for the location of the plots and the recording of information. The crew chief usually employs a compass, careful pacing, and aerial photographs for locating plots and supervises the task of rating various conditions on the plots or in the stands visited. Stands are rated separately for site quality, reproduction adequacy, physiographic variables, and accessibility. The second crew member is responsible for physical measurements on the plot; one task is measuring tree diameters, heights, and ages.

## Growth and Yield Projection

Repeated surveys together with site-index concepts allow accurate characterization of future stand con-

**Figure 10.14** Field crew in the process of observing and recording species and tree diameters on a plot. Diameters are being measured with a Biltmore stick held at a fixed distance from the eye. Observations with this tool are based on the geometric principle of similar triangles.

ditions and associated yield. Growth projection models may also be used to predict stand yield for specific management practices. Table 10.2 illustrates a yield table constructed for southern pine stands under a particular set of management alternatives—in this case in terms of stand-density alternatives. Note that the model on which this table is based provides estimates of both growth rates and future product yields. The economics of the alternatives will then affect the choice. It is important to stress that the growth and yield information for this particular forest stand type represents an estimate based on a sample of observations from various study plots. Many other types of yield tables are available (10).

A variety of individual tree growth models have been developed to characterize stand growth and dynamics. It is possible with some of these models to help locate optimal solutions and choices for stand treatments by simulation and/or mathematical programming techniques. Examples of treatments are choices among tree-size class distributions, stand densities or thinnings, series of fertilization treatments, and rotation ages.

## Urban Forest Inventory Practice

Inventories of the forest resource in small communities frequently take the form of a complete census of all trees. Typical information collected for each tree is species, diameter, location (perhaps by block or lot), position (such as boulevard or interior lot), ownership, and condition (notably in terms of vigor classification, including mortality, insect and disease conditions, hazard, etc.). For larger cities, a 5 to 10 percent systematic sample of trees of city blocks may be used. This is sometimes combined with classifications of blocks into two or three tree density classes based on aerial photos. Because of the diversity of species in urban areas, the field crews need considerable background in dendrology.

Given the above information, the urban forest manager is in a good position to estimate future tree removal and replacement needs and to develop subsequent plans for these activities.

## PRIMARY-PRODUCTS ESTIMATION

The primary wood products used by forest industry take many forms—from individual logs and stacked roundwood to chips and residues. As discussed earlier, when trees are cut into lengths of 2.5 meters or more, the sections are referred to as logs. For many products, logs and bolts have some specified minimum small-end diameter.

## Scaling and Grading

The product volumes for felled trees or logs are frequently determined by a *scaling* and *grading* process. A step in the scaling process is illustrated in Figure 10.15, which depicts a scaler determining the inside bark diameter of the small end of a log. Together with measurements of the length of the log and defect extent, the scaler can refer to tables or equations for estimating the product contents of logs of such dimensions (Table 10.3). Such tables or equations are called *log rules*. This scaling procedure may be repeated for a sample or for all of the logs in the particular sale or logyard. Scaling can serve as a means of estimating the products that may actually be sawed or produced from these logs and for establishing payment (value) for the sale.

In addition to scaling, the logs may also be graded. *Grading* involves assessing the surface and internal log characteristics that may affect log quality. These same characteristics will also affect the quantity of certain products that may be cut from the log. The defects fall into two main categories: (1) those that reduce the volume of sound wood or lower its durability, and (2) those that lower its strength, take away from its appearance, or otherwise limit its utility. The first are *scaling defects* (heartrot, ringshake—which is separation of wood along annual rings—etc.), and the second are *grading defects* (knots, stain, etc.). "Grade defect indicators" are outside features of the log; they indicate imperfections in the underlying wood. For example, a branch stub is an indicator of a knot in the product to be sawed from the log (17, 18).

**Table 10-2**

Variable-Density Growth and Yield Table for Managed Stands of Natural Slash Pine. (Cubic meter yields and basal area as projected from various initial ages and stockings.)

| Initial Basal Area | From Age | To Age | Site Index (m)[a] 20 | 25 Projected Yield (m³/ha) | 30 | Projected Basal Area (m²/ha) |
|---|---|---|---|---|---|---|
| | | 20 | 73 | 106 | 136 | 16 |
| | 20 | 30 | 134 | 194 | 248 | 22 |
| | | 40 | 181 | 262 | 336 | 25 |
| | | 50 | 217 | 315 | 403 | 28 |
| | | 30 | 102 | 147 | 189 | 16 |
| 16 m² | 30 | 40 | 147 | 213 | 273 | 20 |
| | | 50 | 184 | 267 | 341 | 23 |
| | | 40 | 120 | 174 | 222 | 16 |
| | 40 | 50 | 156 | 226 | 289 | 19 |
| | | 20 | 89 | 129 | 166 | 20 |
| | 20 | 30 | 153 | 222 | 284 | 25 |
| | | 40 | 200 | 290 | 371 | 28 |
| | | 50 | 235 | 341 | 436 | 30 |
| | | 30 | 124 | 180 | 230 | 20 |
| 20 m² | 30 | 40 | 171 | 248 | 318 | 24 |
| | | 50 | 207 | 301 | 385 | 26 |
| | | 40 | 146 | 212 | 272 | 20 |
| | 40 | 50 | 183 | 265 | 340 | 23 |
| | | 20 | 105 | 152 | 195 | 24 |
| | 20 | 30 | 171 | 247 | 316 | 28 |
| | | 40 | 217 | 315 | 403 | 31 |
| | | 50 | 251 | 364 | 466 | 33 |
| | | 30 | 146 | 212 | 271 | 24 |
| 24 m² | 30 | 40 | 193 | 280 | 359 | 27 |
| | | 50 | 229 | 332 | 425 | 29 |
| | | 40 | 172 | 250 | 320 | 24 |
| | 40 | 50 | 209 | 302 | 387 | 27 |

*Source.* Adapted from equations given by F. A. Bennett, "Variable-density yield tables for managed stands of natural slash pine," U.S.D.A. For. Serv., Res. Note SE-141, 1970.

[a]Base age of 50 years.

**Figure 10.15** A first step in scaling: determining log small-end diameter inside bark.

Log grading depends on what type of material the log might be converted to. Not all hardwood logs that exceed minimum specifications are equally suitable for all products, even though the quality requirements may be similar. Rules for grading hardwood logs or factory lumber emphasize defects such as knots that affect the amount of clear lumber that might be recovered from the log. Grading rules for structural lumber, however, emphasize defects that detract from the strength or durability of the potential products (Table 10.4). Four log-use classes have been designated to cover current hardwood utilization practices (17). They are as follows (see page 255):

**Table 10-3**

Board Foot Volume of 16-foot (4.85 meters) Logs for International Rule and Other Log Rules in Percent of the International Rule[a]

| Scaling Diameter | | International[b] | Scribner | Scribner Decimal C | Doyle |
|---|---|---|---|---|---|
| (in) | (cm) | (board feet) | | percent | |
| 6 | 15 | 20 | 90 | 100 | 20 |
| 8 | 20 | 40 | 80 | 75 | 40 |
| 10 | 25 | 65 | 83 | 92 | 55 |
| 12 | 30 | 95 | 83 | 84 | 67 |
| 14 | 36 | 135 | 84 | 81 | 74 |
| 16 | 41 | 180 | 88 | 89 | 80 |
| 18 | 46 | 230 | 93 | 91 | 85 |
| 20 | 51 | 290 | 97 | 97 | 88 |
| 22 | 56 | 355 | 94 | 93 | 91 |
| 24 | 61 | 425 | 95 | 94 | 94 |
| 26 | 66 | 500 | 100 | 100 | 97 |
| 28 | 71 | 585 | 99 | 99 | 98 |
| 30 | 76 | 675 | 97 | 98 | 100 |
| 32 | 81 | 770 | 96 | 96 | 102 |
| 34 | 86 | 875 | 91 | 91 | 103 |
| 36 | 91 | 980 | 94 | 94 | 104 |
| 38 | 96 | 1095 | 98 | 98 | 106 |
| 40 | 102 | 1220 | 99 | 98 | 106 |

*Source.* D. L. Williams and W. C. Hopkins, ''Converting factors for southern pine products,'' U.S.D.A. For. Serv., Tech. Bull. No. 626, Southern Forest Expt. Sta., New Orleans, 1969.
[a] Terms used in the table are defined later in this section.
[b] Quarter-inch kerf (cut made by saw).

**Table 10-4**

Classification of Hardwood Log Surface Abnormalities

| Abnormalities | Factory Logs | Construction Logs | Local-Use Logs |
|---|---|---|---|
| *Log surface* | | | |
| Bulges | | | |
| Butt | Defect | Defect | No defect |
| Stem | Defect | Defect | No defect |
| Bumps | | | |
| High | Defect | V [a] | V |
| Medium | Defect | V | V |
| Low | | | |
| Burl | Defect | Defect | |
| Butt scar | Defect | V | No defect |
| Butt swell | No defect | V | V |
| Canker | Defect | Defect | No defect |
| Conk | Defect | Defect | No defect |
| Dormant buds | V | No defect | No defect |
| Epicormic branches | V | No defect | No defect |
| Flanges | No defect | No defect | No defect |
| Flutes | V | V | No defect |
| Fork | Defect | Defect | No defect |
| Gum lesions | V | No defect | No defect |
| Holes | | | |
| Large | Defect | V | V |
| Medium | | | |
| Bark scarrer, fresh | No defect | No defect | No defect |
| Bark scarrer, old | Defect | No defect | No defect |
| Birds, light | No defect | No defect | No defect |
| Birds, heavy | Defect | No defect | No defect |
| Grub | V | No defect | No defect |
| Increment borer | Defect | No defect | No defect |
| Tap | Defect | No defect | No defect |
| Small | V | No defect | No defect |
| Log knots | | | |
| Sound | Defect | V | V |
| Unsound | Defect | V | V |
| Limbs | Defect | V | V |
| Overgrowths | | | |
| Knots and bark pockets | Defect | V | No defect |
| Insects | Defect | No defect | No defect |
| Bird peck | Defect | No defect | No defect |
| Bark distortions | | | |
| Heavy or medium | Defect | No defect | No defect |
| Light | No defect | No defect | No defect |
| Seams | V | V | No defect |

**Table 10-4** *(continued)*

| Abnormalities | Factory Logs | Construction Logs | Local-Use Logs |
|---|---|---|---|
| *Log surface* | | | |
| Splits | V | V | No defect |
| Surface rise | No defect | No defect | No defect |
| Wounds | | | |
| New | No defect | No defect | No defect |
| Old | V | V | No defect |
| *Log end* | | | |
| Bird peck | V | No defect | No defect |
| Bark pocket (crotch) | Defect | Defect | No defect |
| Double pith | No defect | Defect | No defect |
| Grease spots | V | No defect | No defect |
| Grub channels | V | V | No defect |
| Gum spots | V | No defect | No defect |
| Loose heart | b | Defect | No defect |
| Rot | V | Defect | No defect |
| Shake | | | |
| Ring | V | Defect | No defect |
| Wind | V | Defect | No defect |
| Soak | V | No defect | No defect |
| Spider heart | V | Defect | No defect |
| Stain | V | No defect | No defect |
| Wormholes | | | |
| Pin, flag and shot | Defect | No defect | No defect |

*Source.* Adapted from E. D. Rast, D. L. Sonderman, and G. L. Gammon, "A guide to hardwood log grading," U.S.D.A. For. Serv., Gen. Tech. Rept. NE-1, Northeast Forest Expt. Sta., Upper Darby, Pa., 1973.

[a] V = variable depending on extent of defect.

[b] Defect if not confined to heart center and inner quality zone.

5140 8:15

1. *Veneer Class.* Very high-value logs as well as some relatively low-value logs. Many logs that qualify for factory-lumber grades 1, 2, and 3 can be utilized as veneer logs.

2. *Factory Class.* Adapted to the production of boards that later can be remanufactured so as to remove most defects and obtain the best yields of clear face and sound cuttings.

3. *Construction Class.* Logs suitable for sawing into ties, timbers, and other items to be used in one piece for structural purposes.

4. *Local-Use Class.* In general, suitable for products not usually covered by standard specifications. High strength, great durability, or fine appearance are not required for the following types of products: crating, pallet parts, mine timbers, industrial blocking, etc.

Since logs of the same size and species may differ substantially in value because of grade, grading and scaling are considered integral procedures in many areas. Given the determination of log and tree contents through scaling or mill processing, it is then possible to develop convenient tree-volume equations for a wide range of products of interest (see Tables 10.1 and 10.3).

## Volume Estimation

Similar to the scaling of individual logs and stacked roundwood in terms of cubic volume or weight, pulpwood chips and residues such as bark and sawdust may also be assessed by cubic volume or weight. A wide variety of conversion factors have also been developed to convert primary volume and weight measures to product contents. The *board-foot* measure of product volume, however, merits further discussion.

The board foot is a dated but commonly used unit of measure for logs. Since tree volumes today are less frequently converted into 1-inch thick boards, this unit is becoming inappropriate and cumbersome. The board-foot content of a log also varies by taper of the stem and width of the saw used in converting the log to lumber. There are many rules (log rules) for converting log dimensions into estimated board-foot contents. The most common conversion rules in the United States are the Scribner, Doyle, and international ¼. There are substantial differences among the rules and the estimates they provide, especially for smaller log sizes (Table 10.3) (19). A wise buyer or seller will study the differences before completing agreements.

The *Scribner log rule* was developed from diagrams of board positions on circles of various sizes representing log ends. Board ends were drawn with allowance for the saw kerf (¼ inch), shrinkages, and with the assumptions that boards would be 1 inch thick and not less than 8 inches wide. The logs were also assumed to be cylinders of a diameter equal to that at the small end (i.e., no adjustments were made for log taper). A commonly used equation developed to describe this rule for 16 foot logs is

$$V = 0.79D^2 - 2D - 4$$

where $V$ is log volume in board feet and $D$ is the small-end scaling diameter (in inches) of the log. The Scribner rule is often converted into a *decimal rule* by rounding to the nearest 10 board feet and dropping the last unit. Thus a 16-foot long, 18-inch-diameter log would scale as 216 board feet or 22 by the *Scribner decimal C rule*.

The *Doyle log rule* for 16-foot logs is based on the simple formula

$$V = (D - 4)^2$$

This rule was derived mathematically from consideration of large logs and allowances made for slabs, saw kerf, and shrinkage. Its simplicity favors its use, but it grossly underestimates volumes for logs less than 20 inches in diameter.

The *international log rule* is one of the most accurate log rules. In its basic form it allows for a ⅛-inch saw kerf and 1/16 inch for shrinkage plus an allowance for slabs and edgings. Further, the basic rule treats only a 4-foot log section. Subsequent 4-foot lengths of a log are treated as having a ½-inch larger diameter. In this way the rule incorporates consideration of taper. The basic formula for the board-foot volume of a 4-foot log section is

$$V = 0.22 D^2 - 0.71 D$$

For a ¼-inch saw kerf this equation or its result is multiplied by 0.905. Further details on these and other log rules may be found in Husch et al. (4).

In contrast to scaling and grading, as applied to individual logs, pulpwood and firewood scaling also frequently involve the assessment of volumes on the basis of stacks or piles of wood. Stacked wood is measured in *cords* or cubic meters. A *standard cord* of wood is a stack 4 by 4 by 8 feet and contains 128 cubic feet (3.6 cubic meters) of wood, air, and bark. Pulpwood is rarely stacked in exactly one-cord piles, but it is possible to convert any pile of known dimensions to cords by dividing the product of the pile width, height, and length by 128. Cordwood is frequently cut into lengths shorter than 8 feet, such as 4 feet or as short as 16 inches, and these are referred to as *short cords* or *face cords* or a variety of local names. An example of a standard and face cord is shown in Figure 10.16. Where the metric system is employed, stacked wood is measured in terms of cubic meters. One cubic meter is equivalent to 35.3 cubic feet of wood, air, and bark.

The actual wood content of a stack varies according to the bark thickness, the diameter and length of the bolts, the straightness and freedom from knots, and the degree of care taken in piling. The proportion of wood in a cord is usually 58 to 66 percent of the cord volume. Consequently, there are various regional and local conversion factors, with many agencies and mills developing their own criteria for assessing the actual amount of wood in given stacks.

Pulpwood and sometimes sawlogs may also be scaled on a weight basis. In this case, entire truckloads of wood may be weighed, both loaded and unloaded, with the difference being converted to cubic contents of wood or to dry weight. Ratios of cubic contents versus dry weight depend on factors such as species, specific gravity, moisture content, and piling.

## ASSESSMENT OF NONTIMBER RESOURCES AND THEIR USE

The use of forests as wildlife habitats, as watersheds, and for recreation activities involves a set of sampling and measurement principles similar to those indicated for the timber resource. In the area of wildlife resources, management surveys usually involve census techniques to determine animal population levels or to develop indexes to indicate relative population levels. Examples of such indexes are pellet counts or flush counts for deer and birds, respectively. There is also increasing interest in relating the forest-habitat conditions, often described by the timber inventory, to the population numbers and the health of the herds inhabiting or potentially inhabiting the area. A further discussion

**Figure 10.16** Examples of stacked wood units from left to right: standard cord, face cord (pieces 16 inches long), split-face cord, and a split-face cord as commonly piled in a small truck.

of the interactions of the forest with wildlife is given in Chapter 16.

With water resources we are primarily interested in measuring quantity, quality, and the timing of the water resource for particular locations. Forest characteristics affect water yield in terms of these variables. Timber-harvest operations are one example of a use that could increase water yield. There is also interest in nonpoint pollution[3] and how it might be controlled by forest-management practices. In this area we may be concerned with sampling and characterizing the forest resource, much as in the timber-resource inventory, or in sampling and measuring streamflow characteristics from a particular watershed. The statistical aspects of this sampling and measurement process are fundamentally like those used for the timber resource. Computer modeling of watersheds in forest ecosystems was discussed in Chapter 6, and a further discussion of watershed management is given in Chapter 11.

Management of recreation areas also involves surveys that are primarily concerned with the numbers of users and the physical impact they have on particular sites. Thus we may be sampling a population of users or a population of sites used by people engaged in outdoor recreation. In sampling the resource users, we frequently use questionnaires and followups intended to get at the attitudes and likely response of the users to various kinds of recreation-resource management. Such surveys may consider the forest as a visual resource to be harvested by the user or visitor. With such concepts it is possible to map or characterize and subsequently manage the forest environment in terms of scenic cover types and attributes that contribute to user response. A further discussion of forest recreation management is given in Chapter 14.

---

[3] "Nonpoint pollution" derives from a dispersed source such as agricultural activity, as compared with "point pollution" where a single pollution source can be identified (i.e., a factory drainspout).

## STATUS AND FUTURE OF RESOURCE ASSESSMENT

There are definite trends toward greater use of statistical concepts in forest sampling and measurement tasks, and in integrating computer capabilities to ease the processing and analysis of usually very large sets of observations. Coupled with this, there is a trend toward measuring fewer sampling units—for example, trees or plots—but measuring them more carefully and using new tools and statistical concepts to increase the accuracy and precision of the survey. In particular there are strong efforts to reduce the amount of fieldwork and rely more heavily on remote sensing capabilities. At the same time, management interests appear to be growing in terms of the desired detail and amount of information requested about the forest and its likely response to treatment. Further, an increasing number of variables are of interest, caused, in part, by the increasing use of the forest for a wider range of activities. We should look forward to greater use of computers in forestry and related models to assess management alternatives and to analyze survey information.

A look around the world at forest-assessment practices suggests similar trends. Practices do differ, however, depending on the level of economic development within a country and the vastness of its forests. Regions with a vast resource and a relatively short period of resource exploitation tend toward extensive surveys emphasizing regional statistics. On the other hand, regions such as Europe with a long history of management emphasize intensive, management-oriented surveys. These traditionally involve a careful description of forest stands by cover type, condition, present growth, and potential yield. Much of the cost in forest inventory is related to transportation—that is, the movement of field crews from one plot to the next. Consequently, there are also large differences in inventory practice because of road-network characteristics and other transportation considerations. Worldwide remote sensing efforts should lead to some reduction in the amount of fieldwork and travel required. Sound statistical approaches, however, will require continued careful descriptions of the forest resource from the ground.

# REFERENCES

1. A. R. Stage, "Prognosis model for stand development," U.S.D.A. For. Serv., Res. Pap. INT-137, 1973; "A generalized forest growth projection system applied to the Lake States region," U.S.D.A. For. Serv., Gen. Tech. Rept. NC-49, 1979.

1a. A. R. Ek, "Development of individual tree-based stand growth simulators: Progress and applications," Dept. of Forest Resources, Univ. of Minnesota, Staff Paper Ser. No. 20, 1980.

1b. J. W. Moser, Jr., "Historical chapters in the development of modern forest growth and yield theory," In *Forecasting Forest Stand Dynamics*, Proc. of Workshop, R. M. Brown and F. R. Clarke, eds., School of Forestry, Lake Head Univ., Thunder Bay, Ont., 1980.

2. F. A. Bennett, "Variable-density yield tables for managed stands of natural slash pine," U.S.D.A. For. Serv., Res. Note SE-141, 1970.

3. S. R. Gevorkiantz and L. P. Olsen, "Composite volume tables for timber and their application in the Lake States," U.S.D.A. For. Serv., Tech. Bull. No. 1104, 1955.

4. B. Husch, C. I. Miller, and T. W. Beers, *Forest Mensuration*, Second Edition, Ronald Press, New York, 1972.

5. T. E. Avery, *Natural Resources Measurements*, Second Edition, McGraw-Hill, New York, 1975.

6. Anon., "Manual of Surveying Instruction," U.S.D.I. Bureau Land Mgmt., 1973.

7. Anon., "Public Land Statistics," U.S.D.I. Bureau Land Mgmt., 1969.

8. H. J. Hovind and C. E. Rieck, "Basal area and point sampling. Interpretation and application," Wisconsin Dept. Natural Res., Tech. Bull. No. 23, Madison, 1970.

9. L. T. Carron, *An Outline of Forest Mensuration*, Australian National University Press, Canberra, 1968.

10. R. D. Forbes and A. B. Meyer, *Forestry Handbook*, Ronald Press, New York, 1955.

11. P. R. Laidly, "Metric site index curves for aspen, birch and conifers in the Lake States," U.S.D.A. For. Serv., Gen. Tech. Rept. NC-54, St. Paul, 1979.

12. T. E. Avery, *Interpretation of Aerial Photographs*, Second Edition, Burgess Publishing Co., Minneapolis, 1968.

13. V. G. Zsilinszky, "Photographic Interpretation of Tree Species in Ontario," Ontario Dept. of Lands and Forests, 1966.

14. T. M. Lillesand and R. W. Kiefer, *Remote Sensing and Image Interpretation*, John Wiley & Sons, New York, 1979.

15. L. R. Grosenbaugh, *J. For.*, 50, 32 (1952).

16. J. R. Dilworth and J. F. Bell, *Variable Probability Sampling*, Oregon State Univ. Bookstores, Corvallis, 1978.

17. E. D. Rast, D. L. Sonderman, and G. L. Gammon, "A guide to hardwood log grading," U.S.D.A. For. Serv., Gen. Tech. Rept. NE-1, Upper Darby, PA, 1973.

18. C. R. Lockard, J. A. Putnam, and R. D. Carpenter, "Grade defects in hardwood timber and logs," U.S.D.A. For. Serv., Agriculture Handbook No. 244, 1963.

19. D. L. Williams and W. C. Hopkins, "Converting factors for southern pine products," U.S.D.A. For. Serv., Tech. Bull. No. 626, New Orleans, 1969.

# 11

# MULTIPLE-USE MANAGEMENT OF THE FOREST

# WILLIAM A. LEUSCHNER, HAROLD W. WISDOM, AND W. DAVID KLEMPERER

The forest is a living system with many species of flora and fauna interacting together. These flora and fauna form the forest ecosystem and provide forest products desired by society. The trees provide not only timber for paper, lumber, or plywood, but also food and shelter for game and nongame wildlife species. The combined ecosystem can provide recreational and aesthetic experiences also valued by society (Figure 11.1). These can range from high-density experiences, such as organized campgrounds and picnic areas, through dispersed use and wilderness experiences, such as back-country hiking and camping.

All the products obtained from the forest ecosystem are too numerous to mention. However the entire ecosystem is needed to produce them because they are jointly produced. For example, growing oak-hickory forests automatically produces habitat for squirrels (Figure 11.2), and clearcutting timber automatically produces forest openings that provide habitat for deer and some songbirds. This joint production means that the forest must be managed as a system if all products are desired. It also sometimes causes hard decisions or conflict when the production of one product causes the destruction of another. An extreme example is clearcutting in a campground.

Society is interested in the forest because it produces desired forest products. Society begins to manage the forest when there are insufficient products to meet desires or when it becomes too costly to obtain the products. For example, suppose a society was harvesting raspberries from forest openings created by lightning fires. These people are using forest products but not managing the forest because they simply gather the fruits. Suppose that the forest openings grow over and there are too few raspberries, so that people must now walk a day to reach

**Figure 11.1** Uneven-aged stand of ponderosa pine in central Oregon. Note thicket of pine seedlings in left foreground and older group of pine saplings in right background. (Courtesy of U.S.D.A. Forest Service.)

**Figure 11.2** A chestnut oak stand, with some black oak, on a ridge in West Virginia. (Courtesy of U.S.D.A. Forest Service.)

forest stand. These variables determine the production possibilities for any forest. External influences include federal and state legislation, taxation, and the market for forest products. These external variables will be discussed in more detail in a later section.

The external and internal variables do not always absolutely prohibit or automatically produce the maximum of any one forest product. However, some sites are better suited to producing one forest product than another. For example, some sites produce greater yields from conifers than hardwoods for the same amount of resources used. Further, different products often have different relative values to society. Lumber for housing is relatively more important than wild raspberries for jam on most forest acres. Balancing the relative productivity of a forest site with the relative net value of the product determines which forest-management alternative is chosen. Modern forest management has come to mean the application of analytical techniques to aid in choosing the management alternatives that contribute most to society's (or an organization's) objectives. This is the context within which we will discuss forest management.

## BASIC MANAGEMENT CONCEPTS

Forest-management concepts should encompass the multiple uses made of the forest. These goods and services include recreation, wildlife, watersheds, rangeland, and timber. The management of forest watersheds, rangeland, and timberland is discussed in this chapter; forest-recreation management and forest-wildlife interactions are discussed in separate chapters.

### Range Management

Range management is the science of the management of rangeland for the production of goods and services valued by society (1). Rangeland makes up almost one-half of the total land area of the United States, and the grazing of rangeland by livestock is

them. The people may then decide to start their own fires to create openings so raspberries will grow in the desired location and quantity. This society is now *managing* the forest for its products.

This example shows the historical biological meaning of forest management. Forest management formerly meant only the biological manipulation of trees and forest stands, primarily for timber. Biological manipulation still provides many forest-management alternatives, but it is now usually taught in silviculture and forest ecology courses. Forest management now has a broader meaning.

The forest manager is constrained in manipulating the forest by the external and internal variables present. Internal variables include such things as temperature, rainfall, soil type, and species in a the single largest land use in the United States.

Livestock production in the United States normally follows a cycle of breeding and rearing the young animals on pasture and range feed, followed by a brief fattening period on grain, mainly in feed lots in the Midwest (2). The pasture and grazing phase follows a seasonal pattern, which varies by region, according to the pattern of land ownership and climatic conditions (see Figure 12.5). The two major livestock grazing regions of the United States are the Rocky Mountains and the South.

**Rocky Mountains.** The pattern of livestock grazing in the Rocky Mountains is a legacy from one of the most colorful periods of American history: the settling of the West. In the typical arrangement, a base ranch is supplemented by a substantial amount of rangeland leased from private owners or, more commonly, public land grazed under a permit. In many cases, the supplemental rangelands are essential to the economic survival of the ranch since the base ranch is incapable of supporting the livestock on a year-round basis.

The public land grazing permit establishes when the livestock may be grazed, where they may be grazed, and how many and what kind may be grazed (e.g., cattle or sheep). The livestock owner normally must also pay a monthly grazing fee per head of livestock. Virtually all of the public rangeland is under the administration of two federal agencies, the Bureau of Land Management and the Forest Service, which issue and administer the permit and fee systems on the lands under their jurisdiction.

Range grazing normally begins in the late spring, at the lower elevations, progressing to the alpine meadows by mid-summer. There the livestock are moved from one grazing unit to the next under a carefully developed schedule, with the length of stay on each unit determined by the carrying capacity of the range and the number of livestock. As winter weather begins to move into the upper meadows, the cattle are moved to lower elevations, reversing the pattern followed in the spring. Finally, as winter closes in, the breeding cattle are moved onto the home ranch, and the beef cattle are shipped to feedlots in the Midwest and are fed grain to prepare them for market.

**South.** Livestock grazing in the South can be traced back to the days of the Spanish explorers in Florida and the English settlers in Jamestown, Virginia. The clearcutting and subsequent abandonment of millions of acres of southern pine land in the first third of the twentieth century substantially increased the supply of open range in the South and open-range grazing.

Following World War II, much of the cutover pine land was purchased by forest industry, fenced, and planted to pine. Fencing of the range was often dictated by law as most southern states abandoned the open-range policy. The fencing and regeneration led to a substantial reduction in grazing land, and the era of abundant, free-grass and open range in the South was gone (3). Today, forest grazing appears to be making a comeback in many areas of the South as landowners discover that cattle grazing can significantly increase total forest income and that grazing damage can be kept at acceptable levels or even eliminated by following proper range management (4).

Although grazing occurs in every forest type in the South, the longleaf—slash—pine type is the most important region. Forage is most abundant during a period of perhaps 10 years after pine regeneration becomes established and before the pine canopy closure reduces forage production. During this period, the nutritional value of the forage is best in spring and early summer. Livestock ususally require feed supplements the rest of the year (5).

The vast areas of hardwoods provide scant forage for grazing, and the scarcity of forage encourages the livestock to eat the young hardwood seedlings. Thus timber management and livestock grazing generally are not considered to be compatible in the hardwood types (3).

**Forest Grazing.** Forests supply a significant, and often critical, portion of the forage available to grazing livestock, especially in the western states. In fact, receipts from grazing fees were equal to or greater than revenues from timber sales on national forests until about 1930 (6).

The forest manager's concern with forest grazing is directed, first, to the impact of grazing on the forest and other forest benefits, and, second, to the economic benefits from grazing. Experience with controlled forest grazing indicates that when the numbers of livestock and duration of grazing are in accord with modern range-management practices, forest damage will be negligible and, in fact, in certain cases may even enhance other values of the forest. For example, moderate grazing may be helpful in reducing fire hazard and competition from undesired hardwood species. Cattle grazing in alpine forest meadows may add to the aesthetics of the forest and enhance its recreation value. Controlled grazing may increase water quantity and may be beneficial to many wildlife species (7).

Forest grazing, using modern range-management techniques to prevent overgrazing, often can contribute significantly to the forest owner's economic return from forestlands and, perhaps more important, provide the owner with a source of income from these lands during at least a part of the long period of waiting for the timber to mature. However, large expanses of rangeland and a significant portion of the forest grazing land continues to suffer from past overgrazing. These lands must be returned to their natural level of productivity before significant economic returns can be earned from grazing.

Range improvement is one way to increase forage production on the rangelands with little or no adverse side effects on other forest and rangeland uses. In many cases range improvement could be achieved by providing the native grasses and forbs with an opportunity to accumulate a food supply adequate to ripen seed and tide the plants over the winter months. This can be achieved by delaying grazing in the early spring until the plants have had the oppor-

tunity to replenish their reserve food supply. On severely depleted rangeland, it may be necessary to rest the land for one or more seasons. This can be achieved by adopting a pattern of rotation grazing where each year some grazing units are permitted to rest (2). The reseeding of severely damaged rangelands may be necessary in some cases. Overabundant wildlife, especially elk, can degrade a range just as severely as livestock (8). Thus the control of wildlife to prevent overpopulation—wildlife management—can be an important part of a range-management program (see Chapter 16, "Forest-Wildlife Interactions").

Forest-management techniques can be also used to enhance forage production on forestland. For example, the selection and spacing of trees can improve forage production by controlling the amount of light reaching the forest floor, with wide spacings generally encouraging more forage production. Isolated patches of low-quality soils can be left unplanted to form meadows. The selection of harvesting technique will influence subsequent forage production on the cutover site. Clearcutting followed by burning normally produces the heaviest forage response. Partial cuts and thinnings may stimulate some additional forage, but less than after clearcutting (9).

## Watershed Management

A watershed is the land area draining into a stream or river. Such areas may be a few acres for a small creek or several states draining into a large river. Since many watersheds are fully or partially forested, and since vegetation patterns can strongly influence downstream water quality and quantity, foresters are concerned with watershed management.

Watershed management deals with land-use practices designed to change or maintain the quality and quantity of water for purposes such as residences, industry, irrigation, fish, wildlife, and recreation (10–12).

**Water Quantity.** Given a fixed amount and distribution of annual precipitation falling on a watershed, land-management practices can radically affect the amount and timing of water available to downstream users. In Chapter 6 it was noted that trees and plants in general consume water and return it to the atmosphere through transpiration. Thus, if we wanted to maximize downstream runoff of surface water, we would remove all vegetation in the watershed. The result, however, is likely to be severe flooding and soil erosion during rainy periods, with deficient streamflow and groundwater in the dry season.

Increasing the amount of vegetation will stabilize soil and slow surface runoff. This allows water to percolate through the soil and recharge groundwater supplies. Although vegetation is likely to reduce total water runoff, flood danger is lessened, and waterflow throughout the year (the ''regimen'') is more even. In addition, groundwater for wells will be increased. By manipulating timber harvest patterns and species, forest managers can improve the water regimen for downstream users.

In many mountainous areas, especially in the western United States, snow is the major form of precipitation, and significant downstream water supplies come from snowmelt. In such regions, insufficient shade from trees and shrubs will result in rapid snowmelt and floods in the spring, with not enough water later in the year.

In snowy regions, watershed managers often experiment with patterns of partial timber cutting that will maximize the snowpack but will provide enough shade to reduce the rate of snowmelt. Such patterns include clearcutting in strips, patches, T-shapes, and L-shapes and selective removal of individual trees (12).

**Water Quality.** Chapter 4 notes the relationships between the amount of soil particles in water and the upstream vegetation and forestry practices. Excessive sediment and turbidity in rivers and streams can be caused by insufficient vegetation or logging and road building which unduly disturb soil. The result

can be increased municipal water purification costs, siltation of lakes and dams, fish kill, and reduced quality of water-based recreation.

Forest managers often take measures to lessen soil disturbance that reduces water quality. Such practices will vary with the soil type, slope, and climate; they include limiting size of clearcuts, limiting the area and slope of roads, seeding old roads with groundcover plants, scattering logging slash over exposed soil, and installing drains and physical barriers to reduce soil erosion on roaded areas.

Removal of streamside trees reduces shade and sometimes elevates water temperature enough to kill certain valuable fish. In such cases, forested streamside strips are recommended to maintain lower water temperatures.

**Difficult Trade-offs.** In order to obtain more water—say, for irrigation in arid regions—the density of trees in the surrounding mountains may have to be reduced. So we increase water benefits at the expense of decreased timber income. For each incremental reduction in timber stocking, one should estimate whether added water benefits exceed the loss in timber income. This involves difficult questions of prediction and valuation.

Forested streamside strips present other interesting management questions. Up to a point, if we leave longer and wider strips, we may gain larger fish populations but will lose timber income. There is some optimal level of streamside harvest restriction that will maximize the combined value of fish and timber benefits.

Another thorny trade-off is that of requiring more costly road building and logging practices that reduce siltation and turbidity of downstream water. Eventually, added expenses of, say, more culverts and more use of expensive cable logging will bring smaller improvements in water quality. At which point will added benefits no longer exceed the costs?

In each of the above examples, much information is needed to predict the effects of management practices and to estimate costs and benefits—information that is usually not very precise. Thus the question of optimal watershed management strategies is an excellent area for continued research.

For many decades researchers have been monitoring the effects of different forest management methods on water quality and quantity in carefully controlled experimental watersheds. These forests include a wide range of soils, species, climates, and geologic formations and are located in areas such as New Hampshire, North Carolina, Pennsylvania, Oregon, and Arizona (12). Continued work of this type will provide useful knowledge for forest managers.

Most forest-management concepts were developed for timber management because timber was perhaps the forest product in shortest supply at that time. However, many of the concepts can be applied equally to all the multiple-use products. Timber management is emphasized in the rest of the chapter for simplicity.

## Timber Management

**The Regulated Forest.** Forest products are usually desired over a continuous time period and in about the same or increasing amounts if a population is stable or increasing. However, tree age and size may not be distributed so trees will be ready for harvest throughout that period. For example, some trees may be too small to saw into lumber, and there may be some years when no trees are really suitable for cutting.

In these cases the forest owner or society may decide to change the forest structure to meet their needs. The forest may be manipulated so trees of all ages are present for continuous harvesting. A forest that produces a continuous flow of products of about the same size, quality, and quantity over time is called a *regulated forest*. This definition could apply as well to wildlife game species or recreational opportunities as to timber.

**Sustained Yield.** *Sustained yield* requires a more or less continuous flow of forest products over multi-year periods. Regulated forests, by definition, provide a sustained yield. However, sustained yield becomes a problem during the period when an unregulated forest is converted to a regulated forest. Imagine that a forest has trees all the same age (Figure 11.3). This means that the trees will be more or less ready for harvest at the same time. However, no timber will be available between the time the trees are harvested and the time new ones grow to maturity. Forest managers may thus begin to convert the forest to one that has all ages present. They will want a sustained yield during the time they are converting to a regulated forest, but they will have to cut fewer trees per year to change the forest. Thus, attaining sustained yield, or maintaining the volume of sustained yield, can be difficult during the conversion period.

Sustained yield may apply to a single forest owner or to a broad geographic area, such as a county, state, or even the nation. Sustained yield is difficult

**Figure 11.3** A stand of longleaf pine about 125 years old in Mississippi. (Courtesy of U.S.D.A. Forest Service.)

for small landowners unless they use uneven-aged management, discussed later. The larger the ownership, the easier sustained yield becomes because there is more flexibility in timing timber harvests. The reason for the enhanced flexibility is that with the larger area there is greater variation in age classes, which occur for a variety of reasons including past management activities as well as natural disasters. Sustained yield may not be limited to a single landowner, however. It often occurs in state or multicounty areas over all owners even though, as an extreme, no one owner may have sustained yield. For example, during a 30-year period all timber may come from federal forests during the first 10 years, from industrial forests during the second 10, and from small private forests during the third 10-year period.

Conceptually, yield need not take place on a particular forest or ownership each and every year to be "sustained." A forest could be harvested every two, three, or five years and be both regulated and have sustained yield. However, as a practical matter, there must be a continuous daily yield over a wide geographic area. Industrial mills must have raw material daily or they cannot operate economically, and people in less developed nations need daily supplies of firewood for cooking and heating.

## Even-Aged and Uneven-Aged Management

The forest may be regulated by using either even-aged or uneven-aged management or a combination of the two. The concept of even-aged and uneven-aged forest stands was discussed in Chapter 9. In an oversimplified example of *even-aged management*, suppose trees take 25 years to mature in a 25-acre forest. Then the even-aged regulated forest would have 25 timber stands of equal productivity, each one acre and each one year older than the next (Figure 11.4).

The acre with the 25-year-old stand is harvested each year and immediately regenerated. For example, the acre in the far lower right of Figure 11.4a is cut in 1975, the acre to its left in 1976, and so on in perpetuity. Each year an acre is harvested and each

year the yield is the same because we have assumed equal productivity. The conversion to even-aged management from, for example, a 25-acre forest with trees all the same age would take 25 years; this is the conversion period discussed previously.

Even-aged management in practice is seldom so simple. The first problem is deciding on the desired age structure. Then one must decide on how to manipulate the existing forest to obtain it. Further, the existing tree species may not be those desired and so the forest manager must decide whether the site can biologically and economically support conversion to the desired species. Or, one must decide how to manage the undesired species so as to obtain the maximum return if conversion is unfeasible.

An *uneven-aged* stand is one where "trees differ markedly in age . . . . By convention, a minimum of 10 to 20 years is generally accepted." (13). Suppose a stand had sufficient age classes that some trees were mature every four years. Then the stand could be harvested every four years, and only four different stands would be needed to obtain regulation. One of these stands would be cut each year and each stand would be cut every four years, thus producing a regulated forest and a sustained yield (Figure 11.5).

*Rotation age* and *cutting cycle* are terms used to designate when stands are cut. Rotation age is the length of time from final harvest cut to final harvest cut in even-aged management. The rotation age in the preceding example is 25 years. Rotation age applies only to even-aged management because there is no *final* harvest cut in uneven-aged management. With the latter method a stand always exists and is only partially harvested each time the stand is cut. The length of time between these major cuts is called the cutting cycle. This term applies only to uneven-aged stands. The cutting cycle in the preceding example is four years. Analytical forest-management techniques are often used to determine rotation age and cutting cycle.

**The Normal Forest.** Perhaps the earliest concept of the ideal, regulated, even-aged forest was the

1975

| 1 | 2 | 3 | 4 | 5 |
|---|---|---|---|---|
| 6 | 7 | 8 | 9 | 10 |
| 11 | 12 | 13 | 14 | 15 |
| 16 | 17 | 18 | 19 | 20 |
| 21 | 22 | 23 | 24 | 25 |

(a)

1976

| 2 | 3 | 4 | 5 | 6 |
|---|---|---|---|---|
| 7 | 8 | 9 | 10 | 11 |
| 12 | 13 | 14 | 15 | 16 |
| 17 | 18 | 19 | 20 | 21 |
| 22 | 23 | 24 | 25 | 1 |

(b)

1977

| 3 | 4 | 5 | 6 | 7 |
|---|---|---|---|---|
| 8 | 9 | 10 | 11 | 12 |
| 13 | 14 | 15 | 16 | 17 |
| 18 | 19 | 20 | 21 | 22 |
| 23 | 24 | 25 | 1 | 2 |

(c)

1999

| 25 | 1 | 2 | 3 | 4 |
|---|---|---|---|---|
| 5 | 6 | 7 | 8 | 9 |
| 10 | 11 | 12 | 13 | 14 |
| 15 | 16 | 17 | 18 | 19 |
| 20 | 21 | 22 | 23 | 24 |

(d)

**Figure 11.4** Map of a simplified even-aged, regulated forest over time. Each cell is a separate stand and numbers in cells are stand age.

"Normal Forest," developed in Germany and Austria in the mid-1800s. The model was predicated on cutting fairly small, uniform blocks of even-aged timber and had three requirements. These were that the forest have (1) normal increment (growth), (2) normal age-class distribution, and (3) normal growing-stock levels.

Increment was considered normal if it was the maximum attainable for a particular species on the site. The normal age-class distribution was one with a series of equally productive stands that varied in age with the oldest age class equal to the rotation age. These stands were not necessarily the same size because of differences in site productivity. Figure 11.4 is a diagram of a normal age class distribution if all sites are equally productive, the stands are square, and the rotation is 25 years. Normal growing stock is automatically obtained when the increment and age-class distribution is normal.

The normal forest does not exist in the field but has influenced the thinking of forest managers for many generations. It is the *conceptual model* on

| | |
|---|---|
| Stand 1<br>Cut in:<br>1980<br>1984<br>1988<br>.<br>.<br>. | Stand 2<br>Cut in:<br>1981<br>1985<br>1989<br>.<br>.<br>. |
| Stand 3<br>Cut in:<br>1982<br>1986<br>1990<br>.<br>.<br>. | Stand 4<br>Cut in:<br>1983<br>1987<br>1991<br>.<br>.<br>. |

**Figure 11.5** Map of a simplified, uneven-aged, regulated forest.

which many even-aged forests are based and contains several ideas that are prevalent in modern forest management—for example, manipulating the stand's age distribution to obtain an equal annual yield of timber, maximum increment or growth, and uniform rotation age.

**Allowable Cut.** The *allowable cut* is the amount of timber considered available for cutting during a specified time period, usually one year. It is based on the biological possibilities of the existing stands and the alternatives chosen to obtain a regulated forest. The allowable cut is the amount and species of timber the forest manager would like harvested, but there are many reasons why the cut is not reached. These include fluctuations in the demand for forest products (discussed further later), weather conditions that prevent access to the timber or require cutting timber prematurely to replace inaccessible timber, availability of labor, and so on. The real goal is to achieve the allowable cut over multiple-year periods—for example, a five-year av-

erage, which allows for natural fluctuations. Undercutting one year is thus balanced by overcutting in other years.

## HOW FORESTS ARE MANAGED

Forests are usually managed either by even-aged or uneven-aged systems although sometimes the two forms are combined in the same forest. Chapter 9, "Silviculture," contains a detailed discussion of these management forms and of *clearcutting*, which is the predominant way even-aged stands are obtained. Briefly, *even-aged management* is the most common management form because: commercially desirable species are often shade-intolerant or susceptible to wind-throw and so grow best in even-aged stands; there is less expense per unit of volume harvested when clearcutting; there is less expense to regenerate artificially a clearcut stand, using, for example, site preparation and planting;[1] and wildlife habitat is created by creating forest openings.

There are, of course, several reasons why *uneven-aged management* may be preferred, as long as the tree species can tolerate the shade generated by this management system. First, small landowners may desire as much of a sustained yield as possible to generate cash more frequently. This is better accomplished with uneven-aged management on small individual holdings. Second, other forest products, such as aesthetic and recreational values, may require continuous forest cover. Finally, tree-species diversity may be enhanced and wildlife habitat improved by providing both food and shelter.

The choice of even-aged or uneven-aged management depends, in the final analysis, on the *landowner's objectives*. Another of the forest manager's jobs is to assist the landowner in analyzing which management form would best suit the owner's objectives. We will emphasize even-aged manage-

---

[1] Artificial regeneration is often preferred to natural because it usually provides fuller stocking on the site and establishes the new stand more rapidly. On the other hand, it requires a large capital investment that usually is not returned until the end of the rotation. Many small landowners are not willing to bear this cost.

ment because it is the most prevalent and because the concepts are best developed.

## Even-Aged Management

Even-aged management conceptually begins with determining *rotation age*. A forest stand grows first at an increasing rate and then at a decreasing rate until it finally levels off and begins to lose volume because of mortality exceeding growth (Figure 11.6). The rotation age must be chosen to accom-

modate both the landowner's objectives and this growth curve.

Rotation age is determined by first identifying the landowner's objective. The value of this objective is then calculated at each year of a stand's life; the year that produces the *maximum value*[2] is the rotation age. The two most common single objectives are

[2]There are various measures of maximum value—for example, maximum average annual value, maximum periodic value, maximum absolute value.

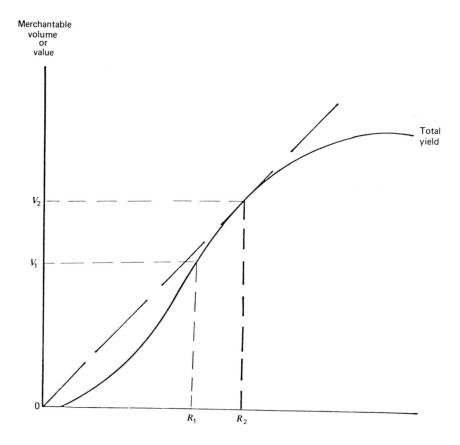

**Figure 11.6** Total volume or value growth of merchantable aspen timber on 1 hectare of land in the Great Lakes states.

maximizing wood cut and net cash flows, including imputed interest charges.

Maximum wood flow is obtained by maximizing the average annual yield, called *mean annual increment* (MAI) by foresters. MAI is simply the total volume available for harvest in a particular year divided by the number of years since the stand was established. It would be, for example, the volume found at point $V_2$ divided by the stand age found at point $R_2$ in Figure 11.6. MAI is calculated for all stand ages, and the age where it is greatest is chosen as the rotation age.

Maximum cash flow is obtained by maximizing the *land expectation value* (LEV) (14). LEV is basically the residual value of a perpetual forestry investment at a stated interest rate after accounting for all operating and holding costs. Therefore it sets the maximum price an investor could pay for the bare land and still earn the stated interest rate. Many forest economists believe that maximization of LEV is the correct rotation age criterion for both publicly and privately owned forests. LEV is a more complex criterion than MAI because it includes costs and revenues from perpetual forestry activities, all of which are discounted to allow for the time value of money.

More precisely, if yield ($Y$) is a function of time ($T$), then $Y = f(T)$ and MAI $= f(T)/T = Y/T$. A condensed LEV formulation is

$$LEV = \frac{R_t - C_t}{(1 + i)^t - 1}$$

where: $t$ = rotation age; $R_t$ = all revenues from the forestry investment compounded forward from the year they are received to year $t$; $C_t$ = all costs, except land purchase price, compounded forward from the year they are incurred to year $t$; $i$ = stated interest rate. The multiplier $1/(1 + i)^t - 1$ calculates the present value of a perpetual periodic payment occurring $t$ years in the future and every $t$ years thereafter. Note that the land is assumed bare with no trees on it, and the same revenues and costs are assumed to occur throughout the perpetual rotations.

Rotation age is, again, that stand age where LEV is the greatest. A further discussion of rotation age in which interest rates are taken into account is given in the section on "Timber Culture" in Chapter 20, "The Forest-Products Economy."

Rotation ages are for individual stands, but forests are made up of many stands. Further, regulating the entire forest is usually desired, regardless of whether the objective is maximizing the volume of wood harvested, the cash flows, or some other item. The optimal forest structure for age classes, species, and stocking may be identified in advance. This in itself can be a difficult task. In addition, the manipulation of the forest during the conversion period, when it is being brought to the regulated state, must also be specified. In fact, a forest may never be fully regulated because of additions and subtractions of acreage, changes in owner objectives, changes in technology and utilization standards, and other considerations.

*Harvest scheduling* specifies the year, or multiyear period, in which specific stands will be cut. The sum of the cut from all the stands during any time period is the allowable cut for that time period. There are several different ways to determine the harvest schedule and allowable cut. One way is to use *area control*, where cutting is controlled by specifying the number of acres to cut. The basic idea can be expressed using an oversimplified case where the rotation age is the same for all stands in the forest. In this case, the total acres in the forest are divided by the rotation age to determine the number of acres per year to be cut. One acre is cut each year in the preceding example with a 25-acre forest to a 25-year rotation. However, this still does not tell us which stand to cut. Usually, the oldest stand is cut first, but this can be modified by the various factors previously discussed.

Another way to determine the harvest schedule is to use *volume control,* where cutting is controlled by specifying the volume of timber to cut. There are many different formulas to calculate the volume to cut (for example, see reference 15). Most formulas calculate the cut as the sum of the net annual growth on the forest plus or minus an adjustment to increase or decrease the growing stock. Cutting growth and manipulating growing stock seem more in concert with uneven-aged management, discussed later, although volume control can also be used for even-aged management. In any case, the individual stands must again be identified in the forest and scheduled for cutting.

In practice, and particularly for privately owned forests, a combination of area and volume control is used. As mentioned, private owners are often interested in the continuous flow of wood or dollars from their land. This may lead to specifying a minimum acceptable level of annual cut with which to modify the acreage cut under an area-control scheme. Strict area control may not provide the desired volumes because of under- or overstocking, differences in site quality and hence yield, and other reasons.

A management plan may be written for all or part of the land owned, depending on the size of ownership. The management plan contains the harvest schedule but is usually broader than a harvesting plan. Management-plan contents will vary by organization, management objectives, and the size of ownership. In fact, some large landowners may have no formal management plan but simply have an idea of which stands will be cut next. Other owners may depend on market demand to determine when they will cut.

The breadth of management plans is indicated by Davis's "checklist" of items, as follows (15): (1) purposes of management; (2) markets, labor, and general economic situation; (3) forest organization and subdivision; (4) accessibility; (5) correlation with other forestland uses; (6) protection against fire, insect, and diseases; (7) silviculture; (8) inventory information; (9) regulatory framework; (10) provision for plan continuity; (11) cutting budget (harvest schedule). Some sections of the management plan are updated continuously, such as records of cutting and land acquisitions. The entire plan is usually updated on a 3- to 5-year cycle, usually following the latest continuous forest inventory.

## Uneven-Aged Management

The scheme behind uneven-aged management is to determine the desirable level of growing stock for an uneven-aged stand, allow it to grow for a relatively short time (say, 5 or 10 years), and then cut a volume of timber equal to the growth. The forest is regulated by manipulating the stands so that an equal volume of timber is due for cutting each year.

These ideas are expressed in Figure 11.7a, which shows a hypothetical stand with a 5-year cutting cycle. The *reserve growing stock* is that part of the growing stock reserved (uncut) to produce growth for future cuts, distance *a*. It is 350 cubic meters per hectare in our example. The stand grows to 450 cubic meters during the 5 years (point *b*) and then is

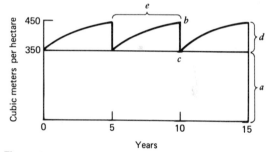

**Figure 11.7 a** The cutting cycle for a single stand.

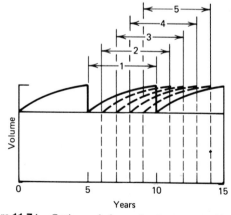

**Figure 11.7 b** Cutting cycle for regulated, uneven-aged forest.

cut back to 350 cubic meters (point *c*). The harvest is 100 (450 − 350) cubic meters (distance *d*) and the cutting cycle is 5 years (distance *e*). The cycle continues for as long as the stand is being managed.

The graph for a regulated forest (Figure 11.7*b*) is just a series of the individual stands overlayed on each other. In this example the graphs for five individual stands are overlayed, one stand being cut each year. In practice, 10, 20, or 100 stands might be cut in any one year.

The concept of uneven-aged management is simple, just like living off the interest from money in the bank. The implementation is far more difficult. Hann and Bare's (16) list of "major decisions" the forest manager must make indicates the complexity. These are

1. The optimal, sustainable diameter distribution for a given stand, expressed as number of trees in each diameter class.

2. The optimal species mix for a stand.

3. The optimal cutting-cycle length for each stand.

4. The optimal conversion strategy and conversion-period length for each stand.

5. The optimal scheduling of compartment treatments and the date of entry for each compartment.

## Mathematical Harvesting Scheduling

Computers, quantitative analyses, and mathematical planning techniques are firmly a part of both public and industrial forest management. Financial analyses, often in the form of benefit-cost analyses in the public sector, are frequently made to assess investment possibilities ranging from equipment purchases through cultural practices (such as thinning) to land acquisition. We will limit discussion in this section to harvest scheduling and simply mention some applications to multiple-use planning.

Mathematical harvest scheduling has been most widely adopted in even-aged management, although developmental work continues in uneven-aged man-

agement (see reference 16 for a discussion). The different stands, or classes of stands, must first be identified for use in even-aged management. Then, all likely management regimes for each stand or stand class are identified. The management regimes detail thinnings, rotation ages, or any other cultural practices that may be performed on the stand. The practices are usually detailed for multiyear periods so that, for example, period 1 is the first 5 years of a stand's life, period 2 the second 5 years, and so on. The next step is to calculate the values of the *management objectives* for each management regime for each stand. These objectives might be, for example, wood flow and present net worth (PNW). Thus, the forest manager has specified the most likely alternatives for managing the individual stand and has done this for each stand in the forest (Figure 11.8).

These data are then entered into a mathematical program that optimizes an objective or variable. *Linear programs* are most often used because they

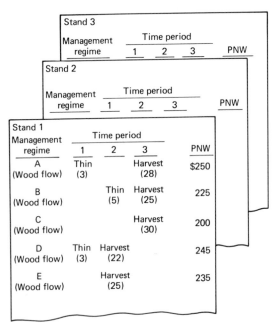

**Figure 11.8** Specification of alternative management regimes and objectives values for each stand.

can efficiently calculate answers for large data sets, are readily available on most computer systems, and are well documented and understood. The linear program will then either maximize or minimize an objective, such as maximizing present net worth or minimizing cost. The linear programs are also constrained to obtain other management objectives, such as a sustained yield or a fairly constant number of hectares harvested per time period. The answer will tell the forest manager the proportion of each stand to cut by each management regime during each time period to optimize that objective. This becomes a harvest schedule for the forest. The harvest schedule is then checked and modified by the field forester to allow for conditions in the forest that could not be included in the mathematical programming solution.

Several computer programs are available for mathematical harvest scheduling. These include MAX MILLION II (17), Timber RAM (18), Model I and Model II (19), and TREES (20). Mathematical programs have also been used for *multiple-use planning*, most frequently in the national forests. Both linear and goal programming techniques have been utilized for these applications (21–24). *Goal programming* is a variant of linear programming that allows stating several management goals at one time and has the advantage that these goals do not have to be measured in the same units. For example, board feet of timber, visitor-days recreation, and animal unit-months of grazing can all be stated. This is particularly important for multiple-use planning where many different forest products must be considered.

## FOREST OWNERS AND ORGANIZATION

Roughly one-third of the land area of the United States is classified as *forestland* (Table 11.1). Approximately 195 million of 296 million hectares of forestland, or two-thirds, is classified by the Forest Service as commercial forestland. Commercial forestland includes all land "which is producing or is capable of producing crops of industrial wood and not withdrawn from timber utilization by statute or administrative regulation" (25). *Commercial* is, perhaps, a misleading term because the classification is not limited to forests used for commercial purposes. Instead, it includes all lands *capable* of producing a commercial timber crop, whether or not they are producing it. Thus, the classification both includes some forestlands not available for commercial use and excludes some forestland devoted to other commercial purposes, such as hunting or outdoor recreation.

**Table 11.1**

Area in the United States, by Major Class of Land and Section (million hectares)

| Section | Total Land Area | Forestland[a] | | | Rangeland | Other Land |
| | | Total | Commercial[b] | Other | | |
| --- | --- | --- | --- | --- | --- | --- |
| North | 250.8 | 72.3 | 68.3 | 4.0 | 29.3 | 149.2 |
| South | 204.2 | 82.8 | 75.4 | 7.5 | 41.6 | 79.8 |
| Pacific Coast | 228.4 | 85.8 | 28.3 | 57.5 | 122.4 | 20.2 |
| Rocky Mountain | 221.9 | 55.1 | 23.1 | 32.0 | 133.5 | 33.3 |
| Total, United States | 905.3 | 296.0 | 195.1 | 100.9 | 326.9 | 282.5 |

*Source.* "Forest statistics of the U.S.," U.S.D.A. For. Serv., Review Draft, 1978.

[a] Land at least 10 percent stocked by forest trees of any size, or formerly having had such cover and not currently developed for non-forest use.

[b] Forestland that is producing or is capable of producing crops of industrial wood and not withdrawn from timber utilization by statute or administrative regulation.

## Land Ownership and Distribution

Commercial forestland is unevenly distributed across the United States, with the northern and southern regions together accounting for almost three-fourths (Table 11.2). About 72 percent of the nation's commercial forest land is privately owned, and 58 percent is held by private nonindustrial landowners. National forests, on the other hand, account for only 18 percent of the total. Eighty-three percent of the total national forestland is located in the West, where it accounts for over half of the total western commercial forestland.

Eighty-nine percent of the private commercial forests are located in the eastern United States, with the South accounting for 49 percent and the North 40 percent of the total. Accordingly, privately held forests comprise a more important part of the forestry sector in the North and South, whereas public forests are more important in the West.

The private nonindustrial forests dominate all other forestland ownerships in the East, accounting for 71 percent of the commercial forestland area. Industrial forestland, on the other hand, is heavily concentrated in the South (53 percent of the total) and to a lesser extent in the North and the West. The location of forestland is only a part of the story, however, and one must also examine the distribution of the growing stock on these forestlands to fully understand the forestry situation in the United States.

Figure 11.9 shows the distribution of *growing stock* by ownership category and major species group. Almost one-half (46 percent) of the entire softwood growing stock is located on national forestlands, even though the national forests make up only 18 percent of the total forestland area. The private nonindustrial forests, on the other hand, contain only 27 percent of the nation's softwood growing stock, on 58 percent of the forestland area. The bulk of the nation's hardwoods growing stock (70 percent) is located on the private nonindustrial forestlands.

The apparent inconsistency between the distribu-tion of the forestland and growing stock among ownerships can be explained by comparing the average age of stands on the two ownerships. A substantial portion of the western national forests are high-volume, old-growth, softwood forests. In contrast, most of the private nonindustrial forests, are immature, low-volume hardwoods forests. The net annual growth on the national forests is less than that on the private nonindustrial forests, reflecting these age differences. The Forest Service estimates that the national forests are producing at only 48 percent of their timber potential compared to 68 percent for industrial forests (25). (See Chapter 13 for a further discussion of growing stock and forest-site produc-tivity.)

An important reason for classifying our forest-lands by ownership is that management objectives tend to differ by owner. We can expect that the forest management practiced on a particular tract will reflect the landowner objectives because man-agement objectives largely determine management practices.

Forest organization tends to vary by management objective just as management objectives tend to vary by ownership. The organization of large forestland holdings, such as public and industrial forestlands, reflects their wide geographic distribution and the products produced. Thus they are organized along regional and product lines. In contrast, small forestland-holding organizations tend to be quite simple, if, indeed, any formal organization exists at all.

## Public Forest-Management Agencies

Public forests are administered by a variety of public agencies. Most are national forests, administered by the U.S. Department of Agriculture, Forest Service. Others are administered by the Bureau of Land Management and Bureau of Indian Affairs, both in the U.S. Department of Interior; by the U.S. De-partment of Defense; and by state forestry agencies. The Forest Service has the most sophisticated and advanced forest-management system among the fed-

**Table 11.2**

Area of Commercial Timberland in the United States, by Ownership and Section (million hectares)

| Type of Ownership | Total United States | (%) | Section North | South | Pacific Coast | Rocky Mountains |
|---|---|---|---|---|---|---|
| Total, all ownerships | 195.1 | | 68.3 | 75.4 | 28.3 | 23.1 |
| Total public | 54.7 | 28.0 | 12.5 | 7.1 | 17.8 | 17.3 |
| Total federal | 39.9 | 20.4 | 4.5 | 5.7 | 14.4 | 15.3 |
| National forest | 35.6 | 18.2 | 4.0 | 4.4 | 12.6 | 14.6 |
| Bureau of Land Management | 2.3 | 1.2 | a | a | 1.6 | 0.7 |
| Other federal | 1.9 | 1.0 | 0.5 | 1.3 | 0.2 | 0.1 |
| Other public (state, county, municipal) | 14.8 | 7.6 | 8.0 | 1.4 | 3.4 | 2.0 |
| Total private | 140.4 | 72.0 | 55.8 | 68.3 | 10.5 | 5.8 |
| Forest industry | 27.2 | 13.9 | 7.1 | 14.3 | 4.9 | 0.8 |
| Nonindustrial private forests | 113.2 | 58.0 | 48.7 | 54.0 | 5.6 | 5.0 |

*Source.* "Forest statistics of the U.S.," U.S.D.A. For. Serv., Review Draft, 1978.
a Fewer than 20,000 hectares.

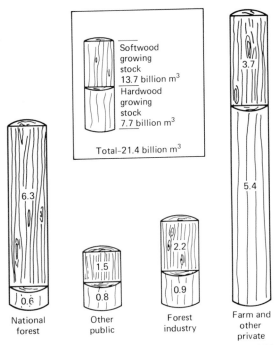

Softwood growing stock 13.7 billion m³
Hardwood growing stock 7.7 billion m³
Total—21.4 billion m³

3.7

5.4

6.3

1.5

2.2

0.9

0.6

0.8

National forest

Other public

Forest industry

Farm and other private

**Figure 11.9** Timber growing stock in United States in 1976, by ownership class and species group (billions of cubic meters). (U.S.D.A. Forest Service data.)

eral land management agencies, and also manages the largest commercial forest acreage.

The Forest Service's planning process attempts to balance national and local interests. Broad national forest-policy goals are established at the national level and implemented at the local level. Whereas national goals reflect general public interest, implementation at the local level must ensure that no one locality shoulders an unfair share of the burden in meeting the national goals.

The *Forest Service planning* occurs at the national, regional, and local forest level. There is a continuous flow of information along the three levels (26). The chief of the Forest Service develops the long-term national goals and programs to achieve those goals, based on a thorough assessment of the demand and supply situation and long-term

projections for each of the major forestry uses. National goals are assigned to each region, based on local supply and market conditions.

Each regional forester develops a regional plan incorporating the program direction and goals established by the national level. Regional goals, in turn, are assigned to each national forest within a region. The assignments are based on national-forest supply capabilities, socioeconomic assessments, potential environmental effects, economic-efficiency criteria, and community-stability objectives.

The basic planning unit is the *national forest,* and regional plans are implemented here. Forest plans are prepared for all lands in the national forest system. One integrated plan—including, for example, timber, wildlife, recreation, and watershed—may be prepared for all lands for which a forest supervisor is responsible, or a separate plan may be prepared for each national forest. In most cases a forest supervisor is responsible for a single national forest; hence most forest plans are prepared for a single forest.

The Forest Service's planning process reflects both the complexity of public demands on the national forests and the need for effective public participation in national forest planning. The regional and forest planning process has ten basic steps.

1. Identify issues, concerns, and opportunities.
2. Develop planning criteria.
3. Collect inventory data and information.
4. Analyze management situation.
5. Formulate objectives.
6. Estimate effects of alternatives.
7. Evaluate alternatives.
8. Select alternative.
9. Implement plan.
10. Monitor and evaluate implementation.

A further description of forestry at the national level is given in Chapter 12.

Considerable variation exists among the state

forestry agencies, depending on the importance of the state forestlands. Oregon, California, and Washington, for example, have large forestry agencies and quite advanced and comprehensive planning systems, reflecting the great value of the forests in those states. Several midwestern and eastern states have more modest forestry organizations and only minimal planning, reflecting the minor importance of those state forestlands.

Activities directed toward private forestlands—for example, fire and pest control, education, and forestry incentives—tend to dominate many state forestry agencies. Accordingly, the organization of state forestry agencies tends to emphasize these activities. For example, the location of field offices may be dictated by the geographic distribution of private instead of state forestlands. Staffing also may be dominated by fire-control and cooperative forest management (CFM) foresters instead of by forest-management personnel.

## Industrial Forests

Owners of industrial forests are those with wood-processing plants. Some may have only one mill and a few thousand forest hectares, while others may have various types of mills throughout the nation and own millions of hectares.

While one might surmise that the major forestry objective is to produce wood for company mills, a broader objective is to provide *acceptable profits* for the firm. Thus, in some cases, a paper company may sell its higher-value timber for poles and veneer and purchase lower-value pulpwood from other landowners. Similarly, a firm may develop or sell some of its forestlands for higher-valued nontimber uses. However, most firms have a policy of providing a part of their wood needs from company lands.

Sometimes the firm's processing facilities dictate what species and size trees to grow; for example, a firm may need loblolly pine pulpwood to supply a paper mill. But in the long run, these decisions are flexible. Timber growth goals can change as mar-

kets change and processing plants with new technology are built. Emphasis may shift from pulpwood to sawlogs and veneer logs, or vice versa.

Forestry organization varies among firms. Smaller companies may have a chief forester and assistants implementing company forest policies. Larger firms will have a timberlands division with a vice-president and even regional headquarters in some cases. The degree of autonomy of the timberlands division varies among firms, but final management responsibility rests with the board of directors. Some firms are operated as company or regional "profit centers" that have to show acceptable financial returns on all forestry investments. Others may be required to meet certain production goals at minimal cost.

Because of the size, complexity, and importance of private nonindustrial forestlands, Chapter 13 is devoted to this aspect of forest management.

## EXTERNAL INFLUENCES ON FOREST MANAGEMENT

So far we have been discussing forest management and determination of management objectives as if they were solely determined by either the landowner's personal objectives or by the biological and physical limitations of the forest. Another set of factors external to the forest must be considered by forest managers in making decisions. These external influences include the market for forest products, federal and state legislation, and taxation.

### The Market

A major stimulus for private production of salable forest products is their current and prospective price. Just as we see farmers raising more cattle when beef prices are high, forest owners have begun to manage timber more intensively as wood prices have increased.

Some timber-output responses to price are very

slow because trees take a long time to mature (see Chapter 20, "The Forest Products Economy"). However, many firms and public agencies are making current reforestation and timber stand-improvement investments based on projections that real wood prices will be significantly higher in several decades.

In addition, there can be immediate output responses to increased wood prices. For example, in the Northwest red alder was once considered a useless "weed tree." When the furniture industry began using alder, prices rose, and a new resource was available immediately. Similarly, the cut-and-haul cost of some material was more than the selling price, so this material was left in the woods. Much of this material is now harvested because rising wood prices exceed costs. Examples where this has happened include small trees, thinnings, treetops, and, in some cases, even branches used in whole-tree chippers. When wood prices are low, such material is best left in the forest. For example, society is poorly served if $200 is spent on labor, fuel, and equipment to remove and process wood products for which consumers would only pay $150.

Market factors also apply to resources needed to grow trees. We see less hand planting of trees and more machine planting when labor prices rise relative to equipment prices.

Prices also affect the production of certain non-timber products. Increased willingness to pay for forest-based recreation has stimulated sale of hunting permits and leases on private forestlands and more management to improve wildlife. Some landowners have sold or leased forestlands for recreation cabins and campsites.

Certain outputs such as clean air and water, scenic beauty, and dispersed recreation are not so easily sold in the market and are thus not likely to be supplied in optimal quantities from private forests. Thus, public agencies tend to concentrate on producing many of these so-called nonmarket goods. But we also have laws to increase the production of such goods on private lands.

## Legislation

One of the most fundamental ways in which the public influences and provides direction to forest management is through legislation. In a broad sense, all of society's laws affect forest management; however, it is possible to identify at least four classes of legislation that have a direct and profound impact on forest management: (1) environmental legislation, (2) health and safety legislation, (3) federal forest-management legislation, and (4) state forestry legislation.

### Environmental Legislation.

As discussed in Chapter 1 and in Chapter 12, the impact of environmental legislation on public forest management has been profound. The most important environmental law affecting forest management is the National Environmental Policy Act (NEPA) of 1969, which requires environmental impact statements (EIS) on "every recommendation or report on proposals for legislation and other major Federal actions significantly affecting the quality of the human environment." The need to prepare an EIS and submit it to public review has led to more careful consideration of the broad impacts of forest-management practices, a greater emphasis on public participation in the forest-planning process, and greater attention to alternative ways to achieve project objectives.

NEPA is perhaps the most far-reaching single piece of environmental legislation; but legislation to control water and air pollution, although more restricted in scope, imposes important constraints on forest-management practices. The objective of these laws is to maintain or restore water and air quality at some established level by restricting activities that reduce quality. The practical effect of water and air pollution-control legislation is to eliminate some kinds of forestry activities and restrict others.

### Safety and Health Legislation.

Forest-management activities characteristically are labor intensive. All of the laws concerning the safety, health, and working conditions of workers apply to forest-management activities as well. One of the most important labor laws affecting forest-management practices is the Occupational Safety and Health Act of 1970 (OSHA). Perhaps the most important aspect of OSHA for forest management is the health and safety operating standards it imposed on crews involved in planting, stand improvements, and timber-harvesting activities.

## Federal Forest-Management Legislation.

Broad direction and goals for managing public forests are provided by specific legislation at the federal level in the case of federal forestlands and the state level in the case of state lands. Three federal laws are particularly important in the management of the national forests: the Multiple Use—Sustained Yield (MU—SY) Act of 1960, the Forest and Rangeland Renewable Resources Planning Act (RPA) of 1974, and the National Forest Management Act (NFMA) of 1976. A detailed description of the effect of these acts on forest management is given in Chapters 1 and 12.

## State Forestry Laws.

A number of states have state forestry laws regulating forestry practices on private forestlands. The scope of these laws ranges from the very broad forest-practices laws of California, Oregon, and Washington—which regulate forestry practices from the harvesting and regeneration of timber to environmental protection—to laws for achieving a specific, limited goal, such as the reforestation of forestlands. This causes forest management practices to vary by state because of differences in the forestry laws.

## Taxation

Taxes yield revenues for governments to supply goods and services that citizens feel are best provided by the public sector. Forest owners share in this responsibility by paying local property taxes on their land, state and federal income taxes on forest revenues, and death taxes on inherited forests.

Some foresters have long sought the ideal combination of tax incentives to stimulate "needed" forest production. However, others have pointed out that the same argument can be made for stimulating production of all "needed" products. The difficulty arises in identifying how badly a product is needed in relation to other products. Consumer needs are usually expressed through higher product prices, which in turn stimulate production. Many economists have suggested neutral taxes that do not favor one industry over another for the price mechanism to work most efficiently.

## Local Government Taxes.

The *property tax* levied annually on real-estate values is a major source of local government revenue. In principle such values include forests, but in practice much timber value has escaped property taxation. Taxing authorities often have problems in determining and keeping pace with constantly changing timber values. Forest owners have sometimes harvested timber prematurely to reduce taxes where full timber values have been taxed annually.

Practical experience and theoretical studies have demonstrated that an annual property tax on full forest value is usually more discouraging to forestry than to other land uses with annual incomes. Thus the property tax on forests is almost always reduced, modified, or supplemented by another form of tax. One property-tax modification is to allow forestland to be taxed at *forestry values* instead of at higher development values. This is often done to encourage open-space land use.

Another modification is the *yield tax* levied in several states in place of the timber property tax. This tax is levied as a percent of harvest value when timber is cut. Yield taxes are often advocated because they do not stimulate premature timber cutting.

Another alternative is the *productivity tax*. This tax is paid annually at a different level for each productivity class of forestland; the higher the land productivity, the higher the tax. In theory, this tax does not penalize good management because the tax is always the same for any given site, no matter how much timber is grown or harvested. Proponents therefore claim it is an incentive for good forest management.

**Income Taxes.** Harvest income from timber held more than one year is taxed by the federal government at 28 percent for corporations and at 40 percent of the ordinary income tax rate for individuals. These are the reduced rates on gains from selling any asset held longer than one year—the long-term capital gains. Most states also levy taxes on timber harvest income, with maximum rates usually in the 5 to 10 percent range.

**Death Taxes.** A federal estate tax is paid on a decedent's forest property starting effectively at about 33 percent of amounts over $175,000 to 70 percent of amounts over $5 million. Up to certain limits, federal estate taxes are reduced by the amount of state death taxes. However, several states levy taxes beyond these limits.

Corporations are unaffected by death tax laws, but there has always been concern that individuals might have to harvest or sell timberlands to pay death taxes. The result could be premature cutting or fragmentation of properties into uneconomic units. To help prevent this problem, federal and some state laws now permit delayed payment of death taxes on certain managed woodlands. Also, some laws allow land valuation, for tax purposes, based on forest values instead of on higher potential development values.

# HARVESTING[3]

Partially or totally harvesting timber stands is a major tool for forest manipulation to obtain man-

[3]The authors are indebted to Dr. T. A. Walbridge, School of Forestry and Wildlife Resources, Virginia Polytechnic Institute and State University, for his substantial contributions to this section, including Tables 11.3 and 11.4.

agement objectives. Harvesting in the eastern United States is usually done by independent private contractors, although some are crews employed directly by industrial forest landowners. A combination of independent contractors and company crews is found in the western United States. The forest manager may be personally responsible for recommending management-related contract conditions, designating timber for cutting, and inspecting for contract compliance. Alternatively, these tasks may be performed by someone in the wood procurement function or someone attached to the corporate harvesting division. A brief discussion of harvesting is included because of its central place in forest management.

## Harvesting Objectives

A major harvesting objective is cost minimization while preventing undue delays, damage to remaining and harvested timber, and damage to soil, water quality, fish, and scenery. Difficult trade-offs must often be made. For example, highly mechanized systems may excessively damage harvested timber, the residual stand, and/or the environment. On the other hand, labor-intensive systems or exotic systems using balloons or helicopters minimize damage but may cost more than the trees are worth. Principles of engineering, economics, and operations research are applied to design optimal logging systems that maximize net benefits for a particular logging job.

The location and engineering of *logging roads* are often important in reaching harvesting objectives. Logging roads must be built because much timber is away from public roads. These roads are often maintained after harvesting is completed to provide access for management practices and fire control. The roads must be carefully located and engineered for minimal damage to soil and water quality, efficient equipment operation, and minimal aesthetic impact. Factors considered are drainage, steepness, surfacing, sharpness of curves, erosion control, bridges, and expected traffic volume.

**Table 11.3**
Phases and Functions of Harvesting Operations

| Phase | Function | Description |
|---|---|---|
| Preparing tree | Felling | Sever tree from its stump |
| | Limbing | Remove limbs and top from felled tree |
| | Bucking | Cut tree into segments |
| | Debarking | Remove bark from tree |
| | Chipping | Make chips from tree or segments |
| Moving tree to concentration point | Piling | Pile tree segments for in-woods loading |
| | Bunching | Put trees or segments in bunches before skidding, prehauling, or yarding |
| | Skidding | Move tree or segment, part of load on ground |
| | Prehauling | Move tree or segment, whole load off ground |
| | Yarding | Move tree or segment using wire rope and stationary machine |
| Loading tree for hauling | Sorting | Divide trees or segments into products before loading |
| | In-woods loading | Load tree or segment on prehauler in woods |
| | Unload at landing | Remove trees or segments from prehauler at landing. Landing is concentration point where trees are loaded for hauling |
| Hauling tree to market | Load for haul | Place trees or tree segments on trucks for haul to market point |
| | Hauling | Drive truck from landing to market point |
| | Unloading | Remove tree or segments from haul truck at market point |
| | Scaling | Measure or weigh tree or segments to determine volume of wood delivered |

*Source.* Prepared by T. A. Walbridge.

## Harvest Systems

Harvesting has four major phases: (1) preparing the tree, (2) moving the tree or its segments to a concentration point, (3) loading the tree or its segments for transport, and (4) hauling the tree or its segments to market. Each of these phases may in turn be subdivided into one or more functions (Table 11.3). Harvesting systems are then designed by combining these functions and performing them with different types of equipment to achieve harvesting objectives. Harvesting systems will vary in functional configuration depending on the terrain, tree size, and product being harvested. They are often defined by the delivered product's form, such as short-wood or long-wood systems (Table 11.4).

**Gentle Terrain.** The most traditional system is to *fell trees* with a gasoline-powered chain saw, limb the tree with a saw and/or an axe, and skid the tree to the landing for loading. The tree may be bucked at either the stump or the landing, or it may be hauled "tree-length" to the mill where it is bucked mechan-

ically by several different methods. Smaller trees, up to 18 to 20 inches stump diameter, are often felled or felled and bunched by powerful hydraulic shears mounted on rubber-tired or crawler tractors (see Figure 9.13). These are considered highly mechanized systems.

*Skidding* is usually performed by rubber-tired, four-wheel-drive tractors, not by metal-treaded crawler tractors, unless trees are very large (see Figure 4.5). Some tractors are equipped with grapples that can lift the front end of bunched trees off the ground while they are being skidded (Figure 11.10). Others are equipped with the standard choker-cable system—cables fastened around individual logs and then combined to form a bunch. The larger the logs, the smaller the load, and some western old-growth timber is so large that only one log is skidded at a time. On many western old-growth clear-cuts, huge winches pull logs with wire rope cables from the stump to the landing. In the South, pulpwood bucked at the stump may be hand or mechanically loaded onto prehaulers for transport to the landing or onto trucks for hauling.

**Table 11.4**
Harvesting Systems Classified by Product Form

| Function Performed | Shortwood | | Longwood | | Full Tree | |
|---|---|---|---|---|---|---|
| | Woods Bucking | Landing Bucking | Random or Multiple Length | Tree Length | Partial Tree Chipping | Total Tree Chipping |
| In woods | Fell, limb, buck | Fell, limb | Fell, limb | Fell, limb | Fell | Fell |
| | Load, prehaul, or yard | Skid or yard | Skid, prehaul, or yard | Skid, prehaul, or yard | Skid, prehaul, or yard | Skid, or yard |
| At landing | Unload, load, haul | Buck, load, haul | Buck, load, haul | Load, haul | Limb, debark, chip, load, haul | Chip, load, haul |

*Source.* Prepared by T. A. Walbridge.

**Figure 11.10**   Grapple skidder with moving boom used in thinning operation of Douglas fir stand. (Courtesy of M. Wotton.)

**Figure 11.11**   Full-tree chipper in use with hardwoods. (Courtesy of U.S.D.A. Forest Service.)

Sometimes *"whole-tree logging"* is used. Here, the whole tree, including stem, limbs, and tops (but not the roots) is either transported to the processing site or is skidded to a chipper located at the landing. The entire tree is then fed into the chipper. The resulting mixture of wood, bark, and leaves is blown into trailers for hauling to the pulp mill (Figure 11.11). High-quality saw logs are usually cut from the whole tree before it is chipped.

*Loading* is also performed by a variety of machines. These can range from the "big stick" loader for pulpwood (roughly, a wire rope with a pair of tongs or slide hook on one end and a small power takeoff winch on the other) through large

heel-boom loaders, built on excavator bases, which load one big old-growth log at a time. Much loading is done by hydraulic knuckle-boom loaders with rotating grapples. These are often mounted on trucks and provide versatile, mobile units.

**Steep Terrain.** *Yarding* replaces the skidding function on terrain too steep for safe or economical tractor operation or where tractors would cause excessive soil disturbance. It is also sometimes used on flat terrain that is too wet to log with conventional skidders. On rare occasions balloons or helicopters are used on the very steepest areas to lift logs to the landing (Figure 11.12). *Cable logging* is often

**Figure 11.12** *a*  Harvesting by helicopter in inaccessible area or steep terrain.

**Figure 11.12** *b*  Helicopter yarding operation. (Courtesy of U.S.D.A. Forest Service.)

identified with the western United States, but smaller, mobile systems are sometimes used in mountainous eastern regions.

The basic cable logging scheme is that logs are attached to a wire rope that is either run through an elevated pulley (block) or attached to a carriage mounted on yet another wire rope (skyline), as schematically depicted in Figure 11.13. The logs are then transported to the landing by reeling in the wire ropes with large stationary yarders. The elevation is provided either by large standing trees that have been limbed and topped or by portable steel towers. *High-lead systems* are those where a block is elevated and a wire rope run through this pulley. *Skyline systems* are those where a carriage is attached to a wire rope that is suspended between two trees or towers. Logs are then attached to the carriage by other wire ropes, and the carriage is pulled to the landing with the logs attached (Figure

**Figure 11.14** High-lead logging uses spar tree to support cables and pulleys for moving logs from stump to central deck powered by stationary diesel unit and winches. (Courtesy of American Forest Institute.)

11.14). There are many variations of the two systems.

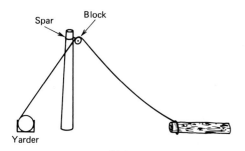

High-lead system

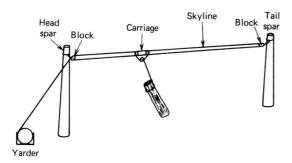

Skyline system

**Figure 11.13** Schematic diagram of basic high-lead and skyline yarding system.

# REFERENCES

1. L. A. Stoddart, S. W. Smith, and T. Box, *Range Management,* Third Edition, McGraw-Hill, New York, 1975.
2. H. L. Shirley, *Forest and Its Career Opportunities,* Third Edition, McGraw-Hill, New York, 1973.
3. H. E. Grelen, *J. Range Mgt., 31* (4), 244 (1978).
4. H. L. Haney, "Economics of integrated cattle-timber land use," In *Proceedings of the Southern Forest Range and Pasture Symposium,* New Orleans, March 13−14, 1980, 165−183.

5. H. A. Pearson and L. B. Whitaker, *J. Range Mgt., 26* (2), 85 (1973).
6. B. H. Kosco and J. W. Bartolome, *J. Range Mgt., 34* (3), 248 (1981).
7. J. L. Holechek, *J. Range Mgt., 34* (3), 251 (1981).
8. R. M. Hansen and L. D. Reid, *J. Range Mgt., 28* (1), 43 (1975).
9. H. F. Heady, *Rangeland Management,* McGraw-Hill, New York, 1975.
10. D. R. Satterlund, *Wildland Watershed Management,* Ronald Press, New York, 1972.
11. G. W. Sharpe, C. W. Hendee, and S. W. Allen, *Introduction to Forestry,* McGraw-Hill, New York, 1976.
12. W. E. Sopper, *Watershed Management,* National Water Commission, Arlington, Va., 1971.
13. F. C. Ford-Robertson, *Terminology of Forest Science, Technology, Practice and Products,* Soc, Am. Foresters, Washington, D.C., 1971.
14. W. Linnard and M. Gane, "Martin Faustmann and the evolution of discounted cash flow: two articles from the original German of 1849," Commonwealth Forestry Institute, Univ. of Oxford, Oxford, 1968.
15. K. P. Davis, *Forest Management: Regulation and Valuation,* Second Edition, McGraw-Hill, New York, 1966.
16. D. W. Hann and B. B. Bare, "Uneven-aged forest management: state of the art (or science?)," U.S.D.A. For. Serv., Gen. Tech. Rep. INT-50, Intermountain For. and Range Ex. Sta., Odgen, Utah, 1979.
17. J. L. Clutter, J. C. Fortson, and L. V. Pienaar, "A computerized forest management planning system, user's manual," Univ. of Georgia, Athens, 1978.
18. D. I. Navon, "Timber RAM: a long-range planning method for commercial timber lands under multiple-use management," Res. Paper PSW-70, Berkeley, 1971.
19. K. N. Johnson and H. L. Scheurman, "Techniques for prescribing optimal timber harvest and investment under different objectives—discussion and synthesis," *Forest Sci. Mono. 18,* 1977.
20. P. L. Tedder, J. S. Schmidt, and J. Gourley, "TREES: timber resource economic estimation system, Vol. I, a user's manual for forest management and harvest scheduling," Res. Bull. 31a, School of Forestry, Oregon State Univ., Corvallis, 1980.
21. W. A. Leuschner, J. R. Porter, M. R. Reynolds, and H. E. Burkhart, *Can. J. For. Res., 5,* 485 (1975).
22. A. Schuler and J. C. Meadows, *J. Environ. Mgt., 3,* 351 (1975).
23. E. F. Bell, "Goal programming for land use planning," U.S.D.A. For. Serv., Gen. Tech. Rpt. PNW-53, Portland, Ore., 1976.
24. R. C. Field, "Timber management planning with timber RAM and goal programming," In *Compiler, Operational Forest Management Planning Methods,* Proc. of Meeting of Steering Systems Project Group, D. Navon, ed., IUFRO, Bucharest, Romania, June 1978. Gen. Tech. Rep. PSW-32, U.S.D.A. For. Serv. Berkeley, 117 pp.
25. Anon., "Forest Statistics of the U.S., 1977," Review Draft, U.S.D.A. For. Serv., 1978.
26. Anon., "National Forest System Land and Resources Management Planning," U.S.D.A. For. Serv., *Federal Register,* Vol. *44* (181): 53927−53999, Part IV, Sept. 17, 1979.

# 12

# FORESTRY AT THE NATIONAL LEVEL

## R. Max Peterson and Robert D. Gale

- DEFINING FORESTRY FROM A NATIONAL PERSPECTIVE
- AGENCIES AND ORGANIZATIONS WITH NATIONAL INTEREST IN FORESTRY
  Agencies
  Forest Service
  National Interest Groups
- THE FUNCTIONING OF FEDERAL AGENCIES AND FORESTRY

- INCORPORATING PUBLIC INTERESTS INTO FORESTRY AT THE NATIONAL LEVEL
- COOPERATIVE FORESTRY ACTIVITIES
- FORESTRY RESEARCH
- SUMMARY AND A LOOK AHEAD
- REFERENCES

The question is often asked, "What do all those bureaucrats and lobbyists do in Washington?" While many other chapters in this text cover technical forestry, this one will attempt to answer that question by highlighting another aspect of forestry—forestry at the national level. Together, the national focus and the technical focus are equally important aspects of forest management.

This chapter examines national forestry in two ways. First, a general overview is presented. Diverse groups and agencies with interests in forestry issues and policies are examined. Second, the chapter discusses specific examples of national activities. The U.S. Department of Agriculture *Forest Service* is used as an example to explain national policymaking and the dynamics of interaction between groups and agencies (Figure 12.1).

Much of what distinguishes forestry at the national level is its political and administrative context. This is where the chapter concentrates. Laws, executive orders, and histories of forestry policy are touched on where relevant. Others chapters, such as Chapter 1, provide a more in-depth legal and historical overview of forestry in the United States.

## DEFINING FORESTRY FROM A NATIONAL PERSPECTIVE

Applied technical forestry concentrates on a forest's potential to produce resources and the relationships among these resources. Forestry at the national level concentrates on the relationships between forestry and other public policy issues, such as inflation, unemployment, environmental quality, or international trade, and the opportunities that forest resources provide to address these national issues.

It is often thought that forestry policy is established only at the national level; this is not really true. Forestry at the national level sets the goals and overall direction for practicing forestry, but this must be done with full recognition of the physical, biological, and social constraints facing forestry at the field level; the two aspects are interdependent. Also, to a degree, forest policy is actually set at all levels of management—national, regional, state, and local.

What distinguishes forestry at the national level is the context within which it is practiced, especially with regard to federal forestry. Foresters must view forest-resource management needs and opportunities in terms of their relationships to national issues, while not losing sight of local situations. The Forest Service, like other agencies, develops a general program that it feels will best protect, improve, and utilize forest resources, while also attempting to serve local, regional, and national needs. The Department of Agriculture, working with the president's Office of Management and Budget (OMB), must mesh this program with other resource and nonresource programs, which must be done within the framework of a national budget that meets the goals and objectives of the administration. This requires almost continuous interaction with other agencies, special-interest groups, Congress, and foresters in the field. Forestry becomes a job of balancing the goals of an administration with the professional aspects of resource management's existing laws.

*National policy* often depends on the political climate in our nation's capital. To illustrate this, we will examine the role of the Forest Service in the activities of the president's anti-inflation task force. In a speech to the nation in June 1979, President Jimmy Carter outlined four steps to try to curb inflation. One directed the Forest Service to explore opportunities to increase the supply of timber from the nation's forests.

Sharp escalation of prices for new houses and increasing lumber and plywood prices led the president's Council on Wage and Price Stability (in 1979) to see timber inventories in national forests as a nationally controlled asset that could be used to help the nation's inflation problems. At the same time, the Council on Environmental Quality and the Environmental Protection Agency expressed their concerns about the loss of nontimber values that would result from increased timber production. OMB was concerned with the budgetary implica-

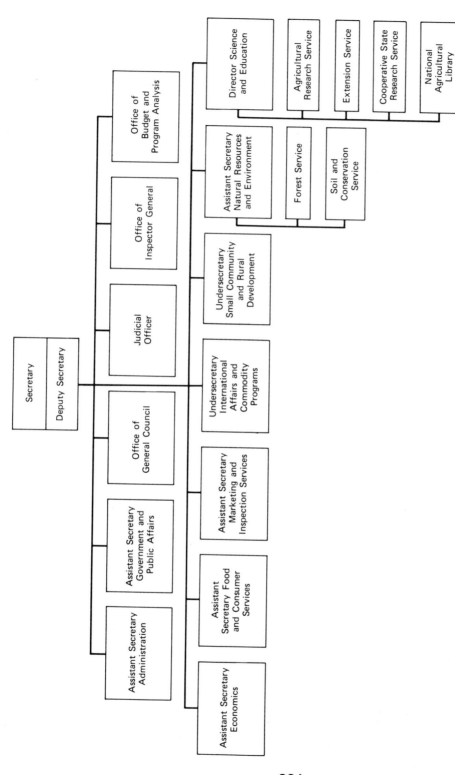

**Figure 12.1** Abbreviated organization chart of the U.S. Department of Agriculture. (Note: The Science and Education Administration (SEA) was dissolved under the Reagan Administration.

tions of increasing timber production. The Washington office of the Forest Service, in consultation with its field units, contributed technical expertise by outlining what the options were and the consequences of alternative policy directions. The president's Domestic Policy Council was assigned responsibility to work with the president's economic advisors and the concerned agencies to try to arrive at a reasonable solution to the issue.

After several months of analysis, discussion, and negotiation, a decision was reached by the president.

*I hereby direct the Departments of Agriculture and Interior, consistent with existing legal requirements, to use maximum speed in updating land management plans on selected National Forests with the objective of increasing the harvest of mature timber through departure from the current nondeclining even-flow policy. In updating land management plans, all relevant economic and environmental implications must be taken into account. A schedule for rapid completion of this process on those forests with substantial inventories of mature timber should be developed with regular progress reports to me. (a memorandum for the secretary of agriculture)*

It was a *compromise* that provided for an increase in timber production from public lands by permitting a short-term departure from even-flow timber management practices, but within the context of the existing laws and planning process.

Three important points that should be noted about forestry at the national level: (1) there is no single, fixed, overall forestry policy; (2) national responsibility for providing forestry leadership and technical information is charged to the Forest Service; (3) there are important international dimensions of forestry as practiced in the United States.

There are several reasons why there is not a single, overall *forestry policy* in the United States. Despite several generations of exploitation and use,

our country still has large expanses of forests with significant variations in the intensity of forest management. Also, forestry policy in a national perspective is dynamic and ever-changing. People use forests in many ways. Forestry policy must be flexible enough to respond to society's changing needs and demands, even when the demands conflict with each other. Many people and interest groups focus their demands on forestry at the national level—individual citizens, resource professionals, politicians, and citizens' groups representing common and vastly different interests. These interests must all be taken into account. This does not mean that there is any lack of national policy, only that policy must be *dynamic* and capable of accommodating many interests and changes. Currently, Forest Service policies are best articulated in the Resources Planning Act, a 5-year program, and related policy statements.

Demands and new opportunities for forest resources are continually changing as society changes. Newly emerging needs for protecting wild ecosystems (Figure 12.2), for wood as a structural and energy resource, and forestry in urban environments—to name but a few—have been incorporated into national forestry policy for the 1980s. By 1990, there will be new needs, many as yet unforeseen. Many of the needs that persist throughout the decade will change in scope and focus. Forestry at the technical level changes with advances in knowledge about how to manage resources. Forestry at the national level changes with changing societal needs.

Another reason for a *diversified national policy* is that our system of government was designed to spread authority across separate but equal branches of government. Both Congress and the executive branch have active roles in forestry, and the judicial branch is often employed to seek a balance between various aspects of forestry and differing interests. (The relationship between these branches of government are discussed more completely later in the chapter.) The diversity of both resources and social interests means that forest policy is actually a

**Figure 12.2**   Old-growth redwood on a ridge top site in Del Norte County, Calif. (Courtesy of U.S.D.A. Forest Service.)

collection of policies addressing many concerns. Although possibly cumbersome, the multifaceted nature of national forestry policy is more flexible than a single policy could be in meeting the range of social demands that forestry faces.

The Forest Service has an expanded national role in forestry. The agency, as directed by laws and regulations of the secretary of agriculture, is a national *source of information* about forestry. The Forest Service has two major programs that deal directly with the development and transfer of technical information—a research program and a major program area that cooperates with state and private forest owners. The national functioning of both research and state and private forestry activities is discussed in greater detail later in the chapter. Those two programs, along with a third that deals with management of the national forests and human

resource programs, comprise the Forest Service. Drawing on expertise from these program areas, the Forest Service provides technical advice on forestry matters to the Congress and the executive branch. The U.S. Department of the Interior's Fish and Wildlife Service has a similar advisory role specific to migratory and endangered fish and wildlife aspects of forest management.

Forestry at the national level also has *international implications*. Many of the forests in developing nations are publicly managed (Figure 12.3). The manner in which our public and private forests are managed and influenced by a nationally guided agency is often used as an example of how to structure forest management in other countries. In addition, the United States provides technical knowledge for increasing the utilization and productivity of the natural resources of developing nations.

**Figure 12.3** Plantation of *Pinus patula* on the Stapleford Forest near Umtali, Zimbabwe (formerly Rhodesia). The stand is about 17 years old and was thinned at 8 and 14 years and pruned to 22 feet with crop trees to 36 feet. (Courtesy of M. Wotton.)

In summary, forestry at the national level is characterized by the comprehensive context within which it is practiced. Forestry becomes a component of important national and international policies and issues. Forestry policy is shaped by the overall executive program, Congress, the courts, and the opportunities that exist at the technical level where it is to be applied. National forestry also includes providing technical assistance to Congress and developing nations.

## AGENCIES AND ORGANIZATIONS WITH NATIONAL INTEREST IN FORESTRY

### Agencies

The nation's forestlands total about 300 million hectares. Approximately 72 percent[1] of the commercial forestland is controlled by nonfederal owners. Several agencies directly administer forest- and rangelands for various purposes, depending on the agency's particular responsibilities. Approximately 10 percent of the forestland and rangeland is administered by federal agencies whose forestry functions are generally minor or incidental to their major responsibilities. The Department of Defense, for example, manages forestland on military reservations. While activities such as grazing, timber production, and wildlife management are permitted on some of these lands, they are primarily managed for defense purposes.

Four federal agencies have land management as their primary responsibility: the Forest Service of the Department of Agriculture, the Bureau of Land Management, the Fish and Wildlife Service, and the National Park Service of Department of the Interior. Of these four agencies, the Forest Service manages 25 percent of the federally controlled forest and rangeland and the Bureau of Land Management (BLM) 62 percent. However, the Forest Service is responsible for approximately 80 percent of the federal *commercial* timberland, while the BLM

---

[1]Recent estimates are closer to 80 percent.

manages fewer than 25 million hectares of these forests. All of the BLM lands are located in the 13 western states, with most located in the two states of Alaska and Oregon.

Federal agencies, such as the Soil Conservation Service, Agricultural Stabilization and Conservation Service, Forest Service, and Science and Education Administration[2] of the Department of Agriculture also advise and assist private landowners in forest management.

The Forest Service was established in 1905 to protect and manage forest- and rangelands and to ensure a continuous flow of natural-resource benefits for the growing nation (Figure 12.4). The term *conservation* was used to characterize the management that was intended to be practiced on forested lands. It was defined as wise use and has since been clarified to mean the production of *multiple products* to ensure a sustained flow of goods and services to the public.

*National park* management is probably the oldest federal forestland-management program. In 1872, Congress established Yellowstone National Park by withdrawing it from public-domain lands open to entry for homesteading. The early parks were under the protection and administration of the Department of the Army. In 1916, Congress created the National Park Service in the Department of the Interior to manage the growing system of national parks. The mission of the National Park Service is to preserve unique American cultural and landscape heritages. These resources are managed primarily for recreation use and enjoyment, while maintaining their existing natural quality.

The *Fish and Wildlife Service* of the Department of the Interior manages approximately 400 wildlife refuges. The management of these refuges aids in the conservation of migratory birds, certain mammals, and sport fish.

The *Bureau of Land Management* of the Department of the Interior manages the largest segment of the nation's public lands. Its management goals are similar to those of the Forest Service. However, the vast majority of its lands are rangelands instead of forests (Figure 12.5).

Most land-management agencies have, as part of their mission, other responsibilities. These include educating the public in their field of resource management and assisting and encouraging good management practices on private lands with characteristics similar to the public lands they manage. In addition to the land-managing agencies, there are a host of departments and agencies with responsibilities that have an impact on forestry activities. They include the Departments of Commerce and Treasury, the State Department, the Environmental Protection Agency, the Agency for International Development, the Agriculture Research Service, the Soil Conservation Service, and the Science and Education Administration. Because of the national importance of the Forest Service to forest management, the organization of this federal agency is further discussed.

## Forest Service

As outlined previously, the Forest Service is divided into three main parts, the national forest system, forestry research, and state and private forestry (Figures 12.6 and 12.7). The *national forest system* is the dominant part of the agency and the part responsible for managing the national forests. *Forestry research* provides basic and applied research support on all aspects of forest management. *State and private forestry* covers a variety of services to the state and private forestry sectors, such as technical and financial assistance in forest-fire and pest control, tree planting, and timber-stand improvement (1, 2).

The *field organization* of the Forest Service has four main levels. At the top is the Washington office, headed by the chief of the Forest Service. Although general policymaking and planning takes

---

[2]SEA was dissolved under the Reagan Administration. The director of Science and Education is now responsible for the Agricultural Research Service, the Cooperative State Research Service, and the Extension Service (see Figure 12.1).

**Figure 12.4** Oldest ranger station in the United States, Bitterroot National Forest, Montana. (Courtesy of U.S.D.A. Forest Service.)

place in the Washington office, most Forest Service operations,—including substantial policymaking authority—are delegated to Forest Service field offices.

The national forest system field offices are divided into nine regions. This is the second level. Each *regional office* is headed by a regional forester, who exercises broad authority over all activities in the region. Immediately below the regional office at the third level is the *national forest,* headed by a forest supervisor. Except for Alaska, with only two—albeit large—national forests, there are from 13 to 33 national forests within a region. In addition to the national forests, there are 19 national grasslands in the prairie states, administered by national forest supervisors.

The lowest administrative unit within the Forest Service is the *ranger district,* headed by a forest ranger who directly supervises forest-management activities within the district. The district ranger is the primary line officer of the Forest Service—an operating officer, not a policymaker.

The *research field organization* has eight experiment stations and a separate forest-products laboratory (Figure 12.8). Each of these has a director, several assistant directors, and a staff that performs the research. *State and private forestry* consists of two area offices reporting directly to the chief. In the West, state and private forestry is organized as a division within the regional offices. The regional offices of the Forest Service administer all the affairs of their respective regions with the exception of the eight research stations and the two eastern field offices of state and private forestry.

**Figure 12.5** Sheep grazing in Midway Valley, Dixie National Forest, Utah. (Courtesy of U.S.D.A. Forest Service.)

## National Interest Groups

So far we have spoken only of formal government at the national level. Of equal importance is the vast array of national interest groups. They are often referred to as the "lobby," although many would not consider that as their primary objective. These groups can be classified into four general categories: (1) the commodity-user group, (2) the noncommodity-user group, (3) the professional group, and (4) the special-issue group. It is important to recognize that specific organizations may have activities in more than one group. However, one overriding interest usually tends to be reflected.

The commodity and noncommodity groups are both forest users. Both groups try to promote forest policies and budgets that favor their interests. The *commodity group* is composed of those organizations associated with an industry that produces a marketed product such as paper, lumber, or beef. Examples are the American Plywood Association and the National Forest Products Association.

The *noncommodity group* is also a user of the forest, but their use does not involve the production of a forest product. They primarily use the forest for enjoyment. Examples of the noncommodity groups are the National Wildlife Federation, the Sierra Club, Forests Unlimited, and the All-Terrain Vehicle Association.

The third group, referred to as the *professional group*, represents those organizations whose primary purpose is to maintain and advance the technical and scientific level of the forestry profession.

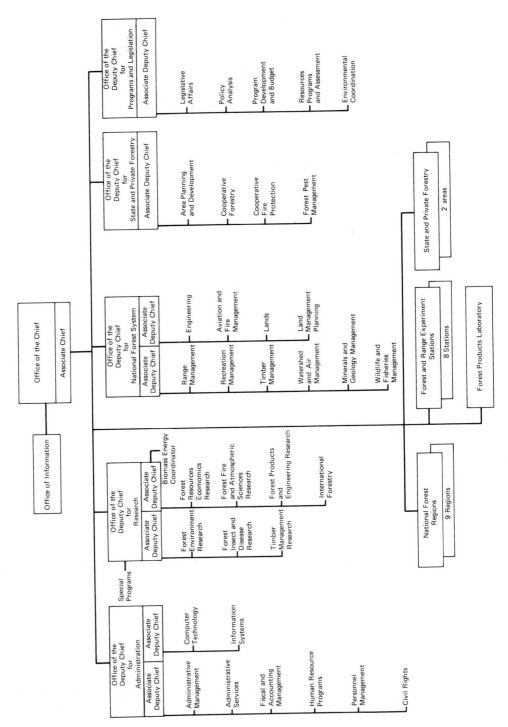

**Figure 12.6** Management responsibility of Forest Service.

# THE NATIONAL FOREST SYSTEM

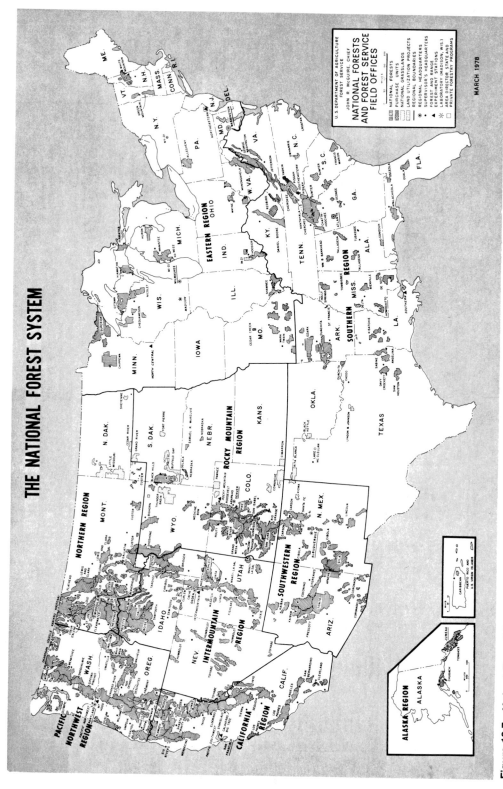

**Figure 12.7** National Forest System and Related Data Map. (Courtesy of U.S.D.A. Forest Service.)

**Figure 12.8** Forest Products Laboratory, Madison, Wisc. (Courtesy of U.S.D.A. Forest Service.)

This group includes such organizations as the Society of American Foresters, Resources for the Future, and the Society for Range Management.

The final category has been called the *special-issue group*. These are organizations that formally support or oppose a single issue. Their existence is usually limited to the duration of the issue. However, on occasion, they take on new issues and evolve into organizations with broader interests. Examples of special issue groups are Citizens Against Toxic Substances and Friends of the Boundary Waters Wilderness.

All of these national interest groups contribute to formulation of national policy. However, the Society of American Foresters plays an additional significant role in the development of the forestry profession.

The Society of American Foresters (SAF) was founded in 1900 with the objectives of advancing the science, technology, education, and practice of pro-fessional forestry in America and of using the knowledge and skill of the profession to benefit society. SAF publishes the monthly *Journal of Forestry* and *Forest Science,* a quarterly research journal.

The functions of the agency also include the formulation of a code of professional ethics for foresters, promotion of international forestry relations (for example, SAF recently hosted a Chinese delegation to the United States), preparation of descriptions of forest-cover types, preparation of cutting practice guides for different regions of the country, and classification of forestry literature, to name a few. Another important function of the agency is the study and development of standards in forestry education and accreditation of forestry schools. A listing of forestry schools in the United States is given in Appendix V, with those accredited by SAF denoted by an asterisk.

The society sets standards for curricula in forestry

**300**

schools in the study of basic forestry principles. The society states that "specialization should be built upon a foundation of general academic and professional education and should include interdisciplinary work pertinent to the individual student. It is essential that graduates have the ability to communicate effectively, both orally and in writing, with a wide range of people."

According to SAF, each professional curriculum should do the following:

1. Recognize that forestry is "managing and using for human benefit the forestlands and natural resources that occur on and in association with forestlands, including trees, other plants, animals, soil, water and related air and climate."

2. Provide significant concepts, multiple-use principles, and working knowledge of the following areas of study.
   (a) *Forest Biology.*
   (b) *Forestry in the Social Context.*
   (c) *Forest-Resources Measurements.*
   (d) *Forest-Ecosystem Management.*
   (e) *Forest-Resources Administration.*

3. Teach technical skills to the extent that they contribute to professional education.

4. Include field and laboratory instruction conducive to an understanding of concepts, principles, and methods and their applications.

5. Maintain an appropriate balance among forestry and nonforestry courses.

6. Emphasize the dynamic nature of the sciences and technologies by teaching new concepts and methods.

7. Stress understanding instead of rote learning of facts, principles instead of routines.

8. Promote continuing professional growth.

9. Provide challenging programs to develop individual talents and interest.

The *Office of Personnel Management* also provides a similar set of standards for forestry school curricula.

## THE FUNCTIONING OF FEDERAL AGENCIES AND FORESTRY

In order to understand forestry in a national frame of reference, we need to understand how the groups discussed in the previous section function and interrelate with the three branches of government to help formulate forestry policy. As discussed previously, there are several departments and agencies in the *executive branch* with direct interest in forestry matters. They develop procedures and establish direction for managing forest resources under their jurisdiction. In the process they must interact with and seek approval from the president's staff, the OMB, and Congress. This section will examine the "give and take" within government necessary to develop a forest-management program.

Within an agency, there are staff units, each sometimes having different concepts about what forestry policy should be. Informal discussions, staff meetings, and other means are employed to hammer out policy direction. Constraints are set by the limitations of the resources to be managed, laws, regulations, tradition, and executive orders from the president. This process goes within a legal framework established by Congress in a single charter act or by a series of acts for different components of the agency's program.

The management program of an agency such as the Forest Service is part of an overall *executive program*. It is also part of one finite budget. Forestry programs must be balanced with other programs such as health care, transportation systems, and defense matters. The central issue is how much should be allocated to forestry programs in relation to other programs to best serve the American public.

The unenviable task of recommending to the president how to slice the pie falls to the president's *Office of Management and Budget*. OMB must take all the agency and department budget proposals and fit them into one or more cohesive packages. OMB operates under the president's overall program direction and with no allegiance to any one agency or department. Generally, staff members at OMB referred to as "examiners" are assigned responsibility for one agency (at most three or four). The examiner analyzes the agency's budget proposal, for use in program balancing deliberations. The agency must provide full information and justification to its examiner. Analyses and assessments must accompany each program request. If support is not deemed adequate, the OMB representative may challenge or even recommend dropping a specific program. Effective interaction with the examiner, as well as support by the secretary and departmental staff is critical to an agency in maintaining its position within an adminstration's budget.

In addition to budget planning, OMB monitors the agency's programs. Programs, policies, and activities are watched for results within the president's program context. The agency faces detailed scrutiny at budget time if OMB questions have not been resolved during the year. The role of OMB in this sense is not punitive.

Forestry issues and policy are then incorporated into several parts of the president's annual program budget proposal. Implementation of any part of that plan must await *congressional action* to approve the activity and its funding. Congress may, of course, increase, decrease, or otherwise change the president's budget proposal. Congressional interest in forestry issues is evidenced by both individual members of Congress and by committee or subcommittee members. No single committee or subcommittee has overall jurisdiction over forestry matters; for example, committees on foreign trade consider log exports, while committees on energy issues may consider wood fiber as an alternative energy source.

A representative or staff member may have expertise in forestry matters or may rely on an agency for specific knowledge. Congressional committee staffs have recently increased their forestry expertise. Although most members of Congress have little background in forestry, they still may take a strong interest in particular forestry issues. The Forest Service manages land in many state and congres-

sional districts. As a result, it is not unusual for legislators to represent the interests of their constituents in specific forestry matters during the annual congressional budget-review process.

Congress's overall role in forestry issues is somewhat similar to that of a local forest manager. Congress tries to resolve disputes over conflicting uses, but on a broader scale—the scale of forestry in a national context. Congress carries out its role in two ways, first by reviewing and revising the president's program budget requests. It often provides direction in the annual appropriation act and the appropriation committee reports. The budget-review process provides an overview of an agency's plans and policies; here congressional direction is restricted to existing laws. The direction usually alters funding or alters the manner in which funds may be used.

Congress performs another role in national policy matters by *passing legislation*. Laws define, redefine, or clarify the context within which agencies administer policy. Congress tends to legislate infrequently regarding forestry, although the 1970s were an exception to this rule. The legislature has generally set broad guidelines or frameworks but prefers that the agencies develop and carry out specific policy. This happens for three reasons. First, as discussed previously, forests in the United States are very diverse and must respond to many often-changing needs. Second, Congress is not a very appropriate forum to produce specific direction because of its size and diverse membership. Third, many members of Congress consider it unwise to legislate on professional forestry matters. Congress' position on forestry also leads to support for, and strong reliance on, the agencies that are heavily staffed and run by professional resource managers.

A final but important role performed by Congress is monitoring and reviewing the day-to-day activities and occasional crises that occur during agency operations. These tasks are performed by the *General Accounting Office* and the *Congressional Budget Office*, both arms of Congress, and also through congressional oversight hearings. The results of these activities take the form of reports to or from Congress.

The executive and legislative branches sometimes employ subtle methods of reaching an agreement when establishing programs and setting program direction. The executive branch may omit programs from its budget recommendation that are enthusiastically supported by members of Congress because they are considered of lower priority. Then, in return for congressional compromise on another issue, the executive branch will include a portion or all of the omitted program. This process may also work in reverse. It must be remembered that the key national issues of compromise often are not forestry matters, but other matters of domestic or foreign policy. Professional foresters generally participate at the fringes of this process. They provide factual information on forestry opportunities and the consequences of various actions to the forest resources and the public who rely on those resources.

The *judicial branch* of the federal government is concerned with forestry issues only at the request of an interested party. Its role is to interpret and clarify actions and policies in terms of existing law and to offer redress to petitioners. The courts can either approve or prohibit specific activities and policies according to legal interpretation. They cannot intitiate new direction unless an existing basis can be shown to support it. However, if this base exists, an agency's operating policies may need to be changed in order to comply with the court's decision. Where the law is overly broad or unclear or where controversy touches on constitutional matters the courts may, in fact, provide considerable directions that the agency must follow. Each time a law is tested in court, new case law or precedent is established. If the law or action being tested is confirmed as being appropriate, then the law or action takes on new support or strength for similar future actions.

This section has stressed the *functional roles* of the three branches of the federal government and the way they *interact* to produce and interpret laws and policies. Perhaps an example may help to provide a clearer picture of the processes. In very general terms, we will follow public interest and government action in the evolution of forestry management policy for the Forest Service. A key point is that forestry policy has changed with social needs and demands over the past nine decades. These processes and relationships are summarized in Table 12.1 and are discussed below.

In the 1860s and 1870s, public opinion grew to favor federal management of forests. In 1879, the American Forestry Association (AFA) and the American Association for the Advancement of Science (AAAS) both petitioned Congress to reserve or set aside forested lands from public entry. In 1891, Congress passed a bill for general revision of the public land laws. When the bill emerged from House-Senate Conference, Section 24 had been added. It provided authority for a president to reserve forestlands from public entry. One month later, President Harrison set aside the Yellowstone Park Forest Reserve, south of Yellowstone Park. Executive reserves were proclaimed, but direction on how or for what purpose they were to be managed was unspecified.

In 1896, the president requested the National Academy of Sciences to study what had become known as the forest reserves. Congress incorporated the concepts of forestry management resulting from the study into an amendment to an appropriation bill. This action, in 1897, called the Organic Act, laid the groundwork for how the reserved federal forestland would be managed and used.

In 1905, the president, with congressional approval, transferred the Bureau of Forestry from the Department of the Interior to the Department of Agriculture and changed its name to the Forest Service. Two years later, the former forest reserves became known as national forests. Throughout the 1900s, the Forest Service managed the national forests and set specific policy based primarily on the Organic Act and the annual budget review. In 1960, Congress stepped back into center stage by passing a

**Table 12.1**
Major Events and Participants in the Evolution of Forest Policy

| Date | Public Interest | Legislative | Executive | Judicial |
|---|---|---|---|---|
| 1889 | AFA and AAAS petition Congress to reserve forest-lands[a] | | | |
| 1891 | | Reservation Act | President establishes reserves | |
| 1896 | NAS reserve-management report to president[b] | | | |
| 1897 | | Organic Act | Establishment of reserves continued; forestry-management concepts stated | |
| 1905 | | | Establishment of Forest Service | |
| 1960 | | Multiple Use–Sustained Yield Act | | |
| 1973 | Public petition of courts to review compliance with organic act | | | Court rules noncompliance |
| 1974 | | Renewable Resources Planning Act (RPA) | | |
| 1976 | | National Forest Management Act | Forest Service produces first national inventory and long-range programs based on RPA | |

[a] AFA: American Forestry Association; AAAS: American Association for the Advancement of Science.
[b] NAS: National Academy of Sciences.

new law to ensure that national forests would be managed for multiple uses at levels providing a sustained yield for the future (Figure 12.9). This was a codification of policies already followed by the Forest Service.

In the early 1970s several groups of people became concerned about how forestry was being practiced in some national forests. These groups petitioned the courts in 1973. The courts ruled that forestry practices were not in accordance with the law of 1897. Congress reentered the scene in 1974 with the Renewable Resources Planning Act (RPA). This bill requires the secretary of agriculture to assess natural resources periodically and to submit a five-year renewable-resources program to Congress, based on this assessment of future supplies and demands.

In 1976, Congress amended the RPA legislation and enacted the National Forest Management Act (NFMA), also in response to the 1973 court action. This bill provides general guidelines for the agency by establishing the general content and process to be followed in developing national forest plans.

Over the century from 1879 to 1979, forestry policy has moved into the spotlight several times and has been scrutinized and reshaped by public interest, the executive branch, the legislature, and the judiciary. By reviewing this long time span from a national perspective, it should be easier to see how the policy for managing our national forests was forged.

## INCORPORATING PUBLIC INTERESTS INTO FORESTRY AT THE NATIONAL LEVEL

Forestry at the national level, as we have seen, is concerned with the public interest in forest resources. This section of the chapter considers how

**Figure 12.9** Properly managed forest stands can offer a multiplicity of uses to both people and animals. Shown is a mature stand of eastern white pine in Minnesota with an understory of hardwood saplings. (Courtesy of U.S.D.A. Forest Service.)

people express their common interests and how those interests become input for forestry policy. There are many ways by which people can make themselves heard by policymakers. Individuals and groups can contact management agencies and their congressional representatives, or they can resort to some form of public expression. Concern with the public interests and the integration of diverse interests into the formulation of public policy are not new to our political scene.

In 1789, James Madison discussed in the *Federalist Papers* the role and importance of what we call *public interest* or *pressure groups*. Madison indicated that a major function of the governmental process was to integrate opposing interests and reconcile conflicting views. Almost 50 years later, Alexander de Tocqueville, the eminent French publicist, in his classic assessment of American culture and government entitled *Democracy in America*, commented on the tendency of Americans to form and join organizations, which in turn, often had agendas for political action.

In more recent times, political scientists have suggested the "group basis of politics" as one fundamental characteristic of American government. Economists have recognized "countervailing power" and interactive forces as important elements in public-policy decision making. Matters of the environment, natural resources, and forestry are not exempt with respect to the importance of interest groups in developing public policy.

Two related developments in recent years have intensified both individual and group involvement in questions of forestry policy and management. One of these is the widespread and growing interest in issues concerning the environment; the other is statutory requirements reinforced in court decision making and agency responses to public views and comments.

Numerous court challenges to government agency actions have occurred. A preliminary step to such action often is the formation of an ad hoc group, where a permanent group did not exist. In this context, the National Environmental Policy Act (NEPA) of 1969 as discussed in Chapters 1 and 11, has had major significance in providing the basis for legal challenges to government agencies (and thus has indirectly contributed to group formation and growth). Among other things, NEPA requires federal agencies to prepare impact statements assessing the consequences of alternatives to major federal actions affecting the environment. Citizens dissatisfied with the content and rationale of such statements have filed suits challenging findings and other aspects of agency decisions.

Citizen-court surveillance has considerably sharpened the awareness of decision-makers to consequences and alternatives of action and has stopped or delayed actions as well. In many cases this has contributed to wiser decisions. Most observers would agree that this emphasis on impact analysis has been materially advanced by the willingness of the federal courts to give "standing to sue" to a variety of interest groups. One result has been that federal agencies have taken the requirements of NEPA and other statutes more seriously than might otherwise have been the case. A few law professors have, in fact, asserted that this access to the courts is crucial to democratic government in this technocratic age. In any case, these developments have undoubtedly contributed to the growth and expansion of group activities with respect to environmental policy and administration.

It has also been pointed out, however, that on any issue or set of issues neither the involved groups nor the individual participants are likely to represent all people and all possible interest configurations. In part, the problem is one of span of attention. People cannot possibly get involved in all the issues that will affect them and their interests, nor is it clear that the decision to get involved is always rational or deliberate. Many factors, including personality, friendship, and presence, as well as preferences, may determine both the fact and the degree of involvement. Failure to be involved with issues that affect one's interests may mirror a lack of commitment, time, money, or understanding. As a result, it is crucial to recognize that less vocal citizens must also be considered and might not remain silent if a wrong decision is reached. By exercising informed judgments on what they perceive are the interests of the expressed and the silent publics, professionals and their agencies must begin to approximate the overall *public interest*.

In forest management, as in many resource and environmental decisions, the articulation of the public interest is often complicated by the fact that decisions made today have very *long-term* consequences. The responsible professional public servant must attempt to address the future. To be sure, the crystal ball is always clouded, and there is a tendency to address the immediate crisis. Hence analysis must substitute for prophecy and foreknowledge. If public agencies respond only to current public outcry, the real potential public interest may be overlooked.

It should be recognized that the very multiplicity of interests in forestry at the national level ensures a high level of conflict and controversy. In many situations, one set of interests will run counter to another. A major task of Congress and agencies is conflict resolution—seeking to reconcile and choose the appropriate solution among a wide range of possible outcomes.

## COOPERATIVE FORESTRY ACTIVITIES

Millions of hectares of forestlands are not administered by federal agencies. Nonfederal owners include forest industries, states, local governments, and small landowners (see Table 11.2 and Chapter 13). There are several formal programs to facilitate forest management on these various ownerships. Some programs provide forestry assistance to landowners, primarily small, nonindustrial owners. Other programs coordinate the activities of large land managers, primarily public agencies and forest industries. The term *cooperative forestry activities* is often used in referring to these types of programs.

The Forest Service has a major program (state and private forestry) specifically dedicated to cooperative forestry activities. A major effort is made to work with state forestry agencies either in facilitating the state programs or in funneling assistance to small forest owners. An example of assistance would be the Forest Service distribution of federal money for state wildfire prevention and suppression. This money is available under the *Clark-McNary Act*.

Coordination between larger landowners and agencies is often achieved by formal groups, which tend to be national or regional in scope. An example of a national group is the National Wildfire Coordination Group. Members are state and federal forestry representatives with wildfire prevention and suppression responsibilities. The purpose of this group is to coordinate programs in order to eliminate needless duplication and to share limited facilities, personnel, and supplies.

Currently there is great interest in *private nonindustrial* forestlands. While currently contributing a great deal, they have an even greater potential to contribute to future forest resource production in the United States. Nearly 60 percent of the commercial forestland in the United States is in farm and other private nonindustrial ownership. These owners also have millions of acres of noncommercial forest. Private nonindustrial lands produce a significant share of the nation's timber, support livestock herds, and provide recreational opportunities for many people. The majority of these forest ownerships are small parcels, less than 400 hectares (1000 acres).

Much is known about the extent of private nonindustrial forest ownership and about the resource-production capabilities of these lands. However, not enough is known about the landowners themselves. Their motivations for retaining forest tracts are quite diverse, and forest management may not be a major consideration. Returns from the forest are often from the sale of stumpage prior to selling the land itself.

Some controversy now surrounds private nonindustrial forestry at the national level—just as it did forestry on public lands 100 years ago. Policies from the national perspective for small woodlot owners will be in a state of flux during the 1980s. The first area of discussion is whether or not these lands are a matter of significant national forestry concern. Should private nonindustrial lands be part of the national effort to intensify forest management or are they outside that effort? How can forestry management be encouraged on these lands? Work is underway to determine how forest-management objectives might coincide with ownership objectives for small private forest parcels. Not only the Forest Service, but also state forestry agencies, the forest industry, forestry consultants, and universities are currently discussing these issues and examining the alternatives. There is a close parallel between this process for nonindustrial private lands and the one that went on 100 years ago and resulted in a program of conservation for public forest lands. A further discussion of private nonindustrial forests is given in Chapter 13.

## FORESTRY RESEARCH

Research has long been associated with the national concern for forest-resource management. Currently forestry management is a blend of basic and applied research investigation. Research projects are initiated to examine particular management questions, often at the request of resource administrators.

The need for research is not a recent phenomenon. Reports and recommendations on the nation's forests specifically called for national research initiatives before 1890. The Reverend Frederick Starr, Jr., called for "extensive, protracted, and scientific experiments in the propogation and cultivation of forest trees" in 1865. The "Report on Forestry" by Franklin B. Hough in 1882 called for research on the effect of forests on climate and for the establishment of experiment stations.

Forestry research at the national level has three functions: (1) to assist in identifying *areas of major concern* that require research, (2) to establish and *maintain continuity* between research and evolving management policy, (3) to provide *coordination* and *management* of the research program.

As previously discussed, national forestry policy and direction change with fluctuating social conditions and needs. Quite often, management policy options depend on new ways of monitoring uses and impacts, new methods of doing old jobs, new means of incorporating and balancing resource needs, etc. National forestry policy and the national research agenda are closely related. National forestry policies must be based on sound scientific information. Also, research findings may indicate a need to change national policy.

The research staff at the national level maintains the links between needed research and current policy. The link to policy helps determine which areas of study have high priority. High-priority research is not simply a matter of which forest problem is the greatest. The national staff encourages research that has applicability beyond a particular problem in a particular area. The other area of national responsibility for research is coordination. The national staffs seek to coordinate regional research to avoid duplication and research voids.

Many agencies and groups have national interests in forestry research. These programs vary considerably in size and diversity. The Fish and Wildlife Service studies the protection and management of animal resources (Figure 12.10). The National Park Service studies resource protection and management (especially in terms of opportunities to produce products from the forests and how to protect and enhance noncommodity values) and forest product improvement. The Environmental Protection Agency sponsors research on environmental protection and the consequences of forest activities on air and water quality.

Several special-interest groups also support research. They often do not have a national program of study, but concentrate on the interests of the organization. The National Wildlife Federation has a program of grants to sponsor research by university students. The National Forest Products Association sponsors research of interest to its members. Organizations such as these study forest technology,

**Figure 12.10** Wildlife such as the majestic moose are carefully managed in Yellowstone National Park, Wyo. (Photograph by R. A. Young.)

the resource base, changing social needs, and interactions between social demands and renewable resources.

Several national organizations seek to focus and direct research to current and future areas of concern and, when appropriate, to develop a greater understanding of current knowledge in the state of the art. Examples of these groups are Resources for the Future and the Society of American Foresters.

University studies often depend on an individual investigator's interests and funding sources with or without overall department programs. Their studies may involve social demands and needs and improved product utilization (Figure 12.11). National research coordination is much harder to achieve between agencies, organizations, and universities than within an agency or organization. Some umbrella-type organizations formally link different research bodies. These linkages facilitate communication more than they set national priorities. An example is the Forest Service's Eisenhower Consor-

tium, which seeks, primarily through planning and funding, to coordinate research at various universities. Where formal connections do not provide a national network between scientists, coordination may frequently be initiated by individual scientists.

The Forest and Rangeland Renewable Resources Planning Act of 1974 requires that forestry research planning be a continual process with ample opportunity for public participation. In compliance with this act there has been an enhanced effort to coordinate research at the national level. At the request of the Agricultural Research Policy Advisory Committee, a "National Program of Research for Forests and Associated Rangelands" was developed by a joint task force of the U.S. Department of Agriculture and the National Association of State Universities and Land-Grant Colleges (3).

The program was designed to satisfy several needs. First, to provide a guide for forestry research planning in the Science and Education Administration (SEA) and the participating forestry schools as required by Title XIV of the Food and Agricultural Act of 1977. Second, to provide the basis for the research portion of the 1980 to 1985 program under the 1974 RPA. Third, to provide a guide for coordinated annual program development among the Forest Service, cooperative research of SEA, the university community, and others.

The need was recognized for certain overall policy changes to strengthen the forestry research effort. Some recommendations were for more emphasis on research already underway, while others pointed to new directions. The specific recommendations outlined in the report not only give a perspective on possible future directions for forestry research but also provide an insight into current operations of national research planning. The recommendations were as follows (3).

1. *Place More Emphasis on Technology Transfer.*

2. *Improve Research Planning and Coordination.*

**Figure 12.11** A large part of university research is government sponsored. Academic research involves work in the *(a)* greenhouse and *(b)* at the "bench," as well as fieldwork. Photographs by R.A. Young.

3. *Achieve a Better Balance in Research Programs.*

4. *Use Interdisciplinary Approach in Research.*

5. *Increase Research at Forestry Schools.*

6. *Innovate to Get More From the Research Dollar.*

7. *Enlarge International Forestry Research and Development Programs.*

Table 12.2 shows the combined university-USDA (U.S. Department of Agriculture) research effort for the base year 1975 with projections for 1980 and 1985 (3).

People use forest environments in many ways. New knowledge is continually needed to manage the complex and changing relationships between people and forests. Research provides this knowledge.

## SUMMARY AND A LOOK AHEAD

Forestry at the national level is different from that practiced at the field or technical level. It focuses on forestry issues as components of many diverse national policies. Many groups, agencies, and individuals are involved in shaping national policy—some solely to carry out or influence certain aspects

**Table 12.2**

Present and Projected Forestry Research by Research Area, 1975, 1980, and 1985

| Research Area | Scientist Years[1] | | | |
|---|---|---|---|---|
| | 1975 | 1980 | 1985 | Increase 1975 to 1985 |
| Multiresource inventory, appraisal, and evaluation | 112 | 261 | 291 | 179 |
| Timber management Biology, culture and management of forests Genetics and breeding of forest trees Economics of timber production | 396 | 548 | 597 | 201 |
| Forest protection Control of insects, diseases, and fire | 323 | 368 | 365 | 42 |
| Harvesting, processing, and marketing of wood products | 328 | 419 | 449 | 121 |
| Forest watersheds, soils, and pollution | 220 | 326 | 410 | 190 |
| Forest range, wildlife, and fisheries habitat development | 109 | 189 | 273 | 164 |
| Forest recreation and environmental values | 64 | 99 | 204 | 140 |
| Total | 1552 | 2210 | 2589 | 1037 |

*Source.* "National Program of Research for Forests and Associated Rangelands," Report of the Joint Task Force of the U.S. Dept. of Agriculture and National Assoc. of State Univ. and Land-Grant Colleges, August 1978.

[1] A scientist year includes all technical and clerical support, together with facility, administrative, and other operational costs necessary to support one scientist for one year.

of forestry. However, for most individuals concerned with national activities, forestry is only a small part of their mission. By necessity, forestry from a national perspective must be viewed in a context of larger, national concerns such as employment, housing, energy, and international relations. Much effort goes into identifying how forestry can address these major national concerns.

In concluding this chapter, it might also be helpful to look ahead to the future of forestry from a national perspective. Forest resources—both commodity and noncommodity—are renewable. This should increase their importance as nonrenewable resources continue to dwindle. The ways in which forestry issues are important to national policies will become even more complex and diverse in the coming decades as we increase our knowledge of forest ecosystems.

Increasing public interest in and access to forestry issues will lead to questions about the roles of both resource professionals and interested citizens. Forestry professionals will need to develop better ways of analyzing alternative actions and displaying the decision-making process. People with little forestry background whose interests may be narrowly defined must be able to understand these processes. An increased awareness of international forestry will create new demands and will result in a broader range of issues and problems for foresters to address.

People will increasingly employ available means of influence (through all branches of government—executive, legislative, and judicial) as they become more involved with national forestry issues. Competing interests and uses for forest resources will require new approaches to balance social needs and resource capabilities. This is the future realm of forestry at the national level. The possibilities are challenging and intriguing. To serve the public in this future scenario foresters will need to

- Grow more trees.
- Use more reconstituted wood products.
- Improve public understanding and management of the ecosystem.
- Compensate private landowners for providing public values.
- Learn to accommodate additional segments of society in managing forests.

The future of forestry issues in national and international policies promises to be active and controversial. The coming decades will be perplexing and frustrating to those professionals who continue to see forestry solely in terms of applying technical forestry principles. On the other hand, the coming decades can be a time of challenge and excitement for the professional who understands the national perspective of forestry. For this professional, the times ahead will provide the opportunity to make valuable contributions to forestry in the tradition of Bernhard Fernow, Franklin Hough, and Gifford Pinchot.

## REFERENCES

1. G. O. Robinson, *The Forest Service*, Resources for the Future, Washington, D.C., 1975.
2. M. Frome, *The Forest Service*, Praeger, New York, 1971.
3. "National Program of Research for Forests and Associated Rangelands," USDA, SEA, Ag. Rev. and Manual Series, ARM-H-1, 1978.

# 13

# PRIVATE NONINDUSTRIAL FORESTS

## Gordon R. Cunningham

313

As indicated in the previous chapters, about 60 percent of land currently defined as commercial forestland is in private nonindustrial forests (PNFs). These are privately owned forestlands not owned by the forest industry. The major consideration is whether or not the large proportion of commercial forestland in PNFs makes them the "key" to future timber supplies; or does the uncertainty of ownership interests reduce their importance below that of public or industrial forests? A wide array of opinions exist on the purposes and values of PNFs. PNF owners represent a broad spectrum of socioeconomic classes with a concomitant wide variety of reasons for PNF ownership, ranging from purely aesthetic values to intense timber production for economic gains. Most observers agree, however, that PNFs are in a continual transition related to changing ownership, the changing interests of those owners, the changing interests of other fellow citizens, and the changing natural resources and energy supplies. In this chapter, facts about and opinions regarding PNFs will be presented.

## SIZE AND DISTRIBUTION

PNF ownerships include more commercial forestland than all other ownerships: forest industry, federal, state, county, and municipal. In 1977, by combining the most recent forestland estimates for all states, the Forest Service reported about 113.2 million hectares, or 58 percent of all commercial forestland in the United States, were in private nonindustrial ownerships (see Tables 11.1 and 11.2). Almost the same share of total forestland was reported by the Forest Service in 1952 and 1962 (60 percent both years). However, within this ownership group, a major shift is occurring. In 1952, farmers owned 35 percent of all commercial forestland, and nonfarmers owned 25 percent. In 1970, the percentages had about reversed: 33 percent owned by nonfarmers, and 26 percent by farmers. This trend probably will continue as long as a growing nonfarm population, with an increasing amount of investment

and discretionary money, competes for a fixed amount of land (Figure 13.1)(1).

National figures show the importance of PNFs in terms of overall area, but such conglomerating obscures other equally important characteristics of these ownerships: numbers and sizes of the forests as well as state and regional differences. Much of the controversy over the importance of PNFs revolves around these differences. For example, some economists consider the relatively small size of most of these forests to be a barrier to their effective management, while others believe owners of small forests are more willing and able to absorb the fixed annual expenses of taxes and interest that can comprise a major share of forest ownership costs.

While some people quote national data as evidence that PNFs are not as productive or well managed as forest industry land, others quote state and regional data from the same sources as evidence of productive and managerial similarities.

Unfortunately, a detailed national description of the numbers and sizes of PNFs has not been reported since 1952 (2). At that time, most of the PNF ownerships were small: 2,962,000 (two-thirds) were 20 hectares (50 acres) or less in size, and almost nine out of ten were 40 hectares (100 acres) or less in size. However, these ownerships of 40 hectares or less represented only 25 percent of the area in PNF. The other 75 percent of the area was in the remaining ownerships larger than 40 hectares: 623,000 ownerships accounting for only 14 percent of all PNF owners.

Whether the number and size of PNFs has increased or decreased since 1952 is conjecture. However, recent studies in nine eastern states (Connecticut, Delaware, Kentucky, Massachusetts, New Hampshire, New Jersey, Rhode Island, Vermont, and West Virginia) show increasing numbers and decreasing sizes (3–8). An eastern bias is evident, but 90 percent of the private forestland is located in the eastern states, so the changes in ownership in these states should indicate changes in numbers and sizes of most PNFs. On the basis of this assump-

**Figure 13.1** Western white pine timber, most privately owned, viewed from Elk Butte in Clearwater National Forest in Idaho. (Courtesy of U.S.D.A. Forest Service.)

tion, considerable changes have occurred in the sizes and numbers of PNFs since 1952. Between 1952 and 1978, the *numbers* of private nonindustrial owners increased in all nine states, from a 15 percent increase in Rhode Island to a 249 percent increase in Massachusetts. If the average annual increase in number of private nonindustrial forest owners for the nine states, 2.4 percent, were applied to the total number of PNF owners in all states, the approximate 4.5 million owners reported in 1952 would have almost doubled to about 8.3 million by 1978.

The *area* of commercial forestland in PNFs in the nine states increased 4 percent between 1952 and 1978. Here again, the combined data obscured differences among the states: the areas in more rural Kentucky, New Hampshire, Vermont, and West Virginia increased, while the areas in more urban Connecticut, Delaware, Massachusetts, New Jersey, and Rhode Island decreased. The average size of PNFs decreased in the nine states, from 23.5 hectares (58 acres) to 13.4 hectares (33 acres); Massachusetts had the largest decrease: from 35.5

hectares (89 acres) to 9.3 hectares (23 acres). This reflects the great increase in number of owners, while total area changed only a small amount during this time period.

If the increase in numbers and decrease in average size are real, they will intensify the discussions about the importance of smaller PNFs as sources of wood and other benefits, and the means to assure continued provision of those benefits to present and future users of these forests.

The *geographic distribution* of PNFs is important because of their concentration in the eastern United States. In 1970, 90 percent of all private nonindustrial forestland was east of a line drawn down the western borders of North Dakota, eastern South Dakota (excluding the Black Hills area), Nebraska, Kansas, Oklahoma, and Texas (Figure 13.2). These forests represent almost three-fourths of the commercial forestland in the eastern states. In the western states, PNFs account for only 17 percent of the commercial forestland. Because of this imbalance of ownership location, comparing forests of

**315**

**Figure 13.2** Distribution of ownership of private nonindustrial forests in the United States.

different ownerships by state or regions reveals information about them that is obscured when comparing only national data.

## FOREST PRODUCTIVITY, GROWTH, AND REMOVAL

Clawson believes six "myths" about PNFs are perpetuated by making comparisons among different ownerships with national data instead of with state or regional data (9). He also presents the "realities" revealed by state and regional data as follows.

### Myths

1. The PNFs have a low biological productive capacity.
2. They are poorly stocked.
3. Wood growth is low in relation to productive capacity.

4. Owners are unresponsive, in their timber growing, to timber prices.
5. These forests are poorly managed.
6. The owners are unwilling to sell their timber, preferring to retain their trees for personal enjoyment.

### Realities

1. When comparison is made on a state-by-state basis, PNFs have almost the same per hectares biological capacity to grow wood as do industrial forests.
2. When comparison is made on a state-by-state basis, PNFs in 1977 had almost as much growing stock per hectare as did industrial forests, but this gap has narrowed progressively at each forest-survey date since then. Comparisons of sawtimber volume per hectare of percentage of stands in sawtimber, and

percentages of stand with high and with low stocking all show PNFs today closely resemble industrial forests and that any past gaps have narrowed over the years.

3. PNFs in 1977 grew wood at 61 percent of biological capacity compared to national forests, which grew wood at 48 percent of capacity. When comparisons are made region by region, PNFs grew wood at about the same proportion of productive capacity per hectare as did the industrial forests.

4. For the period since 1952, PNF owners in the South have responded well to rising prices of timber by growing more timber. Similar relationships exist for the Pacific Northwest. PNF owners have responded to many factors as their wood output per hectare increased, but a response to higher wood prices seems clear.

5. The problems of managing PNFs, most of which are small and all of which lack wood-processing capacity, are indeed difficult. But per hectare wood output of such forests is good compared to that of either industrial or national forests in the same state or region, and the costs of growing such wood are in general low. One cannot fairly describe such results as those of poor management.

6. Availability of markets for species and grades of timber grown are decisive—PNF owners cannot sell their timber if there is no interested buyer. While many present owners will say, with complete honesty, that they will not sell timber from their forests, the probability is very great that over the life of the timber stand, during which its ownership will often change several times, some owner will accept a good offer, if one is made, for merchantable volumes of timber when these have developed. Over the long run, very little really merchantable timber will go unharvested.

Separate investigators (10) have also concurred with that last sentence and stated that rates of change in intention and ownership suggest that eventually most of the merchantable timber will be harvested, although at any one time about a third of the total volume may be off the market.

## Growing Stock

Growing-stock trees are those that qualify as usable for the owner's purposes. For the periodic surveys by the Forest Service and state forestry agencies, growing-stock trees are defined as live trees of commercial species qualifying as desirable or acceptable trees, excluding rough, rotten, and dead trees (1).

Growing-stock trees represent the capital of a forest. The share of total growing stock in PNFs in the United States increased slightly between 1952 and 1976: 37 percent in 1952, 38 percent in 1962, and 43 percent in 1976. Softwood growing stock is of more concern, because demands for softwood products have been relatively much heavier than for hardwood products. Estimates of *softwood growing stock* in PNFs were 2.6 billion cubic meters or 22 percent of the total in 1952, 2.8 billion cubic meters or 23 percent of the total in 1962, and 3.7 billion cubic meters or 27 percent of the total in 1976 (see Figure 11.9). This represents a small increase in softwood growing stock in PNFs nationally. However, regional changes varied considerably. For example, between 1962 and 1970, softwood growing stock in PNFs in south-central states increased from 33 percent of total softwood growing stock to 54 percent. During the same period, softwood growing stock in PNFs in northeastern states declined from 66 percent of the total to 57 percent. In the Pacific Northwest the share of softwood growing stock was essentially unchanged from 1952 to 1970, from only 8 percent to 9 percent.

*Hardwood growing stock* in PNFs represented almost three-fourths of *all* hardwood growing stock (Figure 13.3). This is because almost 90 percent of all hardwood growing stock is in eastern states, where 74 percent of the commercial forestland is in PNFs. In 1952, the 3.6 billion cubic meters in PNFs was 71 percent of all hardwood growing stock in the United States. The volume of hardwood growing stock in PNFs increased in 1962 and again in 1976,

**Figure 13.3** Mixed hardwood stands represent a large proportion of timber stock in private nonindustrial forests. (Courtesy of U.S.D.A. Forest Service.)

species, quantities, and qualities depends on environmental factors such as soil, precipitation and other weather phenomena, altitude, latitude, topography, aspect, other plants and animals, and the activities of humans, as discussed in other chapters. All of these environmental factors comprise the "site" for trees. Productivity of a site for growing sawtimber, pulpwood, and other fiber crops is stated in terms of volume produced per area unit per year. The Forest Service states site productivity in classes, based on cubic meters per hectare or cubic feet per acre. These classes are listed from the most productive to least productive in Table 13.1. PNFs include the largest share of land in every productivity class. The assumed average productivity per hectare per year for each productivity class is shown in the parentheses in Table 13.1. From these figures, an average annual site productivity for all private nonindustrial forestland is calculated at about 5.0 cubic meters per hectare. This compares with the average productivity per hectare per year for industrial forestland at 6.0 cubic meters per hectare, and of national forestland at 4.8 cubic meters per hectare. Thus, average productivity of all private nonindustrial forestland is about 82 percent of the productivity of all industrial forestland and is about 104 percent of all national forestland.

Again, wide differences exist among regions. For example, in the northeastern states, productivity of PNFs is 5.5 cubic meters per hectare, only 4 percent less than industrial forestland. In contrast, productivity of PNFs in the Pacific Northwest, although 30 percent more than in the Northeast, is only about 81 percent that of industrial forestland. These differences reflect the site quality of land in different ownerships. In the northeastern states, the proportions of land in different productivity classes were about the same for PNFs and industrial forests. On the other hand, in Pacific Northwest states, only one-third of private nonindustrial forestland is in the two highest productivity classes, while more than half of the industrial forestland is in those two highest productivity classes. National comparisons *do* obscure state and regional differences.

but because growing stock increased in other ownerships also, the share in PNFs declined slightly: in 1962, 4.0 billion cubic meters was 71 percent of all hardwood growing stock, and in 1976, 5.4 billion cubic meters was 70 percent of the total (see Figure 11.9).

In summary, about one-fourth of all softwood growing stock and about three-fourths of all hardwood growing stock is in PNFs, 90 percent of which are in eastern states.

## Forest-Site Productivity

In addition to watershed protection, climate amelioration, and aesthetic benefits, forests provide many valuable products, including sawtimber, pulpwood, and other wood-based crops. The ability of any stand of trees to produce fiber crops of different

**Table 13.1**

Site Productivity for Private Nonindustrial Forests, 1970

| Class | Productivity[a] (m³/ha) | Area of Commercial Forestland (ha) | Percent of U.S. in PNFs |
|-------|-------------------------|-------------------------------------|-------------------------|
| I | Greater than 11.55 (12.8) | 5,482,000 | 33 |
| II | 8.40–11.55 (10.0) | 15,418,000 | 47 |
| III | 5.95–8.40 (7.2) | 47,029,000 | 64 |
| IV | 3.50–5.95 (4.7) | 79,128,000 | 62 |
| V | Less than 3.50 (1.8) | 53,206,000 | 60 |

*Source.* "The Outlook for Timber in the U.S.," U.S.D.A. For. Serv., Res. Rept. No. 20, 1973.
[a] Numbers in parentheses are an approximate average productivity for each class.

## Growth and Removal

While forest-site productivity data can suggest *potential* growth possibilities, the current volumes of wood grown and removed present the real situation of the moment. As number of days of use can measure recreational pressure on an area of forest, the comparison between growth and removal can measure the wood-harvesting pressures on a forest. If growth and removal are balanced over the same period of time, a forest can be perpetuated. Because PNFs include such a major segment of commercial forestland, trends in the relationship between growth and removals for this ownership group could determine in large part the future availability of wood. In 1975, the Forest Service predicted that relatively constant proportions of roundwood harvests will be maintained from the national forests and other public ownership through 2020. The share of output from industrial forestlands is projected to drop about 7 percentage points, with farm and miscellaneous (i.e., private nonindustrial) owners sharing a corresponding increase (11).

What has been the relationship between growth and removals on private nonindustrial forestlands? In 1952, more softwood was removed than grew that year: removals were 106 percent of growth. However, the trend since has been for growth to exceed removals considerably: only 71 percent of growth was removed in 1962, and 74 percent in 1970. This will counteract in part, the excess of removals over

growth from industry and national forestlands, where softwood removals were 148 percent, 101 percent, and 121 percent of growth in 1952, 1962, and 1970, respectively. However, a considerable amount of those apparent excess removals were harvests of centuries of accumulated growth in old-growth western forest stands (Figure 13.4). Decreasing shares of hardwood growth were removed during the same years; 73 percent of growth was removed in 1952, 64 percent in 1962, and 62 percent in 1970. All in all, growth of both softwoods and hardwoods appears to be increasing at a decreasing rate, while removals appear to be increasing at an increasing rate.

## CHARACTERISTICS OF PNF OWNERS

Knowledge about the areas and numbers, geographic distribution, growing stock, productivity, and growth and removal of PNFs is important to understanding the changing natural resources that are the physical foundation of this civilization. Knowledge about the *owners* of those forests is critical to understanding how their part of that natural-resources foundation will change and will contribute to civilization.

Types of PNF owners vary greatly, and a number of different classification methods have been used to determine percentages of owner types. PNF owners include farmers, business and professional people,

**Figure 13.4** Old-growth ponderosa pine in eastern Oregon in the Fremont National Forest. (Courtesy of U.S.D.A. Forest Service.)

retired people, laborers, clerical workers, homemakers, people who do not earn wages, clubs, institutions, resort operators, dealers in forestland, municipal utilities, etc. A brief summary of the distribution of owner types is given in Table 13.2 for four different regions of the country. The distribution changes over time as well as with the region.

It is clear that extreme variation exists among the PNF owners relative to individual characteristics such as educational level, occupation, size of ownership, and objectives of ownership. Marler and Graves (12) divided the owners of PNFs into apparent homogeneous subgroups and classified their objectives relative to the probability of investment in forestry programs. They specified the following categories:

1. *Commercial farmer.* Full-time farming involves substituting capital for labor, and specialized commodity production. This may result in underutilization of land and timber,

although capital will still flow into the farm business because of higher returns. The opportunity to practice timber management exists because the return would be considered profitable. The commercial farmer's ability to hold and manage large capital assets is obvious. In order to be most effective, some mechanism is needed to allow the development of an opportunity that complements (other enterprises of a) farm business and does not compete with it (them) for labor and capital (unless more profitable).

2. *Part-time farmer.* Supplements nonfarm income by working the most productive land. Usually there is a minimal investment in machinery. Income is usually low, ability to hold capital low, and alternative rate of return high. Land and timber holdings are apt to be large enough to warrant management practices, but because of a higher and more im-

**Table 13.2**

Summary of Private Nonindustrial Forest Owner Types

| | Total Number of Owners (%) | | | | |
|---|---|---|---|---|---|
| | Central Wisconsin 1959 | Northern Idaho 1960 | Missouri 1964 | Southern New England 1973 | Kentucky 1975 |
| Farmer | 52 | 39 | 28 | 4 | 25 |
| Business-professional | 9 | 8 | 26 | 31 | 6 |
| Retired | 8 | 8 | 31 | 19 | 23 |
| Nonwage earner | 2 | — | 3 | a | 4 |
| Wage earner | 26 | 26 | 6 | 35 | 23 |
| Other | 3 | 19 | 6 | 11 | 19 |

*Source.* "The Forest-Land Owners of . . . ," U.S.D.A. For. Serv., Res. Bull. NE-38, NE-39, NE-41, NE-51, NE-57, NE-58, 1975–1978.
[a] Included in another classification

mediate rate of return, the farm business receives priority.

3. *Rural nonfarm resident.* Similar in some respects to the part-time farmer—not likely to be able to afford investments in forest management. May have a considerable acreage of forestland but primarily uses land for residence because employed elsewhere. Research indicates the nonfarm resident has an interest in his forestland and would not be opposed to timber sales.

4. *Absentee, business/professional.* This owner uses land primarily for nonfinancial purposes and generally is not opposed to harvesting except where conflicts with other uses occur. Income and asset level are such that investment in forestland would be possible. However, because of special needs and interest in the land, unique approaches to management will be needed.

5. *Absentee, retired.* Most likely, safety of capital with income is one of the most important objectives in use of capital. Planning horizon is limited and investments in forest management will not take place unless benefits can be shown to accrue to heirs, and capital can be protected.

6. *Absentee, wage earner/homemaker.* This group tends to be preservationist. Other characteristics involve limited income, a lack of desire to hold forest capital, and perhaps an aversion to any active management.

7. *Other (rural poor, speculators, etc.).* These persons usually have little investment potential and no interest in practicing any form of forest management.

A considerable number of studies have been performed in practically all regions of the United States to assess the characteristics of PNF owners. Most of the studies were to determine if forestry management practices were utilized on the forest-land holdings. In the interpretation of these investigations, designation as "well-managed" usually implied the PNF was managed for timber production and not for purely aesthetic characteristics. This apparent conflict of perceived value for PNFs will be discussed later in this chapter.

Although considerable variation exists from region to region and over time, the following generalizations seem to be characteristic for most PNFs based on a large number of surveys:

*Size of ownership.* Owners of large PNFs had a greater tendency to apply forestry management practices, generally had PNFs with greater productivity, and had a greater interest in timber value.

*Absentee ownership.* Management of PNFs by absentee owners was about as good as that of resident owners.

*Length of time of ownership.* No general conclusions can be made for this category (variable effects).

*Economic status of owner.* The better the economic status of the owner, the better the PNFs were managed.

*Reasons for ownership.* The most often cited reasons include investment, aesthetic value, recreational use, and timber value.

Most public and private programs for PNFs have had as their objective the enhancement of timber supply with very little attention directed toward landowners with objectives other than timber production. In Table 13.3 part of the results of a survey of owners of PNFs in nine eastern states during 1972–1976 are summarized (3–8). It is clear that a considerable number of the landowners place *aesthetic value* high, even to the extent of having an antilogging attitude. Aesthetics and speculation should be included among key objectives around which management rationale should be developed. According to Marler and Graves (12), a program that includes maintenance and improvement of satisfaction and speculation probably stands a greater chance of acceptance and implementation by the largest percentage of landowners. These authors suggested two realistic approaches for developing a timber management rationale, as follows.

1. Timber management can be expected to increase if programs equate management with achieving or maintaining the satisfaction objective.

2. Timber management can be expected to increase if programs equate management costs with an equivalent or larger increase in speculative gain.

Marler and Graves further suggested that the individual landowners cannot be expected to respond favorably to so-called public-good programs aimed at increasing timber production from their land if they must sacrifice either (or both) psychological (satisfaction) or economic benefits for the good of society. However, this does not mean PNF owners do not receive satisfaction from actions that benefit society. For example, in the nine states surveyed recently (3–8), from one-third to three-fourths of the PNF land is open to the public, although some of the land may be open because of requirements for receiving special property tax treatment.

After a review of many studies and surveys of PNFs and forest owners over the 50 years prior to 1979 (13), it was concluded that the key determinants of landowner behavior and thus timber supply are likely to be *broader socioeconomic variables* such as land turnover rates, tax policies, and markets; from a geographic or social perspective, these impart value to the forest resources of a given landholding (Figure 13.5). It was also suggested that past surveys have fostered the perception of substandard landowner performance by repeatedly evaluating landowner behavior in terms of deviation from publicly desirable actions. Important sociogenic determinants such as turnover in ownership and changing attitudes have been largely ignored.

The preceding viewpoint raises the question of which determinants, or group of determinants, have precedence? Should perpetuation of renewable forest resources be ensured more or less by such determinants as turnover in landowners and changing attitudes than by publicly desirable actions? Economic and/or aesthetic self-interest? Or, like the three branches of our federal government, should several determinants each have ascendancy—but only to some limit beyond which ascendancy would

**Table 13.3**

Perspectives and Attitudes of Owners of Private Nonindustrial Forests

| State | Reasons for Ownership of Two Largest Shares of Total Area | % Area | Major Reasons for Harvesting, Two Most Frequent | % Area | Major Reasons for NOT Harvesting, Two Most Frequent | % Area | Major Benefits for Past 5 Years, Two Most Frequent | % Area |
|---|---|---|---|---|---|---|---|---|
| New Jersey | Land investment | 38 | Timber mature | 27 | Antilogging[a] | 20 | Land value increase | 38 |
| | Part of residence | 28 | Need money | 19 | Timber immature | 17 | Aesthetics | 35 |
| Massachusetts | Part of residence | 26 | Timber mature | 26 | Antilogging | 30 | Aesthetics | 37 |
| | Recreation | 21 | Need money | 24 | Timber immature | 25 | Land value increase | 26 |
| New Hampshire[b] | Recreation | 28 | Timber mature | 35 | Antilogging | 30 | Aesthetics | 24 |
| | Land investment | 25 | Need money | 17 | Timber immature | 28 | Land value increase | 22 |
| Kentucky | Part of farm | 21 | Timber mature | 22 | Timber immature | 34 | Farm and domestic use | 25 |
| | Farm and domestic use | 18 | Need money | 22 | Antilogging | 13 | Land value increase | 23 |
| West Virginia[b] | Farm and domestic use | 14 | Timber mature | 32 | Timber immature | 27 | Land value increase | 22 |
| | Part of farm | 14 | Owner use | 24 | Antilogging | 23 | Aesthetics | 21 |

*Source.* "The Forest-Land Owners of . . . ." U.S.D.A. For. Ser., Res. Bull. NE-38, NE-39, NE-41, NE-51, NE-57, NE-58, 1975–1978.

[a] Antilogging reasons include: would destroy scenery, distrust loggers, opposed to harvesting, would destroy hunting.

[b] Estimates based on assumption that industrial forestland was primarily for timber production.

**Figure 13.5** Private landowners have found that growing Christmas trees can yield periodic cash crops.

pass to another determinant? This assumes publicly desirable actions to be those by one individual or group of citizens that will have no ill effects on other individuals or groups of citizens.

## PRESENT MANAGEMENT OF PNFS

The Forest Service estimates that perhaps *only 5 percent* of the land in private nonindustrial ownerships is intensively managed on a continuing basis where tree crops are grown for harvesting and manufacture, with owners using all or most practices considered practicable. About one-third of the PNF owners have some interest in forestry for timber production and manage their lands under extensive forestry practices that are usually unplanned or accomplished at random. However, owners of nearly half of these holdings display no interest in intensified forestry practices for timber production, although from time to time owners sell timber grown without management. Possibly 15 percent of these

ownerships are held essentially for nontimber purposes. This includes land held for speculation as well as land held for recreation or other nontimber values (1). Speculation could be concerned with timber as well as land and space.

Why is so little PNF land intensely managed? Zivnuska (14) questions the definition of the problem.

*If this is a problem it is not one of "poor" management, rather it is that the private nonindustrial owner's objectives are not the same as those who believe they should invest more time and money into the management for improved timber production of their forest lands.*

LeMaster (15) asks:

*With timber production being a minor objective for many private nonindustrial owners, is the problem the use of the standard of management performance* [which is] *the same as that given to forest industry lands, whose owners must respond to market forces to try to maximize profits?*

Certainly this standard of management performance is suitable for PNF owners whose primary income over time is from timber crops. However, if maximization of profits for present owners were the only management criteria for PNF owners whose primary income is from other, considerably more profitable enterprises, harvesting of all salable timber to acquire investment funds, instead of managing for future crops, would be the best use of their woods. Such self-interest would be injurious to the concept of renewable forest resources if the sum of all those harvests were greater than the growth possible within a rotation and the harvests were completed in fewer years than rotation length. Shortening rotations would appear to prevent a supply gap, but when would the shortening end? Of course, if enhancement and enjoyment of nontimber purposes became the sole objectives of many PNF owners, the supply of wood-based products and energy would shrink. The majority of PNF owners may have disregarded forestry because they have heard some foresters equating it with only part of forestry—that is, *timber production*. Having little interest in timber production, they have not learned about forestry and the skills useful in managing their forests for their own satisfaction.

The current situation of most PNFs might be analogous to a human community and giving blood: some people are too small to give a usable amount of blood without endangering their health, and others just do not want to give blood. Likewise, some woodlands are too small to give a usable amount of wood for industrial use without endangering other benefits, and some woodland owners just do not want trees to be harvested from their woods. However, most healthy people can give blood regularly if the amount and frequency of blood removal are determined by a physician and the blood is taken with care by a skillful person. For a brief time the donor may not be "up to par." Between donations, community members continue healthy, living, and growing. Likewise, most PNFs can give periodic crops of timber as long as the amount and frequency of timber to be taken are determined by a forester and the trees are removed with care by skilled loggers. For a brief time the harvested area of the forest can be less attractive. Except for this short time, the many other benefits of a forest can be enjoyed between harvests. In the community, as some people grow too old to give blood, younger people grow old enough to give. In the forest, when periodic harvests remove older trees, younger trees grow or are planted in the space they occupied. Perhaps the analogy can be carried one step further: if the people in the community do not become overcrowded, care for themselves, and stay healthy and resistant to diseases, they can give blood as long as the community exists. Likewise, if the forest does not become overcrowded, is taken care of, and is protected from fire, animals, insects, diseases, and overcutting, it can give timber crops as long as it exists.

Finally, as members of the community understand the processes of blood formation and blood giving and appreciate the benefits to themselves (blood will be available if they need it) and to the community, they cultivate good health for the satisfaction of being healthy, and so they can contribute to the community blood-giving program if they wish. Likewise, as PNF owners understand the principles of forestry and appreciate how management of their forests can benefit their own psychic, physical, and/or economic needs, they begin to manage their forestlands for the satisfaction of having healthy woods and so they can contribute to the needs of the community if they wish.

## Management Assistance for PNF Owners

Forestry assistance for PNF owners can be provided through the formation of *cooperatives* or *associations,* or assistance can be obtained from public, consulting, or industrial foresters. This topic was briefly alluded to in the previous chapter. Cooperatives and associations can provide other benefits for members besides management services. Buying and selling positions are strengthened by consolidation of purchases and of products to sell. Social benefits incur from associating with other PNF owners and political clout is enhanced.

After a worldwide study of forestry cooperatives, it was concluded that the difficulties that caused the demise of those begun in the 1930s and 1940s in the United States included the following (16).

1. The markets for the different forest products were too widely scattered, and little information was available concerning them.
2. The land holdings were too small and the harvest period (5–10 years) too long.
3. There was a lack of equipment and/or transportation facilities.
4. There was a lack of knowledge at both the managerial and technical level.

The limited progress of forestry cooperation contrasts with the massive success of agricultural cooperation in the United States.

Among *management-service* associations still functioning are the New England Forestry Foundation, with sixteen management centers in Massachusetts, New Hampshire, Vermont, and Maine, and Connwood, Incorporated, in Connecticut. State woodland owner or forestry associations exist in many states. Their bylaws might read:

*The objectives of this association shall be to advance the interest of woodland owners and the cause of forestry and to develop public appreciation for the value of (state) woodlands and their importance in the economy and overall welfare of the state; to foster and to encourage the wise use and management of the woodlands and all related resources in (state).*

The *American Forestry Association* was estab-lished in 1875 as "a national conservation organization—independent and nonpolitical—for the advancement of intelligent management and use of our forests, soil, water, wildlife, and all other natural resources necessary for an environment of high quality and the well-being of all citizens." Membership in the American Forestry Association is open to nonforest owners as well as owners. Headquarters are in Washington, D.C. The association furnishes a wide variety of information about woodlands via a monthly magazine, *American Forests*. It also sponsors conferences, tours, and workshops concerning forest conservation.

## Group Education

Group education has been provided to PNF owners through extension programs; individual assistance has been given by state, industrial, and consulting foresters; and financial incentives have been available via public cost-sharing programs, special forest-land taxes, and helpful income tax treatment.

Group education through extension programs began with the passage of the *Clarke-McNary Act* of 1924, which authorized the U.S. Department of Agriculture to cooperate with state land-grant universities in providing forestry educational programs similar to highly successful agricultural extension programs. *University extension* faculty members in the counties, some with forestry training, "extend" current knowledge through literature, movies and slides, media releases, indoor and outdoor meetings, tours, demonstrations, exhibits, etc. The county extension faculty members are supported by one or more extension forestry specialists, who help prepare material, present forestry information that county faculty members feel inadequately prepared to present, and enlist the aid of research colleagues if they also feel inadequately prepared to present a subject. Extension faculty members extend new research findings to their fellow foresters, forest owners, and forest users, and carry back new problems in need of research solutions. At present about 160 extension forestry specialists and agents attempt to provide group forestry education to the forest-using public and to possibly 8 million owners of 113 million hectares of private nonindustrial forestland—that is, one specialist or agent for about 50,000 owners or 700,000 hectares.

The group educational activities and individual assistance activities of state, industrial, and consulting foresters overlap cooperatively, especially during meetings, field days, and tours, when extension foresters enlist the state, industrial, and consulting foresters to present parts of the programs (Figure 13.6). These opportunities provide for landowners to meet the foresters who can assist with their individual forest management.

## Legislated Assistance

The first public individual "assistance" to PNFs was fire protection. Green (17) has reviewed this

major first step in forest management assistance, which included private lands. "Federal cooperation with the states in protecting forest lands from fire originated with the passage of the Weeks Law in March 1911. Although the intent of the law was to acquire and protect the headwaters of navigable streams, cooperative fire control was included." The Clarke-McNary Act authorized the secretary of agriculture to cooperate with states and other private agencies in the protection of forestlands from fire, as indicated in Chapter 12. Levels of cost sharing by the federal government were not to exceed 50 percent. Cost sharing has now decreased nationwide to about 15 percent. The Clarke-McNary Act also provided for low-cost planting stock and expanded reforestation. This act is further discussed in Chapter 1. In 1975 a total of more than 293 million hectares of land in the 50 states and Guam were protected under the act. Based on actual fire losses

**Figure 13.6** Extension foresters present forestry information to private landowners.

of these lands from 1965 to 1972, the states have lost only 0.31 of 1 percent of protected areas to wildfires.

The first public management assistance began in 1937 with enactment of the *Norris-Doxey Cooperative Farm Forestry Act,* authorizing establishment of demonstration forests and assistance to forest owners. In most states, these activities were performed by the state forestry agency. In Kansas and New Hampshire, they were combined with existing extension forestry programs, so each area or county forester was both extension forester and "service" forester. The individual service programs were expanded with passage of the *Cooperative Forest Management (CFM) Act* of 1950. A branch of the Forest Service, State and Private Forestry, was assigned responsibility for administration of the program through cooperative agreements with state forestry agencies. The *Cooperative Forestry Assistance Act* of 1978 consolidated assistance programs authorized by seven congressional acts dating back to 1924, and assigned responsibility for administration of the consolidated programs to the State and Private Forestry branch of the Forest Service. State CFM foresters may provide one to five days of management assistance to a PNF owner. Most states set a maximum forest size, formally or informally, above which owners are referred to consulting foresters. Although the ideal assistance program for owners would include preparation of management plans, most CFM foresters have so many requests for advice and assistance with reforestation, stand improvement, and harvesting activities that little time is available for any such detailed assistance. At present CFM foresters in 50 states, Puerto Rico, and Guam are providing about 660 work-years of forestry guidance annually to about 143,000 PNF owners on about 2.5 million hectares of forestland. Assuming the number of owners to be about 8 million, about 1 in 56 would receive some assistance annually. The total area in private nonindustrial ownership is 113 million hectares; therefore, forestry assistance is received by only 2 percent of the PNF land annually.

*County soil and water district conservationists* incorporate forestry recommendations in farm conservation plans. The recommendations usually are general and refer landowners to state foresters for specific forestry recommendations. Woodland conservationists on state soil conservation service staffs provide district conservationists with woodland productivity information.

Since its beginning in 1941, the *Tennessee Valley Authority* has provided forestry information to landowners within the watershed of the Tennessee River. In particular, the TVA Division of Forestry Relations established over 500 forest-management demonstrations in all seven valley states in cooperation with the owners, the states cooperative extension services, and forestry agencies. A current project by the division concerns the efficient use of wood for heating by woodland owners and by public and commercial establishments in the valley.

## Commercial Assistance

Industrial foresters offer forestry guidance and assistance as part of several kinds of agreements with PNF owners. An agreement can be *informal and verbal,* with the industrial forester offering management assistance in return for "first-refusal" rights on mature timber—that is, the privilege of making a first offer to buy the timber. The woodland owner is free to accept more lucrative offers. Of course, if a landowner accepts the offer of another company, the company that provided the management services would have no obligation to continue providing the services.

Other agreements include more *binding commitments* by landowner and company; for example, a timber purchase agreement could bind the the company to buy marketable timber at current market prices and the landowner to sell them only to the company. Sizemore (18) has suggested a leasing agreement in which the lessee would be licensed by the federal government and landowners would transfer forest management rights to the lessee. Lessees could be wood-based firms, state agencies, conservation groups, hunting clubs, consulting firms, individuals, or cooperatives.

A number of companies have organized tree-farm families (Figure 13.7). The *Tree Farm System* is sponsored by the forest industry through the *American Forest Institute*. Its purpose is to give recognition to private forest owners who are managing their woodlands for multiple use, including growing timber crops. The Tree Farm Program will be described more fully later.

A company with a Tree Farm family agrees with Tree Farmers in its purchasing area to provide management services and to purchase marketable timber. The agreement can be informal and verbal, or formal and binding on both company and tree-farmers. Usually the company will hold at least one annual event for Tree Farm family members: a picnic, tour, or field day.

*Consulting foresters* are self-employed foresters who offer a variety of forestry services, many of which public foresters are not allowed to offer, such as appraisal of property before purchase or bargaining with timber buyers. Other services range from planting of trees and pest control for the absentee owner of a small forest to development and supervision of comprehensive long-range plans for large estates, companies, and even countries. They are paid to manage a forest owner's resources in the same way a lawyer is employed to manage legal affairs. The recent surveys in the nine eastern states (3–8) reported that from 19 to 53 percent of PNF owners had received forestry assistance of some kind.

### Financial Assistance

Indirect financial assistance is given to owners of PNFs through such tax-supported activities as fire

**Figure 13.7** The tree farm sign on a woodlot signifies a certified Tree Farmer.

protection, insect and disease control, low-cost planting stock, and management assistance programs already described. *Direct financial assistance is given in the forms of special property taxes and treatment of income from sale of forest crops as capital gains, as discussed in Chapter 11, low-cost loans, and cost-sharing payments. Special property taxes are intended to encourage owners not to harvest timber prematurely (19).

Low-cost loans are available from the *Farmers Home Administration* and the *Federal Land Bank* to landowners for which managed timber can be used as collateral. "Cost-sharing" payments to landowners help defray the expenses involved in establishing, protecting, or improving private forests. Cost sharing is subsidization, as is public financial assistance given to any individual or firm when such support seems justified by societal benefits. These include: paying cost overruns, limiting importation of competing products, maintaining minimal agricultural crop prices, and providing highways and airports.

Two examples of cost-sharing assistance to PNF owners are the *Agricultural Conservation Program* (ACP) and the *Forestry Incentives Program* (FIP). In 1936, the Soil Conservation and Domestic Allotment Act provided cost-sharing payments to help farmers defray the costs of carrying out conservation and erosion-control practices. Provisions of the act are administered by the Agricultural Stabilization and Conservation Service (ASCS) of the U.S. Department of Agriculture in cooperation with county ASCS committees. Two forestry practices were included: tree planting and timber-stand improvement (TSI). The amount of cost sharing has been usually between 50 and 75 percent of actual expenses, up to some maximum limit. Before a woodland owner undertakes planting or TSI, a forester, usually a state CFM forester, must inspect the planting area or woods and state whether or not this is feasible. Before payment is made for the practice, the forester must reinspect the area for satisfactory completion of the practice. However,

ACP cost-sharing has been primarily for agronomic and livestock enterprises.

Title XX of Public Law 93-86 authorized the *Forestry Incentive Program* (FIP). As Green (17) describes it, "the Forestry Incentives Program provides cost-sharing assistance to private nonindustrial forest landowners holding tracts of less than 500 acres for carrying out prescribed forestry measures primarily for timber production purposes." To be eligible, tracts must have an approved management plan and have a growth potential of at least 3.5 cubic meters per hectare per year. The legislation authorizing FIP specifically directed the secretary of agriculture to encourage the use of private agencies, firms, and businesses furnishing services and materials needed in applying forestry practices. The states of Mississippi and Virginia have cost-sharing programs of their own to encourage planting and TSI, and planting, respectively.

Regarding subsidization of forestry practices in PNFs and alternatives to present the cost-sharing approval, Gregersen (20) feels that

First, *we need to be much more concerned with the relative efficiency of investing in different regions, on different types of properties, and under different situations. Given a limited budget for subsidizing small woodlands, we have to make sure that the money is used in the most efficient fashion. Actually, one factor in getting greater funding is to show that present funds are efficiently utilized, albeit in a politically acceptable fashion. Second, what many landowners need is more practical technical advice and help in developing management plans and simple cash flows for their forest land operations and not more outright cost-share subsidies. For many woodland owners the effective returns they can expect to get without subsidies should be large enough to encourage investment, if they really are interested in investment. Increased practical information through technical assistance is the key. Several studies and discussions with foresters support this point.* Third, *if we are going to subsidize initial forestry practices we should also commit ourselves to better programs all the way through harvest, processing and marketing–it is the end product which interests us and not merely getting stands established. Continuity is a key to success.* Fourth, *we need to consider other, more flexible, and more locally oriented programs of public support for increasing effective timber supplies from the small woodlands. Such programs need to be tailored to local conditions and attitudes and might include expansion of tax subsidies, long term contracts, low interest credit with extended repayment, public or private direct forestry activities instead of cost subsidies, and regulations such as those found in several states today. And, of course, there must be an expansion of technical information support or extension.* Finally, *we need to reassess the future role of small woodlands relative to the opportunities for stimulating and increasing timber output from other categories of lands, including a detailed assessment of the economics of wood supplies from federal, state and county lands. We need to redefine commercial forest land on the basis of more economic variables.*

## Recognition Programs

Recognition of achievement encourages both recipients and others with potential for similar achievement. Several recognition programs have the purpose of encouraging the practice of forestry by PNF owners. The most widely known recognition program is the *American Tree Farm System* of the *American Forest Institute,* which is supported by the forest industry. Because the forest industry knows that much of its wood must be obtained from PNFs, the industry encourages multiple-use management of those forests by giving recognition to owners who

practice such multiple-use forestry. Evidence that a PNF owner has received recognition as a *"Tree Farmer"* is a green and white diamond-shaped sign displayed at the owner's woods or home (Figure 13.7). In 1975, state 4-H organizations at land-grant universities joined with the National 4-H Council and the American Forest Institute in recognizing annually several 4-H members or camps whose woodlands have been certified as Tree Farms. Each year one state is featured in national publicity. Several state Soil and Water Conservation District Associations and state Tree Farm committees jointly or separately select state Tree Farmers each year, who receive public recognition, and gifts such as chain saws and trips. A national Tree Farmer is selected annually and receives publicity as well as an extensive award trip.

## PRIVATE NONINDUSTRIAL FORESTS IN THE FUTURE

Over 9 million PNFs could exist in the United States by 1982 if the 2.4 percent annual increase between 1952 and 1978 in nine recently surveyed eastern states were replicated in all states. Assuming the total U.S. population would be about 230 million by 1982, the owners of PNFs would represent less than 4 percent of the total population. Many of the other 96 percent would want some forestland of their own. Those not willing to and those not financially able to purchase some forestland can influence the future of PNF lands through political and financial activities. Forest owners can wield similar influence individually and through associations and cooperatives. The need for such activities rests on the perceptions of PNF owners, and of nonowners who want to influence their use, concerning these forestlands. For example, are PNFs being adequately managed to meet the perceived needs from these forests? Sedjo and Ostermeier (21) expressed two perceptions that evolved from a workshop on policy alternatives for PNFs. One, described as the traditional view, perceived

PNFs as being inadequately managed. The other, rejecting the traditional view, perceived present management as adequate. Five policy alternatives for PNFs were discussed during the workshop. Based on the amount of governmental involvement, they ranged from "benign neglect" (by government) to increased government involvement.

Self-help through private associations and cooperatives could be recommended by both the benign-neglect advocate and the increased-government-involvement advocate. Members of effective *associations* and *cooperatives* can employ their own foresters; can pool purchasing, silvicultural, and selling activities; and can lobby for lower taxes on forest property, income, and transfer. Also, associations and cooperatives can lobby for more public protection, managerial, and cost-sharing funds and for laws to proscribe buyer activities. Nonowner individuals and organizations that would benefit by little or no governmental assistance to PNF owners could be advocates of benign neglect. Nonowner individuals and organizations wanting more public regulation of private nonindustrial forests could be advocates of increased government involvement.

A clearer view of private nonindustrial forests must wait for a more precise definition of *commercial forestland,* a more accurate and detailed *survey* of the forests and the owners, and a more *homogeneous (and harmonious?) perception* of their present and future contributions to the physical, psychic, and economic welfare of present and future beneficiaries. Because PNFs include such a major share of commercial forestland (as now defined) the ultimate ethical question regarding the use of natural resources is particularly applicable to them: *how can present owners and users meet their needs and wants while conserving resources for future generations?*

## REFERENCES

1. Anon., "The Outlook for Timber in the United States," U.S.D.A. For. Serv., Res. Rept. No. 20, Washington, D.C., 1973.

2. Anon., "Timber Resources for America's Future", U.S.D.A. For. Serv., Res. Rept. No. 14, Washington, D.C., 1958.

3. N. P. Kingsley and J. C. Finley, "The Forest-Land Owners of Delaware," Northeastern Forest Exper. Sta., U.S.D.A. For. Serv., Resource Bull. NE-38, Broomall, Pa., 1975.

4. N. P. Kingsley, "The Forest-Land Owners of New Jersey," Northeastern Forest Exper. Sta., U.S.D.A. For. Serv., Res. Bull. NE-39, Broomall, Pa., 1975.

5. N. P. Kingsley, "The Forest-Land Owners of Southern New England," Northeastern Forest Exper. Sta., U.S.D.A. For. Serv., Res. Bull. NE-41, Broomall, Pa., 1976.

6. N. P. Kingsley and T. W. Birch, "The Forest-Land Owners of New Hampshire and Vermont," Northeastern Forest Exper. Sta., U.S.D.A. For. Serv., Res. Bull. NE-51, Broomall, Pa., 1977.

7. T. W. Birch and D. S. Powell, "The Forest-Land Owners of Kentucky," Northeastern Forest Exper. Sta., U.S.D.A. For. Serv., Res. Bull. NE-57, Broomall, Pa., 1978.

8. T. W. Birch and N. P. Kingsley, "The Forest-Land Owners of West Virginia," Northeastern Forest Exper. Sta., U.S.D.A. For. Serv., Res. Bull. NE-58, Broomall, Pa., 1978.

9. Marian Clawson, "Nonindustrial Private Forest Lands: Myths and Realities," *Proc. of 1978 Joint Convention of Society of American Foresters and Canadian Institute of Forestry,* Society of American Foresters, Washington, D.C., 1979.

10. B. J. Turner, J. C. Finley, and N. P. Kingsley, *J. For.,* 75, 498 (1977).

11. Anon., "The Nation's Renewable Resources—An Assessment," U.S.D.A. For. Serv., Rept. No. 21, Washington, D.C., 1977.

12. R. L. Marler and P. R. Graves, "A New Management Rationale for Small Forest Owners," Applied Forestry Res. Inst., Rept. No. 17, SUNY College of Environmental Science & Forestry, Syracuse, N.Y., 1974.

13. J. Royer, "Conclusions from a Review of 50 Years of Small Woodland Owner Studies," Address to Southern Forest Economics Workshop, Center for Resource and Environmental Policy Research, Duke University, 1979.

# REFERENCES

14. J. A. Zivnuska, "Forestry Investments for Multiple Uses Among Multiple Ownership Types," Background Paper Prepared for Resources for the Future Forum on Forest Policy for the Future: Conflict, Compromise, Consensus, Resources for the Future, Inc., Washington, D.C., 1974.

15. D. C. LeMaster, "Timber Supply, Nonindustrial Private Forest Land, and the Conventional View," *J. For.*, 76, 365 (1978).

16. M. Digby and T. E. Edwardson, "The Organization of Forestry Cooperatives," Occasional Paper No. 41, The Plunkett Inst. for Cooperative Studies, Parchment (Oxford) Ltd., London, 1976.

17. D. L. Green, "The Extent of Subsidy Programs Today," *Proceedings of the 1976 National Convention*, Society of American Foresters, Washington, D.C., 1977.

18. W. R. Sizemore, "The Private Nonindustrial Forest Resource: Forest Industry—Leasing and Other Corporate Approaches," *Proceedings of the 1975 National Convention*, Society of American Foresters, Washington, D.C., 1976.

19. R. O. McMahon, "Private Nonindustrial Ownership of Forest Land," Bulletin 68, School of Forestry, Yale University, 1964.

20. H. M. Gregersen, "Can We Afford Small Woodland Subsidies? It Depends," *Proceedings of the 1976 National Convention*, Society of American Foresters, Washington, D.C., 1977.

21. R. A. Sedjo and D. M. Ostermeier, "Policy Alternatives for Nonindustrial Private Forests," *Proceedings of the 1977 National Convention*, Society of American Foresters, Washington, D.C., 1978.

# 14

# FOREST-RECREATION MANAGEMENT

## Robert H. Becker and Alan Jubenville

To the casual observer outdoor recreation appears deceptively easy to understand. To hunt you need an area with game, to boat you need access to water, and to camp you need a site in a natural area. Too simplistic? Absolutely. Think of an outdoor recreational activity and the forms it can take. Camping, for example, includes use of both large motor-home recreation vehicles and featherweight tents. Fishing can take the form of dry—fly-fishing in mountain streams and pan-fishing with several rods on a reservoir or in surf. No matter what form a recreation activity may take there is a common element among participants—a search for quality.

## INTRODUCTION

*Quality* as applied to outdoor recreation is hard to define and to measure; yet everyone with any experience, as consumer or as manager of a recreation area, will agree that it exists (Figure 14.1). Some outdoor experiences are inspirational, educational, or simply enjoyable. Others are mediocre in one or more respects, and still others are inferior, some to the point of negative value or dissatisfaction (1).

The extent to which a person achieves *satisfaction* from an activity depends on expectations brought to the activity and the degree to which those expectations are met. A person who goes fly-fishing expecting to be alone in the stream may seek areas known for isolation instead of for an abundance of fish. The person camping who enjoys meeting other campers and making new acquaintances may feel uneasy and even dissatisfied in an empty campground. Conversely, the camper preferring to be with just a group of friends would relish that same empty campground.

Thus the qualities, values, and desired attributes of any outdoor recreation sites are perceived differently by various user groups in society. As beauty is in the eye of the beholder, the quality of the recreation experience is in the mind of the user.

Managers of forests, rivers, and parks are faced with a complex set of conditions. Managing agencies must consider a wide range of activities that frequently compete for use of the same parcel of land and are in conflict with one another. They must also provide for a variety of users—old, young, active, passive, etc.—and provide opportunities for expression of a wide range of values, many of which are incompatible with one another. To offer varied recreational experiences there must be a commitment to provide and continue to improve the full spectrum of outdoor recreation: resources, experiences, and activities that now exist or may exist in the future.

## Recreation

The recreational experience is often considered to be actual participation in an activity. The experience is much broader than this, and can be separated into four categories (2).

1. *Anticipation.* The period of foreseeing and awaiting a trip or occasion involves imagination and develops enthusiasm. Events may never occur but still contribute to one's happiness through anticipation.

2. *Planning.* Actual preparation for the event includes gathering equipment and supplies, packing, and preparing other logistics. Sometimes this involves physical training.

3. *Participation.* The activity and the events surrounding it extend from departure to return. It is the heart of the experience, the time of encounter with the resource and activity opportunities.

4. *Recollection.* After participation, an experience is not usually over. Participation is relived through pictures, stories, and memories. At times, the experience develops new significance and gains embellishments during the recollection phase.

Figure 14.2 is a diagram of an individual's decision to participate in a specific recreation activ-

**Figure 14.1** A "quality" recreational experience may be in many varied forms—here the Lower St. Croix River. Wisconsin-Minnesota border.

ity (3). Three factors are associated with that decision: (1) individual characteristics, (2) social relationships and societal influences, and (3) available opportunities for recreation. The outcome of the process is an individual's participation in a specific activity at a specific time and place.

Every person has *goals* for the use of leisure time. Clearly, the ordering and importance of values—such as physical fitness, family togetherness, solitude, achievement, teammate camaraderie—vary among individual groups (3). Specific recreational activities may be viewed as tools or a means by which an individual's goals or motivations can be fulfilled. Very little is known, however, about how an individual's goals are formed.

Five postulates have been presented to explain a *behavioral approach* to recreation (4).

1. Recreation is an experience that results from recreational engagements.

2. Recreational engagements require commitment by the recreationist.

3. Recreational engagements are self-rewarding: the engagement is pleasant in and of itself, and recreation is the experience.

4. Recreational engagements require personal and free choice on the part of the recreationist.

5. Recreational engagements occur during nonobligated time.

The first postulate states what recreation is. The remaining four serve as descriptors to separate recreation from other forms of human behavior.

The key words are *nonobligated time, personal choice,* and *rewarding* (not negative) *engagements.* The word *engagement* is used instead of *activity* to incorporate the psychological dimension; we might be mentally engaged and not physically engaged. Recall that anticipation and recollection were previ-

INDIVIDUAL RECREATION CHOICE

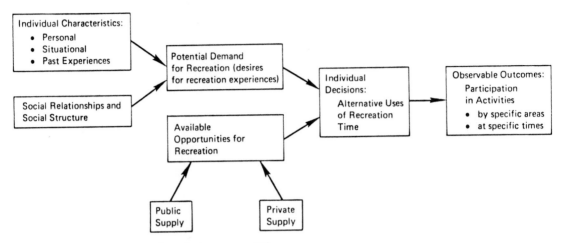

**Figure 14.2** Inputs into the recreation selection process. (After the National Academy of Sciences.)

ously identified as part of the recreation experience.

We can observe a person's behavior—but experiences are personal. "Experience is man's invisibility to man . . . [However] we must not be content with observation [of behavior] alone. Observations of behavior must be extended by inference to attributions about experience. . . . In a science of persons, I shall state as axiomatic that: behavior is a function of experience (5)."

For a growing number of persons, the quality of recreation experience is linked to the use and enjoyment of forests, lakes, rivers, and coastlines. The popularity of resource-based recreation has made it necessary for area managers to be as capable of managing the *social use* of the resource as they are capable of managing the *physical-site* characteristics—an interesting challenge.

## FOREST-RECREATION MANAGEMENT

Forest-recreation management is a phase of resource management aimed at providing recreational opportunities in the nonurban setting. Thus its applicability extends from small public-resource areas near

urban centers, through large, commercial forestlands, to even larger public lands managed by such agencies as the Bureau of Land Management, the Forest Service, the National Park Service, etc. The emphasis is on the resource base as the primary planning element, with sufficient development and/or special services to provide or enhance the particular recreational opportunities. Since many resource uses may be accommodated by a single management agency or a mosaic of land ownerships, any management planning must stress *coordination* of programs. Plus, there must be one other ingredient or philosophy that any good land manager must strive to attain: creativity in meeting the expanding needs of the public on a stable to shrinking resource base. In recreation management, we need to search for ways of making heretofore incompatible uses compatible. We need to handle large numbers of people on a smaller resource base without alteration of the experience, and to maintain these experiences over extended periods of time with the minimum necessary direct management control because of lower budgets and the participants' preferences. While that is certainly the direction management should be moving, this chapter does not profess to have the answers to such ambitious goals. With those goals as targets, however, the remainder of this chapter will focus on a management framework that we hope will move us in that direction.

## Recreation in a Multiple-Use Framework

Recreation competes with and complements other forest products and as such must relate to these other uses. Planning and management of forest recreation is as important as managing timber, wildlife, or watersheds. Yet wildlife managers know more about their subjects than is currently known about recreation users (Chapter 16). Similarly, timber management has well-established objectives and practices (Chapter 11), while recreation management is often a reaction to a problem instead of the result of systematic planning. The recreation component in the total resource-management concept, however, may be the most visible component and the one to which most people relate. After all, the product of forest recreation is not the placement of picnic tables or number of campsites; the product of forest recreation is the *satisfaction* of individual visitors. Figure 14.3 places recreation in the context of other forest products. The outline assumes that for all forest-related products, two production stages can be identified, the first in converting the raw, basic forest resource into intermediate goods (forest product/resources) and second in converting these immediate goods into final goods that can be utilized directly by the consumer. In actual practice, many more than one intermediate good may be produced (more than two production stages) before a final commodity emerges; however, the simple structure described is sufficient to illustrate product relationship. It is also important to note that in the case of producing the recreation experience, the consumer is performing a production role in converting the recreation resource into a directly consumable commodity. The soundest justification for this assumed structure is that no recreation can generally take place at a given site without the other factors (travel, equipment, etc.) and that these factors are clearly combined and employed to create recreation by the consumer, and no one else (6).

## Basic Management

As mentioned earlier, the resource base is a primary element; the other two elements are the visitor or user of that resource base and the development or services provided to offer or enhance the particular pattern of recreational use. These three elements are combined to define the forest-recreation management subsystem (Figure 14.4). It is called a subsystem because it would typically fit into a larger system of land management that may also include timber, water, wildlife, range, and natural areas.

The manager must then choose those options that will, through the manipulation of the resource (i.e., improved road access, forest-campground development, winter-sports site complex, etc.), provide or enhance the recreational opportunity and protect the resource itself (avoidance of sensitive areas, site hardening, zoning, etc.). While this may describe a classic forest-recreation management system, how does one apply such principles to the typical dispersed types of recreational opportunities available on public-domain lands? While the answer is not simple, it is not nearly as complex as one would think. *First,* recreation-area managers are not going to spend much staff time and budget dollars in continually manipulating the resource base, such as fertilizing to increase the vigor of overstory and understory vegetation so it can sustain a higher level of use, even though this may be necessary on a few intensively used sites. *Second,* managers are not going to spend similar kinds of efforts for the direct manipulation of the visitor, even though this may be done on a few specific sites. There will be a need for enforcement of rules and regulations, for dispersal of concentrated use, and for dissemination of information through environmental interpretation; but even with all the possible programs available to the manager, the dispersed nature of most forest recreation would preclude the use of such rules and regulations

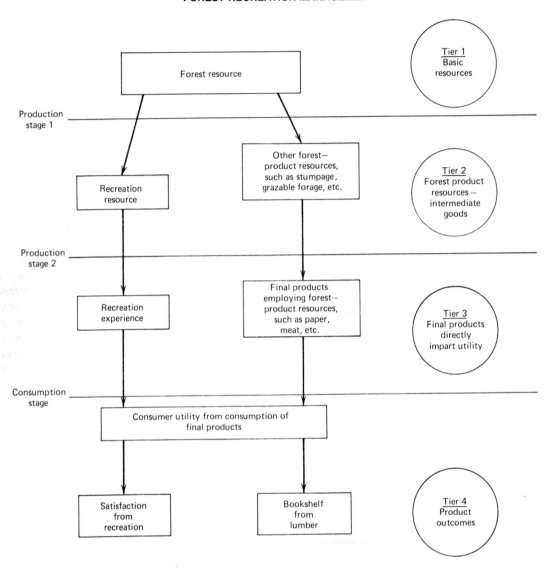

**Figure 14.3** Structure of the recreation experience with other forest products. (After Hof (6).)

except at the more heavily used locations where the use is causing resource and/or social conflicts. The direction is therefore the periodic manipulation of the resource base to achieve certain recreation-program objectives, commonly called recreation-area or unit planning, or *master planning*. The manipulation of the resource is in the form of access such as the development, improvement, or maintenance of transportation system (roads, trails, airstrips, etc.) and site/facility development associated with the transportation system. The recreational experience can be enhanced by proper location of the transportation system so that the high-quality landscape features are visually available. The same transportation system

**340**

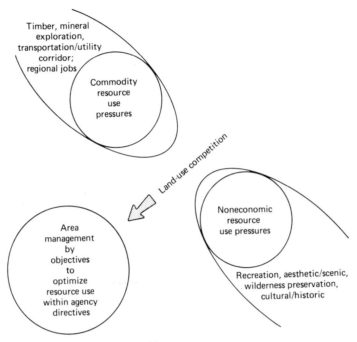

Timber, mineral
exploration,
transportation/utility
corridor;
regional jobs

Commodity
resource
use
pressures

Land-use competition

Area
management
by
objectives
to
optimize
resource use
within agency
directives

Noneconomic
resource
use pressures

Recreation, aesthetic/scenic,
wilderness preservation,
cultural/historic

**Figure 14.4** Land-use competition-amelioration and mitigation through management by objectives.

can also be used to avoid areas that may be socially congested or environmentally sensitive, have negative visual impacts, or may possibly be hazardous to the participant. The location of specific sites and/or facility development along the transportation system can do the same and also be used to enhance the experience (whether it is a visitor center or a campground) or to avoid locations that are sensitive or hazardous. In sum, the process described is called *management by design*, and it is basically accomplished through the planning process.

## AREA MASTER PLANNING

Area master planning is a process of allocating space for specific recreational opportunities or programs based on *program objectives*. The process involves land-use zoning for specific recreational opportunities and the careful development of the access transportation system and specific sites to encourage

the type and level of recreational use specified in program objectives. Rarely would one plan an area today that did not already have an existing access transportation system and some site development; consequently there will always be some level of recreational use of the area. This is particularly true on multiple-use lands where much of the access and developments have been established for the management of all land-resource uses. Planning should therefore address the fact that while some changes may be possible, the existing situation is primarily a given in the equation. Furthermore, planning should proceed only if there is need—that is, a problem exists and we need to solve it. We do not need to implement some change just because we were hired as a planner. At the same time, planning is a continuous process, and any actions taken should be based on program objectives. Thus any changes that take place over time should be based on changes in objectives. Even if we decide not to do something in

**Figure 14.5**  Hiking in the Cascade Mountains near Mt. Shuksan. (Photograph by R. A. Young.)

an area, we should develop program objectives to maintain that *status quo;* otherwise, casual encroachment may change the access/development, which changes the recreational experience offered, or may cause some social or resource conflict that must be resolved through active "hands-on" management. Four concepts related to area planning will be discussed: recreation-opportunity spectrum, visitor norms, management by objectives, and social succession. From the perspective of the total mission of an agency, there should be a district or forest-wide plan that coordinates specific land uses to ensure a balance of resource products and services from the land within the goals of the agency and that considers the capability of the land to provide and sustain the products and services over time.

## Plan for District or Forest

Before area planning can take place, one must have an *umbrella plan* or *coordinating document* that establishes targets for the district or forest to meet in supplying identified products and services. Depending on the agency, the district plan attempts to establish an overall mix of products and services and assigns targets to individual areas within the district. Under a typical multiple-use framework, each land area is evaluated based on a resource inventory of its potential for providing specific products and services. Then those areas with the highest potential for a specific product/service would be targeted to provide that product or service. This type of planning would make efficient allocation of resources and theoretically would provide maximum available supply of the products/services. In terms of recreation, the district plan would also coordinate the continuity of the recreational experiences where two or more adjacent land areas share a common recreational experience, such as a hiking trail, a river corridor, or a main travel route (Figure 14.5).

With an expanding demand for various products and services and a diminishing resource base, simple allocation of the resource to any and all uses is not possible. Certain *trade-offs* will have to be made. If you increase recreational use, you may have to modify timber production; if you increase developed recreation, you may have to forego some dispersed recreational opportunities. Within that framework, it behooves the manager to seek new, creative ways of making incompatible land uses functionally compatible such that the trade-offs can be reduced to a minimum level.

One such response was in the Warms Springs—Crazy Creek unit of the Bitterroot National Forest, Idaho, where hiking, timber management, and watershed protection were all accommodated in a single, small watershed. The more productive timberlands were in the lower watershed, but they were too steep for conventional logging. They were designated for helicopter logging to protect the soil and watershed, and those lands between the road and logging area were left intact to protect visual qualities and preclude off-road vehicle use. The day-use hiking opportunity started at the end of the road and provided a variety of viewing experiences for the participant. Where the trail passed near the logging it was directed into the buffer zone along the stream to obscure the visual effects of logging and to focus on the detail of the stream environment. It was then directed out of the canyon onto the less steep slopes for a more distant viewing of the upper watershed. The day-use trail looped back, and the wilderness trail angled off the loop and into the more scenic but more environmentally sensitive upper canyon. The upper canyon, although relatively small, was suitable for wilderness designation because it was adjacent to the already-designated Selway-Bitterroot

Wilderness. Furthermore, the upper canyon was deemed to be suitable grizzly bear habitat, and the primitive trail and limited use were compatible with that habitat.

## Spectrum of Recreation Opportunities

Many people have suggested a need for providing a *spectrum* of recreational opportunities. Some experts have offered refinements in the concept by suggesting a *total continuum* from the heavily developed landscape to the totally undeveloped (7). Along this continuum would be identified anchor points (experiences) with specific qualifying descriptors to distinguish one anchor point from another. Thus, the opportunity spectrum would span all activities and would specify the norms of participation for each anchor point. Using the Forest Service manual for descriptions of these anchor points—more aptly termed *segments of the continuum*—the total recreation experience spectrum (RES) is shown in Figure 14.6 (8).

The totally pristine environment with no development offers the antithesis to the urban environment. Moving from a Type 1 to a Type 5 experience, the norms of the experience change as described in the next section. For the resource manager, the most interesting and challenging opportunity is in the intermediate or Type 3 experience. This would occur on most intensive-use zones under multiple-use management. Several resource uses may be accommodated, including recreation; plus, there is sufficient flexibility within that segment of the continuum for the manager to respond to both roaded and roadless recreational opportunities.

## Participation or Experience Norms

Norms are defined as standards or patterns of participation and/or preferences by a group of participants that would distinguish one group from another. Three clusters of norms define the experience along the RES, such that

$$\text{Recreational experience} = \begin{cases} \text{Social norms} \\ \text{Development norms} \\ \text{Management-control} \\ \quad \text{norms} \end{cases}$$

A description for five experience levels associated with the three clusters of norms is given in Table 14.1 (9).

On many multiple-use lands, we have typically viewed management controls as a means of achieving social norms; yet, as shown above, they are part of the experience, not a means of achieving the experience. On these same lands, it is essential that we plan the experiences such that we can, to the maximum degree possible, practice *management by design*, a concept described earlier in the chapter. Using this concept, the integration of the three clusters of norms would take on the following configuration.

Development norms
$\Big\langle$
Social norms

Management-control norms

The norms of development would establish the social norms and the need for certain management controls. For example, if we develop a typical forest campground with the emphasis on a minimum of 100-foot spacing between units; rustic, centralized facilities such as a vault toilet and water point; and the use of native materials such as wood and stone, then the design itself places emphasis in terms of social norms on natural aesthetics, privacy for the camper yet opportunity for informal socialization, and a sense of being close to nature yet secure because of the limited development and the presence of other people (10). Socially it is the style of camping where the automobile-oriented person interfaces with nature because of the limited development. Thus the access transportation system and the facility development tend to attract a person having a certain social norm. That same design subtly directs use (where to park your auto, where to walk, where to pitch your tent, etc.) where the site has been *hardened* to sustain that use. By hardening we mean any planned modifications to the site undertaken to mitigate damage to the site that would accompany high levels of visitor use. Thus if the use is directed such that the social norms are maintained and the resource is basically protected from unacceptable change, there is very little need for hands-on man-

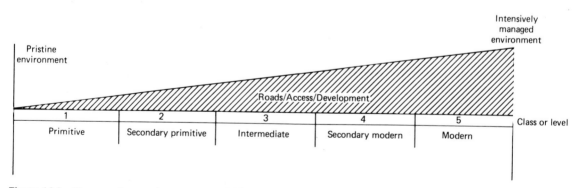

**Figure 14.6** The recreation experience spectrum (RES), using the Forest Service terminology to describe specific opportunities (see Table 14.1 for a discussion of each class or level).

**Table 14.1**

Recreation Experience and Environmental Modification Norms for Resource-Oriented Activities

| Experience/ Development Level | Recreation Experience Norm | Environmental Modification Norm |
|---|---|---|
| 1 *Primitive* | Primary interest is the feeling of achievement, sense of adventure, and challenge to the elements. Small group participation develops camaraderie. Fine opportunities for solitude. Some activities may require a high level of outdoor skills at this level. Outside distractions or influences often very displeasing. | Natural primitive environment is dominant. Minimum site modification. Rustic rudimentary improvements designed for protection of the site rather than comfort of the users. Use of indigenous materials preferred. Water provided by participant. Sanitation provisions spartan. Site maintenance by participants. Minimum controls are subtle. No obvious means of regimentation. Spacing informal and extended to minimize contacts with others. Motorized access not provided or permitted. |
| 2 *Secondary primitive* | Feeling of accomplishment is important, but physical stamina is not essential. Several small groups may socialize briefly, then separate for the majority of the experience. Some activities may require a moderate level of outdoor skills. Outside influences tolerated. | Natural environment is dominant. Little site modification. Rustic or rudimentary improvements designed for protection of the site rather than comfort of the users. Use of synthetic materials avoided. Water and sanitation provisions developed but simple. Site and facility maintenance provided at least seasonally. Minimum controls are subtle. Little obvious regimentation. Spacing informal and extended to minimize contacts with others. Motorized access provided or permitted. Primary access over primitive roads. |
| 3 *Intermediate* | A taste of adventure is important, but a sense of security is present. | Environment essentially natural. Site modification moderate. Facilities about equally for |

**Table 14.1** *(continued)*

| Experience/ Development Level | Recreation Experience Norm | Environmental Modification Norm |
|---|---|---|
| | Considerations for convenience and comfort accepted. Some activities may require a moderate level of outdoor skills. Outside influences accepted. | protection of site and comfort of users. Design of improvements is usually based on use of native materials with contemporary conservation techniques. Water and sanitation provisions adequate and regularly maintained. Inconspicuous vehicular traffic controls usually provided. Roads may be hard surfaced and trails formalized. Primary access to site may be over high-standard, well-traveled roads. Visitor information services, if available, are informal and incidental. Security patrols may be made periodically. |
| 4 *Secondary modern* | Experience provides change of routine and surroundings. Apparent opportunities for socializing with others. Provisions for convenience and comfort expected. Willing to pay for extras. May rely on program services for entertainment as much as exposure to the environment. Outside influences present but not regarded as incongruous. | Environment pleasing but necessarily natural. Site heavily modified. Some facilities designed strictly for comfort and convenience of users, but luxury facilities not provided. Facility designs may tend toward and incorporate synthetic materials. Extensive use of artificial surfacing of roads and trails. Vehicular traffic controls present and usually obvious. Primary access usually over paved roads. Plant materials usually native. Visitor information services frequently available. Maintenance and security checks regular and periodic. Some programming services provided. |
| 5 *Modern* | Pleasing environment attractive to the tourist, novice, or highly gregarious | High degree of site modification. Facilities mostly designed for comfort and convenience of |

**Table 14.1** (*continued*)

| Experience/ Development Level | Recreation Experience Norm | Environmental Modification Norm |
|---|---|---|
| | recreationist. Opportunity to socialize with others very important. Satisfies need for compensation experiences. Obvious to users that they are in secure situation where ample provision is made for their personal comfort. Expect to be entertained by program services; do not expect to find own amusement. Outside influences considered part of the show. | users include flush toilets; may include showers, bath houses, laundry facilities, and electrical hookups. Synthetic materials commonly used. Formal walks or surfaced trails. Regimentation of users is obvious. Access usually by high-speed highways. Plant materials may be foreign to the environment. Formal visitor information services usually available. Designs formalized and architecture may be contemporary. Mowed lawns and clipped shrubs not unusual. Maintenance and security forces usually visible. High degree of programming services. |

*Source.* "Recreation Experience Levels," U.S.D.A., *Forest Service Manual,* 2330.5-3, 1977; "National Forest Camp and Picnic Site Levels of Environmental Modification and Recreation Experiences," U.S.D.A. *Forest Service Manual,* 2331.11c-3, 1978.

agement. In this case, the possible limitation of the length of stay (which is typically done in a forest campground) to ensure reasonable availability of this particular type of camping opportunity may be the only necessary direct management control. This can be done very subtly through simple monitoring to ensure compliance. The arrangement is usually acceptable to forest campers because they typically only stay a few days and move on, or use sites close to home primarily on the weekend.

## Management by Objectives

Management by objectives (MBO) is important in outdoor recreation management if we are to maintain a specific identifiable recreational experience on the ground. A modification of the MBO model has the

following inputs for recreation program objectives (11):

Resource capability
Institutional constraints
Existing situation $\Bigg\}$ = Recreation program objectives
User preferences
Coordination

The relationships between these five inputs are graphically described in Figure 14.7 to show the actual band of operation within which the particular program objectives are made.

Usually the *resource capability* will describe the overall limitations in terms of programs, but typically agencies are more constrained by laws, regula-

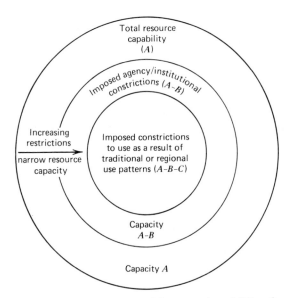

**Figure 14.7** Elements constraining use and capabilities of a specific resource—rarely does the capacity of the resource shape the type and intensity of that area's recreational use. Agencies are often limited by their organic legislation. Similarly, traditional user expectations often constrict the type of area recreational use beyond agency limitations.

dination comes when an experience overlaps two or more landownerships, requiring that the agencies coordinate with each other to ensure continuity of the experience—that is, that they operate in the same band. Negotiation may be necessary to ensure that they operate as nearly as possible within the same band.

## Social Succession

Using the axiom presented earlier that the development norms (expressed in the particular development, either access or facilities) dictate the social and management control norms, any change in that development may, and often does, cause a shift in the social and management control norms. This shift in norms, if too great, usually causes a *social succession* to take place, as shown in Figure 14.8 (12).

The net effect of succession is a *displacement* of one group of users by another and is usually caused by a failure to manage by objectives (13). If the primary objective is to maintain a particular experi-

tions, or policies that effectively reduce the typical band of operation for the particular agency. If one has never managed recreation using program objectives, then a certain clientele has usually developed over time. The *existing situation* (the norms of the existing clientele) will probably dictate the direction of the initial management planning, further constricting the operating bands within which the program objectives will be developed. Beyond this, if other *user preferences* can be accommodated within that narrow band, it is appropriate to include them. Or if the area is geographically large or diverse enough to accommodate preferences outside that band, but within the *institutional constraints* band, it would also be appropriate to include these additional preferences. On occasion, one may plan an area where there has been little past use, and consequently user preferences may play a greater role in determining the actual band of operation. The coor-

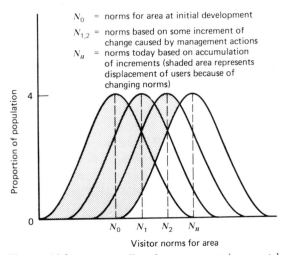

**Figure 14.8** Incrementalism in management-incremental change without regard to objectives and the ultimate effect on the recreational experience. (Modified from Jubenville (12))

ence, the manager may simply not understand the effects of widening the road, improving the trail, or putting in a footbridge. Often these minor modifications of existing development are sufficient (particularly their cumulative effect) to shift the norms to the point that the experience is no longer attractive to the present group of users and they are displaced by a new group whose norms more closely fit the new situation. The total process of succession is shown in Figure 14.9 (14).

Displacement is an actual move away from an *unacceptable situation*, not a move toward a desired one. This distinction is useful in separating displacement, a form of reactive movement, from other forms of movement behavior. Among the other forms of movement behavior are: (1) *active migrations*, where people seek a suitable destination according to their values—for example white-water canoeists who seek a variety of risk and skill testing; (2) *passive migration*, where people select a location because it is convenient, such as visiting areas to meet friends for picnics, or because other members of the participation group desire that location; and (3) *diurnal requirements of an activity*, such as moving to different locations on a lake to fish at

various times of a day. Movement is then a general term, while displacement is a negative reactive movement (15).

## The Area-Planning Process

The sum of the preceding processes should then logically be a product of the following underlying actions.

1. *Inventory Area.* The area should have a complete inventory of the social subsystem (recreational use, history and archeology, nonrecreational use, economics, and legal/political inputs), biological subsystem (flora and fauna, levels and location of sensitive sites, hazards, etc.), and the physical subsystem (natural factors such as water, physiography, etc. and artificial developments such as roads, buildings, etc.). This information will help in determining significant values that should be maintained or enhanced, and in determining the appropriate band of operation.

2. *Determine Band of Operation.* Use the approach described in the section on management by objectives.

3. *Establish Program Objectives.* State the program objectives within the band of operation and the actual clientele group(s) whose norms will be adopted in planning the area. While responding to a particular set of norms, also account for specific management concerns in the planning of the programs (including the access transportation system, specific site developments, and their locations). The program objectives should incorporate the experience(s) to be provided, where they will be provided, and related management concerns such as potential hazards, public safety, environmental impact, etc. (Table 14.1).

4. *Develop and Evaluate Concept Plans.* Concept plans are simply attempts to manipulate the area graphically, based on the detailed

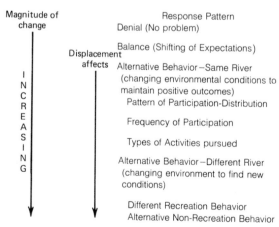

**Figure 14.9** Potential levels of adaptation by the recreationist to changes in the recreation environment. (Modified from Schreyer (14), U.S.D.A. Forest Service.)

inventory, and to test alternative courses of action to meet the program objectives. The following is an example of a concept plan that was considered, although not completed, for Rattlesnake Drainage, a 20,000-hectare area in the Lolo National Forest, Montana (Figure 14.10).

The following is a brief summary of the area.

1. There are 5 alpine lakes; lakes 1, 2, and 3 are used extensively by hikers, usually from the Divide Trail.

2. Lakes 3, 4, and 5 are also used by horseback riders. Some conflicts have occurred between hikers and riders centering around the amount of horse manure and the deterioration of the meadows around the alpine lakes. Lakes 4 and 5 are showing severe loss of vegetation around the lakes and problems of erosion.

3. The Canyon Trail is an old four-wheel-drive road that has been closed for nearly a decade so no vehicles are allowed in the area. It is used during the summer by the horseback riders.

4. Summer and fall trail use is concentrated in the alpine zone. Fall hunting is mainly dispersed throughout the forest zone. Winter use is primarily by cross-country skiers along the Canyon Trail.

A quick review indicates that problems are focused on summer use in the alpine zone, primarily lakes 4 and 5. The objectives for the area, assuming such planning should be problem-oriented, should therefore focus on summer use, primarily horse use, in the alpine zone. The specific objectives are

1. To offer a Class I nonmonitored summer experience in the alpine zone, including the access to the zone.

2. To maintain, as closely as possible, existing patterns of use in the alpine zone and the travel patterns to the zone.

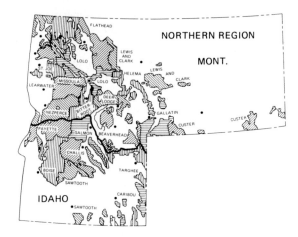

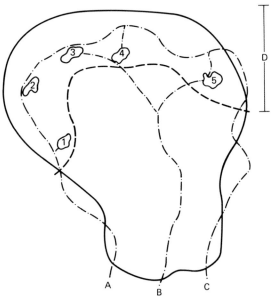

1-5 Alpine lakes
A Divide trail entry point
B Canyon trail
C Divide trail
D Entry zone

**Figure 14.10** Rattlesnake drainage of the Lolo National Forest abstracted for area management plan.

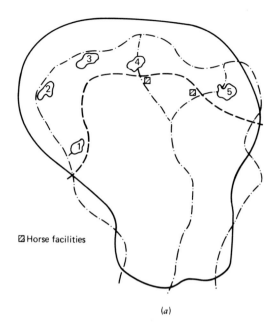

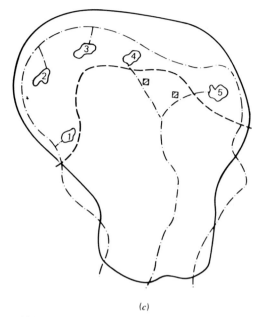

(a)

(c)

Horse facilities

**Figure 14.11** Concept plans (a) and (b); final management plan (c) for Rattlesnake drainage, Lolo National Forest, Montana.

3. To locate minimum horse facilities below the alpine zone that would basically allow the horseback rider to continue use of the lakes, particularly lakes 4 and 5.
4. To allow no camping or fires within 400 meters (¼ mile) of any lake.
5. To maintain current pack-in, pack-out policy.

Note that the program objectives included the maintenance of horse use, even though a simpler response would have been to zone the area for hiking only.

Both concept plans (Figure 14.11 *a & b*) meet the objectives; Plan A places the horse facilities in relatively stable areas near lakes 4 and 5. The centralized facility in Plan B was deemed too far from the lakes for typical day use. However, the bypass concept was initiated in Plan B; the Divide Trail was rerouted to give a greater viewing experi-

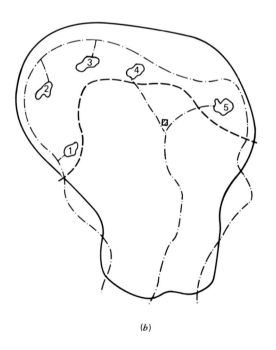

(b)

**351**

ence to the hiker and to make the lakes visually available; lakes 1, 2, and 3 were made accessible via spur trails for people who wanted to spend some time around the lakes. Spur trails from the divide to lakes 4 and 5 were obliterated, and the lakes were made visually accessible at points where steep terrain would effectively eliminate casual use. Where easy access may have been available, the Divide Trail was rerouted to the opposite side of the divide. The actual placement of the dual horse facilities was adjusted to take advantage of well-drained, stable soil locations. Thus, the final plan is a mixture of the two concept plans (Figure 14.11 c).

While trade-offs are usually necessary in any planning effort to solve a problem, ideally we should strive to *maximize the benefits* to the user at minimum cost either in adjustment of the experience or loss of environmental amenities. However, any decision we reach today should maintain the maximum possible future management options. Too often we seem to relish the idea of planning every hectare, yet every hectare is not needed; most of the same philosophy pervades other areas of planning—we have the technology to do it, so let's do it. We do not seem to evaluate the appropriateness of the technology in relation to the situation. In forest recreation, planners do not create the experience through technology. They simply use the technology to make available, to protect, or to enhance that opportunity within the limits described in the norms in Table 14.1. With some creative planning they can provide the desired types of experiences for larger numbers of people on smaller areas.

Another objective for the Rattlesnake Drainage area is to *establish priorities*. It is not feasible to expect any area plan to be immediately funded in its entirety. The planner must establish priorities of programs and capital improvements within those programs. These priorities should be listed as immediate, short-run, and long-run. Immediate items would be implemented immediately within the existing operating budget. Short-run items would be those sites and facilities needed to implement the basic program for the priority programs. Long-run items would be those needed to complete the higher-priority programs and to complete the entire lower-priority programs.

## MANAGEMENT ISSUES

Most recreation-management issues involve some of the concepts introduced earlier: defined recreational experiences, management by objectives, and recreational opportunity spectrum; but they tend to focus on some activity.

### Recreational Experiences

Most of the controversy surrounding recreation planning points to one single issue—the failure to define recreational experiences. We can neither plan nor manage specific programs to provide specific recreational experiences unless we have well-defined social, development, and management-control norms; thus, this chapter has tried to address that void in forest recreation planning.

To be completely responsive, the planner needs to recognize the total spectrum of recreational opportunities and the discrete segments of the spectrum that constitute the particular experience. The planner must then incorporate the recreational experience into the management objectives and be willing to take the necessary steps to ensure implementation of the program. *Administrative zoning* may be one of those controversial actions one needs to implement to maintain the *status quo* of the particular experience. To change the *status quo* would be to change the experience; such change would only be acceptable if it were based on a change in objectives. For example, if an area were established for a Class II hiking experience, yet density of use was low, we might be inclined simply to accommodate off-road vehicle use. As use increased, more hikers would be displaced elsewhere, to the point that the area might be primarily used by recreational-vehicle users. Typically, as use builds up, the more modern forms of recreational travel will invade and displace the more primitive forms. Many public-land managers feel that zoning is inappropriate because it tends to discriminate against specific segments of the user population. Yet, as shown in the example above, the failure to zone constitutes tacit zoning—favoring one user group over another. In that same example, the one we end up favoring because we did not zone is not the one we chose to favor in our objectives. In sum, management by objectives is only as good as the actions taken to implement those objectives.

Wilderness use is one of the activities that the manager has failed to recognize by its unique location on the spectrum—and the associated norms of the experience. Wilderness is not only a Class I experience; it occupies a unique niche within the Class I zone. It defines the extremity of the roadless portion of the spectrum. There are only two well-defined points on the continuum—the extremities: wilderness and inner-city urban development.

The typical scenario in *wilderness* has been incremental development such as external road improvement, internal travel access, facilities at trail heads, bridges across streams, toilets near lakes, etc. With the increase in development, the norms of the experience have changed, causing in many cases a series of visitor displacements (Figure 14.8). The end result is that, although we think we are offering a Class I experience, we are in fact offering at best a Class II experience. Unfortunately, many managers have not recognized this and are continuing to erode the experience by more incremental development. The standard argument is that there is more and more ''demand'' for wilderness so ''we have got to do something.'' First, people's initial response is an attraction to the word *wilderness*, but thereafter they are responding to the norms of the experience we have designed into the system. Thus, the ''demand'' (consumption) is really based on the norms we develop through the area-planning process. In the cases of wilderness we have typically used the term as a catchall for most *roadless experiences*. What is needed now is the development of a variety of roadless recreation experiences; ideally many of them would be located nearer to the participant and

on lands that could sustain higher levels of use. It appears that most people would prefer a Class II or III roadless experience to a Class I wilderness. If we refuse to clear downed timber from trails, there is a good probability that the ''demand'' for wilderness would suddenly drop. Those people who were displaced would be responding to an increment of reverse development—decreased access.

## Carrying Capacity Syndrome

Recreational carrying capacity is a management concept that places recreation into the context of *site capabilities*. Some reasons why carrying capacity has surfaced as a managerial issue are: (1) the growing demand for recreational (particularly outdoor) space is, in some areas, fast outstripping not only the existing and proposed facilities but even the resources. For example, it has been estimated that in New York state the demand for recreational land is growing at a rate four times that of the population (2). Heavily used, depleted, and deteriorating recreational sites already constitute a serious problem in certain areas (Figure 14.12) and have focused attention on the management of recreational land to its carrying capacity (16).

Because the issue concerns escalating demand for a finite resource base, management models that associate demand for recreation with the capacity and limitation of the resource base have become popular. These methods assume a wide variety of approaches and are generically known as recreational carrying capacity.

*Recreational carrying capacity* has been defined as the character of use that can be supported over a specific time by an area developed at a certain level without causing excessive damage to either the physical environment or the experience for the visitor (17). Carrying capacity has also been used to express architectural or design limits. A parking lot may have a designed capacity of 60 cars. That parking lot's carrying capacity is the 60 spaces multiplied by an automobile turnover rate.

In outdoor recreational settings, capacity may be

**Figure 14.12** Heavily utilized campgrounds. (*a*) Campground managed to sustain high use. (*b*) Campground with little man-agement. Both in the Savage River State Forest, Maryland. (Photograph by R.H. Becker.)

expressed in design units such as camping spaces or picnic tables. When the recreational experience is separated from designed limitation, application of a design-capacity concept becomes less precise. Is the carrying capacity of a beach area the number of towels that can be placed next to each other? Probably not—very few people would tolerate such use levels.

The concept of carrying capacity is not new (18–24). It has been implicit, if not always explicitly defined, in many aspects of land use. Carrying capacity developed as a range-management concept, for example, involves a negative consequence to a population as a result of overuse of a feeding range (18). If an elk herd exceeds the capability of its feeding-range regeneration, elements of the herd die—a definite negative impact on the elk. Impacts of recreation overuse do not have similar consequences. In this search for consequences of recreational use, the focus centers on the principle product of recreation: user satisfaction.

Much of the early social carrying-capacity work was based on the assumption that increasing numbers reduced the satisfaction of the visitor. Under this model, average individual satisfaction is reduced with the inclusion of each new user. For a while total satisfaction increases, but later begins to level off and soon declines (25). The use level prior to the leveling off was considered to be the social carrying capacity. By periodically measuring satisfaction in the field, researchers and managers hoped to find the carrying capacity for specific sites. Recent studies (26, 27), however, indicate that the simple satisfaction model based on density of use is not valid, and a more complex, multidimensional model has been suggested. Becker (28) provided an empirical basis by observing user densities as a means of separating users into homogeneous subsets and then statistically testing the perceptions of the desired experiences. His conclusion was that "satisfaction would appear strongly linked with the nature of the experience and is independent of use density levels."

There has been heavy emphasis in research on studying recreational carrying capacity; this obsession with carrying capacity has tended to oversimplify the role of the manager. Many land managers have already spent a large amount of money on research and gathering other data. At Grand Canyon, during a 4-year period, about $500,000 was spent on such studies (29). Grand Canyon personnel spent a considerable amount of time and effort gathering public input through meetings at various major western cities and such things as questionnaires and workbook response to management proposals. Most of the managers generally looked at the research and study programs in combination with public involvement and legislative authority as a means to a "final management plan."

As Grand Canyon managers began the management plan effort, it became evident that they would *never* reach a final management plan because public demand for river trips is dynamic. As new information becomes available and public demands change, managers have to respond with dynamic plans that adapt to changing conditions and pressure. No management plan can be of value if it is "set in concrete." Grand Canyon is currently involved in a court suit because demands have apparently changed and management has not kept up with that change.

Thus success as a manager should not be measured in numbers of people or capacity but in *how well the participants match with the experiences.* The manager should steer away from capacity—a search for a magic number—and develop recreational opportunities based on *management by objectives.* The primary objective should focus on the type of experience to be offered.

## REFERENCES

1. M. Clawson and J. L. Knetsch, *Economics of Outdoor Recreation,* Johns Hopkins Press, Baltimore, 1966.
2. D. M. Knudson, *Outdoor Recreation,* Macmillan. New York, 1980.
3. Anon., "Assessing Demand for Outdoor Recrea-

tion'', Nat. Acad. Sci. Rept., U.S. Dept. of Interior, Bur. of Outdoor Rec., Washington, D.C., 1975.

4. J. Huizinga, *Homoludens: A Study of the Plan Element of Culture*, Beacon, Boston, 1966.

5. R. D. Laing, *The Politics of Experience*, Ballantine Books, New York, 1967.

6. J. G. Hof, "Problems in Projecting Recreation Resources Used Through Supply and Demand Analysis," in *Proc. of I.U.F.R.O. Meeting on Economics of Outdoor Recreation*, Washington, D.C., 1979.

7. P. J. Brown, B. L. Driver, and C. McConnell, "The Opportunity Spectrum Concept and Behavioral Information in Outdoor Recreation Resource Supply Inventories: Background and Application," in *Proc. from National Workshop on Integrated Inventories of Renewable Natural Resources*, Tucson, 1978.

8. Anon., *Forest Service Manual 2330.5-3*, U.S.D.A. For. Serv., Washington, D.C., 1977.

9. M. I. Christiansen, *Park Planning Handbook*, John Wiley & Sons, New York, 1977.

10. J. A. Wagar, "Campgrounds for Many Tastes," U.S.D.A. For. Serv., Intermountain Forest and Range Experiment Sta., Res. Paper INT-6, Ogden, Utah, 1963.

11. P. J. Brown, "Information Needs for River Recreation Planning and Management," in *Proc. of River Management and Research Symposium*, D. Lime, ed., U.S.D.A. For. Serv., St. Paul, 1977.

12. A. Jubenville, "River Recreation Research Needs for the 1980's: Role Segregation/Allocation," in *Proc. of Symposium on Applied Research in the 1980's for Parks and Outdoor Recreation*, Victoria, B.C., 1980.

13. R. Schreyer and J. W. Roggenbuck, "The Influence of Experience Expectation on Crowding Perception and Social-Psychological Carrying Capacity," *Leisure Sci., 1*, 373 (1978).

14. R. Schreyer, "Succession and Displacement in River Recreation, Part I, Problem Definition and Analysis," River Recreation Project Rept., U.S.D.A. For. Serv., North Central Forest Experiment Sta., St. Paul, 1979.

15. R. H. Becker, B. J. Niemann, and W. A. Gates, "Displacement of Users Within a River System: Social and Environmental Trade-Offs," paper presented at *Second Conference on Scientific Research in the National Parks*, San Francisco, U.S. Park Service, 1979.

16. J. Tivy, *The Concept and Determination of Carrying Capacity of Recreational Land in the USA*, The Countryside Commission, Perth, Scotland, 1972.

17. D. W. Lime and G. H. Stankey, "Carrying Capacity: Maintaining Outdoor Recreation Quality," in *Recreation Symposium Proceedings*, U.S.D.A. For. Serv., Syracuse, 1971.

18. H. T. Heady, *Rangeland Management*, McGraw-Hill, New York, 1975.

19. R. C. Lucas, "The Recreational Capacity of the Quetico-Superior Area," U.S.D.A. For. Serv., Research Paper LS-15, 1964.

20. J. A. Wagar, *The Carrying Capacity of Wildlands for Recreation*, Forest Science Monograph No. 7, Society of American Foresters, Washington, D.C., 1964.

21. M. Chubb, "Outdoor Recreation Land Capacity: Concepts, Usage, and Definitions," M.S. Thesis, Michigan State University, 1964.

22. M. Chubb and P. Ashton, "Park and Recreation Standards Research: The Creation of Environmental Quality Controls for Recreation," Recreation Research and Planning Unit, Technical Report #5, Michigan State University, 1969.

23. G. H. Stankey, "Visitor Perception of Wilderness Recreation Carrying Capacity," U.S.D.A. For. Serv., Res. Rept. INT-142, Ogden, Utah, 1973.

24. G. H. Stankey and J. Baden, "Rationing Wilderness Use: Methods, Problems, and Guidelines," U.S.D.A., For. Serv., Res. Paper INT-192, Ogden, Utah, 1977.

25. C. J. Cecchetti and U. K. Smith, *Soc. Sci. Res., 2*, 15 (1973).

26. B. Shelby, "Motors and Oars in the Grand Canyon; River Contact Study," National Park Service, Washington, D.C., 1976.

27. T. A. Heberlein, "Density, Crowding, and Satisfaction: Sociological Studies for Determining Carrying Capacity," in *Proc. of River Management and Research Symposium*, D. Lime, ed., U.S.D.A. For. Serv., St. Paul, 1977.

28. R. H. Becker, *Leisure Sci., 1*, 241 (1978).

29. K. R. Mak, M. O. Jensen, and T. L. Hartman, "Management Response to Growing Pressures in Western White-Water Rivers—The Art of the Possible," in *Proc. of River Management and Research Symp.*, D. Lime, ed., U.S.D.A. For. Serv., St. Paul, 1977.

# 15

# BEHAVIOR AND MANAGEMENT OF FOREST FIRES

## Craig G. Lorimer

In many areas of the world, humans have historically been the principal cause of forest fires, in terms of both the actual number of fires and the total area burned. Yet forest fires have probably occurred for as long as there have been lightning storms (Figure 15.1), regions of dense vegetation, and occasional periods of dry weather. In some regions, bits of charcoal embedded in lake sediments testify to the periodic occurrence of fires over thousands of years (1), and it is likely that at least some of these were caused by lightning. Evidence of fires in the distant past can also sometimes be found on the forest site itself. Long-lived and relatively fire-resistant trees such as coast redwood and ponderosa pine often bear visible external wounds caused by fire (Figure 15.2). When the trunks of such trees are examined in cross section, scars of fires that occurred centuries ago may be evident. Even in forests that show no obvious indication of recent fire, careful examination of the lower layers of the forest floor will often reveal fragments of charcoal from fires that occurred hundreds of years ago.

We need not appeal to historical evidence, however, to establish the importance of fire in natural communities. On a worldwide basis, it is estimated

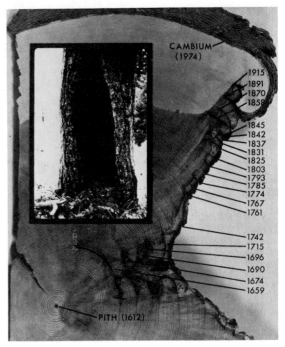

**Figure 15.2** Multiple fire scars visible on a cross-section of this old ponderosa pine tree (inset) in the Bitterroot National Forest, western Montana, reveal that 21 fires occurred on this site between 1659 and 1915. (From Arno (2); courtesy of U.S.D.A. Forest Service.)

that approximately 500,000 cloud-to-ground lightning discharges occur in forested regions each day (3). Most of these discharges probably strike trees, although only about 10 percent of them actually result in fires (4). Hardly a year goes by when foresters in western North America are not busy locating and suppressing lightning fires.

## NATURAL FIRE REGIMES

The frequency of lightning fires is highly variable in different parts of the world, even over relatively short distances. Lightning fires are infrequent in tropical rain forests, and they are relatively uncommon in moist temperate areas such as western Europe and much of eastern North America. The range in natural fire frequency is evident by compar-

**Figure 15.1** Several minutes of lightning activity during a thunderstorm in the Rocky Mountains. In this region lightning causes 60 percent of all fires. (Courtesy of U.S.D.A. Forest Service.)

ing wildfire statistics for the eastern and western United States. In the eastern forests, lightning causes 2 percent or less of all forest fires. The incidence of lightning fires in the western conifer forests, on the other hand, is probably the highest of any region in the world (3). In the Rocky Mountain region, for instance, lightning causes no less than 60 percent of all fires. It is not unusual for a single storm to ignite more than 30 fires in the region over which it passes.

Much of this variability can be attributed to *climate* and *topography*. Lightning fires are obviously more common in regions with a pronounced dry season and in mountainous country that is subject to more thunderstorms. But the nature of the vegetation seems to exert considerable influence as well. Fires are much more common in conifer forests than in stands of broad-leaved deciduous trees. The reason for this is not entirely clear, but it is possibly explained by the chemical makeup of the foliage and wood. According to one hypothesis, conifers have higher quantities of flammable chemical compounds that, after the impact of a lightning bolt, are easily vaporized and ignited (4, 5).

Relatively few lightning fires reach catastrophic proportions. Lightning strikes often occur during periods of high humidity or rain, while fires of human origin are actually more likely to occur in fair weather. For this reason lightning fires are often less intense and more easily suppressed than those caused by humans. Of the 63,050 lightning fires suppressed on U.S. national forests between 1960 and 1969, 97 percent were controlled at a size of 4 hectares (10 acres) or less.

It is clear, however, that under certain weather and fuel conditions, lightning fires can be as large and intense as any other type of fire. "Dry" lightning strikes in the absence of rain are common events, and even under damp conditions, a fire can smolder in leaf litter or a dead tree for days or even weeks until dry conditions return. For example, the lightning-caused Sundance Fire of 1967 in Idaho burned 23,000 hectares (56,000 acres), and the Great Idaho Fire of 1910, set mostly by multiple lightning strikes, engulfed an area of not less than 1 million hectares (almost 3 million acres). Assessment of the possibilities of lightning fires reaching a large size has become increasingly important in recent years as greater attention has been given to restoration of natural fire regimes in parks and wilderness. The estimated annual timber loss due to fires is given in Table 7.1.

## Influence on the Landscape

The frequency and intensity of fires in a particular region may have an important role in shaping the forest landscape. Fire frequency and intensity partly determine whether most forest stands will be young or old, even-aged or all-aged, early successional or climax. These characteristics, in turn, affect wildlife populations, forest growth, and insect and disease conditions.

Parts of western North America have a natural fire regime characterized by frequent light *surface fires* that burn much of the litter layer and may kill some of the understory vegetation, but that have little effect on the mature trees (Figure 15.3). Evidence from fire scars on old living trees indicates that frequency of fires in a given stand of trees, known as the *recurrence interval* or *mean fire interval,* was often as short as 9 to 12 years (Figure 15.2). Since only the more intense surface fires cause scars, this represents a conservative estimate of fire frequency. The more destructive *crown fires* that sweep through the forest canopy were much less frequent, but extensive even-aged stands of "pioneer" species such as lodgepole pine testify that crown fires must have occurred at periodic intervals as well (Figure 15.4).

Northern Minnesota is an example of an area in which crown fires and intense surface fires are fairly common. As a result, the primeval forest landscape was dominated by early successional species such as aspen, jack pine, and red pine, and climax forests were rare. The recurrence interval has been estimated to have been approximately 100 years, which is shorter than the maximum life span of the tree

**Figure 15.3** Surface fire. (Courtesy of U.S.D.A. Forest Service.)

**Figure 15.4** Crown fire. (Courtesy of U.S.D.A. Forest Service.)

species (6). Crown fires also occurred periodically in the northern conifer-hardwoods forests stretching from Wisconsin to Maine, but apparently at much longer intervals. Climax forests dominated the landscape of this region (7, 8), and uneven-aged stands appear to have been common (8, 9). Long intervals may also have elapsed between severe fires in some areas of central and southern hardwoods, as suggested by the low incidence of lightning fires, the humid climate, and the uneven-aged character of virgin forest remnants (10).

## The Natural Role of Fire

Given the fact that lightning fires are common events in some regions, it is not surprising that a number of species show evidence of adaptations to periodic fire. Although the nature of this adaptation varies among species, most fire-adapted species possess characteristics that enable them to colonize rapidly and dominate severely burned areas. Some of the birches and aspens have light seeds that can be transported considerable distances by wind, thus increasing the chances that seeds will reach a burned area. Other species, such as jack pine, lodgepole pine, and pitch pine, have seeds that are held in tightly closed *serotinous* cones. Unlike the cones of most gymnosperms, serotinous cones are sealed by resin, and seeds are not released until high temperatures melt the resin and allow the cones to open. The seeds of fire-adapted species germinate rapidly on charred surfaces or exposed soil, and the seedlings tend to be tolerant of the dry surface conditions and extremes of temperature common to exposed sites. As is typical of shade-intolerant species, they grow rapidly, particularly in the early years, and hence usually outcompete other species that may arrive on the site. In areas prone to repeated surface fires, trees of certain species, such as ponderosa pine and longleaf pine, develop thick bark at maturity that makes them fairly resistant to injury from light fires. Frequent fires may be beneficial to such species by retarding the invasion of these stands by species of later successional stages. Thus in the South, fires in the longleaf pine forests hamper the development of a dense understory of climax hardwood species. The beneficial effects of fire on certain species of trees are paralleled by beneficial effects on the habitat of many wildlife species (see Chapter 16).

Fire may have more subtle beneficial functions as well. In cold dry climates, forest litter and woody debris have a tendency to build up faster than they can be decomposed. Occasional light surface fires can reduce this accumulation of hazardous fuels, which otherwise might build up to a point where catastrophic fires would become more likely. Burning of this debris may release some of the nutrients previously locked up in organic matter into the soil where it can be made available to plants.

## HUMAN INFLUENCE

Human modification of the natural fire regime is not a recent development. It is well documented that primitive societies commonly used fire to improve hunting and overland travel, to aid in land clearance, and to reduce insect and snake populations. The shifting pattern of slash-and-burn agriculture was widely practiced by native peoples of the tropics. Intentional burning was also a common practice among North American Indians, and although most of these fires were probably light surface fires, we can only guess as to what proportion of the even-aged postfire forests at this time were the result of Indian activity. In Massachusetts, a colonist named Thomas Morton wrote the following in 1632.

*The Salvages are accustomed, to set fire of the Country in all places where they come; and to burne it, twize a yeare. . . . And this custome of firing the Country is the meanes to make it passable, and by that meanes the trees grow here, and there as in our parks, and makes the Country very beautifull, and commodius.*

The number of large and destructive fires dramatically increased with the arrival of European settlers. Relatively few of the trees cut down for land clearance were used for lumber or fuel because settlers had much more timber than they could possibly use themselves, and there was little demand for wood elsewhere on the open market. So the settlers developed a quick method of disposing of the trees: setting them ablaze. Early historians reported that the usual approach was either to fell the trees and wait until the fuels dried sufficiently to burn, or else to save some effort by cutting the trees halfway through and letting the wind do the rest of the work. In either case the resulting fires were clearly risky no matter what precautions were taken. Seldom have so many large and disastrous fires occurred over such a short period of time. Typically, the worst fires occurred in the northern forests. In early October 1825 a series of fires raged over 1.2 million hectares (3 million acres) in Maine and New Brunswick. An equal amount of area was burned in 1871 and 1881 in Michigan and Wisconsin. In fact, so many large fires occurred during this time that occasionally the amount of smoke and particulates in the atmosphere was sufficient to cast semidarkness over the land. One such "dark day" in 1780, caused by fires raging in Vermont and New York, was described as follows:

*The legislature of Connecticut was in session at Hartford on that day. The deepening gloom enwrapped the city, and the rooms of the state house grew dark. The journal of the house of representatives reads "None could see to read or write in the house, or even at a window, or distinguish persons at a small distance" (11).*

This scenario set the stage for a policy of vigorous *fire suppression*. Not only did fire frequently destroy a valuable timber resource, but even small smoldering surface fires represented a constant threat to human life and property should weather conditions suddenly create more severe burning conditions. There were too many disastrous fires to allow room for the thought that some fires might have beneficial effects. It is therefore not surprising that one of the top priorities of the American Forestry Association when it convened in 1875 was the "protection of the existing forests of the country from unnecessary waste," of which fire was the leading cause. The fruits of these labors became evident in the Weeks Law of 1911 and the Clarke-McNary Act of 1924, which for the first time provided federal funding to assist the states in developing a cooperative forest-fire control program (see Chapters 1, 12, and 13). Although the actual amount of money provided was small at first, it did allow the construction of fire towers and the hiring of fire wardens and equipment.

Fire control on publicly owned lands has undergone several changes in the current century (12). The 1920s and 1930s were characterized more or less by a policy of attempted fire exclusion, by which all wildfires were suppressed as quickly as possible. In 1935 the "*10 A.M. fire-control policy*" was formulated, setting the objective of rapid and thorough suppression of all fires during potentially dangerous fire weather by 10:00 the next morning. The planned use of fire under carefully specified conditions, known as *prescribed burning*, was nevertheless soon acknowledged to be useful in achieving certain objectives such as fuel reduction and seedbed preparation.

Some modification of the 10 A.M. policy was required in certain cases. In parts of the western United States, labor and equipment were not always sufficient to suppress all fires, and it was recognized that such an attempt had probably passed a point of diminishing returns in terms of costs and benefits. Fire suppression was therefore handled on a priority

basis from about 1940 to 1960. On federal lands, fires burning in areas of highest resource values were attacked first. Remote areas of noncommercial forest with low-hazard fuels were attended to last.

The current widely accepted policy on forest fires is that of *fire management,* not simply fire control. This policy takes advantage of the beneficial effects of some forest fires while still carrying on suppression of fires expected to have undesirable effects. Several features of this policy represent a bold departure from previous policies. *First*, it is recognized that the decision on how to handle a particular fire on federal lands should be based not only on the anticipated behavior of the fire, but also on the long-range management objectives of each unit of land. On some national forests, a management plan is written for each homogeneous unit of vegetation and fuels, and the degree to which fire is necessary to accomplish these objectives is clearly stated. *Second*, there is a provision for allowing certain fires to burn under supervision if the predictions of fire behavior indicate that the fire will help achieve the management objectives. For example, a lightning fire or other unplanned ignition may be allowed to burn under surveillance if fuel reduction is needed on that unit of land, and the fire is predicted to burn as a light or moderate surface fire. *Finally*, fire is acknowledged to be more than simply a management tool. It is considered to be an environmental factor that may serve a necessary function not easily substituted by other methods. Thus, while control of understory hardwoods in southern pine forests can be achieved by cutting down the hardwood stems and applying herbicides to the stumps, it is recognized that all the beneficial effects of fire cannot be feasibly duplicated by mechanical means (13).

## FIRE BEHAVIOR

Anticipation of fire behavior is one of the most critical aspects of fire management. The choice of strategy in wildfire suppression and prescribed burning depends largely on how the fire is expected to behave—its rate of spread, direction of travel, and intensity. These aspects of fire behavior are regulated by a number of interacting factors. The prerequisites for the start and spread of a forest fire are: (1) flammable fuels, (2) sufficient heat energy to bring the fuels to the ignition temperature, and (3) adequate oxygen. Virtually all of the phenomena influencing fire behavior, including those related to weather and topography, can ultimately be attributed to one or more of these three factors. Thus the size, total weight, and moisture content of fuel elements partly determine the amount of heat required for ignition and the heat released by combustion. Their spatial arrangement influences oxygen availability. Variations in these factors are ultimately reflected in the rate of fire spread and its intensity. Grass fires, for example, spread rapidly but are of relatively low intensity, while fires in heavy logging debris spread slowly but burn intensely.

## Fuel Conditions

Fuels are often classified in a general manner by their spatial location in the forest. *Surface fuels* constitute a large, heterogeneous group of fuels found on or close to the surface of the ground. Included are undecomposed leaf litter, fallen twigs and branches, logs, grass, herbs, tree seedlings, and low shrubs. *Ground fuels* are found beneath the loose layer of surface litter. They include partly decomposed organic matter or duff, roots, and muck or peat in wet areas. *Aerial fuels* include all flammable material in the subcanopy layers of the forest and in the tree crowns. Fuels are classified in this manner partly because of the three distinctive types of fires associated with them: surface fires, ground fires, and crown fires.

The most readily available fuels for a forest fire are the dry surface layer of litter on the forest floor, interspersed small dead branchwood, and cured grass in some forests. This is the material consumed in most *surface fires*. Green herbs and understory vegetation are usually a deterrent to fire spread in the spring because of the high moisture content of the foliage, but may contribute significantly to fire intensity and rate of spread when in a cured condition. Although the larger fuels, such as fallen logs, may be partly or wholly consumed by the time a surface fire has died out, such material is too large and often too damp to influence the forward momentum of the fire. Thus, research seems to indicate that the effect of fuels on the forward rate of spread of a surface fire is largely determined by the amount, arrangement, and moisture content of the fine fuels (14). The effect of larger surface fuels such as fallen logs is to cause a more intense fire. For this reason the most intense fires are usually those that start in logging slash or other areas of heavy fuel accumulations. In general, the higher the total weight of fuels, the more difficult the fire will be to control.

In finely divided ground fuels such as peat or duff, oxygen is often limiting to the point that only glowing combustion is possible. As a result, *ground fires* are often of low intensity and spread slowly. They are, however, remarkably persistent, often smoldering for days or weeks. For this reason they present an especially serious problem, and it is often difficult to judge whether suppression activities have been successful in completely extinguishing the fire.

The susceptibility of tree crowns to ignition varies somewhat among species. Especially pronounced is the difference between coniferous species and broad-leaved deciduous species (hardwoods). *Crown fires* are fairly common in coniferous forests but rare in hardwoods, probably because of differences in chemical makeup and average moisture content of the foliage. Yet even in conifer forests, the probability of a crown fire is low if the understory is sparse and the trees are mature. The presence of a well-stratified understory layer provides a means for an intense surface fire to climb into the crowns of the dominant trees. Susceptibility to crown fire is increased if this understory is coniferous and if a large accumulation of dead fuel is present.

## Weather Conditions

Within a given fuel type, fire behavior is regulated largely by the state of the weather. Particularly important are the effects of *atmospheric moisture* and *wind*. Fuel moisture is determined not only by the amount and duration of precipitation, but also by relative humidity during rainless periods. As humidity increases, fuels absorb moisture from the air, and more of the fire's energy is used to drive off this moisture prior to combustion. Evaporation of water vapor from the surface of the fuel also has a smothering effect by limiting the amount of oxygen available for combustion. As humidity decreases, fuels give off moisture to the air. The rapidity of response to humidity depends on the size of the fuel elements. The "flashy" fine fuels respond quickly to changes in relative humidity, while the larger fuels respond much more slowly. The rapidity with which fine fuels respond to atmospheric moisture is evident in the diurnal variations in fire intensity caused largely by normal fluctuations in relative humidity. Fire intensity and the probability of ignition are closely related to relative humidity and fuel moisture (Table 15.1).

*Wind* has a dramatic effect on the rate of fire spread and intensity. It has long been a rule of thumb among fire-control officials that the rate of spread is approximately proportional to the square of the windspeed; hence, a doubling of windspeed will quadruple the rate of spread. Winds, especially if they are gusty and turbulent, also increase the chances of a crown fire and various types of erratic behavior.

The effect of wind on the pattern or shape of fires is illustrated in Figure 15.5. Under conditions of moderate or strong winds, fires tend burn in elliptical patterns with the long axis in the direction of the wind. The strategy of fire suppression is partly based on estimates of the increase in perimeter of this elliptical zone of flames per unit time. The pattern of spread, however, can be greatly changed by abrupt wind shifts, which can turn the flank of a fire into a much expanded burning head. This greatly increases the area burned by the fire. It is not uncommon for fires to undergo one or more moderate shifts in direction (15).

## Topography

Fires burn more quickly up steep slopes, largely because heat generated by the fire front is directed more closely to the surface of the ground, thereby decreasing the moisture and increasing the temperature of the fuels ahead of the fire. Topography also has many effects on the microclimate of a particular site. Slopes facing toward the south and southwest, for example, tend to be the warmest and driest slopes because they are exposed to the direct rays of the sun during the hottest part of the day. As a result fires are more frequent and spread more quickly on south slopes. Topography also modifies and channels airflow patterns. Rugged, mountainous topography often induces turbulent winds that increase fire intensity and the possibility of erratic behavior.

## Erratic Behavior

It is not uncommon for crown fires at some point in their development to exhibit a sudden increase in intensity, which may be visibly apparent from the development of a powerful convection column of rapidly rising smoke and hot gases. Such fires are often called *blowup fires* and represent an unfavorable turn of events for firefighters because they are often uncontrollable by conventional firefighting techniques (Figure 15.6). The development of a dynamic convection column appears to require that the fire exceed a certain threshold intensity, for which the initiating factor may be a sudden increase in windspeed or the start of crowning (16). The convection column tends to create its own "draft," which helps maintain fire intensity at a high level. Blowup fires frequently exhibit erratic behavior. They may generate high winds in excess of 350 kilometers per hour, further increasing fire intensity, as well as whirlwinds of hot air and flames that may

**Table 15.1**

Effect of Relative Humidity and Fuel Moisture on Fire Behavior

| Relative Humidity (%) | Moisture Content (%) | | Fire Behavior |
|---|---|---|---|
| | Forest Litter | Small Branchwood | |
| >95 | >25 | | Little or no ignition |
| >60 | >20 | >15 | Very little ignition. Fire smolders and spreads slowly |
| 45–60 | 15–19 | 12–15 | Low ignition hazard, but campfires become dangerous; glowing brands cause ignition when relative humidity <50%. Spreads slowly but readily; many prescribed burns conducted in this range |
| 35–45 | 11–14 | 10–12 | Medium ignitibility; matches become dangerous. "Easy" burning conditions |
| 25–35 | 8–10 | 7–10 | High ignition hazard; matches always dangerous. Occasional crowning, spotting caused by gusty winds. "Moderate" burning conditions |
| 15–25 | 5–7 | 5–7 | Quick ignition, rapid buildup, extensive crowning; any increase in wind causes increased spotting, crowning, loss of control; fire moves up bark of trees igniting aerial fuels; long-distance spotting in pine stands. Dangerous burning conditions |
| <15 | <5 | <5 | All sources of ignition dangerous. Aggressive burning; spot fires occur often and spread rapidly, extreme fire behavior probable. Critical burning conditions |

*Source.* Adapted from Albini (36).

hurl burning debris far ahead of the main fire front. Such behavior, known as *spotting,* can result in many new fires.

## Prediction of Fire Behavior

A fire researcher named H. T. Gisborne remarked at a conference in the 1940s, "I doubt that anyone will ever be able to sit down to a machine, punch a key for every factor of the situation, and have the machine tell him what to do" (17). Be that as it may, the advent of *computer simulation techniques* in recent years has proved to be very useful to fire managers. Clearly it would be desirable to at least have an estimate of the rate of spread and intensity of a fire given certain weather and fuel conditions.

The quantitative study of fire behavior and prediction has been intensively carried out at the U.S.

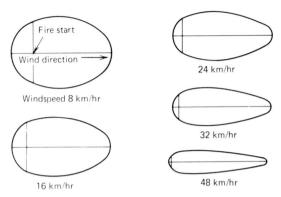

**Figure 15.5** Approximate fire shapes that result from a constant wind direction at various windspeeds (the different fires are not drawn to the same scale). (From Albini (20).)

Forest Service's Northern Forest Fire Lab in Missoula, Mont., for the past two decades. One of the basic aims of this research has been to use physical laws, such as the law of conservation of energy, to describe the process of combustion and fire spread in mathematical terms (18, 19). The use of basic principles of physics to predict fire behavior has some advantages over statistical correlations between past fire behavior and various independent variables because the former approach is more universal in its applicability; that is, it can be used to predict fire behavior in a wide variety of forest types, shrublands, and even grasslands. Developing these equations required much elaborate experimentation with fire behavior in a laboratory environment, because some of the mechanisms of heat transfer and combustion were not known, and carefully controlled experiments were the only way to determine empirically the required factors.

This type of research has had handsome payoffs in practical application, one of the most useful of which has been the development of a revised *National Fire-Danger Rating System* (21). Various forms of fire-danger rating had long been used to indicate the relative severity of fire-weather conditions, probable suppression forces needed, and other information. With the new system, much more specific and accurate predictions are possible. Included are predictions of the number of fires expected per unit area, ease of ignition, rate of spread, and burning intensity. A current limitation of the system is that it applies only to surface fires; however, it is possible to infer the likelihood of crown fire and spotting from the surface fire ratings. As with all theoretical models of natural phenomena, these predictions must be compared with the observed behavior of many fires before proper interpretation can be made.

Fire-danger ratings are computed daily and utilize measurements of such variables as windspeed, fuel moisture, precipitation amount and duration, lightning activity, and the condition of the herbaceous vegetation. Although some of the needed measurements can be obtained from stations maintained by the Weather Service, the stations do not ordinarily make measurements of such important fire variables as fuel moisture or vegetative conditions, and the locations of ordinary weather stations (usually in valleys) are often not representative of vast tracts of forestland. A network of fire-weather stations in forested areas has been established in recent years to meet these needs. Once the necessary data have been obtained, tables or graphs based on the fire-spread equations are used to obtain predictions for various aspects of fire behavior.

The adoption of a standardized National Fire-Danger Rating System has simplified administrative procedures and improved communication among government agencies. In 1954 eight different systems were in use; by 1977 the new national system had been adopted by all federal agencies and by 38 state agencies.

## FIRE PREVENTION

Because humans are the leading cause of forest fires in most areas, fire-prevention campaigns have been vigorously promoted to reduce the number of these fires. The most visible efforts are public education campaigns via conventional media—radio mes-

**Figure 15.6**  Aftermath of a blowup fire, showing numerous snags that can serve as a major source of fuel for subsequent intense fires. (From Anderson (22); courtesy of U.S.D.A. Forest Service.)

sages, signs, magazine articles, news releases, etc. Such efforts as the Smokey Bear and Keep America Green programs have relied heavily on public education.

In order for fire-prevention programs to be highly effective, the relative importance of specific causes needs to be known. This information is usually collected from standard fire reports prepared for each fire by state forestry departments. A 50-year statistical compilation of these reports (16) indicates that in the United States, the leading cause has been incendiarism, which has accounted for 26 percent of all fires. Other major causes have been smoking (19 percent), debris burning (18 percent), lightning (9 percent), machine use (8 percent), and campfires (6 percent). Regional variations are pronounced. Incendiary fires are much less important in the North and West than in the South. Smoking is the leading cause in the northeastern states, with debris burning most important in the north-central states.

This information helps indicate where the thrust of prevention campaigns should be directed. The high frequency of fires caused by smoking, for example, has led to regular appeals to crush cigarettes and use ashtrays, especially along highways where most cigarette fires occur. A high frequency of fires attributable to escaped campfires in some localities may indicate the need for installation of outdoor fireplaces in popular but undeveloped recreation areas. *Incendiarism* is a more difficult problem to tackle, although it is probable that education has some effect. But particularly in the South, annual or periodic burning has long been a deeply ingrained custom among rural people; it is intended to improve cattle forage, kill ticks, chiggers, and snakes, and to improve wildlife habitat and hunting prospects.

Whatever positive results such fires may have, the fact remains that they are unsupervised wildfires, usually initiated without adequate knowledge of fuel and weather conditions. For this reason they often cause substantial damage to living trees and always have the potential for becoming uncontrollable. They are usually set without the landowners' knowledge or consent. In the late 1920s, the American Forestry Association obtained funds for a traveling road show known as the ''Dixie Crusaders'' to educate rural southern residents about fire protection. Although such programs have achieved positive results, incendiarism is still the principal cause of wildfires in the South, accounting for 39 percent of all fires in the region.

In some cases the appropriate contact is not with individuals but with organizations. A high frequency of railroad fires or those caused by power lines can lead to negotiations with the appropriate agency to remedy the situation. Fires caused by sparks from mechanized equipment can be reduced by strict enforcement of regulations pertaining to the installation of spark arresters.

Fire prevention can also be accomplished by *hazard reduction,* commonly by reducing accumulations of particularly hazardous fuels or by constructing barriers to the spread of fire. Controlled burning in areas of heavy logging slash, along railroad tracks, and even in some forests can reduce particularly serious accumulations of fuel. One of the most hazardous types of fuel is the blackened remnants of trees left in the wake of a crown fire (Figure 15.6). These snags are highly susceptible to further ignition, especially by lightning. Ironically, burned-over areas are actually among the most susceptible areas to fire. Brown and Davis (16) report that examples of repeated fires in the same location ''can be cited almost endlessly.'' Where felling of snags is economically justifiable, as on highly productive timberlands, fire damage can be reduced because fallen snags decay more quickly and have a higher moisture content than those left standing. Even in these areas, however, some snags should be left standing

to provide habitat for cavity-nesting birds and mammals.

## FIRE CONTROL

Wildland fire control in the United States is administered as a cooperative venture by the Forest Service, the Bureau of Land Management, the National Park Service, and the various state governments. In some areas private owners and industrial firms also participate in the suppression of fires. Fire-control activities on large fires are usually very tightly organized, and the suppression activity itself may resemble a military campaign.

### Detection

In the early years of the century, lookout towers formed the backbone of the fire-detection system. Sufficient numbers of lookouts were placed on higher points of land in the area to provide reasonably thorough coverage of the landscape. Aerial detection of forest fires by systematic airplane flights, however, has gradually overshadowed fixed-pointed lookouts, partly because it is cheaper and allows for more complete and detailed coverage. Over 5000 lookouts were in use in the United States in 1953, compared to only 3500 in 1968. Most agencies continue to use a skeletal system of lookouts, however, in order to supplement the aerial reconnaissance.

More recent developments in fire detection have included the aerial use of *infrared sensing equipment* that photographically records the location of heat sources. Although some problems in heat source identification remain, the use of infrared sensing equipment in aerial reconnaissance experiments has shown that it is possible to detect the presence of small targets such as glowing buckets of charcoal beneath a forest canopy. This technique has considerable potential for identifying small, smoldering fires that do not produce enough smoke to be detected by the unaided eye.

## Suppression of Wildfires

When a fire has been spotted by a lookout or aerial observer, its location is reported by two-way radio to the dispatcher at the fire-control headquarters. The dispatcher plots the location of the fire on a map, estimates the probable size of the attack force needed to contain the fire, and sends the needed people and equipment to the fire site.

Fire suppression can be accomplished by removing any one of the three essential "ingredients" of fire: (1) fuel, (2) oxygen, and (3) heat. Removal of fuels is accomplished by digging, scraping, or plowing a strip of earth known as a *fire line* in advance of the fire to halt its progress (Figure 15.7). The application of dirt, water, or fire-retardant chemicals serves to reduce both fuel temperature and the supply of oxygen.

If the fire is not too intense, the preferred method of control is *direct attack*, where the fire line is constructed near the fire edge and the flames are knocked down by water, dirt, or other means (Figure 15.7). If the fire cannot be safely approached at close range, the fire line must be constructed at a distance. In such cases fires will usually be set just inside the line and allowed to spread toward the wildfire in order to rob the fire of fuel. This is known as *indirect attack*.

Although the suppression of large forest fires generally requires the use of hand tools, bulldozers, and water pumps over a period of many hours or days, significant contributions to the overall suppression effort can be made by aerial techniques. Just as small airplanes can be used to spray insecticides on crops, so too can they be used to apply water or fire-retardant chemicals to active forest fires. The usual effects of water on a fire can be augmented by the addition of flame-inhibiting chemicals or other additives that enhance the "wettability" of water or increase its smothering effect on the combustion of fuels. Fine clays are often mixed with water to increase the cohesiveness of the mixture and prevent excessive dissipation during its descent.

These mixtures of clay and liquids are known as *slurries*. The application of slurries from the air is particularly helpful as a delaying tactic that allows time for people and equipment to arrive on the scene, especially when the fire occurs in a remote location. However, aerial retardants and slurries are not usually sufficient to extinguish a forest fire, and follow-up work by ground crews is almost always necessary.

The more intense the fire, the more problematic spotting is likely to be for the ground crews. Because spotting may cause the fire to jump the line in many places (Figure 15.8), constant surveillance for spot fires by the suppression crew is necessary. Experienced firefighters realize that under blowup conditions, spread of a fire is seldom restricted by the location of firebreaks. Conflagration fires in the north country routinely jump scores of streams, bogs, and even lakes.

The job of fire suppression is not finished when the fire line is completed and the flames have been extinguished. The tedious process of "mop-up," which involves extinguishing all smoldering fires and firebrands near the inside edge of the fire line, is necessary to ensure that the fire will not flare up again and cross the line. Many flare-ups in the early years of firefighting furnished ample evidence of the need for thorough mop-up.

## PRESCRIBED BURNING

The controlled use of fire to accomplish specific objectives is known as *prescribed burning*. The most common objectives are: (1) reduction of logging debris or slash following clearcutting, which typically leaves behind large volumes of mixed fuels: (2) preparation of a seedbed for tree species that require exposed mineral soil; (3) reduction of fuel accumulations in standing forests to lessen the probability of crown fire; (4) control of understory vegetation in certain forest types, such as hardwood saplings in southern pine stands; and (5) improvement of wildlife habitat (Figure 15.9) (see Chapter 16).

**Figure 15.7** Construction of a fire line (*a*) by hand tools in western conifer forest and (*b*) by a tractor and plow unit in southern pine forest. (Courtesy of U.S.D.A. Forest Service.)

Prescribed burning requires careful planning to minimize risk and to enhance the likelihood that objectives will be met. Topography and fuel conditions on the treatment area should be assessed in terms of probable effects on fire behavior and

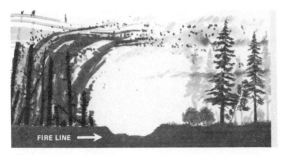

**Figure 15.8** Careful surveillance is necessary to control spot fires caused by burning embers hurled across the fire line. (Reproduced with permission of the Robert J. Brady Co. from its copyrighted work "Wildfires," 1974.)

desirable location of fuel breaks. It is frequently useful to obtain quantitative estimates of fuel weights and depths by standardized sampling techniques. Samples of woody material and duff can also be transported back to a lab to determine fuel moisture content as a percentage of oven-dry weight. This information can then be used to write the *fire prescription*, which outlines the desired effects of the burn—the approximate amount of duff and fuels to be removed, the proportion of the area to have exposed mineral soil, the proportion of understory stems to be killed, etc. The fire prescription will include estimates of the level of fire intensity and spread rate needed to accomplish these objectives and the range of weather conditions under which the burning would be feasible (23). The National Fire-Danger Rating System can provide help in identifying suitable days. Use of available fire-behavior models can provide guidance in anticipating probable effects. The final planning steps involve deciding the method of burning and sequence of ignitions, the placement of fire crews, and the equipment and supplies needed.

Prescribed fires are commonly set with a drip torch (Figure 15.10) within preestablished fire lines to minimize the risk of escape. Risk may be further reduced by burning the area in consecutive strips, each delimited by a fire line. Regulation of fire intensity is achieved not only by selecting days with desired weather conditions but also by the sequence of ignitions and the direction of spread. Fires allowed to burn in the direction of the wind are known as *head fires* and are characterized by relatively fast rates of spread and high temperatures. Fires can be induced to burn against the wind by igniting the fuels on the inside edge of a fire line. Spread in the direction of the wind is therefore prevented by the fire line, and the flames move slowly against the wind. Such *backfires* are somewhat easier to control and may be preferable to head fires on days of relatively high fire hazard.

Although some of the common objectives of prescribed burning can be accomplished by other means (for example, seedbed preparation by mechanical scarification), prescribed burning is often the most economical option available and the one least demanding of petrochemical energy. The main disadvantages of prescribed burning are the risks involved, the problem of air pollution from the smoke, and the fact that the number of days per year suitable for burning may be few in some regions.

## ENVIRONMENTAL IMPACTS OF FOREST FIRES

Early observers of the aftermath of severe forest fires frequently commented on the seemingly destructive effect on the productivity of the site. Land surveyors in 1826 reported that a conflagration in a spruce-northern hardwoods forest in New England had caused the soil to be "burnt off" in places, leaving behind a "bed of stones." Thoreau visited the site of a similar holocaust more than 40 years

**Figure 15.9** Before (*a*) and after (*b*) prescribed burning in a sequoia-mixed-conifer forest in California. In addition to reducing the amount of fuels present as litter and fallen logs, the fire killed most of the pole-sized white fir trees shown in these photos. (National Park Service photographs by Bruce M. Kilgore (*a*) and Don Taylor (*b*).)

**Figure 15.10** Prescribed burning with a drip torch for fuel reduction and seedbed preparation. (National Park Service photograph by Bruce M. Kilgore.)

after the fire, and found it to be still "exceedingly wild and desolate, with . . . low poplars springing up" (24). Although these early observations represent a "prescientific" assessment of the effects of fire, possible detrimental effects on environmental quality must be considered to understand how fire can best be managed to achieve the beneficial effects discussed earlier.

There seems to be little doubt that massive blowup fires can indeed have detrimental effects on soils. The burning of humus down to bedrock on poor sites, resulting in a conversion of stunted forest to bare rock and shrubs, has been observed in recent times (25, 26). Intense fires have also been known to cause erosion on good sites as well. But the effects

of fire on site productivity are so variable that generalizations are difficult to make. Some authors have noted that almost any effects of fire—positive, negative, or neutral—can be documented by the results of reputable researchers (27). Clearly the intensity of the fire, characteristics of the site, and weather conditions after the fire have much bearing on the outcome.

In most cases, erosion following fire can be traced to either or both of the following causes: (1) exposure of bare soil because of burning of the protective litter layer; (2) reduction of soil porosity (and hence increased runoff of water) because of either intense heating or clogging of soil pores by fine particles carried in runoff. Light or moderate fires such as most prescribed burns do not expose enough soil to cause serious erosion. Rarely do such fires burn down to mineral soil. Likewise soil temperatures during prescribed burning are rarely hot enough to cause structural changes in the soil.

Crown fires or fires burning in logging slash, on the other hand, may be intense enough to alter soil structure as well as leave bare patches of unprotected soil. Erosion will be more severe on steep slopes than on gently sloping or level sites. Following a severe wildfire in Idaho, about 30 percent of the sample plots on gently sloping sites showed significant erosion, compared to over 80 percent on steep slopes (28). A burned area is usually revegetated by shrubs and tree seedlings within a few years, so the critical period of susceptibility to erosion does not last long.

The influence of fire on soil fertility is also somewhat variable. Even though burning of organic matter theoretically releases nutrients in a form that is more available for plant uptake, in many cases the addition of ash to the soil does not seem to stimulate the growth of plants, or else the effect is very short-lived (29, 30). For example, twenty years of annual or periodic prescribed burns in South Carolina had little effect on the total amount or availability of nutrients (30). Severe fires can result in some losses of nutrients by leaching, but the total loss may actually be rather small (31).

Forest fires often have some effects on insect and disease conditions. The susceptibility of trees to insect and disease outbreaks is sometimes increased and sometimes decreased by fire. Injury from fire frequently predisposes trees to insect and disease infestations that otherwise might have been avoided. Coniferous trees weakened by fire, for example, may become more susceptible to bark beetle attack. On the other hand, the mosaic of vegetation types and age classes created by frequent fire may act as a deterrent to the spread of large-scale epidemics. Fire is also known to inhibit certain pathogens directly. In forests of the southern coastal plain, frequent surface fires kill spores that cause brown spot needle blight of longleaf pine.

Smoke from forest fires has come under scrutiny in recent years as a significant contribution to the overall air pollution problem. One ton of burning forest fuel releases approximately 1 ton of $CO_2$, 25 kilograms of carbon monoxide, 5 kilograms of hydrocarbons, 5 kilograms of particulates, and small amounts of nitrogen oxides. Forest fires are responsible for about 8 percent by weight of all atmospheric pollutants in the United States (32). Although open burning is restricted in many states and counties, exceptions are often granted for prescribed burning partly because it does not constitute a major source of pollutants. It is probable that prescribed burning will be more closely regulated in the future; even now air quality considerations are often used in selecting suitable days for burning.

## FIRE IN THE WILDERNESS

In 1968, without much fanfare and on an experimental basis, the National Park Service began to allow certain lightning fires to burn unhindered in parts of Sequoia and Kings Canyon national parks in California. This marked the beginning of an official policy to restore natural fire to certain wilderness areas.

This alteration of the long-established policy of suppressing all forest fires came about partly in response to the obvious changes that were occurring in the national parks as a result of overprotection from fire. For example, in the nineteenth century many forests in the Sierra Nevada were open and parklike with little undergrowth because of frequent surface fires. By 1963 the Leopold Committee, assigned by the Department of the Interior to make recommendations on elk habitat and management in the parks, noted that much of the west slope of the Sierra Nevada was a "dog-hair thicket" of young trees and brush. The committee wondered: "Is it possible that the primitive open forest could be restored, at least on a local scale? And if so, how? We cannot offer an answer. But we are posing a question to which there should be an answer of immense concern to the National Park Service."

Other pressing problems dictated a prompt response. The giant sequoia, with which the Park Service was entrusted with preservation, was not regenerating because of a lack of a suitable seedbed and because of competition with the dense understory of white fir. Moreover, understory fuels were accumulating to the point where conflagrations were likely. In 1965, prescribed burning was initiated in some sequoia groves to remedy this situation.

If the goal of park and wilderness management were merely to maintain certain desirable forest environments, it is likely that the policy of fire suppression would have merely been modified to allow for an active program of prescribed burning. But such action would seem to violate the spirit and intent of wilderness preservation. The congressional act of 1916 that created the National Park Service, to be sure, emphasized mainly protection of parklands in order to leave them "unimpaired" for future generations. But the Wilderness Act of 1964 was much more explicit in defining wilderness to be an area retaining its "primeval character and influence," where "man himself is a visitor who does not remain," and which is managed so as to preserve natural conditions.

Neither prescribed burning by itself nor total fire suppression seems appropriate under this concept of wilderness—the former because it is manipulative and somewhat arbitrary and the latter because it constitutes major indirect human modification of the vegetation in naturally fire-prone environments.

## The Approach

Full restoration of the natural fire regime in wilderness areas is usually not feasible, because some fires would inevitably threaten to burn beyond the park boundaries onto private land, or endanger human life inside or outside the park. The current intent of the natural fire-management policy is to allow fire to "more nearly play its natural role" whenever possible. In most areas, several management zones corresponding to different vegetation types and fuel conditions have been established. Each lightning fire is monitored, and a particular fire may be allowed to burn, or its spread may be blocked in one direction, or it may be totally suppressed. The decision will be based on the vegetation type, fuels, projected fire weather, and location of the fire in relation to human development or private property. Most fires caused by humans continue to be suppressed. Prescribed burning is sometimes used in zones where natural fire management is not feasible or where heavy, unnatural accumulations of fuels must be reduced artificially in preparation for natural fire management.

## Interim Results

Fire restoration programs have been established primarily in the high-elevation zones of some major western wilderness areas, such as Yellowstone, Yosemite, Sequoia, Kings Canyon, and Grand Teton national parks and the Selway-Bitterroot Wilderness Area in Idaho. Everglades National Park in Florida is an example of an eastern park firmly committed to natural fire management, having allowed or conducted over 200 fires between 1968 and 1974 (33). The more general policy of allowing fires to burn on nonwilderness public lands if the fires meet land-management objectives is also in effect in some national forests and national parks. Results to date have not revealed serious problems with the policy. In Sequoia and Kings Canyon national parks, for example, 80 lightning fires were allowed to burn between 1968 and 1973. Of this number, 80 percent were less than 0.1 hectare (¼ acre) in size, and only four exceeded 120 hectares (300 acres) (34). Crowning, except in isolated patches of trees, has not been common. But, as might be expected, some large fires have already occurred. A lightning fire in Grand Teton National Park in 1974 burned 1400 hectares (Figure 15.11), and a 600-hectare fire occurred in spruce-fir and lodgepole pine forests of Yellowstone National Park in 1976. Crowning in the second fire occurred on about half the area (35). In 1977 and 1979, several natural fires in California and Idaho each spread slowly over more than 2000

**Figure 15.11** A lightning fire allowed to burn in Grand Teton National Park, Wyoming, as part of a program to restore the natural occurrence of fires in wilderness areas. (Denver Post photograph by Bill Wuensch.)

hectares (5000 acres). Some potentially more severe fires were suppressed during this time.

Administrative tolerance of crown fires may seem surprising, but some intense fires are necessary for the regeneration of certain species. Surface fires may not be sufficient. Yet the incorporation of crown fires into management plans shows to what degree opinions have changed since the time it was thought that fires do no good whatever, are totally destructive, and should be stopped.

## REFERENCES

1. A. M. Swain, *Quat. Res., 10,* 55 (1978).
2. S. F. Arno, "The historical role of fire on the Bitterroot National Forest," U.S.D.A. For. Serv., Res. Pap. INT-187, 1976.
3. A. R. Taylor, *J. For., 68,* 476 (1971).
4. A. R. Taylor, "Lightning and Trees," *In: Lightning,* Vol. 2, *Lightning Protection,* E. A. Golde, ed., Academic Press, London, 1977.
5. R. W. Mutch, *Ecol., 51,* 1046 (1970).
6. M. L. Heinselman, *Quat. Res., 3,* 329 (1973).
7. R. W. Finley, "Original vegetation cover of Wisconsin (map)," U.S.D.A. For. Serv., North Central Forest Exper. Sta., St. Paul, 1976.
8. C. G. Lorimer, *Ecol., 58,* 139 (1977).
9. F. C. Gates and G. E. Nichols, *J. For., 28,* 395 (1930).
10. C. G. Lorimer, *Ecol, 61,* 1169 (1980).
11. S. Perley, *Historic Storms of New England,* Salem Press and Printing Co., 1891.
12. W. R. Moore, *Western Wildlands, 1* (3), 11 (1974).
13. R. W. Mutch, *Western Wildlands, 3* (1), 13 (1976).
14. W. Fons, *J. Agr. Res., 72,* 93 (1946).
15. R. W. Sando and D. A. Haines, "Fire weather and behavior of the Little Sioux Fire," U.S.D.A. For. Serv., Res. Pap. NC-76, 1972.
16. A. A. Brown and K. P. Davis, *Forest Fire: Control and Use,* Second Edition, McGraw-Hill, New York, 1973.

17. D. Noble, "An Updated National Fire-Danger Rating System," *In: Forestry Research: What's New in the West*, U.S.D.A. For. Serv., Fort Collins, Col., 1978.

18. W. H. Frandsen, *Combust. and Flame, 16*, 9 (1971).

19. R. C. Rothermel, "A mathematical model for predicting fire spread in wildland fuels," U.S.D.A. For. Serv., Res. Pap. INT-115, 1972.

20. F. A. Albini, "Estimating wildfire behavior and effects." U.S.D.A. For. Serv., Gen. Tech. Rept. INT-30, 1976.

21. J. E. Deeming, R. E. Burgen, and J. D. Cohen, "The National Fire-Danger Rating System—1978," U.S.D.A. For. Serv., Gen. Tech. Rept. INT-39, Intermountain Forest and Range Exper. Sta., Ogden, Utah, 1977.

22. H. E. Anderson, "Sundance Fire: An analysis of fire phenomena," U.S.D.A. For. Serv., Res. Pap. INT-56, 1968.

23. W. C. Fischer, "Planning and evaluating prescribed fires—a standard procedure," U.S.D.A. For. Serv., Gen. Tech. Rept. INT-43, 1978.

24. H. D. Thoreau, *The Maine Woods*, Ticknor and Fields, Boston, 1864.

25. F. H. Bormann and G. E. Likens, *Pattern and Process in a Forested Ecosystem*, Springer-Verlag, New York, 1979.

26. S. H. Spurr and B. V. Barnes, *Forest Ecology*, Second Edition, Ronald Press, New York, 1973.

27. C. W. Ralston and G. E. Hatchell, "Effects of prescribed burning on physical properties of soil," *In: Prescribed Burning Symp. Proc.*, U.S.D.A. For. Serv., Southeastern Forest Exper. Sta., Asheville, N.C., 1971.

28. C. A. Connaughton, *J. For., 33*, 751 (1935).

29. I. F. Ahlgren and C. E. Ahlgren, *Bot. Rev., 26*, 483 (1960).

30. C. G. Wells, "Effects of prescribed burning on soil chemical properties and nutrient availability," *In: Prescribed Burning Symp. Proc.*, U.S.D.A. For. Serv., Southeastern Forest Exper. Sta., Asheville, 1971.

31. N. V. DeByle and P. E. Packer, "Plant nutrient and soil losses in overland flow from burned forest clearcuts," *In: Watersheds in Transition, Proc. Amer. Water Resources Assoc.*, 1972.

32. J. H. Dieterich, "Prescribed burning and air quality," *In: Southern Pine Management—Today and Tomorrow*, 20th Ann. For. Symp., La. State Univ., Div. Contin. Educ., Baton Rouge, 1971.

33. B. M. Kilgore, "Fire management in the national parks: an overview," *Proc. Tall Timbers Fire Ecology Conf. and Fire and Land Management Sympos., 14*, 45−57, 1974.

34. R. W. Mutch and G. S. Briggs, "The maintenance of natural ecosystems: smoke as a factor," *In: Air Quality and Smoke From Urban and Forest Fires, Proc. Int. Symp. Nat. Acad. Sci.*, Washington, D.C., 1976.

35. D. G. Despain and R. E. Sellers, *Western Wildlands, 4*, 20 (1977).

36. F. A. Albini, "Spot fire distance from burning trees—a predictive model," U.S.D.A. For. Serv., Gen. Tech. Rept. INT-56, 1979.

# 16

# FOREST-WILDLIFE INTERACTIONS
## Gordon W. Gullion

Forests provide the basic habitat for a large proportion of the world's wildlife, including amphibians, reptiles, birds, and mammals. Trees singly or in forests provide food and protection from the weather and from other animals. Forests also have a stabilizing effect on streamflow that provides habitats for fish. Taken together these elements constitute *wildlife habitat,* which may be a specific forest type such as a beech-maple forest, or a mixed forest such as a spruce-fir stand intermixed with pine and aspen-birch. Within each habitat each species of wildlife uses a particular portion, or its niche. The *ecological niche* of an organism depends not only on where it lives but also on what it does.

Some forms of wildlife need the stems and leaves of woody plants growing in full sunlight within a meter or two of the forest floor. Young trees are especially important as food for deer, wapiti (or elk), and moose. These *primary consumers* or *herbivores* feed on the succulent stems and leaves of the growing shoots in summer and on the dormant stems in winter. Predators are *secondary consumers* or *carnivores* that consume little plant material but use trees as cover for their hunting, and for nests or dens while feeding on the herbivores or other carnivores.

## INTRODUCTION

The relationship between forest and wildlife is so intertwined and complex that little can be done to a forest that does not have impact on some form of wildlife. One obvious impact is the effect of clearcutting or burning a forest. The habitat of some animals can be harmed—cover is removed, nesting or denning sites are damaged, and seed- or fruit-producing trees are destroyed. Clearcutting also creates habitats for other species, as will be discussed later.

There is also an impact on wildlife populations when a forest is allowed to proceed toward climax through normal succession (see Chapter 6). The larger herbivorous species dependent on low-growing plant forms diminish and are replaced by a

greater diversity of smaller animals feeding mostly on other animals.

Thus the concept of what is "good" and "bad" forest management for wildlife depends on the situation. A practice bad for one group of species may be good for others. The forest-management scheme favorable for ruffed grouse, woodcock, and white-tailed deer in the Great Lakes states, for example, would be detrimental to wood ducks, bald eagles, and Kirtland warblers.

## Wildlife Values

Animals are an integral part of the forest scene, but a monetary value cannot be assigned to a bald eagle or a flying squirrel, for example. Yet several hundred forms of American wildlife are so valued that millions of hectares of timberland are reserved from commercial harvesting in the United States, partly to preserve wildlife habitats.

A national survey of participants in wildlife-associated recreation showed that nearly 19.8 million Americans hunted big and small game in 1975 (1). Their expenditures for equipment, lodging, food, and transportation in pursuit of forest-associated game exceeded $3 billion. This does not include the cost of licenses, tags and special permits. A 1971 study in the southeastern United States showed that 11 million out of 16 million households received enjoyment from 472 million days of fishing, hunting, bird-watching, and other wildlife-related activities (2). A similar analysis on the Bridger-Teton National Forest in Wyoming indicated that 188,700 recreation days of hunting had a value of $9.3 million during the fall 1977 season. This compares with an estimated timber harvest value from Wyoming of about $14 million statewide in 1975 (3).

In addition to the value generated by hunting game animals, the nonconsumptive use of wildlife has become increasingly important. The 1975 national survey showed that over 95 million Americans participated in wildlife-associated recreation

(1). An estimated $500 million were spent in 1974 by persons interested in nongame wildlife, and it is believed that more than $185 million were spent for backyard bird feeding and bird nest boxes (4).

While it is difficult to place a dollar value on finding an osprey nest, hearing a pileated woodpecker call, or attempting to bag an elusive white-tailed deer, these intangible values have a very real influence on how forest managers treat the woodlands.

## Characteristics of Wildlife

The primary drive for each animal is to survive long enough to *perpetuate its kind*. The animal must consume water and sufficient nutritious food to sustain it in a thrifty condition until that goal is accomplished. Every animal requires some form of protection, either from the physical environment or from other animals, and usually from both. Few animals smaller than adult black bears, bald eagles, wolves, and mountain lions terminate their existence with a quiet, painless death. Most animals die violent deaths to provide nourishment for another animal.

One important difference between plants and animals is the latters' mobility, which allows an animal to move about seeking food, a mate, and shelter. This mobility brings a need for a higher food intake along with problems of competition and predation. A concept underlying the discussion throughout this chapter is that the less an individual animal has to move to meet its basic needs, the longer it is likely to survive, and the greater the opportunity to pass its genetic constitution on to a succeeding generation. The value of a forest habitat depends on a juxtaposition of the lifelong needs of a particular animal in such a manner that they can be utilized safely and efficiently.

**Population Dynamics.** Wildlife has annual *cycles of abundance* much like those of annual plants. Numbers are greatest following the hatching of eggs or the birth of young, usually in late spring or early summer. Then numbers decline, the rates varying from year to year and from species to species.

If a population is to remain static, there must be as many alive to produce young the next season as were alive the previous year. This means that from the parents and fourteen eggs in a wood duck nest, only two need be alive the following spring, a 12 percent survival. Among ruffed grouse two out of ten must survive, a 20 percent survival; but for bluebirds two of seven need to survive, a 28 percent survival.

In addition to the annual population cycle there are longer-term cycles among wildlife populations. In North America the best known of these is the *10-year cycle*, which is most evident among snowshoe hares and ruffed grouse (5). These cycles are most dramatic in regions where environmental stresses are most severe, such as cold northern or arid western regions. Lynx and other predators feeding largely on the hares or grouse also fluctuate in numbers, usually lagging a year or two behind the population changes in the prey species.

The regularity of these cycles is shown by the history of ruffed grouse in Minnesota. During the past half century, numbers of these birds peaked in 1923, 1933, 1941–1942, 1951, 1960–1961, and 1971–1972. Populations are usually lowest about 4 to 5 years after the peaks (Figure 16.1).

Although much attention has been given to these periodic fluctuations for many years, the basic causes are still being questioned. Earlier these fluctuations were believed to be the result of overhunting or disease epidemics, but as wildlife research expanded, it became evident that hunting was least likely to be a factor.

*Cyclic fluctuations* of animal populations have been associated with a number of different factors and include sunspot activity and lunar cycles, periodic variations in the nutrient quality of the primary forage plants, and genetic constitution of the animals. A number of other possibilities exist and include predator-prey interaction, fire and forest succession, and climate and weather factors (6).

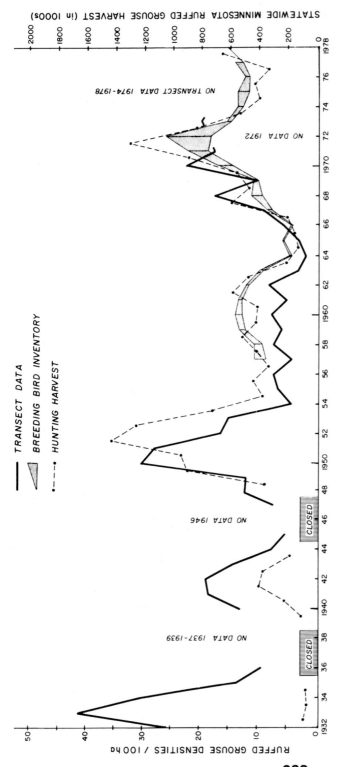

**Figure 16.1** Ruffed grouse breeding population levels at the Cloquet Forestry Center, Minnesota. Populations were determined by walking a series of transects from 1932 to 1973, and by a census of breeding males from 1957 to 1978. The populations for the 1360 hectare Cloquet Forest are compared with the estimated Minnesota statewide grouse harvest for the years when the hunting season was open. The shaded portion shows total populations for the years from 1957 to 1977: it includes males present but not occupying breeding territories in those seasons.

382

Although the causes for these long-term cycles may be beyond our control, it is important to be aware of these periodic fluctuations. The best-planned habitat-management scheme may appear to fail if timing coincides with a region-wide, cyclic decline of the target species.

## Interactions Among Forest Wildlife

Just as trees compete with one another for space, food, water, and sunlight, wildlife living in the forest interact with one another. These interactions occur at two levels, *intraspecifically* and *interspecifically,* and may be expressed as either *competitive* or *consumptive interaction.* At both levels the character of the forest habitat has an influence on how wildlife succeeds.

Most wildlife requires certain amounts of space or *territory* to meet its needs. Animals usually have to maintain an aggressive stance to defend territories, and this is the purpose of most bird songs in the spring. Many mammals, and some reptiles and amphibians, leave scent posts or other signs to mark territorial boundaries.

The territory may be that of a single individual, a pair, or even a flock or pack, depending on the species. This behavior can serve to isolate a pair to allow undisturbed reproductive activity or to reserve sufficient food and cover resources to allow an animal or a pair to survive the winter. Thus, territorial behavior limits animal abundance and density. Mountain lions in Idaho may need from 200 to 400 square kilometers for their territory (7), whereas a red squirrel in Alaska may need only 0.65 hectares (8). Territorial behavior usually represents intraspecific interaction, but interspecific competition also occurs. As timber wolves have expanded their range in northern Minnesota, coyotes have disappeared from those areas.

Consumptive interaction is predation and most often is interspecific. But most predators occasionally kill and eat their own kind. Cannibalism among siblings appears to be of frequent occurrence in the nests of hawks and owls.

The effect of predation on wildlife populations has long been controversial. For many years it was felt that all predators (anything that killed other animals) were "bad." Then various studies, especially those of Errington (9), began to suggest that predation was less important than some other factors in limiting wildlife abundance. These studies reinforced the concept of *carrying capacity* expressed by Leopold in 1933 (10).

Basically, carrying capacity is the number of individuals of a species that can survive in a given unit of habitat secure from predation. It is a measure of the adequacy of food and other resources in relation to secure cover. Once a prey species has been reduced to carrying capacity, it is no longer profitable for predators to continue hunting those animals. But carrying capacity is not a fixed entity; it varies from site to site, and on the same site it may vary from year to year depending on food production, cover quality, and even snow conditions and depth.

Predators enforce carrying capacity, and in the absence of predators some wildlife becomes more abundant in habitats that otherwise would be marginal. When big-game animals are living in the absence of their normal predators, carrying capacity commonly refers to the quantity of adequate forage resources needed to maintain the animals in a thrifty, productive condition. Among small-game species territorial behavior supplants carrying capacity as a factor limiting population size in the absence of effective predation. Under these conditions the food and cover resources may have the capacity to support a considerably higher population of a species than intraspecific aggression will permit. In the Cloquet Research Forest in northern Minnesota, ruffed grouse reach greater abundance in an aspen-pine forest when goshawks are not nesting in that forest.

Predation is largely *opportunistic*. It most often occurs when prey is in a situation where the predator has an advantage. There is much more rapid loss to predation (and hunters) among young animals than among adults. Minnesota ruffed grouse studies have shown that the percentage loss among young grouse over a 7-month period from mid-September to mid-April is as great as the loss among adult grouse over a 12-month period, and numerically is about 3.4-fold greater on a monthly basis (11).

## WILDLIFE USE OF FORESTS

### Dependency on Forests

Wildlife use of a forest may be *obligatory*, meaning that the animal cannot exist in its wild form without trees; or use may be *discretionary*, implying the animal may use trees if they are available, but can survive without them. The obligate forest users are further segregated into *stenotopic* forms limited to a very specific habitat niche and the *eurytopic* species able to successfully use a broader range of forest situations.

**Obligatory Use.** Among North American terrest-

rial wildlife about one-half of the birds and several mammals have an obligatory relationship to trees or forest cover. Among some 567 species of birds on the continent at least 272 can be considered to have an obligatory relationship with trees. Similarly, among the 348 species of mammals in North America north of Mexico, about 49 have an obligatory relationship to trees (Table 16.1).

Trees provide all the needs of many birds and some mammals. Most woodpeckers nest in holes excavated in trees, and usually their food consists of insects collected on or in trees. Chickadees and nuthatches also nest in tree cavities, and their food consists largely of eggs, larvae, pupae, and adult insects taken from the bark, branches, and foliage of trees. Similarly, gray, flying, red, and pine squirrels depend on trees for their dens as well as for most of their food. But the common flicker does much of its feeding on the ground, while depending on trees for nesting. Two species of swallows, purple martins, and swifts use cavities in trees for nesting, but all of their feeding is on insects in flight.

**Table 16.1**
Numbers of Species of North American Warm-Blooded Vertebrates Dependent on Trees[a]

| Normal Habitat | Total | Birds Tree Obligates | | Total | Mammals Tree Obligates | |
|---|---|---|---|---|---|---|
| | | Food | Nest | | Food | Nest |
| Aquatic | 82 | 0 | 13 | 4 | 1 | 0 |
| Shoreline | 65 | 0 | 11 | 5 | 0 | 0 |
| Marshes | 19 | 0 | 0 | 37 | 0 | 0 |
| Grasslands and tundra | 83 | 0 | 27 | 184 | 0 | 0 |
| Brush | 91 | 0 | 14 | 42 | 0 | 0 |
| Trees | | | | | | |
| Single or groups[b] | 0 | 0 | 41 | 6 | 6 | 0 |
| Forests | 178 | 159 | 160 | 34 | 27 | 23 |
| Aerial foragers | 49 | 0 | 29 | 39 | 1 | 6 |

*Source.* Original compilation.
[a] This table differs from Yeager (12) primarily in the separation of brush inhabiting species from tree-associated species.
[b] These are primarily animals depending on grasslands or brush for their food resources and using trees for nesting.

**Discretionary Use.** Several animals utilize trees when use is convenient but they can survive quite well in the absence of a forest. Ravens will nest in heavy forest cover or on cliffs and rock outcrops, and both black ducks and mallards occasionally use trees for nesting but normally nest on the ground.

Some other species use isolated trees or small groves, but avoid a forest consisting of more than a few dozen or hundreds of trees. Examples are mourning doves, magpies, and sharp-tailed grouse.

## Nutritional Needs Supplied to Wildlife by the Forest

**Plant Materials Consumed by Wildlife.** Probably few trees are not used as food by some form of wildlife at one time or another. Among 224 herbivores (birds and mammals) studied in the most comprehensive wildlife study of food habits made in North America, resources provided by trees constituted an important part of the diet of 89 species, or 40 percent of the total (13).

In this study oak acorns were the most used and provided a part of the diet for at least 96 species of wildlife. Other trees used as food by more than 25 species of animals include pines, cherries, hackberries, junipers, mulberries, maples, blackgum, beech, and aspen. The fruit or seeds of these trees are the parts usually used as food by wildlife (except for aspen). Collectively these are called *mast,* and for many species of wildlife the annual mast crop is a major factor determining their abundance from year to year.

A reduction in the mast crop can result in a scarcity of the less mobile squirrels, and in some forest situations deer may suffer. Several species of birds are nomadic in their behavior, and their wanderings and even breeding activities depend on the regional vagaries of mast production.

Where snow is an important part of the winter environment, resident wildlife depends on other parts of plants for sustenance. The herbivorous mammals such as hares, deer, and moose depend on shrubby plants or young growth of trees for their food resource, and take the stems and twigs of these throughout the winter. Beavers and porcupines feed mostly on the bark and cambium layer of various trees.

Because the seeds of most northern deciduous trees are shed when mature and are buried under the snow, only birds such as siskins and crossbills, which extract seeds from cones, can survive as seed consumers. The remaining birds permanently resident in these regions are typically the insectivorous chickadees, nuthatches, and woodpeckers, the scavenging jays and ravens, the predatory hawks and owls, and the needle- and bud-eating grouse.

**Food Provided by Forest Litter and Debris.** Dead portions of the forest provide important or even critical resources for many species of wildlife. Decaying litter on the forest floor provides the organic material to nourish many invertebrate animals, ranging from microscopic nematodes to quite large insects. Also, many saprophitic plants ranging from bacteria to the various fungi, and even a group of higher ericaceous plants, utilize these nutrient resources. These are also primary consumers, at the base of a *food chain* that supports a pyramid of secondary consumers.

Although ruffed grouse are normally herbivores their newly hatched chicks are wholly dependent on the invertebrate fauna on the forest floor for their first five or six weeks of life (14); lacking this resource the chicks will perish.

But all types of forest litter are not equally valuable as a nutrient base for the primary consumers and their predators. An important portion of the summer diet of young and adult woodcock consists of a few species of earthworms that live in the forest litter atop the mineral soil. The concentration of these earthworms in the rich litter under aspen is associated with a marked summer preference for aspen stands by woodcock. Most amphibians (salamanders, frogs, and toads) as well as several species of snakes and lizards also depend on the invertebrate animals living among decaying forest debris.

## Cover Provided by the Forest

**Protection from Environmental Factors.** The protection trees provide from weather, including shade on a hot summer day or protection from a heavy rainstorm, is important. Forest cover also provides less obvious but more important benefits.

A large part of North America's forestland lies in cold regions where snow usually covers the ground for three to six months each winter, so it is appropriate to examine how animals dependent on the forest survive this season. Forest wildlife has several strategies for surviving winter. Many birds and bats simply migrate to warmer climates, some going as far as South America. In mountain areas this migration may be no more than moving downslope a few kilometers to snowfree lower elevations.

The cold-blooded amphibians and reptiles, and many mice, chipmunks, ground squirrels, raccoons, and bears hibernate for the winter. These animals accumulate fat in the fall, enter a burrow, cave, or den, and reduce body functions (including heartbeat, respiration, and temperature) to such a level that stored fat will meet their energy needs all winter. White-tailed deer enter a state of semihibernation, with a marked reduction in the pace of body function.

Animals that are active all winter rely on other means of coping. Tree squirrels store supplies of cones, acorns, or nuts; beavers store a winter's food supply in the mud on the bottom of their pond; ruffed grouse cope with winter cold by spending as much time as possible in a snow burrow made by plunging headlong into the snow from full flight (Figure 16.2). Voles, pocket gophers, and other rodents remain active all winter, making a labyrinth of tunnels on the surface of the ground under the snow and feeding on dried vegetation, seeds, and the bark of shrubs and small trees.

The forest environment must meet two energy-related needs to maintain wildlife in winter. It must provide *adequate energy resources* for species that remain active, and it must provide protection against *excessive energy dissipation*. An adequate energy resource means sufficient mast, woody stems, twigs, or flower buds to meet the needs of the animals living there. This may be some 18 kilograms of acorns from sixteen 36 centimeter dbh white oaks to feed one gray squirrel in the southeast, or about 1100 kilograms of balsam fir and hardwood twigs per square kilometer to meet the winter-long needs of moose in Quebec, or about 9 kilograms of aspen flower buds per hectare to maintain a ruffed grouse population at a breeding density of 50 birds per 100 hectares in Minnesota.

Although conifer cover tends to be detrimental to ruffed grouse, it is essential for larger animals such as deer and moose. The overhead cover serves as a barrier to the loss of body heat to the night sky.

**Protection from Predation.** From the standpoint of wildlife cover, forest growth can be roughly divided into two categories. One is *vertical cover*, the other *horizontal cover*. This identifies the physical characteristics of the vegetation; the species of plants or trees are unimportant, except to the extent that they most readily develop as one or the other of these categories of cover.

Ideal vertical cover consists of small-diameter stems of sapling trees or shrubs evenly spaced and growing straight from the ground to form a closed canopy 3 to 10 meters overhead (Figure 16.3). It must be open enough to allow the desired wildlife to move about easily but not provide concealment for mammalian predators, and too dense for raptors (hawks and owls) to fly through. Vertical cover provides protection for ground-dwelling forest wildlife such as woodcock, ruffed grouse, and snowshoe hares.

Horizontal cover favors the predators by providing them a concealed site from which they can ambush prey moving into a vulnerable position (Figure 16.4). The branches of evergreens, especially the conifers, provide this sort of cover. Fallen

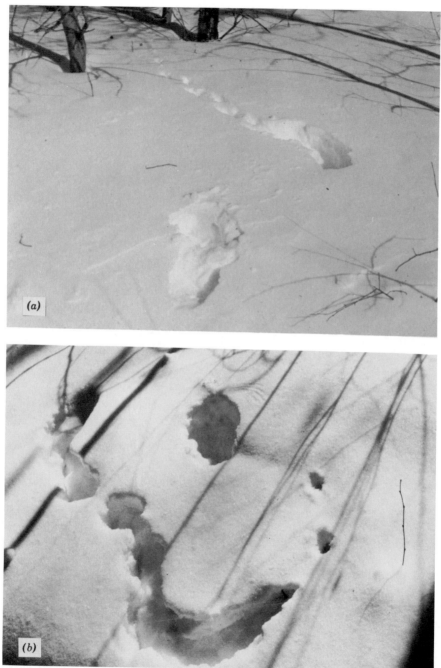

**Figure 16.2** Snow-burrow roosting by ruffed grouse. (*a*) The bird plunged into the snow in the foreground and moved about 1 meter in the snow to its overnight roosting position. This bird walked out of its burrow the following day—an unusual departure, they usually fly out. (*b*) The bird dived into the snow at the upper left, and as it moved through the snow having a depth of only 20 centimeters for a distance of about 2 meters the burrow collapsed behind it. Wing marks on the snow show that this bird flew from its overnight roost.

**Figure 16.3** Good vertical wildlife cover in a 10-year-old aspen stand resulting from clearcut logging. In 1970 to 1978 this quality of cover supported populations of ruffed grouse exceeding 48 breeding grouse per 100 hectares.

logs, brush piles, and logging debris on the ground are hazardous horizontal cover for some species, but a necessary habitat niche for other wildlife.

### Nesting Sites

Among the 567 species of birds in North America, at least 254 species use trees for nesting. A recent Forest Service publication lists 85 species of birds from 17 families that use tree cavities (15), including wood ducks, buffleheads, American and Barrow's goldeneyes, and hooded mergansers. Orioles weave pendulant nests on the tips of limber branches, and many birds build nests in the forks of limbs. The tree creeper usually nests behind a piece of loose bark; wrens sometimes use a similar site, although they prefer cavities.

The larger hawks, eagles, owls, ravens, and herons require large trees to support their heavy nests. For example, bald eagles living around the lakes in the level country of northern Minnesota must have tall, sturdy trees with strong branches so arranged that the adult eagles, having wingspans exceeding 1 meter, can enter and leave the nests without damaging their wing feathers. This means that the nesting tree must have some special attributes, most often provided by large, mature red and white pines in this region (Figure 16.5).

### USE OF FOREST ECOSYSTEMS BY WILDLIFE

Forests are dynamic ecosystems, seldom remaining static. There has probably been more stability in North American forests in the current century than at any other time in their recent history. With this stability we have become accustomed to extensive areas of what should properly be considered "un-

**Figure 16.4**   Mature conifers standing over a hardwoods forest provide optimum hunting cover for the hawks and owls, which are major predators on grouse, hares, and other small animals in Great Lake states forests.

natural'' forest. Much of the information about forest-wildlife interactions obtained during the past half century has dealt with wildlife populations living in these ''unnatural'' forest environments.

In the primeval forest, periodic catastrophic ecological change was quite frequent. For example, the wilderness forests of the Great Lakes states and New England were affected by fire about every 36 years, as discussed in Chapter 15. Forest wildlife has evolved over thousands of centuries to survive in this system of changing forest habitats. Regardless of the stage of forest development, some forms of wildlife have adapted by utilizing the resources provided.

## Wildlife in Changing Forests

**Hardwoods Succession.**   A hardwoods forest developing through primary succession usually is invading an area dominated by grass, forbs, and shrubs, as described in Chapter 6. Early in the succession there is a considerable mixture of habitat niches, such as grassy openings, dense berry-bush thickets, and low trees. This provides a wide assortment of seeds and browse, and the animals using this stage are largely primary consumers feeding on plant materials. The *granivorous* (seed-eating) sparrows and various small mammals such as deer mice, chipmunks, and ground squirrels are a part of this seral stage. This is also a productive habitat for deer, rabbits, and hares, since the shrubs and young trees provide leafy browse in summer and small-diameter twigs in winter within reach of these browsers. Bears also benefit from the abundance of berries produced in this situation.

The young forest stage is the least diverse in wildlife species of any stage of forest development, but the numbers of individuals of the species present

**389**

**Figure 16.5** Bald eagle nest in a large red pine in the Chippewa National Forest, Minnesota. A large tree is required to support the massive nests of these raptors. (Photograph courtesy of J. Mathisen.)

usually is quite high, and their biomass is large. This is the stage of forest succession supporting the species having the cyclic population levels discussed earlier.

Primary forest succession can require several decades between the initial establishment of tree seedlings and the development of a closed-canopy forest, providing habitat for stenotopic wildlife for a comparatively long time. By contrast, the development of secondary succession proceeds quite rapidly, and the niches satisfactory for these species may persist only a few years.

If the original forest preceding secondary succession was a northern hardwoods forest with aspen prominent in the canopy, successional development will proceed as illustrated in Figure 16.6. For the first several years the site will be dominated by a high density of rapidly growing aspen root sprouts, together with stump sprouts from the birches, maples, oaks, and other hardwoods. The aspen stand then goes through a natural thinning at about 10 years, and the site becomes more open under a tight canopy 8 to 10 meters overhead, Now the stand becomes an acceptable covert for adult, breeding, and wintering ruffed grouse, a summer habitat for red-eyed vireos, catbirds, and several species of thrushes, and a nesting and brood habitat for woodcock; it is less useful for hares, deer, and moose, however, because the foliage grows out of reach. Beavers prefer a stand of this character, and a beaver colony will consume about 0.2 to 0.4 hectares of aspen of this age in a year.

After about a quarter century the aspen thins to the density of a mature stand. The trees are 12 to 19 meters tall and there may be fewer than 4000 stems per hectare, but the other tolerant hardwoods continue to grow and begin to overtop the aspen. Canopy closure limits sunlight penetration to the forest floor, so the intolerant berry and browse plants die. Low shrub cover deteriorates, exposing wildlife on the forest floor to increased predation risk. This forest has lost its value as cover for ruffed grouse and as forage for deer, moose, and other browsers.

The aspen is now becoming important as food for ruffed grouse, and the litter continues to provide food for woodcock. Ovenbirds become common on the forest floor and sapsuckers, and downy and hairy woodpeckers use this type of forest. Several species of warblers and vireos live in the canopy, and least flycatchers, goshawks, broad-winged hawks, and barred owls can hunt efficiently under this parklike forest canopy. The composition of the wildlife population has changed from a concentration of biomass in a few species of larger primary foragers to a spread of the biomass among many smaller species, which are secondary foragers that prey on other animals.

Depending on the site, the aspens begin de-

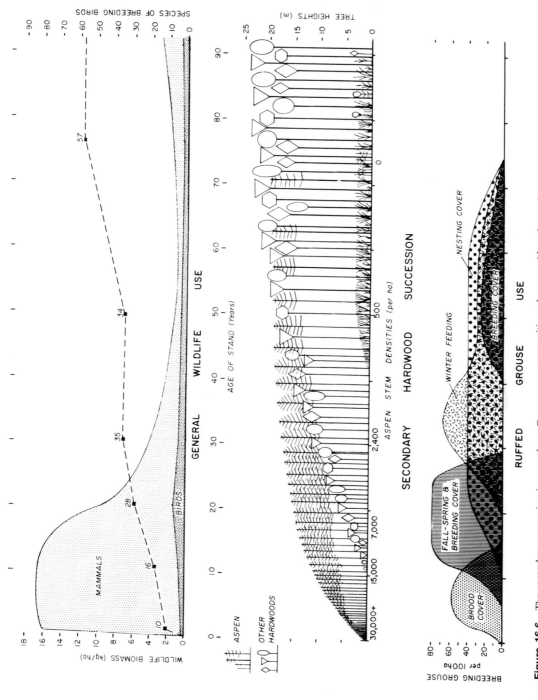

**Figure 16.6** The secondary succession in a northern Great Lakes region hardwoods forest, showing the sequence of dominant vegetation and how ruffed grouse respond as the forest composition changes. Also shown is the change in animal biomass (per hectare) and bird species diversity associated with this succession.

teriorating at 40 to 60 years of age. Heartrot and other types of decay become frequent in the decadent aspen and provide opportunities for the excavation of nesting cavities. The larger woodpeckers such as the pileated and flickers take advantage of this opportunity to develop nesting cavities. Thus nesting sites are provided for chickadees, nuthatches, bluebirds, swallows, various owls, flying squirrels, and other small mammals.

As this northern hardwoods succession proceeds toward climax, changes in the wildlife composition continue. Big-game mammals occur only rarely, and as the last aspens disappear ruffed grouse live at low densities on the edges or around scattered holes in the forest canopy. Woodcock make little use of this older forest. But gray squirrels increase in numbers, and if winter snow is not too deep turkeys should reach a maximum abundance, for many of the longer-lived hardwoods are important mast producers. With the more open understory thrushes become less common, but an abundance of insectivorous warblers and vireos feed among the leaves of the forest canopy and trunk foragers include black-and-white warblers and white-breasted nuthatches. The size and strength of the trees in the mature forest provide solid support for the heavy nests of larger birds such as the hawks and owls, eagles, ravens, and herons.

As decadence increases and tree mortality begins to open the forest canopy, some of the aerial foragers such as swallows, swifts, martins, and kingbirds find the proper combination of nesting sites, perches, and space in which to forage. With more sunlight reaching the forest floor, intolerant berry and browse shrubs reappear. The wildlife biomass gradually shifts from many small individuals of many species of secondary consumers back to fewer forms of the larger primary consumers associated with a young forest.

## Wildlife Associated with Conifer Succession. Succession in a coniferous forest goes

through the same stages as in a hardwoods forest, with a similar change in the forest. Blue grouse on Vancouver Island require various ages of coniferous forest in much the same manner as ruffed grouse require different ages in an aspen-hardwood forest. In a logged and burned Douglas-fir forest blue grouse begin using the area for breeding soon after the forest is destroyed (16). This use continues for about 8 years, until the canopy begins to close in and the forest loses its value as breeding habitat. Each fall during this period these grouse move up in the mountains to spend the winter feeding on the needles of mature firs. Blue grouse require an early seral stage for breeding and a mature forest to provide a winter food resource.

The Kirtland warbler is a stenotopic species dependent on a specific stage of succession in a jack pine forest. They are found only in 30-hectare or larger homogeneous blocks of dense pines 2 to 5 meters tall, having a patchy arrangement with nearly as much area in small openings. This niche exists while the pine stand is from 5 to 20 years old and fades when the lower branches begin to die at 15 to 20 years of age (17).

In a study of the avifauna associated with the successional development of a Douglas-fir forest, Meslow (18) found that only 38 of the 84 species in western Oregon's coniferous forests use the earliest (grass-forbs) seral stage, with 6 nesting (Figure 16.7). But as the succession proceeds into the shrub-sapling stage at 8 to 15 years, bird use increases markedly, with 73 (87 percent) of the species present. At least 40 are nesting in this seral stage. In the next stage at 16 to 40 years old the number of species declines to 61, but several efficient predators become part of the nesting component. As the firs grow larger the avifaunal composition changes little, but in the older forest at least 30 bird species find suitable nesting sites lacking in forests less than 40 years old. A similar pattern of animal use was found in a different conifer succession in the Blue Mountains of Oregon and Washington (Figure 16.7) (19).

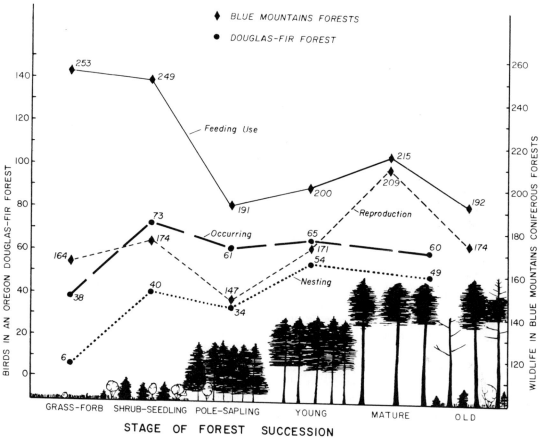

**Figure 16.7** Wildlife use of western coniferous forests in two regions. Songbird use of an Oregon Douglas-fir forest shows the increasing species diversity as succession proceeds toward climax (after Meslow (16)), while the wildlife use in the Blue Mountains shows use by all species of wildlife in an intermountain pine forest. (Reproduced with permission from Thomas et al. (17).)

## Wildlife Associated with Interspersed Age Classes or Composition

Forest successions do not always proceed as simply as has just been described. Coniferous forests in the Pacific Northwest remain coniferous as they move toward climax, but in the Southeast coniferous forests represent a *subclimax stage* and are eventually replaced by hardwoods. Aspen forests at higher elevation in the central and southern Rocky Mountains succeed to spruce-fir forests, and aspen-birch stands in boreal forests have the same fate. In eastern deciduous forests succession proceeds from a forest of intolerant hardwoods to one of longer-lived, tolerant hardwoods.

Forests succeeding from hardwoods to conifers or vice versa have more wildlife than either the hardwoods or the coniferous forests alone (20). This mixture in the ecotone between the northern hardwoods and the boreal coniferous forest in the Great Lakes–St. Lawrence region produces an avifaunal diversity ranging from 129 to 142 species.

Some forms of wildlife require an interspersion of tree age classes or species composition. Primary consumers or *herbivores* are most dependent on interspersion of forest resources because they use forest vegetation in several ways. Conditions favorable for the production of food resources usually differ from those providing secure cover. Additionally the forest-dwelling herbivores tend to be non-migratory and therefore require year-round food and cover from the habitats they occupy. Some herbivores, such as hares, grouse, and deer in the Great Lakes region forests, require this diversity within comparatively small areas. But deer and wapiti in western mountainous regions find needed forest diversity by being migratory, often moving many kilometers from summer to winter ranges.

Moose require an interspersion of forest types, with the addition of streams, ponds, or lakes to provide the aquatic vegetation for their summer diet. In Minnesota the proper mixture on an area of 9300 hectares is given as 40 to 50 percent open land less than 20 years old, 5 to 15 percent in spruce-fir, and 35 to 55 percent aspen-birch stands over 20 years old, and ponds, lakes or streams (21).

The larger the herbivore and the more severe the climate, the greater the diversity needed in the habitat resources provided by the forest. The same general rule applies for predators as well, except that the secondary consumers have larger foraging ranges, and many are migratory. Goshawks, for example, prefer to nest and hunt in relatively mature forests having an open understory (Figure 16.8). But the bulk of their prey consists of the medium-sized herbivores (squirrels, hares, and grouse), which require a mixed-forest composition for their livelihood.

## Wildlife Associated with Forest Edges

At various times this discussion of forest-wildlife interactions has referred to "properly interspersed" habitat conditions, which means two different types of forest or two seral stages of the same forest type abutting each other in a manner that best meets the needs of wildlife. The place where these differing types come together is known as an *edge*, and edges have had a special significance in wildlife management for the past half century.

Aldo Leopold, widely considered the founder of modern game management in the United States, first emphasized this relationship in 1933 when he wrote (10):

*Game is a phenomenon of edges. It occurs where the types of food and cover which it needs come together, i.e., where their edges meet. . . . We do not understand the reason for all of these edge effects, but in those cases where we can guess the reason, it usually harks back either to the desirability of simultaneous access to more than one environmental type, or the greater richness of border vegetation, or both.*

Much emphasis has been directed toward understanding the *edge effect* since 1933, and it is quite well understood today. Most forest wildlife-management plans emphasize maintaining edge, but it may be stated as "habitat diversity," "interspersion," or "a mosaic of types."

Edges are placed in two categories (22): (1) *inherent edges*, created by differences in physical features, such as an upland forest against a sphagnum bog, or a pine stand dominating a dry, south-facing slope, abutting a mixed Douglas-fir–spruce stand on a more moist, north-facing slope; (2) *induced edges*, the relatively temporary break between two seral stages of one forest type or between two forest types, resulting from fire, windstorm, avalanche, or timber harvesting. These edges could persist for several centuries, but there is no physical reason why the forest on both sides of an induced edge should not eventually be the same.

For some animals, edges are important as the places where they are most likely to find a meal; for other species edges are where they are most likely to die. But even for these latter species an edge is critical for they may have to cross it frequently when they travel from secure cover to their food or water resources.

**Figure 16.8** Nesting habitat for goshawks in northern Minnesota. The occupied nest is in the upper center of this figure. A mature pine forest such as this provides optimum hunting habitat for these raptors and a poor habitat for prey animals.

When resources essential to a herbivorous prey species are concentrated in an edge, the predators know where they may find a meal when hungry; if essential resources are well scattered over a broad area, however, giving the prey species a choice of sites providing food and cover, the "cost" of hunting becomes excessive, and predators can seldom "afford" (in terms of energy expenditure) to hunt that prey.

## Riparian Forest Habitats

Forest growth along stream courses, or the *riparian forest*, is an especially important wildlife habitat. In the conifer-dominated Blue Mountains of Oregon and Washington, the deciduous riparian forests have the highest diversity of wildlife species. The arid southwestern riparian forests are fragile and require special attention. They frequently consist of a vegetation type unique for that region and no more than 200 to 300 meters wide, but many kilometers in length.

Although riparian habitats in eastern forests lack the unique character they have in the West, they still receive special recognition for their importance as wildlife habitat, stream-bank maintenance, and particularly as fisheries resources.

## WILDLIFE IMPACTS ON FORESTS

### Beneficial Influences

**Seed Dispersal and Planting.** Wildlife plays an important role in the distribution of seeds of many trees. Very few of the birds that feed on the fruits of cherries, mountain ash, junipers and others crush or damage the seeds. The seeds pass through the birds' digestive systems intact and ready to germinate wherever they are dropped. The frequent occurrence of fruit-producing shrubs and trees along fences and under telephone wires or power lines attests to this function. If the fruits have been taken by a bird in migration, the seeds may be deposited many kilometers from where they were consumed.

Turtles, tortoises, lizards, and fish also transport seeds from one site to another, and if one of these animals happens to be preyed on by a bird, seeds may be moved a considerable distance. Even seeds taken by granivores may become scattered some distance from the point of origin as a result of predation. Birds commonly carry seeds in a storage pouch, or crop, for some time before the food passes into the stomach or gizzard to be ground and digested. Predators feeding on a bird usually consume the fleshy part of the crop and leave the contents scattered at the site.

Recent studies concerning the mycophagous (fungus-eating) habits of mice and chipmunks in western forests suggest that the transmission of fungal spores from one site to another may promote the establishment of conifer plantations through distribution of the mycorrhizae important to nutrient absorption by tree roots (see Chapters 4 and 8).

**Pest Control.** There can be little question that the consumption of insects, their eggs, larvae, and nymphs by insectivorous birds and small mammals represents some control over insect abundance, but this feeding seems to be more a matter of cropping the insecure surplus than reducing arthropod populations. Insectivorous birds in the Great Lakes states have had little impact on the growth and spread of tent caterpillar infestations when environmental conditions are satisfactory for the latter, nor did the bark foragers and hole-drillers halt the spread of the Englemann spruce beetle, which destroyed more than 9.43 million cubic meters of spruce in Colorado forests from 1942 to 1948.

Another indication of the negligible influence birds have in controlling insect epidemics is given by studies that find no response on the part of bird populations to insecticide applications (23). These studies suggest that insect numbers exceed the capacity of birds to consume them by so much that the loss of a major portion of the insect population to the insecticide has no effect on the food resources of the insectivores.

On the other hand, because of the conflict with human values, we have reduced to ineffective levels some of the predators that at one time probably were fairly effective in controlling what are now serious forests pests. Our reduction of the larger predators such as wolves, bears, mountain lions, wolverines, and fishers has favored increased abundance of deer, wapiti, moose, porcupines, and beavers, all of which can have serious impact on forest development. This does not imply that increases in numbers of these herbivores were due solely to reduction of predators, for human-induced changes in forest structure and composition also had a profound effect.

### Detrimental Influences

**Browsing.** Wildlife use of trees can be detrimental to the forest in several ways. Most prominent among these is browsing on seedlings, sprouts, and saplings by deer, moose, wapiti, snowshoe hares, and various rodents. In some regions the primary forage for wildlife is the trees that should develop into a new forest. This occurs in all parts of the continent and is often a major factor hindering forest regeneration.

Destructive use of tree regeneration by wildlife may be quite selective, virtually destroying the new growth of one species, while allowing unimpeded regeneration of another nearby species. This is illustrated by the differential browsing pressure exerted by white-tailed deer on aspen regeneration on an experimental ruffed grouse management area in Vermont's Green Mountains in 1977. As shown in Figure 16.9, summer use by deer kept big-toothed aspen regeneration browsed to ground level, while on a similar site only 500 meters distant root sprouts of quaking aspen grew unimpeded. Even within the

**Figure 16.9** An example of differential browsing on aspen regeneration by deer in Vermont. These two sites were both clearcut in the winter of 1976−1977 and the photographs taken in September 1977. (*a*) This site was dominated by a clone of big-toothed aspen, but deer kept the root-sprouts browsed almost to the ground in the background allowing only a few quaking aspen sprouts in the foreground to reach a height of about 45 centimeters. (*b*) Quaking aspen 500 meters distant unaffected by deer browsing, with a high density of aspen root-sprouts reaching heights of 1.5 to 1.8 meters during the first growing season.

block severely browsed by deer, quaking aspen was much less heavily used than big-toothed aspen.

**Feeding on Bark.** Porcupines are most often associated with damage from feeding on bark, for the cambium layer of trees provides much of their winter-long food resource. The amount of damage done to a forest by porcupines varies depending on the region and the value of the tree species preferred for feeding. In a Maine forest, losses were estimated to be about 0.5 percent of the total volume in a mixed forest of merchantable red spruce, balsam fir, and red and white pines, but in a nonmerchantable black spruce bog damage represented 2.4 percent of the stand (24). Porcupines were responsible for the destruction of an estimated 72,500 cubic meters of merchantable aspen in one 1200-hectare stand and 18,000 cubic meters of aspen in another Michigan forest in the early 1950s (25).

Rodents and rabbits also do a great deal of damage to forest regeneration by feeding on the tender bark of young trees. During periods of high populations of mice, stands of seedlings or sprouts may be almost completely destroyed by rodent girdling.

**Seed Destruction.** Earlier the importance of seeds to wildlife was discussed, and the dependency of some wildlife on seeds, or the mast crop, was emphasized. Wildlife destruction of seeds scattered for reforestation has been so serious that considerable effort has gone into developing methods for protecting seeds from consumption. This includes dyeing to make seeds look unacceptable to color-sensitive birds, treating with chemicals to make seeds unattractive to taste-sensitive mammals, or enclosing seeds in pellets of clay or other materials to make the seeds inaccessible until they germinate.

**Felling.** The impact of beavers is most severe in forests where aspen is an important forest resource. In northeastern Minnesota lake country beavers have nearly eliminated aspen as a part of the forest composition for a distance of 100 to 150 meters from

the shorelines, most often leaving a residual hardwoods forest dominated by paper birch and red maple. In a study of aspen in Michigan in the 1950s it was found that beavers had so depleted aspen stands near waterways that researchers could not study the effects of beavers on aspen (25).

Beavers not only fall any size of aspen they encounter, but they also feed on sprouts that develop from the roots of the felled trees. This type of utilization soon eliminates aspen from the forest stand (Figure 16.10). In addition, aspen stands often

**Figure 16.10** Two examples of beaver destruction of aspen stands. (*a*) A stand of mature aspen in the Cloquet Forest, Minnesota, felled by beavers in the fall of 1962. This site was converted to a grassy meadow still devoid of forest cover 16 years later. (*b*) Beaver destruction of an aspen stand along a small stream in the Toquima Range in central Nevada.

do not regenerate as readily following cutting by beavers as they do following destruction by fire or logging. Once the beavers have felled all the aspen, they may turn to other trees. But more often when the aspen stand has been destroyed these rodents will abandon the site.

In regions where aspen does not occur, beavers may fell a variety of trees such as cottonwoods, alders, and willows. In Louisiana, for example, beavers feed on loblolly and spruce pine, sweet gum, southern sweetbay, tupelo gum, bald cypress, and blue beech and also make some use of fifteen other hardwoods, including four species of oaks (26).

The role of the beaver in the forest-wildlife picture is more complex than simply being a feller and consumer of trees. Their damming of streams, and subsequent development of impoundments, affects the welfare of a number of other forms of fish and wildlife. In eastern Canada beaver ponds were found to be very important for black duck broods, with ponds larger than 2 hectares being most important (27). Beaver ponds also provide habitat for various fish, turtles, frogs, and other amphibians and for other prized furbearers such as mink and otter. Many of the aquatic plants favored by moose in the summer thrive in beaver ponds. The flooding of woodlands frequently kills many trees in addition to these felled by the beaver. This mortality provides snags for cavity-nesting wildlife and openings in extensive forest tracts that favor flycatching swallows, kingbirds, and waxwings.

**Miscellaneous Damage.** While most of the deleterious impact on the forest is the result of feeding on trees or their seeds, a certain amount of other damage occurs, mostly related to behavioral traits of different wildlife species. For example, trampling of small trees can be important on sites where deer or wapiti concentrate.

In late summer, as antler growth is completed on male deer, wapiti, and moose, the "velvet," which contains the blood vessels providing nutrition to the developing antlers, withers and begins to shed. Then these animals rub the dead velvet off and "polish" their antlers on small-diameter trees or large shrubs. A study in New England forests showed that most of the damage by white-tailed deer was to trees 1.2 to 12 centimeters in diameter and usually extended from about 30 to 80 centimeters above the ground (28) (Figure 16.11).

The damage often affects only one side of the tree, but an occasional tree may be girdled. Sometimes small red pines (up to 3 meters tall) are torn from the ground by especially vigorous buck deer. In northern Minnesota the most severely damaged trees are those that have been pruned or otherwise have lost their lower branches while still less than 10 to 15 cm in diameter.

## IMPACT OF FOREST MANAGEMENT ON WILDLIFE

### Fire Management

**Fire Suppression.** The place of fire in the forest ecosystem is currently a controversial subject. While there is little argument concerning the place of wildfire in an accessible, commercially valuable timber stand, the issue becomes clouded when a forest has little commercial value such as in a wilderness setting where a forest's value as wildlife habitat is greater than its timber value. A large proportion of forest wildlife depends on the *periodic destruction and renewal* of the forest for survival. We have already discussed the species that require young forests or two or more stages in the seral development of a forest stand. Stoddard recognized this in relation to bobwhite quail living in southeastern Georgia forests 40 years ago (29), and later the same belief was expressed in relation to wildlife in northern forests.

Successful prevention and suppression of fire have had a profound effect upon forest wildlife resources. The most obvious effect is allowing millions of hectares of forestland to proceed toward

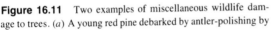

**Figure 16.11** Two examples of miscellaneous wildlife damage to trees. (*a*) A young red pine debarked by antler-polishing by a male white-tailed deer. (*b*) Damage to a paper birch by a sapsucker making holes to obtain access to the tree's sap.

climax, usually with the loss of the intolerant plants that provide the bulk of the wildlife habitat resources.

In New England forests some 1.2 million hectares went this route between 1953 and 1970. In the Rocky Mountains about 462,000 hectares are faced with this prospect, and in Minnesota undisturbed succession on 1.8 million hectares of overmature aspen forests has already had a major impact on the white-tailed deer population. This is associated with a decline in Minnesota deer harvests of from 95,000 to 127,000 deer annually in the 1959 to 1968 period, to only 46,000 to 48,000 in the 1977 to 1978 period.

**Prescribed Burning.** Depending on the goal, prescribed burning may be either beneficial or destructive to wildlife resources. If the goal of burning is to set back succession to an earlier seral stage it will probably be of considerable value to wildlife. For the past half century prescribed fire has been used routinely in pine forests of the southeastern United States to maintain bobwhite habitats.

Another outstanding example of the use of prescribed fire to maintain a wildlife population has been the restoration of a prairie from an aspen–jack pine forest on the Crex Meadows Wildlife Area in northwestern Wisconsin. By using fire on a regular basis, some 4800 hectares of scrub forest have been converted back to a prairie habitat favored by cranes, geese, ducks, pinnated and sharp-tailed grouse, and a number of other grassland species.

On the other hand, if prescribed fire is being used for purely silvicultural purposes, it can be detrimental to wildlife resources. Summer burning of young aspen regeneration in planting site preparation eliminates an important wildlife habitat in Great Lakes states forests. In southeastern pine forests burning may also have a detrimental impact on wildlife. Wood and Niles (30), assessing the effects of longleaf and slash pine management on non-gamebirds habitats, conclude:

*Prescribed burning is a necessary practice in longleaf–slash pine management, but when*

**400**

*carried out with the objective of eradicating understory rather than controlling it, the practice has a highly detrimental effect on nongame bird habitat.*

**Effects on Wildlife Food.** The most obvious impacts of fire on forest wildlife are the changes wrought in the structure or composition of the forest. If a fire destroys a mature pine forest, which is replaced by a vigorous growth of early seral deciduous browse species, a dramatic change will occur in the wildlife population. One such fire in northern Minnesota in 1971 resulted in a fivefold increase in moose abundance on the burned area within two years (31) as well as a marked change in the composition of the songbird population.

But less obvious effects also occur. For example, a fourfold increase was recorded within a month in deer mouse abundance on a burned area as compared to an uncut jack pine forest (32). This response was due to increased availability of seeds exposed by fire. A prompt, marked increase in herbivorous wildlife on burned areas seems to be the general pattern of response, usually accompanied by a decline in species diversity. Of more importance are the longer-duration changes that occur in the nutrient values of browse. Generally the forage quality and quantity of both woody browse and grasses increase markedly after burning.

**Timber Cutting**

Any discussion of the impact of timber cutting upon wildlife is complex and somewhat tentative for several reasons. Not the least of these is the scarcity of long-term research to evaluate the impact of various treatments on wildlife. Few studies have lasted more than a few years, yet in the Great Lakes states it takes 8 to 12 years after logging or fire before a regenerating aspen forest becomes most valuable as ruffed grouse cover, and a quarter century before the stand begins to be most useful as a food resource for these grouse. Most studies have looked at wildlife use of existing habitats during a

brief time span without regard for change or consideration that the animals might be using the best habitats available, although not the preferred habitats.

Silviculturists classify the various types of timber cutting as thinnings, release cuttings, clearcutting, seed-tree cuttings, shelterwood cuttings, or selection cuttings (see Chapter 9). For wildlife purposes all of the cutting schemes are best lumped into two categories: *clearcutting*, with less than about 5 to 10 percent of the canopy trees remaining, and *partial cutting*, with more than 5 to 10 percent of the canopy remaining intact. For most species of herbivorous wildlife, how much sunlight reaches the forest floor following silvicultural treatment is most important.

**Clearcutting.** When one examines the impact of clearcutting on wildlife, various questions arise because the term *clearcut* has several connotations. A commercial clearcut having certain diameter limits, or limited to certain species, may really be a partial cut having either little effect on the faunal composition or a very profound effect, depending on the trees cut. A complete clearcut in which all trees are removed will always have a marked impact on wildlife populations (Figure 16.12).

Depending on the scale, shape, and dispersion of cutting the result may be either clearly detrimental or highly beneficial, but *seldom neutral*. Cutting ten dispersed 10-hectare blocks from a 1000-hectare compartment will affect wildlife differently than cutting the same amount of forest in one 100-hectare block. If the 10-hectare blocks are rectangular strips, the value to wildlife may be quite different than if they are square or circular in shape.

The farther an animal is forced to range from cover to feed, the less likely it is to escape an encounter with a predator. Ruffed grouse are unlikely to make much use of winter cover in the central part of a 10-hectare clearcut block because of the 150-meter distance to the food resource in the surrounding uncut forest; if that clearing is 50 meters wide by 200 meters long, however, all of the 10 hectares would be used, probably by 20 percent

**Figure 16.12** Commercial clearcut logging designed to improve the forest habitat for wildlife on a wildlife-management area in Minnesota.

more grouse than would be associated with the same size of block in a square shape (33).

Deer feeding on new growth in a cutover area dislike ranging too far from cover of the older forest, and wapiti concentrate their activity in a clearcut within 300 meters of the uncut forest. Obviously, *configuration* of a clearcut is as important as size in determining its value to wildlife.

Although forest clearcutting has been much maligned by some segments of the American public, it is the most satisfactory method for maintaining an abundance of many forest wildlife species. The other management alternative is to use fire, which is usually less acceptable and often means wastage of woodland resources. In the absence of properly dispersed and timed periodic destruction of forest stands, by either logging or fire, the existence of many forest wildlife species is threatened.

**Partial Cutting.** When compared to properly executed clearcutting, partial cutting, which main-

tains an uneven-aged forest, is less likely to be *beneficial* to wildlife, and conversely will seldom be as damaging to wildlife as improper clearcutting.

Each of the several types of partial cutting may have a different impact on wildlife. A *thinning operation* could be undesirable if the trees removed were primary mast producers supporting a squirrel, turkey, and deer population in the Ozarks. Removal of large overstory trees may also destroy the potential snags or decadent trees most likely to provide the cavities essential to much wildlife. A study of wildlife and cattle use of aspen groves in the Southwest has shown that thinned stands, even though they produced more forage, were less used by deer and wapiti than nearby unthinned aspen stands.

A partial cut may be a *selection cut* in which trees of selected species or certain diameter limits (basal areas) are harvested. A study of the effects of four degrees of partial cutting in an Adirondack hardwoods forest in New York provides a good indication of the effect of this type of logging on a songbird population (34). The logging removed 25, 50, 75, and 100 percent of the merchantable trees 30 to 36 centimeters dbh or larger. The residual timber volume on the 100-percent removal area was about one half that of the stand in the 25-percent removal area. All four logged areas had *greater bird species diversity* than the unlogged control area, with the most heavily cut blocks showing the greatest increase in diversity.

Some stenotopic species dependent on closed-canopy or high-density mature forests were adversely affected by the disturbance of the forest canopy. Removal of only 25 percent of the hardwoods forest in this New York study discouraged continued use by blackburnian warblers and least flycatchers. Five other species of songbirds disappeared as the logging intensity increased toward 100 percent of the merchantable stand.

*Group selection cutting,* which opens a hole in the forest canopy, is the partial cutting method most likely to be generally beneficial to wildlife. This procedure may create enough of an opening to stimulate dense young growth on the forest floor and improve both food and cover. However, caution must be exercised with this type of cutting. If the clearings are in locations with large big-game populations, excessive browsing may destroy all regeneration and create a fairly permanent opening in the forest (Figure 16.13). It may be necessary to make a considerable number of these cuttings to provide sufficient browse to satisfy the herbivores and still allow regeneration to occur. In a Michigan aspen forest having a density of ten deer per square kilometer, about 6 hectares of aspen per square kilometer would have to be cut at one time to ensure that enough of the aspen regeneration survived browsing by deer to stock the stand adequately (25).

The size of the group selection clearing may be critical as well. Recent studies in Minnesota have shown that clearings less than about 0.4 hectares in size provide too little cover to be acceptable for yearround occupancy by ruffed grouse. In an Alaska white spruce forest a shelterwood harvest had a detrimental impact on a red squirrel population, reducing numbers 66 percent in two seasons (8).

Usually one should expect a favorable response by most wildlife to *shelterwood* or *seed-tree* cuttings, for not only are mature trees left as habitats for trunk and aerial foragers, but also sunlight reaches the forest floor to stimulate increased growth of the understory vegetation. More browse of higher quality becomes available, and various fruit-producing plants are stimulated to produce the food resource important to many rodents, foxes, raccoons, bears, and birds. Dead or decadent trees left standing as sites for cavity-users maintain a forest having greater value to wildlife than if dead and defective stems are felled.

## Chemical Treatments

**Effects of Herbicides.** Much controversy has revolved around the effects of herbicides on wildlife. It has mostly considered whether or not various species of wildlife are harmed directly or genetically by herbicide applications. Generally the conclusion has been that there is *seldom direct* damage to wildlife by herbicide application (35). Still, many forms of wildlife suffer *eventual losses* when herbicides are used, for the same reason that some wildlife suffers when a forest moves toward climax. Most often herbicides are used to release conifers from the competition of deciduous vegetation.

The wildlife most vulnerable to impaction by herbicide use are the *larger herbivores.* But ruffed grouse, woodcock, and other animals dependent on brush, deciduous vegetation, or mast crops also lose their resources.

**Effects of Pesticides.** The destruction of wildlife resulting from the use of pesticides is well documented (35). Use of the persistent pesticides is banned or sharply curtailed in the United States, and use has shifted to pesticides that degrade rapidly. But when we recognize that nearly every bird in the

**Figure 16.13** Two examples of group-selection cutting presenting management problems. (*a*) A 0.2 hectare clearing designed to preserve a clone of aspen in a beech-maple forest in Vermont's Green Mountains. This cutting was made a season after several similar cuttings were made and the deer attracted by the other clearings destroyed all sprout growth on this later cutting. (*b*) A clearing made in a Colorado lodgepole pine forest to favor the few aspen scattered through this forest. A small band of wapiti summering here were cropping the aspen regeneration as fast as it appeared, defeating the purpose of this management.

forest (except for the hawks and owls) and many mammals depend on insects as a food resource at some time in their lives, one would suspect that an insecticide application that is effective in reducing insect populations would have an adverse effect on wildlife.

However, several studies have shown that this does not necessarily happen. Giles, for example, found little change in wildlife populations following aerial application of *malathion* to an Ohio forest (23). In these situations it appears that insect populations are so far in excess of the consumptive abilities of the insectivorous wildlife that a marked reduction in insect abundance had no effect.

On the other hand, Moulding (36), in study of the effects of *Sevin* spraying in a New Jersey forest in June, found a significant 55 percent decline among birds over an 8-week period in the sprayed forest, but no change in the unsprayed forest. Here insect numbers may have been closer to the abundance necessary to sustain the songbird population.

## STRATEGIES FOR INTEGRATING WILDLIFE- AND FORESTRY-MANAGEMENT PRACTICES

At the beginning of this chapter we pointed out that any management action in a forest will have an impact on the component wildlife, It is seldom economically feasible to alter much forestland to benefit wildlife, especially when we are talking about affecting hundreds of thousands of hectares to have a significant effect in regional abundance. Most of this alteration must be achieved through commercial timber management. Thus, it is necessary to integrate wildlife- and forest-management practices.

The Forest Service currently has two approaches to the integration of forestry and wildlife management. In the southern region the *featured-species* concept has been adopted (37). This approach involves selecting certain wildlife species to be featured on each unit of forestland, and managing the forest in such a manner that the year-long food and

cover needs are provided within the normal foraging range of that species. The objective of the management plan has been reached when "food and cover support the population without waste, without unduly suppressing other necessary habitat features, or without sacrifice of other multiple-use objectives."

Turkeys may be the featured species in one compartment or district, with the management goal directed toward maintaining mature stands of mixed hardwoods, scattered groups of conifers, relatively open understories, and scattered clearings. Water must be available, and the area should be remote from areas of human activity.

This management is directed toward optimizing benefits for the featured species and incidentally the other forms of wildlife that have similar needs. This scheme should produce relatively high populations of the featured species at some cost to a diversity of other wildlife.

In contrast to the plan in the southern region is that in the eastern region, where the goal is for *diversity*. Siderits and Radtke (38) feel that the concept of diversity considers species richness in the ecosystem instead of richness in individual species. Management under this concept recognizes wildlife on a community basis, not the needs of individual species.

This concept is being applied in the Ozark Mountains (39). The forests are divided into compartments of about 400 hectares each, and desired diversity is developed for each compartment. The management guides call for establishing short- and long-range cover objectives for oak, oak-pine, and pine types, balancing size classes of oak and oak-pine and of pine stands if they exceed 10 percent of each compartment.

To develop diversity the guides call for 20 percent of each compartment to be in a productive forage condition; in oak and cedar-hardwood compartments 40 percent should be mast producing, or 30 percent if the compartment is predominantly pine; and 10 percent of each compartment should be in old growth. The plan also calls for one permanent water source on each 260 hectares of habitat.

A variation is the management guidelines being developed for the Blue Mountains of Oregon and Washington (40). This variation sets as a minimum goal "that habitat for all existing species of wildlife be retained in quantity and quality sufficient to maintain at least *self-sustaining populations* of each existing species." This plan differs from the other two programs by indicating the *general abundance* of wildlife to be maintained in a certain sized area (about 2000 to 2400 hectares), and then habitat management objectives are tailored to create the diversity necessary to attain that goal. This approach addresses the problem of how much wildlife is to be sustained by forest management.

In addition to these guides to the general management of wildlife habitats, more specific guides apply to certain endangered species. In the Great Lakes states forests, bald eagle nesting sites and Kirtland warbler habitats receive special attention; in southern forests habitat for the red-cockaded woodpecker is a special feature, and in most forest areas the preservation of snags is becoming an important consideration. In western forests the preservation of riparian habitat receives special attention, and the western Blue Mountains program is unique in placing emphasis on preservation of logs and debris on the ground as a vital habitat for a number of small mammals, lizards, and amphibians.

## REFERENCES

1. Anon., "1975 National Survey of Hunting, Fishing and Wildlife-Associated Recreation," U.S.D.I. Fish & Wildl. Serv., Washington, 1977.
2. J. C. Horvath, "Economic Survey of Southeastern Wildlife and Wildlife-Oriented Recreation," *Trans. 39th No. Amer. Wildl. and Nat. Resour. Conf.*, Wildl. Mgmt. Inst., Washington, 1974.
3. Personal communication from J. J. Harju.
4. B. R. Payne and R. M. DeGraff, "Economic Values and Recreational Trends Associated With Human Enjoyment of Nongame Birds," U.S.D.A. For. Serv., Gen. Tech. Rept. WO-1, Washington, 1975.
5. L. B. Keith, *Wildlife's Ten-Year Cycle*, Univ. of Wisconsin Press, Madison, 1963.
6. G. W. Gullion, *Ecology, 41*, 518 (1960).
7. J. C. Seidensticker IV, M, G, Hornocker, W. V. Wiles, and J. P. Messick, "Mountain Lion Social Organization in the Idaho Primitive Area," *Wildl. Monogr. No. 35*, Wildl. Soc., Washington, 1973.
8. J. O. Wolff and J. C. Zasada, "Red Squirrel Response to Clearcut and Shelterwood Systems in Interior Alaska," U.S.D.A. For. Serv., Res. Note PNW-255, Portland, 1975.
9. P. L. Errington, *Of Predation and Life*, Iowa State Univ. Press, Ames, 1967.
10. A. Leopold, *Game Management*, Scribners, New York, 1933.
11. G. W. Gullion and W. H. Marshall, *The Living Bird, 7*, 117–167 (1968).
12. L. E. Yeager, *J. For., 59*, 671 (1961).
13. A. C. Martin, H. S. Zim, and A. L. Nelson, *American Wildlife and Plants, A Guide to Wildlife Food Habits*, McGraw-Hill, New York, 1951.
14. R. O. Kimmel and D. E. Samuel, "Feeding Behavior of Young Ruffed Grouse in West Virginia," *Trans. Northeastern Fish and Wildl. Conf.*, in press.
15. V. E. Scott, K. E. Evans, D. R. Patton, and C. P. Stone, "Cavity-Nesting Birds of North American Forests," U.S.D.A. For. Serv. Agric. Handb. 511, Washington, 1977.
16. J. F. Bendell and P. W. Elliot, *Condor, 68*, 442 (1966).
17. R. Radtke and J. Byelich, *Wilson Bull., 75*, 208 (1963).
18. E. C. Meslow, "The Relationship of Birds to Habitat Structure—Plant Community and Successional States." U.S.D.A. For. Serv., Gen. Tech. Rept. PNW-64, Portland, 1978.
19. J. W. Thomas, R. Miller, C. Maser, R. Anderson, and B. Carter, "The Relationship of Terrestrial Vertebrates to Plant Communities and Their Successional Stages," *Proc. Symp. on Classification, Inventory, and Analysis of Fish and Wildlife Habitat*, U.S.D.I. Fish & Wildl. Serv., Office Biol. Serv. Washington, 1977.
20. D.W. Johnston and E. P. Odum, *Ecology, 37*, 50 (1956).
21. J. M.. Peek, D. L. Urich, and R. J. Mackie, *Wildl. Monogr. No. 48*, Wildlife Soc., Washington, D.C., 1976.
22. J. W. Thomas, C. Maser, and J. E. Rodiek, "Edges," *In: Wildlife Habitats in Managed Forests,*

# REFERENCES

*The Blue Mountains of Oregon and Washington.* J. W. Thomas, ed., U.S.D.A. For. Serv., Agric. Handb. No. 553, Washington, 1979.

23. R. H. Giles, Jr., "The Ecology of a Small Forested Watershed Treated With the Insecticide Malathion-S³⁵," *Wildl. Monogr. No. 24,* Wildl. Soc., Washington, 1970.

24. J. D. Curtis, *J. Wildl. Mgmt., 8,* 90 (1944).

25. S. A. Graham, R. P. Harrison, Jr., and C. E. Westell, Jr., *Aspens: Phoenix Trees of the Great Lakes Region,* University of Michigan Press, Ann Arbor, 1963.

26. R. H. Chabreck, *J. Wildl. Mgmt., 22,* 181 (1958).

27. R. N. Renouf, *J. Wildl. Mgmt., 36,* 740 (1972).

28. H. J. Lutz and H. H. Chapman, *J. Wildl. Mgmt., 8,* 80 (1944).

29. H. L. Stoddard, *The Bobwhite Quail, Its Habits, Preservation and Increase,* Scribners, New York, 1950.

30. G. W. Wood and L. J. Niles, "Effects of Management Practices on Nongame Bird Habitat in Longleaf-Slash Pine Forests," U.S.D.A. For. Serv., Gen. Tech. Rept. SE-14, Asheville, N.C., 1978. (1975).

31. L. L. Irwin, *J. Wildl. Mgmt., 39,* 653 (1975).

32. C. E. Ahlgren, *J. Forestry, 64,* 614 (1966).

33. G. W. Gullion, *Improving Your Forested Lands for Ruffed Grouse,* Ruffed Grouse Society, Coraopolis, Pa., 1972.

34. W. L. Webb, D. F. Behrend, and B. Saisorn, "Effects of Logging on Songbird Populations in a Northern Hardwood Forest," *Wildl. Mongr. No. 55,* Wildl. Soc., Washington, 1977.

35. A. W. A. Brown, *Ecology of Pesticides,* John Wiley & Sons, New York, 1978.

36. J. D. Moulding, *Auk, 93,* 692 (1976).

37. W. D. Zeedyk and R. B. Hazel, "The Southeastern Featured Species Plan." *Timber-Wildlife Management Proceed., Occ Paper 3,* Missouri Acad. Science, Columbia, 1974.

38. K. Siderits and R. E. Radtke, "Enhancing Forest Wildlife Habitat Through Diversity," *Trans. 42nd No. Amer. Wildl. and Nat. Resour. Conf.,* Wildl. Mgmt. Instit., Washington, 1977.

39. R. D. Evans, "Wildlife Habitat Management Program: A Concept of Diversity for the Public Forests of Missouri," *Timber-Wildlife Management Proceed., Occ. Paper 3,* Missouri Acad. Science, Columbia, 1974.

40. R. Miller, "Guidelines for Wildlife Management in Western Coniferous Forests," U.S.D.A. For. Serv., Gen. Tech. Rept. PNW-64, Portland, 1978.

# PART 4

## FOREST PRODUCTS

In this section the use of wood as a raw material is emphasized. The unique characteristics and comparative abundance of wood have made it a desirable natural material for homes and other structures, furniture, tools, vehicles, and decorative objects. The multitude of uses for wood are summarized in Table P4.1.

Wood is mainly composed of three polymers; cellulose, hemicelluloses, and lignin formed in a cellular structure. Variations in the characteristics and volume of the components and in the cellular structure result in differences in wood properties, for example, hardness, weight, flexibility, etc. For a single species, the properties are relatively constant within limits; however, to use wood to its best advantage and most effectively in engineering applications, the effect of specific characteristics or physical properties must be considered (1).

Throughout history different types of wood have served many purposes. The tough, strong, and durable white oak, for example, was a well-proved wood for ships, bridges, cooperage, barn timbers, farm implements, railroad crossties, fenceposts, flooring, paneling, and other products. In contrast, woods such as black walnut and cherry became primarily cabinet woods. Hickory was manufactured into tough, hard, resilient tool handles. Black locust was used for barn timbers and treenails. What the early artisan learned by trial and error became the basis for intelligent decisions as to which species was best suited to a given purpose and also what characteristics to look for in selecting trees for different applications. It was known that wood from trees grown in certain locations was stronger, more durable, and more easily worked with tools than wood from the same species grown in different locations. Modern wood-quality research has sub-stantiated that location and growth conditions significantly affect wood properties (1).

With the decline of the virgin forests in the United States the available supply of large clear logs for lumber and veneer has been reduced. However, the importance of high-quality logs has diminished as new concepts of wood use have been introduced. Second-growth timber, the balance of the old-growth forests, and imports continue to fill the needs for wood in the quality required. Wood is still a very valuable engineering material (1). The inherent factors that keep wood in the forefront of raw materials are many and varied. The structure and chief attributes that give wood these special properties are discussed in Chapter 17, "Properties of Wood."

In the United States more than 100 kinds of wood are available to the prospective user, but it is very unlikely that all are available in any one locality. About 60 native woods are of major commercial importance. Another 30 wood types are commonly imported in the form of logs, cants, lumber, and veneer for industrial uses, the building trades, and crafts (1).

An increasing percentage of harvested wood is used for production of pulp and paper. Thousands of paper products are produced every year for household and industrial use. Since smaller-size logs are suitable for pulp production, the second-growth timber in the United States is very suitable for production of these important commodities (Figure P4.1). In addition, many different species of hardwoods are proving suitable for paper manufacture. Chapter 18, "Chemistry and Pulping of Wood," describes the chemical nature of wood and the methods for paper manufacture.

With the 1980s came an acute public awareness of

**Table P4.1**

Summary of Uses for Wood

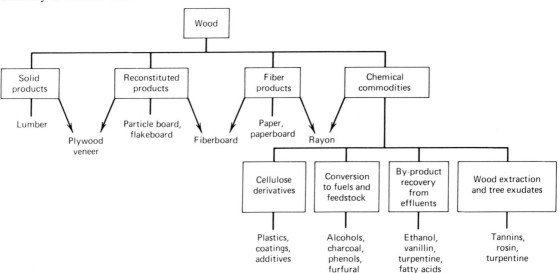

**Figure P4.1** Wrestling Douglas-fir logs on Oregon's Coos River, using long pike poles and a short peavey. These logs will roar downstream to be processed in a pulpwood mill. (Courtesy of Life Picture Service)

the potentially severe energy problems facing the United States. The role of wood as a raw material for energy and chemicals is outlined in Chapter 19, ''Energy and Chemicals from Wood.'' Wood once was a significant primary energy source for the United States but will probably never regain such status. However, up to 15 percent of our energy needs could be potentially derived from biomass, probably through more efficient use of urban, agricultural and forest residues.

Wood is both imported into and exported from the United States. Thus, both the U.S. and the world economies are affected by the marketing of wood and wood products. Chapter 20, ''The Forest-Products Economy,'' gives details on the market value of forest products and how this affects timber-management practices.

## REFERENCES

1. Anon., *Wood Handbook: Wood as an Engineering Material*, Agricultural Handbook No. 72, U.S.D.A. For. Serv., Washington, D.C., 1974.

# 17

# PROPERTIES OF WOOD

## Hans Kubler

Forest stands are managed and trees are harvested because people want and need wood. Through the ages wood has been used for thousands of purposes, ranging from toothpicks to floor joists, and it is a part of life from the cradle to the coffin.

Industrial societies could survive without wood because this natural material is replaceable in nearly all uses, the options being metals, plastics, concrete, stone, and clay. In some cases people accept substitutes, in others they prefer wood. Wood properties, the demand for wood, and the fate of forests are closely related. In the following section, we will first consider wood properties from a physiological viewpoint.

## WOOD AS PART OF THE TREE

Trees are extraordinary living organisms; they live the longest, grow the tallest, and as forests dominate the vegetation wherever conditions favor rich growth. The largest parts of trees—roots, trunk, and branches—consist mainly of wood (Figure 17.1). Without this tissue, trees could not grow tall and survive through cold winters when herbaceous plants wither to the ground. Obviously wood serves the tree extremely well and must have properties tailored to its needs (1).

## The Function of Wood in Trees

As discussed in Chapter 3 on tree physiology, wood serves some obvious function to the tree (Figure 17.2). Wood supports the tree mechanically to give strength to carry the tree crown high above ground level, and wood conducts water from the soil to the crown. Wood also serves for transverse and longitu-

**Figure 17.1** Cutaway view of a Douglas-fir tree trunk showing outer bark, inner bark, cambial layer, sapwood, and heartwood. (From *The Secret Life of the Forest* by Richard M. Ketchum; copyright 1970 by McGraw-Hill Inc. Photograph courtesy of St. Regis Paper Company.)

412

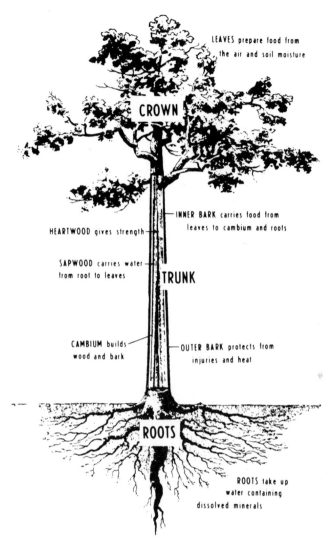

**Figure 17.2**   Parts of the tree and their function.

dinal transport of carbohydrates and their storage—so important to the growth of trees.

## Function-Related Wood Properties

The tree trunk, carrying the tree crown, needs strength predominantly in the direction of the stem axis. Wood is indeed many times *stronger longitu-*dinally than transversely. Although the ratio of longitudinal to transverse strength varies with the type of strength measured (bending, compression, etc.) and with different tree species, on the average wood resists a ten-times-greater force longitudinally than transversely. Therefore tree cross sections (tree rounds) break much more easily than lengthwise sections (boards) of equal thickness. The longitudi-

**413**

nal strength favors many uses of wood. Wall studs, for example, need mainly longitudinal strength for carrying the upper parts of the building.

The tree trunk has adequate strength to support the crown even when snow and ice double the crown's weight. Bending by wind creates even greater stresses. This strength required for bending is important because bending pressure is the primary stress exerted on joists that carry the loads on floors, in beams under bridges, and in shovel handles.

Wood must be *porous* to conduct water and carbohydrates throughout the tree. Because many times more liquid (water) flows longitudinally in the tree trunk than flows (as a sugar solution) transversely, wood is much more permeable longitudinally than transversely. This permeability is illustrated by the fact that glue, varnish, wood preservatives, and water soak relatively rapidly into the ends of lumber, and lumber and firewood dry through *end* surfaces much faster than through *lateral* surfaces.

Trees grow upright to orient the crown for good utilization of light, although in heavy winds a low profile is usually adopted. Wood meets these two conflicting demands with *flexibility*. Trunks and branches bend in the wind and reorient to the light as soon as the wind ceases. They return to their normal position by virtue of wood's resiliency or elasticity. Since wood is flexible and elastic it yields to loads by bending, stretching, compressing, and distorting and recovers when the deforming force ceases. The ability of materials to endure deformation without rupture is termed *toughness*. Materials that do not yield but break without deformation are *brittle*. The toughness of wood combined with resiliency is crucial for baseball bats and diving boards, ax and hammer handles, archery bows, support beams, railroad ties, guardrails, posts, frames of buildings exposed to wind and earthquakes, and many other items made from wood. When the deforming forces reach dangerous magnitudes, the stressed wood begins to sag, crack, and splinter before complete failure—a warning feature that is essential for mine props and other structural uses of wood (2).

## Wood Structure

Materials such as wood whose properties vary according to the direction of measurement are *anisotropic*. Wood's anisotropy also appears in its microscopic structure—that is, in the shape and orientation of the billions of tiny wood cells in each large tree. The minute structure of wood reflects the primary function of wood in the tree, as previously described.

Hollow cylinders, or pipes, are structures useful for both liquid transport and load support. People use pipes to carry water and as columns or posts to support floors and roofs. Wood tissue consists essentially of pipe-shaped cells arranged parallel to each other in the longitudinal direction. The tissue contains a mass of aligned fiber cells, the length of which measures up to 100 times greater than the width (Figure 17.3). Hence *fiber direction* or *grain direction* is oriented in the longitudinal direction in wood (*grain* stands here for *fiber*). The longitudinal alignment of the fibers makes wood anisotropic and is the reason nearly all wood properties depend on the grain or fiber direction. This longitudinal alignment also explains a number of physical characteristics of wood; for instance, the fact that lumber tends to be much rougher and more difficult to machine on the end faces than on the lateral surfaces, and the fact that splitting and checking occur on the end grain.

Approximately 90 percent of the wood tissue of coniferous trees consists of *tracheids*, a special kind of fiber (Figure 17.3*a*), which gives strength and conducts water. Broad-leaved trees, which appeared later on earth, produce special *vessel* cells for conducting water (Figure 17.3*b*). Vessels are much wider than the fibers, a feature that facilitates water flow. Each vessel consists of numerous vessel segments or members that are drum-shaped cells with open ends and are stacked one above the other to form a continuous vessel pipeline from the tips of the roots up to the leaves. Vessel width in oaks and other broad-leaved trees greatly exceeds that of the

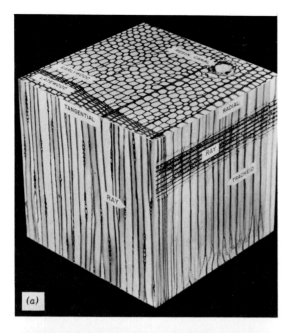

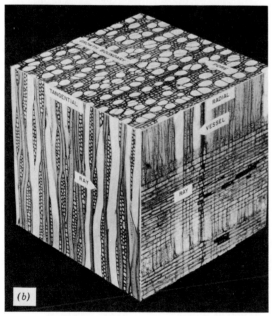

**Figure 17.3** Photomicrographic model of (*a*) coniferous wood and (*b*) wood from a broad-leaved tree. (Courtesy of Kollmann and Côté (1968)).

species in Figure 17.3*b* (see Figure 17.4*a*). Indeed, their vessels are sufficiently large to be seen with the unaided eye as round pores at the cross section and as needlelike grooves on the lateral section (3–6).

In some hardwoods, the vessels in the springwood are much larger than those farther out in the ring, and the transition from one type to the other is more or less abrupt. Such timbers are designated *ring-porous*—as, for example, oak (Figure 17.4*a*). In *diffuse-porous* woods, such as maple and birch, on the other hand, the vessels do not vary appreciably in size throughout the ring (Figure 17.4*b*). Since vessels do not occur in the coniferous woods, they are sometimes designated *nonporous*, while the hardwoods are *porous woods* (4).

Carbohydrates are transported from the inner bark through the cambial layer into wood through radially oriented *rays* (Figure 17.3); the term *radial* originates from the *radius* of the circular tree cross section and growth rings. Rays resemble knife blades, stuck horizontally into the vertical trunk between the fibers. In many broad-leaved trees the rays are quite large in the vertical direction, about 1 inch high in white oak, and thick enough to be seen with the unaided eye on all wood-plane sections (see Figure 17.5). On tree cross sections, rays appear like spokes of a wheel, originating in the bark and terminating in the wood at various distances between bark and pith.

The rays consist mainly of thin-walled, brick-shaped cells (parenchyma) that lack the strength of the fibers. Hence wood is more easily split in the planes of the rays and fails under tangential tension in the rays. The term *tangential* (Figure 17.5) derives from the tangent to the rings, and thus tangential and radial are both transverse directions. Since rays are oriented radially, they provide some strength in this direction; for this reason most wood species are stronger radially than tangentially.

Fibers and vessels die at an age of several weeks, after they attain their final shape and chemical composition. Parenchyma cells live much longer, although the oldest die as part of the conversion of

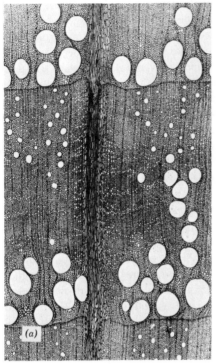
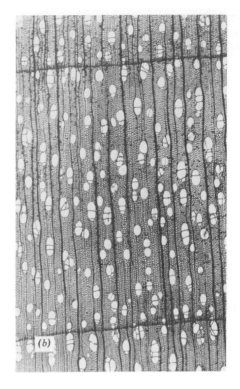

**Figure 17.4** Photomicrograph of hardwood cross-section depicting (*a*) ring porous and (*b*) diffuse porous wood. (Courtesy of U.S.D.A. Forest Products Laboratory.)

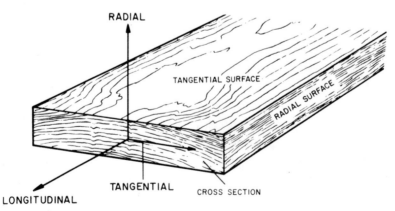

**Figure 17.5** The three principal axes and surfaces of wood with regard to fiber direction and growth rings. (Modified from U.S.D.A. For. Serv., Forest Products Laboratory.)

**416**

sapwood into heartwood (Figure 17.1). Conversion of sugars and the starch is the task of the living parenchyma cells. The fact that sapwood contains food reserves is one reason why most wood-damaging organisms prefer sapwood over heartwood and why heartwood is at least a little more durable than sapwood—except in living trees, where sap can drown attacking organisms.

Practically all wood cells are interconnected through tiny openings in the cell walls. The openings in the overlapping ends of fibers, particularly of tracheids, provide a vertical passageway for water rising from one fiber to another, while thin walls between ray cells are perforated for the transport of carbohydrates. Growing cells need connections also in the tangential direction. Hence wood is permeable in all three of its cardinal directions. However, because of the longitudinal orientation of the vessels and fibers, liquids and gases move many times faster in fiber direction than transversely. Of the two transverse directions, the radial orientation of rays allows radial movement of liquids and gases up to twice as rapidly as tangential movement.

## Wood Density as an Indicator of Wood Quality

Wood as porous material consists of cell walls and air- or water-filled cell cavities. The cell wall substance differs very little from species to species and among the various parts of the tree and has a density always near 1.5 grams per cubic centimeter. The density of wood thus depends on the proportion of the cell wall volume to the volume of the whole wood.

The densest commercial North American wood species is pignut hickory. With a density of 0.75 grams per cubic centimeter in the dry state, the cell walls occupy one half (0.75/1.5) of the volume. Douglas-fir, the most common lumber and plywood species, weighs about 0.5 grams per cubic centimeter, corresponding to a cell wall proportion of 0.5/1.5 or one-third. The density of the lightest wood, balsa from South America, averages 0.17 grams per cubic centimeter, which means the cell walls comprise little more than 10 percent of the volume. *Lignum vitae*, also from South America, is the heaviest commercial species, with a density around 1.25 grams per cubic centimeter. It is comprised of more than 80 percent cell walls and sinks rapidly in water even in the dry state (the density of water is 1.0 grams per cubic centimeter by definition) (5).

Most wood properties, particularly strength and stiffness, depend on density. Relatively dense species are hard and strong, as one might expect from the fact that they contain much cell wall substance. Wood density is *the* indicator of nearly all wood properties and of wood quality. For example, dense woods have relatively little cell cavity space and cannot contain much water, but the water they contain migrates slowly through the narrow cavities; thus dense wood dries slowly. Dense woods tend to split when nailed because they lack cavity spaces. With less dense woods (more cavity spaces) the cell walls compress away from the nail, so that the piece is not forced apart.

People have always been aware of the relationship between density and wood properties. However, they have paid more attention to *hardness*, the resistance to indentation, which depends heavily on density. Hardness is easy to estimate—for example, by pressing wood surfaces with a fingernail or with a small tool. Wood sections of any size, including huge logs too heavy to be weighed, are suited for the hardness test. Also, water in wood effects hardness less than it affects density. In earlier times in Europe practically all commercial coniferous trees were soft and the commercial broad-leaved trees hard; therefore coniferous trees were called *softwoods* and the broad-leaved trees *hardwoods*. Today we utilize a wider range of tree species, including many from tropical forests, but we have retained these terms even though the wood of many broad-leaved trees such as balsa and aspen is softer than the wood of most coniferous trees, and conifers such as yew are heavier than the wood of most broad-leaved tree species (2−4).

Wood species also vary in features not related to density, such as color, composition and arrangement of cells, and to some extent chemical composition. Therefore woods of the same density are likely to differ, and the various properties—including strength—may vary more than the densities. People were always aware of these variations and preferred a particular wood species for many uses, such as hickory for baseball bats and ax handles, redwood and western red cedar for house siding, and hard maple for cutting boards and roller skating rinks.

## FURTHER ADVANTAGEOUS PROPERTIES

Features that are irrelevant in the tree's life may or may not meet our desired uses for wood. This section deals with features that are appreciated in most use categories, while the following section is concerned with undesirable properties.

### Strength and Stiffness

When strength is evaluated in terms of force per unit cross section, no wood species is as strong as steel or aluminum. However, on basis of weight or mass, wood outperforms most other materials with the exception of fiberglass and some synthetic fibers such as nylon. In the fiber direction, 1 kilogram of wood, for example, can carry a greater load than 1 kilogram of steel.

The *strength/mass ratio* is quite meaningful. Pole-vaulters, for example, want a strong pole of low weight. The ratio has equal significance in construction, where most wood is used. In any building the structural members carry not only inhabitants, furnishings, and equipment, but also the upper structure, which typically weighs more than the contents of the building. High strength in a small mass permits construction with a reduced amount of expensive material. Wood's high strength/mass ratio is not surprising; it is also important in trees because the trunk carries not only leaves, snow, and ice, but also all the wood of branches and twigs.

Load-bearing joists and beams under floors should not bend noticeably under the weight of people and heavy items. The members need to be stiff, a property in which wood again compares favorably, even with steel (weight for weight).

### Availability and Workability

Wood is readily available in most parts of the world. In many North American states and provinces the bulk of lumber on the market comes from Oregon, Washington, British Columbia, and the South, but with little effort it can also be procured from local forests. By contrast, metals, glass, concrete, and plastics have to be manufactured in elaborate facilities from relatively rare raw materials.

Wood is easy to work with. People lost in the wilderness without any equipment and tools, in desperate need of protection from adverse elements, can somehow assemble a primitive shelter from stems and branches of trees. Primitive people could shape chunks of wood into valuable products by means of sharp stones, which are rather useless for working present-day metals. The ease of woodworking is even more obvious with modern power tools.

### Appearance

All sapwood is pale in color, in some species nearly white and in others yellowish. Heartwood color varies in a much wider range between white and red; in many species it appears brown. People perceive these colors as pleasant and warm, especially if the tone is enhanced by a clear finish. Since some tropical species grow heartwood in interesting green and blue shades, wood can be procured in almost any color. In addition, the colors can be enhanced or altered; wood, as a porous material, readily absorbs stain (6).

Some species such as basswood and poplar appear very uniform, showing hardly any variation. But most woods feature visible growth rings and rays that give each piece a *figure*. No two pieces of wood exhibit a figure exactly alike because no tree grows exactly cylindrical; the growth rate varies from year

**418**

to year, and the appearance of each surface depends on the cut. Knots also add very special conspicuous configurations. This variability appeals to people, who perceive wood as a fascinating, intrinsically beautiful natural material with which they feel familiar and comfortable (1). Manufacturers of automobile bodies and plastics employ wood-grain imitations for good reason.

## Thermal Insulation

Most frames, sashes, and casements of windows consist of either wood or aluminum. Wood has the big advantage because it is a *thermal insulator*. If in winter the window frame outside is colder than the inside surface, the aluminum will conduct 1200 times more heat to the outside than Douglas-fir wood of the same size. In reality the heat losses differ less because air layers at the surfaces contribute to the insulation, and the aluminum frame has a smaller surface than the wood frame.

Thermal insulation has significance also for studs in outside walls of houses because wood studs insulate many times better than studs of steel. The significance is moderated by the fact that studs occupy only a fraction of walls that may be filled with rock wool or other insulation that carries no load.

*Low thermal conductivity* contributes to wood's image of a pleasant warm material. Wood handles of coffeepots do not feel hot. Similarly, cold wood flooring under bare feet is perceived to be warmer than concrete of the same temperature. Wood always seems comfortable to the touch, no matter what its temperature, because wood conducts little heat in or out of the skin (our nerves sense the skin temperature, not the wood temperature).

## Fuel and Fire Performance

Wood was the first human fuel and still serves as the main source of heat for many people in nonindustrialized countries (see Chapter 20). Small pieces of dry wood burn readily to few ashes and create gases that are much less obnoxious than the combustion gases of coal. In fireplaces, burning wood fascinates by the ever-changing flames and crackling sounds. However, in furnaces wood can rarely compete with natural gas, oil, and coal because it is bulky and not well suited to automatic feeding.

It is well known that wood species differ in *burning quality*. Some people go so far as to consider aspen and boxelder, for example, not suitable as firewood. Actually all species burn very well if the wood is dry because they all have nearly the same heat value on the basis of weight. This should not be surprising; all species consist essentially of the same cell wall substance and differ little in chemical composition. The heat value on the basis of volume is another matter, because this depends on density. A cubic meter of pignut hickory with a density of 0.75 grams per cubic centimeter has twice the heat value of aspen with a density of 0.38 grams per cubic centimeter. Thus density is a good indicator of the heat value of wood. Table 17.1 lists the densities of some common wood species along with their heat values. Dense species not only give relatively more heat, but also burn longer. Thick pieces of light wood, however, burn as long as thin pieces of dense wood and give the same amount of heat (5, 6).

The fact that wood burns does not mean that structural lumber is a fire hazard. First, it should be noted that most fires start on room contents, such as beds, papers, furniture, and fabrics, and not on the building itself. Second, the smoke generated by the burning contents usually kills the inhabitants. Whether the structural material burns has little consequences in the early stages of the fire. Later, it is crucial whether the building retains its integrity or whether it collapses, and in this regard wood outperforms metals (Figure 17.6). Steel and aluminum heat rapidly over their whole cross section and become soft enough to bend under the load. By contrast, structural wood has relatively large cross sections in which the temperature rises very slowly. The surface layers of wood char and conduct little heat. Besides, a high proportion of the conducted

**Table 17-1**

Densities and Heat Values[a] at 12 Percent Moisture Content[b] of Some Important Woods Grown in the United States

| Official Common Tree Name | Density (g/cm³) | Heat Value (Joule/cm³) | Heat Value[c] (million Btu/cord) |
|---|---|---|---|
| *Hardwoods* | | | |
| Live oak | 0.99 | 17,290 | 39.6 |
| Shagbark hickory | 0.81 | 14,140 | 32.4 |
| White oak | 0.76 | 13,360 | 30.6 |
| Honeylocust | 0.72 | 12,570 | 28.8 |
| Sugar maple | 0.71 | 12,380 | 28.4 |
| Northern red oak | 0.71 | 12,380 | 28.4 |
| Yellow birch | 0.69 | 12,170 | 27.9 |
| White ash | 0.67 | 11,750 | 26.9 |
| Sweetgum | 0.58 | 10,170 | 23.3 |
| American sycamore | 0.58 | 10,170 | 23.3 |
| Black cherry | 0.56 | 9,820 | 22.5 |
| American elm | 0.56 | 9,820 | 22.5 |
| Southern magnolia | 0.56 | 9,820 | 22.5 |
| Black tupelo | 0.56 | 9,820 | 22.5 |
| Sassafras | 0.52 | 9,030 | 20.7 |
| Yellow poplar | 0.47 | 8,240 | 18.9 |
| Red alder | 0.46 | 8,070 | 18.5 |
| Eastern cottonwood | 0.45 | 7,890 | 18.1 |
| Quaking aspen | 0.43 | 7,450 | 17.1 |
| *Softwoods* | | | |
| Longleaf pine | 0.66 | 11,860 | 27.2 |
| Western larch | 0.58 | 10,440 | 23.9 |
| Douglas-fir | 0.54 | 9,650 | 22.1 |
| Bald cypress | 0.52 | 9,240 | 21.2 |
| Western hemlock | 0.50 | 9,040 | 20.7 |
| White fir | 0.48 | 7,840 | 18.0 |
| Eastern white pine | 0.39 | 7,030 | 16.1 |
| Engelmann spruce | 0.39 | 7,030 | 16.1 |
| Western red cedar | 0.36 | 6,460 | 14.8 |

*Source.* In part from the *Wood Handbook: Wood as an Engineering Material,* U.S.D.A. Agr. Handbook 72, U.S.D.A. For. Serv., Forest Products Laboratory, 1974.

[a] Heat values include latent heat of water vapor.
[b] Based on weight of ovendry wood.
[c] One cord is 128 ft³; it is assumed that the pile is two-thirds wood and one-third air (between the pieces).

heat is consumed in evaporation of wood moisture. Also, because of wood's high specific heat, many calories are required to raise its temperature. When wood finally reaches high temperatures, the resulting reversible softening is partly offset by the gain in strength due to the drying.

Strictly speaking wood does not burn, but high degrees of heat decompose it irreversibly into combustible gases, whereby it loses its strength and finally disintegrates into pieces of charcoal. The process is controlled by the penetration of heat and progresses slowly from the surface to the core so that

**Figure 17.6** Burned-out structure showing lumber carry loads long after steel has collapsed. (Courtesy of U.S.D.A. For. Serv., Forest Products Laboratory.)

thick timbers in fires carry their load for several hours.

### Electrical Properties

Occasionally people receive severe and at times lethal electrical shocks. Charges of voltage *per se* do no harm; only currents cause shocks. Electricity flows through people if they touch the voltage with one part of their body and a conductor with another part—for example, when holding a defective electrical appliance with one hand and a water faucet with the other. Dry wood does not conduct electricity, and therefore wood floors, counters, furniture, and walls in kitchens and bathrooms do not contribute to dangerous electric shocks. The *insulating qualities* of wood are also advantageous in power-line poles, although after a rain the water at the pole surface and in the pole can conduct electricity to some extent.

In homes and offices people generate static electricity while brushing against various insulating materials and then receive minor annoying shocks from the currents produced when they touch doorknobs and other conductors. Friction with wood does not generate such charges because the moisture present, even in air-dry wood, has some conducting capacity. Touching wood after being charged also causes no shocks because wood insulates sufficiently.

### DISADVANTAGEOUS PROPERTIES

In past decades wood has been replaced in many uses, most conspicuously in the manufacture of vehicles. The first carriages, railroad cars, boats, and airplanes consisted solely or mainly of wood. Up to the turn of the century, steel in carriages was restricted to rims and axles of wheels and a few bolts, while today's automobiles retain only an occasional reminder of wood in the form of wood-grain imitations. Railroad freight cars utilize steel throughout, and all large boats and airplanes are constructed of metals and plastics, many completely without wood.

The replacement has continued in spite of wood's outstanding properties. Obviously wood must have features that are unfavorable for these purposes. The undesirable features vary from case to case. Many people consider *swelling* and *shrinkage* as wood's main drawback, while this author ranks the *lack of plasticity* first, even above variability and deterioration.

## Lack of Plasticity and Fusibility

Automobile bodies are molded by pressing plane sheet metal over a form of the desired shape. Plastics can be similarly molded into spoons and dishes, for example, although the material may first have to be heated. Wood treated in this fashion breaks before reaching the desired curvature. Wood can be press-bent a little, but on removal of pressure it "springs back" and reverts to its original form; thus the deformation is *elastic*, not *plastic*. Paper clips show the difference between elasticity and plasticity very nicely. When utilized for their intended function the clips bend elastically and hold papers together, but if bent too much the two loops remain apart without "spring" because of the plastic nature of the deformation. Many materials feature elasticity at small deformations and plasticity at large deformations. Wood shows a trace of this characteristic when it is bent close to the breaking point because then a part of the bend remains.

Plastic shaping is very efficient. For the casing and trim of doors and windows, manufacturers bend metals and plastics into a U-shaped casing-trim unit, whereas with wood three sections must be nailed together. For structures, steel is simply "rolled" into I-beams, a shape that provides high strength and stiffness with a minimum of material. U-shaped wall studs made from bent steel and aluminum make use of the material equally efficiently. In wood the favored I- and U-shapes would have to be carved out of the solid wood or assembled from wood sections with glue.

Hot, moist wood can be bent a considerable amount before breaking; cooling and drying in the desired shape sets the bend (a technique resembling ironing a crease into a pair of cotton pants). But the curvature is limited and the process is time-consuming. Skis of hickory and ash were formerly made this way, while the curved parts of many chairs are still steam-bent. Bending renders a stronger product than cut-shaping, because in the bent section the fibers run parallel to the long axis over the whole length.

Many metal, plastic, and glass products such as motor blocks, plastic foam packaging, and ashtrays are manufactured by casting the liquified material into a form. Wood cannot be cast because it disintegrates before melting when heated; in other words, it lacks *fusibility*.

The wood industry has developed an alternative to sawing or routing out the desired form from solid wood. The wood is separated into sections and then rebonded into the desired shape. The pieces may be whole boards as in glued laminated beams, veneer as in plywood chairs, planer shavings as in some toilet seats, fibers as in imitation louver doors, delignified fibers as in paper cups, or cellulose molecules as in viscose rayon (see Chapter 18). But such separation and rebonding can cost more than the press-forming of plastic material.

## Deterioration

All tissue of living organisms (organic material) serves as food for other living organisms. Wood belongs in this category, but in nature it is in relatively low demand because most animals and plants cannot utilize it. Human limitations are typical in this respect; people can digest grain, flour, eggs, meat, and all kinds of vegetables, but not wood, even when the wood is ground into flour. The human digestive system lacks the ability to break the wood down and to dissolve wood components. However, a small proportion of living organisms have adapted so that they can utilize wood, and thus they impose limits on *wood durability*.

The destruction of wood by organisms has the advantage that discarded wood is automatically recycled by nature through conversion to carbon dioxide and water. Wood thrown away or left on the forest ground fades away within a few years. This automatic recylcing can be accelerated by simply burning the wood.

## Wood-Damaging Fungi.

Among the organisms that live on wood, fungi have the greatest impact, particularly the kinds that cause wood *rot*, as described in Chapter 8. Like all plants, wood-inhabiting fungi need moisture and cannot grow on dry wood. In the presence of moisture or under damp conditions it is only a question of time until some fungi decompose wood, the rate depending on temperature, availability of oxygen for respiration, and the wood species.

Some wood-inhabiting fungi lack the ability to decompose wood, but live on food reserves stored in sapwood and discolor the sapwood. Under favorable conditions these *stain* fungi infect whole piles of lumber within a few days. The stainers widen the openings between wood cells, making the wood more porous, more absorptive for water, and hence more disposed to decay. For a further discussion of fungal infection of wood, see Chapter 8.

## Wood-Damaging Insects.

Many insects feed on wood and/or use wood for shelter. Since these creatures digest the material inside their gut and not by external secretion of enzymes, they need less moisture than fungi. Some insects live on dry wood, but most species prefer it damp, for it is then soft and provides a comfortable humid environment for the thin-skinned larvae.

By far the most destructive wood feeding insects are termites. As well-organized social creatures, a termite colony can ruin a house within a few years. Termites prefer warm climates and do most damage in the southern states but occur as far north as Vermont, Ontario, Wisconsin, Colorado, and British Columbia. The subject of the damaging effects of insects on wood was discussed in Chapter 7.

## Durability and Preservation.

Wood of low density offers relatively little resistance to damaging organisms because insects find it easy to chew and fungi have plenty of space for oxygen and water. As mentioned earlier, food reserves in sapwood attract the organisms. However, wood density and food reserves are minor factors compared with the chemicals or extractives the tree deposits when sapwood becomes heartwood. In many species the extractives are poisonous to wood-damaging organisms and protect the wood. In all species, the sapwood of tree stems left on the forest ground rots within a few years, while in numerous species the heartwood "poisons" retard the decay for many years. Even underground, redwood and western red cedar heartwood fence posts resist decay. It should be emphasized that not all wood species deposit heartwood chemicals and not all deposited chemicals are poisonous, although most give the heartwood a particular color. Heartwood, which visually looks different from sapwood, is often more durable in many tree species. Alaska cedar and Port-Orford-cedar, however, have very durable heartwood that does not appear visually different from the sapwood.

Wood can be *protected* from damaging organisms by "poisoning" with preservatives. The most common preservative is creosote, which is a group of coal-tar distillates. When applied, the creosote gives utility poles and railroad ties their dark brown appearance and obnoxious smell. For interior use, researchers have found a series of waterborne preservative salts that become insoluble in wood. The preservatives are brushed on or applied by soaking, but special pressure treatment achieves much deeper penetration and longer-lasting protection. Since 1967 the industry has offered treated studs and plywood for wood foundations of homes that have significant advantages over concrete foundations and are expected to become quite common.

## Variability

Unfortunately wood properties vary from tree to tree of each wood species and even within each tree. For example, one Douglas-fir stud may be only 0.45 grams per cubic centimeter in density, while another may be 0.55 grams per cubic centimeter. When considering smaller and thinner pieces the variations are even greater. In species whose *earlywood* (formed early in the growing season) is much more porous than *latewood* (Figure 17.3a) the earlywood-latewood density contrast may be 1/3. Thus small pieces differ more than thick lumber or whole trunks whose properties are averaged out (2–6).

By far the largest variations within each wood species result from knots in which the fibers deviate from the normal direction parallel to the axis of the stem. Knots are formed from branches and thus have the fiber orientation of the branch, which is nearly at right angles to the stem axis. The fiber deviation affects practically all wood properties, including workability. For many purposes knotty lumber is either not serviceable or the knotty sections must be removed. In structural lumber, knots are permitted but allowances are made for the lower strengths.

The effect of knots and other growth variations on strength cannot be assessed accurately without physically testing the wood, particularly when the defect is invisible. Therefore, structures have to be designed for the potential weakness of each section and require much more lumber than would be necessary with an ideal material of uniform strength.

## Shrinkage and Swelling

In wood technology shrinkage means contraction because of loss of moisture, while swelling is expansion because of moisture adsorption. Shrinkage and swelling annoy both the manufacturers and the users of wood products. Green wood when exposed to dry air loses moisture and shrinks both tangentially and radially. With most species, the wood shrinks tangentially by several percent—radially about one-half as much as tangentially—and in fiber direction the wood shrinkage is almost negligible. The large transverse shrinkage opens joints between edges of boards, causes loosening in items such as drawers and the handles of tools, leads to surface checks in fast-drying lumber, and causes warp where the shrinkage is one-sided.

**Moisture Equilibrium**  Many annoying effects of shrinkage can be avoided by properly drying the wood before cutting to specified sizes and shapes. However, the moisture content (MC) of dried wood does not remain constant; it is subject to atmospheric humidity and attains an *equilibrium moisture content* (EMC). For example, wood has a MC of 12 percent at 65 percent relative humidity (RH) but only 7 percent MC at 35 percent RH. Wood dimensions vary with the humidity because moisture changes cause swelling or shrinkage.

The EMC of wood is affected by two basic properties: (1) wood is hygroscopic (it attracts moisture), and (2) wood loses moisture due to escape of the vibrating moisture molecules into the surrounding air. Wood is continually absorbing and releasing moisture, but during drying the release exceeds the adsorption. With dry wood under humid conditions, adsorption exceeds the release of moisture to the point where adsorption and release are equivalent, or the EMC has been attained (2–4).

Hygroscopy and moisture equilibrium are common features of organic substances. All plant tissue, including fruits and seeds, and nearly all organic compounds, among them sugar and honey, contain moisture depending on the humidity of the surrounding atmosphere. Their equilibrium moisture contents have the same order of magnitude as that of wood. The interaction of moisture with the wood cellulose is further discussed in Chapter 18.

**Free and Bound Moisture.** Moisture adsorbed by dry wood penetrates the cell walls and forces the cell-wall components apart, thereby causing the walls and the whole wood to swell. The water in the cell walls is termed *bound water*, and it weakens the wood as well as affecting most other wood properties. *Free water* occurs in the cell cavities (lumen) and has no effect on the cell-wall components, causes no swelling or shrinkage, and does not affect wood strength. Green and wet wood begin to shrink only after the free water is dried out of the cell cavities, when the bound cell-wall moisture begins to escape. This point at which the wood contains maximum bound (cell wall) water but no free water is termed the *fiber saturation point* and occurs at about 30 percent moisture content based on weight of dry wood.

Free water and bound water differ in the moisture equilibrium; when exposed to humid air the moisture content of originally dry wood can rise only to the fiber-saturation point. The cell walls do not pull water into the cell cavities from the surrounding air; instead, free water soaks in as liquid by capillary forces.

**Real Dimensional Changes in Service.** Wood dimensions also vary because of temperature changes, but temperature increases are usually associated with decreasing humidity of the air, and the resulting shrinkage opposes the *thermal expansion*. Wood expands very little in the fiber direction because of thermal expansion—less than steel, aluminum, and plastics—so that in service lumber maintains a constant length. For all practical purposes wood-frame houses do not change in height, length, or width.

Transverse shrinkage does occur to some extent in wood structures, however. In buildings, where the humidity fluctuates between the conditions of very high humidity in summer and very low humidity at the peak of the heating season, the actual tangential dimension changes of dense wood can exceed 2 percent. Under outside exposure the moisture contents vary much more. The consequential swelling and shrinking impose heavy stress on glue joints and contribute to the limited life of paints and other finishes. Finish coats reduce the moisture fluctuations by exclusion of liquid water, but the finishes still allow vapor to pass and therefore do not totally prevent dimensional changes.

## WOOD-BASED PANEL PRODUCTS

For house sheathing, siding, paneling, etc., lumber boards are far from ideal. Carpenters and cabinetmakers prefer wide panels that are strong in both length and width so that the thickness can be low. Plywood, particleboard, and fiberboard meet these requirements and have found increasing use in the past decades, mostly as $4 \times 8$-foot panels. Panel consumption has increased dramatically in recent years, as discussed in Chapter 20. Among the three types of panels, plywood is the oldest and still used in the largest quantities.

### Plywood

Plywood consists of layers of wood joined with adhesive. In each panel some or all layers are *veneer*, thin sheets of wood (Figure 17.7). Other layers, particularly in the core, may consist of lumber strips, particleboard, or fiberboard. The fiber direction is roughly at right angles to that of the adjoining layer. This *crossbanding* dictates the primary desirable feature of plywood: that the properties in the direction of panel length resemble those in the direction of panel width. Thus plywood is less anisotropic than lumber.

Crossbanding affects strength in a simple way. In each direction the panel is as strong as the combined layers. Since transverse layers contribute practically no strength, plywood is in length and in width one-half as strong as lumber lengthwise. But by the same principle plywood is stronger than lumber transversely, and for this reason it does not readily split like solid wood products. Plywood properties equal those of lumber in the thickness direction only, provided that the adhesive bonds are adequate.

**Figure 17.7** Five-ply plywood opened to show crossbanding; black bands indicate fiber direction.

Crossbanding gives plywood dimensional stability. To understand this effect, consider the fiber direction of the face veneers in Figure 17.7. Both face veneers tend to swell and shrink very little, whereas the two transverse veneers, the two *crossbands*, have a very strong tendency to swell. The adhesive bonds compel all five veneers to shrink and swell by the same amount, somewhere between the small longitudinal shrinkage and the large transverse shrinkage of lumber. However, since wood is many times stiffer in the fiber direction than transversely, longitudinal shrinkage dominates and the panel shrinks and swells only very little. In the other direction of the plane, the two crossbands likewise dominate and restrain the movements. According to a rule of thumb, plywood shrinks and swells in both plane directions about twice as much as lumber does lengthwise. However, this amount of shrinkage is small, and for most practical purposes plywood is considered to be essentially dimensionally stable. Although crossbanding stabilizes in the length and width of the panel, it has practically no effect on the dimensional stability of the panel thickness.

Plywood thicknesses range from less than 1 millimeter to several centimeters, with 6 millimeters (1/4 inch) the most typical product. Great quantities of plywood are used for sheathing of wood-frame houses, cabinets, bookshelves, concrete forms, skins of flush doors, paneling, chairs, boxes, and in construction of mobile homes and trailers.

## Particleboard

Particleboard appears in many versions and under many names such as *chipboard*, *chipcore*, *shavingsboard*, and *splinterboard*. To illustrate its features, let us make a panel from toothpicks: spray adhesive on the picks, sprinkle them on a steel plate to form a mat, cover the mat with another steel plate, and press until the glue has bonded. The result is that the picks are oriented at random in the panel's plane, and none point in the thickness direction. This variable orientation amounts to a crossbanding effect similar to plywood. Common particleboard, like plywood, is a crossbanded panel of uniform strength and good dimensional stability in the plane.

The strength of particleboard is less than that of plywood of the same density; when utilized for the same purpose, the particleboard panels must be thicker, commonly 19 millimeters (3/4 inch). This is because the particles contact each other only at points and not over their whole length. Furthermore, adhesives are too expensive to coat each particle completely and must be applied sparingly.

Industry produces some boards from slivers that resemble toothpicks, but in North America most of the raw material consists of crushed planer shavings. The particles vary in size and in form ranging from wood flour to small pieces of veneer residues. Many good boards feature coarse particles in the core, flat flakes under the two surfaces, and *fines* at the surface. One type of panel is made of flat, veneer-like wood pieces and is marketed as *waferboard*.

Particleboard represents the youngest among the three types of panels and has achieved the fastest growth in past years. In some European countries that have a shortage of timber and prefer brick houses, particleboard consumption by far exceeds that of plywood and reached that of lumber in 1980 (see Chapter 20).

## Fiberboard

Fiberboard evolved from paper manufacture and may be considered as an extremely thick, crude cardboard (see Chapter 18). It consists essentially of fibers from mechanically disintegrated wood held together by interfelting, natural bonds, and a few percent of binder. Otherwise fiberboard resembles particleboard. The fibers, fiber bundles, and fiber fragments lie at random in the plane and provide crossbanding.

The boards appear as two main types; *insulating board* and *hardboard* and differ in manufacture and properties. Insulating board factories equalize the mat of loose fibers for bonding between screens and rollers, whereas hardboard factories press-bond the mat between hot plates into a dense strong panel. The dividing line between the two types of boards lies at a density of 0.5 grams per cubic centimeter. Both types are manufactured in wide ranges of properties for many specific purposes.

Insulating board has a density of at least 0.16 grams per cubic centimeter and is typically 13 millimeters (1/2 inch) thick. *Exterior* insulating board for house sheathing is black from asphalt impregnation, which is applied to impart water repellency and durability, whereas *interior finish* board for wall sheathing has a white factory finish. Grey untreated insulating board is used inside walls as sound-deadening board. *Acoustical tiles* with numerous holes or fissures for sound absorption represent one of many other versions.

Hardboard densities range from 0.5 to 1.3 grams per cubic centimeter. Best known under the brand name *Masonite*, hardboard serves for cabinet backs, drawer bottoms, and many other hidden parts. It is typically 4 to 5 millimeters (3/16 inch) thick. Some panels are smooth on both surfaces, but the majority show a *screen-back* imprint from the screen holding the fiber mat, which allows the escape of vapors during hot-pressing. When drilled or punched with holes the hardboard is used as *pegboard*, room dividers, and backing for television and radio cabinets. Hardboard with imprinted wood grain looks almost like natural wood and is much cheaper than plywood paneling. Hardboard panels can feature pressed imitations of basket weave, weathered lumber for siding, and many other special patterns.

*Medium-density hardboard*, in the density range between 0.5 and 0.8 grams per cubic centimeter, is made specifically for house siding in large patterned panels or as long one-foot-boards.

## Significance of Wood-Based Panels to Forests

The good properties of wood-based panels and their engineering for specific end uses has not only caused partial replacement of lumber in the market, but also opened entirely new markets for wood. This would suggest that the panels created an enhanced demand for timber, but a close look reveals just the opposite.

All three types of panels use timber more *efficiently*. First, they are relatively thin, roughly one-half and even less than one-fourth as thick as lumber. Second, only about one-half the timber volume is utilized in lumber production, with the other half lost as trim ends, sawdust, slabs, and edgings. Plywood is not better in this respect, but manufacture of particleboard and fiberboard results in very little wood waste. Third, particleboard and fiberboard are manufactured mainly from wood waste such as sawmill residues from lumber production, plywood mill residues, and forest residues (the small, crooked, and defective stems as well as branches that otherwise would rot away on the forest ground).

## SUMMARY AND CONCLUSION

Wood has good and bad properties for human use; it excels in features that play important roles in the life of the tree, whereas the features people do not prefer are irrelevant to the tree. Whenever one wonders how well wood may function in a certain use, the question of *"how important is this property for the tree"* gives a clue.

People appreciate wood's strength in fiber direction, the high strength/mass ratio, its resiliency, wide variety, availability, ease of working, beauty and warmth, fuel value, and electrical properties. On the negative side, wood cannot be plasticized economically, a property needed for mass production; it lacks dimensional stability, is highly variable, and must be kept dry or should be treated with preservatives to enhance endurance.

## REFERENCES

1. W. M. Harlow, *Inside Wood—Masterpiece of Nature*, American Forestry Association, Washington, D.C., 1970.
2. F. F. P. Kollmann and W. A. Côté, *Principles of Wood Science and Technology*, Vol. 1, *Solid Wood*, Springer-Verlag, Berlin, 1968.
3. H. Kubler, *Wood as Building and Hobby Material*, Wiley-Interscience, New York, 1980.
4. A. J. Panshin and C. de Zeeuw, *Textbook of Wood Technology*, Vol. 1, *Structure, Identification, Uses, and Properties of the Commercial Woods of the United States and Canada*, Fourth Edition, McGraw-Hill, New York, 1980.
5. Anon., *Wood Handbook: Wood as an Engineering Material*, U.S.D.A. Agr. Handb. 72, U.S.D.A. For. Ser., Forest Products Laboratory, U.S. Government Printing Office, Washington, D.C., 1974.
6. Anon., *Wood—Colors and Kinds*, U.S.D.A. Agr. Handb. 101, U.S.D.A. For. Ser., Forest Products Laboratory, U.S. Government Printing Office, Washington, D.C., 1956.

# 18

# CHEMISTRY AND PULPING OF WOOD

# John N. McGovern,  Bjorn F. Hrutfiord, Raymond A. Young

The importance of wood as a raw material for fiber production and for a number of important chemical commodities is of a similar magnitude to the use of wood as a solid material. In 1976, lumber accounted for about 49 percent of roundwood usage, plywood and veneer about 10 percent, and pulp products almost 38 percent. This compares to 1950 when pulpwood was only 19 percent of the roundwood production. Obviously an increasingly greater share of roundwood usage has been for pulpwood (Figure 18.1).

In this chapter we discuss the chemical nature of wood, the characteristics of pulping and papermaking processes, and the kinds of chemicals derivable from wood.

## CHEMICAL NATURE OF WOOD

As described in Chapter 3, wood is like all other plant material in that it begins with the basic photosynthetic equation in which carbon dioxide and water are combined by means of the sun's energy to produce glucose and oxygen as follows:

$$\text{light energy}$$
$$6\ CO_2 + 6H_2O \rightarrow C_6H_{12}O_6 + 6O_2$$
$$\text{carbon dioxide} + \text{water} \rightarrow \text{sugar} + \text{oxygen}$$

In order to understand the chemical nature of wood, it is necessary to trace the developments in the plant starting with glucose, a basic sugar.[1]

Glucose, as produced in equation (1), is only one of a series of sugars that occur in nature. The sugars are generally classified according to the number of carbon (C) atoms in their structure; thus, sugars with six carbons are referred to as hexoses, and those with five carbons are pentoses. The important sugars in wood structure are the hexoses (glucose, mannose, and galactose) and the pentoses (xylose and arabinose). The importance of sugars in our lives

[1]Sugars are common sweet-tasting substances, such as glucose or dextrose (grape sugar), fructose (fruit sugar), or sucrose (cane sugar), and are classed as carbohydrates because of their empirical formula, $C_y(H_2O)_x$.

has resulted in a separate field of chemistry devoted totally to sugar derivatives, termed carbohydrate chemistry.

Sugars generally do not occur as simple compounds in wood but as higher-molecular-weight structures known generally as *polymers*. The concept of a polymer can be visualized if one sugar unit is considered one link (the monomer) in a long chain (the polymer). Thus with each link an identical sugar, a chain of sugar units is formed—a polymer of sugars known commonly as polysaccharides. This is depicted schematically as follows.

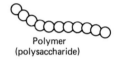

Monomer                     Polymer
(sugar)               (polysaccharide)

Polysaccharides are characterized by the number of sugars in the chain or the *degree of polymerization* (DP).

Because there are many different sugars, many different polysaccharides can be formed. A polysaccharide formed from glucose is a glucan, from xylose a xylan, from mannose a mannan, etc. If combinations of sugars occur in one polysaccharide, a mixed polymer is formed, usually named for its predominant sugars. Thus if glucose and mannose are present, the polysaccharide is a glucomannan, if arabinose and galactose are present, arabinogalactan, etc.

Polysaccharides are of paramount importance in wood and to the uses of chemically processed wood. *Cellulose* is the common term used for the glucan present in wood; it comprises about 42 percent of wood's dry weight. Cellulose is the primary cell-wall component of wood fibers and is the main structural material of wood and other plants. Paper, paperboard, and other wood-fiber products are therefore also composed mainly of cellulose. The chemical structure of the cellulose macromolecule is shown in Figure 18.2. In the plant, the DP of cellulose is approximately 14,000.

Closely associated with cellulose in the wood

**Figure 18.1** Unloading at a pulpmill in Kingsport, Tenn. (Courtesy of U.S.D.A. Forest Service.)

structure and in paper products are other polysac-charides termed *hemicelluloses*. The hemicelluloses have often been labeled as the matrix material of wood. In hardwoods the primary hemicellulose is a xylan (polymer of xylose), while in softwoods the primary hemicellulose is a glucomannan, although both of these polysaccharides occur to some extent in both types of wood. The DP of the hemicelluloses is much less than cellulose, in the range of 100 to 200.

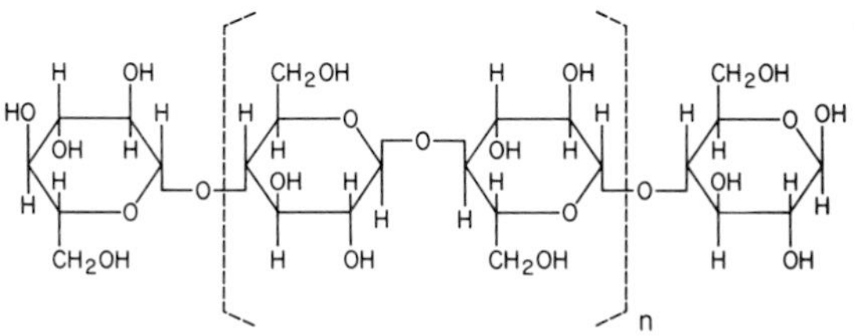

**Figure 18.2** Chemical structure of cellulose (cellulose repeat unit in brackets).

Table 18.1 gives a comparison of the chemical composition of extractive-free hardwoods and softwoods (1−3). (The nature of wood extractives is treated later under "silvichemicals.") Since cellulose and the hemicelluloses are both polysac-charides, it is obvious that the polysaccharide component of wood is by far the dominant one, comprising approximately 70 percent of both hardwoods and softwoods. Additional polysaccharides may occur as extraneous or noncell-wall components of wood; for example, the heartwood of species of larch can contain up to 25 percent (dry weight) of arabinogalactan, a water-soluble polysac-charide that occurs only in trace quantities in other wood species.

The third major component of wood shown in Table 18.1 is lignin. Although lignin is also a polymer, it has a definitely different chemical structure when compared to the polysaccharides. The monomeric units in this case are phenolic-type

**Table 18-1**

Chemical Composition and Fiber Characteristics of Extractive-Free Wood

| Component | Hardwood (Red Maple) (%) | Softwood (Balsam Fir) (%) |
|---|---|---|
| Cellulose | 44 | 42 |
| Hemicelluloses | | |
| Xylan | 25 | 9 |
| Glucomannan | 4 | 18 |
| Lignin | 25 | 29 |
| Pectin, starch | 2 | 2 |
| Average fiber length, mm | Hardwoods 0.8−1.5 | Softwoods 2.5−6 |

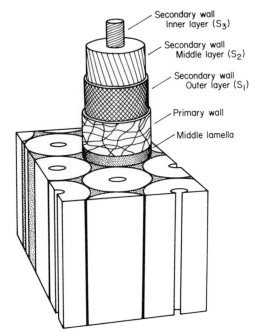

Figure 18.3 Structure of a fiber in wood showing microfibrillar orientation in different layers of the cell wall (6).

compounds, the structures of which are shown below. The phenol with one methoxyl group ($OCH_3$) attached to the ring is termed a *guaiacyl unit*, while the phenol with two methoxyl groups present is a *syringyl unit*.

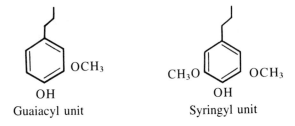

Guaiacyl unit                Syringyl unit

Lignin is an extremely complex polymer of guaiacyl units in softwood lignin and of both guaiacyl and syringyl units in hardwood lignin. In addition, hardwoods generally contain less lignin compared to softwoods, as shown in Table 18.1. The exact chemical structure of lignin is still not known after 100 years of intensive research. The space between fibers in wood is almost pure lignin and is termed the *middle lamella* in Figure 18.3 (3−5). Lignin is also considered the gluing or encrusting substance of wood and adds mechanical strength (stiffness) to the tree and to wood. Higher plants are commonly referred to as lignocellulosic

because of the typical occurrence of lignin and cellulose.

A fourth class of wood components is known as *extraneous material* and is present in wood in the amounts of 3 to 10 percent. These materials comprise a vast array of chemical compounds that are not constituents of the cell wall. Most of these compounds can be extracted with water or organic solvents or volatilized with steam and are called *extractives*. They are considered in detail subsequently. A small portion of the extraneous materials (starch, pectins, and inorganic salts) are not extractable.

The basic monomeric units such as sugars and phenols are constructed into larger molecules known as polymers; thus cellulose, hemicelluloses, and lignin have been defined. However, wood fibers are comprised mainly of cellulose; therefore it is necessary to discuss wood structure further from the polymer through the fiber.

**432**

## Structure of Wood and Wood Fibers

In the plant, the cellulose polymers are laid down uniformly (parallel), and the long-chain molecules associate strongly through secondary forces that develop between hydroxyl (OH) groups, known as *hydrogen bonds*. These bonds create very strong associations between the cellulose macromolecules. This association between the cellulose chains gives a very uniform crystalline structure known as *micelles* or *microcrystallites*, shown in Figure 18.4.

The micelles are also associated in the plant to give long threadlike structures termed *microfibrils*, also shown in Figure 18.4. The structure of the microfibrils is not completely uniform in terms of the alignment of the cellulose macromolecules. The regions of nonuniformity btween the micelles in the microfibrils are the amorphous regions; the cellulose microfibril therefore has a crystalline-amorphous character (1−5). Water molecules enter the amorphous regions and swell the microfibrils; ultimately this is the mechanism by which fibers and wood swell in moist or wet environments.

The final fiber structure is essentially layers of the microfibrils aligned in several different directions, as shown in Figure 18.3. The microfibrils that comprise the wood fiber are visible under the scanning electron microscope, which magnifies beyond the light microscope (Figure 18.5) (5).

The structure of wood can thus be simplified to

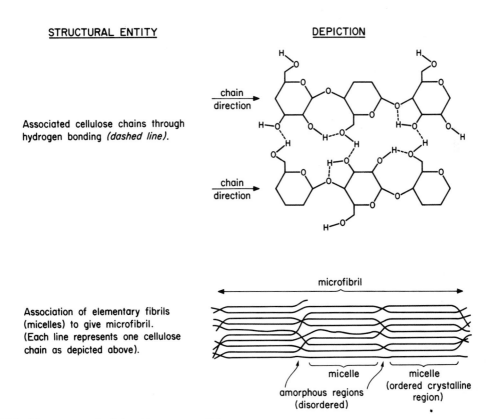

STRUCTURAL ENTITY          DEPICTION

Associated cellulose chains through hydrogen bonding *(dashed line).*

chain direction

chain direction

Association of elementary fibrils (micelles) to give microfibril. (Each line represents one cellulose chain as depicted above).

microfibril

micelle

amorphous regions (disordered)

micelle (ordered crystalline region)

**Figure 18.4** Fine structure of cellulose fibers; many cellulose chains associate to give microfibrils oriented in various directions in the cell wall.

**433**

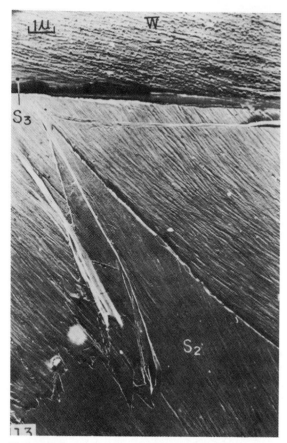

**Figure 18.5** A scanning electron micrograph of a replica of a spruce earlywood tracheid showing the microfibrillar orientation in S₂ and S₃ layers of the secondary wall (See Figure 18.3). (Courtesy of Wilfred Côté and Syracuse University Press.)

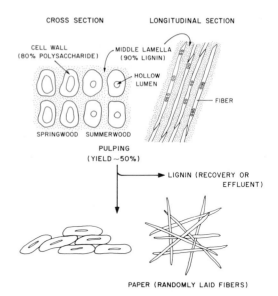

**Figure 18.6** Simplified schematic of wood structure and pulping of wood.

the schematic shown in Figure 18.6. The fibers are composed primarily of polysaccharides (80 percent), crystalline-amorphous cellulose intermixed with amorphous hemicelluloses, with some lignin present in the cell wall (4–6). Two types of cell-wall structures are shown for the fibers in Figure 18.6: the *springwood* type with a large lumen (capable of handling heavy sap flow in the spring) and the *summerwood* type with a much narrower lumen. The summerwood fibers are stiffer as a result of the thicker cell wall (1–3).

The entity holding the fibers together, the middle lamella, is almost pure lignin (90 percent), as mentioned before. In order to separate the cellulose fibers, the middle lamella lignin must be chemically removed or mechanically degraded to free the fibers for papermaking (Figure 18.7). A paper sheet can then be formed from the separated cellulose fibers by depositing them from a water slurry onto a wire screen. The water drains away, leaving a fiber mat that derives its main strength from reassociation of the fibers through many hydrogen bonds—the same type of bond that gives mechanical integrity to the fibers (Figure 18.8).

## PULPING AND PAPERMAKING HISTORY AND DEVELOPMENTS

Pulping (fiber separation) and papermaking (reforming of fibers) were invented simultaneously in an integrated system in China in A.D. 105, a development attributed to T'Sai Lun, a court official. Bast fibers from the inner bark of the mulberry tree (still employed for hand papermaking in Japan), fishnets, and hemp rags were macerated in water into a pulp

**Figure 18.7** Scanning electron micrograph of a cluster of eastern white pine elements after pulping or maceration of a small wood cube. (Courtesy of Wilfred Côté and Syracuse University Press.)

**Figure 18.8** Scanning electron micrograph of paper surface showing random arrangement of coniferous tracheid fibers in the sheet. Note the flattened or collapsed nature of the fibers in the cross section cut with a razor blade. (Courtesy of Wilfred Côté and Syracuse University Press.)

slurry that was formed into a wet mat on a bamboo frame equipped with a cloth screen to drain the water. The mat was then dried in the sun into a finished piece of paper. The invention was based on the necessity for a low-cost writing material. The development was closely guarded for many years, but spread to the West when a Chinese papermaker was captured by marauding Muslims in a battle at Samarkand in western China (now in the U.S.S.R.) in 751. Papermaking was introduced to the United States in 1690. The chronological journey of papermaking to the West is as follows.

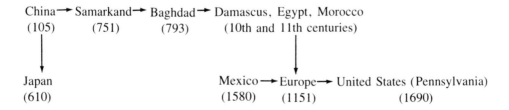

**435**

Paper was made by hand essentially as above through the advent of the Gutenberg printing press (1455) until the invention of the long, continuous wire screen machine by Louis Robért in France in 1798. The machine was subsequently developed commercially in England by the *Fourdrinier* brothers, whose name is associated with it to this day (see Figure 18.11). The pulping of rags was mechanized by the introduction of the stamp mill in 1151 and the *Hollander beater* (1680s) (see Figure 18.10). Also during the period of hand papermaking, pulp bleaching to give a whiter sheet was initiated in 1790 following the discovery of chlorine in 1774. The fiber supply was dependent on cotton and linen rags until the 1840s, when mechanical grinding of wood to make *groundwood pulp* was introduced in Germany, based on experimental work at the turn of the nineteenth century. The chemical separation of wood fibers using sodium hydroxide (caustic soda, *soda process*) was invented in 1854 in England. Another important wood-pulping process, *sulfite*, was invented in the United States in 1867 and in Sweden in 1874 using a reagent of calcium bisulfite in sulfurous acid. The present dominant pulping process for wood, the sulfate or *kraft* process (sodium hydroxide and sodium sulfide), was conceived in Germany in 1874 and introduced into the United States in 1911. The process became important following the developments of chemical recovery of the pulping reagents in the 1920s, multistage bleaching of the dark kraft pulp in the 1930s, and the "packaging revolution" starting in the 1940s. In 1979, kraft pulps accounted for almost 72 percent of the total United States pulp production, 34 million metric tons out of a total of 47.6 million metric tons.

Another important process, the *semichemical* process (part chemical and part mechanical), came about in 1925 using sodium sulfite buffered with sodium bicarbonate. In the last 50 years many combinations have been developed from these basic pulping processes. Production from the other processes in 1979 was: groundwood and thermomechanical 8.3 percent, semichemical 7.7 percent, sulfite 3.4 percent, dissolving 2.5 percent, and miscellaneous 5.9 percent. The major operations and developments in pulp and papermaking are discussed in more detail in the following sections.

## Fiber Resources

Up to about 1850, fibers for paper manufacture in the United States were chiefly derived from cotton and linen rags. After this date, however, wood was increasingly used as the fiber source for paper products. In 1978, fibers for production of pulp for making paper and paperboard were obtained from pulpwood (including chips from sawmill residues) (76 percent), recycled paper (23 percent), and nonwood plant fibers (1 percent). The total pulpwood consumption in the United States increased from about 2 to 74 million cords from 1899 to 1974. The annual rate of increase during this period was 4.9 percent. The annual rate of increase slowed to 3.4 percent between 1976 and 1979. This reduced rate is typical of the general trends in the U. S. economy.

Long-fibered softwoods were the predominant species used for pulp until 1950, amounting to 20.4 million cords or 84 percent of the total pulpwood (including chips) in that year (see Table 18.1 for fiber lengths). After 1950, however, the short-fibered hardwoods were used in increasing volumes and reached 20.9 million cords or 26 percent of the pulpwood in 1979 (74 percent for softwoods). This advance came from technological improvements and the recognition of the availability of excess volumes of hardwoods in the forests.

Roundwood has been diminishing in relative importance as a fiber source because of increasing use of chips from sawmill slabs and edgings and other forest and logging residues. In 1950 chips accounted for 6 percent of the total pulpwood volume but were almost 38 percent by 1979. In fact, roundwood pulpwood furnished only about 40 percent of the total paper fiber supply if recycled fiber is taken into account. The consumption of *recycled fiber* increased from 3.6 million metric tons in 1935 to 14.6 million metric tons in 1978, or 23 percent of the total fiber consumed for papermaking. Recycled fiber represented 25 percent of the total fiber consumption in 1950, and the figure was as high as 45 percent during World War II. The percentage decreased to about 18 percent in the early 1970s but has risen since that time with fiber-shortage situations, as well as environmental pressures to reduce municipal solid wastes in recent years. The use of recycled fibers depends on its price competitiveness with virgin fibers, regional availability, quality of paper stock (sorted waste paper), technological developments, and other use demands. Other countries deficient in wood recycle higher percentages of fiber—35 percent in Poland and Japan, for example. These countries import waste paper, while the United States is an important exporter.

## Wood Preparation

After harvesting the standing timber (Chapter 11), the tree-length or shorter logs are transported to the pulp mill for *debarking*. In a few instances, the logs are debarked and chipped in the woods for transporting in vans to the mill. A recent development involves chipping of the whole tree, including branches, with partial extraneous matter separation for transporting to the mills (see Figure 11.11). This practice increases greatly the yield of harvested material, though with reduced chip quality. Drums and ring barkers are used for debarking the rough logs. Logs are tumbled against one another in a large rotating drum causing the bark to be removed by impact and abrasion. The ring barker employs a rotating head with projections to scrape the bark loose. The debarked bolts are then slashed into suitable lengths for stone grinding or chipped for chemical, semichemical, and refiner pulping using multiknife chippers. After chipping, the mass of chips is passed over perforated screen plates to remove over- and undersize chips and transported to storage or to the pulp mill. In certain cases the chips are washed and drained to remove abrasive material such as sand and grit. The optimum dimensions for chips are approximately 16 to 25 millimeters (⅝ to 1

inch) in grain direction, 25 millimeters (1 inch) wide, and 2 to 5 millimeters (0.08 to 0.2 inch) thick.

Pulp mills normally carry a reserve supply of pulpwood and chips to offset procurement irregularities caused by adverse weather and logging conditions and other contingencies. The storage period may vary from one month for chips or roundwood in the South to considerably longer periods for pulpwood in the North. Chips produced at the pulp mill or received from sawmills or other sources tend to deteriorate in storage at a rate dependent on storage conditions such as temperature rises from chip respiration, oxidation, and action of microorganisms. These effects result in wood weight loss and sometimes poorer pulp quality. Treatments to minimize these losses are under development.

## Pulping

The pulping or fiber separation stage of the total papermaking system entails breaking the lignified fiber bonds by mechanical or chemical means or a combination, generally at elevated temperatures and pressures. The historical macerating, stamping, or beating actions applicable to cotton and linen and certain bark materials are inadequate for fiberizing wood. The historical developments of wood pulping by mechanical, chemical and semichemical methods were described previously, and the modern application of these methods is given in the following sections. The processes in use are summarized in Table 18.2 (3, 7–9).

*Mechanical pulping* is conducted on wood bolts for stone groundwood pulp and chips for *refiner* (RMP) or *thermomechanical* (TMP) refiner pulps. A stone grinder consists of a round grindstone rotating in a housing equipped with piston arrangements for feeding the bolts continuously to the grinding surface (Figure 18.9a). Refiner-type pulping is conducted on chips fed through the hub of one of two parallel disks usually vertically mounted with one or both disks rotating. The disks contain protruding bars in various designs to create the fiberizing

**Table 18-2**
Summary of Present Pulping Processes

| | Treatment | | pH | Pulp Yield[a] |
|---|---|---|---|---|
| | Mechanical | Chemical | | |
| *Mechanical processes* | | | | |
| Stone groundwood | Grindstone | None | | 93–95 |
| Refiner mechanical (RMP) | Disk refiner | None | | 93–95 |
| Thermomechanical (TMP) | Disk refiner (pressure) | Steam | | 91–93 |
| Coarse fiber | Disk refiner | Steam | | 80–90 |
| *Chemimechanical processes (CMP)* | | | | |
| Cold soda | Disk refiner | Sodium hydroxide | >9 | 80–90 |
| Alkaline sulfite | Disk refiner | Sodium sulfite (alkaline) | 9–10 | 80–90 |
| *Chemithermomechanical* | Disk refiner | Steam + sodium sulfite | 3–10 | 65–85 |
| *Semichemical processes* | | | | |
| Neutral sulfite (NSSC) | Disk refiner | Sodium sulfite + sodium carbonate | 6–8 | 70–85 |
| Green liquor nonsulfur | Disk refiner | Sodium carbonate + sodium sulfide | >10 | 65–86 |
| Nonsulfur | Disk refiner | Sodium carbonate + sodium hydroxide | 6–8 | 65–85 |
| *Chemical processes* | | | | |
| Kraft | None | Sodium hydroxide + sodium sulfide | >10 | 40–55 (55–65)[c] |
| Acid sulfite | None | Calcium[b] bisulfite + sulfur dioxide | <2 | 45–55 (55–70)[c] |
| Bisulfite | None | Magnesium (ammonium) bisulfite | 2–5 | 45–60 |
| Soda | None | Sodium hydroxide | >10 | 40–55 |
| Soda-oxygen | None | Sodium hydroxide + oxygen | >10 | 45–60 |
| Soda-additive | None | Sodium hydroxide + anthraquinone | >10 | 45–55 |
| *Dissolving pulp processes* | | | | |
| Prehydrolysis kraft | None | Steam and kraft | >10 | 35 |
| Acid sulfite | None | Acid sulfite | <2 | 35 |

[a] The pulp yield is a percent of oven-dry original wood.
[b] Calcium, magnesium, sodium, or ammonium.
[c] Yields given in parentheses are for *high yield chemical processes* which require additional mechanical defiberizing (disk refiner).

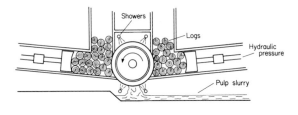

a. Stone grinder

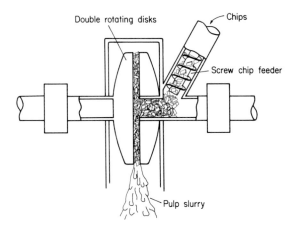

b. Double disk refiner

**Figure 18.9** Schematic of (*a*) stone grinder (wood bolts) for groundwood pulp and (*b*) disk refiner (wood chips) for refiner and thermomechanical pulp (TMP) pulps. Showers provide water for both methods.

action (Figure 18.9*b*). In the case of TMP, the chips are presteamed under pressure, and the defibering is also done under steam pressure. The addition of heat helps to soften the lignin bond, thus aiding the fiberizing and producing an improved quality pulp. The groundwood and refiner pulps are next passed through a screening system to remove coarse, unde-fibered fiber bundles; these rejects are defibered in another refiner or discarded.

The production of TMP has expanded greatly in North America and Europe since paper-grade pulp was first made in 1968—from 0.2 million metric tons in 1970 to 6 million tons in 1978. TMP requires approximately 40 percent more energy than stone pulping for the same grade of pulp (7.9 versus 5.8 megajoules per kilogram). Mechanical pulps are

made primarily from softwoods and soft hardwoods (e.g., poplars), except for insulating and hard-pressed boards (see Chapter 17), which utilize mostly mixed hardwoods. Stone grinding under pressure is being developed for energy saving and improved pulp quality.

*Chemical pulping* is conducted using chips sub-jected to the chemical reagents indicated in Table 18.2, in vessels called digesters under heat and pressure. In the kraft batch process, the digester is simply a large steel cylinder capable of holding volumes up to 200 cubic meters of chips (32–40 metric tons, dry basis) and having daily pulp capacities of 15 to 20 metric tons (dry basis) for kraft pulp, for example. Continuous vertical kraft diges-ters are also commonly used and have a capacity of up to 900 air-dry metric tons of pulp per day.

The lignin-removal and fiber-separation mechanisms involved in chemical pulping are al-kaline hydrolysis (lignin bond cleavage) in *soda pulping* and additionally the formation of soluble sulfur-containing lignin (thiolignins) in *kraft pulp-ing*. The chemical mechanisms in *sulfite pulping* also involve lignin bond hydrolysis and formation of soluble sulfur-containing lignin derivatives, termed *lignosulfonates* (10). Polysaccharide reactions are secondary to fiber separation in chemical pulping, although their retention, solution, or modification profoundly affects pulp yield and properties. Neutral sodium sulfite reactions in *neutral sulfite semichem-ical* (NSSC) pulping are also based on sulfonation for partial dissolution of lignin and a partial modifi-cation of the fiber bond to permit a clean separation of the fibers by mechanical action in disk refiner mills. The pulping chemicals are applied in water solutions (white liquor) at various concentrations and ratios of liquids to solids under different condi-tions of temperature and pressure to achieve the desired degree of delignification. An early advan-tage of sulfite pulping was its use of low-cost starting chemicals, sulfur and limestone, which could be economically discharged as used (spent) liquor directly into millstreams. For environmental and economic reasons this is not possible now, and all U.S. sulfite mills recover the chemicals or otherwise reduce the pollution load to an acceptable level. Because the kraft and soda process are based on the higher-priced sodium compounds, it was early found necessary to recover these chemicals for use. As pointed out previously, the development of a successful recovery method of the pulping chemicals from the kraft black (spent) liquor contributed greatly to the dominance of this process. Other important advantages of the kraft process are high strength of the paper products and flexibility or universality in pulping practically all wood species. Pine woods are generally resistant to sulfite pulping (1−3, 7−9).

The digesters are discharged under pressure at the end of the pulping cycle into vessels called blow-tanks, and the spent liquor is recovered through washing by displacement or diffusion. The washed pulp is then screened to remove unpulped chips, knots, and other extraneous matter, and the pulp is then ready for bleaching or papermaking. The recovered black liquor is evaporated to 60 percent total solids to become combustible and burned. Excess heat is generated and recovered as steam, as discussed later. The major kraft pulping and chemical recovery operations can be depicted as follows.

Another type of high-purity pulp, *dissolving pulp*, is produced for preparation of regenerated cellulose and cellulose derivatives. In this case, care is taken to remove essentially all the hemicelluloses and lignin for preparation of a wide variety of cellulose products. The list includes rayon fibers and cellophane (both regenerated cellulose), cellulose acetate fibers (i.e., cigarette filters), cellulose nitrate (smokeless powder) and cellulose acetate and nitrate plastics, films, and lacquers (11). Approximately 1.2 million metric tons of dissolving pulp were produced in 1979 by the processes outlined in Table 18.2.

## Recycled Fiber

The production of pulp from sorted waste paper (paper stock) involves separation of bonded fibers in the recovered paper and paperboard by mechanical action. This is done in water in a hydrapulper, which is a tub equipped with a powerful propeller rotor and auxiliary equipment to separate rags, wire, and other coarse contaminants. Treatment with sodium hydroxide to loosen ink is also often utilized in the

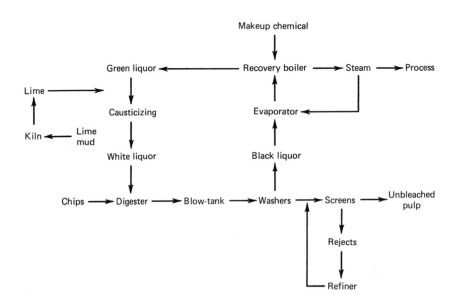

repulping operation and called *deinking*. The coarse contaminants are removed by screening and cleaning equipment, and the pulp is given an extra fiberizing and finally subjected to fine screening and cleaning (7–9). These steps are as follows.

latter is located in the cell wall and is difficult to remove. If the pulping processes themselves are carried to complete lignin removal, the polysaccharides are degraded and dissolved, and the pulp yield and quality are lowered (3, 8).

Steam, chemicals

Paper stock →Hydrapulper → Coarse screen, cleaner → Fiberizer → Screen, cleaner → Washer→ Pulp from recycled paper

## BLEACHING AND BRIGHTENING

Although pulpwood is generally light-colored and can retain its brightness in acid and neutral sulfite pulping, the dominant alkaline kraft pulping results in dark-colored pulps. This is evident in unbleached kraft packaging paper and boards. About one-half of the 37 million metric tons of chemical pulps produced in the United States in 1979 were bleached to different degrees of brightness (whiteness relative to magnesium oxide as 100 percent). Substantial tonnages of mechanical and chemimechanical pulps are also brightened to intermediate brightness levels. In *bleaching*, as discussed later, the residual colored lignin in pulp is dissolved chemically, whereas in *brightening* the lignin is altered to a lighter-colored compound without removal.

The exact nature of the colored compounds in pulps has not been totally elucidated. It is generally agreed that the lignin portion of the pulp represents the principal site of the colored or chromophoric groups. The extraneous constituents of wood can also contribute to the color of certain pulps, especially mechanical pulps. Heavy metals such as ferric (iron) and cupric (copper) ions may form colored complexes with extractives and lignin and thus deepen the color. Whatever the cause, it is necessary to treat unbleached pulps chemically for further removal of lignin and coloring matters in order to obtain the desired product brightness. The lignin content of unbleached sulfite pulp is 4 to 5 percent and that of kraft pulp 6 to 8 percent. A portion of the

Up to 1930 pulp bleaching was conducted with an oxidizing reagent, calcium hypochlorite (bleaching powder) or the sodium hypochlorite counterpart in one or two stages. This procedure was effective with sulfite pulps, kraft pulps being of secondary importance in the early 1920s. About 1930 elemental chlorine, a well-known delignifying agent, was introduced along with the necessary development of the corrosion-resistant stainless steels. Since chlorolignins are relatively insoluble in water, an alkaline extraction stage with sodium hydroxide (caustic soda) was added. This was generally followed with an oxidizing, bleaching stage using hypochlorites. It was also learned during this period that a stepwise removal of lignin in bleaching was more effective than single large dosages of chemicals. In time mills operated with as many as nine stages. This trend was changed with the application in 1946 in Scandinavia of another oxidizing agent, chlorine dioxide ($ClO_2$). This compound is much more effective and milder in action than hypochlorites. Developments in its manufacture made this bleaching agent economically available. By 1960 kraft pulps with brightness levels of 90 percent were being made with a stage sequence of chlorination (C) alkaline extraction (E), $ClO_2$ bleach (D), alkaline extraction (E), $ClO_2$ bleach (D)—the CEDED sequence. Multistage bleaching has the serious disadvantage of high capital investment for large, corrosion-resistant equipment with high maintenance costs. Extraneous matters in unbleached pulp such as bark and undefibered bundles, knot pieces, etc., are highly undesirable in bleached pulp, and their removal is an important function of bleaching. Development of centrifugal pulp cleaners has made this function less critical than it was formerly.

Another oxidizing agent, sodium or hydrogen peroxide, is used as a final stage in kraft pulp bleaching to improve brightness stability. These reagents are also used for brightening mechanical pulps. The mechanical pulps are also brightened by application of a reducing agent, sodium or zinc dithionite, formerly called hydrosulfite. Bisulfites have also been used for brightening mechanical pulps. The peroxide and dithionite treatments are usually conducted in chests or towers (3, 7−9).

A recent development has been the use of oxygen in bleaching. The oxygen is both a delignifying and oxidizing reagent and has the advantage over chlorine of producing an effluent without objectionable chlorinated compounds. There may be a somewhat lower pulp quality with oxygen bleaching.

## PAPERMAKING OPERATIONS

### Stock Preparation

The separated fibers obtained are generally not fully suitable for direct use in papermaking (except mechanical pulp). To obtain the optimum paper properties, additional treatment is necessary to obtain interfiber bonding and to impart special paper characteristics. The treatment to increase fiber bonding is called *beating* or *pulp processing*, and it is part of a subsystem called *stock preparation* (7−9).

The steps in the subsystem are illustrated as follows.

The objectives of stock preparation are as follows.

1. Develop fiber bonding potential (beating).
2. Introduce additives (size, dyes, pigments, etc.).
3. Blend different pulps and mix additives.
4. Adjust fiber length.
5. Clean and disperse fibers.

Beating, a basic step in the transition from pulp to paper, is accomplished by imparting cutting (shortening), rubbing (abrading), and crushing (bruising) actions to the pulp fibers by passing them between the rotating and stationary bars of a beater, as shown in Figure 18.10, or the disks of a refiner (Figure 18.9b). These actions serve to increase fiber flexibility and the area of contact between the wet fibers through exposure of the fibrils and microfibrils on external and internal surfaces. The close contact enables formation of hydrogen bonds between the adjacent fibers on drying, as explained earlier in this chapter.

Paper is rarely made from 100 percent pure fibers; the color is altered by dyes, the writing and printing capacity is improved by internal and surface sizing agents (rosin and starch, respectively); the wet strength is enhanced with resins; required opacity is obtained with pigments such as clay and titanium dioxide; the pH of the pulp slurry is controlled with alum (aluminum sulfate). These additives can be introduced during the beating operation or in blending chests before the paper machine.

Paper is also seldom made from 100 percent of any one kind of fiber. Furthermore, the pulp may enter the stock preparation system as a pulp slurry (slush pulp) from an adjoining pulp mill integrated

Additives

Slush pulp → Beater (refiner) → Blender → Jordan → Screen, cleaner → Papermaking

**Figure 18.10** Original Hollander beater, which is similar to modern equipment. (Photograph contributed by Netherlands Open Air Museum, Arhem, Holland.)

with the paper mill or as bales of dried pulp. It is necessary to repulp the dried pulp, usually in an arrangement of a tub equipped with a powerful, propeller-like rotor. As indicated previously, fiber morphology and surface characteristics can vary widely between and within hardwoods and softwoods, nonwood plant materials, and synthetic

fibers. These different pulps, selected to give in combination the desired paper properties, are blended in mixing chests as part of the stock-preparation system.

Another objective of stock preparation is a final, fine control of the fiber length for uniformity of paper formation, paper properties, and drainage—achieved through use of a conical refiner, the *jordan*, which is similar in action to the beater and disk refiner but more finely tuned. The last step of pulp treatment before papermaking is the cleaning and dispersing of the fibers.

## Papermaking

The cleaned and dispersed fibers are formed or combined into a fibrous mat in the papermaking stage of the system by deposition from a dilute headbox suspension (0.3 to 0.9 percent solids) onto the traveling continuous wire screen of the Fourdrinier paper machine mentioned earlier. The surplus water is removed by drainage from this wire screen aided by vacuum boxes, foils, and a vacuum "couch" roll, by pressing between rolls, and by drying on steam-heated drums or in a hot-air chamber. Other functions of the papermaking stage are to control the sheet density and surface smoothness through application of pressure and some friction in the calender (Figure 18.11). Another func-

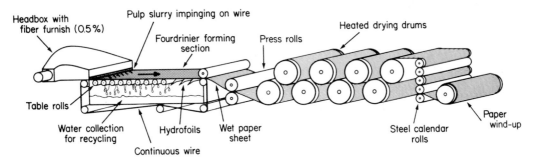

**Figure 18.11** Schematic of modern Fourdrinier paper machine.

tion is the application of a surface coating. The solids contents following each drying step are: drainage 15 percent, pressing 40 percent, and drum-drying 95 percent. The sequence of operations in papermaking can be depicted as follows.

on the sheet resulting in glossing of the sheet surface.

$$\text{Pulp} \rightarrow \text{Headbox} \rightarrow \underset{\text{wire}}{\text{Forming}} \rightarrow \underset{\text{section}}{\text{Press}} \rightarrow \underset{\text{section}}{\text{Dryer}} \rightarrow \underset{\text{section}}{\text{Size, coating}} \rightarrow \underset{\text{section}}{\text{Dryer}} \rightarrow \underset{\text{stack}}{\text{Calender}} \rightarrow \text{Reel} \rightarrow \text{Paper}$$

Recent improvements in the Fourdrinier-type of paper machine have been (1) a combination of a synthetic wire screen and a synthetic material foil to improve water drainage and (2) the development of a twin-wire forming section to improve paper surface. The latter involves impinging the dilute pulp flow from a jet into the nip of twin continuous wire screens. Fourdrinier forming sections can be fitted with a secondary headbox to permit a second sheet to be formed on the primary web (7—9). Another type of paper machine is composed of a series of vats with cylinder wire screen formers to enable a laminated sheet to be formed. This is called a *cylinder paper machine*.

## Finishing and Converting

The objectives in the final stage of the total papermaking system are to improve the paper surface, to reduce rolls and sheets in size and package for shipping, to modify paper for special properties (coat or emboss), and to convert to finished products (corrugated boxes, bags). Paper is generally coated to improve printing properties. A surface coating of a pigment (mostly kaolin or china clay, calcium carbonate, titanium dioxide) and an adhesive (starch, casein, and others) is applied to the partially dried web by brush, blade, spray, or other method and dried during papermaking (on-machine) operation or in a separate operation. The paper surface is brought to a high finish by passing through calenders or supercalenders. These are stacks of alternate steel and densified fiber rolls that create a rubbing action

## PRODUCTION/CONSUMPTION IN THE PAPER INDUSTRY

The situation regarding pulpwood and chips was discussed earlier under "Fiber Resources." The production of *wood pulp* increased nearly tenfold between 1935 and 1974, from 4.4 to 43.6 million metric tons, at an annual rate of increase of 6 percent. The 1976—1978 rate of increase was about 3 percent, in line with reduced rates in the 1980 economy to reach 45 million metric tons.

Total *paper* and *paperboard* production increased from 13.5 million metric tons in 1939 to almost 60.0 million metric tons in 1974, at an annual rate of increase of 4.4 percent. The rate dropped to 3.5 percent between 1976 and 1979, with the production of 58.9 million metric tons in the latest year. This was 58.9 percent of the world production, with North America and Europe together accounting for 81 percent of the world production in 1979. The difference in paper consumption between developed and less developed countries shows up strikingly in the per-capita consumptions of paper and paperboard in 1979 (kilograms per capita): United States 290, West Germany 205, Australia 133, U.S.S.R. 33, Egypt 7, Indonesia 3, and Afghanistan 0.3. The production and consumption of paper and paper products are treated further in Chapter 20, "The Forest Products Economy."

## ENVIRONMENTAL PROTECTION

The manufacture of pulp and paper is a chemical process industry and produces effluents, air emissions, and solid wastes that are potential environmental hazards. The industry uses large volumes of process water (25,000–300,000 gallons per metric ton of bleached paper, for example) that has become contaminated in use. Noxious fumes may emanate from chemical recovery furnaces. Solid wastes are produced in mill operations and especially in effluent-treatment systems. The general nature of these emanations, their sources, and their treatments are summarized in Table 18.3. Although a detailed discussion of the sources and control methods for pollutants from the pulp and paper industry is beyond the scope of this chapter, it is pertinent to note that considerable effort has been made by the industry to clean both air emissions and water effluents from the mills. This has been mainly because of government legislation that requires installation of pollution treatment facilities by specified dates. Compliance by industry has been good.

Most mills have historically had some type of *primary effluent treatment;* that is, the removal of settleable material, such as fiber fragments and clay, by holding the wastewaters for a period in settling tanks or ponds. By 1980, however, the mills were required to have *secondary treatment* facilities installed for handling the oxygen demand of the

effluents. This represented a considerable investment by the industry (10 to 15 percent of total mill capital cost) because it was necessary to install facilities to settle suspended solids and also to treat organic compounds that result in consumption of oxygen in the receiving lakes and streams. Such typical organic compounds from wood are sugars or sugar acids derived from degraded polysaccharides (cellulose and hemicelluloses). Removal of the compounds that create a *biological oxygen demand* (BOD) is accomplished by inoculation of the holding lagoons with microorganisms that consume the sugars and thus decrease the BOD of the mill effluent. Other specific treatment methods are shown in Table 18.3.

When the objectionable constituents of pulp and paper mill effluents are removed by treatments described, a solid waste called *sludge* is the result. Satisfactory methods for disposal or utilization of sludge have been incompletely devised up to the present.

Two *air emissions* have characterized pulp mills: the sulfur dioxide of the sulfite mill and the very odorous organic compounds (mercaptans and sulfides) of the kraft mill. These have been reduced to manageable limits in most cases by recovering the sulfur dioxide through scrubbing and absorption and

**Table 18-3**

Summary of Pollution from Pulp and Paper Mill Operations

| Type of Pollutant | Mill Operation | Treatment |
|---|---|---|
| Effluents | | |
| Suspended solids (SS) (fiber fragments, inert additives, i.e., clay) | Papermaking | Primary—clarification |
| Biochemical oxidation demand (BOD) | Pulping residuals | Secondary—biological treatment and clarification |
| Air emissions | | |
| Total reduced sulfur (TRS) | Kraft liquor recovery | Oxidation, precipitation, scrubbing, incineration |
| Particulates | Steam generation | Precipitation, scrubbing |
| Solid wastes | Effluent clarification | Landfill, utilization |

by oxidizing and incinerating the environmentally nonacceptable kraft mill emission. Investigations have been undertaken in recent years to develop alternatives to kraft pulping (12).

## SILVICHEMICALS

The term *silvichemicals* refers to wood-derived chemicals analogous to petrochemicals. These wood chemicals are produced by (1) scarification of living pine trees to yield oleoresin for naval stores (Figure 18.12), (2) extraction or mild processing of wood, (3) drastic hydrolytic and pyrolytic treatments of wood (Chapter 19), and (4) recovery as by-products of wood pulping. Leaves and needles can also be sources of certain silvichemicals. Silvichemicals are derived from the polysaccharide, lignin, and extractive components of wood.

Pitch and tar from pine-tree oleoresin (called naval stores) were essential for wooden ships in early American history. The uses of the chemicals from the oleoresin have changed, and many chemicals with a diversity of applications have been added to the list of silvichemicals. The scarification and extraction methods for obtaining naval stores have waned in recent years, and the basic turpentine and rosin necessary to meet the new product demands have been obtained as pulping by-products. The value of silvichemicals in the United States in 1977 was $528 million. This value has increased modestly at about 3 percent per year since 1963, if the negative effect of the diminishing naval stores is excluded. The three major silvichemicals, crude tall oil from kraft pulping of pines, lignosulfonates from sulfite pulping, and charcoal briquettes (see Chapter 19), have increased in production from approximately 1.0 million metric tons in 1963 to 1.7 million metric tons in 1977 for an annual rate of increase of 4.2 percent.

Attention is being directed toward wood as a renewable source of additional chemicals in view of decreasing availability of other resources for chemicals. This subject is further treated in Chapter 19, "Energy and Chemicals from Wood."

**Figure 18.12** Scarification of pine trees for collections of oleoresin. (*a*) View of stand (*b*) Close-up of tree wound. (Courtesy of University of Georgia, College of Agriculture.)

## Wood Extractives

All species of wood and other plants contain small (mostly) to large quantities of substances that are not constituents of the cell wall, as pointed out previously. The entire class is called *extraneous components*. Extractives are the largest group by far of this class. The extractives embrace a very large number of individual compounds that often influence the physical properties of wood and play an important role in its utilization. Colored and volatile constituents provide visual and olfactory aesthetic values. Certain phenolic compounds lend resistance to fungal and insect attack with resulting durability, and silica imparts resistance to the wood-destroying marine borer (1). A wide variety of extractives are utilized commercially. For example, tannins for manufacturing leather were previously extracted from chestnut wood in the United States before the blight devastation. The heartwood of the South American tree, quebracho, is now used to obtain tannins for this purpose (1, 2).

Extractives can also have a detrimental effect on the use of wood. Alkaloids and some other physiologically active materials may present health hazards. Certain phenols present in pine heartwood inhibit the calcium-base sulfite pulping process and cause pitch problems. The loss of water absorbency properties of wood pulps can also be due to extractives. Extractives from cedar wood and a number of other species can cause severe corrosion problems in the pulping operation (1).

Two broad classes of extractives occur in wood: those soluble in organic solvents, such as wood resins including turpentine, rosin, fat, and fatty acids, and those soluble in water, mostly polyphenolic material including flavanoids and tannins.

## Naval Stores

Of all the silvichemicals produced in the United States, those from the pine woods, commonly referred to as naval stores, have the largest aggregate volume and value. There are several methods of production, each of which confers specific characteristics on the two common products, turpentine and rosin.

The three common classes of naval stores—gum, wood, and sulfate—contributed 6, 27, and 67 percent, respectively, to current U.S. production in 1975 (combined rosin and turpentine). *Gum naval stores* are those produced by wounding pines and collecting the *oleoresin*, which is processed into rosin and turpentine.[2] In this country the gum naval-stores industry is based on two southern pine species, slash and longleaf, and is centered in the state of Georgia (1, 8, 13). While very important in the past, this method today accounts for only a small percentage of U.S. oleoresin production. Typically the oleoresin is collected in containers by cutting grooves in the tree so that the wound opens the resin ducts (Figure 18.12). Various means are used to stimulate oleoresin production such as repeated wounding and spraying with sulfuric acid. In recent years oleoresin production has been enhanced over 1000 times by application of the herbicide paraquat to the tree wound. The so-called *light wood* (high-oleoresin-content wood) then contains up to 40 percent resin (13).

*Wood naval stores* are obtained by organic solvent extraction of chipped or shredded aged pine stumps. The old pine stumps have lost most of the outer sapwood and are comprised primarily of the resin-rich heartwood where the extractives are mainly deposited. Turpentine, pine oil, and crude resin fractions are obtained by this method (13).

*Sulfate naval stores* are derived as by-product streams from the kraft pulping process. As pine chips are cooked in the digester to produce pulp, the volatilized gases are released and condensed to yield a sulfate turpentine. Fatty acid and resin acid fractions are also obtained from the waste (black) pulping liquor (8, 13).

**Uses of Turpentine.** Turpentine was used as a solvent in its early history, particularly as a paint solvent. Today this use is small, and the majority is used as a feedstock for manufacture of many products, including synthetic pine oil, resins, insecticides, and a variety of flavor and fragrance chemicals. Most of this synthetic activity is based on α-

[2]Oleoresin has two major components, an essential oil (turpentine) and a resin (rosin).
[3]The term *light wood* relates to the use of the high-oleoresin-content wood as torches in earlier times.

and β-pinene, the major components of the turpentine.

The major use of α-pinene is hydration to synthetic pine oil used in pine-scented disinfectants and cleaners. The chlorinated insecticides toxaphene and strobane are also made from α-pinene. β-pinene is used in the manufacture of resins of high quality for such things as bonding aids. It is also converted to basic intermediates for the manufacture of many flavor and fragrance chemicals such as lemon, lime, spearmint, peppermint, menthol, or lilac. The α-pinene is also converted to synthetic pine oil, which can be further converted to terpin hydrate, the well-known expectorant. Obviously, turpentine has become a valuable by-product of the forest and pulp and paper industry (13).

**Tall Oil.** The term *tall oil* is derived from the Swedish word *tallolja* ("pine oil"). A literal translation would have caused confusion with the essential oil known as pine oil, so the simple transliteration to tall oil has been utilized. Crude southern-pine tall oil contains 40 to 60 percent resin acids, 40 to 55 percent fatty acids, and 5 to 10 percent neutral constituents. The major portion of tall oil is fractioned into tall oil *rosin* and *fatty acids* (13).

About two-thirds of the rosin produced in the United States today comes from the tall oil produced as a by-product in the kraft pulping industry. The rosin components are freed from the wood in the digester and remain in the waste pulping (black) liquor. After the black liquor is concentrated in evaporators, the fatty and rosin acids form soaps that rise to the top as a brown mass. They are then skimmed from the surface of the liquor and acidified to produce crude tall oil. The crude tall oil is then separated from the pitch and fractionated to rosin and fatty acids (7, 8). The pitch is frequently used as fuel in the distillation plants to bring it close to energy self-sufficiency.

**Uses of Rosin.** Rosins are mostly used in a form modified by further chemical reaction. The largest use is in the sizing of paper to control water absorptivity. Rosin found considerable use at one time in laundry soap (38 percent of rosin was used for this purpose in 1938), but this use is almost negligible today. Rosin soaps are presently important as emulsifying and tackifying agents in synthetic rubber manufacture. Rosin is also used in adhesives, surface coatings, printing inks, and chewing gum. The United States produces about 37 percent of current world rosin supply, followed by the U.S.S.R., China, Portugal, and Mexico (13).

**Fatty Acids.** A valuable fraction of tall oil is the fatty acids, which are mostly the unsaturated type. These compete with fatty acids from other sources, mainly edible oil production, and enjoy wide markets as chemical intermediates and in protective coatings such as alkyd resins. A specific example of a chemical intermediate is in the formation of polyamide or nylon types of resin. In the protective coating area, the acids are condensed with other chemicals to form alkyd resins, which when used in paints form strong films by air oxidation and polymerization (13).

## Additional Pulping By-product Chemicals

**Sulfite Spent Liquor (SSL).** The spent liquor from sulfite pulping contains 55 percent calcium (or magnesium, sodium, ammonium) lignosulfonate, 30 percent sugar and related products, 8 percent residual pulping chemicals, and minor amounts of unknown material. The spent liquor is recovered from the blow pits or washers with the highest efficiency possible (95 percent) to reduce the effluent discharged from the mill.

The SSL is first stripped of sulfur dioxide for recycling as pulping chemical. The remaining SSL, which contains lignosulfonates and sugars, can then be used as a dispersant, binder, emulsifier, sequestering agent, resin extender, tanning agent, animal feed binder, well-drilling mud thinner (modified with iron and chromium salts), etc. The sugars contained in the SSL from pulping of softwoods are mostly hexoses (C6), which can be fermented to ethanol (19 million liters in 1977). The SSL from hardwood pulping also has a high content of pentoses (C5) which, together with the hexoses, furnish nutrient for torula yeast growth (7300 metric tons in 1977). The torula yeast has a high protein and vitamin B content and is marketed as a food additive and flavor enhancer. The SSL has also been tested as a wood adhesive.

**Vanillin.** The major chemical produced by degradation of lignin is vanillin, the flavoring compound. About 2,542 metric tons of by-product vanillin were produced in the United States in 1977. Vanillin is the main ingredient of synthetic vanilla flavoring, as compared to the natural product fermented from vanilla beans. The synthetic material replaced the natural product for economic and resource supply reasons. Vanillin is made from desugared softwood lignosulfonate by an alkaline oxidation using air or oxygen under pressure in the presence of catalysts followed by extraction with an organic solvent.

In addition to the widespread use of vanillin as a flavoring agent, it also has application as a chemical intermediate for important drugs. Two of these are L-DOPA used in Parkinson's disease and α-methyl DOPA for control of hypertension.

**Kraft Pulping.** The major by-product chemicals from kraft pulping, sulfate turpentine, and tall oil were described previously under extractives. The black liquor (BL) also contains saccharinic acids and lignin organic sulfide compounds. Dimethyl sulfide (DMS) is recovered from the BL by flash drying after increasing the DMS content by addition of sulfur. DMS is an odorant for natural gas and a solvent. DMS is also oxidized to give dimethyl sulfoxide (DMSO), an important solvent and a medicinal of current interest for treatment of arthritis. Small amounts of kraft lignin compounds are used as dispersants and emulsifiers.

**Semichemical Pulping.** Acetic acid is recovered from NSSC spent liquor by a special solvent process.

**Coarse-Fiber Pulping.** Pulping to produce coarse fiber for hardboard and insulating board (Table 18.2) produces a waste solution rich in hemicellulose material suitable after evaporation as a cattle food. Hardwood extracts are high in xylose, a starting material for furfural production, further described in Chapter 19.

## REFERENCES

1. B. L. Browning, ed., *The Chemistry of Wood*, Robert E. Krieger Pub. Co., Huntington, N.Y., 1975.
2. E. Sjöström, *Wood Chemistry Fundamentals and Applications*, Academic Press, New York, 1981.
3. S. A. Rydholm, *Pulping Processes*, Wiley-Interscience, New York, 1965.
4. K. Kratzl and G. Billek, eds., *Biochemistry of Wood*, Pergamon Press, London, 1959.
5. W. A. Côté, ed., *Cellular Ultrastructure of Woody Plants*, Syracuse Univ. Press, Syracuse, 1965.
6. H. Meier, *J. Polym. Sci., 51*, 11 (1961); *Pure and Appl. Chem., 5*, 37 (1962).
7. K. W. Britt, ed., *Handbook of Pulp and Paper Technology*, Second Edition, Van Nostrand Reinhold, New York, 1970.
8. J. D. Casey, ed., *Pulp and Paper, Chemistry and Chemical Technology*, Third Edition, Wiley-Interscience, New York, 1980.
9. R. G. MacDonald, ed., *Pulp and Paper Manufacture*, Vol. I—III, McGraw-Hill, New York, 1969.
10. K. V. Sarkanen and C. H. Ludwig, eds., *Lignins—Occurrence, Formation, Structure and Reactions*, Wiley-Interscience, New York, 1971.
11. R. M. Rowell and R. A. Young, *Modified Cellulosics*, Academic Press, New York, 1978.
12. R. A. Young and J. Gierer, *J. Appl. Polym. Symp., 28*, 1213 (1976).
13. D. F. Zinkel, *J. Appl. Polym. Symp.*, 28, 309 (1975).

# 19

# ENERGY AND CHEMICALS FROM WOOD

# Roger M. Rowell, George J. Hajny, Raymond A. Young

451

It is generally agreed that the era of abundant, cheap energy is over and that continuing dependence on foreign energy sources could threaten national security. However, the direction of the energy future of the United States is a controversial matter. This is because the United States can follow several different sets of alternatives or paths that involve different technological, social, economic, and political costs, risks, and benefits in the solution of its energy problems (1). In this chapter several alternatives will be briefly reviewed, and the use of biomass, particularly woody biomass, as a source of energy, liquid fuels, and chemicals will be discussed and put in proper perspective.

## INTRODUCTION

During the past 150 years the patterns of energy consumption have changed dramatically in the United States. The patterns of energy consumption relate to what form the energy takes, who uses it, and for what purposes. The forms of energy are the primary fuels specifically, wood, coal, petroleum, and natural gas, and also electricity, which converts the primary fuels or other inputs (such as hydroelectric, geothermal, and nuclear) into energy (1).

As shown in Figure 19.1, prior to 1880 wood was the primary energy form but was then gradually replaced by coal. Coal retained one-half of the energy market until after World War II with the peak period of coal usage around 1920. The petroleum share of consumption increased steadily although at a decreased rate since 1950. Today oil represents close to 50 percent of the share of primary fuels for energy. Natural gas represented only 4 percent of the energy usage in 1920 but jumped markedly in the postwar years to about 25 percent in 1960 and like oil has leveled off. The present heavy dependence on the three primary fossil fuels (petroleum, natural gas, and coal) amounts to over 90 percent of the use of all primary fuels. The remaining contribution to the nation's energy supply is from nuclear plants (4 percent), wood (direct and indirect, 2 percent), and a

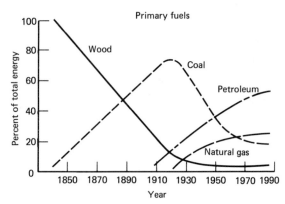

**Figure 19.1** Relative usage of primary fuels in the United States from 1850 to 1980 (1).

number of other sources such as solar, hydroelectric, geothermal, etc. (1 percent) (1).

The levels of energy consumption for the past 150 years are shown in Figure 19.2 (1). The pattern of energy consumption spells an ominous future if it continues at the current rate. In 1880 the nation consumed only about 4 quads[1] of energy. As a result of industrialization and mechanization the energy consumption increased dramatically. About 80 quads of energy are now consumed in the United States per year; at the current rate energy consumption is doubled every 10 years. Even to the casual observer several points should be obvious from the above observations (1).

1. The rate of energy consumption in the United States must be reduced considerably.

2. Energy conservation should be an important component of daily living.

3. Alternate energy sources must be explored and instituted.

The government already has a stepped-up program for energy conservation, and we can expect further emphasis on conservation measures in the

[1] A quad is a measure of energy with 1 quad $= 1 \times 10^{15}$ British thermal units (Btu).

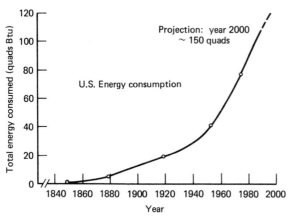

**Figure 19.2** Energy consumption in the United States from 1850 projected to the year 2000 (1) (Because of recent energy conservation measures some experts now believe the United States will use closer to 100 quads of energy in the year 2000.)

years to come. A number of energy experts feel that sufficient energy conservation can be achieved without a dramatic decrease in the American standard of living. Representatives of the Office of Technology Assessment have suggested that conservation should be regarded as substituting new technology or different procedures for energy without reducing the amenities (1). They feel we should avoid heroic measures of curtailment to reduce energy consumption quickly by the cheapest means available. Denis Hayes, the former director of the Solar Energy Research Institute, has pointed out the differences between energy conservation and curtailment with the analogy that curtailment means a cold house while conservation means a well-insulated house with an efficient heating system; or curtailment means giving up automobiles while conservation means trading in a 7-mile-per-gallon status symbol for a 40-mile-per-gallon commuter vehicle. Thus energy conservation will not necessarily require curtailment of vital services but merely will require the curtailment of energy waste (1).

Conservation alone, however, is not the solution to the energy crisis. Alternate energy sources must be explored, but what are those alternate sources and

what possible paths are available to reduce foreign imports of petroleum? A few of these alternatives are explored in the next section.

## ALTERNATE ENERGY SOURCES

According to a recent estimate by the Exxon Corporation, by the year 2000 petroleum and natural gas usage should drop from the current combined level of about 75 percent of the primary fuels to approximately 45 percent (2). The percentage of each of the alternate energy sources that will make up the difference is still a matter of speculation at this point.

The United States possesses about 31 percent of the world's known *coal reserves*, accounting for about 393 billion metric tons of coal; it is fairly certain that about 225 billion metric tons of this are recoverable. Thus coal is a very important domestic energy resource capable of considerable expansion. Many energy experts feel that the use of coal will enable the United States to bridge the gap between present dependence on foreign oil imports and the development of alternate synthetic fuels. However, the use of coal has many negative features such as environmental pollution with burning and potential unsightly strip-mining for recovery. Synthetic fuels derived from coal offer considerable promise for the future (1).

*Nuclear power* is a relatively clean energy alternative, but public pressure may limit extensive exploitation. Certainly, the near melt-down at Three Mile Island in Pennsylvania in 1979 emphasized the potential for more far-reaching disasters in the proliferation of nuclear power plants. Thus, public concern and rising capital costs could restrict expansion of nuclear energy. Another significant factor in the future use of nuclear energy is the limitation of the natural resource, uranium, necessary to fuel the plant. Recent estimates suggest that there will not be sufficient uranium past the year 2000 for nuclear power plants to make any significant energy contribution in the distant future.

There is also considerable controversy over whether or not it is feasible that *solar energy* can make a significant contribution to the energy needs of the nation in the future. Estimates for the contribution of solar energy in the year 2000 range from 1 to 20 percent (1). Clearly, a very large financial investment, on the order of billions of dollars annually, will be necessary to bring solar-generated electricity to fruition on a commercial scale. An intriguing concept in this respect is the use of solar-power satellites that would capture the sun's rays and focus them back to earth via lasers (1).

An important "passive" form of solar energy is the production of *plant biomass* through the photosynthetic process as described in Chapters 3 and 18. The net photosynthetic productivity (NPP) of the earth has been estimated at $140 \times 10^9$ metric tons of dry matter per year. Forests account for about 42 percent or 59 billion metric tons of the NPP, which is equivalent to more than the world consumption of fossil fuels (3) (Table 19.1).

In the United States the equivalent of 80 quads of energy is produced each year as total plant biomass; however, much of this is inaccessible, uneconomical to collect, or already utilized for agricultural crops or forest products. It has been estimated that there are approximately 200 quads of standing timber in the nation's forests today. Thus if an attempt were made to have wood as the sole source of energy in the United States, the country would be totally depleted of this reserve in roughly 2 years (4). Woody biomass will therefore never be a panacea to the energy crisis, but certainly a greater contribution to the overall energy diet can be supplied by this important resource.

Probably the most significant advantage of biomass is the *renewability*. The U.S. Department of Energy has estimated that the equivalent of about 8 quads of energy in the form of biomass is produced annually in the nation's forests, but roughly one-half or the equivalent of 4 quads is already harvested annually for timber and paper products (4). Much of the forest that is not harvested is inaccessible or under harvesting restrictions. Thus the major con-

tribution from woody biomass will probably be in the form of more efficient use of *residues* and *waste*.

If all types of waste are included in the scenario of biomass utilization, including urban and agricultral wastes in addition to wood wastes, then these wastes and residues represent close to 1 billion metric tons or the equivalent fuel value of approximately 15 percent of the total energy needs of the United States. Wood, in the form of logging and manufacturing residues, accounts for about 25 percent of this figure (5). In addition, roughly 50 percent of most municipal waste is comprised of waste paper, which represents the wood cellulose ultimately derived from the forest. Thus a significant energy contribution could be made by efficient utilization of waste material. The nature of wood residues and the predominant areas of accumulation are discussed in the following section.

## Available Forest Residues

The continual increase in wood usage also increases the availability of residues suitable for fuel. Greater utilization of these forest residues would provide distinct environmental advantages and decrease the cost of subsequent forest-management activities. The largest potential source of residues is the large inventory of rough, rotten, and salvable dead trees. *Rough trees* are those commercial species that do not contain at least one 3.6-meter (12-foot) sawlog, or two noncontiguous sawlogs each 2.4 meters (8 feet) or longer or are deformed. It also includes live trees of noncommercial species which are 12.7 centimeters (5 inches) at breast height or larger. *Rotten trees* are those having more than 50 percent of their volume classified as rotten. *Salvable dead* are standing or downed trees that are considered merchantable. Total inventory in these three classes is approximately 900 million metric tons, with the largest inventory of rough trees in the South, of rotten trees in the North, and of salvable dead in the Rocky Mountains (3).

Residues from logging operations result in another large inventory of potential fuel. This in-

**Table 19-1**

Land Area and Net Photosynthetic Production of Dry Matter per Year

| Geographic Division | Area (% of total) | | Net Productivity (% of total) | |
|---|---|---|---|---|
| Forests | | | | |
|   Tropical rain | 3.3 | | 21.9 | |
|   Raingreen | 1.5 | | 7.3 | |
|   Summer green | 1.4 | | 4.5 | |
|   Chaparral | 0.3 | | 0.7 | |
|   Warm temperate mixed | 1.0 | | 3.2 | |
| Boreal (Northern) | 2.4 | | 3.9 | |
|   Subtotal | | 9.8 | | 41.6 |
| Woodland | | 1.4 | | 2.7 |
| Dwarf and scrub | | | | |
|   Tundra | 1.6 | | 0.7 | |
|   Desert scrub | 3.5 | | 0.8 | |
|   Subtotal | | 5.1 | | 1.5 |
| Grassland | | | | |
|   Tropical | 2.9 | | 6.8 | |
|   Temperate | 1.8 | | 2.9 | |
|   Subtotal | | 4.7 | | 9.7 |
| Desert (extreme) | | | | |
|   Dry | 1.7 | | 0.0 | |
|   Ice | 3.0 | | 0.0 | |
|   Subtotal | | 4.7 | | 0.0 |
| Cultivated land | | 2.7 | | 5.9 |
| Freshwater | | | | |
|   Swamp and marsh | 0.4 | | 2.6 | |
|   Lake and stream | 0.4 | | 0.6 | |
|   Subtotal | | 0.8 | | 3.2 |
|   Continents total | | 29.2 | | 64.6 |
| Reefs and estuaries | | 0.4 | | 2.6 |
| Continental shelf | | 5.1 | | 6.0 |
| Open ocean | | 65.1 | | 26.7 |
| Upwelling zones | | 0.08 | | 0.1 |
|   Oceans total | | 70.8 | | 35.4 |
|   Grand total earth | | 100.0 | | 100.0 |

*Source.* J. F. Saeman, Proceedings of Institute of Gas Technology Symposium on Clean Fuels from Biomass and Waters, Orlando, Fla., 1977.

cludes wood and bark from growing stock, non-growing stock, and uncut small and undesirable trees. Logging residues account for about 100 million metric tons of wood and 18 million metric tons of bark each year. The southern United States contains the largest fraction of this residue, and a significant amount is unsalvaged hardwood material owing to stringent hardwood product requirements and limited markets for hardwood pulpwood. The distribution of logging residues in the U.S. is shown in Figure 19.3.

About 18 million metric tons of softwoods and hardwoods are removed from inventory annually in the United States by such operations as timber-stand improvement, land clearing, and changes in land use; these usually are not utilized for timber products. Residues from primary manufacturing, excluding pulp and paper, are estimated at 10 million metric tons of wood and 7 million metric tons of bark. These represent the unused by-products and residues from manufacturing lumber and wood products. The largest amount of this residue is also in the South.

It is difficult to estimate the exact amount of wood residue that is or could be available for energy generation. Some wood stock is on land with a low volume per acre, some located long distances from potential use sites, and some located in inaccessible areas where the removal costs would be prohibitive. Estimates of costs of delivered residues to plant sites vary greatly for different geographic locations. Estimates of the average costs of collecting and transporting wood residues to a central location for processing range between $13 and $31 per oven-dry metric ton. Figures from 1975 show that wood residue could compete with other fuels when its fuel

**Figure 19.3** Distribution of logging residues in the United States. (U.S.D.A. Forest Service Data)

price was below $22 per oven-dry metric ton. This cost represents the minimum price that this residue can have if used for any other purpose.

The economics of using forest residues for energy depends to a great extent on efficiency in harvesting, transportation to the point of use, pretreatments such as drying necessary to upgrade its quality, and the sustained availability to justify new capital expenditures (6). Current combustion technology is, for the most part, capable of utilizing forest residue as fuel.

Whether the woody biomass is recovered as waste and residues or directly as timber from the forest, it is important to understand the processes for utilization of this important renewable resource in energy applications.

## ENERGY AND FUELS FROM WOOD

The use of wood for energy and fuels can be conveniently divided into four major categories.

1. Direct combustion.
2. Saccharification-fermentation (SF).
3. Thermal decomposition.
4. Thermochemical liquefaction.

Each of these methods is discussed in more detail in the following sections.

### Direct Combustion

The concept of using wood as a source of energy by direct combustion dates back to the very beginning of human existence. As soon as early people learned to use fire, wood became the major source of energy. It is important to note that even now approximately one-half of all the wood harvested worldwide is used for fuel by direct combustion (see Chapter 20). Thus direct combustion is probably the most important method for deriving energy from wood.

Wood has certain *advantages* over fossil fuels. The most important, of course, is that it is a renewable resource; but it also has a low ash content

that is easily and usefully disposed of on land as mineral constituents essential for plant growth. The sulfur content of wood is low, usually less than 0.1 percent, so air pollution from this source is negligible, although particulates may cause a serious problem (7). Generally, wood fuel is used close to where it is grown; thus the need for energy in long distance transport is reduced. The use of fossil fuels unlocks the carbon that has been stored in them for ages and increases the carbon dioxide content of the atmosphere. In contrast, wood fuel releases the same amount of carbon dioxide that the forest has recently fixed.

Wood does have *disadvantages* as a fuel. It is a bulky material, and, in contrast to other fuels, it has a low heat of combustion. Bituminous coal, fuel oil, and natural gas have heats of combustion of 28,600, 39,600, and 40,700 Btu per kilogram, respectively, while dry wood of most species has a heat of combustion of about 18,920 Btu per kilogram. When harvested, green wood has a high moisture content (50 percent), and the heat of vaporization of this water in the furnace further reduces the heat recoverable from a given weight of wood to 9350 Btu per kilogram. Most manufacturers of combustion equipment recommend burning wood at below 15 percent moisture. The high moisture content also adds to shipping costs. The capital cost of a wood-burning system is considerably higher than a comparable gas-burning installation because of the need for storage and handling facilities. In addition, labor requirements for operating the equipment are greater. The heat values of important woods grown in the United States are shown in Table 17.1.

The Wisconsin Department of Natural Resources recently completed an evaluation of the costs for heating with wood compared to fossil fuels. An analysis was made for both industrial fuel uses in the form of chips (Table 19.2) and for residential space heating with cut logs (Tables 19.3 and 19.4). Based on this evaluation, industrial fuel costs could be reduced approximately sixfold and the residential heating costs reduced threefold by substituting wood for fuel oil. With the rising costs of foreign oil, this

**Table 19-2**
Present Cost of Wood Chips[a] and Comparative Fossil Fuel Costs[b]

| | |
|---|---|
| Delivered cost of green wood chips, per ton | $12.00 |
| Energy value, million Btu | 8.5 |
| Cost per million Btu | $2.01 |
| Delivered cost of oven-dry wood chips, per ton | $16.00 |
| Energy value, million Btu | 17 |
| Cost per million Btu | $1.34 |
| Cost of #1 and #2 fuel oil, per barrel | $42.00 |
| Energy value, million Btu | 5.88 |
| Cost per million Btu | $8.40 |
| Cost of natural gas, per 100 ft³ | $3.00 |
| Energy value, million Btu | 1 |
| Cost per million Btu | $3.89 |
| Cost of coal, per ton | $55.00 |
| Energy value, million Btu | 26 |
| Cost per million Btu | $2.49 |

*Source.* Wisconsin Dept. of National Resources Data, Madison, 1980.
[a] Chips are the most likely form of wood energy to be used by industry in the foreseeable future. The technology already exists to produce and deliver wood chips and will be improved in the future.
[b] Average boiler efficiencies are accounted for in costs: 65 percent for wood, 85 percent for oil, 77 percent for natural gas and 85 percent for coal. Cost per million Btu indicates comparative heating costs for "usable" heat.

**Table 19-3**
Comparative Present Costs of Wood, Oil, and Natural Gas for Residential Space Heating

| Type of Fuel | Quantity | Cost | Usable Btu | Costs Per Million Usable Btu |
|---|---|---|---|---|
| Wood—delivered[a] stove length & air-dry | 1 std. cord | $100 | 17,000,000 | $5.88 |
| Wood—delivered in 8-ft length (pulpwood size)[b] | 1 std. cord | $40 | 17,000,000 | $2.35 |
| #1 and #2 fuel oil[c] | 1 gallon | $1 | 119,000 | $8.40 |
| Natural gas[d] | 1000 ft³ | $3 | 770,000 | $3.89 |

*Source.* Wisconsin Dept. of National Resources Data, Madison, 1980.
[a] One standard cord of air-dry mixed hardwoods contains 34 million gross Btu or 17 million net or "usable" Btu if thermal efficiency is 50 percent.
[b] Assumed wood would be fired air-dry, even though price reflects green wood.
[c] Assumed a thermal efficiency of 85 percent; also, comparing usable Btu, 123 gallons equals 1 standard cord.
[d] Assumed a thermal efficiency of 77 percent.

**Table 19-4**

Comparative Heating Costs for an Average Wisconsin Household[a]

| | Oil | Wood[b] | Savings with Wood |
|---|---|---|---|
| Situation A | $1000 | $813[c] (@ $100/cord) | $187 |
| Situation B | $1000 | $325[d] (@ $40/cord) | $675 |
| | Natural Gas | Wood | Savings (Loss) with Wood |
| Situation A | $420 | $813 (@ $100/cord) | ($393) |
| Situation B | $420 | $325 (@ $40/cord) | $95 |

*Source.* Wisconsin Dept. of National Resources Data, Madison, 1980.

[a] Costs are for heating season of 1979–1980; average household used $140 \times 10$ Btu, equivalent to 1000 gallons of fuel oil at $1.00 per gallon, or 140,000 cubic feet of natural gas at $3.00 per 1,000 cubic feet, or 8.13 standard cords of air-dry wood.

[b] Wood was fired as "air-dry" with an average thermal efficiency of 50 percent.

[c] Price of wood was $100 per standard cord (delivered, stove-wood length, air-dry).

[d] Price of wood was $40 per standard cord (delivered in 8-foot or pulpwood lengths).

cost difference will probably be even greater in the future.

## Saccharification-Fermentation

The saccharification-fermentation (SF) method is based on the breakdown or hydrolysis of the polysaccharides in wood to the constituent monomeric sugars (see Chapter 18). The six-carbon or hexose sugars (glucose, galactose, and mannose) are then fermentable to *ethyl alcohol* (ethanol or grain alcohol, $C_2H_5OH$) by yeast fermentation in much the same way that ethanol is produced from grains or fruits. Obviously the concept is not a new one; the polysaccharide character of wood has been known for over 100 years. The limitations to the use of wood for ethanol production have been primarily the difficulty in separating and hydrolyzing the crystalline cellulose component in wood. Much of the technology was developed during World War II when ethanol production from wood was anticipated in this country to supplement industrial alcohol supplies. The only ethanol-from-wood operation in this country was built as a pilot plant in Springfield, Ore., but was closed shortly after the war and never attained commercial production. Synthetic ethanol is easily produced from petroleum feedstock by direct catalytic hydration of ethylene.

Interest in producing alcohols from wood in the United States was revitalized by the dramatic increase in petroleum prices and the push to decrease oil imports by substituting gasohol (one part alcohol in ten parts gasoline) for 100 percent gasoline at the gas pumps. Both ethanol and methanol can be used in gasohol blends. A number of methods can be used for production of ethanol from wood; these are briefly reviewed.

**Ethanol from Wood.** During World War II, the *Scholler process* (developed in Germany) was used in Europe for ethanol production. The method employed dilute sulfuric acid for hydrolysis of the wood polysaccharides in a batch process. This method yielded about 170 liters of 190-proof ethanol per oven-dry metric ton (50 gallons per ton oven-dry) of wood chips. Later, the *Madison process* was developed at the U.S.D.A. Forest Products Laboratory to give an improved yield of about 222 liters per metric ton (65 gallons per oven-dry ton). In the Madison process wood waste in the form of sawdust, shavings, or chips is loaded into a large steel container called the digester. When filled, steam is admitted to the digester to bring the charge up to a temperature of about 140°C. Dilute sulfuric acid (0.5 percent) at 140°C is then pumped into the digester until the wood is completely covered. Dilute acid is then continuously pumped into the digester, and the hydrolysis solution is continuously pumped out. This *percolation process* as opposed to the *batch process* (Scholler) is the main innovation provided by the U.S.D.A. Forest Products Laboratory. The total hydrolysis time is about 3 to 4 hours; at the end, the lignin-rich residue is discharged and recovered for its fuel value (8).

The liquor from the hydrolysis reaction is neutralized, blended with yeast, and passed to fermentation tanks. The fermentation is carried out by a strain of *Saccharomyces cerevisiae* yeast. Following fermentation, the ethanol is stripped from the dilute solution and the remaining solution is concentrated. From this solution, the five-carbon or pentose sugars (xylose and arabinose) are separated and concentrated to a 65-percent solution and sold as feed supplement or used for the production of furfural, an additional chemical derivable from wood (discussed in a later section). A number of modifications of the original Madison process have been proposed in recent years.

Saccharification of wood polysaccharides to sugars can be accomplished by enzymatic techniques instead of acid hydrolysis. The U.S. Army Natick Laboratories have developed a method for conversion of cellulose to glucose with a cellulose enzyme from an active strain of the fungus *Trichoderma viride*. However, extensive pretreatment of wood is necessary before sufficient enzymatic hydrolysis will take place (9).

Enzymatic methods show the biggest promise for conversion of waste paper from municipal waste into glucose for ethanol production. Because paper is primarily composed of wood cellulose fibers, the enzyme inhibition due to lack of accessibility with whole wood is partially alleviated. As mentioned previously, waste paper can represent up to 50 percent of typical municipal waste. Currently the separated paper from the waste is burned for fuel value.

The Gulf Oil Company developed a method called simultaneous saccharification and fermentation (SSF) for enzymatic conversion of waste paper to ethanol (10). In this process the cellulose is enzymatically hydrolyzed and the glucose is yeast fermented in one operation. This modification, along with improved enzyme production and performance, has made the enzymatic technique more economically viable for conversion of waste paper to ethanol. Research is currently active on this method of alcohol production.

## Thermal Decomposition

A number of terms are used interchangeably for thermal decomposition of wood and generally refer to similar processing methods: *carbonization, pyrolysis, gasification, wood distillation, destructive distillation,* and *dry distillation*. All result in the thermal breakdown of the wood polymers to smaller molecules in the form of char, a condensible liquid or tar and gaseous products. A liquid fuel derivable from wood by this method is *methyl alcohol* (methanol or wood alcohol, $CH_3OH$). A wide variety of other chemicals are also derivable from wood by thermal decomposition, a method with a long history of applications.

During World War II in Germany, automobiles were fueled by the gases produced from thermal decomposition of wood, and research is active today on more efficient gasification of wood. Destructive distillation has been used throughout most recorded history to obtain turpentine from pinewood, as discussed in Chapter 18. Some additional chemicals derivable from thermal decomposition of wood will be discussed in this section.

**Methanol.** Similar to the situation with ethanol, the concept of producing methanol from wood is not new. Methanol obtained from the destructive distillation of wood was the only commercial source until the 1920s. The yield of methanol from wood by this method is low, only about 1 to 2 percent or 20 liters per metric ton (6 gallons per ton) for hardwoods and about one-half that for softwoods. With the introduction of natural gas technology, the industry gradually switched to a synthetic methanol formed from a synthesis gas (syngas)[2] produced from reformed natural gas.

About 50 percent of the methanol produced goes into production of formaldehyde; the remaining half is used for solvents (10 percent), acrylics (10 percent), insecticides (10 percent), fungicides (10 percent), textile fibers (5 percent), and miscellaneous uses (2 percent); about 3 percent is exported (11). The large use of methanol for production of formaldehyde and the concomitant large use of formaldehyde in plywood adhesives links the demand for methanol directly to fluctuations in home construction. Large volumes of plywood are used for building homes.

Methanol is produced from syngas with the use of catalysts at high pressure. Coal, lignite, or wood waste can also be utilized to produce methanol by this method. For any solid carbonaceous material to be converted to syngas, it is first necessary to burn or oxidize partially the material to produce a crude gas consisting of $H_2$, CO, and $CO_2$. If air is used to oxidize or burn the material, the crude gas will contain about 46 percent nitrogen, which must be removed. Thus, reforming the gasification products obtained at high temperatures is a second method for production of methanol from wood. This is in contrast to the older method (destructive distillation) which directly yields small quantities of methanol (lower temperatures) as previously described.

Several types of *gasifiers* have been developed for the partial oxidation of wood, wood waste, and garbage. These are designed to operate at atmospheric pressure, in contrast to coal gasifiers, which can operate at pressures up to 400 pounds per square inch gage (psig). Also, about 2 percent of the wood (dry basis) is converted to an oil-tar fraction. A comparison of the crude gas from two types of gasifiers is shown in Table 19.5.

Although the feed material for the UCC Purox

**Table 19-5**

Comparative Crude Gas Compositions, Volume (%)

| Raw Gas (Dry Basis) | Moore-Canada (Wood Waste) | UCC Purox (Garbage) |
|---|---|---|
| Hydrogen | 18.0 | 26.0 |
| Carbon monoxide | 22.8 | 40.0 |
| Carbon dioxide | 9.2 | 23.0 |
| Methane | 2.5 | 5.0 |
| Hydrocarbon | 0.9 | 5.0 |
| Oxygen | 0.5 | 0.5 |
| Nitrogen | 45.8 | 0.5 |
| | 100.0 | 100.0 |

*Source.* "Chemicals from Wood Waste," Katzen Report, U.S.D.A. For. Serv., Forest Products Laboratory, 1975.

reactor is municipal solid waste, it is expected that the crude gas composition will be essentially the same for wood waste because municipal solid waste has been found to have practically the same composition with regard to carbon, hydrogen, and oxygen.

Because of the simplicity of the conversion of natural gas to methanol, investment cost for such a plant is about one-third that of a comparable wood waste facility. Conversion efficiency of natural gas to methanol (91 percent) is significantly greater than that of wood waste (51 percent). It takes 150 cubic feet of natural gas (containing more than 95 percent methane) or 22 kilograms (4.9 pounds) to make 3.8 liters (1 gallon) of methanol. Conversion of coal to methanol, while considerably more efficient than that of waste wood (coal, 85 percent), involves more processing facilities because of the greater amount of ash and sulfur. Coal conversion to syngas is more efficient because it has a higher carbon content and less oxygen than wood. It is technically feasible but not yet economically attractive to produce methanol from wood residues. The yield of methanol from wood is about 38 percent or 342 liters per metric ton (100 gallons per oven-dry ton). This yield is based on all process energy required coming from the wood residues. At a wood residue cost of $13.50 per

[2]Synthesis gas or syngas is a gas produced synthetically by combining two parts hydrogen ($H_2$) with one part carbon monoxide (CO).

metric ton ($15 per ton), the selling price of methanol is estimated at $0.20 per liter ($0.77 per gallon); at $30.60 per metric ton ($34 per ton), selling price is $0.25 per liter ($0.96 per gal.). The 1979 selling price of methanol was $0.12 per liter ($0.44 per gallon) (12).

**Charcoal and Other Chemicals.** Production of charcoal and tars by destructive distillation is the oldest of all chemical wood-processing methods. Charcoal was probably first discovered when the black material left over from a previous fire burned with intense heat and little smoke and flame. For centuries, charcoal has been used in braziers for heating purposes. Destructive distillation of hardwoods has been carried out with charcoal being the product sought and volatiles being by-products; with softwoods (pines), volatiles were the principal products (naval stores), with charcoal considered a by-product.

In the United States, charcoal production began in the early colonial days. During this period, principal uses of charcoal were as a fuel in blast furnaces for production of pig iron and as an ingredient of gunpowder. Charcoal needed by the iron industry required that it have a high crushing strength, and therefore it was made from dense hardwoods such as maple, birch, oak, and hickory. A softer charcoal was preferred for making gunpowder and thus was produced from willow and basswood. The first successful blast furnace was built in Saugus, Mass., in 1645. Other furnaces were started in close proximity to iron-ore deposits. These early furnaces were small, usually producing only 1 to 3 metric tons of pig iron per day. In the late 1880s, wood charcoal lost its metallurgical market to coke, which was better suited to the demands of the larger furnaces then being built.

In 1812, the additional collection by condensation of the volatile substances from hardwood carbonization began. Products were now charcoal, crude pyroligneous acid, and noncondensible gases. The *pyroligneous acid* was refined to produce methanol, acetate of lime, which in turn was used to make

either acetic acid or acetone and tar. The *noncondensible gases* in a normal wood distillation consisted of about 50 percent carbon dioxide, 30 percent carbon monoxide, 10 percent methane, 3 percent heavier hydrocarbons, and 3 percent hydrogen (13). Table 19.6 gives the yields of products from an industrial operation. The tars and noncondensible gases were usually used as fuel. In the late 1800s and until the 1920s, destructive distillation of hardwoods was an important source of industrial acetic acid, methanol, and acetone. This market was lost when these materials were made synthetically from petroleum. In 1920, there were approximately 100 plants recovering these products from hardwood distillation; the last of these plants ceased operation in 1969.

In the early 1900s, charcoal from by-product recovery plants was usually used for cooking and heating in low-income areas and was known as a "poor man's fuel." Beginning in about 1950, there was an upturn in demand for charcoal for recreational use. In this era of suburban living, the use of charcoal briquettes for cookouts represents a significant market. The charcoal briquette can now be

**Table 19-6**

Yield of Products from Destructive Distillation of 1 Ton of Dry Hardwood

| Product | Quantity |
| --- | --- |
| Charcoal | 270 kg (600 lb) |
| Noncondensible gas[a] | 150 m³ (5000 ft³) |
| Soluble tar | 83.6 $l$ (22 gal) |
| Pitch | 29.7 kg (66 lb) |
| Creosote oil | 12.5 $l$ (3.3 gal) |
| Methanol | 11.8 $l$ (3.1 gal) |
| Acetone | 2.7 $l$ (0.7 gal) |
| Allyl alcohol | 0.2 $l$ (0.05 gal) |
| Ketones | 0.8 $l$ (0.2 gal) |
| Methyl acetate | 3.8 $l$ (1.0 gal) |
| Acetic acid | 45.5 kg (101 lb) |

*Source.* U.S.D.A. Forest Service Data.
[a] Composition in order of highest to lowest $CO_2$, $CO$, $CH_4$, $H_2$, others.

considered a luxury fuel, since it is too expensive for heating.

Basic techniques for producing charcoal have not changed over the years, although the equipment has. Charcoal is produced when wood is burned under conditions in which the supply of oxygen is severely limited (14). *Carbonization* is a term that aptly describes the thermal decomposition of wood for this application. Decomposition of carbon compounds takes place as the temperature rises, leading to a solid residue that is richer in carbon than the original material. Wood has a carbon content of about 50 percent, while charcoal of a quality suitable for general market acceptance will be analyzed as follows: fixed carbon 74 to 81 percent, volatiles 18 to 23 percent, moisture 2 to 4 percent, and ash 1 to 4 percent. Charcoal with a volatile content over 24 percent will cause smoking and is undesirable for recreational uses.

Earthen "pit kilns" were originally used to produce charcoal. A circular mound-shaped pile of wood (15 to 45 cords) was built up with an open core 30 to 60 centimeters (1 to 2 feet) in diameter to serve as a flue. The entire surface of the pile, except for the top flue opening and several small openings around the bottom periphery, was then covered with dirt or sod sufficiently thick to exclude air. The mound was then allowed to "coal" for 20 to 30 days to give the final product.

In the second half of the nineteenth century, brick or masonry "beehive" kilns came into widespread use (Figure 19.4). The capacity of many of these kilns was from 50 to 90 cords, and operation was essentially the same as for the pit kilns. Many other types of kilns have come into use from time to time. Small portable sheet-metal kilns of 1 to 2 cords have been widely used, as have rectangular masonry block kilns of various designs. These were predominantly used by farmers and small woodlot owners.

Large-scale production of charcoal was done by distilling the wood in steel buggies in long horizontal ovens. The buggies rode on steel rails that carried the cars in line from predriers to the ovens and then to coolers. Charcoal was produced by this method in a matter of 24 hours. The latest types of charcoal-producing equipment are designed for continuous operation and make use of residues instead of roundwood (15). An example is the *Herreshoff multiple hearth furnace* in which several hearths or burning chambers are stacked on top of one another, the number depending on capacity. Production in this type of furnace is from 1 to 2½ metric tons of charcoal per hour.

## Thermochemical Liquefaction

Although a reasonable amount of research effort has been expended on thermochemical liquefaction of wood, extensive commercialization of this process is not anticipated in the near future. The basis of the method is a high-pressure and high-temperature treatment of wood chips in the presence of hydrogen gas or syngas to produce an oil instead of a gas. The low-grade oil produced could potentially be substituted for some present petroleum uses.

An oil of a heating value of about 35,200 Btu per kilogram can be obtained by reaction of wood waste for 1 hour with syngas, a catalyst, a temperature of 750°F, and a pressure of 5000 psi. The feasibility of the process has been tested in a pilot plant in Albany, Ore., based on laboratory work conducted at the U.S. Bureau of Mines. So far, it has been determined that a barrel of oil equivalent to No. 6 bunker fuel can be produced from about 405 kilogram of wood chips (16).

A similar process was developed in Japan in the 1950s specifically to degrade lignin. Named the *Noguchi process,* it was thought to hold promise for production of phenols from lignin. By 1955, the Japanese investigators had discovered superior catalysts that converted a substantial portion of the lignin into a relatively few phenols. The Crown-Zellerbach Corporation subsequently obtained an option on the process and initiated their own trials. Despite several improvements they were able to make, the process did not prove profitable at the time. However, the company was routinely able to obtain a yield of 55 percent (and up to 65 percent) of

**Figure 19.4** ''Beehive'' type kiln for making pine tar and charcoal depicted on medicine revenue stamp of the 1870s.

distillable products. The major drawback was the inability to separate cleanly even the few different phenols remaining after the reactions (17).

## Furfural from Wood

An additional, potentially important chemical derivable from wood as a result of hydrolytic (acid) treatment is furfural. Furfural is derived from the hemicellulose fraction (see Chapter 18) of wood—specifically from the five-carbon or pentose sugars (primarily xylose). The pentose sugars are not yeast fermentable by standard methods to ethanol but can be treated with acid, which causes dehydration and yields furfural.

$$\text{Hemicellulose} \xrightarrow{\text{Acid}} \text{Pentosans} \xrightarrow{\text{Acid}} \text{Furfural} \xrightarrow{\text{Reduce}} \text{Furfuryl alcohol}$$

Most furfural is produced from corncobs and oat and rice hulls, primarily by the Quaker Oats Company. The product is used in the chemical industry as a solvent and in wood rosin refining. A large amount of furfural is further treated to give furfuryl alcohol. The furfuryl alcohol is added to urea-formaldehyde resins in applications for adhesives and foundry core binders.

## INDUSTRIAL USE OF ENERGY

In 1972 when the total U.S. energy consumption was 64.6 quads, the energy use by categories was divided as shown in Figure 19.5. Of the industrial sector, the largest single user was primary metals (21.2 percent), followed by chemical and allied products (19.7 percent), petroleum and related products (11.3 percent), and forest industries (5.8 percent). Although the forest-industry portion represents only 2 percent of the total national energy, it is a major identifiable segment of energy usage (18).

As described earlier, if the total annual growth of

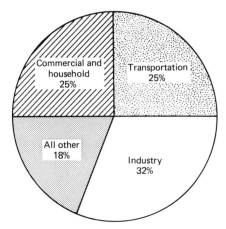

**Figure 19.5** Distribution of energy consumption by user.

paper industry and is about 1/3 as energy intensive. At present, it is estimated that plywood manufacturing is approximately 50 percent energy self-sufficient.

Attainment of energy self-sufficiency in the pulp and paper industry would have the largest impact on reducing purchased energy within the forest industries. A detailed examination of this segment has shown that it is possible to increase the present 40 percent self-sufficiency significantly. Most of the additional energy would be supplied through whole-tree chipping (see Chapter 11) and efficient use of residues (18).

## ENERGY PLANTATIONS

Concern over future supplies and cost of fossil fuels has stimulated interest in growing wood for use solely as an energy source. The average yield on commercial forestland is only about 2.3 metric tons per hectare per year. However, the definition of commercial forestland includes, for statistical purposes, much land, such as mountain slopes, that is not very productive, so that the national norm might be closer to 3.4 to 6.8 metric tons per hectare if these marginal lands were excluded (18). Advocates of the use of forest fuels for production of electricity maintain that by short-rotation forestry, yields of 7.9 to 33.8 metric tons per hectare can now be achieved and that by selection and genetic improvement, potential yields can be 45 to 67 metric tons per hectare (Figure 19.6). A further discussion of the applications of forest genetics is given in Chapter 5. Short-rotation forestry has a number of names, including *energy plantations, biomass farms, minirotation forestry, puckerbush, sycamore silage,* and *coppicing.*

Management of an energy plantation would more closely resemble a farming operation than conventional forestry. Selected tree species with rapid early growth characteristics for the climate and soil type would be planted at very close spacing and harvested at appropriate times, perhaps at 5- to 8-year intervals. Harvesting would be done mechanically, simi-

timber on all commercial forestlands were used for energy, it would supply only a small percentage of our total annual national energy needs. If, however, residues and unused inventories from these lands were used by the forest industries for energy, it is possible that this industrial segment could become energy self-sufficient. The forest industries already have the land, equipment, and knowledge of handling to use wood in their plants and many already do utilize their residues to a certain extent.

Of the three largest users of purchased energy in the forest industries, the pulp and paper sector accounts for 92 percent of the energy purchased. The pulp and paper industry has already achieved 40 percent *energy self-sufficiency* as a result of continuing improvements in recent years by consuming spent pulping liquors and burning some hogged wood and bark. Less detailed information is available from sawmilling operations, but it is estimated that energy self-sufficiency may range from 20 to 40 percent. From these estimates, it may be inferred that the pulp and paper segment uses about fifteen times as much energy to produce a comparable tonnage of product; hence the sawmill operations are much less energy intensive and are much smaller users of total energy. Plywood manufacturing purchases about 1/50 as much energy as the pulp and

**Figure 19.6** Cutting of eastern cottonwood about 16 feet tall in 6 months growing in Mississippi. (Courtesy of U.S.D.A. Forest Service.)

lar to corn or hay crops, and regeneration would be by *vegetative reproduction* such as *coppicing* (Figure 19.7) (see Chapter 3 and 9). Thus planting of seedlings need only be done at the start of the operation. For maximum biomass yields, intensive crop management with fertilization, weed control, and (possibly) irrigation would be necessary.

Selection of tree species for energy plantations differs from that in conventional forestry. Forest species are now selected based on desirable wood properties such as strength, freedom from defects, color, fiber length, etc. For energy production, the most important factor is the ability to grow rapidly with no regard for strength properties or shape of stem. The usual criteria for selection of species for biomass production are rapid juvenile growth, ease of establishment and regeneration, freedom from

major insect and fungal pests, climate, and site qualities. Species generally considered as having high potential for energy plantations are sycamore, hybrid poplars, red alder, eucalyptus, and loblolly pine (Figure 19.8). Table 19.7 shows yields achieved from experimental work as reported in the literature as well as estimates of yields that can now be achieved by intensive management (19). The national average yield from intensive silviculture can be approximately 17.9 dry metric tons per hectare, and in the near future it could be 33.6 metric tons.

Because the biomass is grown for its energy content, it is of interest to compare energy consumed (except for solar energy) to energy output. Energy input consists of fuel used in harvesting, loading, hauling, irrigation, manufacture of fertilizers and pesticides, and their transport (19). From this analysis, energy from the biomass is from ten to fifteen times the primary energy consumed. Cost of production of biomass under intensive management is estimated at from $1.20 to $2.00 per million Btu, which is generally competitive with fuel-oil prices.

Many of our fossil fuels are used to produce electricity, so we can determine whether *land requirements* for an energy plantation to fuel a moderately sized electric utility plant would be at all practical (7, 20). Assuming that dry wood and bark have an energy content of 16 million Btu per ton, that it would be burned green at an energy efficiency of 68 percent, and that the plant would operate at 60 percent of rated capacity, a 150-megawatt steam generator would have an overall efficiency of 27 percent. On this basis, approximately 558,000 metric tons of dry wood would be required per year to power the plant. Land area required depends on productivity; at 11.3 metric tons per hectare per year, the area required is about 504 square kilometers (194 square miles). A 150-megawatt plant would supply electricity needs for a community of 150,000.

Wood requirements of a 150-ton megawatt plant are about 1530 metric tons per day. A pulp mill rated at 900 metric tons of pulp per day at a 50

**Figure 19.7** Circle of basswood trunks formed by vegetative reproduction (Courtesy of University of Wisconsin Press.)

**Table 19-7**

Annual Productivity, Actual and Estimated, of Short-Rotation Species

| Species | Productivity (metric tons per hectare per year) | |
| --- | --- | --- |
| | Literature (20) | Projected (19) |
| Sycamore | 2.3–13.3 | 13.5 |
| Eucalyptus | 3.8–8.3 | 27.0 |
| Hybrid poplar | 1.1–11.0 | 22.5 |
| Black cottonwood | 2.3–14.2 | 13.5 |
| Red alder | 2.9–36.0 | 20.3 |
| Loblolly pine | 2.3–6.8 | 11.3 |

*Sources.* R. S. Evans, "Energy Plantations—Should We Grow Trees for Power Plant Fuels?" Can. For. Serv., Rept. No. VP-X-129, Western Forest Products Laboratory, Vancouver, 1974; R. E. Inman, et al., "Silvicultural Biomass Forms," Vol. I–VI, Mitre Tech. Rept. No. 7347, The Mitre Corp., McLean, Va., 1977, Forest Products Laboratory Data.

**Figure 19.8** View of extensive plantations of *Pinus patula* on former high elevation grassland between Sabie and Helspruit, East Transvaal, Republic of South Africa. To the right *Eucal-* *pytus sp.* was planted on either side of the railroad tracks in the (since disproven) belief that this would reduce fire hazard from the steam-powered locomotives. (Courtesy of M. Wotton.)

percent pulp yield requires 1800 metric tons of wood per day. In 1974, there were 52 pulp mills in the United States with rated capacities of 900 metric tons or more (17). Thus the wood requirements of a 150-megawatt electric plant are within the realm of possibility.

Energy plantations can make a contribution to the nation's energy budget. Major considerations that must be addressed are biomass productivity and land availability. Even in the event that suitable land is available, much research is still needed to: (1) optimize productivity through species selection and improvement, (2) improve silvicultural methods for short-rotation forestry, and (3) develop equipment for harvesting the crop economically.

## REFERENCES

1. M. Kranzberg, T. A. Hall, and J. L. Scheiber, eds., *Energy and the Way We Live*, Boyd & Fraser Pub. Co., San Francisco, 1980.

2. Anon., "U.S.A.'s Energy Outlook 1978–1990," Exxon Company, Houston, Tex., 1978.

3. J. F. Saeman, *Proceedings of Institute of Gas Technology Symposium on Clean Fuels from Biomass and Wastes,* Orlando, Fla., 1977.

4. P. Koch and J. Karchesy, "Processes For Producing Energy From Hardwoods Growing on Southern Pine Sites," *Proceedings on the National Convention of the Society of American Foresters,* 1978.

5. K. V. Sarkanen, *Science, 191,* 773 (1976).

6. J. I. Zerbe, R. A. Arola, and R. M. Rowell, *AICHE Symposium Series 177,* Vol. 74, 58 (1978).

7. Anon., *National Council of the Paper Industry for Air and Stream Improvement,* Tech. Bull. No. 96, Washington, D.C., 1978.

8. E. E. Harris and E. Beglinger, *Ind. Eng. Chem., 38,* 890 (1946).

9. M. Mandels, L. Hontz, and J. Nystrom, *Biotechnol. Bioeng., XVI,* 1471 (1974).

10. R. G. H. Emert and R. Katzen. "Chemicals from Biomass by Improved Enzyme Technology," *Symposium on Biomass as a Non-Fossil Fuel Source,* Am. Chem. Soc. Mtg., Honolulu, 1979.

# REFERENCES

11. Anon., *Chemical Economics Handbook,* Stanford Res. Inst., Section 674.5022T, Stanford, Cal., 1971.

12. R. M. Rowell and A. E. Hokanson, "Methanol From Wood: A Critical Assessment," *In: Progress in Biomass Conversion,* K. V. Sarkanen and D. A. Tillman, eds., Academic Press, New York, 1979.

13. A. J. Stamm and E. E. Harris, *Chemical Processing of Wood,* Chemical Publishing Co., New York, 1953.

14. Anon., "Charcoal Production, Marketing, and Use," U.S.D.A. For. Serv., Forest Products Laboratory Rept. No. 2213, 1961.

15. P. Koch, ed., "Utilization of the Southern Pines," U.S.D.A. For. Serv., *Agricultural Handbook No. 420,* 1972.

16. H. R. Appell, "The Production of Oil From Wood Waste," *In: Fuels From Waste,* Academic Press, New York, 1977.

17. K. V. Sarkanen and C. H. Ludwig, ed., *Lignins,* Wiley-Interscience, New York, 1971.

18. Anon., "Feasibility of Utilizing Forest Residues for Energy and Chemicals," U.S.D.A. For. Serv., NTIS Publication PB 258−630, 1976.

19. R. E. Inman, et al., "Silvicultural Biomass Farms," Vol. I−VI, Mitre Tech. Rept. No. 7347, The Mitre Corporation, McLean, Va., 1977.

20. R. S. Evans, "Energy Plantations—Should We Grow Trees for Power Plant Fuels?" Can. For. Serv., Rept. No. VP-X-129, Western Forest Products Laboratory, Vancouver, 1974.

# 20

# THE FOREST-PRODUCTS ECONOMY

# Jeffrey C. Stier and Joseph Buongiorno

The early colonists viewed the forests of the new nation almost exclusively as a resource to be exploited for economic development. The first ships returning to England from Jamestown reportedly carried "clapboards and wainscott," and export of lumber was a regular feature of the Plymouth economy by 1621. The very first patent issued in America for a mechanical invention was granted in 1646 for design of an improved sawmill, and sawmills were established in the United States well over a century before their adoption in England. Wood was the principal natural resource of the United States until the middle of the nineteenth century, serving both as fuel and as an industrial raw material. By 1860, the lumber industry was surpassed only by the cotton industry in terms of its contribution to the national economy (1).

Today, the U.S. economy is much less dependent on wood as a raw material. Nevertheless, timber remains an important resource. On the basis of weight, forest products were estimated to comprise 96 percent of all renewable resources used as industrial materials in 1972. The industrial consumption of forest products is, by weight, more than twice that of all metals combined (2).

If one examines the composition of domestic timber production since 1900, a somewhat surprising pattern emerges (Figure 20.1). Total production of all timber products, as well as the volume that is processed into lumber, has varied remarkably little since 1900. Indeed, the volumes for 1900 and 1970 for these two categories are very similar. However, the same cannot be said for the remaining timber-processing industries. Production of veneer and pulp

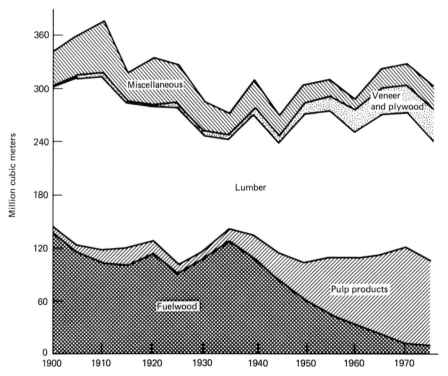

**Figure 20.1**  Composition of U.S. timber harvest, 1900 to 1975 (3).

products was negligible prior to 1900, whereas fuelwood absorbed fully 40 percent of all timber.

The declining importance over time of fuelwood is not difficult to understand; wood was largely replaced by coal and petroleum (see Figure 19.1). But who in 1900 could have foreseen the tremendous increase in timber going into pulp products, or even the smaller absolute growth of the veneer and plywood industries? A mere glance at the changes that have taken place during the past 75 years is sufficient to impart a sense of the difficulty encountered when forecasting demand and supply very far into the future.

How is timber used today? The consumption of forest products in 1976 is shown in Table 20.1. Softwoods account for about three-quarters of total consumption, and, among softwood products, lumber is dominant with pulp products a distant second. In contrast, lumber and pulp products comprise about equal proportions of the total consumption of hardwoods. The minor importance of fuel-wood in the United States is readily apparent for both hardwoods and softwoods.

Employment in the forest products industry exceeded 1.3 million persons in 1977, or about 7 percent of all manufacturing employment. Value added amounted to 38 billion, which was approximately 2 percent of the U.S. gross national product (GNP). In the following section, three groups of industries involved in the manufacture of wood products are considered: lumber, wood-based panels, and paper and allied products. This is followed by a brief examination of the economics of producing the timber on which the wood-products industries depend.

A basic understanding of the U.S. forest economy is necessary for the modern forestry professional, but in today's world it is not sufficient. The highly complex structure of interrelationships among the nations of the world makes it equally important to gain an understanding of the world forest economy and how the U.S. situation com-

**Table 20-1**

Apparent Consumption of Forest Products in the United States in 1976, by Species Group[a]

| Species Group and Product | Apparent Consumption | |
|---|---|---|
| | Million Cubic Meters[b] | Percent of Total |
| Softwoods | 291.5 | 77 |
| Lumber | 156.0 | 41 |
| Plywood and veneer | 32.1 | 8 |
| Pulp products | 92.6 | 25 |
| Fuelwood | 3.0 | 1 |
| Miscellaneous | 7.8 | 2 |
| Hardwoods | 86.6 | 23 |
| Lumber | 29.4 | 8 |
| Plywood and veneer | 7.6 | 2 |
| Pulp products | 31.6 | 8 |
| Fuelwood | 11.9 | 3 |
| Miscellaneous | 6.1 | 2 |
| Totals | 378.1 | 100 |

*Source.* "The demand and price situation for forest products," U.S.D.A. For. Serv. Misc. Publ. No. 1357, Washington, D.C., 1977.
[a] Apparent consumption = domestic production plus net imports.
[b] Roundwood equivalent.

pares to that of most other nations. This world view is presented in the third section.

## AMERICAN FOREST-PRODUCTS INDUSTRIES AND MARKETS

### Lumber

**Structure of the Industry.** The lumber industry is generally considered to be quite competitive. The number of firms is large—about 7000 in 1977—and no one firm or group of firms controls a very large share of the market. More than 80 percent of all firms employ fewer than twenty persons; nevertheless, some are quite large. The twenty largest firms produce about one-third of the total value of all industry shipments (5).

Competition is enhanced when producers are unable to establish consumer loyalty to brand names and when no significant barriers exist to entry of new firms. Product differentiation among lumber producers is difficult; a construction-grade Douglas-fir stud is pretty much the same regardless of which firm produced it. Likewise, entry into the industry is generally easy, in part because of the absence of product differentiation, but also because the capital costs of building and equipping a new sawmill are not prohibitive. However, small mills are likely to be less efficient, and entry into the industry does not ensure economic survival. U.S. Commerce Department records indicate that between 1967 and 1972, exits and mergers accounted for the loss of over 1000 firms from the industry.

The lumber industry is actually composed of two relatively distinct subsectors. One subsector consists of firms that manufacture hardwood lumber, the other of firms that produce softwood lumber. The softwood sector is the more important; annual production is four and one-half times that of hardwood lumber.

The location of sawmills is determined primarily by the availability of timber. Hence, the Pacific Coast region—Washington, Oregon, and Califor-

nia—which contains 63 percent of the nations softwood sawtimber inventory and almost 50 percent of all softwood growing stock, is the center of the softwood lumber industry. Hardwoods are grown primarily in the eastern half of the United States, with hardwood lumber production divided about equally between the North and the South. This unequal distribution is reflected in the disproportionate timber harvest shown by region and species group in Figure 20.2 (also see Table 11.2).

Geography is not the only characteristic differentiating the two sectors. Softwood sawmills tend, on average, to be larger than hardwood mills. The largest softwood mills are capable of producing in excess of 2 million cubic meters of sawed lumber annually, although economic studies have not revealed any significant cost advantages beyond an annual output capacity of about 100,000 cubic meters (7). Many of the larger mills, especially softwood mills, are part of an integrated wood-products organization consisting of, for example, a sawmill, a plywood mill, and a pulp or particle-board mill.

Hardwood sawmills frequently have an annual capacity of less than 120 cubic meters of sawed lumber. Firms with such a limited capacity are often able to remain viable by supplying local markets that are too small to attract larger competitors and by concentrating on production of specialty items.

**Prices, Demand, and Supply.** Aggregate *price indexes* for "all-lumber" and "all-commodities" are shown for the years 1950–1978 in Figure 20.3. The latter index reflects the general level of prices in the economy; year to year changes in it are a measure of the annual rate of inflation. Several distinct trends in lumber prices are evident in Figure 20.3. From 1950 through 1967 lumber prices were really quite stable; there were even a few years during the late 1950s when prices declined slightly. Although the lumber price index exhibited somewhat greater variation than the general price level, during the period 1950–1967 movements in the former largely reflected the general rate of inflation.

**Figure 20.2** U.S. timber harvest in 1976 by region and species group (millions of cubic meters of roundwood) (10).

Since 1967, however, the picture has changed dramatically. These later years have been characterized by high rates of inflation, as evidenced by the rapid rise of the "all-commodities" price index. But lumber prices have risen even faster; in fact, they more than tripled between 1967 and 1976. This phenomenon—an increase in the price of one commodity relative to the general price level—is what economists refer to as a *real* price increase; it is one signal that a commodity is becoming scarce in an economic sense. The rapid rise of the price of petroleum in recent years is another example of such a signal. Note that neither timber nor oil is truly scarce in an absolute physical sense; yet both are becoming economically scarce as evidenced by their rising prices.

The "all-lumber" price index is constructed as a weighted average of the prices of most of the individual sizes and species of lumber. The volume

of softwood lumber consumed is more than five times that of hardwood lumber and the "all-lumber" price index incorporates this information. The weighting procedure causes the "all-lumber" price index in Figure 20.3 to reflect primarily what has happened to softwood lumber prices. Separate price indexes for softwood and hardwood lumber are shown in Figure 20.4.

The indexes in Figure 20.4 are relative price indexes; that is, for each year the wholesale price index for softwood and hardwood lumber has been divided by the corresponding "all-commodities" price index for that year. The adjustment is done to remove the impact of general inflation on price movements. Thus the direction and magnitude of changes in a relative price index indicate price movements that differ from general inflationary trends. Note in Figure 20.4 that although the two price indexes generally move in the same direction,

**475**

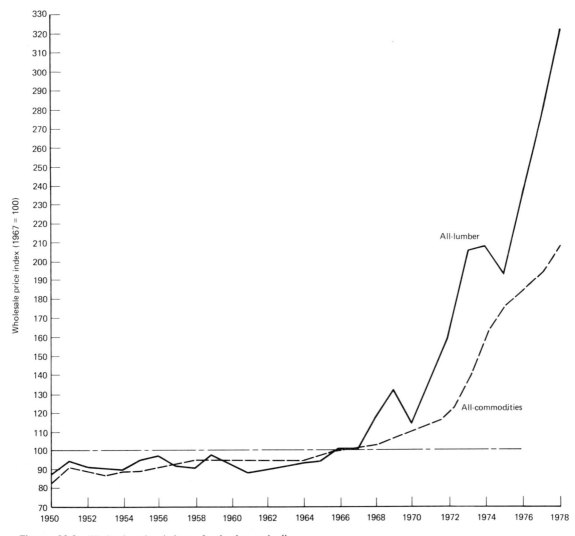

**Figure 20.3** Wholesale price indexes for lumber and all commodities, 1950 to 1978 (4).

softwood lumber prices have exhibited far more variation and in particular have risen much faster than either hardwood prices or the general price level since 1967. Note, also, that in addition to the two longer-term trends in prices that correspond to the periods before and after 1967, several shorter cyclical price movements have occurred, from 1954 to 1958, 1958 to 1961, 1967 to 1970, and 1970 to 1975.

What economic factors account for the price movements evident in Figures 20.3 and 20.4? Prices are determined by the interaction of *demand and supply*. The short-term cyclical swings are caused mainly by variations in demand coupled with a

**476**

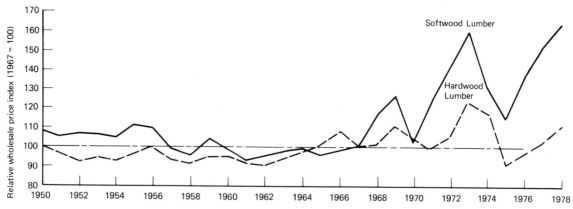

**Figure 20.4** Relative wholesale price indexes for hardwood and softwood lumber, 1950 to 1978 (4).

relatively inflexible supply. The demand for lumber, especially softwood lumber, is derived principally from the demand for new construction. Residential construction accounts for slightly less than one-half of the U.S. consumption of softwood; if nonresidential construction is included the proportion is increased to two-thirds.

In economics, as in ecology, diversity enhances stability. It is partly because hardwood lumber enjoys a secondary market for manufacture of furniture that hardwood lumber prices have tended to be less volatile than softwood prices. Dependence on a narrow market, particularly one as notoriously cyclical as the housing industry, results in wide variations in demand.

The economic health of the construction industry is determined primarily by national economic policies, especially *monetary policy,* which largely determines the interest rate buyers must pay for home mortgages. Thus, the short-run instability in lumber demand could not be reduced without changing monetary policy, which in turn would have major impacts on the rest of the economy. But demand is only one side of the picture. If supply were very responsive to price, an increase (decrease) in demand would cause price to rise (fall), which would in turn cause supply to increase (decrease).

This linkage would tend automatically to dampen the initial price change and restore equilibrium.

Unfortunately, lumber supply responds weakly to price changes, and then only after a certain delay. The sluggish response of supply to price is due to the high cost of maintaining large inventories of lumber, to short-run constraints on mill capacity and the availability of labor and timber, and to the time required to harvest and process additional timber. Increases in imports do augment domestic supplies during periods of peak demand, but, on balance, supply is not sufficiently flexible to meet the rapid variations in demand that result from the housing cycle.

What of the future? Historically, the average consumption of lumber per person—that is, per-capita consumption—has been declining in response to higher real lumber prices. Yet demographic and economic trends suggest that aggregate lumber demand will continue to grow at least through the mid-1980s, by which time the population bulge caused by the World War II baby boom will have passed through the stage of household formation. The supply picture is not likely to improve. Federal timber harvest policies preclude any significant increases in supply from public lands, and additional withdrawals of public land could reduce current

**477**

harvest levels. Intensified management on private lands is not likely to expand supply fast enough to prevent further price increases. What remains to be seen is the extent to which continued price increases will stimulate further substitution of other wood or nonwood materials for lumber, thus dampening expected increases in the demand for lumber.

## Wood-Based Panels

Wood-based panels include the following specific types: (1) plywood, which is further subdivided into softwood and hardwood plywood, (2) particle board, (3) compressed fiberboard, commonly called hardboard, which has a density of approximately 0.4 grams per cubic centimeter, and (4) noncompressed fiberboard or insulation board, which is less dense than compressed fiberboard. All four types of panels are used in construction, although, as its name implies, insulation board is not used as a structural material (see Chapter 17).

**Plywood.** Large-scale production of plywood was not possible until the development of mechanical veneer cutting techniques sometime around 1900. However, it was not until the discovery of waterproof glues in the late 1920s that plywood began to gain market acceptance as a construction material. World War II brought increased demand, especially for molded hardwood plywood products. The market for both softwood and hardwood plywood expanded after the war, but the hardwood plywood industry never experienced the sustained rapid growth of the softwood industry. Between 1945 and 1974, softwood plywood production increased tenfold, while the number of softwood plywood mills rose eightfold (4). The hardwood plywood industry has suffered greatly from a lack of domestic timber of veneer quality. During the 1950s over one-half of all hardwood plywood was produced from domestic timber; by 1977 the proportion had fallen to one-quarter (8).

*Structure of the Industry.* The economic characteristics of the plywood industry are very similar to those of the lumber industry. The geographic distribution of plywood mills parallels that of the nation's timber resources, although, somewhat surprisingly, Oregon is the nation's leading producer of both hardwood and softwood plywood. Hardwood mills tend to be smaller and less efficient than softwood mills. In 1972 the average increase in the value of the final product was $6.51 per hour worked in a hardwood mill, whereas a softwood mill averaged $10.99 per hour worked. Hourly wages in the two sectors reflect this disparity; workers in the softwood sector earn approximately 32 percent more than those in the hardwood sector (8).

In 1979, softwood plywood was produced in 192 mills in 18 states; for hardwood plywood the figures were 133 mills in 27 states. In the hardwood industry a substantial number of mills are independently operated. For softwood, however, the number of firms is only about one-half the number of mills. The ownership of two or more mills that engage in the same stage of production is referred to as *horizontal integration*. The softwood plywood industry is integrated to a greater degree than the hardwood industry, although both have remained quite competitive in terms of pricing behavior.

*Prices, Demand, and Supply.* The uses of plywood are virtually the same as those of lumber; consequently the demands for the two products are determined by the same forces. As a building material, softwood plywood is used mainly for wall sheathing and subflooring; hardwood plywood is used primarily for decorative paneling.

Hardwood lumber and plywood also enjoy a second market, stemming from their use in the manufacture of wood furniture, that is generally insignificant for softwood products. Since the furniture industry is not subject to the cyclical demand that characterizes the construction industry, demands and prices for hardwood lumber and hardwood plywood tend to be more stable than those for softwood.

Figure 20.5 shows the relative price indexes for softwood and hardwood plywood for the period since 1950. Hardwood plywood prices remained virtually constant until 1973 when strong demand, combined with the removal of national price controls, contributed to a price rise. The relative price index has declined steadily, however, and in fact declined most dramatically in 1974–1975. These trends indicate that hardwood plywood prices have not risen as fast as the general rate of inflation. This result is due almost entirely to the flexibility in supply provided by imports. Since 1950 consumption has risen steadily, whereas domestic production has declined by over 40 percent. Only by increasing imports has supply been expanded fast enough to meet demand and thereby prevent real price increases.

For softwood plywood the price picture is not so favorable. Prices did decline between 1950 and 1967, but they have almost tripled since then. During the latter period the price of softwood plywood increased much faster than the general rate of inflation. Note also that since 1967 the relative price indexes for softwood lumber (Figure 20.4) and softwood plywood (Figure 20.5) show a strikingly similar pattern. This is because the two products have virtually the same uses. Thus, in a sense, they are really alternative forms of the same product.

For softwood plywood, imports have not been an effective mechanism for mitigating upward pressure on prices during periods of strong demand. The United States has been a net exporter of softwood plywood and veneer since 1969, and exports have actually increased substantially during peak demand periods. Hence foreign demand may actually contribute somewhat to price increases in the softwood plywood market.

It was noted earlier that softwood lumber and

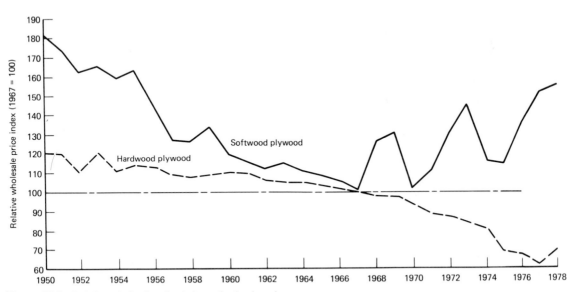

**Figure 20.5**  Relative wholesale price indexes for hardwood and softwood plywood, 1950 to 1978 (4).

**479**

softwood plywood are excellent substitutes for each other and that their prices tend to move in tandem. However, because it is manufactured in large sheets instead of individual boards, plywood has become less expensive to install as the price of labor has risen. This has produced an increase in the per-capita consumption of softwood plywood that is in stark contrast to the concomitant decrease in per-capita consumption of softwood lumber. Thus even though the prices of both products have risen, the consumption patterns have been quite different over time.

*Prospects for the Future.* Currently about four-fifths of all plywood produced in the United States is made from softwoods, and over 60 percent of all softwood plywood is Douglas-fir. The mature stands of this species in the Pacific Northwest could supply sufficient veneer logs to meet demand for several decades. Large logs are not necessary for production of plywood, however. If public land-management policies curtail harvests in the Pacific Northwest, there may occur greater emphasis on use of southern pines.

On the demand side, the possibilities for substituting plywood for lumber in housing are pretty much exhausted; indeed the current trend is toward increasing use of particleboard to replace the more expensive plywood. However, Forest Service projections are for plywood consumption to double by the year 2020 (9, 10). This projection is contingent on the relative price of plywood remaining at its 1970 level, but if past trends in prices of plywood and particleboard continue, the demand for softwood plywood will probably grow at a slower rate than the Forest Service has projected.

Forest Service projections are for consumption of hardwood plywood to grow at about the same rate as for softwoods. The domestic supply of hardwood veneer logs is limited, and the public lands do not contain a reserve inventory. The implication, therefore, is continued growth of imports, which already account for the bulk of total consumption.

**Particleboard.** Although wood particleboard was patented in the United States as early as 1905, commercial development of the product is usually credited to either Germany or Czechoslovakia in 1941. Production was restricted by a shortage of gluing resins during most of World War II but in 1945 the first American plant began operation (11). Particleboard did not really begin to gain market acceptance until the 1960s. From 1964 to 1979 consumption increased at an average annual rate of 34 percent. In terms of total consumption of wood-based panels, however, particleboard held only about 11 percent of the market in 1976.

*Structure of the Industry.* Particleboard is among the *most concentrated* of all the wood-products industries. An industry is usually considered concentrated if four firms produce more than 50 percent of the industry's total output. In 1972, four firms did account for almost one-half of the total production of particleboard. However, the industry appears to remain strongly price competitive. The product is quite homogeneous, and technological improvements have caused the cost of production to decline during recent years. During the early history of the industry, production capacity was divided almost equally between the South and the West. Although several very large plants have been built in the West during recent years, in 1976 the South still held 49 percent of the market.

Particleboard plants are frequently integrated with lumber and plywood mills from which they derive much of their raw material. Approximately 65 percent of all wood used in particleboard manufacture consists of shavings produced when lumber is planed. An additional 10 percent and 9 percent come, respectively, from plywood mill residue and sawdust. Softwood is the preferred species group, comprising slightly more than 80 percent of the total raw material output.

*Prices, Demand, and Supply.* When it was first introduced, particleboard was used as a core material for furniture. Gradually it began to capture from plywood the market for floor underlayment. Recently it has been used as a backing for plastic overlay paneling and for mobile-home decking. In 1979, industrial use and floor underlayment accounted for 83 percent of total output while mobile-home decking consumed another 9 percent.

Because particleboard is manufactured largely from sawmill residues, it has contributed significantly to the total utilization of timber. Improved bonding techniques and large-scale plants have gradually lowered the cost of production. The relative price index for particleboard fell by almost 50 percent between 1966 and 1978, from 108 to 68.

*Prospects for the Future.* The factor most significantly limiting the market for particleboard has been the availability of inexpensive plywood (12). Plywood is no longer inexpensive relative to particle board, and the future must be considered bright for the particleboard industry. The pattern of growth of the industry in other countries suggests that particle board may ultimately become the dominant wood-based panel. Whether plywood continues to remain competitive will probably depend on whether the structural properties of particleboard can be guaranteed. If they can, further substitution can be expected.

The projected increase in the demand for particle board—a threefold rise by the year 2020—cannot be met solely by utilizing wood residues, especially if mills begin to use wood residue as a fuel source on a greater scale. Supply therefore will probably depend on greater use of timber and especially hardwoods. This should create a market for low-quality hardwoods and thereby permit forest managers to recover some or all of the costs of upgrading hardwood stands.

**Fiberboard.** In terms of total use, insulation board and hardboard are relatively unimportant. Both products are produced by a small number of firms, but pricing patterns in both industries appear to be competitive.

In 1950, consumption of hardboard was, by weight, roughly 50 percent that of insulation board; by 1976 the percentages were almost exactly reversed. This has come about because although total use of insulation board has increased over the past 25 years by 73 percent, per-capita consumption has remained constant, whereas for hardboard it has doubled (4). These figures indicate the faster growth rate of the hardboard industry, which has been brought about because favorable prices have stimulated substitution of hardboard for plywood and lumber in construction and furniture. About 85 percent of all insulation board is used in construction, but because it is a nonstructural material, it is not readily substituted for either plywood or hardboard.

The demand for hardboard is expected to parallel closely that for plywood, but the demand for insulation board may increase at a faster pace in the future if higher energy costs increase the demand for insulating materials. Roundwood can be expected to assume greater importance as a source of wood fiber for both products as competition for wood residue intensifies. Like particleboard, the fiberboards hold great promise for increasing utilization of wood fiber and for providing markets for low-quality timber.

## Paper and Allied Products

**Structure of the Industry.** What is commonly referred to as the pulp and paper industry is actually a loose conglomeration of firms that encompasses three stages of production: (1) pulping of wood, wastepaper, and other raw materials, (2) production of paper and paperboard from wood pulp, and (3) manufacturing of paper into final commodities. The science and technology of pulp and paper manufacture are discussed in Chapter 18. Only about 10 percent of all wood pulp is marketed without further processing. About 70 percent of all firms are vertically integrated—that is, they operate at more than one of the three stages of production. Vertically integrated firms frequently grow some or all of their own pulpwood timber, process pulpwood into pulp, and convert the pulp into paper products. The newer mills are also frequently integrated with lumber or plywood mills and are thus able to utilize the residues from those facilities.

The history of the pulp and paper industry and the nature of each region's wood resource have produced a *distinct geographic pattern* in the industry. The Northeast contains the oldest, smallest, and generally least efficient mills. The newest and largest mills are found in the West and the South. Many of the newer installations, especially in the South, utilize the kraft (sulfate) process (see Chapter 18). The characteristics of the Great Lakes states' industry tend to be intermediate between those of the Northeast and those of the South and West.

The market structure of the pulp and paper industry can be characterized as one with a few very large firms that can to some degree influence the prices of their products, and a much greater number of smaller firms that have little or no control over the prices they receive. Although this description is probably appropriate for the industry as a whole, a wide range of market conditions does exist among the various sectors within the industry. For example, dissolving market pulp (see Chapter 18) is produced by only eight U.S. firms, four of which account for over three-quarters of total output. In contrast, the recycled paperboard sector contains over 100 firms and together the four largest control only one-quarter of total production. The combination of a few large firms and many smaller firms often leads to a pricing pattern that is referred to as *price leadership* in which the larger firms establish their price, and the remaining, smaller firms are more or less forced to adopt it if they are to remain economically viable. This pricing pattern is also attributed to the steel and automobile industries.

Much of the specialization that has taken place within the industry is regional in nature. For example, in the South and West, where supplies of

inexpensive softwoods are readily available, production of kraft paper and paperboard is prominent. Industries in the Northeast, and to a somewhat lesser extent the Great Lakes states, have generally concentrated on the production of high-quality, more valuable papers in which they have a competitive advantage. Thus, although the South dominates the industry in terms of production capacity (Figure 20.6), the northeastern and north-central regions combined greatly outweigh the South in terms of the *value of output*; the leading state on this basis is Wisconsin.

Concentration within the pulp and paper industry is likely to increase for several reasons, the most significant of which is probably the cost of entry. Although relatively small mill scales—for example, 100 metric tons per day—may be economically viable for production of some specialty papers, the average daily capacity of unbleached kraft paper mills is approximately 1400 metric tons.

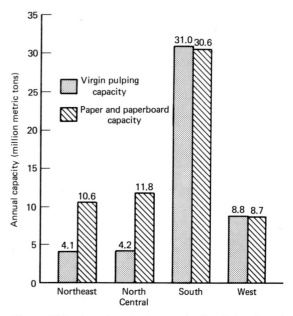

**Figure 20.6** Annual production capacity for virgin pulp and paper and paperboard mills in 1976, by region (13). (West includes the Rocky Mountain states, which have a combined capacity of less than 2 percent of U.S. production capacity.)

The effect of inflation on the capital requirements for constructing and operating such large plants is enormous. A kraft linerboard mill with a daily output of 746 tons could be put into operation in 1964 for about 40 million; by 1974 the cost had increased to 135 million. During the same 10-year period, the cost of land necessary to supply 20 percent of the mill's wood requirements increased from 17 million to 102 million (14). Small entrepreneurs may still be able to find a niche in the lumber industry, but even established firms sometimes find it difficult to raise the capital needed to finance expansions in the pulp and paper industry. Considering the size of the investments required, it is perhaps surprising that the industry is not even more concentrated.

**Price, Demand, and Supply.** During the 1960s the wholesale price index for paper products remained virtually constant. New production capacity was added at an annual rate of 4 percent, and by the middle of the decade the combination of capacity expansion and increased productivity of existing production facilities began to generate excess capacity. Typically, paper firms have been reluctant to reduce output because the cost per ton of output tends to increase as production is decreased. The industry was characterized by fierce competition as firms attempted to maintain production levels. This competition held down potential price increases but it also eroded industry profits, a process that was exacerbated by the recession of 1970–1971.

Since 1970 the industry has undergone a major transition. Capacity expansion has slowed to 2.5 percent per year and in some years dropped below 2 percent. The overcapacity problem was further alleviated by the closure of more than 100 mills in the early 1970s. These mills were generally of marginal efficiency and unable to meet the combination of strong price competition and rising costs of pollution control.

When the economy began to strengthen in 1972 the industry was unable to meet the demand. Utilization rates for existing capacity climbed to 97 percent in 1973, well above the 93 percent level at which prices generally begin to rise. And rise they did—by 16 percent per year in 1973 and 1974! However, the price increases were completely in line with the movement of other prices, and the relative wholesale price index for paper products has fallen since 1973.

The paper industry learned much about basic economics in the early 1970s. Firms began to employ professional managers in the top executive positions, and profitability replaced volume of production as a management goal. These changes appear to have been effective. Despite a sharp drop in demand during the 1975 recession, the industry was able, by reducing supplies, not only to maintain prices but actually to raise them and thus maintain profitability.

The range of products manufactured by the pulp and paper industry is so diverse as to preclude consideration of each product. The two main categories of finished products are (1) *paper*, which includes newsprint, writing and printing papers, packaging papers, and sanitary papers, and (2) *paperboards*, of which the largest production is in the form of corrugated container boards—that is, cardboard boxes. These products are used so pervasively throughout all stages of the economy that aggregate demand for paper products generally parallels movements in *real GNP* at a ratio of about 24,000 tons of paper and paperboard products consumed for every million dollars of GNP. Hence, the industry undergoes periods of alternating strong and weak demand as the nation undergoes economic expansions and recessions. However, since per-capita real GNP has increased almost continuously over time, so too has per-capita consumption of paper products.

**Prospects for the Future.** The paper industry is a *mature industry*; that is, the majority of products have not changed appreciably in recent years, the production technology is generally available to all firms, and prospects for uncovering large, untapped markets are limited. The long-term growth rate for demand is projected at 3 percent per year. The industry also faces very large capital costs for new investment in mills, land, and pollution-control equipment. These characteristics suggest that entry by new firms will be restricted and that consolidation within, and competition among, firms will increase.

A particular consequence of the new management philosophy brought about by events in the early 1970s is greater scrutiny of land-management policies. Instead of owning timberland merely to ensure pulpwood supply, firms are undertaking comprehensive land-use plans in an effort to increase returns. On lands that are to remain in timber production, management is continually being intensified, especially in the South where gains in productivity have already been impressive.

The future wood supply situation for the pulp and paper industry is far more favorable than that for the lumber and plywood industries. Pulp products do not require large or high-quality timber as raw material. Moreover, the industry has been making increasing use of hardwoods, of which there are ample supplies. Since 1950, domestic output of softwood pulp products has doubled while that from hardwoods has increased fivefold. Should these trends continue, the industry will not face the shortage of timber that might plague the lumber and plywood industries.

The forest-products industries have been examined prior to discussion of the economics of timber production for a very important reason. The demand for timber is a *derived demand*; that is, it is derived from the demand for the final products in which timber is used. Forest economists often make much of the concept of derived demand, perhaps imparting the impression that it is unique to their discipline. Such is not the case, however. Derived demand characterizes primary commodity industries ranging from milk to iron ore. In all these cases, the demand for the raw product is derived directly from the demand for the end product, be it ice cream or automobiles. Thus it is important to have a firm grasp of the current status and projected changes in the demands for wood products because they have

important implications for how and what types of timber will be grown. We now turn to the latter subject.

## TIMBER-PRODUCTION ECONOMICS

The timber-production process includes all steps necessary to grow trees, from timber culture to harvesting (see Chapters 9–11). Although decisions regarding the culture and harvest of timber are inextricably intertwined, it is convenient to consider the two separately.

### Timber Supply

As noted previously, many firms in the timber-processing industries are *integrated backward* into timber production. The extent of this integration can be seen in Figure 20.7 (see also Table 11.2 and Figure 11.9). Industry owns only 14 percent of all commercial forestland, but contributes more than one-third of the total softwood harvest, whereas other private owners, who hold almost 60 percent of the land, supply only 36 percent of the softwood harvest. For hardwoods, the percentage of the total harvest from industry-owned lands is approximately in line with the percentage for land area ownership, but private owners harvest a disproportionate share of the total. On publicly owned lands softwood and hardwood harvest percentages are roughly the same as those for landholdings.

The disparities between the percentages of land owned and the percentages of timber harvested could be due merely to concentration of holdings in a particular species group. The data on holdings of growing stock (see Figure 11.9) indicate that this is indeed the case among private nonindustrial owners; they own and harvest the greatest proportion of hardwood timber. However, the forest industries own far less softwood growing stock than is suggested by their contribution to the total softwood harvest.

Comparison of Figures 11.9 and 20.7 also reveals that the national forests contain the bulk of the

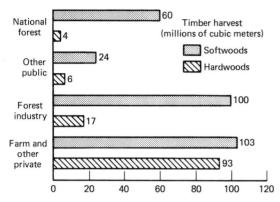

**Figure 20.7** Timber harvest in the United States in 1976, by ownership class and species group (10).

softwood timber inventory, especially for sawtimber, but furnish less than one-quarter of the total softwood harvest.

The forest industries have been able to harvest more softwoods from their lands by liquidating more rapidly their stocks of very old timber in the Pacific Coast region. By harvesting the slow-growing, mature timber and regenerating the areas with fast-growing young stock, productivity as measured by net annual growth per unit area is increased. In the Pacific Coast region the current productivity of industry-owned forestland is almost two and one-half times greater than that of the national forests. Potential growth on national forestland is over three times current growth, but still only about 82 percent of that possible from industry lands and about 92 percent of the potential on other privately owned land. The greater potential of industry-owned lands is due primarily to the fact that forest-products firms have tended to purchase the best sites in an effort to increase profitability.

Differences in the amount, inherent productivity, and current timber inventory cannot account for all of the differences in harvest among the various groups of landowners. The decisions on when and how much to harvest are strongly influenced by the objectives of the owner. There is no reason to suppose that all owners will choose to pursue the

same objectives, and indeed they do not. The forest industries expect their forestland to contribute to the overall profitability of the enterprise, either directly if timber production proves to be profitable, or indirectly if such production lowers the cost of timber used and ensures a source of supply. Because profitability is an important objective of industry, timber-production decisions depend strongly on prices and costs. For the national forests, the land-management objective is sustained production of an array of outputs. Profitability is not the only, or even most important, criterion of timber-production decisions. Indeed, some critics contend that economic considerations are ignored almost totally in management decision-making for the national forests (15).

The objectives of nonindustrial private forest land owners are diverse and not well understood, as discussed in Chapter 13, but profitability certainly does not appear to be the sole objective of timber production, nor is timber production necessarily the only purpose of landownership. The impact of market conditions on the timber-production decisions of this group of forest landowners is therefore very difficult to predict. Suffice it to say, though, that when the profitability of timber production becomes great enough, owners usually do respond to economic incentives.

The aggregate harvest (supply) of timber in any time period will be the sum of the harvests from privately and publicly owned forestland. Because hardwoods are harvested mainly from private lands, it is reasonable to expect supply to be responsive to price. The same can be said for the supply of both softwood and hardwood timber for pulpwood. However, softwood lumber and softwood plywood and veneer are manufactured primarily from timber grown in the Pacific Coast region, an area in which a large proportion of the forestland is publicly owned.

The national forests of the Pacific Coast region supply 27 percent of the nation's softwood sawtimber. On these forests the timber harvest is governed by the National Forest Management Act of

1976, which limits harvests to "a quantity equal to or less than a quantity which can be removed from such a forest annually in perpetuity on a *sustained-yield basis*" (16). The rationale for sustained yield is the desire to avoid overcutting, similar to that which occurred in the Great Lakes states at the turn of the century. The Forest Service has interpreted the sustained-yield requirement to mean that harvest volumes should be virtually constant from year to year (Figure 20.8). Some critics have argued that this is too rigid an interpretation and that the Forest Service actually has greater discretion than it chooses to exercise in setting harvest volumes. This argument is not likely to be settled for some time. In the meantime, the supply of timber from the national forests remains almost totally unresponsive to price signals; that is, the supply of timber from the national forests is *price inelastic*. Because the total softwood supply is merely the sum of the harvests from public and private forestland, the aggregate supply is also relatively price inelastic. This price-inelastic supply of softwood sawtimber, coupled with the wide fluctuations in softwood lumber demand that parallel the peaks and troughs of housing activity, result in timber, lumber, and plywood prices that are extremely volatile. If harvests from public lands were more responsive to initial price changes, the ultimate variations in prices of timber and derived products could probably be reduced. This potential for dampening price swings lies behind the persistent efforts of the forest-products industries to persuade the Forest Service to increase timber harvests. It also prompted President Carter to order a study in 1978 of the potential for dampening inflationary trends in the economy, and in particular in the construction industry, by increasing the harvest from public forestland (see Chapter 12). However, as noted previously, prospects for actual increases in the harvest are remote.

The supply of timber in any time period is a function of existing stocks; in order to harvest more it is necessary to have available timber of merchantable size. Thus supply, as used here, is a short- to medium-run concept. But what of the longer run?

Surely prices and costs also affect a landowner's decisions whether and how to grow timber.

## Timber Culture

Let us suppose that there is available 1 hectare of forestland from which all timber has just been harvested. The management objective is to maximize the income from this land. We wish to examine how economic factors affect management decisions.

We can begin our examination with a very simple case in which the land is located in the Great Lakes states and previously contained a stand of bigtoothed aspen. The site is of slightly better than average productivity, which suggests that pulpwood is the most profitable timber product to grow. Accordingly, the stand is allowed to regenerate itself naturally. Figure 11.6 illustrates the general relationship that might be expected between the volume of harvestable pulpwood and stand age. Note that the curve does not begin at the origin because trees must be of some minimum size before they are merchantable. If we assume that the real price of aspen pulpwood stumpage—that is, standing trees—does not vary with time or stand volume, the yield curve can be thought of as representing either physical volume or gross income. To keep this illustration simple we will also assume that gross income and net income are equal—there are no management costs or taxes of any kind.

The most important management decision for aspen is deciding when to harvest. *Maximization of income* (or harvest volume) per unit of time would lead to harvesting the stand at the age $R_2$ (as discussed in Chapter 11), defined by the point of tangency of the yield curve with a straight line from the origin. This is the traditional way of determining the *rotation age* and it is still often advocated. However, the procedure ignores the existence of *interest rates*—that is, the fact that income received at an earlier date than $R_2$ can be invested in other ventures and generate yet more income. Moreover, the interest effect influences not just the first rotation

**Figure 20.8** Reforested area on the Kaniksu National Forest in Idaho. Foreground is stocked with western larch and Douglas-fir reproduced naturally. The central area, edged by mature timber, is a field-planted western white pine plantation (Courtesy of U.S.D.A. Forest Service.)

but all future rotations. Taking interest rates into account leads to an economic rotation $R_1$ that is significantly shorter than $R_2$. We will ignore details of the procedure by which $R_1$ is determined, but we note that for aspen growing on moderately good sites in the Great Lakes states, $R_2$ is about 40 years; even at very low interest rates, $R_1$ would generally be at least 5 years less (17). The *economic rotation* is especially sensitive to the rate of interest chosen. The higher the interest rate, the shorter the economic rotation, and at very high interest rates timber production may not be profitable at all.

The previous example, although exceedingly simple, is quite representative of aspen management in the Great Lakes states. It demonstrates very well the influence that an important economic variable, the interest rate, has on rotation length. But what about more complex management situations?

Suppose now that our hectare of land is located in Georgia, that the species to be grown is slash pine,

and that the stand must be regenerated artificially. The first question to be decided is how much site preparation to undertake prior to planting. Obviously, it is least expensive to do none, but unprepared sites are likely to experience considerable ingrowth of hardwoods and, consequently, greater mortality among the pine. Intensive site preparation is expensive and can only be justified if it will result in significantly greater timber value at the time of harvest. A second decision must be made on the spacing between seedlings. Closer spacings produce a greater total wood volume per unit area but they are more expensive; the final product also tends to be of smaller diameter and therefore less valuable. In order to determine the most profitable combination of site preparation and spacing, it is necessary to compare the present worth of costs and returns that are likely to result from each of a range of alternatives. A recent study (18) doing just that arrived at the following general conclusions.

1. If it is profitable to plant slash pine on unprepared sites, it is even more profitable to plant on intensively prepared sites.

2. The most profitable tree spacing becomes closer as the site index and the degree of site preparation increase.

3. Optimum spacing is relatively insensitive to the interest rate, but quite sensitive to product values. The optimum spacing increases as the price of sawtimber rises relative to the price of pulpwood.

Aspen and slash pine are managed as even-aged species. Let us briefly examine how economic factors affect the culture of an all-aged forest of, for example, mixed species of northern hardwoods. As with the determination of the rotation, the economic variable most significantly affecting management of uneven-aged stands is the interest rate. The value of the trees in the stand comprises a capital investment since the option always exists of harvesting them and putting the income received into some alternative investment. Consequently, the stand should return at least as much as could be earned by investing in the best alternative available or it would be more profitable to get out of the timber-growing business.

By what means can the profitability of timber production from an uneven-aged stand be increased? The variables most directly under the control of the forest manager are the *length of cutting cycle* (time interval between harvests), the *stocking level,* the *size (diameter) class distribution* of trees in the stand, and the *species composition.*

Altering the species composition to favor the most valuable species is an obvious management strategy. But what choice of cutting cycle, stocking level, and diameter distribution will contribute most to profitability? The answer is not at all obvious because maximum volume and value productivity are not necessarily identical, and both are jointly dependent on all three variables. For example, volume growth would be greatest if an annual cutting cycle were employed, harvesting each year the annual increase in volume. Such frequent harvests are usually not economical, however, because the volume harvested is quite small. As the cutting cycle is lengthened, maximizing both volume and value productivity calls for a lower stocking level and perhaps also a smaller average tree size. Similarly, a stand that is managed solely for sawtimber and veneer would tend to have a larger average tree diameter than one that is managed for pulpwood because large trees would be more valuable in the former case.

Each of the three management situations discussed involves slightly different *decision variables.* A number of additional variables could be included: whether and how much to fertilize, to plant genetically superior stock, to thin, to prune, or to control fire, insects, and disease. It is not possible to consider all of the many possible management situations. Nor is it necessary to do so. Our three examples illustrate well the general manner in which economic factors affect timber culture.

The variables that a forest manager seeks to control can all be expected to produce the same general effect—to maintain or increase the quantity or quality of timber that is produced. But not all actions that produce this result are profitable. Just which are and which are not is determined by comparing the additional income attributable to a particular practice with the additional cost that is incurred, including the cost of waiting until the income is received. Analysis usually indicates, for example, that pruning is not a profitable cultural practice except for very valuable veneer species. In contrast, thinning, even when it produces no immediate revenue, frequently increases the rate of value growth of the remaining trees enough to be worthwhile (Figure 20.9).

## FOREST PRODUCTS IN THE WORLD ECONOMY

The previous discussion of forestry and forest-product economics dealt exclusively with the situation in the United States. The modern student of

**Figure 20.9** A 40-year-old Douglas-fir stand marked prior to thinning, Pe E11, Washington. (Courtesy of M. Wotton.)

forestry would be ill-advised to assume that the U.S. forest economy is representative of the situation in other nations. Forestry problems in industrial countries may be somewhat similar to those of the United States, but they are very different in the rest of the world where at least two-thirds of the human population lives. It is the objective of this section to provide a general overview of the forest economy of several world regions. Particular attention will be paid to the enormous differences between the rich industrialized countries and those of the third world.

## Forest Resources of the World

Forests cover 30 percent of the world's land area, most of which is closed forest with a small percentage as open woodland. As discussed in Chapter 2, three major types of forest can be distinguished: *coniferous forest* below the Arctic tundra and extending along the major mountain chains, *tropical*

*hardwoods* heavily concentrated in the hot, humid equatorial regions, and the more widely scattered *deciduous types*. The most heavily forested (closed) areas by far are in the U.S.S.R., Latin America, and North America, all of which contain greater than 2 hectares of forestland per capita. But the numbers can be very misleading. The nature of the resource varies considerably from region to region in terms of timber quality, forest accessibility, and distribution. Coniferous timber found in North America is an all-purpose, homogeneous wood. In contrast, humid tropical forests contain hundreds of species, of which only a few are currently being used. While the average forest area per capita in Europe (0.3 hectares per capita) is similar to those in Asia (0.2 hectares per capita) and Africa (0.5 hectares per capita), this ignores the fact that 95 percent of all European forests are under some form of use and geographically well distributed. Vast areas of Africa and Asia are almost bare of trees, while the future of the highly concentrated tropical forests in the Ama-

**489**

zon, West Africa, and Southeast Asia is somewhat uncertain.

Data are very scarce and often inaccurate, but it is generally thought that forest area is stable or increasing in the developed world where some balance between agriculture and forestry has been struck. However, tropical forest area appears to be *declining* by about 1.2 percent annually, a figure that corresponds to deforestation of an area the size of Cuba each year.

Some observers claim that at their present rate of decline, the moist tropical forests will be gone in 50 years. It should be recognized that given the pressures of population growth and poverty, some transformation of a forest domain that is currently underused is necessary to generate badly needed capital and agricultural land. On the other hand, the methods used should ensure maintenance of the long-term productivity of the soil. Shifting cultivation, whereby people clear a parcel of forest and cultivate the soil until it is impoverished before moving on to another area, is a frequent practice in developing countries. This problem is particularly serious in the subtropical regions where increasing population density is leading to an overexpansion of agriculture and excessive grazing and fuelwood harvests. Removal of an already light forest cover is

leading to the accelerated desertification of a naturally fragile environment.

Because about 80 percent of the world's forest area is under some form of public ownership, it may seem that the future of world forests is merely a matter of policy easily settled by rule of law. This is not generally so, however, particularly when the law is not compatible with the immediate needs or long-time traditions of the people. Under these conditions forest laws may be unenforceable, even by a well-trained and well-staffed forestry corps. In India, for example, illegal use of state forests is so great that it almost precludes planned management.

## World Timber-Products Output, Trade, and Consumption

As indicated in Table 20.2, the current world harvest (about 2.5 billion cubic meters) is divided evenly between *fuelwood* and *industrial roundwood*. The importance of fuelwood in the world forest economy, to which we will return later, is probably underestimated by offical figures. Logs used in the manufacture of lumber and plywood represent 60 percent of industrial wood production, while the remaining 40 percent consists of pulpwood, the main raw material of the pulp and paper industry.

**Table 20-2**

World Wood Production

| | 1978 | | 1963–1978 Growth (%/year) |
|---|---|---|---|
| | (million m³) | (%) | |
| Total removals | 2510 | 100 | 1.6 |
| Fuelwood | 1170 | 47 | 1.0 |
| Industrial roundwood | 1340 | 53 | 2.2 |
| Logs | 800 | 32 | 1.8 |
| Pulpwood | 340 | 14 | 4.4 |
| Other | 200 | 7 | 0.2 |

*Source.* K. F. S. King, "The Forestry Sector and Economic International Relationships," Weyerhaeuser Lecture Series, Univ. of Toronto, 1975, UN-FAO.

However, pulpwood harvest is growing twice as fast as log production. Pulp and paper manufacturing is rapidly becoming the major user of the world's industrial roundwood harvest.

Forest industries are heavily concentrated in the developed nations of the Northern Hemisphere (19). This may seem surprising in view of the somewhat larger volume of timber stock available in developing countries (170 million cubic meters versus 140 million in developed countries). It underlines the fact that many variables affect the growth of timber-based industries. We have already indicated the technological advantages of softwoods, particularly over mixed tropical hardwoods. *Capital* is a factor of production that is relatively scarce in developing countries, as are skilled labor and the general infrastructure needed to support modern industry. Besides adequate supplies of factors of production, a new industry needs sufficient *markets* to be successful. Very often domestic markets are small in developing economies, and international markets are inaccessible because of combinations of high production and transportation costs and import tariffs. For these reasons there is very little pulp and paper production in the developing world. Pulp and paper manufacturing requires large amounts of capital, technical knowledge, a good economic infrastructure, and large markets. Lumber and plywood industries have been much more successful. They require less capital, use simple skills, and because of the availability of local raw material and cheap labor, have been able to compete on the international market despite heavy import duties levied by importing countries. Nevertheless, the average value of all wood products manufactured in developing countries does not exceed 9 percent of the total value of world output. Furthermore, this share has not increased during the last two decades, an alarming situation given the fact that population growth has increased at least twice as fast in developing countries as in the rest of the world during the same period.

As suggested above, competitiveness in international markets is the acid test of development. There is ample evidence that the lumber and plywood industries of several third-world countries have achieved such competitiveness. Nevertheless, 80 percent of all world forest-products trade is between developed countries. Softwood lumber, wood pulp, and newsprint dominate this trade. Developing nations export mostly logs to developed nations and import almost all the paper and paperboard they need, usually with an overall trade deficit. The system of trade preferences is heavily biased against potential exports of manufactured products from developing countries. While logs are usually imported duty-free into industrial countries, heavy tariffs are levied on processed products. For example, the United States imposes a 20 percent duty on hardwood plywood imports, regardless of origin, thereby effectively limiting the ability of Southeast Asian producers to penetrate the American market. Domestic producers are also favored by recent laws prohibiting export of a large part of the timber harvest in the western United States. The percentages of total timber harvest prohibited from export for Washington, Oregon, and California in 1975 were 17.8, 47, and 37, respectively. Such regulations represent a subsidy to domestic producers and an encouragement to inefficiency relative to foreign competitors who would be willing to pay much higher prices for the raw material involved.

Because of differences in income there are tremendous differences between levels of timber-products consumption in the developed and developing world. Developing countries, which make up 70 percent of the world population, consume only 10 to 15 percent of the lumber and paper produced in the world (Table 20.3). Individual country figures reveal even greater disparities, with consumption of lumber per capita 50 times higher in Canada than in Mali. Consumption of paper and paperboard is more than 200 times higher in the United States than in Mali or in the Philippines. Econometric studies reveal a systematic relationship between the growth of income per capita and the resulting growth of

**Table 20-3**

World Distribution of Forest Products Consumption, 1977

| | Population | | Lumber | | Paper | |
|---|---|---|---|---|---|---|
| | Million | % | Million m³ | % | Million tons | % |
| Developed countries | 1100 | 29 | 390 | 88 | 131 | 89 |
| Developing countries | 2730 | 71 | 54 | 12 | 16 | 11 |
| World | 3830 | 100 | 444 | 100 | 147 | 100 |

*Sources.* K. F. S. King, "The Forestry Sector and Economic International Relationships," Weyerhaeuser Lecture Series, Univ. of Toronto, 1975; and "Forestry for Rural Communities," FAO, United Nations, Rome, 1978.

wood-products consumption per capita. Figure 20.10 represents this relationship for structural wood consumption in France, the United States, and Japan. These consumption functions allow us to estimate the impact of expected economic and demographic growth on long-term wood requirements. The results tend to indicate that as a whole, the world does not face an immediate wood shortage. This is because in North America, for example, more wood is being grown than harvested. Furthermore, there is ample room for improving productivity in most forests. However, local problems, already serious in parts of the developing world, will increase directly with the growth of population. One problem that is particularly relevant to the world forest economy is the *fuelwood crisis*.

## The Fuelwood Crisis

Fuelwood is the basic heating and cooking fuel for at least one-third of the world's people (21). In the third-world close to 90 percent of the timber harvest is for fuelwood (Figure 20.11). It is the source of up to 70 percent of all energy of the developing world (Table 20.4). In largely rural societies fuelwood does not enter the monetary economy and is therefore taken for granted and ignored in economic calculations. Nevertheless it has been observed in parts of the Andean Sierra and Africa that fuelwood sold on the market absorbs as much as 25 to 30 percent of the average household income. This high

price leads individual households to do their own collection, but this necessarily restricts the land available for collection to a family's immediate vicinity. High population densities, coupled with overgrazing, inevitably lead to deforestation, which in turn causes increased erosion. In the fragile ecosystem of the Sahel, deforestation is currently leading to rapid desertification. The decrease in fuelwood supply requires ever-increasing efforts to collect a minimum amount of fuel. It has been observed in Tanzania that fuelwood collection necessitates some 300 days of labor per year for a single household. Fuelwood shortages also lead to the search for substitutes such as cow dung and crop

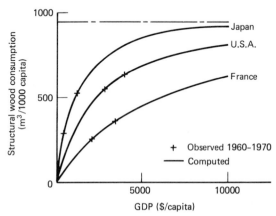

**Figure 20.10** Consumption functions showing the relationship between gross domestic product (GDP) growth and structural wood consumption growth in selected countries.

**Figure 20.11** Fuelwood collection and supply is a critical problem in developing countries. (UN-FAO Photograph.)

residues. But this removal of natural manure results in lower productivity of existing arable land. As a result the remaining forest has to be cleared, which inevitably decreases the fuelwood supply even further. This dismal unending circle has spurred fresh thinking in the area of development aid, with ever more emphasis being given to community development.

**Table 20-4**

Estimated Use of Wood for Energy as a Percent of Total Energy (Other than Animal and Human)

| Region | Percentage |
| --- | --- |
| Asia and Pacific | 29 |
| Near East | 6 |
| Africa | 66 |
| Latin America | 20 |

*Source.* J. E. M. Arnold and J. Jongma, *Unasylva, 29,* 2 (1978). UN-FAO Publication.

## Forests for People

A large portion of past efforts in forestry development aid centered on the idea that the creation of industrial centers, coupled with large-scale national planning, was the key to getting a national forest economy started. This industrial activity would create demand from and supply for other sectors that would have a snowball effect ever-increasing the economic impact of the starting project. Coupled to the large industrial centers were equally large forest estates either publicly or privately owned. Apart from a few success stories, the policy did not work. As indicated previously, the gap between developed and developing countries has not decreased. Worse perhaps, the differences between rich and poor within developing countries have increased. The domestic urban elites, together with the foreign investors who have participated in the industrial ventures, have reaped considerable benefits, but the fate of the common people has remained unchanged.

**493**

In fact, it has often been made worse by the lure of urban industrial jobs that have not materialized. It is now recognized that continuous migration to urban slums can only be stopped by improving the quality of life in small rural communities, and that forestry has a key role to play in this venture. It requires a different view of forestry, however; not big forestry, not industrial forestry, not timber forestry—instead, small, communal, *multiple-use forestry* (20, 23). In this view the forest would be a source of goods and services for the local community, providing firewood, some grazing, poles, and small construction materials. It would also be used for windbreak and erosion control. To avoid competition between forestry and agricultural use of land, traditional stands would be replaced, when possible, by *agri-silvicultural systems* that integrate trees and other agricultural crops.

*Community forestry*, as its name implies, requires community acceptance and involvement. Villagers must be convinced that a village woodlot will really serve them; otherwise it is difficult to expect them to keep their starving herd from eating the seedlings as soon as they are planted. There is ample evidence from very successful community forestry programs in Korea and China that such community support can be secured. However, it entails a firm commitment by governments to rural development. It may require far-reaching reforms in the land-tenure system of a country at the expense of the ruling elite. But a successful program may contribute substantially to a more equitable distribution of social well-being between the urban and rural areas. Only through such redistribution can the massive migration of the rural poor to the slums of most third-world cities be reversed.

This new, grass-root view of development forestry seems to be slowly gaining creditability within the bureaucracies of national and international development agencies. A number of nations are operating *bilateral assistance* in forestry. The United States program, particularly through the Agency for International Development and the Peace Corps, is probably the greatest contributor in absolute amount, although other nations such as Canada, Sweden, Great Britain, and France contribute more in proportion to their gross national product. However, these bilateral programs have their usual political biases in favor of the donor country instead of the receiver. *Multilateral aid* is a better approach. International multilateral aid in forestry development is offered by the Food and Agricultural Organization (FAO) of the United Nations operating from Rome through individual country projects funded by various agencies including the United Nations Development Program. FAO's field operations seem to be at least in part committed to the concept of forestry for community development, but its resources are totally inadequate. FAO's staff of professional foresters, particularly those working in field projects, is ridiculously small compared, for example, to the staff of the U.S. Forest Service. Much more important programs will be required to affect seriously the course of forestry in the developing world. This should not discourage any individual of goodwill from embracing the field of development forestry, for it is by far the most important challenge facing our profession now and in the coming decades.

## SUMMARY

The economy of colonial America was marked by a strong dependence on the production, largely for export, of basic food and fiber commodities. Over the years, growth expanded and diversified the American economy; today the forest-based industries constitute a smaller absolute, but perhaps no less important, segment of the aggregate economy.

Important changes have also taken place within the forest-based sector. With the exception of the Douglas-fir in the Pacific Northwest, the virgin stands of large, high-quality timber have been cut. Technological advances have expanded the timber resource. Lumber and plywood are produced today from smaller logs, though at an increase in cost. The discovery of the kraft pulping process enlarged the pulpwood base to include northern hardwoods and southern pines, and the development of reconstituted wood products such as the fiberboards has created markets for what were once unutilized residues. Rising stumpage prices permit exploitation of more remote timber stands and make more intensive timber culture profitable.

The "timber resource" is not some fixed inventory but instead a *dynamic concept* defined by the current state of technology and by costs and prices. Given the relatively long time period required to produce timber and the large proportion of commercial forestland that is under public ownership, it is quite possible that the supply and demand for timber will be balanced in the future only if prices increase substantially. Whether such a result will be acceptable to the American people is a question that is sure to spark much debate.

The most striking characteristic of the world forest economy is the staggering difference that exists between industrially advanced countries and the third world. Developing countries either have little forest or what they have is difficult to manage. They also have few industries, and those that could compete on international markets face high tariff barriers from importers. Consumption of all forest products in these countries is extremely low. Basic materials such as fuelwood are becoming very scarce in some regions. The view that forestry for community development is more important than industrial forestry is slowly being adopted by development agencies. But to achieve some success in that area, rich countries must give much more consideration to the plight of the third world than they do currently.

# REFERENCES

1. N. Rosenberg, *Perspectives on Technology*, Cambridge Univ. Press, Cambridge, 1976.
2. National Commission on Materials Policy, *Material Needs and the Environment, Today and Tomorrow*, U.S. Govt. Printing Office, Washington, D.C., 1973.
3. Anon., "The Demand and Price Situation for Forest Products, 1964," U.S.D.A. For. Serv., Misc. Publ. No. 983, Washington, D.C., 1964.
4. Anon., "The Demand and Price Situation for Forest Products, 1976–77," U.S.D.A. For. Serv., Misc. Publ. No. 1357, Washington, D.C., 1977.
5. Anon., "Census of Manufacturing, 1977," Vol. I, U.S. Dept. of Comm., Bur. of the Census, Washington, D.C., 1981.
6. Anon., "Annual Survey of Manufacturers, 1976," U.S. Dept. of Comm., Bur. of the Census, Washington, D.C., 1977.
7. W. J. Mead, *Competition and Oligopsony in the Douglas-Fir Lumber Industry*, Univ. of California Press, Berkeley, 1966.
8. Anon., "Summary of Trade and Tariff Information. Hardwood Plywood," U.S. International Trade Commission, Washington, D.C., 1978.
9. Anon., "The Outlook for Timber in the United States," U.S.D.A. For. Serv., For. Res. Rept. No. 20, Washington, D.C., 1973.
10. Anon., "Forest Statistics of the United States," U.S.D.A. For. Serv., Review Draft, Washington, D.C., 1977.
11. A. A. Moslemi, *Particleboard*, Vol. I, *Materials*, Southern Illinois Univ. Press, Carbondale, 1974.
12. G. R. Gregory, *Forest Resource Economics*, Ronald Press, New York, 1972.
13. Anon., "Statistics of Paper and Paperboard, 1978," American Paper Inst., 1978.
14. A. D. Little, Inc., *Economic Impacts of Pulp and Paper Industry Compliance with Government Environment Regulations*, Vol. I, U.S. Environmental Protection Agency, Washington, D.C., 1977.
15. M. Clawson, *Science, 191*, 4227, 762 (1976).
16. Pub. L. 94-588, 90 Stat. 2949 (1976), Sec. 13.
17. D. A. Perala, "Manager's Handbook for Aspen in the North Central States," U.S.D.A. For. Serv., Gen. Tech. Rept. NC-36, St. Paul, 1977.
18. H. D. Smith and G. Anderson, "Economically Optimal Spacing and Site Preparation for Slash Pine Plantations," North Carolina State Univ., School of Forest Resources, Tech. Rept. No. 59, 1977.
19. K. F. S. King, "The Forestry Sector and Economic International Relationships," Weyerhaeuser Lecture Series, Univ. of Toronto, 1975.
20. Anon., "Forestry for Rural Communities," FAO, United Nations, Rome, 1978.
21. E. P. Eckholm, *Ceres*, Nov.-Dec., 44 (1975).
22. J. E. M. Arnold and J. Jongma, *Unasylva, 29*, 2 (1978).
23. Anon., *Forestry for Local Community Development*, FAO, United Nations, Rome, 1978.

# APPENDIX I

## SEED PLANT STRUCTURE: A REVIEW

## Norah J. Cashin[1]

- **PLANT GROWTH**
  Primary Growth
  Secondary Growth
  Cell Wall Development
- **TISSUE ORGANIZATION**
  Organization of the Plant Body
  Ground Tissue System
  Vascular Tissue System
  Dermal Tissue System
- **ORGAN STRUCTURE**
  Root
  Stem
  Leaf
- **CONCLUSION**
- **REFERENCES**

[1]Department of Forestry, University of Wisconsin, Madison, Wisconsin.

Seed plants are the most highly evolved members of the plant kingdom. They are classified into two distinct groups, the *gymnosperms* and the *angiosperms*. The two categories are distinguished by the manner in which the seeds are borne. The word *gymnosperm*, derived from Greek, means "naked seed" and includes plants in which the seeds are produced on scales or fleshy structures (for example, scales of cones). The seeds of angiosperms (from Greek meaning "seed vessel") are enclosed in a matured fruit or ovary (1−5).

The gymnosperms are of ancient lineage, with many species extinct and known only through fossils. There are over 800 forms of gymnosperms grouped in four divisions: conifers, cycads, gnetophytes, and ginkgos. By far the most numerous and widespread are the conifers, with about 550 species. The cycadophyta and gnetophyta are much more diverse even though each division is represented by fewer than 100 species. The division with the fewest number of living species is the ginkgos, with only one representative, *ginkgo biloba*, the maidenhair tree. Ginkgo is the sole living survivor of an evolutionary line extending back to the Paleozoic era (1, 2, 4).

In contrast, the angiosperms are comprised of about 250,000 species, by far the largest number of any group. The flowering plants are the dominant features of our present landscape, except in cool temperate regions with extensive stands of conifer trees. The major reasons for the success of the angiosperms include the ability to survive and reproduce in almost all kinds of environments and the production of flowers, fruits, and seeds that facilitate reproduction (1, 4).

The two classes of angiosperms are *monocotyledons* with one seed leaf and parallel-veined leaves (grasses, palms, lilies, etc.) and *dicotyledons* with two seed leaves and generally net-veined leaves. Dicotyledons include almost all herbs and woody plants other than gymnosperms.

## PLANT GROWTH

A vascular plant begins life as a unicellular fertilized egg, the zygote. Cell divisions then transform the unicellular zygote into a multicellular plant (2). The embryonic plant contained in a seed consists of a cylindrical axis and one or more leaflike appendages, the cotyledons. The lower end of the embryonic axis forms the basis for the root system, and the upper end forms the shoot system.

After germination of the seed, new cell tissues and organs of the plant body are produced almost exclusively by *meristems*. Meristematic tissue, which is perpetually embryonic and undifferentiated, is responsible for plant growth.

Growth of the plant body involves both cell division and cell enlargement. Cell division in the meristems is carried on by certain self-perpetuating cells called *initials*. As these cells divide, one sister cell remains in the meristem while the other, called a *derivative*, is incorporated into the plant body. The initials perpetuate the meristem. The derivatives begin to enlarge and differentiate to form the tissues of the maturing plant body.

### Primary Growth

*Apical meristems* occur at the tips of shoots and roots and produce growth in length, which results in elongation of the plant body. Such growth is called *primary growth*, and tissues formed at this stage are *primary tissues*. The portion of the plant made up of primary tissues is referred to as the *primary plant body*. A complete plant consisting of roots, stems, leaves, flowers, and seeds is produced by primary growth alone (Figure A.1). Most monocotyledons and herbaceous dicotyledons complete their entire life cycle exclusively through primary growth. In temperate regions, either the shoot or the entire plant dies back after one season. Woody plants, however, have persistent stems; they resume primary growth

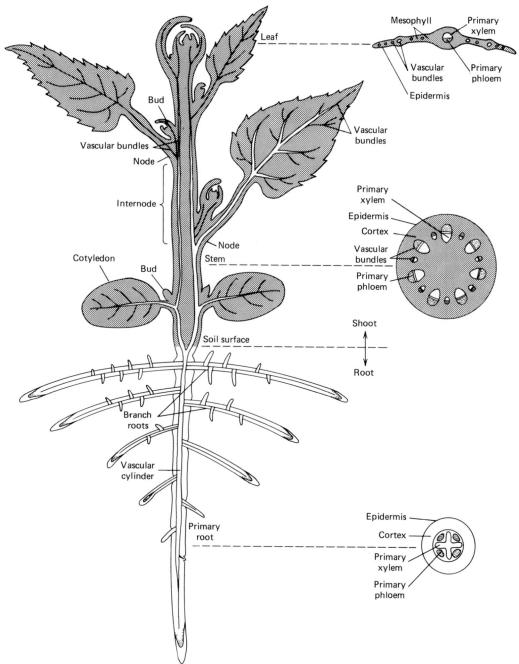

**Figure A-1.** A diagram of a dicotyledonous plant, showing the principal organs of the primary plant body. The tissues of each organ are shown in transverse sections of (a) leaf, (b) stem, and (c) root. In all three organs, the dermal tissue system is represented by the epidermis, and the vascular tissue system, consisting of xylem and phloem, is embedded in the ground tissue system. The ground tissue system in the leaf is represented by mesophyll tissue (not shown in this leaf section); in the stem it is divided into cortex and pith; and in the root it is represented by the cortex only. The leaf is specialized for photosynthesis; the stem for support of the leaves and for conduction; and the root for absorption and anchorage. (From *Biology of Plants*, Third Edition, P. H. Raven, R. F. Evert, and H. Curtis, 1981, courtesy of Worth Publishers, Inc.).

each year and add secondary tissues to the older plant parts, increasing the accumulated bulk (diameter) of the plant body. Although lacking secondary growth, some monocots, such as palms, may develop thick stems by primary growth alone.[1]

## Secondary Growth

The stems and roots of gymnosperms and woody dicots increase in diameter through secondary growth as a result of activity of the *lateral meristems* (vascular cambium and cork cambium). These meristems occur as thin cylindrical sheaths from the roots to the growing shoot tips and produce growth in girth (Figure A.2). Although nearly all tissues and organs of the plant are produced by primary growth, the bulk of the plant body in gymnosperms and woody dicots is produced by secondary growth.

## Cell Wall Development

Another type of primary-secondary development occurs at the level of the cell wall. The cell wall deposited before and during active growth of the cell is known as the primary wall (see Figure 18.3). This cell wall contains cellulose, hemicellulose, and some pectin that makes stretching and growth of the cell possible. Many cells have only a primary wall. Among these are actively dividing cells and mature cells involved with processes such as photosynthesis, respiration, and secretion. Cells with only primary walls are able to de-differentiate (lose specialized form), divide, and re-differentiate (regain form); consequently this class of cells includes those involved in wound healing and regeneration. Primary cell walls are not of uniform thickness, but have thin areas called *primary pitfields* that facilitate the interchange of materials between cells (5−7).

---

[1]The terms *woody plants* and *trees* do not correspond to any specific taxonomic category. A woody plant accumulates secondary xylem and includes gymnosperms, some dicots, but no monocots. A tree is a tall, usually single-stemmed plant represented by species in the conifers, ginkgos, dicotyledons, and a few monocotyledons.

After the cell has ceased to grow, some cells deposit a secondary wall. Cellulose is more abundant in secondary than in primary walls, making the secondary wall more rigid. In addition, the cell wall may become impregnated with lignin, a macromolecular substance that stiffens the cell wall. This is particularly important in cell walls with functions such as conduction or support. In these cells, the protoplast often dies at maturity.

Conduction is facilitated by gaps in the secondary wall over the sites of the primary pitfields. These gaps, termed *pits*, usually occur opposite a pit in an adjoining cell (see Figure 18.7). Adjoining pits are separated by a pit membrane, across which materials may diffuse. Another structure of the cell wall that functions in the transfer of substances is the *perforation*. This is an area lacking a pit membrane; it is literally a hole in the cell wall. Cells with perforations occur in the xylem of angiosperms (cell wall structure is also discussed in Chapter 18).

## TISSUE ORGANIZATION

### Organization of the Plant Body

The developing cells of the plant body differentiate and specialize, taking on a variety of forms and functions. Associations form between cells based on similar structure or function. These groups form the various plant tissues. Some tissues such as parenchyma, collenchyma, and sclerenchyma are structurally simple in that they are composed of only one type of cell. Complex tissues (xylem, phloem, and epidermis) consist of two or more cell types (Table A.1) (1, 2).

Plant organs are structurally interdependent; specific groups of tissues are continuous throughout all of the organs of the plant as a result of functional interrelationships such as conduction, support, or storage. To highlight this organizational unity, these larger groupings of tissues are referred to as tissue systems. The three tissue systems—ground, vascular, and dermal—occur in a continuous pattern through all the plant organs.

# TISSUE ORGANIZATION

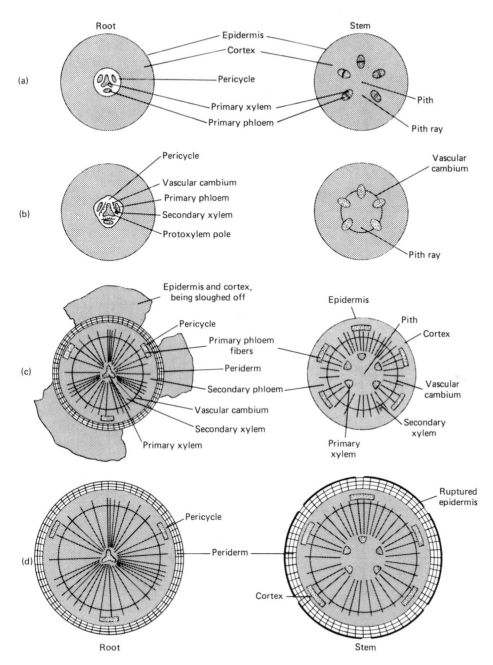

**Figure A-2.** Comparison of primary and secondary structure of a woody dicot. (a) Root and stem at completion of primary growth. (b) Origin of vascular cambium. (c) After formation of some secondary xylem and secondary phloem in the root and stem and periderm formation in the root. (d) End of first year's growth, showing effect of secondary growth. (From *Biology of Plants,* Third Edition, P. H. Raven, R. F. Evert, and H. Curtis, 1981, courtesy of Worth Publishers, Inc.).

**501**

**Table A.1**

Organization of Tissue Systems, Tissues, and Cell Types

| Tissue System | Tissue | Cell types |
|---|---|---|
| Ground | Parenchyma | Parenchyma cells |
| | Collenchyma | Collenchyma cells |
| | Sclerenchyma | Fibers or sclereids |
| Vascular | Xylem | Tracheids (most gymnosperms) |
| | | Vessel members (most angiosperms) |
| | | Parenchyma cells |
| | | Sclerenchyma cells |
| | Phloem | Sieve cells (gymnosperms) |
| | | Sieve-tube members (angiosperms) |
| | | Albuminous cells (gymnosperms) |
| | | Companion cells (angiosperms) |
| | | Parenchyma cells |
| | | Sclerenchyma cells |
| Dermal | Epidermis | Parenchyma cells, including guard cells, root hair cells |
| | | Sclerenchyma cells |
| | Periderm | Parenchyma cells |
| | | Sclerenchyma cells |

*Source.* P. H. Raven, R. F. Evert, and H. Curtis, *Biology of Plants,* Third Edition, Worth Publishers, New York, 1981.

## Ground Tissue System

The ground tissue system forms the fundamental substance of the plant. It is comprised of simple tissues, parenchyma, collenchyma, and sclerenchyma.

*Parenchyma tissue,* the main component of the ground tissue system, is comprised entirely of parenchyma cells. It forms a continuous tissue in shoot cortex and pith, root cortex, and leaf mesophyll. Parenchyma cells are generally living and usually have only a primary cell wall (Table A.2). These cells are involved in metabolic functions, photosynthesis, wound healing, and formation of adventitious structures such as prop roots. Pieces of parenchyma tissue, even single cells, are capable of reproducing entire plants (2).

*Collenchyma tissue* is also composed of living cells with primary walls. Collenchyma cell walls are unevenly thickened, nonlignified, and capable of stretching. This type of wall is well adapted for support of young, growing organs; for example, the strings in celery stalks are composed of collenchyma tissue.

*Sclerenchyma tissue* is characterized by cells with thick, often lignified secondary walls capable of supporting plant parts that have ceased elongating. Although sclerenchyma tissue is not a complex tissue, two types of sclerenchyma cells are recognized: *fibers* and *sclereids.* Fibers are long, slender cells that occur in strands or bundles. They are economically important as bast fibers—for example, hemp, jute, and flax. Sclereids are "stone cells" that form extremely hard tissue such as fruit pits and the gritty cells in pears.

## Vascular Tissue System

The water- and food-conducting system of the vascular plants, the vascular tissue system, is composed of xylem and phloem tissues.

*Xylem tissue* conducts water and minerals from the roots to the leaves. It is also involved in food storage and in support. Xylem may be primary (derived from the apical meristem) or secondary (derived from the vascular cambium) in origin. The principal conducting cells of the xylem are tracheids in gymnosperms and vessel members in angiosperms.[2] Vessel members are joined end-to-end into vessels. Water and minerals pass vertically from cell to cell through pits or perforations in the cell walls of tracheids or vessels.

Xylem tissues contain parenchyma cells that store substances. These cells occur in vertical strands and, in secondary xylem, in horizontal strands called *rays*. Fibers and sclereids also occur in xylem tissue. Many of these fibers are living at maturity and function in storage and support. The fibers used in papermaking are xylem fibers.

*Phloem tissue* transports sugars manufactured in the leaves throughout the plant. Phloem may be primary or secondary in origin. As with xylem tissue, the principal conducting cells are of two types: sieve cells (generally in gymnosperms) and sieve-tube members (in angioperms). Sieve-tube members join end-to-end in long vertical columns called sieve tubes. Characteristically associated with sieve cells are specialized parenchyma cells called albuminous cells. The sieve-tube members exhibit a similar association with companion cells. These parenchyma cells secrete into, and remove substance from, the sieve elements (1−4).

Other parenchyma cells occur in the phloem as axial (vertically oriented) or ray parenchyma. Fibers and sclereids are also present in phloem tissue.

## Dermal Tissue System

The dermal tissue system is the protective sheath around the plant body and regulates the rates of transpiration and aeration.

The *epidermis* is the outermost layer of cells in the primary plant body and constitutes the dermal system of leaves, flowers, fruits, and seeds. The epidermis may contain such specialized structures as stomata, root hairs, or stinging cells.

*Periderm* replaces the epidermis in stems and roots having secondary growth. The periderm consists of cork, cork cambium, and phelloderm. Both epidermal and peridermal tissue may also contain sclerenchyma cells.

The three tissue systems (ground, vascular, and dermal) occur in all plant organs, in basically similar patterns. Generally, the vascular tissue is embedded in the ground tissue and the dermal tissue forms the protective outer coating. Variations in this pattern occur in the relative distribution of vascular and ground tissues (1, 2).

## ORGAN STRUCTURE

### Root

The roots of seed plants perform many functions. Roots anchor the plant in the soil where water and minerals are absorbed and conducted through the primary and secondary xylem to the crown. Sugars produced by photosynthesis in the leaves are transported down to the roots through phloem tissue. Excess sugars manufactured in the leaves can thus be stored as starches underground. Hormones necessary for shoot growth and development are also synthesized in the roots.

The first root of the plant develops from the apical meristem at the lower end of the embryonic axis. In gymnosperms and dicotyledons, this primary root elongates to form a taproot; smaller lateral roots branch out from this primary root forming a taproot system. In monocotyledons, the primary root is short-lived and is replaced by adventitious roots developing from the stem. These roots and their branch roots are known as a fibrous root system. Some large woody plants have also evolved adventitious root structures for enhanced support. Examples include banyan, bald cypress, and mangrove (Figure 2.8).

---

[2]There are exceptions: gnetophytes (gymnosperms) contain vessels, and most angiosperms contain at least some tracheids.

**Table A.2**
Summary of Cell Types

| Cell Type | Characteristics | Location | Function |
|---|---|---|---|
| Parenchyma | Shape: commonly polyhedral (many-sided); variable<br>Cell wall: primary, or primary and secondary; may be lignified, suberized, or cutinized<br>Living at maturity | Throughout the plant, as parenchyma tissue in cortex, as pith and pith rays, or in xylem and phloem as axial or ray parenchyma | Such metabolic processes as respiration, digestion, and photosynthesis; storage and conduction; wound healing and regeneration; adventitious structures |
| Collenchyma | Shape: elongated<br>Cell wall: unevenly thickened; primary only—nonlignified<br>Living at maturity | On the periphery (beneath the epidermis) in young elongating stems; often as a cylinder of tissue or only in patches; in ribs along veins in some leaves | Support in primary plant body |
| Fibers | Shape: generally very long<br>Cell wall: primary and thick secondary—often lignified<br>Often (not always) dead at maturity | Sometimes in cortex of stems, most often associated with xylem and phloem; in leaves of monocotyledons | Support |
| Sclereids | Shape: variable; generally shorter than fibers<br>Cell wall: primary and thick secondary—generally lignified<br>May be living or dead at maturity | Throughout the plant | Mechanical, protective |
| Tracheid | Shape: elongated and tapering<br>Cell wall: primary and secondary; lignified; contains pits, but not perforations<br>Dead at maturity | Xylem | Chief water-conducting element in gymnosperms and lower vascular plants; also found in angiosperms |
| Vessel member | Shape: elongated, generally not as long as tracheids<br>Cell wall: primary and secondary; lignified; contains pits and perforations; several vessel members end-to-end constitute a vessel<br>Dead at maturity | Xylem | Chief water-conducting element in angiosperms |

**504**

**Table A.2** (*continued*)

| Cell Type | Characteristics | Location | Function |
|---|---|---|---|
| Sieve cell | Shape: elongated and tapering<br><br>Cell wall: primary in most species; with sieve areas<br><br>Living at maturity; either lacks or contains remnants of a nucleus at maturity; lacks distinction between vacuole and cytoplasm | Phloem | Chief food-conducting element in gymnosperms and lower vascular plants |
| Albuminous cell | Shape: generally elongated<br><br>Cell wall: primary<br><br>Living at maturity; associated with sieve cell, but generally not derived from same mother cell as sieve cell | Phloem | Believed to play a role in the movement of food into and out of the sieve cell |
| Sieve-tube member | Shape: elongated<br><br>Cell wall: primary, with sieve areas; sieve areas on end wall with much larger pores than those on side walls; this wall part is termed a sieve plate; callose often associated with wall and pores<br><br>Living at maturity; either lacks a nucleus at maturity, or contains only remnants of nucleus; contains a proteinaceous substance known as slime, or P-protein, in dicots and some monocots; several sieve-tube members in a vertical series constitute a sieve tube | Phloem | Chief food-conducting element in angiosperms |
| Companion cell | Shape: variable, generally elongated<br><br>Cell wall: primary<br><br>Living at maturity; closely associated with sieve-tube members; derived from same mother cell as sieve-tube member; has numerous connections with sieve-tube member | Phloem | Believed to play a role in the movement of food into and out of the sieve-tube member |

*Source.* P. H. Raven, R. F. Evert, and H. Curtis, *Biology of Plants*, Third Edition, Worth Publishers, New York, 1981.

Growth and branching of roots is a nearly continuous process. To protect the apical meristem and aid in penetration of the soil, the growing root tip is covered by a layer of cells, the root cap (Figure A.3). Behind this cap, the apical meristem and its immediate derivatives are known as the region of cell division. This region grades into the region of cell elongation. This is the only area in which the root increases in length. The epidermal cells of this young root produce root hairs, which greatly increase the surface area of the roots. Absorption of

water and minerals is performed by these young feeder roots. As the root matures, the root hairs die, and the root becomes involved with conduction and support (1, 2).

Tissues of the root in the primary state of growth are: the cortex (ground tissue system), primary xylem and phloem (vascular tissue system), and epidermis (dermal tissue system) (Table A.3). In the roots of some plants the vascular tissue surrounds a core of pith (ground tissue system) instead of forming a solid cylinder. The vascular tissue is surrounded by a layer of cells called the pericycle, which gives rise to the vascular cambium and cork cambium. Lateral roots originate in the pericycle.

The vascular cambium forms between the primary xylem and phloem and pushes the primary phloem outward (see Figure A.2). With secondary growth the epidermis and cortex are sloughed off and replaced by the periderm (Figure A.4).

### Stem

The stem of the plant supports the leaves, stores polysaccharides, and conducts water and food throughout the plant.

The embryonic shoot apex consists of the stem, one or more leaf primordia, and an apical meristem. This shoot expands from the embryo during germination utilizing food stored in the cotyledons or the seed endosperm. The stem elongates into an orderly sequence of nodes and internodes, and new leaves develop from the edges of the apical meristem (Figure A.5). Bud primordia form in the axis of the leaves and are capable of following a sequence of growth similar to the shoot apex (2–5).

As the shoot develops, the primary vascular tissue forms a ring, sometimes discontinuous, around a pith of primarily parenchyma tissue. The vascular tissue is surrounded by cortex, which is composed of parenchyma cells (containing chlorophyll) and collenchyma cells. In plants where the vascular tissue is discontinuous, the areas of ground tissue between vascular bundles are known as pith rays. As in the

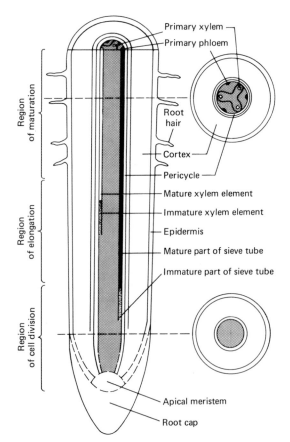

**Figure A-3.** A diagram illustrating early stages in the primary development of a root tip. (From *Biology of Plants*, Third Edition, P. H. Raven, R. F. Evert, and H. Curtis, 1981, courtesy of Worth Publishers, Inc.).

Primary xylem
Primary phloem
Root hair
Cortex
Pericycle
Mature xylem element
Immature xylem element
Epidermis
Mature part of sieve tube
Immature part of sieve tube
Apical meristem
Root cap

Region of maturation
Region of elongation
Region of cell division

**Table A.3**

Summary of Stem and Root Development

| | Primary Tissue | Lateral Meristems | Secondary Tissue | Tissue System |
|---|---|---|---|---|
| **Stem apical meristem** | Epidermis | | | Dermal |
| | Primary phloem | Vascular cambium | Secondary phloem | Vascular |
| | Primary xylem | | Secondary xylem | |
| | Pith rays | | | |
| | Pith | | | Ground |
| | Cortex | Cork cambium | Cork [a] | Ground |
| | | | Phelloderm [a] | |
| **Root apical meristem** | Epidermis | | | Dermal |
| | Primary phloem | | | |
| | Primary xylem | Vascular cambium | Secondary phloem | Vascular |
| | Pericycle | | Secondary xylem | |
| | | Cork cambium | Cork [a] | Ground |
| | | | Phelloderm [a] | |
| | Cortex | | | Dermal |

[a] Components of periderm.

root, the epidermis is a primary tissue that is shed following the onset of secondary growth.

The vascular cambium forms between the primary xylem and phloem and in the pith rays (see Figure A.2). As the cambial initials divide, new cells formed toward the inside of the plant become xylem (Figure A.6). Cells produced in the spring growing season are usually much larger and thin-walled to carry the sap necessary for bud and leaf growth. The smaller size and increased density of summerwood cells make them look dark. It is the alteration of the darker *summerwood* with the lighter *springwood* that produces the pattern of annual rings in trees (see Figure 3.4). In dicotyledons, the vessels produced in the springwood may be larger than vessels produced later in the year, forming a distinct ring of pores in cross section. Such wood is referred to as *ring-porous* wood. Trees that form vessels of fairly uniform size throughout the growing season have *diffuse-porous* wood (see Figure 17.4) (6, 7).

With age, the inner part of the xylem ceases to function as a conductive tissue. The cells die and often become infused with tannins or resins, darkening in color. This tissue, known as *heartwood*, serves only for support and is the portion of the tree that is most desirable for use as lumber, because it is more durable than the outer xylem or *sapwood* and frequently of better color (e.g., black walnut).

Tissue formed outside the vascular cambium becomes phloem. Phloem tissue does not accumulate as xylem does, because it is crushed by the newly forming periderm. It is believed that only the current year's growth of secondary phloem is active in the long-distance transport of food through the stem, although the parenchyma cells in the inner bark may continue to function as storage cells (1, 2).

In addition to xylem and phloem, the cells of which are vertically oriented, certain initials in the vascular cambium produce horizontally oriented parenchyma cells in strands called *rays*. The rays

**507**

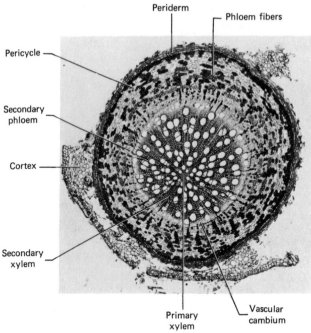

Periderm

Phloem fibers

Pericycle

Secondary
phloem

Cortex

Secondary
xylem

Primary
xylem

Vascular
cambium

**Figure A-4.** Transverse section of the willow *(Salix)* root at end of first year's growth, showing effect of secondary growth on primary plant body (X45). (Photomicrograph courtesy of Ray Evert).

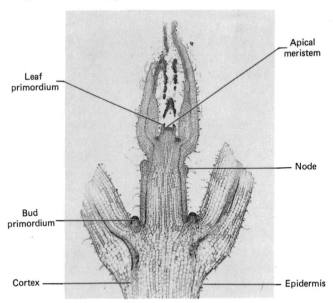

Apical
meristem

Leaf
primordium

Node

Bud
primordium

Cortex

Epidermis

**Figure A-5.** Longitudinal section of a shoot tip of common houseplant *Coleus blumei,* a dicot (X25). (Photomicrograph courtesy of Ray Evert).

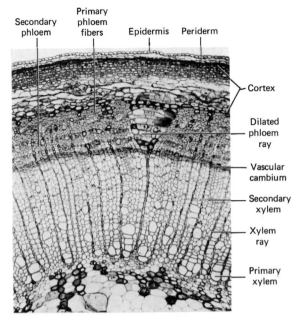

Secondary phloem | Primary phloem fibers | Epidermis | Periderm

Cortex

Dilated phloem ray

Vascular cambium

Secondary xylem

Xylem ray

Primary xylem

**Figure A-6.** Transverse section of 1-year-old linden *(Tilia americana)* tree stem (X110). (Photomicrograph courtesy of Ray Evert).

ensure the horizontal distribution of water and sugars.

The cork cambium forms outside the ring of phloem fibers. It produces mostly cork, or outer bark. As the tree grows in girth, the outer bark splits in a manner characteristic of the species. Many trees can be identified by the bark pattern. Cork cells, which protect the tree from water loss and parasites, build up a layer of fatty suberin, making the tissue highly impermeable to water and gases. The lateral exchange of gases necessary to the inner tissues of stems and roots is carried through *lenticels,* corky portions of the periderm with large intercellular spaces.

## Leaf

Leaves are the primary photosynthetic organs of the plant. The leaf begins development as leaf primordia originating at the sides of the apical meristem (see Figure A.5). A portion of the vascular tissue of the

stem diverges away from the rest of the vascular cylinder and enters the developing leaf. This vascular bundle is called the *leaf trace.* The gap in the vascular cylinder of the stem above the leaf trace is filled with ground tissue and is termed the *leaf gap.* The upper portion of union of leaf and stem, the *axil,* usually contains a bud or bud primordium (1–4).

The leaf is formed as an organ of the primary plant body and generally does not undergo secondary growth. These generalized concepts apply to all vascular plant leaves, although the outward structure and arrangement of tissues occurs in many varied and sometimes bizarre forms throughout the seed plants. This discussion will be confined to plant groups in which trees occur.

In spite of their varied form, the three tissue systems occur in all vascular plant leaves. The epidermal cells of the leaf are covered with a cuticle to reduce water loss but minute openings called *stomata* occur in the epidermis to facilitate oxygen and carbon dioxide exchange. Specialized guard cells that surround the stomata open and close the pore by means of water pressure within their cell walls. In conifers and dicotyledons adapted to dry conditions, the stomata are sunken below the surface of the leaf to avoid dehydration. The stomata occur in rows parallel to the long axis of the leaf in monocotyledons; while in dicotyledons, the stomata are arranged in random patterns.

The ground tissue of the leaf, the *mesophyll,* is specialized for photosynthesis (see Figure A.1). It is primarily made up of chlorophyll-containing parenchyma cells. The rapid gas exchange necessary for photosynthesis is facilitated by large intercellular spaces that form continuous channels with the stomatal openings. Resin ducts are also distributed throughout the mesophyll of conifer leaves.

The vascular tissue of the leaf is continuous with the vascular-tissue system in the stem. Vascular bundles or *veins* are integrated throughout the mesophyll of most vascular plants. The veins in ginkgos occur in a forked or *dichotomous* pattern. Most monocotyledon leaves have veins of similar size oriented parallel to one another, a pattern referred to as *parallel veination*. In most dicotyledons the veins are arranged in a branching pattern known as *netted veination*.

The xylem and phloem contained in the veins are generally all primary in origin. Strength and support are imparted to the leaves by a number of factors. The epidermal cells are compactly arranged, and the cuticle provides some rigidity. In monocotyledons, the veins and leaf edges may be bordered by fibers. Collenchyma cells may occur along the larger veins and edges of dicotyledon leaves.

Many plants with persistent stems shed their leaves during the cold or dry season. These are the *deciduous* plants. The separation or *abscission* of the leaf from the stem is preceded by certain chemical and structural changes near the base of the leaf, resulting in the formation of an abscission zone. The zone of separation is made up of short cells with poorly developed wall thickenings, which make the layer structurally weak and cause leaves to fall (1, 2). After the leaf falls, this area forms a distinct protective layer called a *leaf scar*. The pattern of the leaf scar varies from species to species and may aid in plant identification.

The main factor in tree identification, however, is leaf morphology. Leaves vary greatly in form. Conifers produce needlelike or scaly leaves, frequently arranged in bundles. Ginkgos are easily recognized by distinctly veined, fan-shaped leaves. In most monocotyledons and some dicotyledons, the base of the leaf broadens into a *sheath* that encircles the stem. Dicotyledonous leaves commonly consist of an expanded *blade* and a stalklike *petiole*. Leaves that lack petioles are referred to as *sessile*. Small scalelike *stipules* develop at the base of some leaves.

The arrangement of the leaves on the stem differs from plant to plant. The pattern may be *alternate* (spiral), *opposite* (pair), or *whorled* (three or more at a node).

The leaves of dicotyledons may be either simple or compound. The blade of a simple leaf is a single unit. Compound leaves are divided into leaflets, each with its own small stalk, or *petiolule*. Leaves may be compounded in two patterns: *pinnately compound* with leaflets arising from either side of an extended petiole, or *palmately compound* with leaflets diverging from a single point at the tip of the petiole. A leaflet can be distinguished from a leaf by the fact that buds only occur in the axils of leaves (1–7).

## CONCLUSION

All of the growth and resulting tissue described above comprise the vegetative growth stage in the life of a seed plant. However, a living being does not complete its life cycle without reproducing more of its kind. Therefore, at an appropriate time, determined by a complex interaction of light, temperature, and plant maturity, certain vegetative apical meristems of the shoot become reproductive apical meristems that produce flowers or other reproductive structures and ultimately seeds; thus the cycle begins anew.

## REFERENCES

1. P. H. Raven, R. F. Evert, and H. Curtis, *Biology of Plants,* Third Edition, Worth Publishers, New York, 1981.
2. K. Esau, *Anatomy of Seed Plants,* Second Edition, John Wiley & Sons, New York, 1977.
3. W. W. Robbins, T. E. Weier, and C. R. Stocking, *Botany,* Third Edition, John Wiley & Sons, New York, 1965.
4. C. L. Wilson and W. E. Loomis, *Botany,* Third Edition, Holt, Rinehart and Winston, New York, 1962.
5. D. von Denffer, et al., *Strasburger's Textbook of Botany,* English Edition, Longman, New York, 1976.
6. M. Busgen, *The Structure and Life of Forest Trees,* English Edition, Chapman and Hall, London, 1929.
7. G. I. Torora, D. R. Cicero, and H. I. Parish, *Plant Form and Function,* Macmillan, New York, 1970.

# APPENDIX II

## COMMON AND SCIENTIFIC NAMES OF TREE SPECIES MENTIONED IN THE TEXT

| Common Names | Scientific Names |
| --- | --- |
| Acacia | *Acacia spp.* |
| Achin | *Pistacia mexicana* |
| Ailanthus or tree of heaven | *Ailanthus altissima* |
| Alder, common or European | *Alnus glutinosa* |
| red | *Alnus rubra* |
| Aliso | *Alnus jorullensis* |
| American hornbeam (see Beech) | |
| Ash, American mountain | *Sorbus americana* |
| common | *Fraxinus excelsior* |
| flowering | *Fraxinus ornus* |
| green or red | *Fraxinus pennsylvanica* |
| mountain | *Eucalyptus regnans* |
| oregon | *Fraxinus latifolia* |
| white | *Fraxinus americana* |
| Aspen (Europe) | *Populus tremula* |
| largetooth or bigtooth | *Populus grandidentata* |
| quaking or trembling | *Populus tremuloides* |
| Bald cypress (see Cypress) | |
| Bamboo | *Cephalostachyum pergracile* |
| Basswood, American or American linden | *Tilia americana* |
| small-leaved linden | *Tilia cordata* |
| white | *Tilia heterophylla* |
| Beech, American | *Fagus grandifolia* |
| blue, or American hornbeam | *Carpinus caroliniana (Carpinus betulus virginiana)* |

| Common Names | Scientific Names |
| --- | --- |
| common or European | *Fagus sylvatica* |
| eastern hornbeam | *Carpinus orientalis* |
| European hornbeam | *Carpinus betulus* |
| southern | *Nothofagus spp.* |
| Bigcone Douglas-fir (see Fir) | |
| Birch, gray or field | *Betula populifolia* |
| river | *Betula nigra* |
| silver | *Betula verrucosa* |
| sweet or black | *Betula lenta* |
| white or paper | *Betula papyrifera* |
| yellow | *Betula alleghaniensis (Betula lutea)* |
| Blackgum (see Gum) | |
| Bluebeech (see Beech) | |
| Boxelder (see Elder) | |
| Buckeye, yellow | *Aesculus octandra* |
| Butternut | *Juglans cinerea* |
| Camaron | *Alvaradoa amorphoides* |
| Caoba | *Swietenia humulis* |
| Carob tree | *Caratonia siliqua* |
| Castano bellota | *Sterculia mexicana* |
| Catalpa, northern or hardy | *Catalpa speciosa* |
| southern | *Catalpa bignonioides* |
| Cedar, Alaska yellow | *Chamaecyparis nootkatensis* |
| Atlantic white | *Chamaecyparis thyoides* |
| eastern red | *Juniperus virginiana* |
| incense | *Libocedrus decurrens* |
| Japanese | *Cryptomeria japonica* |
| northern white, or eastern arborvitae | *Thuja occidentalis* |

**511**

# COMMON AND SCIENTIFIC NAMES OF TREE SPECIES

| Common Names | Scientific Names | Common Names | Scientific Names |
|---|---|---|---|
| Port Orford | *Chamaecyparis lawsoniana* | Gum, black or black tupelo | *Nyssa sylvatica* |
| prickly juniper | *Juniperus oxycedrus* | red or sweet | *Liquidambar styraciflua* |
| western juniper | *Juniperus occidentalis* | swamp tupelo | *Nyssa sylvatica biflora* |
| western red | *Thuja plicata* | tupelo or water tupelo | *Nyssa aquatica* |
| Cherry, black | *Prunus serotina* | Gumbo-limbo | *Bursera simaruba* |
| cornelian | *Cornus mas* | Hackberry | *Celtis occidentalis* |
| Chestnut, American | *Castenea dentata* | Hazel, European or filbert | *Corylus avellana* |
| Spanish | *Castenea sativa* | Hemlock, eastern | *Tsuga canadensis* |
| China tree | *Melia azedarach* | mountain | *Tsuga mertensiana* |
| Chinkapin, golden | *Castanopsis chrysophylla* | western | *Tsuga heterophylla* |
| Chokeberry | *Aronia spp.* | Hickory, bitternut | *Carya cordiformis* |
| Coffeetree, Kentucky | *Gymnocladus dioicus* | mockernut | *Carya tomentosa* |
| Cottonwood (see Poplar) | | shagbark | *Carya ovata* |
| Crape myrtle | *Lagerstroemia indica* | Holly, American | *Ilex opaca* |
| Cucumber tree or cucumber magnolia | *Magnolia acuminata* | Honeylocust (see Locust) | |
| Cypress, bald | *Taxodium distichum* | Hoja fresca | *Gilbertia arborea* |
| monterey | *Cupressus macrocarpa* | Hophornbeam, eastern | *Ostrya virginiana* |
| Montezuma | *Taxodium mucronatum* | European | *Ostrya carpinifolia* |
| Dogwood, flowering | *Cornus florida* | Hornbeam (see Beech) | |
| Douglas-fir (see Fir) | | Horsechestnut (Buckeye) | *Aesculus hippocastanum* |
| Doveplum | *Coccoloba diversifolia* | Huisache | *Acacia farnesiana* |
| Eucalyptus | *Eucalyptus spp.* | Ironwood | *Dialium guianense* |
| Elder, box | *Acer negundo* | Judas tree | *Cercis siliquastrum* |
| Elm, American or white | *Ulmus americana* | Juniper (see Cedar) | |
| English | *Ulmus procera* | Kentucky coffeetree (see Coffeetree) | |
| Japanese | *Ulmus japonica* | Larch, American, eastern, or Tamarack | *Larix laricina* |
| rock or cork | *Ulmus thomasii* | European | *Larix decidua (Larix europaca)* |
| Siberian | *Ulmus pumila* | | |
| False mastic | *Sideroxylon foetidissimum* | subalpine | *Larix lyallii* |
| Filbert (see Hazel) | | western | *Larix occidentalis* |
| Fir, alpine or subalpine | *Abies lasiocarpa* | Laurel, bay | *Laurus nobilis* |
| bigcone Douglas | *Pseudotsuga macrocarpa* | California, Oregon-myrtle | *Umbellularia californica* |
| balsam | *Abies balsamea* | Leadwood | *Krugiodendron ferreum* |
| California red | *Abies magnifica* | Lignum vitae | *Guaiacum sanctum* |
| Douglas | *Pseudotsuga menziesii* | Linden (see Basswood) | |
| grand or lowland white | *Abies grandis* | Locust, black or yellow | *Robinia pseudoacacia* |
| noble | *Abies procera (Abies nobilis)* | honey | *Gleditsia triacanthos* |
| Pacific silver | *Abies amabilis* | Madrone, Pacific | *Arbutus menziesii* |
| silver | *Abies alba* | Magnolia, southern | *Magnolia grandiflora* |
| white | *Abies concolor* | Mahogany, West Indies | *Swietenia mahagoni* |
| Fish poison tree, Florida | *Piscidia piscipula* | Mangrove, black | *Avicennia nitida* |
| Ginkgo tree | *Ginkgo biloba* | Maple, bigleaf | *Acer macrophyllum* |
| Goldenrain tree | *Koelreuteria paniculata* | | |

512

# COMMON AND SCIENTIFIC NAMES OF TREE SPECIES

| Common Names | Scientific Names | Common Names | Scientific Names |
|---|---|---|---|
| Norway | *Acer platanoides* | white | *Quercus alba* |
| red (including trident) | *Acer rubrum* | willow | *Quercus phellos* |
| silver | *Acer saccharinum* | Olive | *Olea europaea* |
| sugar | *Acer saccharum* | Oriental plane | *Platanus orientalis* |
| sycamore | *Acer pseudoplatanus* | Oyamel | *Abies religiosa* |
| vine | *Acer circinatum* | Paulownia | *Paulownia tomentosa* |
| Melina | *Gmelina arborea* | Pecan | *Carya illinoensis* |
| Metasequoia | *Metasequoia glyptostroboides* | Persimmon, common | *Diospyros virginiana* |
| | | Pine, aleppo | *Pinus halepensis* |
| Monkeypod, monkey puzzle | *Araucaria araucana* | apache | *Pinus engelmannii* |
| | | bishop | *Pinus muricata* |
| Mulberry, red | *Morus rubra* | black or Austrian | *Pinus nigra* |
| white | *Morus alba* | bristlecone | *Pinus aristata* |
| Nettle tree, European | *Celtis australis* | Caribbean | *Pinus caribaea* |
| Oak, black | *Quercus velutina* | Chihuahua or piño | |
| blackjack | *Quercus marilandica* | chino | *Pinus lieophylla* var. *chihuahuana* |
| bur | *Quercus macrocarpa* | | |
| California black | *Quercus kelloggii* | Coulter | *Pinus coulteri* |
| California live | *Quercuus agrifolia* | Digger | *Pinus sabiniana* |
| California white | *Quercus lobata* | eastern white | *Pinus strobus* |
| canyon live | *Quercus chrysolepis* | foxtail | *Pinus balfouriana* |
| cherry bark | *Quercus falcata pagodaefolia* | jack | *Pinus banksiana* |
| | | Jeffrey | *Pinus jeffreyi* |
| chestnut | *Quercus prinus* | knobcone | *Pinus attenuata* |
| cork | *Quercus suber* | limber pine | *Pinus flexilis* |
| durmast | *Quercus petraea* | loblolly | *Pinus taeda* |
| English | *Quercus robur* | lodgepole | *Pinus contorta* |
| holm | *Quercus ilex* | longleaf | *Pinus palustris* |
| Hungarian | *Quercus frainetto* | maritime | *Pinus pinaster* |
| live | *Quercus virginiana* | Monterey | *Pinus radiata* |
| northern red or eastern red | *Quercus rubra (Quercus borealis)* | Norfolk Island | *Araucaria heterophylla* |
| | | pinabete | *Pinus ayacahuite* |
| | | piño de Montezuma | *Pinus montezumae* |
| Oregon white | *Quercus garryana* | piño prieto | *Pinus oocarpa* |
| overcup | *Quercus lyrata* | piño colorado | *Pinus teocote* |
| pin | *Quercus palustris* | pinyon | *Pinus edulis* |
| post | *Quercus stellata* | pitch | *Pinus rigida* |
| pubescent | *Quercus pubescens* | pond | *Pinus serotina* |
| scarlet | *Quercus coccinea* | ponderosa or western yellow | *Pinus ponderosa* |
| silky | *Grevillea robusta* | (Rocky Mountain form) | *Pinus ponderosa* var. *scopulorum* |
| southern red | *Quercus falcata* | | |
| swamp chestnut | *Quercus michauxii* | | |
| turkey (U.S.) | *Quercus laevis (Quercus catesbaei)* | red or Norway | *Pinus resinosa* |
| | | sand | *Pinus clausa* |
| turkey (Europe) | *Quercus cerris* | Scotch | *Pinus sylvestris* |
| water | *Quercus nigra* | | |

# COMMON AND SCIENTIFIC NAMES OF TREE SPECIES

| Common Names | Scientific Names | Common Names | Scientific Names |
|---|---|---|---|
| shortleaf | *Pinus echinata* | blue | *Picea pungens* |
| slash | *Pinus elliotti* | Engelmann | *Picea engelmannii* |
| southwestern white | *Pinus strobiformis* | Norway | *Picea abies* |
| spruce | *Pinus glabra* | red | *Picea rubens* |
| stone | *Pinus pinea* | sitka | *Picea sitchensis* |
| sugar | *Pinus lambertiana* | white | *Picea glauca* |
| Tenasserim | *Pinus merkusii* | St. Johns bread (see Carob | |
| Virginia or scrub | *Pinus virginiana* | tree) | |
| western white | *Pinus monticola* | Strangler fig, Florida | *Ficus aurea* |
| whitebark | *Pinus albicaulis* | Strawberry tree | *Arbutus unedo* |
| Poplar, California or | | Sugarberry | *Celtis laevigata* |
| black cottonwood | *Populus trichocarpa* | Sugi (see Cedar, | |
| eastern or eastern | | Japanese) | |
| cottonwood | *Populus deltoides* | Sweetbay, southern | *Magnolia virginiana* |
| swamp cottonwood | *Populus heterophylla* | Sycamore, American | *Platanus occidentalis* |
| yellow, or tuliptree | *Liriodendron tulipifera* | Tamarack (see Larch) | |
| Prickly ash, lime | *Zanthoxylon fagara* | Tamarind, wild | *Lysiloma bahamensis* |
| Redberry eugenia | *Eugenia confusa* | Tanoak | *Lithocarpus densiflorus* |
| Redcedar (see Cedar) | | Teak | *Tectona grandis* |
| Redwood | *Sequoia sempervirens* | Torreya, California | *Torreya californica* |
| Rompezapata or | | Trumpet wood | *Cecropia mexicana* |
| saffron-plum | *Bumelia celastrina* | Tuliptree (see Poplar) | |
| Rosewood | *Dalbergia spp.* | Karri | *Eucalyptus diversicolor* |
| Royal palm, Florida | *Roystonea elata* | Tupelo (see Gum) | |
| Sassafras | *Sassafras albidum* | Walnut, black | *Juglans nigra* |
| Sequoia, giant | *Sequoia gigantea* | Willow | *Salix spp.* |
| Silk-cotton tree | *Ceiba pentandra* | Yellow-poplar (see | |
| Silktree | *Albizzia julibrissin* | Poplar) | |
| Soapberry, windleaf | *Sapindus saponaria* | Yew, common | *Taxus baccata* |
| Sourwood | *Oxydendron arboreum* | pacific | *Taxus brevifolia* |
| Spruce, black | *Picea mariana* | | |

# APPENDIX III

## COMMON AND SCIENTIFIC NAMES OF WILDLIFE SPECIES MENTIONED IN THE TEXT

| Common Names | Scientific Names | Common Names | Scientific Names |
|---|---|---|---|
| | | Raccoon | *Procyon lotor* |
| | | Wolf, gray or timber | *Canis lupus* |
| | | Wolverine | *Gulo luscus* |

### Insectivores

| Common Names | Scientific Names |
|---|---|
| Mole, eastern | *Scalopus aquaticus* |
| Shrew | *Sorex spp.* |

### Hares and Rabbits

| Common Names | Scientific Names |
|---|---|
| Hare, snowshoe | *Lepus americanus* |
| Cottontail, eastern | *Sylvilagus floridanus* |

### Rodents

| Common Names | Scientific Names |
|---|---|
| Beaver | *Castor canadensis* |
| Gopher, pocket | *Thomomys spp.* |
| Mouse, white-footed deer | *Peromyscus maniculatus* |
| Porcupine | *Erethizon dorsatum* |
| Squirrel, flying (southern) | *Galucomys volans* |
| Squirrel, ground | *Spermophilus spp.* |
|   chipmunk least | |
|     (western) | *Eutamias minimus* |
| Squirrel, tree | |
|   gray, eastern | *Sciurus carolinensis* |
|   pine or chickaree | *Tamiasciurus douglasi* |
|   red | *Tamiasciurus hudsonicus* |
| Voles | *Microtus spp.* |

### Carnivores

| Common Names | Scientific Names |
|---|---|
| Bear, black | *Ursus americanus* |
| Coyote | *Canis latrans* |
| Fisher | *Martes pennanti* |
| Fox, gray | *Vulpes fulva* |
|   red | *Urocyon cinereoargenteus* |
| Lynx | *Lynx canadensis* |
| Mink | *Mustela vison* |
| Mountain lion | *Felis concolor* |
| Otter | *Lutra canadensis* |

### Even-Toed Ungulates

| Common Names | Scientific Names |
|---|---|
| Deer, mule | *Odocoileus hemionus* |
|   white-tailed | *Odocoileus virginianus* |
| Elk (wapiti) | *Cervus canadensis* |
| Moose | *Alces alces* |

### Birds

| Common Names | Scientific Names |
|---|---|
| Bluebird, eastern | *Sialia sialis* |
| Catbird | *Dumetella carolinensis* |
| Chickadee, black-capped | *Parus atricapillus* |
| Cranes | *Grus spp.* |
| Creeper, brown tree | *Certhia familiaris* |
| Crossbill | *Loxia spp.* |
| Dove, mourning | *Zenaida macroura* |
| Duck, American | |
|   golden-eye | *Glaucionetta clangula* |
|   Barrow's golden-eye | *Bucephala islandica* |
|   buffle-head | *Bucephala albeola* |
|   black | *Anas rubripes* |
|   hooded merganser | *Lophodytes cucullatus* |
|   mallard, common | *Anas platyrhynchos* |
|   wood | *Aix sponsa* |
| Eagle, bald | *Haliaeetus leucocephalus* |
| Flycatcher, least | *Empidonax minimus* |
| Goose, Canada | *Branta canadensis* |
| Grouse, blue | *Dendragapus obscurus* |
|   prairie chicken or | |
|     pinnated | *Tympamuchus cupido* |
|   ruffed | *Bonasa umbellus* |

## COMMON AND SCIENTIFIC NAMES OF WILDLIFE SPECIES

| Common Names | Scientific Names | Common Names | Scientific Names |
|---|---|---|---|
| sharp-tailed | *Pedioecetes phasianellus* | southern pine | *Dendroctonus frontalis* |
| Hawk, broad-winged | *Buteo platypterus* | western pine | *Dendroctonus brevicomis* |
| goshawk | *Accipiter gentilis* | Borer, bonze birch | *Agrilus anxius* |
| Kingbird | *Tyrannus spp.* | hemlock | *Melanophila fulvoguttata* |
| Magpie | *Pica pica* | poplar | *Saperda calcarata* |
| Martin, purple | *Progne subis* | two-lined chestnut | *Agrilus bilineatus* |
| Nuthatch, white-breasted | *Sitta carolinensis* | Budworm, jack pine | *Choristoneura pinus* |
| Oriole, Baltimore | *Icterus galbula* | spruce | *Choristoneura fumiferana* |
| Osprey | *Pandion haliaetus* | Casebearer, larch | *Coleophora laricella* |
| Ovenbird | *Seiurus aurocopillus* | Engraver, fir | *Scolytus ventralis* |
| Owl, barred | *Strix varia* | pine | *Ips pini* |
| Quail, bobwhite | *Colinus virginianus* | Looper, hemlock | *Lambdina fiscellaria* |
| Raven | *Corvus corax* | linden | *Erannis tiliaria* |
| Siskin | *Carduelis pinus* | Moth, gypsy | *Lymantria dispar* |
| Swallow, tree | *Iridoprocne bicolor* | shoot, European pine | *Rhyacionia buoliana* |
| Swift, chimney | *Chaetura pelagica* | Douglas-fir tussock | *Orgyia pseudotsugata* |
| Thrush | *Hylocichla spp.* | pine tussock | *Dasychira plagiata* |
| Turkey, eastern | *Meleagris gallopavo silvestrii* | white-marked tussock | *Hemerocampa leucostigma* |
| Vireo, red-eyed | *Vireo olivaceus* | Pitch nodule maker | *Petrova albicapitana* |
| Warbler, black-and-white | *Mniotilta varia* | Sawfly, European pine | *Neodiprion sertifer* |
| blackburian | *Dendroica fusca* | European spruce | *Diprion hercyniae* |
| Kirtland's | *Dendroica Kirtlandii* | jack pine | *Neodiprion pratti banksianae* |
| Waxwing | *Bombycilla spp.* | | |
| Wren | *Thyrothorus spp.* | larch | *Pristiphora erichsonii* |
| Woodcock | *Philohela minor* | red-headed pine | *Neodiprion lecontei* |
| Woodpecker, downy | *Dendrocopus pubescens* | red pine | *Neodiprion nanulus nanulus* |
| flicker | *Colaptes auratus* | | |
| hairy | *Dendrocopus villosus* | Swaine jack pine | *Neodiprion swainei* |
| pileated | *Dryocopus pileatus* | Sawyer, southern pine | *Monochamas titillator* |
| red-cockaded | *Dendrocopus borealis* | white spotted | *Monochamus scutellatus* |
| yellow-bellied | | Scale, pine tortoise | *Toumeyella numismatica* |
| sapsucker | *Sphyrapicus varius* | Spanworm, elm | *Ennomos subsignarius* |
| | | Spittlebug, pine | *Aphrophora parallela* |
| **Insects** | | Saratoga | *Aphrophora saratogensis* |
| | | Tent caterpillar, eastern | *Malacosoma americanum* |
| Aphid, balsam wooly | *Adelges piceae* | forest | *Malacosoma disstria* |
| Beetle, Douglas-fir | *Dendroctonus pseudotsugae* | Walkingstick | *Diapheromera femorata* |
| | | Weevil, pales | *Hylobius pales* |
| Japanese | *Popillia japonica* | pine root collar | *Hylobius radicis* |
| mountain pine | *Dendroctonus ponderosae* | white pine or | |
| smaller European elm | | Englemann spruce | *Pissodes strobi* |
| bark | *Scolytus multistriatus* | | |

# APPENDIX IV
## UNIT CONVERSION TABLES

Linear Measure

|  | cm | m | km | ft | mile | chain | link |
|---|---|---|---|---|---|---|---|
| 1 centimeter | 1 | 0.01 | $10^{-5}$ | 0.0328 | $6.214 \times 10^{-6}$ | $4.971 \times 10^{-4}$ | 0.04971 |
| 1 meter | 100 | 1 | 0.001 | 3.2808 | $6.214 \times 10^{-4}$ | 0.04971 | 4.971 |
| 1 kilometer | $10^5$ | 1000 | 1 | 3,280.84 | 0.6214 | 49.7097 | 4970.97 |
| 1 foot | 30.4801 | 0.3048 | $3.048 \times 10^{-4}$ | 1 | $1.8939 \times 10^{-4}$ | 0.01515 | 1.5152 |
| 1 mile | 160934.4 | 1609.344 | 1.6093 | 5,280 | 1 | 80 | 8000 |
| 1 chain | 2011.68 | 20.1168 | 0.02012 | 66 | 0.0125 | 1 | 100 |
| 1 link | 20.1168 | 0.2012 | $2.0117 \times 10^{-4}$ | 0.66 | $1.25 \times 10^{-4}$ | 0.01 | 1 |

Mass Measure

|  | kg | m ton | pound | short ton |
|---|---|---|---|---|
| 1 kilogram | 1 | 0.001 | 2.2046 | $1.1023 \times 10^{-3}$ |
| 1 metric ton | 1000 | 1 | 2204.6226 | 1.1023 |
| 1 pound | 0.4536 | $4.5359 \times 10^{-4}$ | 1 | 0.0005 |
| 1 short ton | 907.185 | 0.9072 | 2000 | 1 |

Area Measure

| | m² | ha | ft² | chain² | acre | mile² (section) |
|---|---|---|---|---|---|---|
| 1 hectare | 10000 | 1 | 107639.1 | 24.7105 | 2.4711 | 0.0039 |
| 1 square meter | 1 | $1 \times 10^{-4}$ | 10.7639 | $2.4711 \times 10^{-3}$ | $2.4711 \times 10^{-4}$ | $3.8610 \times 10^{-7}$ |
| 1 acre | 4046.86 | 0.4047 | 43560 | 10 | 1 | $1.5625 \times 10^{-3}$ |
| 1 square mile | $2.5910 \times 10^{6}$ | 258.999 | 27878400 | 6400 | 640 | 1 |
| 1 township | — | 9323.9892 | — | — | 23040 | 36 |
| 1 section | 2589988 | 258.9997 | 27878400 | 6400 | 640 | 1 |
| 1/4 section | 647497 | 64.7499 | 6969600 | 1600 | 160 | 0.25 |
| 1/4–1/4 section | 161874 | 16.1875 | 1742400 | 400 | 40 | 0.0625 |

Volume Measure

| | cm³ (ml) | m³ | in.³ | ft³ | qt |
|---|---|---|---|---|---|
| 1 cubic centimeter | 1 | $1 \times 10^{-6}$ | $6.1024 \times 10^{-2}$ | $3.5315 \times 10^{-5}$ | $1.0567 \times 10^{-3}$ |
| 1 cubic meter | $10^{6}$ | 1 | $6.1024 \times 10^{4}$ | 35.3147 | 1056.688 |
| 1 cubic inch | 16.3871 | $1.6387 \times 10^{-5}$ | 1 | $5.7870 \times 10^{-4}$ | $1.7316 \times 10^{-2}$ |
| 1 cubic foot | 28316.85 | $2.8317 \times 10^{-2}$ | 1728 | 1 | 29.9221 |
| 1 milliliter | 1 | $1 \times 10^{-6}$ | $6.1024 \times 10^{-2}$ | $3.5315 \times 10^{-5}$ | $1.0567 \times 10^{-3}$ |
| 1 liter | 1000 | 0.001 | 61.0237 | $3.5315 \times 10^{-2}$ | 1.0567 |
| 1 quart | 946.3529 | $9.4635 \times 10^{-4}$ | 57.75 | $3.3420 \times 10^{-2}$ | 1 |

# APPENDIX V

## FORESTRY SCHOOLS IN THE UNITED STATES

The following list was prepared from a booklet published by the U.S.D.A. Forest Service (FS-9), 1980. Schools accredited by the Society of American Foresters are noted by an asterisk.

*Department of Forestry
Auburn University
Auburn, Alabama

*School of Forestry
Northern Arizona
    University
Flagstaff, Arizona

*Department of
    Watershed
    Management
University of Arizona
Tucson, Arizona

Department of Forestry
University of Arkansas
Monticello, Arkansas

Natural Resources
    Management
    Department
California Polytechnic
    State University
San Luis Obispo,
    California

School of Natural
    Resources
Humboldt University
Arcata, California

*Department of Forestry
    and Resource
    Management

University of California
Berkeley, California

*College of Forestry and
    Natural Resources
Colorado State University
Fort Collins, Colorado

*School of Forestry and
    Environmental
    Studies
Yale University
New Haven, Connecticut

*School of Forest
    Resources and
    Conservation
University of Florida
Gainesville, Florida

*School of Forest
    Resources
University of Georgia
Athens, Georgia

*College of Forestry,
    Wildlife and Range
    Sciences
University of Idaho
Moscow, Idaho

*Department of Forestry
School of Agriculture
Southern Illinois
    University
Carbondale, Illinois

**519**

*Department of Forestry
University of Illinois
Urbana, Illinois

*Department of Forestry
and Natural
Resources
Purdue University
West Lafayette, Indiana

*Department of Forestry
Iowa State University
Ames, Iowa

*Department of Forestry
University of Kentucky
Lexington, Kentucky

*School of Forestry and
Wildlife Management
Louisiana State University
Baton Rouge, Louisiana

Department of Agriculture
McNeese State University
Lake Charles, Louisiana

School of Forestry
College of Life Sciences
Louisiana Tech
University
Ruston, Louisiana

*School of Forest
Resources
University of Maine
Orono, Maine

*Department of Forestry
and Wildlife
Management
University of
Massachusetts
Amherst, Massachusetts

*Department of Forestry
Michigan State University
East Lansing, Michigan

*Department of Forestry
School of Forestry and
Wood Products

Michigan Technological
University
Houghton, Michigan

*School of Natural
Resources
University of Michigan
Ann Arbor, Michigan

*College of Forestry
University of Minnesota
St. Paul, Minnesota

*School of Forest
Resources
Mississippi State
University
Mississippi State,
Mississippi

*School of Forestry,
Fisheries and
Wildlife
University of Missouri
Columbia, Missouri

*School of Forestry
University of Montana
Missoula, Montana

*Forestry Program
University of New
Hampshire
Durham, New Hampshire

Forestry Section
Cook College
Rutgers State University
New Brunswick, New
Jersey

*College of
Environmental
Sciences and
Forestry
State University of New
York
Syracuse, New York

Division of Renewable
Natural Resources

University of Nevada
Reno, Nevada

*School of Forestry and
 Environmental
 Studies
Duke University
Durham, North Carolina

*School of Natural
 Resources
North Carolina State
 University
Raleigh, North Carolina

Division-Department of
 Forestry
School of Natural
 Resources
Ohio State University
Columbus, Ohio

*Department of Forestry
Oklahoma State
 University
Stillwater, Oklahoma

*School of Forestry
Oregon State University
Corvallis, Oregon

*School of Forest
 Resources
Pennsylvania State
 University
University Park,
 Pennsylvania

*Department of Forestry
Clemson University
Clemson, South Carolina

*Department of Forestry,
 Wildlife and
 Fisheries
University of Tennessee
Knoxville, Tennessee

*Department of Forestry
Stephen F. Austin State
 University

Nacogdoches, Texas

*Department of Forest
 Science
Texas A & M University
College Station, Texas

*College of Forest
 Resources
Utah State University
Logan, Utah

*Department of Forestry
University of Vermont
Burlington, Vermont

*School of Forestry and
 Wildlife Resources
Virginia Polytechnic
 Institute and State
 University
Blacksburg, Virginia

*College of Forest
 Resources
University of Washington
Seattle, Washington

*Department of Forestry
 and Range
 Management
Washington State
 University
Pullman, Washington

*Division of Forestry
West Virginia University
Morgantown, West
 Virginia

*Department of Forestry
University of Wisconsin
Madison, Wisconsin

*College of Natural
 Resources
University of Wisconsin
Stevens, Point, Wisconsin

# GLOSSARY

**Abiotic factors.** Nonliving elements (factors) of the environment—that is, soil, climate, physiography.

**Abscission.** Dropping leaves, flowers, fruits, or other plant parts following the formation of a separation zone at the base of the plant part.

**Adaptation.** Genetically determined character or feature of an organism that serves to increase reproductive potential or chance of survival.

**Advance regeneration.** Young trees that have become established naturally before a clearcut is made.

**Adventitious.** Plant part that develops outside of the usual position and/or time.

**Agrisilviculture.** System of cultivation combining agriculture and forestry when tree plantations are interplanted with agricultural crops (the latter of which can yield a fast return while trees slowly mature).

**Air-dry.** Timber or wood dried to equilibrium with the surrounding atmosphere.

**Albuminous cells.** Certain ray and axial parenchyma cells in gymnosperm phloem; associated with sieve cells.

**Allelopathy.** Suppression of germination, growth, or the limiting of the occurrence of plants as the result of the release of chemical inhibitors by some plants.

**Allogenic.** Ecological succession resulting from factors (such as prolonged drought) that arise external to a natural community and alter its habitat (i.e., changes in the vegetation).

**Amorphous.** Formless.

**Angiosperm.** Vascular flowering plants that produce seeds enclosed in an ovary. Include monocotyledons (grasses and palms) and dicotyledons (herbaceous and woody plants).

**Anisotropic.** Of a material whose properties vary according to the direction of measurement. The anisotropy of wood corresponds to the main features of wood structure and the marked anisotropy of the cellulose long-chain molecules.

**Annual ring.** One growth layer as seen in cross section of a woody plant stem. Formed by contrast of springwood and summerwood.

**Apical meristem.** Growing point at the tip of the root or stem. Gives rise to primary tissues.

**Autoecology.** Study of the relationship between an individual organism and its environment.

**Autogenic.** Involving or resulting from a reaction between or in living organisms.

**Avifauna.** Bird life of a given region.

**Axil.** Angle between the upper side of a leaf or twig and the supporting stem.

**Axis.** Longitudinal support on which organs or parts are arranged; the stem and root; the central line of the body. *Axial*, adj.

**Backfire.** Fire set along the inner edge of a fire line to consume the fuel in the path of a forest fire, and/or to change the direction of the fire.

**Bark.** All tissue outside the cambium.

**Basal area.** Area of the cross section of a tree stem, generally at breast height (1.3 meters or 4.5 feet) and inclusive of bark.

**Bast fiber.** Any of several strong, ligneous fibers obtained from phloem tissue and used in the manufacture of woven goods and cordage.

**Bedrock.** Bottom layer; lowest stratum; unbroken solid rock, overlaid in most places by soil or rock fragments.

**Bilateral aid.** Aid based on a formal agreement between a single donor country and the recipient; in contrast to multilateral aid, which originates from several countries, usually through an international agency.

**Binder.** Extraneous bonding agent, organic or inorganic, used to bind particles together—for example, to produce particleboard.

**Biological control.** Regulation of pest species through the use of other organisms.

**Biomass.** Quantity of biological matter of one or more species present on a unit area.

**Biosphere.** Part of the earth's crust, water and atmosphere where living organisms can subsist.

**Biotic factors.** Relation of living organisms to each other from an ecological viewpoint (as opposed to abiotic or nonliving elements).

**Black liquor.** Liquor resulting from the manufacture of pulp by alkaline processes and containing, in a modified form, the greater part of the extracted lignin and sugar degradation products.

**Blowup fire.** Sudden increase in intensity and rate of flame spread, often accompanied by a violent convection column of smoke and hot gases.

**Board foot.** Unit of measurement represented by a board 1 foot long, 1 foot wide, and 1 inch thick (144 cubic inches), measured before surfacing or other finishing. Abbr. b.f.; bd. ft.; ft.b.m.

**Bole.** Tree stem of merchantable thickness.

**Bolt.** Any short log, as a pulpwood or veneer bolt.

**Boreal.** Of or pertaining to the north.

**Brightness.** Blue reflectance of a sheet of paper; a measure of the maximum whiteness that can be achieved with proper tinting.

**Browse.** Leaves, small twigs, and shoots of shrubs, seedling and sapling trees, and vines available for forage for livestock and wildlife.

**Buck.** To cut a tree into proper lengths after it has been felled.

**Bud primordium.** Embryonic shoot formed in the axil of a leaf.

**Calender.** Machine in which cloth, paper, or the like is smoothed, glazed, etc., by pressing between revolving cylinders.

**Canopy.** More or less continuous cover of branches and leaves formed collectively by the crowns of adjacent trees or shrubs. See *Understory.*

**Capillary water.** Water that fills the smaller pores less than 0.05 millimeters in diameter and that by adhesion to the soil particles can resist the force of gravity and remain suspended in the soil. This water constitutes the major source of water for tree growth, except in soils having a high water table.

**Carbonization.** Decomposition by heat of organic substances in a limited supply of air accompanied by the formation of carbon. See *Destructive distillation.*

**Carnivore.** Organism that consumes mostly flesh.

**Carrying capacity.** Number of organisms of a given species and quality that can survive in, without causing the deterioration of, a given ecosystem.

**Cation.** Positively charged atom or group of atoms. Cation-exchange capacity is the total capacity of soil colloids for holding cations.

**Chipper.** Machine for cutting logs or pieces of logs into chips.

**Chlorosis.** Abnormal yellowing of foliage, often a symptom of mineral deficiency, infection, root or stem girdling, or extremely reduced light.

**Chromosome.** Body in the cell nucleus containing genes in a linear order.

**Clearcutting.** Silvicultural system in which the entire timber stand is cut. See *Seed tree method, Shelterwood method.*

**Climatic release.** Relaxation of environmental resistance factors and the recurrence of favorable weather for several successive years. Together, these conditions allow a pest species to approach its reproductive potential.

**Climax community.** Community which has achieved the maximum possible development. The end point of a sere.

**Clinal variation.** Variation occurring in a continuous fashion along a geographic or environmental gradient.

**Collenchyma.** Supporting tissue containing elongated living cells with irregularly thickened primary cell walls; often found in regions of primary growth in stems and leaves.

**Combustion.** Consumption by oxidation, evolving heat, and generally also flame and/or incandescence.

**Community.** Unit of vegetation that is homogeneous with respect to species composition and structure and occupies a unit area of ground.

**Companion Cell.** Specialized parenchyma cell in angiosperm phloem; associated with sieve tube members.

**Conifer.** Division of gymnosperm, plant producing naked seeds in cones, mostly evergreen, with timber known commercially as softwood.

**Coppice system.** Silvicultural system in which crops regenerate vegetatively by stump sprouts and the rotation is comparatively short.

**Cord.** Volume measure of stacked wood. A standard cord is 4 × 4 × 8 feet and contains 128 cubic feet of space. Actual wood volume varies between 70 and 90 cubic feet per cord. A face cord is a short cord in which the length of the pieces is shorter than 8 feet (Figure 10.16).

**Cork cambium.** Lateral meristem that produces cork toward the outside of the plant and phelloderm to the inside.

**Cordillera.** Entire chain of mountain ranges parallel to the Pacific Coast, extending from Cape Horn to Alaska.

**Cortex.** Ground tissue of the shoot or root that is located between the epidermis and the vascular system; a primary tissue region.

**Cotyledon.** Embryonic leaf, characteristic of seed plants; generally stores food in dicotyledons and absorbs food in monocotyledons.

**Crown fire.** Fire that burns the tops of trees and brush.

**Cruise (timber).** Survey of forestlands to locate and estimate volumes and grades of standing timber.

**Cutting cycle.** Period of time between major cuts in an unevenaged stand. See *Rotation age*.

**dbh (diameter at breast height).** Tree diameter at breast height, 1.3 meters (4½ feet) above the ground as measured from the uphill side of the tree.

**Deciduous.** Perennial plants that are normally leafless for some time during the year.

**Defoliation.** Loss of a plant's leaves or needles.

**Dendrology.** Branch of botany dealing with classification, nomenclature, and identification of trees and shrubs.

**Dendrometer.** Instrument for measuring the dimensions of trees or logs.

**Denitrification.** Process by which nitrogen is released from the soil (as a gas) to the atmosphere by denitrifying bacteria.

**Density.** Proportion of cell-wall volume to total volume of wood. The number of individuals (trees, animals) per unit area at a given time.

**Derived demand.** Demand for a good coming from its use in the production of some other good; for example, timber is demanded not by consumers but by firms that manufacture wood products.

**Desertification.** Exhaustion of the soil, often because of removal of vegetative cover in semiarid regions, leading irreversibly to an unproductive desert.

**Destructive distillation.** Decomposition of wood by heating out of contact with air, producing primarily charcoal, tarry distillates, and pyroligneous acid.

**Diapause.** State of arrested physiological development of an insect.

**Dicotyledones.** One of two classes of angiosperms; a plant whose embryo has two seed leaves.

**Diffuse-porous wood.** Hardwood in which the vessels are small in diameter; vessels in springwood do not have much greater diameters than those in summerwood. See *Ring-porous wood*.

**Dominant.** Trees that project somewhat above the general level of the canopy, having crowns that receive direct sunlight from above and partly from the side. See *Suppressed*.

**Duff.** Organic matter in various stages of decomposition on the forest floor.

**Ecology.** Science that deals with the relation of plants and animals to their environment and to the site factors that operate in controlling their distribution and growth.

**Ecosystem.** Any complex of living organisms with their environment considered as a unit for purposes of study.

**Ecotone.** Transition zone between two adjoining communities.

**Edaphic.** Pertaining to soil conditions that influence plant growth.

**Edge.** Boundary between two or more elements of the environment—for example, field/woodland.

**Elasticity.** Relationship, expressed mathematically, between a percentage change in one variable and the resulting percentage change in another variable, when all other things are held constant. The price elasticity of demand (supply) is the percentage change in quantity demanded (supplied) when price changes by 1 percent, with all other variables such as income, population, etc., held constant.

**Endemic population.** Natural low population level of most species native to an area.

**Energy exchange.** Flow of energy through the ecosystem beginning with the capture of radiant solar energy by photosynthesis and ending when the energy is lost back to the environment as heat through metabolism.

**Entomology.** Study of insects.

**Entomophagous.** Feeding on insects.

**Environmental resistance.** Physical and biological factors that inhibit the reproductive potential of a species.

**Epidermis.** Outermost layer(s) of cells on the primary plant body.

**Ericaceous.** Belonging to the heath family of plants, including the heath, arbutus, azalea, rhododendron, American laurel, etc.

**Ethanol.** Ethyl alcohol, $C_2H_5OH$; a colorless, volatile liquid manufactured from starchy or sugary materials by fermentation; also synthetically produced.

**Evapotranspiration.** Combined loss of water (through evaporation and transpiration) from the soil and vegetal cover on an area of land surface.

**Even-aged stand.** Stand in which relatively small age differences exist between individual trees, usually a maximum of 10 to 20 years.

**Excurrent.** Tree with the axis prolonged to form an undivided stem or trunk (as in spruces and other conifers).

**Exotic.** Not native; foreign; introduced from other climates or countries.

**Extractive.** In wood any part that is not an integral part of the cellular structure and can be dissolved out with solvents.

**Fermentation.** Change brought about by an agent such as yeast enzymes, which convert sugars to ethyl alcohol.

**Fiber.** Narrow cell of wood (xylem) or bast (phloem), other than vessel elements and parenchyma; includes tracheids. Or a cell material with a length to diameter (1:d) ratio greater than 20:1.

**Fiberizing.** Separation of wood and other plant material into fibers or fiber bundles by mechanical (sometimes assisted by chemical) means.

**Fines.** Pulp fractions having very short or fragmented fibers.

**Fire line.** Strip of plowed or cleared land made to check the spread of a fire.

**Food chain, food web.** Chain of organisms existing in any natural community such that each link in the chain feeds in the one below and is eaten by the one above; at the base are autotrophic (green) plants, eaten by heterotrophic organisms including plants (fungi), plant-eating animals (herbivores), plant and animal eaters (omnivores), and animal eaters (carnivores).

**Forb.** Any herbaceous plant that is not a grass or grasslike—such plants as geranium, buttercup, or sunflower.

**Fourdrinier.** Name associated with the wire-forming section or the entire paper-making machine. Originally developed by the Fourdrinier brothers in England (1804).

**Fruit.** In angiosperms, a matured, ripened ovary containing the seeds.

**Furfural.** Oily liquid aldehyde, $C_5H_4O_2$, with an aromatic odor, obtained by distilling wood, corncobs, bran, sugar, etc., with dilute sulfuric acid.

**Gall.** Pronounced, localized, tumorlike swelling of greatly modified structure; occurs on plants from irritation by a foreign organism.

**Gamete.** Male pollen cell or a female egg cell, typically the result of meiosis, capable of uniting in the process of fertilization with a reproductive cell of the opposite sex.

**Gasification.** Conversion of a solid or liquid substance to a gas.

**Gene.** Unit of heredity; portion of the DNA of a chromosome.

**Gene flow.** Migration of genes from one population to another via the dispersal of individuals, or of propagules such as seed or pollen.

**Gene pool.** Sum total of genetic information distributed among the members of an interbreeding population.

**Genetic drift.** Change in gene frequency in small breeding populations because of chance, in contrast to a similar change under selection.

**Genotype.** Total amount of genetic information that an individual possesses. See *Phenotype*.

**Girdle.** To destroy tissue, especially the bark and cambium, in a rough ring around a stem, branch, or root. Girdling often kills the tree.

**Globose.** Tree having the shape of a globe or globule; approximately spherical.

**Grade.** Established quality or use classification of trees, timber, and wood products; to classify according to grade.

**Gross national product (GNP).** Total value at current market prices of all final goods and services produced by a nation's economy, before deduction of depreciation and other allowances for consumption of durable capital goods.

**Ground fire.** Fire that not only consumes all the organic materials of the forest floor, but also burns into the underlying soil itself—for example, a peat fire. See *Surface fire*.

**Growth impact.** Pervasive, ongoing destruction of forests because of growth loss and mortality. See *Growth loss, Mortality*.

**Growth loss.** Difference between potential and actual tree growth, caused by destructive agents such as insects, diseases, weather, etc. See *Growth impact, Mortality*.

**Gymnosperm.** Vascular plants that produce seeds not enclosed in an ovary.

**Habitat.** Immediate environment occupied by an organism. In forestry, habitat usually refers to animal habitat.

**Habitat type.** Unit of land capable of supporting a single climax community type.

**Haemocoel.** General insect body cavity in which blood flows.

**Hard pan.** Indurated (hardened) or cemented soil horizon. The soil may have any texture and is compacted or cemented by iron oxide, organic matter, silica, calcium carbonate, or other substances.

**Headbox.** Final holding container of pulp slurries for regulation of flow onto the moving paper-machine wire.

**Head fire.** Fire spreading, or set to spread, with the wind.

**Heartrot.** Decay in the central core of a tree usually caused by fungus.

**Heartwood.** Inner core of a woody stem, wholly composed of nonliving cells and usually differentiated from the outer enveloping layer (sapwood) by its darker color. See *Sapwood*.

**Hemicellulose.** Any of the noncellulosic polysaccharides of the intercellular layer and of the cell wall that can be extracted with aqueous alkaline solutions and are readily hydrolyzable by acids to give sugars.

**Herb.** Any seed-producing plant that does not develop persistent woody tissue above ground. Includes both forbs and grasses. May be perennial. *Herbaceous*, adj.

**Herbivore.** Organism that consumes living plants or their parts.

**Heritability.** Proportion of any observed variability that is due to genetic effects, the remainder being attributed to environment.

**High-grading.** Type of exploitation cutting that removes only trees of a certain species, or of high value.

**Hogged wood.** Wood reduced to coarse chips—for example, for fuel or manufacture of wood pulp or chipboard.

**Horizon, soil.** Layer of soil roughly parallel to the land surface, distinguished from adjacent layers by different physical, chemical, or biological characteristics.

**Humus.** Decomposed lower part of the soil organic layer, generally amorphous, colloidal, and dark-colored.

**Hydrarch succession.** Primary succession beginning on a substrate of water, usually a pond or lake.

**Hydration.** Chemical combination of water with cellulose or hemicelluloses (usually in fibers) to give a swollen structure; endowing fibres with an increased capacity for water retention through mechanical beating.

**Hydrolysis.** Conversion, by reaction with water, of a complex substance into two or more smaller molecules.

**Hypsometer.** Device for measuring tree height.

**Improvement cutting.** Silvicultural treatment in which diseased or poorly formed trees or trees of undesirable species are removed.

**In-breeding depression.** Loss of vigor that frequently results from mating closely related individuals.

**Increment.** Increase in girth, diameter, basal area, height, volume, quality, or value of individual trees or crops.

**Increment borer.** Augerlike instrument with a hollow bit, used to extract cores from trees for the determination of growth and age.

**Infection court.** Site of infection by a pathogen.

**Initial.** Undifferentiated cell that remains within the meristem indefinitely and adds cells to the plant body by division.

**Inland Empire.** Area lying between the crests of the Cascade Mountains and Bitterroot Mountains, and extending from the Okanogan Highlands to the Blue Mountains of northeastern Oregon. Timber production is very important in this region.

**Integration (economics).** Expansion of a firm into production of other, often closely related, types of products (horizontal integration) or into prior or later stages of the production of a given product (vertical integration).

**Intercellular space.** Space between the cells of a tissue.

**Internode.** Portion of a stem or branch that is between two successive nodes.

**Intolerance, shade.** See *Shade tolerance*.

**Ion.** Electrically charged atom or group of atoms.

**Juvenile wood.** Wood formed close to the central core of the tree that contains a high percentage of thin-walled cells.

**Kiln-dry.** Dried in a kiln to a specified moisture-content range.

**Knot.** Portion of a branch enclosed in the xylem by the natural growth of the tree.

**Kraft pulp.** Chemical wood pulp obtained by cooking—that is, digesting wood chips in a solution of sodium hydroxide (caustic soda) and sodium sulfide.

**Lammas shoot.** Abnormal shoot formed late in the summer from expansion of a bud that was not expected to open until the following year.

**Larva.** Immature, wingless, feeding stage of an insect that undergoes complete metamorphosis.

**Lateral meristems.** Meristems that give rise to secondary tissue; the vascular cambium and cork cambium.

**Lattice.** Crossed strips with open spaces between to give the appearance of a screenlike structure.

**Leaching.** Removal of soluble substances (e.g., from soil or timber) by percolating water.

**Leaf primordium.** Lateral outgrowth from the apical meristem that will become a leaf.

**Lenticel.** Small breathing pore in the bark of trees and shrubs; a corky aerating organ that permits gases to diffuse between the plant and the atmosphere.

**Lesion.** Circumscribed diseased area.

**Lignification.** Impregnation with lignin, as in secondary walls of xylem cells. See *Lignin*.

**Lignin.** Noncarbohydrate (phenolic), structural constituent of wood and some other plant tissues; encrusts the cell walls and cements the cells together.

**Lignocellulosic.** Of materials containing both lignin and cellulose; a characteristic of higher forms of terrestrial plants.

**Lignosulfonic acid.** Soluble derivative of lignin produced in the sulfite pulping process and present—in the form of salts (lignosulfonates)—in the waste liquor.

**Limiting factor.** Environmental factor needed by an organism but in shortest supply.

**Lithosphere.** Crust of the earth.

**Littoral.** Of vegetation growing along a seashore or very large lake. See *Riparian*.

**Loam.** Rich friable soil containing a relatively equal mixture of sand and silt and somewhat smaller proportion of clay.

**Log rule.** Table showing the estimated or calculated amount of lumber that can be sawed from logs of given length and diameter.

**Lumen.** Cell cavity (often hollow).

**Macerate.** To soften, or separate the parts of a substance by steeping in a liquid, with or without heat.

**Mast.** Nuts and seeds of trees, serving as food for livestock and wildlife.

**Mature.** Stage of tree growth when height growth slows and crown expansion and diameter increase and become marked. See *Seedling, Sapling, Pole, Senescent*.

**Mensuration, forest.** Science dealing with the measurement of volume, growth, and development of individual trees and stands and the determination of various products obtainable from them.

**Meristem.** Undifferentiated plant tissue from which new cells arise. See *Apical meristem, Lateral meristem*.

**Mesarch succession.** Primary succession beginning on an intermediate substrate that is neither open water nor solid rock, such as a recent mud flow or glacial moraine. See *Hydrarch, Xerarch succession*.

**Mesophyll.** Parenchyma tissue in a leaf between the upper and lower epidermis.

**Methanol.** Methyl alcohol, $CH_3OH$; a colorless, volatile liquid, a product of the destructive distillation of wood, derived mainly from the lignin; also manufactured synthetically.

**Microclimate.** Climate of small areas, especially insofar as this differs significantly from the general climate of the region.

**Middle lamella.** Layer of intercellular material, rich in lignin and pectic compounds, cementing together the primary walls of adjacent cells.

**Mineralization.** Breakdown of organic compounds in soil releasing inorganic constituents that can be taken up by plant roots.

**Monocotyledones.** One of the two classes of angiosperms; a plant whose embryo has one seed leaf.

**Monoculture.** Crop of a single species, generally even-aged. See *Even-aged stand*.

**Monophagous.** Feeding on a single host species.

**Morphology.** Study of form and its development.

**Mortality.** Volume of trees killed by natural causes, exclusive of catastrophes.

**Mutagen.** Substance known to induce mutations.

**Mutation.** Sudden, heritable change in the structure of a gene or chromosome or some set thereof.

**Mycelium.** Vegetative part of a fungus, as distinct from the fruiting body.

**Mycoplasmas.** Smallest of free-living organisms, lacking a cell wall, but possessing a distinct flexible membrane.

**Mycorrhizae.** Symbiotic association between non-pathogenic or weakly pathogenic fungi and living cortical cells of a plant root.

**Naval stores.** Historical term for resin products, particularly turpentine and rosin from pine trees; previously also pine tars and pitch.

**Nematodes.** Parasitic or free-living, elongated smooth worms of cylindroid shape; roundworms.

**Niche.** Status of a plant or animal in its community—that is, its biotic, trophic, and abiotic relationships. All the components of the environment with which an organism or population interacts.

**Nitrification.** Process whereby protein, amino acids, and other nitrogen compounds in the soil are oxidized by microorganisms with the production of nitrates.

**Nitrogen cycle.** Worldwide circulation of nitrogen atoms in which certain microorganisms take up atmospheric nitrogen and convert it into other forms that may be assimilated into the bodies of other organisms; excretion, burning, and bacterial and fungal action in dead organisms return nitrogen atoms to the atmosphere.

**Nitrogen fixation.** Conversion of elemental nitrogen ($N_2$) from the atmosphere to organic combinations or to forms readily utilizable in biological processes.

**Node.** Part of a stem or branch where one or more leaves or branches is attached.

**Oleoresin.** Group of "soft" natural resins, consisting of a viscous mixture of essential oil (e.g., turpentine) and nonvolatile solids (e.g., rosin) secreted by the resin-forming cells of the pines and certain other trees.

**Organ.** Structure composed of different tissues, such as root, stem, leaf, or flower.

**Oven-dry.** Of wood dried to constant weight in a ventilated oven at a temperature above the boiling point of water.

**Parasite.** Organism that lives in or on another living organism of a different kind and derives subsistance from it without returning any benefit. See *Predator, Saprophyte*.

**Parenchyma.** Tissue composed of living, thin-walled, brick-shaped cells; primarily concerned with the storage and distribution of food materials. Axial parenchyma cells are vertically oriented; ray parenchyma are laterally oriented.

**Pathogen.** Organism directly capable of causing disease in living material. See *Saprogen*.

**Pectin.** Complex organic compound (polysaccharide) present in the intercellular layer and primary wall of plant cells; the basis of fruit jellies.

**Ped.** Visible structural soil aggregate—for example, crumb, block, or prism.

**Perforation.** Gap in the cell wall lacking a pit membrane; occurs in vessel members of angiosperms.

**Pericycle.** Root tissue located between the epidermis and phloem.

**Periderm.** Outer protective tissue that replaces the epidermis; includes cork, cork cambium, and phelloderm.

**Phelloderm.** Tissue formed toward the inside of the plant by the cork cambium.

**Phenol.** Hydroxyl derivative of benzene, $C_6H_5OH$.

**Phenology.** Study of biological events as related to climate (Figure 7.3).

**Phenotype.** Outward appearance or physical attributes of an individual. See *Genotype*.

**Pheromones.** Hormonal substance secreted by an individual and stimulating a physiological or behavioral response from an individual of the same species.

**Phloem.** Tissue of the inner bark; contains sieve elements through which carbohydrates are transported.

**Photosynthesis.** Synthesis of carbohydrates from carbon dioxide and water by green plant cells in the presence of light, with oxygen as a by-product.

**Phototropism.** Growth movement in which the direction of the light is the determining factor, as the growth of a plant toward a light source; turning or bending response to light.

**Physiography.** Science of physical geography.

**Physiology.** Study of the vital functions of living organisms. *Note:* Differences in physiological character may not always be accompanied by morphologial differences.

**Piedmont.** Plateau between the coastal plain and the Appalachian Mountains.

**Pioneer community.** First stage in the ecological development of a community.

**Pit.** Gap or recess in the secondary cell wall that facilitates the interchange of materials between cells.

**Pith.** Ground tissue occupying the center of the plant

stem or root, within the vascular cylinder; usually consists of parenchyma.

**Planer.** Machine for surfacing sawed timber.

**Plasmolysis.** Contraction of the cytoplasm because of removal of water from the protoplast by osmosis.

**Pole.** Still-young tree larger than 4 inches (10 centimeters) dbh, up to about 8 inches (20–23 centimeters) dbh; during this stage height growth predominates and economic bole length is attained. See *Seedling, Sapling, Mature, Senescent*.

**Polymerization.** Transformation of various low-molecular-weight compounds (monomers) into large molecules—that is, polymers.

**Polyphagous.** Feeding on many different host species.

**Predator.** Any animal that preys externally on others—that is, hunts, kills, and feeds on a succession of hosts. See *Parasite*.

**Prescribed burning.** Controlled use of fire to further certain planned objectives of silviculture, wildlife management, fire-hazard reduction, etc.

**Present net worth.** Single amount measuring the net current value of a stream of future revenues and costs.

**Price index.** Price of a good or group of goods in any year divided by the price of the same good or group of goods in a base year. See *Relative price index*.

**Price leadership.** Determination of prices by one or a few firms, with other producers in the industry tacitly accepting the prices thus determined.

**Primary growth.** Growth originating in the apical meristem of shoots and roots. See *Secondary growth*.

**Primary succession.** Succession beginning on a substrate that did not previously support vegetation such as open water, fresh glacial moraine, or bare rock. See *Secondary succession*.

**Profile, soil.** Vertical section of the soil through all its horizons and extending into the parent material.

**Progeny.** Offspring produced from any mating.

**Progeny test.** Evaluation procedure where parents are rated based on the performance of their offspring.

**Protoplasm.** Living substance of all cells.

**Protoplast.** Entire contents of the cell, not including the cell wall.

**Provenance.** Natural origin of seeds or trees, usually synonomous with ''geographic origin,'' or a plant material having a specific place or origin.

**Pulp.** Fibers separated by mechanical or chemical means; the primary raw material from which paper is made.

**Pupa.** (pl. pupae). Insect in the nonfeeding, usually immobile, transformation stage between larva and the adult.

**Pyroligneous acid.** Aqueous portion, after separation of the tar, of the liquor obtained during the destructive distillation of wood; a complex mixture of water (80–90 percent) and organic compounds. See *Destructive distillation*.

**Pyrolysis.** Subjection of wood or organic compounds to very high temperatures and the resulting decomposition. See *Destructive distillation*.

**Quad.** Unit of energy measure; $1 \times 10^{15}$ British thermal units (Btu).

**Ray.** Laterally oriented, ribbon-shaped tissue extending radially in the xylem and phloem; functions in the lateral transport of water and nutrients.

**Recombination.** Formation of new combinations of genes as a result of segregation in crosses between genetically different parents.

**Recurrence interval.** Frequency of fires in a given stand.

**Regeneration.** Renewal of a tree crop, by natural or artificial means.

**Regulated forest.** Forest that produces a continuous flow of products of about the same size, quality, and quantity over time.

**Relative price index.** Price index for one good divided by the price index for another good or group of goods. The divisor is usually the wholesale or consumer's price index.

**Release cutting.** Silvicultural treatment in which larger trees of competing species are removed from competition with desired crop trees.

**Remote sensing.** Collection of data acquired by a device that is not in physical contact with the object, area, or phenomenon under investigation—for example, aerial photography or satellite imagery.

**Reproductive potential.** Ability of a species to multiply in the absence of countervailing forces.

**Resin.** Pitch; the secretions of certain trees, oxidation or polymerization products of the terpenes, consisting of mixtures of aromatic acids and esters insoluble in water but soluble in organic solvents; often exuding from wounds.

**Rhizome.** Horizontal underground stem, usually containing stored food.

**Rickettsia.** Bacteria-like microorganisms of the genus Rickettsia, parasitic on arthropods and pathogenic for humans and animals.

**Ring-porous wood.** Wood (xylem) of hardwoods in which the earlywood vessels are much larger in diameter than vessels in the latewood; the vessels generally appear as a ring in a stem cross section. See *Diffuse-porous wood*.

**Riparian.** Of vegetation growing in close proximity to a watercourse, small lake, swamp, or spring. See *Littoral*.

**Root cap.** Thimble-shaped mass of cells covering and protecting the growing root tip.

**Root hairs.** Tubular outgrowths of epidermal cells of the young plant.

**Rosin.** Solid residue after evaporation and distillation of the turpentine from the oleoresin of various pines, consisting mainly of rosin acids.

**Rotation age.** Period of years required to establish and grow timber crops to a specified condition of maturity. Applies only to even-aged management. See *Cutting cycle*.

**Roundwood.** Timber or firewood prepared in the round state—from felled trees to material trimmed, barked, and crosscut.

**Saccharification.** Conversion of the polysaccharides in wood or other plant material into sugars by hydrolysis with acids or enzymes.

**Sahel.** Semiarid region of Africa between the Savannas and the Sahara extending through Senegal, Mauritania, Mali, Niger, Sudan, northern Nigeria, and Ethiopia. Since the late 1960s this region has been afflicted by devastating drought leading to the starvation of hundreds of thousands of people.

**Sapling.** Young tree at least 1 meter (3 feet) high, but not larger than 10 centimeters (4 inches) dbh; crowns are well elevated and usually many lower branches have started to die. See *Seedling, Pole, Mature, Senescent*.

**Saprogen.** Organism capable of producing decay in nonliving organic material. See *Pathogen*.

**Saprophyte.** Plant organism that is incapable of synthesizing its nutrient requirements from purely inorganic sources and feeds on dead organic material. See *Parasite*.

**Sapwood.** Predominantly living, physiologically active wood; includes the more recent annual layers of xylem that are active in translocation of water and minerals. See *Heartwood*.

**Scale.** Estimated solid (sound) contents of a log or group of logs.

**Scarification.** Wearing down, by abrasion or chemical treatment, of the bark or outer coat.

**Scion.** Detached living portion of a plant grafted onto another plant.

**Sclerenchyma.** Supporting tissue composed of cells with thick, often lignified secondary walls; may include fiber cells or sclereid cells.

**Sclereid.** Sclerenchyma cell with a thick, lignified secondary wall.

**Secondary growth.** Growth derived from lateral meristem; results in increase in girth. See *Primary growth*.

**Secondary succession.** Succession starting after the disturbance of a previously existing plant community. See *Primary succession*.

**Sedimentation.** Deposition or accumulation of mineral or organic matter.

**Seedling.** Youngest trees from the time of germination until they reach a height of 1 meter (3 feet). See *Seedling, Pole, Mature, Senescent*.

**Seed orchard.** Plantation of trees established to provide for the production of seeds of improved quality.

**Seed-tree method.** Silvicultural system in which the mature timber is removed in one cut, except for a small number of seed trees left to provide a source of seed for the next crop. See *Clearcutting, Shelterwood method*.

**Selection.** Any discrimination by natural or artificial means that results in some individuals leaving more offspring than others.

**Selection cutting.** Silvicultural system in which scattered trees or small groups of trees are cut, providing sustained yield from an uneven-aged stand.

**Selection differential.** Difference between the value of a selected individual (or mean value of a selected population) and the mean value of the original unselected population.

**Senescent.** Growing old; aging stands at this stage are overmature; losses from mortality and decay may exceed additions in volume. See *Seedling, Sapling, Pole, Mature*.

**Seral community.** Community that follows the pioneer community in a sere but still does not represent the fully developed mature ecosystem.

**Sere.** Series of communities through time that develop as a result of succession.

**Serotinous cone.** Cones of some species of gymnosperms that are sealed by resin, requiring high temperatures to open the cones and release seeds.

**Serpentine.** Common mineral, hydrous magnesium silicate, $H_2Mg_3Si_2O_2$.

**Shade tolerance.** Capacity of trees to reproduce and grow in the shade of and in competition with other trees. See Tables 6.1 and 9.1.

**Shelterwood method.** Silvicultural system in which the mature timber is removed, leaving sufficient numbers of trees standing to provide shade and protection for new seedlings. See *Clearcutting, Seed-tree method.*

**Shifting cultivation.** Itinerant forms of agriculture, common in tropical regions, whereby a parcel of the forest is cleared and the soil is cultivated until it becomes unproductive, before moving onto another area where the process is started anew.

**Shoot.** Aboveground portion of a vascular plant.

**Shrub.** Woody perennial plant, seldom exceeding 10 feet in height, usually having several persistent woody stems branching from the ground.

**Sieve element.** Cell of the phloem concerned with the long-distance transport of food substances. Classified into sieve cells (gymnosperms) and sieve-tube members (angiosperms).

**Silvichemicals.** Chemicals derived from wood and trees.

**Silviculture.** Manipulation of forest vegetation to accomplish a specified set of objectives; controlling forest establishment, composition, and growth.

**Size, sizing.** Additive introduced to modify the surface properties of manufactured board or paper.

**Skidding.** Loose term for hauling logs by sliding, not on wheels.

**Slash.** Open area strewn with debris of trees from felling or from wind or fire; the debris itself.

**Slurry.** Watery suspension of insoluble matter—that is, pulp slurry.

**Snag.** Standing dead tree from which the leaves and most of the branches have fallen.

**Spot fire, spotting.** Fire set outside the perimeter of the main fire by flying sparks or embers.

**Stenotopic.** Organisms limited to a very specific habitat niche.

**Stomata.** Openings in the surface of a leaf through which water vapor, carbon dioxide, and oxygen pass.

**Structure, soil.** Combination or arrangement of primary soil particles (e.g., sand, silt, clay) into secondary particles called peds. See *Ped.*

**Stumpage.** Value of timber as it stands uncut.

**Suberin.** Fatty material in cell walls of corky bark tissue.

**Subsoil.** Bed or stratum of earth or earthy material immediately under the surface soil.

**Substrate.** Underlying material; the soil beneath plants or animals; the material on which an enzyme or fermenting agent acts, on which adhesive is spread, or on which a fungus grows or is attached.

**Succession.** Change in community composition and structure through time.

**Sulfite pulp.** Chemical wood pulp obtained by cooking—that is, digesting wood chips in a solution of bisulfites and sulfurous acid.

**Suppressed.** Trees with crowns completely overtopped by surrounding trees so that they receive almost no direct sunlight. See *Dominant.*

**Surface fire.** Fire that burns only surface litter, loose debris of the forest floor, and small vegetation. See *Ground fire.*

**Sustained yield.** Yield a forest can produce continuously, such as timber.

**Symbiosis.** Mutually beneficial relationship between two dissimilar living organisms. In some cases, the symbionts form a single body or organ, as in mycorrhizae or lichens.

**Synecology.** Study of the community and its environment.

**Syngas.** Synthesis gas; a synthetically produced gas containing two parts hydrogen ($H_2$) and one part carbon monoxide (CO).

**Systemic.** Of a pathogen, capable of spreading throughout its host. Of a pesticide, absorbed by a plant so as to be lethal to agents that feed on it.

**Systems analysis.** Method of analysis that deals with the movement of energy or materials to different parts or components of a complex system.

**Tall oil.** By-product of the kraft pulping of resinous woods (for example, pine), consisting mainly of resin acids and fatty acids.

**Tannins.** Complex extracellular water-soluble substances, generally formed from a variety of simpler polyphenols; part of wood extractives.

**Terpenes.** Class of hydrocarbons, with their derivatives, commonly occurring in many species of wood and generally having a fragrant odor; characteristically noted with pine trees.

**Texture, soil.** Relative proportion of the various mineral particles such as sand, silt, and clay, expressed as a textural class—for example, sandy loam, clay loam, etc.

**Thermochemical liquefaction.** Decomposition of organic compounds to smaller molecules often in the form of an oil. The reaction is usually carried out in the presence of a catalyst and hydrogen or synthesis gas at high pressure and temperature.

**Thinning.** Silvicultural treatment in which stand density is reduced to accelerate diameter growth in remaining trees.

**Through-fall.** All the precipitation eventually reaching the forest floor—that is, direct precipitation plus canopy drip.

**Tissue.** Group of similar cells organized into a structural and functional unit.

**Tissue system.** Tissue or group of tissues organized into a structural and functional unit in a plant or plant organ.

**Tracheary element.** Tracheid or vessel member.

**Tracheid.** Elongated, thick-walled conducting and supporting cell of xylem. Has tapering ends and pitted walls without perforations. Found in nearly all vascular plants; the main fibrous component of wood. See *Vessel member*.

**Tree.** Woody perennial plant, typically large and with a single well-defined stem and a more or less definite crown.

**Triploid.** Individual having one set of chromosomes more than the typical number for the species.

**Trophic, -troph, Tropho-.** Pertaining to nutrition, feeding.

**Trophic levels.** Steps in the movement of energy through an ecosystem.

**Turgor.** Normal distention or rigidity of plant cells, resulting from the pressure exerted from within against the cell walls by the cell contents.

**Turpentine.** Essential oil that can be obtained by distilling the oleoresin of conifers, particularly pines, consisting of a mixture of terpenes. Most turpentine is now obtained as a by-product of the kraft pulping of pines.

**Understory.** Any plants growing under the canopy formed by others. See *Canopy*.

**Uneven-aged stand.** Stand in which more than two distinct age classes and a range of size classes (seedling, sapling, pole, etc.) are present.

**Uptake.** Amount of water and/or nutrients absorbed by vegetation.

**Vascular cambium.** Cylindrical sheath of meristematic cells, the division of which produces secondary xylem and secondary phloem.

**Vascular tissue.** Specialized conducting tissue in plants forming a vascular system—in woody plants comprising the whole of the xylem and phloem.

**Vector.** Any agent capable of transporting a pathogen or saprogen to a host.

**Veneer.** Thin sheet of wood of uniform thickness, produced by rotary cutting or by slicing.

**Vessel member.** Elongated cell of the xylem characterized by perforations. Its function is to conduct water and minerals through the plant body. Found in nearly all angiosperms and a few other vascular plants. See *Tracheid*.

**Volatiles.** Essential oil distilled from plant tissues, generally characterized by a low boiling point.

**Volume table.** Table showing the average cubic contents of trees or logs by diameter and merchantable length in a specified unit of volume.

**Watershed.** Total area above a given point on a river, stream, etc., that contributes water to the flow at that point.

**Water stress.** Stress or negative pressure exerted on a water column in a plant due to transpiration.

**Water table.** Upper surface of the groundwater. A perched water table is one separated by relatively impermeable material from an underlying body of groundwater; may be seasonally impermanent.

**Wholesale price index (WPI).** Weighed average of wholesale prices of a representative bundle of goods and services produced by the economy. The rate of increase (decrease) in the WPI is one measure of the rate of inflation (deflation) in the economy.

**Wood.** Secondary xylem.

**Woody plants.** Trees or shrubs exhibiting secondary growth.

**Xerarch succession.** Primary succession beginning on a substrate that is solid rock and therefore has minimal water-storing capacity.

**Xylem.** Tissue containing tracheary elements through which water and minerals are transported; wood is secondary xylem.

**Yard.** To haul logs to a central spot to prepare them for transport.

## References

1. F.C. Ford-Robertson, ed., *Terminology of Forest Science, Technology, Practice and Products,* Soc. of Am. Foresters, Wash. D.C., 1971.
2. J. Stein, editor-in-chief, *Random House College Dictionary,* Random House, Inc., New York, 1979.

# Index

# TAXONOMY OF SELECTED FOREST TREES

ANGIOSPERMS (dicotyledones)
Simple leaf[1]
  Willow Family *(Salicaceae)*
    Poplars, Aspens *(Populus)*
    Willows *(Salix)*
  Birch Family *(Betulaceae)*
    Alders *(Alnus)*
    Birches *(Betulus)*
  Beech Family *(Fagaceae)*
    Chestnut, Chinkapins *(Castanea)*
    Beeches *(Fagus)*
    Oaks *(Quercus)*
  Elm Family *(Ulmaceae)*
    Hackberries *(Celtis)*
    Elms *(Ulmus)*
  Magnolia Family *(Magnoliaceae)*
    Tuliptree *(Liriodendron)*
    Magnolia *(Magnolia)*
  Laurel Family *(Lauraceae)*
    Sassafras *(Sassafras)*
  Witch-Hazel Family *(Hamamelidaceae)*
    Sweetgum *(Liquidambar)*
  Sycamore Family *(Platanaceae)*
    Sycamore *(Platanus)*
  Mulberry Family *(Moraceae)*
    Mulberry *(Morus)*
  Maple Family *(Aceraceae)*
    Maple *(Acer)*
  Basswood (Linden) Family *(Tiliaceae)*
    Basswood *(Tilia)*

---

[1]Simple leaves consist of a single blade; compound leaves are composed of three or more leaflets.